The Plays of George Chapman

❖

The Comedies

THE PLAYS OF
GEORGE CHAPMAN

❖

THE COMEDIES

A Critical Edition

General Editor: Allan Holaday

❖

Assisted by Michael Kiernan

UNIVERSITY OF ILLINOIS PRESS
Urbana   Chicago   London

To the memory of MARVIN THEODORE HERRICK

Contents

❖

General Introduction

❖

Collected editions of Chapman's plays — of which the present one is number four — began with *The Comedies and Tragedies of George Chapman,* presumably edited by R. H. Shepherd, and published in 1873 by John Pearson. Essentially a diplomatic reprint of the original quartos, it has slight textual value. But with its immediate successor, *The Works of George Chapman: Plays* (1875), Shepherd did seriously undertake the business of textual correction, perhaps in part as a result of his decision to modernize spelling and punctuation. Forced by this exacting process occasionally to confront textual cruxes, he ultimately produced a text which, though flawed by errors, is, nonetheless, superior to its predecessor.

But the limitations of this second edition prove crippling. Its textual errors result especially from Shepherd's tendency to misread his copy-text, to emend without warrant, and to overlook obvious quarto mistakes. Having made no systematic collation, he was often unaware of corrected states of the quarto texts. And he provided no textual apparatus whatever. Indeed, even a hasty examination of his work convincingly establishes its limited usefulness for any student of Chapman.

Immediate predecessors to the present edition are T. M. Parrott's *The Tragedies* (1910) and *The Comedies* (1914), two volumes in a projected three-volume work, *The Plays and Poems of George Chapman.*[1] Parrott produced much the best complete text then available and supplied as well useful information about early editions, a record of his collations, and discussions of troublesome cruxes. Noting the inadequacy of quarto stage directions, uncritically reproduced by Shepherd, he corrected many of those that he derived from his copy-text and originated others; several of his interpolations which clarify ambiguous scenes have special textual relevance.

But, despite its evident merit, current readers recognize in Parrott's edition serious limitations, the most conspicuous of which result from our changed editorial standards. The inadequacy of Parrott's textual apparatus, for example, often exasperates scholars, many of whom, for quite sound reasons, also object

---

[1] Volume III, *Poems,* was never published.

1

to his modernized text. But even more serious than these shortcomings are his numerous errors, several of which directly resulted from a decision to correct for the printer a copy of Shepherd's second edition. He also chose to collate only two or three quarto copies, thereby missing numerous press-variants. And, inevitably, he overlooked some cruxes, misinterpreted others, and sometimes misread. Thus, though he carried Chapman scholarship a great step forward, Parrott left unfulfilled the critical need for sound texts.

Intent upon satisfying that need, editors of the present edition, in addition to textual introductions, have prepared for each play the following four-part apparatus: a table of press-variants, two "collations," and textual notes. The press-variants (i.e., variations from copy to copy in the copy-text edition) result from changes made in printer's formes during the press run; that is, they derive from printshop efforts to "correct" the quarto text. One of the two collations, recorded in notes at the bottom of each page, lists all emendations made by the editor in deriving his critical text from his copy-text. These include revision of accidentals as well as substantives, excepting only those covered by a general statement on silent emendations. The other, a "historical" collation, lists substantive and semi-substantive (but not accidental) variants which differentiate the critical text from specified earlier versions. The textual notes provide a terse commentary on special cruxes and a defense of editorial decisions. Thus the apparatus records various attempts to correct the text, including original printshop revisions as well as those emendations made or conjectured by succeeding editors and commentators.

Since attention to the distinctions among substantive, semi-substantive, and accidental variants promotes successful use of the apparatus, a brief explanation of these terms seems in order. The basic distinction, of course, is that between substantive variants (i.e., those that affect meaning) and accidental variants (i.e., those that involve spelling or punctuation without altering meaning). The term "semi-substantive" identifies those variations in punctuation or, very occasionally, in spelling that do affect meaning (and hence are substantive) but, because they do not involve diction, resemble accidentals. As a working principle, editors of the present edition follow the now customary practice of accepting as substantive or semi-substantive any emendation which changes copy-text diction, alters copy-text meaning through punctuation, or removes copy-text ambiguity; all other variants are considered accidental.

Recognizing that one rarely reads directly through a collected edition, editors have prefaced each text with whatever information seemed especially pertinent to that play, accepting the duplication of information that occasionally results on the assumption that consequent gains in clarity and convenience for the reader adequately offset the disadvantages. Fortunately, not much information required full repetition; often the complete explanation necessary in one introduction could, in summarized form, serve another. But anyone who does proceed directly through either volume will, on several occasions, recognize that he is covering some of the ground more than once.

Headnotes for each play identify editions cited by sigla in the historical collations; but since variants recorded in the footnotes derive principally from the copy-text, sigla are usually unnecessary here except to distinguish corrected [$Q(c)$] from uncorrected [$Q(u)$] states of the copy-text variant or to identify re-set passages [$Q(r)$] and later quartos (e.g., Q^2, Q^3). Occurrence in a footnote of an editor's name or an appropriate siglum such as $Q(c)$ immediately after the square bracket designates the originator of the emendation recorded in the lemma and hence adopted in the critical text. Thus, the following footnote specifies that the lemma "threed," taken from the critical text, derives from a corrected state of the copy-text; "throat" represents the uncorrected version.

24 threed] $Q(c)$; throat $Q(u)$

Lack of an editor's name or siglum immediately after the bracket in the foot-notes and historical collations implies that the emendation originates with the present text. In the interest of further simplicity, editors, wherever clarity permits, avoid the abbreviation *om.* (omitted) after the bracket to designate an editorial interpolation. Thus, the following footnote,

61 SD *Pointing to D'Olive.*]

indicates that the stage direction comprising the lemma is an interpolation originating with the critical text. To avoid repeating in the variant words found in the lemma, editors usually substitute a swung dash for each omitted word; a caret indicates that a mark of punctuation occurring in the lemma does not reappear in the variant. Thus, the following note indicates that instead of the comma, Shepherd has a semicolon and Parrott no punctuation whatever.

61 more,] $\sim$; S; $\sim \wedge P$

Parenthetical listings, appended to various footnotes, record changes between upper and lower case that result from variations in lineation. Hence, the follow-ing note shows that, in emending the prose lineation of Q to verse (after Parrott), the present editor raised the initial letters of "tel" and "for" to upper case.

65-67 Hast . . . all.] *Parrott; as prose* (tel . . . for)

And finally, an editor identifies cruxes which, because he has accepted the copy-text reading, would otherwise escape mention in the footnotes, by the following device:

81 seasonable] *stet (See Textual Note)*

Unrecorded emendations are few in number and without textual significance. They include the normalization of speech heads, of wrong-font letters, and of wrong-font punctuation; correction of turned letters where no ambiguity exists, of printers' substitutions occasioned by type shortages, and of wrong-font type for complete words in the stage directions; expansion of the tilde and amper-sand; substitutions of standard types for display capitals and of lower case for the capitals that usually follow display letters.

Abbreviations, including abbreviated names and titles, found in the copy-text reappear in the critical texts except for those that prove ambiguous or otherwise confusing. Likewise, editors normally preserve the u-v, i-j spellings of the copy-text, on rare occasions emending to avoid inconvenience to the reader. An example of one such emendation, taken from *The Blind Beggar,* is that from the copy-text spelling, "loud," to the less confusing "lou'd." And, where an "aside" ends mid-speech, editors conventionally mark the conclusion by a dash.

In general, editorial interpolations (i.e., any passages of one word or more in the critical text that are supplied to remedy a copy-text omission) are bracketed; an exception is material added to a stage direction that exists in the copy-text. Completely interpolated stage directions, however, are bracketed. As a means of identifying the source of any substantive emendation, editors record even bracketed interpolations in both the footnotes and the historical collations.

The need to refer in textual introductions to such units of the copy-text as pages, printer's formes, and sheets necessitated the definition within the critical text of the boundaries of each original page. For example, since an editor in presenting his evidence for a change in compositors between sheets B and C in the copy-text of *Monsieur D'Olive* necessarily refers to special characteristics of these sheets, he obligates himself to provide his reader the means by which to identify all relevant passages. Thus, a slash in the critical text marks the point at which one quarto page ends and another begins. And at the right margin opposite the first line or part of a line representing a new copy-text page, a bracketed signature corresponding to that in the copy-text identifies the page. The title-page reproductions that precede the plays have been standardized in size for use in the present volume.

An attempt further to improve Chapman's dramatic texts seems particularly consistent with intense critical interest in this dramatist and, as a response to the evident needs of students, scholars, and critics, to deserve, at the moment, priority over other useful work. Editors of the present edition, therefore, omitting historical and critical commentaries, have sought to establish reliable texts for all of Chapman's plays. Aware of their advantage in being latest to undertake this task, they have provided a record of their predecessors' answers to the common textual problems. Thus, though the critical text represents in each instance its editor's best solution to textual cruxes, the reader has immediate access through the apparatus to requisite information by which he can assess all editorial decisions.

There remains the pleasant task of acknowledging much help generously given. And though to list all our obligations would prove impractical, we can thank those institutions and individuals who gave major assistance to the entire project. Conspicuous among these are the Research Board of the University of Illinois and the Research Committee of the Department of English; without their support, the project would, at best, have required much longer to complete. Also essential was the skilled help of the University of Illinois Library staff, particularly that of Miss Alma DeJordy, who cheerfully assembled for our use hundreds of microfilm copies of Chapman quartos. We are, of course, also indebted to the many libraries throughout Britain and America that supplied those microfilms. And though each institution is identified at an appropriate place in the apparatus, we should like particularly to thank the authorities of the Houghton Library for permission to consult the Chapman proof sheets that survive from a projected, but never published, edition of several plays edited by James Russell Lowell.

Miss Fannie Ratchford kindly provided much helpful information as did Professor Akihiro Yamada, of Shinshu University, Japan, who, over several years, made available to the editors the results of his own investigations of Chapman's comedies. The extent of his assistance is suggested by references to him and his work in the textual introductions. And finally, we take particular pleasure in thanking Mrs. R. J. Menges, of the University of Illinois Press. Her tolerant acceptance of what must often have seemed arbitrary decisions by the editors, her wise advice, and her patient attention to the minutiae of a complex manuscript proved of inestimable help.

The Blind Beggar of Alexandria

edited by Lloyd E. Berry

❖

TEXTUAL INTRODUCTION

The Blind Beggar of Alexandria is the earliest play which is unquestionably by Chapman.[1] The title page states that the play was "sundry times *publickly acted in London,* by the right honorable the Earle *of Nottingham, Lord high* Admirall his seruantes," and a search of Henslowe's *Diary* confirms this fact. *The Blind Beggar* is entered as a new play on 12 February 1595-96:

> 12 of febreary 1595 ne — Rd at the blind beger
> of elexandrea   iij[l12]

The play proved to be a substantial success with no fewer than twenty-two performances recorded between February 1596 and April 1597. This is even more significant when one realizes that there is a hiatus in Henslowe's *Diary* for March and for August-October 1596.[3] *The Blind Beggar* was evidently withdrawn from the stage in 1597, as no further mention is made of the play until 2 May 1601, when there is indication the play was revived on the stage. Henslowe records payments totaling £9. 3s. 4d. for new costumes.[4] Professor Parrott suggests the play was withdrawn in 1597 "to make room for Chapman's next comedy, *An Humourous Day's Mirth,* called by Henslowe *The Comedy of Umers.*"[5] I somewhat doubt the validity of Parrott's suggestion, as after all, at this very time Marlowe had four plays on the stage. It may well be the play had simply run its course.

[1] *Two Italian Gentlemen,* entered in the *Stationers' Register* 12 November 1584, and *The Disguises,* a lost play mentioned by Henslowe under the date 2 October 1595, have been suggested as Chapman's.
[2] R. A. Foakes and R. T. Rickert, eds., *Henslowe's Diary* (Cambridge, 1961), p. 34.
[3] *Henslowe's Diary,* pp. 34 (2), 35 (3), 36 (3), 37 (2), 47 (2), 48, 54 (2), 55 (3), 56 (2), and 57 (2).
[4] *Henslowe's Diary,* pp. 169 (3), and 170.
[5] T. M. Parrott, ed., *The Plays and Poems of George Chapman* (London, 1914), II, 673, fn. 2.

A little over a year later, *The Blind Beggar* was entered in the *Stationers' Register* on 15 August 1598:[6]

William Jones /   Entred for his Copie vnder the handes of bothe the wardens, a booke intituled, *The blynde begger of Alexandrya* / vppon condicon thatt yt belonge to noe other man..............vj d[7]

The Blind Beggar was printed in the same year (Greg, *Bibliography,* 146).

Professor Parrott's remarks concerning the nature of the manuscript which lies behind the printed text have been very influential indeed:

The manuscript from which Jones printed was presumably a stage copy as is shown by the careful stage-directions. . . . The original version seems to have been heavily cut in this manuscript, for the printed play contains only about 1,600 lines, and the omissions are such as to render the serious part of the play almost unintelligible. It is plain, as we may learn from the advertisement of the title-page, that it was the farcical scenes . . . and not the romantic story of Aegiale and Cleanthes, which caught the fancy of the public. It is not unlikely that the former scenes have been enlarged beyond their original form; it is certain that the latter have been cut down. As a consequence the play, as it now stands, totally lacks unity, coherence, and proportion. That the author is to be charged with this lack appears to me more than doubtful.[8]

Dr. Greg accepts most of Parrott's comments but does suggest that "the [stage] directions are no more than what might be supplied from memory of a performance." Greg further suggests that "in spite of its apparently regular publication, the piece if not surreptitiously obtained had at least a somewhat irregular history."[9]

That the present text of *The Blind Beggar* is a "heavily cut" text, there can be no question. Doricles, the principal rival to Cleanthes (the Blind Beggar), appears only twice in the play, and his first speech exhibits a rather wretched example of cutting:

Loue that hath built his temple on my browes
Out of his Battlementes into my hart,
And seeing me to burne in my desire,
Will be I hope appeased at the last.

iv, 28-31

There are other rather striking examples of poor cutting. In scene i, the stage direction reads *"Enter Pego like a Burgomaister,"* but Pego has not left the stage in the present version of the play. The maidens have exited, but that Pego remained is attested to by Irus's instructions to Pego, "Come gird this pistole closely to my side." Again, in scene ix, Euribates says "tell the King of this foule accident [Doricles' murder]." The very next line, Ptolemy enters and says "Oh tell no more"; and he goes on to moan the loss of Doricles.

More generally, the romance between Cleanthes and Aegiale is only hinted at, yet this was surely in the original one of the main plots. The final fate of

[6] As the entry has no date, the date given is that of the previous entry. The subsequent entry is dated August 19th.
[7] Arber, III, 124.
[8] Parrott, pp. 673-74.
[9] W. W. Greg, ed., *The Blind Beggar of Alexandria,* The Malone Society (Oxford, 1928), p. vi. Neither Parrott nor Greg elaborates on his hypothesis as to the manuscript copy for the printed text.

Aegiale is also unknown, as she simply disappears from the play. Cleanthes (as Count Hermes) woos Ptolemy's daughter, Aspasia (the betrothed of Doricles), in what are unquestionably the best lines of the play (ix, 22-34). Aspasia is not tempted by the Count and proceeds to announce to all the murder of Doricles. After this she too disappears from the action. The play that is left is really something of a dramatized version of a picaresque novel. But there are enough indications in the play to demonstrate that this was not originally so and that although the actions of Cleanthes are roguish, he was no rogue.

Another problem raised by both Parrott and Greg is the nature of the manuscript of the play. Parrott suggests that the manuscript was a "stage copy," whereas Greg suggests the possibility of a reported text. Greg also suggests that the play had "a somewhat irregular history" in its progression from manuscript to print. I suspect that Greg may be correct in the first of his suggestions. There is evidence in the text that would argue for a reported text. Almost without exception, verse passages that lapse into prose do so toward the middle or end of the speech (*see* Irus's speech, i, 129-45). There are examples of interpolated phrases in otherwise quite acceptable blank verse or pentameter couplets:

(1) So Ile assure your grace shall meete with him *eare long*

i, 71

(2) My Lord the offer had been to hye a grace *for him,*
For neare did eye behold a fayrer face.

x, 121-22

There are also several rather remarkable examples of transposition:

(1) *Sa.* then do not name it for I feare tis naught.
For yesterday I hard *Menippus* as he was talking (ber doore,
With my mothers maide and I stoode harkning at the cham-
Sayde that, with that woord a mayde was got with childe.

This is the text as it is in Q. First of all, it is set as prose, whereas the passage is blank verse. When it is properly set in verse it becomes apparent that "Sayde" properly follows *"Menippus,"* and the lines should read:

Sa. Then do not name it for I feare tis naught.
For yesterday I hard *Menippus* say
As he was talking with my mothers maide
And I stoode harkning at the chamber doore,
That, with that woord a mayd was got with childe.

i, 202-06

(2) To him that succours him, Ile threaten death,
But he that doth not threaten him shall die.

should read:

To him that succours him, Ile threaten death,
But he that doth not succour him shall die.

i, 96-97

(3) To haue a graces from thy summer darted

should read:

To haue a summer from thy graces darted.

v, 80

(4) hate me not for loue and it is not lust

should read:

> hate me not, for loue it is and not lust
> vi, 29-30

A similar error, which might, however, be an error in hearing occurs in scene x, line 135. Q reads:

> My louing ioy the fresh desire of kinges.

The line should probably read:

> My loues enioy the fresh desire of kinges.

The evidence from the stage directions I do not believe is very conclusive in pointing toward a reported text. Entrances and exits are carefully marked, but there are seldom found the full descriptive directions that are usually associated with reported texts.

Greg's further suggestion that the copy was obtained by the printer through some devious means is of course a possibility, and a reported text would certainly support this theory. Further, since the play had been off the stage for over one year before it was printed, there could scarcely seem any good reason for Henslowe's company to publish a cut version of the play in preference to the original text. The fact that the play was entered in the *Stationers' Register* does not preclude the possibility of a reported text. The play was entered to Jones on the condition that "yt belonge to noe other man," and there is the possibility that it indeed did belong to another person.

It is not known who the printer of the play was. It is possible that the play was printed by the same person who printed Lyly's *The Woman in the Moon* (Greg, *Bibliography,* 142), as the two plays have common ornaments. But as the printer of Lyly's play is also unknown, this information is not very helpful.

The running titles indicate there were two skeletons used in printing the play, but the usual tests employed to determine the number of compositors that set the text have been inconclusive in their results.

The play is not divided into acts or scenes, and I follow Parrott's division of the play into just scenes.

THE BLINDE

begger of Alexan-
dria, moſt pleaſantly diſcour-
ſing his variable humours
in diſguiſed ſhapes full of
conceite and pleaſure.

As it hath beene ſundry times
publickly acted in London.
by the right honorable the Earle
of Nottingham, Lord high Ad-
mirall his ſeruantes.

By George Chapman: Gentleman.

Imprinted at London for William
Iones, dwelling at the ſigne of the
Gun neere Holburne Conduit.
1598.

DRAMATIS PERSONAE

[Ptolemy, King of Egypt
Porus, King of Ethiopia
Rhesus, King of Arabia
Bion, King of Phasiaca
Bebritius, King of Bebritia
Doricles, Prince of Arcadia
Irus, the blind beggar
Pego, his servant
Euribates ⎫
⎬ courtiers
Clearchus ⎭
Antisthenes
Bragadino
Menippus ⎫
Pollidor ⎬ servants
Druso ⎭
A Herald, Councillors, and Lords
Guards, Soldiers, Messengers

Aegiale, Queen of Egypt
Aspasia, her daughter
Elimine
Samathis
Martia
Euphrosyne
Ianthe, Aegiale's maid
Jaquine, Samathis' maid]

THE BLIND BEGGAR

[SCENE I]

Enter Queene *Aegiale, Ianthe* her maid, two counselers.　　　[A2]

AEgi. Leaue me a while my Lordes and waite for me,
At the blacke fountayne, by *Osiris* groue,
Ile walke alone to holy *Irus* caue,
Talking a little while with him and then returne.
Ianthe begone.　　　　　　　　*Exeunt omnes. Manet* Aegiale.
Now *Irus* let thy mindes eternall eye,
Extend the vertue of it past the Sunne.
Ah my *Cleanthes* where art thou become,
But since I saued thy guiltlesse life from death,
And turnd it onely into banishment,　　　　　　　　10
Forgiue me, loue mee, pittie, comfort mee.

Enter Irus *the Begger with* Pego.

Pego. Maister.
Irus. Pego.　　　　　　　　15
Pego. Wipe your eyes and you had them.
Irus. Why *Pego.*
Pego. The Queene is here to see your blindnes.
Irus. Her Maiestie is wel come, Heauens preserue,
And send her highnes an immortall rayne.
AEgi. Thankes reuerent *Irus* for thy gentle prayer,
Dismisse thy man a while and I will lead thee,　　　　　　　　20
For I haue waightie secretes to impart.
Pego. Would I were blind that she might lead mee.　　　　　　*Exit.*
AEgi. Irus thy skill to tell the driftes of fate,
Our fortunes and thinges hid from sensuall eyes,
Hath sent mee to thee for aduertisment,　　　　　　　　25
Where Duke *Cleanthes* liues that was exilde　/
This kingdome for attempting mee with loue,　　　　　　[A2ᵛ]
And offering stayne to *AEgipts* royall bed.

Scene I] *Parrott* ‖ SD maid,] ∼∧ ‖ 6 let] Let ‖ 11 me . . . pittie] *Shepherd*; me∧ loue, mee∧ pittie ‖ 25 aduertisment,] ∼. ‖ 26 exilde] ∼, ‖

Irus. I hope your maiestie will pardon mee,
If Conscience make me vtter what I thinke,   30
Of that hye loue affayres twixt him and you.
   AEgi. I will sweete *Irus* being well assurd,
That whatsoeuer thy sharpe wisdomes sees
In my sad frailtie, thou willt haue regard
To my estate and name and keepe it close.   35
   Irus. Of that your highnes may be well assurde.
Then I am bound madam to tell you this,
That you your selfe did seeke *Cleanthes* loue,
And to aspire it, made away his Dutches,
Which he well knowing and affecting her,   40
Deare as his life denyed to satisfie,
That kindenesse offered twixt your selfe and him;
Therefore did you in rage informe the Duke,
He sought your loue, and so he banisht him.
   AEgi. To true it is graue *Irus* thou has tould,   45
But for my loues sake which not Gods can rule,
Strike me no more of that wound yet too greene,
But onely tell me where *Cleanthes* is,
That I may follow him in some disguise,
And make him recompence for all his wrong.   50
   Irus. *Cleanthes* is about this Cittie oft,
With whom your maiestie shall meete ere long:
And speake with him, if you will vse such meanes,
As you may vse for his discouery.
   AEgi. What shall I vse then, what is in my power,   55
I will not vse for his discouery.
Ile bind the winges of loue vnto myne armes,
And like a Eagle prying for her pray,
Will ouerlooke the earthes round face for him,
Were this sufficient.   60
Or I will Moorelike learne to swimme and diue,
Into the bottome of the Sea for him, /
Least beeing the sonne of *Aegypt* and now set,   [A3]
Thetis in rage with loue would rauish him,
Were this sufficient.   65
   Irus. But Maddam this must be the likliest meane
To seeke him out, and haue him at your will:
Let his true picture through your land be sent

---

33 sees] ∼, ‖ 34 frailtie,] ∼∧ | regard] ∼, ‖ 35 close.] ∼- ‖ 36 assurde.] ∼, ‖ 42 him;] ∼, ‖
51 oft] *Shepherd*; off ‖ 52 your] yonr ‖ 55 then,] ∼∧ ‖ 56 discouery.] ∼, ‖ 64 him,] ∼. ‖ 67
will:] ∼∧ ‖ 68 sent] ∼. ‖

Proposing great rewardes to him that findes him,
And threaten death to them that succour him,   70
So Ile assure your grace shall meete with him eare long.
   AEgi. Happie and blest be *Irus* for his skill
He sweetely plantes in my contentious mind,
For which most reuerent and religious man,
I giue this Iewell to thee, richly worth   75
A kentall or an hundreth waight of gold.
Bestow it as thou list on some good worke,
For well I know thou nothing doost reserue,
Of all thy riches men bestow on thee,
But wouldst thou leaue this place and poore mans life,   80
The court of *Aegipt* should imbrace thy feete,
And toples honors be bestowed on thee.
   Irus. I thanke your highnes for thus raysing mee,
But in this barrennesse I am most renound.
For wisdome and the sight of heauenly thinges,   85
Shines not so cleare as earthlye vanities.
   AEgi. Most rich is *Irus* in his pouertie.
Oh that to finde his skill my crowne were lost.
None but poore *Irus* can of riches boast,
Now my *Cleanthes* I will straight aduance   90
Thy louely pictures on each monument
About the Cittie and within the land,
Proposing twise fiue thousand Crownes to him,
That findes him to be tendered by my handes,
And a kind kisse at my imperiall lipes.   95
To him that succours him, Ile threaten death,
But he that doth not succour him shall die,
For who is worthy, life will see him want. /
To all his pictures when they be disperst   [A3ᵛ]
Will I continuall pilgrimages make,   100
As to the saintes and Idols I adore,
Where I will offer sighes, and vowes, and teares,
And sacrifice a hecatombe of beast,
On seuerall alters built where they are plast,
By them shal *Isis* statue gently stand,   105
And Ile pretend my Iealous rites to her;
But my *Cleanthes* shall the obiect bee,
And I will kneele and pray to none but he.   *Exit.*

---

69 Proposing] *Shepherd;* Opposing *(See Textual Note)* ‖ **75** thee,] ∼∧ | worth] ∼. ‖ **76** gold.] ∼, ‖
81 court] *Parrott;* count ‖ **82** toples] *Shepherd; Toples* | thee.] ∼, ‖ **86** earthlye] *Shepherd;* eathlye ‖
87 pouertie.] ∼, ‖ **92** land,] ∼. ‖ **95** lipes.] ∼, ‖ **97** succour] *Deighton;* threaten ‖ **99** To all his]
Q(c); To his all *Q(u)* | disperst] ∼. ‖ **102** teares,] ∼. ‖ **105** statue] *Shepherd;* stature *Q(c);* statute
Q(u) ‖ **106** her;] ∼∧ ‖

15

Irus. See Earth and Heauen where her *Cleanthes* is.

I am *Cleanthes* and blind *Irus* too,   110

cf. *Tamberlane* And more then these, as you shall soone perceaue,

Yet but a shepheardes sonne at *Memphis* borne,

And I will tell you how I got that name,

My Father was a fortune teller and from him I learnt his art,

And knowing to grow great, was to grow riche,   115

Such mony as I got by palmestrie,

I put to vse and by that meanes became

To take the shape of *Leon,* by which name,

I am well knowne a wealthie Vsurer,

And more then this I am two noble men,   120

Count Hermes is another of my names,

And Duke *Cleanthes* whom the Queene so loues;

For till the time that I may claime the crowne,

I meane to spend my tyme in sportes of loue,

Which in the sequell you shal playnely see,   125

And Ioy I hope in this my pollicie.

         Enter Pego, Elimine, Samathis, *and* Martia *with*

           there men Menippus, Pollidor, *and* Druso.

   Pego. Oh maister, heere comes the three wenches, now strike it

deade for a fortune.

   Irus. These are the nymphes of *Alexandria,*

So called because there beauties are so rare.   130

With two of them at once am I in loue /

Deepely and Equally; the third of them,   [A4]

My silly brother heere asmuch affectes,

Whom I haue made the Burgomaister of this rich towne,

With the great wealth, I haue bestowed on him.   135

All three are maides kept passing warilye,

Yet lately beeing at their Fathers house

As I was *Leon* the rich vserer,

I fell in loue with them, and there my brother too,

This fitly chaunceth that they haue liberty,   140

To visit me alone: now will I tell their fortunes so,

As may make way to both their loues at once,

The one as I am *Leon* the rich vserer,

The other as I am the mad brayne *Count,*

And do the best too, for my brothers loue.   145

   Pego. Thanks good maister brother, but what are they that talke

with them so long, are they wooers trow, I do not like it, would they

would come neare.

118 *Leon,*] ~. ‖ **122** loues;] ~, ‖ **124** sportes] *Q(c)*; spertes *Q(u)* ‖ **126** SD Samathis] Samaphis ‖ **127** maister,] ~∧ | wenches,] ~∧ ‖ **129** *Alexandria,*] ~. ‖ **132** Equally;] ~∧; Equally *Q(c)*; Epually *Q(u)* ‖ **135** him.] ~, ‖ **137-38** Yet . . . vserer,] *Shepherd*; *one line* ‖ **138** vserer,] ~∧ ‖ **145** loue.] ~, ‖ **146-48** Thanks . . . neare.] Thanks . . . that / Talke . . . trow, / I . . . neare. ‖

16

Irus. O those are three seruantes that attend on them,
Let them alone, let them talke a while.   150
   Eli. Tell vs *Menippus, Druso,* and *Polydor,*
Why all our parentes gaue you three such charge,
To waite on vs and ouer see vs still,
What do they feare, thinke you, that we would do.
   Meni. There feare is least you should accompanie,   155
Such as loue wanton talke, and dalliance.
   Eli. Why what is wanton talke.
   Meni. To tell you that were to offend our selues,
And those that haue forbidden you should heare it.
   Sam. Why what is dalliance sayes my seruant then.   160
   Dru. You must not know because you must not dally.
   Sam. How say you by that, well do you keepe it from vs, as much as
you can, weele desire it neuerlesse I can tell ye.
   Mar. Lord, what straite keepers of poore maides are you,
You are so chast you are the worse agayne.   165
   Eli. Pray you good seruantes will you do vs the seruice,
To leaue vs alone a while.
   Meni. We are commaunded not to be from you, /
And therefore to leaue you alone,   [A4ᵛ]
Were to wrong the trust your parentes put in vs.   170
   Mar. I cry you mercy sir, yet do not stand
All on the trust our parentes puts in you,
But put vs in a litell to I pray.
   Sam. Trust vs good seruantes by our selues a while.
   Dru. Lets my masters and you say the woord,   175
Theyle but to *Irus* for to know theire fortunes,
And hees a holy man all *Egypt* knowes.
   Meni. Stay not to long, then mistris and content.
   Eli. Thats my good seruant, we will straight returne.
   Pol. And you mistris.   180
   Mar. And I trustie seruant.
   Pol. Faith then Ile venter my charge among the rest.   *Exeunt servants.*
   Mar. A mightie venture, you shall be cronicled in *Abrahams* asses
catalog of cockscombes for your resolution.
   Eli. Now the great foole take them all.   185
Who could haue pickt out three such liuelesse puppies,
Neuer to venter on their mistrisses.
   Sam. One may see by them it is not meete choise men should haue
offices.

---

154 you,] ∼∧ ‖ **156** dalliance.] ∼, ‖ **160** then.] ∼, ‖ **162** from vs,] *Q(c)*; from, vs *Q(u)* ‖ **163** ye.] ∼, ‖ **164** Lord,] ∼∧ ‖ **169** leaue] leane ‖ **171-73** I . . . pray.] *Parrott;* I . . . the / Trust . . . pray. *Q* (all . . . but) ‖ **175** masters] mastrs ‖ **178** content.] ∼, ‖ **179** seruant,] ∼∧ ‖ **182** SD *Exeunt servants.*] *Parrott subs.; Exeunt.* ‖ **183** venture,] ∼∧ ‖ asses] ∼, ‖ **185-86** Now . . . puppies,] *Shepherd;* Now . . . haue, / Pickt . . . puppies, *Q* (who) ‖ **189** offices.] ∼, ‖

17

Mar. A prettie morrall, work it in the samplar of your hart.　　　190
Eli. But are we by our selues.
Mar. I thinke so vnlesse you haue a bone in your belly.
Eli. Not I, God knowes I neuer came where they grew yet.
Since we are alone lets talke a little merrily,
Mee thinkes I long to know what wanton talke and dalliance is.　　195
Sam. Ile lay my life tis that my mother vses
When she and others do beginne to talke
And that she sayes to me, mayde, get ye hence;
Fall to your needle; what, a mayd and Idle.
Mar. A mayd and Idle, why maydes must be Idle but not another　　200
thing.
Sam. Then do not name it, for I feare tis naught.
For yesterday I hard *Menippus* say
As he was talking, with my mothers maide,
And I stoode harkning at the chamber doore,　　　205
That with that woord a mayd was got with childe.
Eli. How with the very woord.
Sam. I meane with that the woord seemes to expresse.
Mar. Nay if you be so fine you will not name it now, /
We are all alone, you are much too nice.　　　　[B1] 210
Eli. Why let her chuse, let vs two name it.
Mar. Do then *Elimine.*
Eli. Nay doe you *Martia.*
Mar. Why woman I dare.
Eli. Do then I warrant thee.　　　215
Mar. Ile warrant my selfe if I list, but come let it alone, let vs to
Irus for our fortunes.
Eli. God saue graue *Irus.*
Irus.　　　　　　　Welcome beautious Nymphes.
Sam. How know you *Irus* we are beautifull and cannot see.
Irus. Homer was blinde yet could he best discerne,　　　220
The shapes of euery thing and so may I.
Eli. Indeede wee heare your skill can beautifie
Beautie it selfe, and teach dames how to decke,
Their heades and bodies fittest to their formes,
To their complexions and their countenances.　　　225
Irus. So can I beauteous Nimphes, and make all eyes
Sparkle with loue fire from your excellence.
Eli. How thinke you we are tyred to tempte mens lookes,

190 morrall,] ∼∧ | hart.] ∼, ‖ **192** a bone] *Parrott (Brereton conj.*); alone ‖ **193** I,] ∼∧ | yet.] ∼, ‖ **195** is.] ∼∧ ‖ **196-99** Ile . . . Idle.] *Parrott;* Ile . . . others, / Do . . . mayde, / Get . . . Idle. Q (when . . . and . . . fall) ‖ **198** me,] ∼∧ | hence;] ∼∧ ‖ **199** needle; what,] ∼: ∼∧ ‖ **200** Idle,] ∼∧ ‖ **202** Then] then | it,] ∼∧ ‖ **202-5** Then . . . doore,] *Shepherd;* then . . . naught. / For . . . talking, / With . . . doore, Q (as) ‖ **203** say] *Shepherd* ‖ **204** maide,] ∼∧ ‖ **206** That] *Shepherd;* Sayde that, ‖ **211** it.] ∼, ‖ **216** let vs] Let ∼ ‖ **221** I.] ∼, ‖ **222** beautifie] ∼, ‖ **226** beauteous] beateuous | eyes] ∼, ‖

Beeing thus Nimphlike is it not too strange.

   Irus. It is the better so, it doth become.   230

But that I may disclose to you your fortunes,

Tell me first *Pego* their true faces formes.

   Pego. Mary sir, this that speakes to you has a face thinne like vnto

water grewell, but yet it would do your hart good if you could see it.

   Irus. I know and see it better then thy selfe,   235

The blaze whereof doth turne me to a fyre,

Burning mine Intrailes with a strong desire.

   Eli. Why turnst thou from vs *Irus,* tell my fortune.

   Irus. I wonder at the glorie it presentes

To my soules health that sees vppon your heade,   240

A corronet, and at your gratious feete,

Nobles and princes in their highest state,

Which state shal crowne your fortune eare you die,

And eare the hart of Heauen, the glorious sunne,

Shall quench his rosiat fires within the west, /   245

You shall a husband haue noble and rich.   [B1ᵛ]

   Sam. Happie *Elimine,* oh that I myght too.

   Eli. Thankes for this newes good *Irus,* but disclose

The meanes to this, if it be possible.

   Irus. When you come home ascend your Fathers tower,   250

If you see a man come walking by,

And looking vp to you,

Descend and Issue, for you shall haue leaue,

And if he woe, you chuse him from the world;

Though he seeme humorous and want an eye,   255

Wearing a veluet patch vpon the same,

Chuse him your husband, and be blest in him.

   Eli. Ile doe as thou aduisest gentle *Irus,*

And prouing this Ile loue thee whilst I liue.

   Sam. My fortune now sweete *Irus.*   260

   Irus. What face hath this Nimph, *Pego.*

   Pego. Mary sir, a face made in forme like the ace of hartes.

   Irus. And well compard for she commaundes all hartes,

Equall in beautie with that other Nimph,

And equally she burnes my hart with loue.   265

   Sam. Say, say sweete *Irus* what my fortune is,

Thou turnst from me, as when thou didest admire,

The happie fortune of *Elimine.*

229 strange.] ∼, ‖ **230** so,] ∼∧ ‖ **231** fortunes,] ∼∧ ‖ **233** sir,] ∼∧ ‖ **234** it.] ∼∧ ‖ **236** fyre,]
∼. ‖ **238** *Irus,*] ∼∧ ‖ **239** presentes] ∼, ‖ **245** west,] ∼. ‖ **248** *Irus,*] ∼∧ | disclose] ∼, ‖ **250**
tower,] ∼∧ ‖ **252-53** And . . . leaue,] *Parrott*; And . . . descend, / And . . . leaue ‖ **254** world;]
∼, ‖ **257** him.] ∼, ‖ **261** Nimph,] ∼∧ ‖ **262** sir,] ∼∧ ‖ **265** loue.] ∼, ‖

Irus. So might I well, admiring yours no lesse.
Then when the light cround monarch of the heauens   270
Shal quench his fire within the Oceans brest,
Rise you and to your fathers garden hie,
There in an arbour doe a banquet set,
And if there come a man that of him selfe
Sits downe and bids you welcome to your feast,   275
Accept him for he is the richest man,
That *Alexandria* or *AEgypt* hath,
And soone possessing him with all his wealth,
In little tyme you shall be rid of him,
Making your seconde choyse mongst mightie kinges.   280
    Sam. Blest be thy lippes sweet *Irus,* and that light,
That guides thy bosome with such deepe fore sight, /
Sleepe shall not make a closet for these eyes,   [B2]
All this succeeding night for hast to rise.
    Mar. My fortune now sweete *Irus,* but I fayth,   285
I haue some wrong to be the last of all,
For I am olde as they, and big enough
To beare as great a fortune as the best of them.
    Irus. What face hath this Nimph, *Pego.*
    Pego. Oh maister what face hath she not, if I should beg a face I   290
would haue her face.
    Irus. But it is round, and hath it neare a blemmish,
A mouth to wide, a looke too impudent.
    Pego. Oh mayster tis without all these, and without al crie.
    Irus. Round faces and thinne skinde are hapieest still.   295
And vnto you fayre Nimph,
Shall fortune be exceeding gratious too.
When the next morning therefore you shal rise,
Put in your bosome rosemary time and rue,
And presently stand at your fathers doore.   300
He that shall come offering kindenesse there,
And craue for fauour those same holsome hearbes,
Bestowe them on him; and if meeting him,
He keepe the nuptiall Rosemary and time,
And tread the bitter rue beneath his feete,   305
Chuse him your husband and be blest in him.
    Mar. I wil sweete *Irus,* nothing greeues me now,
But that *Elimine* this nyght shall haue,
Her happie husband, and I stay till morning.
    Eli. Nought greeues me *Irus* but that we are maides   310
Kept short of all thinges and haue nought to giue thee,

271 brest,] ∼∧ ‖ 274 selfe] ∼, ‖ 276 richest] rihcest ‖ 287 enough] ∼, ‖ 288 them.] ∼, ‖
289 Nimph,] ∼∧ ‖ 292 round] ronnd ‖ 293 wide,] ∼∧ ‖ 296 Nimph,] ∼. ‖ 297 too.] ∼, ‖
298 rise,] ∼. ‖ 299 rue,] ∼. ‖ 300 doore.] ∼, ‖ 303 Bestowe] bestowe | him;] ∼, ‖ 307 *Irus,*]
∼∧ ‖ 310 maides] ∼. ‖

20

But take our loues and in the wished proofe,
Of these high fortunes thou foretellest vs,
Nothing we haue shall bee to deare for thee.
    Sam. We that are sisters *Irus* by our vow,   315
Will be of one selfe blood and thankefull minde,
To adore so cleare a sight in one so blinde.   *Exeunt the maids.*
    Irus. Farewell most beautious Nimphes your loues to mee
Shall more then gold or any treasure bee,
Now to my wardroppe for my veluet gowne,   320
Now doth the sport beginne. /
Come gird this pistole closely to my side,   [B2ᵛ]
By which I make men feare my humor still,
And haue slayne two or three as twere my mood
When I haue done it most aduisedly   325
To rid them as they were my heauie foes;
Now am I knowne to be the mad braine *Count,*
Whose humours twise fiue summers I haue held,
And sayde at first I came from stately *Rome,*
Calling my selfe *Count Hermes* and assuming   330
The humour of a wild and franticke man,
Carelesse of what I say or what I doe;
And so such faultes as I of purpose doe,
Is buried in my humor; and this gowne I weare,
In rayne or snowe or in the hottest sommer,   335
And neuer goe nor ride without a gowne,
Which humor doth not fit my frencie wel,
But hides my persons forme from beeing knowne,
When I *Cleanthes* am to be discried.

            Enter Pego *like a Burgomaister.*
    Pego. How now maister brother.   340
    Irus. Oh sir you are very well suted.
Now Maister Burgomaister, I pray you remember
To seaze on all *Antistenes* his goods,
His landes and cattels to my propper vse,
As I am *Leon* the rich vsurer,   345
The sunne is downe and all is forfeited.
    Pego. It shalbe doone my noble *Count.*
    Irus. And withal sir I pray you forget not your loue,
To morrow morning at her fathers doore.
    Pego. Ah my good *Count* I cannot that forget,   350
For still to keepe my memorie in order,
As I am Burgomaister, so loue is my Recorder.   *Exeunt.*

313 vs,] ∼. ‖ 315 We] we ‖ 317 SD *Exeunt the maids.] Parrott; Exeunt.* ‖ 318 Farewell] farewell |
mee] ∼. ‖ 320-21 Now . . . beginne.] *Parrott;* one line (now) ‖ 326 foes;] ∼, ‖ 328 twise] ∼, ‖
332 doe;] ∼, ‖ 334 humor;] *Parrott;* ∼ʌ ‖ 337 Which] which ‖ 339 discried.] ∼, ‖ 341-43 Oh . . .
goods,] *Shepherd; as prose* (to) ‖ 342 Maister] M. | Burgomaister,] ∼. ‖ 343 *Antistenes*] *Aleantisthenes*
| goods,] ∼ʌ ‖ 345 vsurer,] ∼. ‖ 352 Recorder] recorder ‖

[SCENE II]

Enter Elimine *aboue on the walles.*

[*Eli.*] Now see a morning in an euening rise.
The morning of my loue and of my ioy,
I will not say of beautie, that were pride;
With in this tower I would I had a torch,
To light like Hero my Leander heather.   5
Who shall be my Leander, let me see, /
Reherse my fortune.   [B3]
When you see one clad in a veluet gowne
And a blacke patch vpon his eye, a patch,
Patch that I am, why that may be a patch   10
Of cloth, of Buckrome, or a fustian cloth,
Say with a veluet patch, vpon his eye,
And so my thoughts may patch vp loue the better.
See where he comes, the *Count*, what girle a countesse?

Enter Count.

See, see, he lookes as *Irus* said he should.   15
Go not away my loue, Ile meete thee straight.   [*Exit.*]
   Count. Oh I thanke you, I am much beholding to you,
I sawe her in the tower and now she is come downe,
Lucke to this patch and to this veluet gowne.

Enter Elimine *and* Bragadino *A Spaniard following her.*

How now shall I be troubled with this rude Spaniard now.   20
   Brag. One worde sweet nimph.
   Count. How now sirra, what are you.
   Brag. I am signeor *Braggadino* the Martiall Spaniardo, the aide of
AEgypt in her present wars, but Iesu what art thou that hast the guts
of thy braines gript with such famine of knowledge not to know me.   25
   Count. How now sir, Ile trie the proofe of your guts with my pistoll
if you be so saucie sir.
   Brag. [*Aside.*] Oh I know him well; it is the rude *Count*, the vnciuill
Count, the vnstayed *Count*, the bloody *Count*, the *Count* of all
Countes; better I were to hazard the dissolution of my braue soule   30
agaynst an host of giantes then with this loose *Count*, otherwise I
could tickle the *Count*. I fayth my noble *Count*, I doe descend to the
crauing of pardon; loue blinded me I knewe thee not.
   Count. Oh sir you are but bonaventure not right Spanish I perceaue; but doe you heare sir, are you in loue.   35

Scene II] *Parrott* ‖ **1** *Eli.*] *Parrott* ‖ **3** pride;] ∼, ‖ **5** Hero] hero | Leander] leander | heather.]
∼, ‖ **6** Leander,] leander∧ ‖ **9-13** And ... better.] *Shepherd;* And ... eye, / A ... cloth, / Of
... patch / Vpon ... better *Q* (A ... patch ... of ... say) ‖ **14** countesse?] ∼, ‖ **15-16** See
... straight.] *Shepherd; as prose* (go) ‖ **15** should.] ∼∧ ‖ **16** SD *Exit.*] *Parrott* ‖ **17** to you,] ∼ ∼∧ ‖
20 *Q repeats stage-heading* "*Count*" | Spaniard now.] spaniard ∼, ‖ **22** sirra,] ∼∧ | you.] ∼, ‖ **23**
Spaniardo,] spaniardo∧ ‖ **26** sir,] ∼∧ ‖ **28** SD *Aside.*] *Parrott* | well;] ∼∧ ‖ **30** Countes;] ∼, ‖ **32**
Count.] ∼, ‖ **33** pardon;] ∼, ‖ **34** Spanish] spanish | perceaue;] ∼∧ ‖ **35** sir,] ∼∧ ‖

Brag. Surely the sodayne glaunce of this lady Nymph hath suppled my Spanish disposition with loue that neuer before drempt of a womans concauitie.

Count. A womans concauitie, sblood whats that.

Brag. Her hollow disposition which you see sweete nature / will [B3ᵛ] 40 supplye or otherwise stop vp in her with solid or firme fayth.

Count. Giue me thy hand we ar louers both, shall we haue her both.

Brag. No, good sweete *Count,* pardon me.

Count. Why then thus it shalbe; weele strike vp a drumme, set vp a tent, call people together, put crownes a peece, lets rifle for her. 45

Brag. Nor that my honest *Count.*

Count. Why then thus it shalbe, weele wooe her both and him she likes best shall lead her home thorow streetes holding her by both her handes, with his face towardes her, the other shall follow with his backe towards her, biting of his thumbes, how sayest thou by this. 50

Brag. It is ridiculous, but I am pleasd. [*Aside.*] For vpon my life I do know this, the shame will light on the neck of the *Count.*

Count. Well to it, lets heare thee.

Brag. Sweete Nimph, a Spaniard is compard to the great elixar or golden medicine. 55

Count. What dost thou come vpon her with medicines, dost thou thinke she is sore.

Brag. Nay, by thy sweete fauour do not interrupt mee.

Count. Well sir goe forward.

Brag. I say a Spaniard is like the Philosophers stone. 60

Count. And I say an other mans stone may bee as good as a Philosophers at all tymes.

Brag. By thy sweete fauour.

Count. Well sir goe on.

Brag. Sweet nimph I loue few wordes; you know my intent, my 65 humor is in sophistical and plaine, I am Spaniard a borne, my byrth speakes for my nature, my nature for your grace; and should you see a whole Battaile ranged by my skil you would commit your whole selfe to my affection, and so sweet nimph I kisse your hand.

Count. To see a whole battaile, ha ha ha; what a iest is that; thou 70 shalt se a whole battaile come forth presently of me, sa sa sa.

[*Draws his pistol.*]

Brag. Put vp thy pistol, tis a most dangerous humor in thee.

Count. Oh is that all, why see tis vp agayne, now thou shalt / see [B4]
Ile come to her in thy humor; sweete lady I loue sweete wordes, but

37 Spanish] spanish ‖ **39** that.] ∼, ‖ **41** firme] (*See Textual Note*) ‖ **42** both.] ∼∧ ‖ **43** No,] ∼∧ | *Count,*] ∼∧ ‖ **44** shalbe;] ∼∧ ‖ **45** peece,] ∼∧ ‖ **50** her,] ∼∧ ‖ **51** pleasd. For] ∼∧ for | SD *Aside.*] *Parrott* ‖ **52** this,] ∼∧ ‖ **53** it,] ∼∧ ‖ **54** Nimph,] ∼∧ | Spaniard] spaniard | to the] to the to the ‖ **56** medicines,] ∼∧ ‖ **58** Nay,] ∼∧ ‖ **60** Spaniard] spaniard ‖ **65** wordes;] ∼∧ | intent,] ∼∧ ‖ **66** plaine,] ∼∧ | Spaniard] spaniard (*See Textual Note*) ‖ **67** grace;] ∼, ‖ **70** battaile,] ∼∧ | ha;] ∼∧ | that;] ∼, ‖ **71** me,] ∼∧ | SD *Draws his pistol.*] *Parrott* ‖ **72** pistol,] ∼∧ ‖ **73** all,] ∼∧ | shalt see] ∼ lee (*catchword correctly has "see"*) ‖ **74** humor;] ∼, ‖

sweete deedes are the noble sowndes of a noble Spaniard, noble by   75
countrie, noble by valour, noble by byrth, my very foote is nobler then
the head of another man, vppon my life I loue, and vpon my loue I
liue, and so sweete Nimph I kisse your hand; why loe heere we are
both, I am in this hand, and hee is in that: handy dandy prickly
prandy, which hand will you haue.   80

    Eli. This hand my Lord if I may haue my choyce.

    Count. Come Spaniard to your pennance, bite your thumbes.

    Brag. Oh base woman.

    Count. Sblood, no base woman but bite your thumbes quickly.

    Brag. Honor commaundes I must do it.   85

    Count. Come on sweete lady, giue me your handes if you are mine,
I am yours, if you take me now at the worst I am the more beholding
to you, if I bee not good enough, Ile mend what would you more.

    Eli. It is enough my Lord and I am youres,
Since I wel know my fortune is to haue you.   90
Now must I leaue the pleasant maiden chase,
In hunting sauage beasts with *Isis* nimphes,
And take me to a life which I God knowes,
Do know no more then how to scale the heauens.

    Count. Well Ile teach you feare not you, what signior not bite your   95
thumbes.

    Brag. Pardon me sir, pardon me.

    Count. By Gods blood I will not pardon you, therefore bite your
thumbes.

    Brag. By thy sweete, let me speake one worde with thee, I do not   100
like this humor in thee in pistoling men in this sort, it is a most dangerous and stigmaticall humor, for by thy fauour tis the most finest thing
of the world for a man to haue a most gentlemanlike carriage of himselfe, for otherwise I doe hold thee for the most tall resolute and accomplisht gentleman on the face of the earth; harke yee weele meete   105
at *Corrucus* and weele haue a pipe of Tobacco, adew adew.

    Count. Do you heare sir, put your thumbes in your mouth with out
any more adoe, by the heauens Ile shoote thee through the mouth. /

    Brag. It is base and ridiculous.   [B4ᵛ]

    Count. Well thou shalt not do it, lend me thy thumbes Ile bite them   110
for thee.

    Brag. Pardon mee.

    Count. Swounes, and you had I would haue made such a wofull
parting betwixt your fingers and your thumbe that your Spanish fistes
should neuer meete againe, in this world; wil you do it sir.   115

    Brag. I will, I will presto and I wil follow thee.

---

75 Spaniard] spaniard ‖ **78** hand;] ∼, ‖ **79** that:] ∼∧ ‖ **81** choyce.] ∼∧ ‖ **82** Spaniard]
spaniard | pennance,] ∼∧ ‖ **84** Sblood,] ∼∧ ‖ **86** lady,] ∼∧ ‖ **89** youres,] ∼. ‖ **90** you.] ∼∧ ‖
96 thumbes.] ∼, ‖ **98** you,] ∼∧ ‖ **100** sweete,] ∼∧ ‖ **105** earth;] ∼, ‖ **106** Tobacco,] ∼∧ ‖
111 thee.] ∼∧ ‖ **113** Swounes,] ∼∧ ‖ **114** Spanish] spanish ‖ **115** world;] ∼∧ ‖

Count. Why so, oh that we had a noyse of musitions to play to this
anticke as we goe; come on sweete lady giue me your handes, weele to
Church and be married straight, beare with my hast now, Ile be slow
enough another tyme I warrant you, come Spagnolo presto, presto,   120
Spagnolo presto.   *Exeunt.*

[SCENE III]

Enter Aegiale, Herald, Euribates, Clearchus *with a picture.*

AEgi. Aduance that picture on this fatall spring,
And Herald speake, vttering the kinges edict.
    Herald. Ptolomie the most sacred king of *AEgypt* first of that name,
desiring peace and amitie with his neighbour princes hath caused this
picture of *Cleanthes* to be set vp in all places, proposing great rewardes   5
to him that findes him, and threatning death to him that sucours him.
    AEgi. [*Aside.*] Which Gods forbid, and put it in his minde
Not so to stomacke his vniust exile
That he conuert the furie of his arme
Agaynst forsaken *AEgypt,* taking part   10
With those foure neighbour kinges that threaten him,
And haue beseiged his most Imperiall towne.
    Clear. Now may it please your highnesse
To leaue your discontented passions,
And take this mornings pride to hunt the Bore.   15
    Ian. We haue attended on your grace thus farre
Out of the Cittie, beeing glad to heare
Your highnesse had abandoned discontent,
And now will bend your selfe to meriment.
    AEgi. So will I louely *Ianthe,* come then,   20
Let vs goe call foorth sacred *Isis* Nimphes,
To helpe vs keepe the game in ceaslesse vew,
That to the busie brightnesse of his eyes,
We may so interuent his shiftes to scape, /
That giddie with his turning he may fall,   [C1] 25
Slayne with our beauties more then swordes or dartes.
            Exit AEgiale *with attendants with a sownd of Horns.*

Enter Leon *with his sworde.*

    Leon. Now am I *Leon* the rich vsurer
And here according to the kinges commaund
And mine owne promise, I haue brought my swoord

117 so,] ∼∧ ‖ 118 goe;] ∼, | handes,] ∼∧ ‖ 120-21 Spagnolo . . . presto.] *Parrott*; spaniola
questo, questo, spaniola questo. ‖ Scene III] *Parrott* ‖ 2 speake,] ∼∧ ‖ 7 SD *Aside.*] *Parrott* |
minde] ∼. ‖ 8 exile] ∼. ‖ 9 arme] ∼, ‖ 10 *AEgypt,*] ∼∧ | part] ∼, ‖ 13-15 Now . . . Bore.]
Parrott; as prose (to . . . and) ‖ 16 your] *Shepherd;* our | farre] ∼, ‖ 17 Cittie,] ∼∧ | heare] ∼,
‖ 18 discontent,] ∼. ‖ 19 meriment.] ∼, ‖ 20 *Ianthe,*] ∼∧ | then,] ∼. ‖ 22 ceaslesse] *Shepherd;*
cealesse ‖ 23 eyes,] ∼. ‖ 24 scape,] ∼. ‖ 26 SD AEgiale *with attendants*] *Parrott* ‖ 27-31 Now
. . . *Cleanthes,*] *Shepherd;* Now . . . according / To . . . promise. / I . . . statue, / She . . . *Cleanthes,*
Q (The . . . and . . . and . . . and . . . By) ‖ 29 promise,] ∼. ‖

And fix it by the statue she set vp,   30
By this am I knowne to be *Cleanthes,*
Whose sodayne sight I now will take vpon mee,
And cause the nobles to pursue my shadowe;
As for my substance they shall neuer finde,
Till I my selfe, do bring my selfe to light.   35
Cleanthes, Cleanthes, stop *Cleanthes,* see *Cleanthes,*
Pursue *Cleanthes,* follow *Cleanthes.*

          Enter three Lordes *with swordes drawne.*

  1 Lord. Where is *Cleanthes, Leon* sawest thou him.
  Leon. I why should I els haue thus cried out on him,
I saw him euen now, heere did he fix his sworde   40
And not for dastard feare or cowardize,
For know all *AEgypt* ringes of his renowne,
But fearing for his noble seruice done,
To be rewarded with ingratitude,
He fled from hence fearing to be pursued.   45
  2 Lord. Come on my Lordes then lets follow him and pursue him to
the death.   *Exeunt the* Lords.
  Leon. Oh do not hurt him gentle Citizens,
See how they flye from him whom they pursue.
I am *Cleanthes,* and whilest I am heare,   50
In vayne they follow for to finde him out.
But here comes my loue Bright *Psamathis,*
Whom I loue Equally with fayre *Elimine,*
See here she comes as I apoynted her.

          Enter Samathis *and her maydes with a banquet.*

  Iaq. But I fayth mistris, is this for a woer.   55
  Sam. Not for a woer onely my *Iaquine,* /
But a quicke speeder girle for this is he,   [C1ᵛ]
That all my fortune runnes vpon I tell thee.
  Iaq. O daintie mistris send for some more banquet.
  Sam. No my fine wench, this and my selfe is well.   60
And let him not sit downe like the oxe and the asse,
But giue God thanks for we are worthie of it
Though we saite.
  Iaq. Mistris tis true. And that he may be good,
I coniure him by these three things a crosse,   65
Now let him come he shalbe good I warrant ye.
  Leon. [*advancing*] Nay do not flye me gentle *Samathis.*

---

30 statue] ∼, ‖ 33 shadowe;] ∼, ‖ 40 now,] ∼∧ ‖ 42 renowne,] ∼. ‖ 44-45 To . . . pursued]
Shepherd; To . . . fled / From . . . pursued, Q (he) ‖ 45 pursued.] ∼, ‖ 47 SD *the* Lords.] *Parrott*
‖ 51 out.] ∼, ‖ 55 mistris,] ∼∧ ‖ 58 thee.] ∼, ‖ 60 wench,] ∼∧ ‖ 62-63 But . . . saite.] *one
line* (though) ‖ 64 Mistris . . . good,] *Shepherd*; Mistris . . . true. / And . . . good, ‖ 66 ye.] ∼,
‖ 67 SD *advancing*] *Parrott* ‖

Sam. Pardon me sir, for if I see a man,
I shall so blush still that I warrant you,
I could make white wine claret with my lookes.   70
   Leon. But do not blush and flie an old mans sight.
   Sam. From whom if not from old men should I flie.
   Leon. From young men rather that can swift pursue,
And then it is some credit to out goe them,
Yet though my yeeres would haue me old I am not,   75
But haue the gentle Ierke of youth in mee,
As fresh as he that hath a maidens chinne.
Thus can I bend the stiffnes of my limbes,
Thus can I turne and leape and hoyse my gate,
Thus can I lift my loue as light as ayre,   80
Now say my *Samathis* am I old or young.
   Sam. I would haue my loue neyther old nor young
But in the middle, Iust betweene them both.
   Leon. Fit am I then for matchlesse *Samathis.*
And will be bould to sit. For batchlers   85
Must not be shamefast when they meet with maids,
Sweete loue now let me intreate you sit,
And welcome you to your owne banquet heere.
   Sam. [*Aside.*] Euen thus did *Irus* say that he should say.
Then by your leaue sir I will sit with you.   90
   Leon. Welcome as gold into my tresurie,
And now will I drinke vnto my loue,
With the same mind that drinking first began
To one another. /
   Sam. And what was that I pray sir.   [C2] 95
   Leon. Ile tell my loue the first kind cause of it,
And why tis vsd as kindnesse still amongst vs,
If it be vsd a right tis to this end,
When I doe say I drinke this loue to you,
I meane I drinke this to your proper good,   100
As if I sayde what health this wine doth worke in mee,
Shalbe imploied for you at your commande
And to your proper vse,
And this was first th'entent of drinking to you.
   Sam. Tis very prettie is it not *Iaquine.*   105
   Iaq. Oh excellent Mistris hees a daintie man.
   Leon. Now to your vse sweete loue I drinke this wine,
And with a merrie hart that makes long life,
Ouer the cup Ile sing for my loues sake.

---

68 sir,] ∼∧ ‖ **70** lookes.] ∼, ‖ **72** flie.] ∼∧ ‖ **83** middle,] ∼∧ ‖ **88** heere.] ∼, ‖ **89** SD *Aside.*]
Parrott | say.] ∼, ‖ **90** you.] ∼, ‖ **93-94** With . . . another.] *Parrott; one line* (to) ‖ **96** it,] ∼. ‖
102-3 Shalbe . . . vse,] *Parrott; one line* (&) ‖ **103** vse,] ∼∧ ‖ **104** th'entent] thentent ‖

Song.

Health, fortune, mirth, and wine,   110
   To thee my loue deuine.
I drinke to my dareling,
   Giue mee thy hand sweeting.
With cuppe full euer plyed,
   And hartes full neuer dryed.   115
Mine owne, mine owne dearest sweeting,
   Oh, oh, myne owne dearest sweeting.

What frollicke, loue; mirth makes the banquet sweete.
  Sam. I loue it sir aswell as you loue me.
  Leon. That is aswell as I do loue my selfe,   120
I will not Ioy my treasure but in thee,
And in thy lookes Ile count it euery hower,
And thy white armes shalbe as bandes to me,
Wherein are mightie Lordshippes forfeited,
And all the dames of *Alexandria,*   125
For their attire shall take there light from thee.
  Sam. Wel sir I drinke to you and pray you thinke
You are as welcome to me as this wine.
  Leon. Thankes gentle *Samathis,* but delitious loue,
Hath beene the figge I eate before this wine, /   130
Which kills the taste of these delitious cates,   [C2ᵛ]
Will you bestowe that banquet loue, on me.
  Sam. Nay gentle *Leon,* talke no more of loue
If you loue God or a good countenance,
For I shal quite be out of countenance then.   135
  Leon. Loue deckes the countenance, speriteth the eye,
And tunes the soule in sweetest harmony,
Loue then sweete *Samathis.*
  Sam. What shall I doe *Iaquine.*
  Iaq. Fayth Mistris take him.   140
  Sam. Oh but he hath a great nose.
  Iaq. Tis no matter for his nose, for he is rich.
  Sam. *Leon* I loue, and since tis foorth, farewell.
  Leon. Then triumph *Leon* richer in thy loue
Then all the heapes of treasure I possesse,   145
Neuer was happie *Leon* rich before,
Nor euer was I couetous till now,
That I see gold so fined in thy haire.
  Sam. Impart it to my Parentes gentle *Leon,*
And till we meete agayne at home farewell.   *Exeunt* Samathis *and maids.*

---

117 *Oh, oh,*] ∼∧ ∼∧ ‖ 118 frollicke, loue;] ∼∧ ∼∧ ‖ 126 thee.] ∼, ‖ 128 wine.] ∼, ‖ 132 loue,] ∼∧ | me.] ∼, ‖ 133 *Leon,*] ∼∧ ‖ 135 then.] ∼, ‖ 143 loue,] ∼∧ | foorth,] ∼∧ ‖ 144 loue] ∼. ‖ 150 SD Samathis *and maids.*] *Parrott* ‖

Leon. Soone will I talke with them and follow thee,
So now is my desire accomplished.
Now was there euer man so fortunate.
To haue his loue so sorted to his wish,
The ioyes of many I in one enioy.   155
Now do I meane to woe them crossely both,
The one as I am *Leon* the rich vsurer,
The other as I am the mad brayne *Count.*
Which if it take effect, and rightly proue,
Twill be a sporte for any emperours loue.   *Exit.*

[SCENE IV]

Enter Ptolomie, Aegiale, Doricles, Aspatia, Ianthe,
Euphrosine, Clearchus, Euribates, *with sound.*

Pto. Prince of *Arcadia* louely *Doricles,*
Be not discouraged that my daughter heere,
Like a well fortified and loftie tower,
Is so repulsiue and vnapt to yeelde; /
The royall siege of your heroycke partes,   [C3] 5
In her acheeuement will be more renound,
And with the greater merite is imployde.
The bewtious queene my wife her mother here
Was so well mand and yet had neuer man,
So mayne a rocke of chast and cold disdayne.   10
AEgi. My Lord what meane ye; go *Aspasia,*
Send for some Ladies to goe play with you,
At chesse, at Billiardes, and at other game,
Ianthe attend her.   [*Exit* Aspasia *and* Ianthe.]
You take a course my Lord to make her coy,   15
To vrge so much the loue of *Doricles,*
And frame a vertue of her wanton hate,
We must perswade her that he loues her not,
But that his seruices and vowes of loue,
Are but the gentle complimentes of court,   20
So would shee thinke that if she would haue lou'd,
Shee might haue wonne him. And with that conceite
Of hardnesse to be wonne, his merites grace
Will shine more clearely, in her turning eyes,
Thinges hard to win with, ease makes loue incited,   25
And fauours wonne with ease are hardly quited,
Then make as If you lou'd her not my Lord.

---

157 vsurer,] ∼. ‖ Scene IV] *Parrott* ‖ **4** yeelde;] ∼, ‖ **6** renound,] ∼. ‖ **11** ye;] ∼, ‖ **12** Ladies]
Ladeis ‖ **14** SD *Exit* . . . Ianthe.] ‖ **21** lou'd] loud ‖ **22-24** Shee . . . eyes,] *Parrott;* Shee . . .
him. / And . . . wonne / His . . . clearely, / In . . . eyes, Q (of . . . will) ‖ **27** lou'd] loud ‖

Dor. Loue that hath built his temple on my browes
Out of his Battlementes into my hart,
And seeing me to burne in my desire,   30
Will be I hope appeased at the last.
   AEgi. Be ruld by me yet, and I warrant you,
She quickly shall beleeue you loue her not.
   Dor. What shall I doe Madam.
   AEgi.   Looke not on her so much.
   Dor. I cannot chuse, my neck standes neuer right,   35
Till it be turnd asside and I behold her.
   AEgi. Now trust me such a wrie neckt loue was neuer sene,
But come with me my Lord and Ile instruct you better.
   Pto. So maddam I leaue you; now from our loue sportes, /
To *Antistenes* and his great sute with *Leon.*   [C3ᵛ] 40

          Enter Antistenes, Leon *and* Burgomaister.
See the *Burgomaister, Antistenes* and *Leon* comes togeather; stay
maister *Burgomaister.* What reason made you vse your office on the
Lord *Antistenes,* seazing on al his moueables, and goodes at the sute
of *Leon.*
   Pego. I will tell your grace the reason of it or any thinge els, for I   45
know you are a wise prince, and apt to learne.
   Pto. I thanke you for your good opinion sir, but the reason of your
office done vpon this noble man and his landes.
   Pego. The reason why I haue put in office or execution, my authori-
tie vpon this nobleman consisteth in three principall poyntes or mem-   50
bers, which indeede are three goodly matters.
   Pto. I pray you lets heare them.
   Pego. The first is the credit of this honest man because he is rich.
   Pto. Why is he honest because he is rich.
   Pego. Oh I learne that in any case, the next is the forfaite of his   55
assurance and the last I will not trouble your grace with all.
   Antis. But this it is whereof I most complaine vnto your grace,
That hauing occasion in your graces seruice,
To borow mony of this *Leon* heere,
For which I morgagd al my landes and goods   60
He onely did agree that paying him foure
Thousand pound at the day I should receiue my statute
Safely, in which now not onely falsely he denies.
But that he hath receiued one penny due,
Which this my friend can wittnes I repayde,   65
Vpon the stone of *Irus* the blinde man,
Foure thousand pound in Iewels and in golde,
And therefore craue I iustice in this case.

---

33 not.] ∼, ‖ **35** chuse,] ∼∧ ‖ **38** better.] ∼∧ ‖ **39** you;] ∼∧ ‖ **40** *Leon.*] ∼, ‖ **41-44** See . . .
Leon.] *Shepherd;* See . . . *Leon.* / Comes . . . *Burgomaister* /. What . . . the / Lord . . . moueables,
/ And . . . *Leon.* ‖ **41** *Burgomaister,*] ∼∧ | *Leon*] ∼. | togeather;] ∼∧ ‖ **43** *Antistenes,*] ∼∧ ‖
45 els,] ∼∧ ‖ **50** consisteth] ∼, ‖ **57-63** But . . . denies *(See Textual Note)* ‖ **62** Thousand]
thousand ‖ **63** Safely] safely ‖ **68** case.] ∼, ‖

Leon. Voutchsafe dread soueraigne an vnpartiall eare
To that I haue to say for my replye,   70
He pleades the payment of foure thousand pounde, /
Vpon the stone before blinde *Irus* caue.   [C4]
To which I answere and do sweare by heauen,
He spake with me at the foresayde place,
And promist payment of foure thousand pound,   75
If I would let him haue his statutes in,
And take other assurance for another thousand,
Some three monthes to come or thereaboutes.
Which I refusing he repayde me none,
But parted in a rage and card not for me.   80
    [*Eur.*] Oh monstrous who euer hard the like.
My Lord I will be sworne he payde him,
On poore *Irus* stone foure thousand pound,
Which I did helpe to tender; and hast thou
A hellish conscience   85
And such a brasen forhead, to denye it
Agaynst my wittnesse, and his noble woorde.
    Leon. Sir agaynst your witnesse and his noble worde,
I plead myne owne and one as good as his,
That then was present at our whole conference.   90
    Antis. My Lord there was not any but our selues,
But who was it that thou affirmst was there.
    Leon. Count Hermes good my Lord a man well known
Though he be humorous to be honorable.
    Pto. And will he saie it.   95
    Leon. He will my gratious Lord I am well assurd,
And him will I send hether presently,
Intreating your gratious fauour if the impediment,
Of a late sickenesse cause me not returne,
For I am passing ill.   100
    Pto. Well send him hether and it shall suffice.
    Leon. I will my gratious Lord and stand
To any censure passing willingly,
Your highnesse shall set downe or commaund
Worshipfull maister *Burgomaister* your officer,   105
To see performed betwixt vs.   *Exit.*
    Pego. We Thanke you hartely, alas poore soule,
How sicke he is. /
Truly I cannot chuse but pittie him,   [C4ᵛ]
In that he loues your gratious officers.   110

---

69 eare] ∼. ‖ **72** caue.] ∼, ‖ **75** pound,] ∼. ‖ **81** *Eur.*] *Parrott; Gen. (See Textual Note)* | like.] ∼, ‖ **84** tender;] ∼ʌ ‖ **85-87** A . . . woorde.] *Parrott;* A . . . forhead. / To . . . wittnesse, / And . . . woorde. Q (and . . . against) ‖ **86** forhead,] ∼. ‖ **92** there.] ∼, ‖ **93-94** *Count . . . honorable.] Shepherd; Count . . .* man / Well . . . honorable, Q (though) ‖ **104** commaund] ∼, ‖ **110** officers.] ∼, |

Enter Count.

Pto. Oh I thanke you sir.

Count. King by your leaue, and yet I neede not aske leaue, because
I am sent for; if not Ile begone agayne without leaue, say am I sent for
yea or no.

Pto. You are to witnesse twixt *Antistenes* and welthy *Leon.*   115

Count. I know the matter and I come from that old miser *Leon,*
who is sodainely fallen sicke of a knaues euill. Which of you are troubled with that disease maisters.

Pto. Wel say what you know of the matter betwixt them.

Count. Then thus I say; my Lord *Antistenes* came to the stone of   120
the blinde foole *Irus,* that day when foure thousand pounds were to be
payde, where he made proffer of so much mony if *Leon* would returne
the morgage of his lands, and take assurance for another thousand to
be paide I trow some three monthes to come or there about, which
Leon like an olde churle as he was most vncourteously refused: my   125
Lord *Antistenes* as he might very well departed in a rage, but if it had
beene to me I would haue pistoled him I fayth.

Antis. But you are wonderously deceiued my Lord,
And was not by when he and we did talke.

Count. Swounes then I say you are deceiued my Lord, for I was by;   130
now by my honor and by all the gods.

Eur. Then you stoode close my Lord vnseene to any.

Count. Why I stood close to you and seene of all, and if you thinke
I am too mad a fellow to witnes such a waightie peece of worke, the
holy begger shall performe as much, for he was by at our whole   135
conference.

Pto. But say *Count Hermes,* was the begger by.

Count. I say he was and he shall say he was.

Eur. But he is now they say lockt in his caue,
Fasting and praying, talking with the Gods,   140
And hath an Iron doore twixt him and you,
How will you then come at him. /

Count. Ile fetch him from his caue in spight of all his Gods and   [D1]
Iron dores, or beate him blinde when as I doe catch him next; far-
well my Lordes you haue done with mee, Ile send the begger presently   145
for I am now ryding to *Corrucus.*   *Exit.*

Pto. I know not what to thinke in these affaires.
I cannot well condemne you my Lord,
And your sufficient witnesse beeing a gentleman,

SD Count.] Coont. ‖ **113** for;] ∼∧ | agayne] ∼. ‖ **114** no.] ∼, ‖ **117** euill.] ∼, ‖ **119** matter⌋
∼, ‖ **120** say;] ∼∧ | Lord] ∼, | came] ∼, ‖ **122** where] Where ‖ **124** I trow] *Q(c);* om. *Q(u)*
‖ **126** rage,] ∼∧ ‖ **128** Lord,] ∼. ‖ **130** for] For | by;] ∼∧ ‖ **132** any.] ∼, ‖ **133-36** Why . . .
conference.] (*See Textual Note*) ‖ **133** if you] ∼ You ‖ **134** worke,] ∼∧ ‖ **137** *Hermes,*] ∼∧ ‖
140 praying,] ∼∧ ‖ **142** him.] ∼, ‖ **144** next;] ∼, ‖ **147** affaires.] ∼∧ ‖

Nor yet the other two, both men of credit,   150
Though in his kinde this *Count* be humorous,
But stay we shall here straight what *Irus* wil depose.

                           Enter Irus.

   Irus. Oh who disturbes me in my holy prayers,
Oh that the king were by that he might heere,
What thundring there is at my farther doore,   155
Oh how the good of *AEgipt* is disturbd
In my deuotion.
   Pto. I am here *Irus* and it was *Count Hermes,*
That was so rude to Interrupt thy prayers,
But I suppose the end of thy repayre,   160
Beeing so waightie could not haue displeasd,
For on thy witnesse doth depend the liuing
Of Lord *Antistenes,* who doth affirme,
That three dayes past he tendered at thy stone
Foure thousand poundes to *Leon,* and desired   165
His morgage quited, which he promising
On such assurance, more as he proposed,
Receiued at that tyme his foure thousand pounds.
   Irus. I then was in the hearing of them both,
But hard noe penny tendred, onely proposed   170
By Lord *Antistenes,* if he would bring him in
His morgage and take assurance for another thousand
Some three monthes to come or there aboutes,
Which *Leon* most vncourteously refused.
My Lord was angrye and I hard no more,   175
And thus must I craue pardon of your grace.   *Exit.*
   Pto. Farewell graue *Irus.*
   Antis. Gods are become oppressors of the right.
   [*Eur.*] Neuer had right so violent a wrong. /
For let the thunder strike me into hell,   [D1ᵛ] 180
If what I haue reported be not true.
   Pto. This holy man no doubt speakes what he hard
And I am sory for *Antistenes.*
But Ile releeue your lowe estate my Lord,
And for your seruice done me gwerdon you.   185
Maister *Burgomaister* let the Lord haue libertie,
And I will answere *Leon* what is due.   *Exeunt.*

152 depose.] ∼, ‖ **156-57** Oh . . . deuotion.] *Parrott; one line* (in) ‖ **158** *Hermes,*] ∼. ‖ **164** stone] ∼, ‖ **166** quited,] ∼∧ ‖ **169** both,] ∼. ‖ **171** *Antistenes,*] ∼,, | in] ∼, ‖ **174** refused.] ∼, ‖ **179** *Eur.*] *Parrott; Euge.* (*See Textual Note*) ‖ **180** hell,] ∼. ‖ **181** true.] ∼, ‖ **185** you.] ∼, ‖

33

[SCENE V]

Enter Elimine, Martia, Samathis.

Eli. Soft Mistris *Burgomaister,* pray you stay,
Your hart is greater then your parson farre
Or your state eyther, doe we not know ye trow,
What woman you are but a Burgomaisters wife,
And he no wiser then his neighbours neyther.   5
Giue me the place acording to my calling.
 Mar. What skill for places, do we not all call sisters.
 Eli. Noe by my fayth, I am a countesse now,
I should haue one to goe before me bare,
And say stand by there to the best of them,   10
And one to come behinde and beare my trayne,
Because my handes must not be put vnto it.
My husband is a Lord and past a Lord.
 Sam. And past a Lord, what is that past I pray.
 Eli. Why hees a what you cal't.   15
 Mar. A what you call it, can you not name it.
 Eli. I thinke I must not name it.
 Sam. And why so I pray.
 Eli. Because it comes so neare a thing that I knowe.
 Mar. Oh he is a Count, that is an Earle.   20
 Sam. And yet he is not knowne to haue much land.
 Eli. Why therefore he is an vnknowne man.
 Mar. I but my husband is the kings officer.
 Sam. I but my husband is able to buy both yours.
 Eli. You say husband, I may saie my Lord.   25
 Mar. And me thinkes husband is worth ten of Lord.
 Eli. Indeede I loue my Lord to call mee wife,
Better then Maddam yet doe I not meane
To lose my Ladies titles at your handes, /
I may for courtesie and to be termd   [D2] 30
A gentle Ladie call you sisters still,
But you must say, and please your Ladishippe,
Tis thus and so, and as your honor please,
Yet shall my husband call me wife like youres,
For why made god the husband and the wife,   35
But that those tearmes should please vs more then others.
New fashion tearmes I like not, for a man,
To call his wife cony, forsooth, and Lambe,
And Porke, and Mutton, he as well may say.

Scene V] *Parrott* ‖ **1-4** Soft . . . wife,] *Shepherd; as prose* (your . . . or . . . what) ‖ **5** neyther.]
∼, ‖ **7** sisters.] ∼, ‖ **8** fayth,] ∼∧ ‖ **13** Lord.] ∼, ‖ **14** Lord,] ∼∧ | pray.] ∼, ‖ **15** cal't] calt
‖ **16** it,] ∼∧ ‖ **19** Because] because | knowe.] ∼, ‖ **20** Count,] ∼∧ ‖ **24** yours.] ∼, ‖ **28** meane]
∼, ‖ **29** Ladies] ∼, ‖ **30** termd] ∼, ‖ **32** say,] ∼∧ ‖ **36** others.] ∼∧ ‖ **37** not,] ∼∧ ‖ **39** say.]
∼, ‖

Mar. Well Madam then and please your Ladishippe,   40
What gownes and head tyres will your honor weare.
 Eli. Twentie are making for me head tyres and gownes,
Head tyres enchast in order like the starres,
With perfit great and fine cut pretious stones,
One hath bright *Ariadnes* Crowne in it,   45
Euen in the figure it presentes in heauen,
Another hath the figure of *Diana,*
And *Berenices* euer bruning haire,
An other hath the bright *Andromica,*
With both her siluer wristes bound to a rocke,   50
And *Perseus* that did lose her and saue her life,
All set in number and in perfect forme,
Euen like the *Asterismes* fixt in heauen,
And euen as you may see in Moone shine nightes,
The Moone and Starres reflecting on the streames   55
So from my head shall you see starres take beames.
 Mar. Oh braue, God willing I will haue the like.
 Sam. And so will I by Gods grace if I liue.
 Eli. Come vp to supper, it will become the house wonderfull well.
 Mar. Well if my husband will not, let him not loke for one good   60
looke of me.
 Sam. Nor mine I sweare.
 Mar. Ile aske my husband when I am with child,
And then I know I shall be sped I fayth.
 Eli. But euery pleasure hath a payne they say,   65
My husband lies each other nyght abrode.
 Sam. And so doth mine which I like but little. /
 Mar. Well time I hope and change of companie,   [D2ᵛ]
Will teach vs somewhat to beare out the absence.
          Exit Martia *with* Samathis.
 Eli. I know not what to say, my husband makes   70
As if each other nyght he had occasion,
To ride from home; at home serues not his turne,
To my good turne it, cupid I beseech you.

     Enter Leon *and* Druso *following him.*

 Leon. [*Aside.*] Now will I trie to make my selfe the *Count,*
An arrant Cuckold and a wittoll too.   75
 Dru. [*Aside.*] Now may I chance to proue a cunning man,
And tell my mistris where my maister hauntes.

---

44 With] *Shepherd*; Which ‖ **47** figure] *Parrott*; fingers ‖ **55** the] their ‖ **56** beames.] ∼, ‖ **57** braue,] ∼∧ ‖ **59** supper,] ∼∧ | well.] ∼∧ ‖ **65** say,] ∼∧ ‖ **66** abrode.] ∼, ‖ **67** And] and | little.] ∼, ‖ **69** absence.] ∼, | SD *Exit . . .* Samathis.] *Parrott*; *Exit.* ‖ **70-71** I . . . occasion,] *Parrott*; I . . . say, / My . . . occasion, Q (as) ‖ **72** home;] ∼∧ ‖ **73** you.] ∼, ‖ **74** SD *Aside.*] *Parrott* | Count,] ∼. ‖ **76** SD *Aside.*] *Parrott* ‖ **77** hauntes.] ∼, ‖

Leon. Bright Nimph I come in name of all the worlde,
That now sustaines dead winter in the spring,
To haue a summer from thy graces darted.   80
Thy loue sweete soule is all that I desire,
To make a generall sommer in this hart,
Where winters duble wrath hath tirrannisde.
   Eli. How dare you *Leon* thus solicit mee,
Where if the *Count* my husband should come now,   85
And see you courting, you were sure to die.
   Leon. Oh but he is safe, for at my house,
Booted and spurd, and in his veluet gowne,
He tooke his horse and rode vnto *Corrucus*,
And therefore beautious Ladie make not strange   90
To take a freind and adde vnto thy Ioyes
Of happie wedlocke: the end of euery acte,
Is to increase contentment and renowne,
Both which my loue shall amplye ioy in you.
   Eli. How can renowne ensue an act of shame.   95
   Leon. No acte hath any shame within itselfe,
But in the knowledge and ascription
Of the base world from whom shall this be kept,
As in a laborinth or a brasen tower.
   Eli. But vertues sole regard must hold me backe.   100
   Leon. The vertue of each thing is in the prayse,
And I will reare thy prayses to the skyes, /
Out of my tresurie chuse the choyse of gold,   [D3]
Till thou finde some matching thy hayre in brightnesse,
But that will neuer be, so chuse thou euer.   105
Out of my Iewelrye chuse thy choyse of Diamondes,
Till thou finde some as bright some as thyne eyes,
But that will neuer be, so chuse thou euer.
Chuse Rubies out vntill thou match thy lippes,
Pearle till thy teeth, and Iuorie till thy skinne,   110
Be matcht in whitnesse but that wil neuer bee.
Nor neuer shall my tresurie haue end,
Till on there beauties Ladies loth to spend,
But that will neuer be, so chuse thou euer.
   Eli. Now what a gods name would this vayne man haue,   115
Do you not shame to tempt a woman thus.
[*Aside.*] I know not what to saye nor what to doe,
He would haue me doe that I feare I should not,
Some thing it is he seekes that he thinkes good,
And me thinkes he should be more wise then I,   120
I am a foolish girle though I be married

80 summer . . . graces] *Parrott (Deighton conj.)*; graces . . . summer ‖ 84 *Leon*] Leon ‖ 86 court-
ing,] ∼∧ ‖ 90 strange] ∼, ‖ 91 Ioyes] ∼, ‖ 94 loue] ∼: | you.] ∼, ‖ 95 shame.] ∼, ‖ 97
ascription] ∼. ‖ 105 neuer be,] ∼, ∼∧ ‖ 106 Diamondes,] ∼. ‖ 108 euer.] ∼, ‖ 114 be,]
∼∧ ‖ 116 thus.] ∼, ‖ 117 SD *Aside.*] *Parrott* ‖

And know not what to doe, the Gods doe know.

    Leon. Are you content sweete loue to graunt me loue.

    Eli. And what then sir.

    Leon. To grant me lodging in your house this night.   125

    Eli. I thinke the man be wearie of his life,

Know you the *Count* my husband.

    Leon. Marueilous well and am assurd of him.

    Eli. Faith that you are as sure as I my selfe,

So you did talke of gold and Diamonds.   130

    Leon. I and gold and Diamondes shal my sweet loue haue.

    Eli. Well Ile not bid you sir, but if you come,

At your owne perill for Ile wash my handes.   *Offer to goe out.*

    Leon. A plague of all sanguine simpliciti.

    Eli. But do you heare sir pray you do not thinke   135

That I granted you in any case.   *[Exit* Elimine.]

    Leon. No I warrant you, Ile haue no such thought.

Oh this is olde excellent.

Now who can desire better sporte.

This nyght my other wife must lie alone, /   140

And next night this wife must doe the like.   [D3ᵛ]

Now will I woe the other as the *Count.*

Which if she graunt and they do breake their troth,

Ile make my selfe a cuckolde twixt them both.   *Exit.*

    Dru. Ile follow him vntill he take the earth, and then Ile leaue him.   *Exit.*

Enter Samathis *alone.*

    Sam. Now if my husband be not all alone,

He is from home and hath left me alone,

So I must learne to lie, as children goe,

All alone, all alone, which lesson now

I am able to beare a childe is worsse to me   150

Then when I was a child, the morall this,

Strength without health a disaduantage is.

Enter Druso.

    [*Dru.*] Mistris what will you say if I can tel you where my maister is.

    Sam. Where *Druso* I pray thee.

    Dru. Euen close with the young countesse I fayth.   155

    Sam. Out on her strumpet; doth she bragge so much

Of her great *Count,* and glad to take my husband.

Hence comes her head tyres and her fayre gownes,

Her trayne borne vp and a man bare before her.

Was this my fortune that should be so good,   160

---

123 loue.] ∼, ‖ **124** And] and ‖ **125** night.] ∼, ‖ **128** him.] ∼, ‖ **130** Diamonds.] ∼, ‖ **131** haue.] ∼, ‖ **132** sir,] ∼∧ ‖ **134** simpliciti.] ∼∧ ‖ **135-36** But . . . case.] *one line* (that) ‖ **136** you] ∼. | case.] ∼∧ | SD *Exit* Elimine.] *Parrott subs.* ‖ **145** then Ile] ∼ ile ‖ **149** now] ∼. ‖ **150-52** I . . . is.] *Shepherd; as prose* (then . . . The . . . strength) ‖ **151** child,] ∼∧ | this,] ∼∧ ‖ **152** without] *Shepherd;* ∼ a ‖ **153** Dru.] *Shepherd* | is.] ∼, ‖ **156** strumpet;] ∼∧ | much] ∼, ‖ **157** husband.] ∼∧ ‖ **159** her.] ∼, ‖

37

I fayth you begger you, you old false knaue,
You holy villaine, you propheticke asse,
Know you noe better what shall come to passe,
Ile be reuenged I fayth, I fayth Ile be reuenged.   *Exit with* Druso.

[SCENE VI]

Enter Aegiale *with the garde.*

AEgi. Oh *Irus* shall thy long approued skill,
Fayle in my fortunes onely; when shall I meete,
With my *Cleanthes*; what a worlde of tyme,
Is it for me to lie as in a sounde,
Without my life *Cleanthes*; can it be,   5
That I shall euer entertayne agayne,
Hauing the habit of colde death in me,
My life *Cleanthes.* /

Count *knocke within.*   [D4]

[*Count.*] Let me come in you knaues, I say let me come in.
1 Guard. Sir, we are set to gard this place as our liues, and none   10
without a warrant from the King or the Queene must enter heere.
Count. Swoundes tell not me of your warrantes, let me come in I
say.
1 Guard. My Lord we are commaunded to keepe out all comers,
because of the branch wherein the kings life remaynes.   15
Count. Let me come in you knaues; [*Enter* Count.] how dare you
keepe me out, twas my gowne to a mantle of rugge, I had not put you
all to the pistoll.
AEgi. Shall we be troubled now with this rude *Count.*
Count. How now Queene what art thou doing, passioning ouer the   20
picture of *Cleanthes* I am sure, for I know thou louest him.
AEgi. Whats that you traytor.
Count. No traytor neyther but a true freind to you, for had I bene
otherwise I should haue disclosed the secret talke thou hadst with
Cleanthes in the arbour, the night before he was banished, whilest I   25
stoode close and hard all.
AEgi. The man is mad, chaines and a whippe for him.
Count. Be patient my wench and Ile tell thee the very words: oh
my *Cleanthes*, loue me, pittie me, hate me not; for loue it is and not
lust hath made me thus importunate, for then there are men enough   30
besides *Cleanthes*; go to tel me were not these your woords, and I like
no traytor to you but a trustie freend; now by this pistol which is Gods
angell, I neuer vttered them till now.

162 villaine,] ∼∧ ‖ Scene VI] *Parrott* ‖ SD *with*] *wiuh* ‖ 2 onely;] ∼, ‖ 3 *Cleanthes*;] ∼∧ ‖
5 *Cleanthes*;] ∼, ‖ 9 *Count.*] *Parrott* | in.] ∼, ‖ 10 liues,] ∼∧ | none] None ‖ 15 remaynes.] ∼,
‖ 16 knaues;] ∼, | SD *Enter* Count.] *Parrott subs.* ‖ 19 *Count.*] ∼∧ ‖ 21 sure,] ∼∧ | him.] ∼,
‖ 27 mad,] ∼∧ ‖ 28 words:] ∼, ‖ 29 not;] ∼∧ | loue it] *Parrott*; loue, and it ‖ 31 *Cleanthes*;]
∼, ‖ 32 freend;] ∼∧ ‖ 33 angell,] ∼∧ | now.] ∼∧ ‖

38

AEgi. I spake them not, but had you beene so bad,
As some men are, you might haue saide as much,   35
By fictions onely; therefore I must needes
Thinke much the better of you to conceale it.

 Count. Oh you'r a cunning wench and am not I a mad slaue to
haue such vertue as secresie in me and none neuer lookt for any such
thing at my handes; and heres a branch forsooth of your little sonne   40
turnd to a Mandracke tree, by Hella the sorceresse.

 AEgi. Tis true and kils me to remember it. /

 Count. Tut tut, remember it and be wise; thou wouldst haue   [D4ᵛ]
Cleanthes, come agayne wouldst thou not.

 AEgi. The king is so aduisd to giue him death.   45

 Count. The King, come come tis you rule the King; now would any
wise woman in the worlde be so hunger starued for a man and not vse
the meanes to haue him; thinkst thou *Cleanthes* will come agayne to
haue his head chopt of so soone as he comes; but had you pluckt vp
this branch wherein the King thy husbandes life consistes and burnt it   50
in the fyre, his olde beard would haue stuncke for't in the graue ere
this, and then thou shouldst haue seene whether *Cleanthes* would haue
come vnto thee or noe.

 AEgi. Oh excreable counsaile.

 Count. Go to, tis good counsaile; take the grace of God before your   55
eyes, and follow it; to it wench corragio; I know I haue gotten thee
with childe of a desire, and thou longst but for a knife to let it out;
hold there tis; [*giving her a knife*] serue God and be thankfull; now
you knaues will you let mee come out trow.

 1 Guard. Please your Lordshippe to bestow something on vs for we   60
are poore knaues.

 Count. Harke, you be euen knaues still, and if you be poore long
you'r foolish knaues, and so Ile leaue you.

 2 Guard. Nay swounes my Lord, no knaues neyther.

 Count. Then he was a knaue that told me so, what doost thou tell   65
mee that.   *Exit.*

 AEgi. This serpentes counsell stinges mee to the hart,
Mountes to my braine and bindes my prince of sence.
My voluntarie motion and my life,
Sitting it selfe triumphing in there thrones,   70
And that doth force my hand to take this knife,
That bowes my knees and sets me by thy branch,
Oh my *Diones,* oh my onely sonne,
Canst thou now feele the rigour of a knife.

---

34 not,] ∼∧ ‖ 35 are,] ∼∧ ‖ 36 onely;] ∼∧ | needes] ∼, ‖ 37 it.] ∼, ‖ 38 you'r] your ‖ 40
handes;] ∼, ‖ 43 tut,] ∼∧ | wise;]∼∧ ‖ 44 not.] ∼, ‖ 46 King;] ∼∧ ‖ 48 him;] ∼, ‖ 49
comes;] ∼, ‖ 51 for't] fort ‖ 55 to,] ∼∧ | counsaile;] ∼, ‖ 56 it;] ∼∧ | corragio;] ∼, ‖ 57
out;] ∼, ‖ 58 tis;] ∼∧ | SD *giving . . . knife*] *Parrott* | thankfull;] ∼, ‖ 62 Harke,] ∼∧ ‖ 63
you'r] your ‖ 64 Lord,] ∼∧ ‖ 65 knaue] knane ‖ 67 hart,] ∼. ‖ 73 *Diones,*] diones ‖ 74 knife.]
∼, ‖

Noe thou art senslesse and Ile cut thee vp,   75
Ile shroude thee in my bosome safe from stormes,
And trust no more my trustlesse gard with thee,
Come then returne vnto thy mothers armes,
And when I / pull thee foorth to serue the fire,   [E1]
Turne thy selfe wholy into a burning tounge,   80
In voking furies and infernall death,
To coole thy tormentes with thy fathers breth.

                                    [*Exit* AEgiale *with the* Guard.]

[SCENE VII]

Enter Elimine *and* Samathis.

  Sam. Now madam countesse, do you make account
To take vp husbandes by your countishippe.
Haue you the broade seale for it, are you so hye,
And stoope, to one so lowe as is my husband.
Hence come your headtyres and your costly gownes,   5
Your trayne borne vp and a man bare before you,
Now fye on pride when women goe thus naked.
I euer thought that pride would haue a fall
But little thought it would haue such a fall.
  Eli. What fall I pray you.   10
  Sam. There you lay last, forsooth there you lay last.
  Eli. Be not so angry woman, you are deceiued.
  Sam. I know I am deceiued for thou deceiuedst me,
Thou mightest aswell haue pict my pursse I tell thee;
Oh would my mother say, when you haue a husband,   15
Keepe to him onely; but now one may see,
How horible a thing it is to change,
Because it angers one so horibly,
You must haue Vshers to make way before you.
  Eli. The dame is madde, Ile stay no longer with her.   *Exit* Elimine.
  Sam. Well madam shorte heeles Ile be euen with you,
See where the mad brayne *Count* her husband comes.

                              Enter Count.

I will begone.
  Count. Heare you Vsurers wife, stay, a plague on you stay, whither
go you so fast, why did I euer hurt any of your sex yet.   25
  Sam. Why no my Lord.
  Count. Why no my Lorde, why the deuill do you turne tayle when

---

78-82 Come . . . breth.] *Shepherd*; *as prose* (and . . . turne . . . in voking . . . to) ‖ 82 SD *Exit*
. . . Guard.] *Parrott* ‖ Scene VII] *Parrott* ‖ 1 countesse,] ∼∧ | account] ∼. ‖ 3-4 Haue . . .
husband.] Haue . . . stoope, / To . . . husband, Q (and) ‖ 4 husband.] ∼, ‖ 7 women] *Parrott*;
woman | thus] thous ‖ 12 woman,] ∼∧ | deceiued.] ∼∧ ‖ 14 thee;] ∼, ‖ 16 onely;] ∼∧ ‖ 19
you.] ∼, ‖ 22 comes.] ∼, ‖ 23 Q *repeats speech-prefix* ‖ 24 wife,] ∼∧ ‖

you should not, when you should you will not be halfe so hastie; a man
must loue you, woe you, spend vpon you and the deuill of one of you is
worthy to kisse the hemme of / my riding gowne heere.   [E1ᵛ] 30

   Sam. Is this your riding gowne my Lord.

   Count. Tis no matter what it is, talke not to me; what the deuill
did I meane to call thee backe agayne.

   Sam. Why my Lord I meane not to trouble you.   *[Offers to go out.]*

   Count. Goe to, stay I say, tis agaynst my will that I vse you so kindly   35
I can tell you.

   Sam. Why you may chuse my Lord.

   Count. I but I cannot chuse, there you lie now; tis loue forsooth
that Intailes me to you, for if it had not beene for loue, I had not
beene heere now, for the Gods do know I hold thee dearer then the   40
Poungranet of mine eye, and thats better by three pence then the aple
of mine eye.

   Sam. My Lord I am sory for your heauinesse.

   Count. Nay tis no matter, I am not the first asse that hath borne
Cupides tresurie.   45

   Sam. My Lord, tis enough to make an asse wise to beare tresure.

   Count. Why then be you that wise asse, and beare me for I haue
some treasure about me, will you loue me.

   Sam. Loue you my Lord, it is strange you wil aske it.

   Count. I am not the first hath desired you.   50

   Sam. Nor you shall not be the last I will refuse.

   Count. Nor are you the fayrest I haue seene.

   Sam. Nor the foulest you haue lou'd.

   Count. Nor the fittest to be beloued.

   Sam. Nor the vnfittest to hate.   55

   Count. Doe and you dare, but sirra and thou wilt not loue, I pray
thee be proud.

   Sam. Why so my Lord.

   Count. Because I would haue thee fall, for pride must haue a fall.

   Sam. Do you delight in my fall so much.   60

   Count. As much as in mine owne rysing I fayth, but do not you
thinke it strange that I doe loue you, for before I did loue you, *Cupid*
pinckt me a Spanish lether Ierkin with shooting at me, and made it so
full of holes that I was fayne to leaue it of, and this losse haue I had
for your sake. /   65
                                            [E2]

   Sam. My Lord Ile bestowe an old Ierkin on you.

   Count. Nay that shall not serue your turne, for I haue had a greater
losse then that, I lost my left eye for your sake.

   Sam. I do not thinke so.

---

28 hastie;] ∼, ‖ 32 me;] ∼, ‖ 33 agayne.] ∼, ‖ 34 you.] ∼, | SD *Offers . . . out.*] *Parrott subs.* ‖
35 to,] ∼∧ ‖ 38 now;] ∼, ‖ 44 matter,] ∼∧ ‖ 46 Lord,] ∼∧ ‖ 49 Lord,] ∼∧ ‖ 50 you.] ∼, ‖
52 seene.] ∼, ‖ 53 lou'd] loud ‖ 56 dare,] ∼∧ ‖ 57 proud.] ∼∧ ‖ 63 Spanish] spanish ‖ 66 you.]
∼, ‖

Count. I but Ile tell you how: as I was hunting in the parke, I saw   70
Cupid shooting a cockhye into your face, and gazing after his arrow it
fell into mine eye.

Sam. A prettie fiction.

Count. I but I finde this no fiction, and you shall make me amends
with loue or by this patch of mine eye, and the patch thou wotest   75
where, I will sweare to all the Cittie I haue layne with thee.

Sam. I hope your Lordshippe will not doe me that wrong.

Count. Then do you me right and let me lie with you, I haue made
the botle nosd knaue your husband so drunke that he is not able to
stand, goe get you home Ile follow you.   80

Sam. Why my Lord what will you do there.

Count. Goe to, make no more questions but say I shall bee welcome
or by mine honor Ile doe as I say, otherwise be as secret as death.

Sam. [*Aside.*] Twentie to one he will; well my Lord if you come
you come.   85

Count. Oh I thanke you hartely, oh exellent or neuer trust mee.   [*Exeunt.*]

Enter Menippus *and* Elimine.

Meni. Madam, your honor is come somewhat to soone.

Eli. Why so *Menippus.*

Meni. Had you stayed neuer so little longer you should haue met
my Lord comming out of *Leons* house and out of his moueables.   90

Eli. How out of his moueables.

Meni. Euen in playne troth, I see him woe her, winne her, and went
in with her.

Eli. Now of mine honor I will be reuenged, fetch me the Burgomaister *Menippus,* Ile haue them both whipt about the towne.   95

Meni. Nay madam you must not dishonor him so.

Eli. What shall mine honor doe then. /

Meni. Do but tongue whip him madam and care not,   [E2ᵛ]
And so I leaue him to the mercie of your tongue.   [*Exit.*]

Eli. My tongue shall haue hell and no mercie in it.   100

Enter the Count.

[*Count.*] Excellent musicke, exellent musicke.

Eli. And the Deuill take the Instrument.

Count. What art thou so nye.

Eli. I and it were a good deede to be a little nier too, you make a
Count asse of me indeede, as if I were too little for you, but bignesse   105
is my fault vnlesse I were a little better vsd at your handes.

Count. Why thou wilt be to perfit if I should vse thee much, for
vse makes perfitnesse.

---

70 how:] ∼∧ ‖ 76 where,] ∼∧ ‖ 80 stand,] ∼∧ ‖ 82 to,] ∼∧ ‖ 84 SD *Aside.*] *Parrott* | will;]
∼, ‖ 86 SD *Exeunt.*] *Parrott* ‖ 87 Madam,] ∼∧ ‖ 90 house] honse ‖ 91 moueables.] ∼, ‖ 94
reuenged,] ∼∧ ‖ 95 *Menippus,*] ∼∧ ‖ 96 dishonor] dshonor | so.] ∼, ‖ 99 tongue.] ∼, | SD
Exit.] ‖ 100 it.] ∼∧ ‖ 101 *Count.*] *Parrott* | musicke,] ∼∧ ‖ 102 Instrument.] ∼, ‖ 107 much,]
∼∧ ‖

Eli. I but I cannot be too perfit and therfore Ile spoyle her
perfections that helpes to spoyle mine, I warrant her.   110

Count. Why may not I lie with her, aswell as thou layest with her
husband.

Eli. I defie you and all the world that can say blacke is mine eye.

Count. I thinke so indeede, for thine eye is gray, but thou didst lye
with him by that same token he gaue thee a carknet, and thou toldst   115
me that thy mother sent it thee, thou didst promise to banquet him
when I was next abroade, thou didst say he could not be so old as he
made himselfe to be, thou didst say twas pittie of his nose, for he would
haue bene a fine man els, and that God did well to make him a rich
man, for a was a good man too, and these tokens I thinke are sufficient,   120
for these a told me with his owne mouth.

Eli. He lyed like an old knaue as he was and that he shall knowe
the next time these lippes open in fayth; [*Aside.*] oh wicked periurd
man would a disclose my secretes. I fayth what woman would trust
any man a liue with her honestie.   *Exit.*

Count. Ha ha ha, I haue sent her in a pelting chafe,
But Ile follow her and make her madde with anger. /   [*Exit.*]

[SCENE VIII]   [E3]

Enter Porus *king of* Aethiopia, Resus *king of* Arabia, Bion *king*
of Phasiaca, Bebritius *king of* Bebritia, *with soldiers and*
drumme and ensigne.

Por. Thus haue we trode the sandy vales of *AEgypt,*
Adioyning to the plaines of *Alexandria,*
Where proud king *Ptolemy* keepes his residence,
Securely trusting to his prophesies,
Which hath foretold him many yeares agoe,   5
That if the young *Archadian Doricles,*
Should linke in marriage with his louely daughter,
He then should conquere all our bordering landes,
And make vs subiect to his tirrannie.

Rhe. Trusting to his fond fantasticke dreames,   10
He hath exild the warlicke Duke *Cleanthes,*
Whose name was terror to our valiant troopes.

Bion. Cleanthes exild giues vs easy way,
To our attemptes; where had he stayed,
And beene a freind to him, yet should he not   15
Excape subiection.

110 mine,] ∼∧ ‖ 111 her,] ∼∧ ‖ 123 fayth;] ∼, | *Aside.*] *Parrott* ‖ 124 secretes.] ∼∧ ‖ 127
SD *Exit.*] *Parrott* ‖ Scene VIII] *Parrott* ‖ SD *ensigne*] ensigue ‖ 7 daughter,] ∼. ‖ 11 *Cleanthes,*]
∼. ‖ 14 attemptes;] ∼∧ ‖

Bebr. We will deuide his kingdome twixt vs foure,
And reaue from him his foure cheife ornamentes,
And for to greeue his aged mind the more,
He shall be kept in lasting seruitude,   20
So to fulfill what fates to him assignde.
 Por. Come let vs march and braue him at the walles,
If *Porus* liue to weild his martiall sworde,
His Citty walles shall not preserue him safe,
But he shall dye by *Porus* and his freindes.   *Exeunt.*

[SCENE IX]

Enter Doricles *and* Aspasia.

 Dor. Sweet madam grant me once a chearful looke
To glad my dying hart with sorow kild,
Your father hath resignd his free consent,
You bound by dutie to obey his will.
 Asp. Nay rather let him hayle me to my death   5
Then gaynst my will constraine me match my selfe. /

    Enter Count.   [E3ᵛ]

 Count. Dye thou vile wretch and liue *Aspatia,*
Euen now I hard thy father *Ptolomy*
With wordes that still do tingle in mine eares
Pronounce him heyre to *Alexandria,*   10
Tis time for me to stirre when such young boyes,
Shal haue their weake neckes ouer poisd with crownes
Which must become resolued champions,
That for a crownes exchange will sel their soules. *He kils him.*
 Asp. Wicked *Count Hermes* for this monsterous deede, 15
AEgypt will hate thee, and thou sure must dye;
Then hye thee to the hils beyond the *Alpes,*
Flye to vnknowne and vnfrequented climes,
Some desert place that neuer sawe the sunne,
For if the king or any of his friendes,   20
Shall finde *Count Hermes* thou art surely dead.
 Count. Ile flye no more then doth a setled rocke,
No more then mountaines or the steadfast powles,
But come sweete loue if thou wilt come with me,
We two will liue amongst the shadowy groues, 25
And we will sit like shepherdes on a hill,
And with our heauenly voyces tice the trees
To eccho sweetely to our coelestiall tunes.
Els will I angle in the running brookes,

20 seruitude,] ∼. ‖ 21 assignde.] ∼, ‖ Scene IX] *Parrott* ‖ 3 consent,] ∼. ‖ 4 will.] ∼, ‖ 9
eares] ∼. ‖ 14 soules.] ∼, ‖ 16 thee,] ∼. | dye;] ∼, ‖ 27 trees] ∼, ‖ 28 tunes.] ∼, ‖

Seasoning our toyles with kisses on the bankes,   30
Sometime Ile diue into the murmering springes,
And fetch thee stones to hang about thy necke,
Which by thy splendor will be turnd to pearle,
Say fayre *Aspasia* wilt thou walke with me.
    Asp. No bloody *Count,* but I will cleare my selfe,   35
And tell thy murders to the amased court.
    Count. Nay if thou wilt not chuse you peeuish girle,
Thou canst not say but thou wert offered fayre.
[*Aside.*] But here must end *Count Hermes* strange disguise,
My veluet gowne, my pistoll and this patch,   40
No more must hide me in the countes attire, /
Now will I turne my gowne to Vsurers Cotes,   [E4]
And thus appeare vnto the worlde no more.
Farewell *Aspasia.*   *Exit* Count.
    Asp. Goe wretched villayne, hide thy hated head,   45
Where neuer heauens light may shine on thee.
Whose there? Come forth for here is murder done,
Murder, Murder of good prince *Doricles.*

                Enter Euribates.
    [*Eur.*] Who cals out murther Lady was it you.
    Asp. As I was walking in the pleasant meades,   50
With *Doricles* the young *Archadian* prince,
Rusht in *Count Hermes* and in desperate wordes,
Hath slayne this prince.
    Eur. A balefull deede, pursue the murderer,
And tell the King of this foule accident.   55

               Enter Ptolemy *and* Lords.
    Pto. Oh tell no more; in stead of teares,
My beating hart dissolues in droppes of blood,
And from mine eyes that stares vpon this corse,
Leapes out my soule and on it I will die.
Oh *Doricles,* oh deare *Arcadian* prince,   60
The bulwarke and supporter of my life,
That by decree of fates was promised,
To adde foure neighbour kingdomes to my crowne,
And shield me from a most abhorred death,
Now shall my kingdome leaue me with my life,   65
And sodainly looke for some monsterous fate,
Shall fall like thunder on my wretched state.

                 Enter a messenger.
    [*Mes.*] Arme arme my Lord, my Lords to instant armes,

31 murmering] murmerrng ‖ **35** *Count,*] ∼∧ ‖ **37** girle,] ∼∧ ‖ **38** fayre.] ∼, ‖ **39** SD *Aside.*]
Parrott | must] *Q(c)*; mnst *Q(u)* ‖ **40** gowne,] ∼∧ ‖ **43** more.] ∼, ‖ **45** villayne,] ∼. ‖ **46** thee.]
∼, ‖ **47** there?] ∼, ‖ **49** *Eur.*] *Parrott* ‖ **50** meades] *Parrott (Brereton conj.)*; weedes ‖ **52** Rusht]
rusht ‖ **54** deede,] ∼∧ ‖ **55** accident.] ∼∧ | SD *Enter ... Lords.*] *Parrott; Enter* Ptolemy. ‖
56 more;] ∼∧ ‖ **58** corse,] ∼. ‖ **59** die.] ∼, ‖ **60** *Doricles,*] ∼∧ ‖ **61** life,] ∼. ‖ **68** *Mes.*]
Shepherd ‖

Foure mightie kinges are landed in thy coast,
And threaten death and ruine to thy land.   70
Blacke *Porus* the *Aethiopian* king,
Comes marching first with twentie thousand men,
Next *Rhesus* king of sweete *Arabia*, /
In warlike manner marcheth after him,   [E4ᵛ]
In equall number and in battaile ray.   75
Next *Bion* king of rich *Phasiaca*,
And sterne *Bebritius* of *Bebritia*,
With each of them ful twentie thousand strong,
All which hath vowd the death of *Ptolomy*,
And thus they hether bend their speedie feete.   80
　　Pto. How sodaynely is weather ouer cast,
How is the face of peacefull *AEgypt* changd,
Like as the smiling flowers aboue the ground,
By keenest edge of *Euras* breath is cut.
　　Clear. To armes my Lord and gather vp your strength,   85
Your bandes in *Memphis* and in *Caspia*,
Ioynd with your power of *Alexandria*,
Will double all the forces of these kinges.
　　Pto. All shalbe done we may; meane while,
Bury the body of this slaughtered prince,   90
Least with the view my senses follow his.
Curst be his hand that wrought the damned deede,
Cold and vncouered may his body lye,
Let stormie hayle and thunder beate on him
And euery bird and beast runne ouer him,   95
That robd poore *Ptolomy* of such a hope.
Pursue the desperate *Count* that murdered him,
A thousand kingdomes shall not saue his life.

　　　　　　　　　Enter Leon.

　　[*Leon.*] A miracle a miracle, a dreadfull miracle.
　　Pto. What miracle, oh what will heauens do more,   100
To punish *AEgypt* and her haplesse king.
　　Leon. As I was walking through the *Serian* groues
I sawe the desperate *Count*, the murderer
Of good prince *Doricles* as I heare say,
Fly through the desarts to the mimphick shades   105
Where hell to interrupt his passage thether,
Rauing beneath the ground worke of the earth
As if ten thousand vapours burst in her,
Seuered her wombe and swallowed quicke, /
The miserable *Count*.   [F1] 110

---

70 land.] ∼, ‖ **78** strong,] ∼∧ ‖ **79-80** All . . . feete.] *Shepherd; as prose* (and) ‖ **79** death] ∼, ‖
88 kinges.] ∼, ‖ **89** may;] ∼∧ ‖ **91** view] *Q(c)*; vew *Q(u)* | his.] ∼, ‖ **96** hope.] ∼, ‖ **98** life.]
∼, ‖ **99** Leon.] *Shepherd* ‖ **101** king.] ∼, ‖ **103** *Count*,] ∼∧ | murderer] ∼, ‖

Pto. Iust are the heauens in his most dreadfull end.
But come my Lords let vs to instant armes,
To driue away more mischiefes from our land.   *Exeunt.*
   Leon. So get you gone and perish all with him,
Now shall you know what want you haue of mee,   115
Now will I gather vp my sommes of money,
And of my creditors borow what I can,
Because as *Leon* Ile be seene no more,
This day they promisd for to meete me heere,
And here comes some of them.   120

            Enter first Messenger.

   [*1 Mes.*] My mayster sir, your friend *Calatius,*
Hath sent you sir your fiue hundreth crownes
For the rich Iewell that he bought of you.
   [*Leon.*] I thanke him hartely;
This Iewell of so many thousand crownes   125
The Queene of *AEgypt* did bestowe on mee,
When that I told her in poore *Irus* shape
Where her *Cleanthes* was, but soft who haue we here.

            Enter second Messenger.

   [*2 Mes.*] *Druso* the *Italian* Marchant here by mee,
Hath sent you sir in Diamonds and in Pearles,   130
So much as mounteth to fiue thousand crownes,
And craues no more assurance but your woord.
   Leon. Theres my bill and thanke thy maister, he shall haue more
then woord.   *Exeunt messengers. Manet* Leon.
Neuer shall he nor they see this agayne,   135
Nor me neyther as I am this present man,
This with the rest I haue wil make a prettie somme
With this will I imploye me in these warres,
Now will I take on me the forme and shape,
Of Duke *Cleanthes;* but what intendes this alarum.   140

        Alarum.   *Enter* Clearchus.

   [*Clear.*] Where may I seeke to finde *Cleanthes* out,
That martiall prince whom *Ptolemy* vnkinde,
Hath banished from out the *AEgyptian* Land,
Our warlike troopes are scatered and ouer throne, /
And his deare freindes *Acates* and *Acanthes,*   [F1ᵛ] 145
Lie in the field besmired in their bloodes.
Ile run through al these groues to find him out.   *Exit.*
   Leon. My sweete *Acates* and *Acanthes* slayne,

---

111 end.] ∼, ‖ **113** mischiefes] mischeiefes ‖ **121** *1 Mes.*] *Shepherd* | sir,] ∼∧ ‖ **122-23** Hath
. . . you.] *Parrott; as prose* (for) ‖ **124** *Leon.*] *Shepherd* ‖ **124-28** I . . . here.] *Parrott; as prose* (this
. . . when . . . where) ‖ **124** hartely;] ∼, ‖ **129** *2 Mes.*] *Shepherd* ‖ **132** woord.] ∼, ‖ **133** maister,]
∼∧ ‖ **134** SD *Exeunt messengers.*] *Parrott; Exeunt.* ‖ **140** *Cleanthes;*] ∼, ‖ **141** *Clear.*] *Shepherd* ‖
146 bloodes.] ∼, ‖

Greife to my hart and sorrow to my soule,
Then rouse thy selfe *Cleanthes* and reuenge   150
Their guiltlesse blood on these base miscreantes.
Oh let the cankred trumpet of the deepe,
Be ratled out and ring into their eares,
The dire reuenge *Cleanthes* will inflicte,
One these foure Kings and all there complices.   [*Exit.*]

Alarum. Excursions.

[SCENE X]

Enter Cleanthes *leading* Porus, Rhesus, Bion, Bebritius,
Pego, Clearchus, Euribates.

Clean. Thus haue you stroue in vayne agaynst those Gods,
That rescues *AEgypt* in *Cleanthes* armes,
Come yeeld your crownes and homages to mee,
Though *Ptolomie* is dead yet I suruiue,
Elect and chosen by the peares to scourge,   5
The vile persumption of your hated liues,
Then yeeld as vanquisht vnto *Aegypts* king.
  Por. First by thy valoure and the strength of armes,
Porus the welthie *Aethiopian* king,
Doth yeeld his crowne and homage vnto thee,   10
Swearing by all my Gods whom I adore,
To honor Duke *Cleanthes* whilst he liue,
And in his ayde with twentie thousand men,
Will alwayes march gaynst whom thou meanst to fyght.
  Bion. *Bion* whose necke was neuer forct to bow   15
Doth yeeld him captiue to thy warlike sworde,
Command what so thou list, we will performe,
And all my power shall march at thy commaund.
  Rhe. *Rhesus* doth yeeld his crowne and dignitie,
To great *Cleanthes, Aegyptes* onely strength,   20
For if *Cleanthes* liues, who euer liued,
More likelier to be monarke of the world. /
Then here accept my vowd allegiance,   [F2]
Which as the rest I render vnto thee.
  Bebr. So sayth *Bebritius* of *Bebritia.*   25
And layes his crowne and homage at thy feete.
  Clean. Hold take your crownes agayne
And kepe your othes and fealties to mee,

---

150 reuenge] ~. ‖ 151 miscreantes.] ~∧ ‖ 155 complices.] ~, | SD *Exit.*] ‖ Scene X] *Parrott*
‖ SD Clearchus,] ~∧ | Euribates] Euribatus ‖ 14 fyght.] ~, ‖ 20 *Cleanthes,*] ~∧ ‖ 22 world.]
~, ‖ 27-28 Hold . . . mee,] *Shepherd; one line* (and) ‖

So shal you liue as free as here to fore,
And neare hereafter stoupe to conquest more.   30

Enter Elimine *and* Samathis *with childe.*

Pego. [*Aside.*] Here comes the two widowes of the begger and the
king, little know they that both their husbandes are turnd into one
king, there would be olde striuing who should bee Queene I fayth.
    Eli. Pittie dread soueraigne.
    Sam.   Pittie gratious Lord.
    Clean. What are your sutes.   35
    Eli. I the poore countesse and the widdow left,
Of late *Count Hermes,* hauing all my goodes
Seazd to our late kings vse for murder done,
Of young prince *Doricles* humbly pray your grace,
I may haue somewhat to mainetayne my state,   40
And this poore burthen which I goe withall,
The haplesse Infant of a haplesse father.
    Sam. And I my Lord humbly intreate your grace,
That where my husband *Leon* is deceast,
And left me much in debt, his creditors   45
Hauing seased all I haue into their handes,
And turnd me with this haplesse burthen heere,
Into the streetes, your highnesse will descend,
To my reliefe by some conuenient order.
    Clean. Poore soules I most extreamely pittie them;   50
But say is *Leon* deade.
    Clear. Men say my Lord he cast his desperate body,
From Thalexandrian tower into the sea.
    Clean. Who saw the sight, or gaue out this reporte,
You maister Burgomaister. /   55
    Pego. I did my gratious Lord.   [F2ᵛ]
    Clean. [*Aside.*] So I deuisd indeede that he should say,
That none should neuer looke for *Leon* more.
But these my widowes here must not be left,
Vnto the mercie of the needy world,   60
Nor mine owne Issue that they goe withall,
Haue such base fortunes and there sire so great.
Widowes in pittie of your widowhood,
And vntymely endes of both your husbandes,
The slaughter of the *Count* your husband madam,   65
Shalbe remitted, and your selfe enioy,
The vtmost of the liuing he possest,
So will I pay your husband *Leons* debt,
And both shall liue fitting there wonted states,

---

30 SD *with childe.*] with childe, ‖ **31** SD *Aside.*] *Parrott* ‖ **36** left,] ∼. ‖ **37** *Hermes,*] ∼∧ | goodes]
∼, ‖ **38** Seazd] seazd ‖ **41** withall,] ∼. ‖ **43** grace,] ∼. ‖ **48** streetes,] ∼∧ ‖ **50** them;] ∼, ‖
51 deade.] ∼, ‖ **57** SD *Aside.*] *Parrott* ‖ **58** more.] ∼∧ ‖ **60** Vnto] vnto ‖ **62** great.] ∼, ‖

Kinges in there mercie come most neare the Goddes,   70
And can no better shew it then in ruth,
Of widowes and of children fatherlesse,
My selfe will therefore be to both your birthes,
A careful father in there bringing vp.
 Ambo. The Gods for euer blesse your maiestie.   75
 Clean. But tell me were your husbandes such bad men,
That euery way they did deserue such endes.
 Eli. Myne was a husband to my hartes content,
But that he vsd the priuiledge of men.
 Clean. What priuiledge of men.   80
 Eli. To take some other loue besides his wife,
Which men think by their custome they may do,
Although their wiues be strictly bound to them.
 Clean. With whom suspect you he was great with all.
 Eli. With this poore widow here, the worlde supposeth.   85
 Sam. So thinkes the world my husband was with you.
 Pego. Fayre dames what will you say to me,
If I can tell you where your husbandes bee.
 Clean. What can you sir.
 Pego. Nay nothing sir, I did but ieast with you. [*Aside.*] I feard   90
him I fayth, but Ile be secret thats flat.
 Clean. Well maister *Burgomaister* see that you restore, /
The goodes and landes you ceasd   [F3]
Both of the countesse and rich *Leons* wife,
Not pittie of their widowhoodes alone,   95
But their rare beauties moue me to this good.
Oh Maister *Burgomaister* see heres your wife
Come to welcome you home from warres.

    Enter Martia *with child.*

 [*Mar.*] Oh husband husband, will you goe to warre, and leaue me
in this taking.   100
 Pego. This taking, why this is a very good taking; how say you is it
not, and like your Maiestie.
 Clean. Tis very wel Maister *Burgomaister.*
 Pego. But shall I intreat one boone of your Maiestie.
 Clean. Whats that Maister *Burgomaister.*   105
 Pego. Mary euen to be god father to my young Burgomaister here.
 Clean. Withall my hart sir.
 Mar. Come on sweete husband for my time drawes neare.
 Pego. Feare not, thou shalt be a ioyfull mother I warrant thee.

---

75 maiestie.] ∼, ‖ **77** endes.] ∼, ‖ **78** content,] ∼. ‖ **80** men.] ∼, ‖ **81** wife,] ∼∧ ‖ **85** here,]
∼∧ ‖ **90** sir,] ∼∧ | you.] ∼, | SD *Aside.*] *Parrott* ‖ **91** fayth,] ∼∧ ‖ **93** ceasd] ∼. ‖ **97-98** Oh
. . . warres.] *Shepherd*; Oh . . . to / welcome . . . warres. Q (come) ‖ **98** SD *with*] *Parrott*; *with*
a ‖ **99** *Mar.*] *Shepherd* | husband,] ∼∧ ‖ **101** taking,] ∼∧ | taking;] ∼∧ ‖ **102** not,] ∼∧ ‖ **104**
shall] Shall ‖ **108** for] fot ‖ **109** not,] ∼∧ ‖

Clean. How say you my Lordes, is not our Burgomaister a tall man   110
euery way, did you not marke how manfully he behaued himselfe in
our late Battayle.

    Por. We did my Lord and wonder at his courage.

    Rhe. His merit doth deserue a better place
Then to be Burgomaister of *Alexandria.*   115

    Clean. Then say my Lordes how shall we deale with him.

    Bion. Had he beene widower he might haue wedded with this
countesse heere.

    Pego. Oh I haue one of mine owne I thanke you sir, heres one has
the sweete of them I fayth.   120

    Por. My Lord the offer had beene to hye a grace for him,
For neare did eye behold a fayrer face.

    Bebr. So sayth mine eye that hath my hart incenst.

    Bion. And *Rhesus* me thinkes this exceedes her farre.

    Rhe. No question of it as the sonne a starre.   125

    Por. As sodaynely as lightning beautie woundes.

    Bebr. None euer lou'd but at first sight they lou'd. /

    Por. Loues dartes are swift as is the lightning fier.   [F3ᵛ]

    Rhe. See he shootes arrowes burning from her eyes.

    Por. Why which loues *Rhesus.*

    Rhe.   This coelestiall dame.   130

    Por. And which loues *Bion.*

    Bion.   Euen the very same.

    Por. Then may I freely Ioy the countesse heere.

    Bebr. No *Porus* for *Bebritius* loues her too.

    Clean. [*Aside.*] Are they in loue, oh Gods would that were true.
My loues enioy the fresh desire of kinges.   135
How now my Lords doth beauty startle you.

    Por. More then dead stockes would startle at such beauty.

    Bebr. In vayne do I resist my passions.
Mightie *Cleanthes* to annex my hart,
In loue to thee aswell as victorie,   140
Grant this fayre countesse here may be my queene.

    Por. No great *Cleanthes* giue her to my hand,
Whose hart was first the subject of her graces.

    Rhe. Then let the *Arabian* king make this his queene.

    Bion. Nay this *Cleanthes* let my loue inioy.   145

    Clean. [*Aside.*] How fatall are these loues; now I perceaue,
Their fortunes that I told as I was *Irus,*
Will now in force I see be come to passe.

---

110 Lordes,] ∼∧ ‖ **112** Battayle.] ∼, ‖ **113** courage.] ∼∧ ‖ **114** place] ∼. ‖ **120** fayth.] ∼:
‖ **121** him,] ∼∧ ‖ **124** farre.] ∼, ‖ **126** woundes.] ∼, ‖ **127** lou'd . . . lou'd] loud . . . loud ‖
133 too.] ∼∧ ‖ **134** SD *Aside.*] *Parrott* | loue,] ∼∧ | true.] ∼∧ ‖ **135** loues enioy] *Parrott*;
louing ioy ‖ **137** beauty.] ∼, ‖ **138** passions.] ∼, ‖ **146** SD *Aside.*] *Parrott* | loues;] ∼∧ ‖ **147**
Irus,] ∼. ‖

Sam. Oh holy *Irus* blessed be thy tongue,
That like an orator hath told our fortunes. 150
   Eli. He told vs we should soone lose our first loues,
Making our second choise mongst greatest kinges.
   Clean. [*Aside.*] I did indeede, but God knowes knew not how.
   Pego. [*Aside.*] How say you maister brother, am not I secret now.
   Clean. [*Aside.*] Thou art and be so still for not the worlde, 155
Shall euer know the mad prankes I haue played.
Now stand fayre my Lordes and let these Ladies view you.
   Eli. In my eye now the blackest is the fayrest,
For euery woman chooseth white and red,
Come martiall *Porus* thou shalt haue my loue. 160
   Bebr. Out on thee foolish woman, thou hast chose a deuill.
   Pego. Not yet sir til he haue hornes, /
   Sam. Tis not the face and colour I regard, [F4]
But fresh and louely youth allures my choyse.
And thee most beautious *Bion* I affecte. 165
   Rhe. Haplesse is *Rhesus.*
   Bebr.   Accurst *Bebritius.*
   Clean. Haue patience gentle Lordes, I will prouide
Other *AEgyptian* Ladies for your turne,
So will we linke in perfit league of loue,
So shall the victorie you lost to me, 170
Set double glorie on your conquered heades.
So let vs goe to frolicke in our Court,
Carousing free whole boules of Greekish wine,
In honor of the conquest we haue made,
That at our banquet all the Gods may tend, 175
Plauding our victorie and this happie end.   *Exeunt.*

FINIS.

153 SD *Aside.*] *Parrott* ‖ **154** SD *Aside.*] *Parrott* | now.] ∼, ‖ **155** SD *Aside.*] *Parrott* ‖ **156** played.] ∼, ‖ **157** you.] ∼, ‖ **161** woman,] ∼∧ ‖ **164** choyse.] ∼, ‖ **167** Lordes,] ∼∧ | prouide] ∼, ‖ **172** Court,] ∼. ‖ **173** Greekish] greekish ‖

HISTORICAL COLLATION

[Editions collated: Shepherd (=*S*, in *The Works of George Chapman: Plays*, 1875, pp. 1-21); Parrott (=*P*, in *The Plays of George Chapman: The Comedies* [1914], pp. 2-43). Only substantive and semi-substantive variants are recorded; obvious errors are not recorded. The lemmata are taken from the present text. Where lemma represents the reading of Q copy-text, omission of siglum indicates agreement with lemma.]

Scene I

Scene I] *P*; *om. Q, S*
11 me . . . pittie] *S, P*; me$_\wedge$ loue, mee$_\wedge$ pittie *Q*
51 oft] *S, P*; off *Q*
69 Proposing] *S*; Opposing *Q, P*
70 threaten] threatening *S*
71 eare long] *om. S*
76 kentall] quintal *S*
81 court] *P*; count *Q, S*
82 toples] *S, P*; *Toples Q*
86 earthlye] *S, P*; eathlye *Q*
96 succours] threatens *Deighton*
97 succour] *Deighton, S, P*; threaten *Q*
105 statue] *S, P*; stature *Q*
182 SD *Exeunt servants.*] *Exeunt the Servingmen P*; *Exeunt. Q, S*
192 a bone] *Brereton, P*; alone *Q, S*
203 say] *S*; *om. Q, P*
206 That] *S*; Sayde that *Q, P*
317 SD *Exeunt the maids*] *P*; *Exeunt Q, S*
334 humor;] *P*; ~$_\wedge$ *Q, S*; ~: *Brereton*
339 discried.] ~. *He disguises himself as* Count Hermes *P*
344 cattels] chattels *S*

Scene II

Scene II] *P*; *om. Q, S*
1 *Eli.*] *P*; *om. Q, S*
14 SD Count.] Count Hermes *P*
16 SD *Exit.*] *P*; *om. Q, S*
28 SD *Aside.*] *P*; *om. Q, S*
41 firme] ~, *S, P*
51 SD *Aside.*] *P*; *om. Q, S*
66 Spaniard a] a Spaniard *Brereton, P*

71 SD *Draws his pistol.*] *P*; *om. Q, S*
73 shalt see] *S, P*; ~ lee *Q*
120-21 Spagnolo . . . presto.] *P*; spaniola questo, questo, spaniola questo. *Q, S*

Scene III

Scene III] *P*; *om. Q, S*
7 SD *Aside.*] *P*; *om. Q, S*
16 your] *S, P*; our *Q*
22 ceaslesse] *S, P*; cealesse *Q*
26 SD AEgiale *with attendants*] *P*; *om. Q, S*
47 SD *Exeunt the* Lords.] *P*; *Exeunt. Q, S*
67 SD *advancing*] *P*; *om. Q, S*
89 SD *Aside.*] *P*; *om. Q, S*
123 bandes] bonds *P*
150 SD *Exeunt . . . maids.*] *P*; *Exeunt. Q, S*

Scene IV

Scene IV] *P*; *om. Q, S*
14 SD *Exit . . .* Ianthe.] *om. Q, S, P*
21 lou'd] *S, P*; loud *Q*
27 lou'd] *S, P;* loud *Q*
40 SD *and*] ~ Pego *as the P*
41 comes] come *S, P*
63 in] *om. S*
77 other] *om. Deighton*
81 *Eur.*] *P*; *Gen. Q, S*
110 SD Count.] Count Hermes *P*
170 proposed] promised *S*
179 *Eur.*] *P*; *Euge. Q, S*

Scene V

Scene V] *P*; *om. Q, S*
44 With] *S, P*; Which *Q*
47 figure] *P*; fingers *Q, S*
55 the] their *Q, S, P*
69 SD *Exit . . .* Samathis.] *P*; *Exit. Q, S*
74 SD *Aside.*] *P*; *om. Q, S*
76 SD *Aside.*] *P*; *om. Q, S*
80 summer . . . graces] *Deighton, P*; graces . . . summer *Q, S*
103 the] thy *P*
117 SD *Aside.*] *P*; *om. Q, S*
136 SD *Exit* Elimine.] *Exit. P*; *om. Q, S*
152 without] *S, P*; ~ a *Q*
153 *Dru.*] *S, P*; *om. Q*
164 SD *Exit with* Druso.] *P*; *Exit. Q, S*

Scene VI

Scene VI] *P; om. Q, S*
9 *Count.*] *P; om. Q, S*
16 SD *Enter* Count.] *Enter* Count Hermes *P; om. Q, S*
29-31 loue it] *P;* loue, and it *Q, S*
38 you'r] *S, P;* your *Q*
51 for't] *S, P;* fort *Q*
58 SD *giving . . . knife*] *P; om. Q, S*
63 you'r] *S, P;* your *Q*
82 SD *Exit . . . Guard.*] *P; om. Q, S*

Scene VII

Scene VII] *P; om. Q, S*
7 women] *P;* woman *Q, S*
22 SD Count.] Count Hermes *P*
34 SD *Offers . . . out.*] *Going P; om. Q, S*
53 lou'd] *S, P;* loud *Q*
63 pinckt] pricked *S*
70 I but] But *S*
84 SD *Aside.*] *P; om. Q, S*
86 SD *Exeunt.*] *P; om. Q, S*
99 SD *Exit.*] *om. Q, S, P*
101 *Count.*] *P; om. Q, S*
123 SD *Aside.*] *P; om. Q, S*
126 chafe] chase *S, P*
127 SD *Exit.*] *P; om. Q, S*

Scene VIII

Scene VIII] *P; om. Q, S*

Scene IX

Scene IX] *P; om. Q, S*
6 SD Count.] Count Hermes *P*
28 to] *om. S*
39 SD *Aside.*] *P; om. Q, S*
49 *Eur.*] *P; om. Q, S*
50 meades] *Brereton, P;* weedes *Q, S*
55 SD *Enter . . . Lords.*] *P; Enter* Ptolemy. *Q, S*
58 stares] starr *S*
68 *Mes.*] *S, P; om. Q*
94 stormie] storm and *S*
99 *Leon.*] *S, P; om. Q*
110 The] *om. S*
121 1 *Mes.*] *S, P; om. Q*
124 *Leon.*] *S, P; om. Q*
129 2 *Mes.*] *S, P; om. Q*
134 SD *Exeunt messengers.*] *P; Exeunt. Q, S*

141 *Clear.*] S, P; *om.* Q
155 SD *Exit.*] *om.* Q, S, P

Scene X

Scene X] P; *om.* Q, S
2 rescues] rescue S
31 SD *Aside.*] P; *om.* Q, S
57 SD *Aside.*] P; *om.* Q, S
90 SD *Aside.*] P; *om.* Q, S
98 SD *with*] P; *with a* Q, S
99 *Mar.*] S, P; *om.* Q
121 for him] *om.* S
127 lou'd . . . lou'd] S, P; loud . . . loud Q
134 SD *Aside.*] P; *om.* Q, S
135 loues enioy] P; louing ioy Q, S
146 SD *Aside.*] P; *om.* Q, S
153 SD *Aside.*] P; *om.* Q, S
154 SD *Aside.*] P; *om.* Q, S
155 SD *Aside.*] P; *om.* Q, S

PRESS-VARIANTS

[Copies collated: BM (British Museum C. 34. c. 11); Bodl¹ (Bodleian Library Malone 240 [1]); Bodl² (Bodleian Library Malone 163 [2]); CSmH (Huntington Library); DFo (Folger Shakespeare Library); Dyce (Victoria and Albert Museum 2028. 26. Box 4. 1); GWU (Glasgow University Library); MH (Harvard University Library)]

Sheet A (inner forme)

Corrected: GWU, Bodl¹, Bodl², Dyce, BM, CSmH, DFo

Uncorrected: MH

Sig. A3ᵛ

I.99 To all his] To his all
105 stature] statute
124 sportes] spertes

Sig. A4

I.132 Equally] Epually
162 from / vs,] from, / vs

Sheet C (outer forme)

Corrected: GWU, Bodl¹, Bodl², Dyce, BM, CSmH, DFo
Uncorrected: MH

Sig. C4ᵛ

IV.124 I trow] *om.*

Sheet E (inner forme)

Corrected: Dyce
Uncorrected: GWU, Bodl¹, Bodl², BM, CSmH, DFo, MH

Sig. E3ᵛ

IX. 39 must] mnst

Sheet E (outer forme)

Corrected: GWU, Bodl¹, Bodl², BM, Dyce, DFo, MH
Uncorrected: CSmH

Sig. E4ᵛ

IX. 91 view] vew

TEXTUAL NOTES

[Scene I]

69 Proposing] Opposing. The *OED* cites this instance as the sole example of "offering" (oppose, *v*, ii, b). However, this is clearly a corruption in the text of the correct form given by the Herald in scene iii, line 5.

[Scene II]

41 firme] ~, Parrott takes "faith" to be an exclamation, but I take it to be the object of the preposition "with."

66 Spaniard a] a Spaniard. Both Brereton and Parrott emend the word order, but as the phrase "Spaniard a borne" is quite acceptable, I see no need for the emendation.

[Scene IV]

57-63 But . . . denies.] The text is so corrupt, I have left the lining as it is in Q.

81 *Eur.*] Q assigns this to *Gen.*, but I agree with Parrott that this must be Euribates, the friend of Antistenes, to whom Q assigns lines 132 and 139-42.

133-36 Why . . . conference.] Parrott sets Count Hermes' speech as poetry, but the Count without exception speaks in prose.

179 *Eur.*] *Euge*. I follow Parrott in assigning the speech to Euribates. *"Euge."* is a possible combination of Euribates and Gentleman.

An Humorous Day's Mirth

edited by Allan Holaday

❖

TEXTUAL INTRODUCTION

Henslowe's reference to "Verones sonnes hosse" and "Labesyas clocke, with gowld buttenes" convinced Fleay that the "comodey of vmers," also mentioned in the *Diary*, is Chapman's *An Humorous Day's Mirth*.[1] According to one notation, it was performed "new" on May 11, 1597, apparently with some success. Certainly Henslowe's record of plentiful receipts from succeeding performances corroborates John Chamberlain's observation that the play was notably popular. Addressing Sir Dudley Carleton about a month after that May performance, Chamberlain wrote: "we haue here a new play of humors in very great request, and I was drawn alonge to yt by the common applause, but my opinion of yt is (as the fellow sayde of the shearing of hogges), that there was a great crie for so litle wolle."[2]

Despite this evident success on the stage, only one early edition, that of 1599,[3] seems to have been published. Hazlitt (*Handbook*, p. 82) mentions an additional issue from that same year, "Printed by Valentine Syms for John Oxenbridge"; but as Greg remarks, if such a variant existed, no known copy survives. Later developments suggest that initial demand for the quarto failed to exhaust even that one edition, for in 1652 remainder sheets from the original printing of *An Humorous Day's Mirth* together with those for five other Chapman plays comprised a nonce edition entitled *Comedies, Tragi-Comedies; and Traegedies: Written by George Chapman*. The title page of a single, dismembered copy survives.[4]

[1] F. G. Fleay, *A Biographical Chronicle of the English Drama, 1559-1642* (London, 1891), I, 55. Henslowe lists these items among various properties belonging to the Admiral's company in 1598. See also R. A. Foakes and R. T. Rickert, eds., *Henslowe's Diary* (Cambridge, 1961), pp. 58, 318, 321, 323.
[2] Quoted by Greg in his Malone Society reprint of *An Humorous Day's Mirth*. The entire letter appears in *Letters Written by John Chamberlain*, ed. Sarah Williams (1861), p. 4.
[3] For description, see W. W. Greg, *A Bibliography of the English Printed Drama to the Restoration*, I, 260-61.
[4] *The Carl Pforzheimer Library. English Literature* (New York, 1940), 142.

In the quarto of 1599 stop-press revision affected, according to my collation, sheets A (inner forme), B (outer and inner), D (outer), F (outer and inner), G (outer), and H (outer and inner). As Professor Akihiro Yamada has discovered, the Bute copy, now in the National Library of Scotland, preserves outer G in proof state and provides us with an otherwise unknown, uncorrected state of that forme. Although none of the stop-press revisions unequivocally derives from the manuscript, they do, for the most part, remove obvious errors. I have, therefore, usually adopted them.[5]

For reasons difficult to discover, type for the final half-sheet H was reset, producing a variant version of sigs. H1-H2, which is preserved in British Museum copy C. 34. c. 14. Although the text came through, except for accidentals, virtually unaltered, the variant particularly contrasts with the original in the printer's use of a different font and a wider measure. Among possible reasons for the resetting, accidental pieing partway through the run seems improbable, since both formes are involved. Greg, by way of explanation, suggested either a short run or the accidental destruction of part of the stock (*Bibliography,* 159). I see little ground for choosing between Greg's alternatives, since the relevant evidence obtainable from the running titles is at best equivocal and since too few copies survive to permit even a guess at the number of sheets printed from the resetting. But because the compositor who reset the type did not return to the manuscript for his copy, I derive my text for this portion of the play from the original printing.

One skeleton served for imposition of all inner, another for all outer formes of sheets B through G, the "regular" sheets of the quarto. But since work began with sheet A, the compositor first constructed special outer and inner skeletons for imposition of this sheet; he concluded by assembling another special pair for the half-sheet H, which completes the quarto. Throughout he practiced the usual economies, transferring the original running titles from the A formes, when these skeletons were no longer required, into those assembled for imposition of sheets B through G; and, when the need arose, he again shifted three titles into the modified skeletons required by the half-sheet H. Presumably in the interest of consistency, midway through press work on the quarto he corrected two instances of the unusual spelling "humerous," both of which occur in the inner skeleton, to "humorous," the version that is always found in the outer forme.

Certainty in discriminating compositors' work stints proves difficult to achieve. Orthographic tests, which ultimately suggest that one workman set most of the type (including the reset half-sheet H) remain, none the less, inconclusive. For example, both final "y" and final "ie" spellings occur in almost every page of the quarto, with no apparent tendency for one to dominate the

---

[5] Akihiro Yamada, "A Proof-Sheet in *An Humorous Day's Mirth* (1599), Printed by Valentine Simmes," *The Library,* Fifth Series, XXI (June, 1966), 155-57. Alice Walker (*Textual Problems of the First Folio,* p. 104), referring to the quarto of *II Henry IV* (1600), thought that "Simmes's proof-reading was clearly done with reference to the manuscript"; and Yamada conceded that evidence from *An Humorous Day's Mirth* suggests on the part of the proof reader "occasional reference to copy."

other. Also, an internal "y" occasionally replaces the usual "i,"[6] and a final "ye" substitutes for the expected "y" or "ie"[7] throughout much of the quarto. Such words as "yong," "countesse," and "yfaith," which might, through variant spellings, indicate a change in compositors, appear often; but variations in their spellings assume no meaningful pattern. A preference for "e" over "ee" in spelling "he," "she," "we," "me," and "be" (i.e., "he" over "hee," "she" over "shee," etc.) and of "ll" over "l" in such words as "shall," "well," "tell," "all," "fall," and "will" is evident throughout the quarto, every forme containing several of the usual spellings and one or more of the less usual. A careful tabulation ultimately failed, however, to identify any section of the book in which variations in these spellings proved clearly significant.

Always a matter for concern when one seeks to determine whether an abrupt variation in orthography signals the intrusion of a new compositor is the fact that such variations may derive from any of several causes. For example, the ampersand appears with some frequency throughout sheet A and the first pages of B, is completely omitted from the final pages of B and from all of C, then reappears in D. But, though such a pattern probably does indicate compositorial preference for "&" over "and," a characteristic that might help to identify a work unit, one supposes that these particular alternations reflect, not changes in compositors, but depletion and replenishment of the printer's case, as, indeed, the failure of several identifiable types found in A to reappear in C also suggests.

Likewise disappointing in the attempt to define work stints are several variations in the speech-prefixes which, theoretically at least, might aid one in such a task. Because most of the twenty-four speakers' names occur in the speech heads sometimes in very short abbreviations (i.e., of one or two letters), sometimes in longer forms, one supposes that a compositor's work might reflect his preference for either the short or the long versions. And a glance at the quarto does show that in some pages the speech heads tend to brevity (e.g., A4^v); in others, to greater length (e.g., D3^v). Indeed, a complete tabulation reveals discernible patterns of this sort in various parts of the text. In every page of sheet A, for example, one finds a mixture of short and long forms, though always with the briefer dominating; sheet B reverses the relationship. But introduction in sheet B of several characters whose names require longer abbreviations effectively invalidates this contrast as evidence of a compositor change. Efforts to identify significant patterns throughout the quarto in the abbreviations used for a particular name (e.g., *Lemot,* which occurs in every sheet) also provide equivocal results. In fact, frequent observation of both short and long abbreviations of the same name in the prefixes of a single page severely erodes one's confidence in the efficacy of such tests for this quarto.

On one brief occasion, however, the presence of a second compositor seems likely. At any rate, such a hypothesis plausibly explains a notable drop in the quality of workmanship in sigs. D1^v-D2. Though misreadings and eye-skips occur throughout the text, they especially cluster here. One might ascribe such

[6] E.g., perceyue (C3^v); clyents (D2); ayde (F4^v); fayre (G2); and frayd (G2^v).
[7] E.g., onelye (A2); dutye (B2); ladye (C2); Ladyesproofe (C3^v); quietlye (D3); anye (D3); and laye (F2^v).

fluctuation to a page or two of damaged copy except that, since the compositor had serious trouble with Latin phrases nowhere but here, he may not have been the same workman who correctly set bits of Latin throughout the rest of the text.

Various characteristics of the quarto suggest that the printer worked from author's papers. For example, the speech head designation of a particular character occasionally changes (e.g., Verone is sometimes called Host, and Moren is called Lord); and similar variations occur in the stage directions (e.g., Florila is identified simply as "the puritane" and Labervele as "her husband"). Furthermore, stage directions are often notably inexplicit;[8] they also tend to be descriptive; and they sometimes ignore the entrance of a principal character — all of which details, when taken together, seem to suggest an author's manuscript.

The printer inserted several stage directions into the margins of the quarto, presumably because he found them in corresponding locations in his copy. None of these, one assumes, derives from Chapman. I take them to be interpolations intended to prevent possible mistakes in staging, as their terseness implies: e.g., "Then hee reades" (B1); "Then he sighes" (C4^v); and "He spies the creame" (F3). That on B2, "Enter Lemot," particularly illustrates its originator's alertness. In the midst of Labervele's excited speech to Florila and Catalian, Lemot enters. Since Labervele's abrupt interjection, "Gods my passion whom do I see . . . ," effectively signals Lemot's approach, Chapman did not mark the entrance. But someone concerned with staging the play, recognizing the need here for a warning notation, inserted a conspicuous direction in the margin.

Six marginal corrections in ink, all, apparently, made by the same seventeenth-century hand, occur in the Clark Library copy. Although the first four correct rather obvious errors in the speech-prefixes, the final two make significant emendations which, though corroborated by their contexts, have been usually overlooked. On D2, "wiues" is corrected by marginal notation to "Wynes" and "house" to "hose."

Because the original compositors printed the entire play, excepting three couplets and two additional lines,[9] as prose, I do not record as variants from the lineation of Q any instances in which the present text is arranged as verse. I have, however, by the following apparatus, identified the originator of lineation that I accept. Since Shepherd's is the first printed text of the play to distinguish verse from prose and since I have usually agreed with Shepherd's lineation, I regard this situation as normal and have not recorded such instances of agreement. In other words, wherever a passage in my text appears as verse without a note assigning some other authority for the lineation, the implication is that, excepting the eight lines just noted, Q is set as prose and Shepherd, among editors, originated the particular lineation that I have accepted. Whenever my text agrees in verse lineation with Parrott against Shepherd, I have assigned credit to Parrott.

[8] E.g., *"Enter the King and all the lords, with the Trumpets"* on C4^v; *"Enter Laberuele, Labesha, and all the rest"* on D1; *"Enter the King and another"* on F1^v; and *"Enter the Queene, and all that were in before"* on G1^v.
[9] I.e., I.iii.12-13, and V.ii.222-23; 227-28; and 248-49.

Because Q, with the exceptions noted above, is set entirely as prose, most upper case letters required to begin lines of verse in my text occur as lower case in Q. I have, therefore, recorded only exceptions to this rule. In other words, an unnoted upper case letter at the start of a line of verse in my text implies that the corresponding letter in Q is lower case unless for some obvious reason other than its function in beginning a line of verse it would normally occur as upper case. Thus, if a proper noun, the pronoun I, or the first word following a full stop also begins a line of verse, the use of the upper case letter would be implied for Q and unrecorded. But other exceptions are recorded (i.e., instances in which a letter in my text raised to upper case to start a line of verse occurs also as upper case in Q but for none of the reasons just listed). Also recorded, of course, are instances in Q of lower case initial letters where upper case would be expected. The ampersand is assumed in all instances to represent lower case.

A pleasant Comedy

entituled :

An Humerous dayes Myrth.

As it hath beene sundrie times publikely acted by
the right honourable the Earle of Nottingham Lord high Admirall
his seruants.

By G.C.

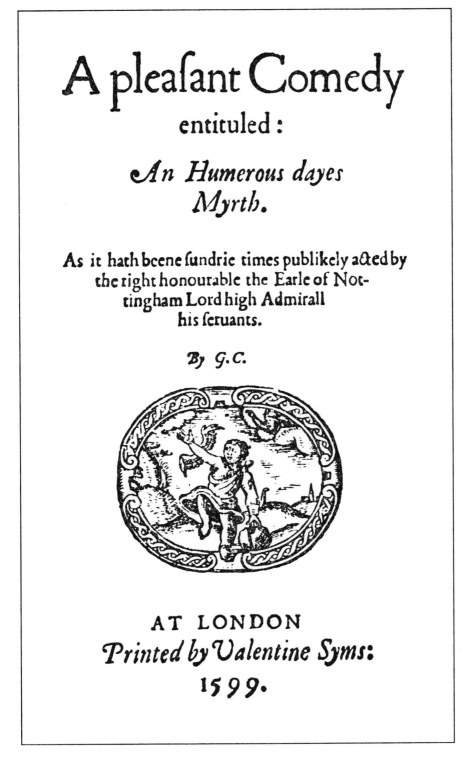

AT LONDON
Printed by Valentine Syms:
1599.

DRAMATIS PERSONAE

[The King   The Queen
Count Labervele   Florila, wife of Labervele
Dowsecer, his son   Countess Moren
Count Moren   Martia
Lemot   Jaquina, Verone's maid]
Foyes
Colinet
Catalian
Blanuel
Labesha
Lavel
Rowley
Berger
Verone, host of the ordinary
Verone's son
Jaques, Verone's man
A Torchbearer

A pleasant Comedie entituled [A2]
An humorous dayes mirth.

[I.i]

Enter the count Laberuele in his shirt and night gowne, with two iewells
in his hand.

Laberuele.

Yet hath the morning sprinckled throwt the clowdes,
But halfe her tincture and the soyle of night
Stickes stil vpon the bosome of the ayre:
Yet sleepe doth rest my loue for Natures debt,
And through her windowe, and this dim twee-light,   5
Her maide, nor any waking I can see.
This is the holy Greene my wifes close walke,
To which not any but her selfe alone
Hath any key, onelye that I haue clapt
Her key in waxe, and made this counterfeite,   10
By the which I steale accesse, to work this rare
And politike deuice:
Faire is my wife and yong and delicate,
Although too religious in the purest sorte,
But pure religion being but mental stuffe,   15
And sence, indeed, al for it selfe,
Tis to be doubted, that when an obiect comes
Fit to her humour she wil intercept
Religious letters sent vnto her minde,
And yeelde vnto the motion of her bloud.   20
Heere haue I brought then two rich agots for her,
Grauen with two poses of mine own deuising,
For Poets Ile not trust, nor friends, nor any:
Shee longs to haue a child, which yet alas
I cannot get, Yet long as much as she,   25
And not to make her desperate, thus I write

I.i] ‖ **2** But] *stet* ‖ **11** By] *Brereton conj.*; to ‖ **13** Faire] *stet* ‖ **15** stuffe,] ∼∧ ‖ **16** sence,] ∼∧ ‖
17 Tis] *Parrott*; is ‖ **20** bloud.] ∼, ‖ **21** Heere] heere ‖

In this faire iewell; though it simple be,
Yet tis mine owne, that meaneth well enough,
           Dispaire not of children,
               Loue / with the longest,   [A2ᵛ] 30
            When man is at the weakest,
              God is at [the] strongest.
I hope tis plain, and knowing; in this other that I write,
           God will reward her a thousand fold,
          That takes what age can and not what age would.   35
I hope tis prety and pathetical:
Wel, euen here
Lie both together til my loue arise
And let her thinke you fall out of the skies,
I will to bed againe.   *Exit.*

[I.ii]

Enter Lemot and Colenet.

Le. How like thou this morning *Colenet?* What, shall we haue a
faire day?

Col. The skie hangs full of humour, and I thinke we shall haue
raine.

Le. Why raine is faire wether when the ground is dry and barren,   5
especially when it raines humor, for then doe men like hot sparrowes
and pigeons open all their wings ready to receiue them.

Col. Why then we may chaunce to haue a faire day, for we shall
spend it with so humorous acquaintance, as raines nothing but humor
al their life time.   10

Le. True *Colenet,* ouer which wil I sit like an old King in an old
fashion play, hauing his wife, his counsel, his children, and his foole
about him, to whome he will sit and point very learnedly as foloweth;
My counsell graue, and you my noble peeres,
My tender wife, and you my children deare,   15
And thou my foole —

Col. Not meaning me sir I hope.

Le. No sir, but thus will I sit, as it were, and point out all my
humorous companions.

Col. You shal do maruelous wel sir.   20

Le. I thanke you for your good incouragement, but *Colinet* thou
shalt see *Catalian* bring me hither an od gentleman presently to be
acquainted withall, who in his manner of taking acquaintance wil
make vs excellent sport.

27 iewell;] ∼∧ ‖ **28** owne,] ∼∧ | enough] *Parrott*; in nought ‖ **29** Dispaire] dispaire, *Q(c)*;
tis spare, *Q(u)* ‖ **32** God] god | the] *Shepherd* | strongest.] ∼, ‖ **33** knowing;] *Shepherd*; ∼∧ ‖
35 would.] ∼, ‖ **37** Wel] *stet* ‖ I.ii] ‖ **16** foole—] ∼. ‖ **21** *Colinet*] roman ‖ **22** *Catalian*] roman ‖

Col. Why *Lemot* I thinke thou sendst about of purpose for yong   25
gallants to be acquainted withal, to make thy selfe merry in the
maner of taking acquaintance. /

Le. By heauen I do *Colenet,* for there is no better sport then to   [A3]
obserue the complement, for that's their word, complement, do you
marke sir?   30

Col. Yea sir, but what humor hath this gallant in his maner of
taking acquaintance?

Le. Marry thus sir, he will speake the very selfe same word, to a
sillable after him of whome he takes acquaintance, as if I should say,
I am marueilous glad of your acquaintance, He will reply,   35
I am meruailous glad of your acquaintance,
I haue heard much good of your rare parts and fine cariage,
I haue heard much good of your rare parts and fine cariage.
So long as the complements of a gentleman last, he is your complete
ape.   40

Col. Why this is excellent.

Le. Nay sirra here's the iest of it: when hee is past this gratulation,
he wil retire himself to a chimny, or a wal, standing folding his armes
thus: and go you and speake to him so farre as the roome you are in
wil afford you, you shal neuer get him from that most gentlemanlike   45
set, or behauior.

Col. This makes his humor perfit, I would he would come once.

Enter Catalian and Blanuel.

Le. See where he comes, now must I say, *Lupus est in fabula,* for
these latine ends are part of a gentleman and a good scholler.

Cat. O good morrow *Monseur Lemot,* here is the gentleman you   50
desired so much to be acquainted withal.

Le. He is marueilous welcome; I shall be exceeding prowd of your
acquaintance.

Blan. I shal be exceeding prowd of your acquaintance.

Le. I haue heard much good of your rare parts and fine cariages.   55

Blan. I haue heard much good of your rare parts and fine cariages.

Le. I shall be glad to be commanded by you. /

Blan. I shall be glad to be commanded by you.   [A3ᵛ]

Le. I pray do not you say so.

Blan. I pray do not you say so.   60

Le. Well Gentlemen, this day let's consecrate to mirth; and *Colenet*
you know no man better, that you are mightily in loue with louely
Martia daughter to old *Foyes.*

Col. I confesse it; here are none but friends.

29 that's] thats ‖ 38 cariage.] ~, ‖ 39 So] so ‖ 42 here's] heres | it:] ~, ‖ 43 wal,] ~∧ ‖ 52
welcome;] ~, ‖ 61 mirth;] ~, ‖ 62 louely] *Parrott, Deighton conj.*; loue, by ‖ 64 it;] ~∧ ‖

Le. Wel then, go to her this morning in Countesse *Morens* name,   65
and so perhaps you may get her company, thogh the olde churle bee
so iealous that he will suffer no man to come at her, but the vaine
gull *Labesha* for his liuing sake, and he as yet she will not be acquainted withall.

    Col. Well this Ile do whatsoeuer come on it.   70

    Le. Why nothing but good wil come of it, nere doubt it man.

    Cat. [*Aside to Lemot.*] Hee hath taken vp his stand, talke a little
further and see and you can remoue him.

    Le. [*Aside.*] I wil *Catalian*; — nowe Monsieur *Blanuele* marke I
pray.   75

    Blan. I do sir very well I warrant you.

    Le. You know the old Count Laberuele, hath a passing faire yong
Lady, that is a passing foule Puritane.

    Blan. I know her very well sir, she goes more like a milke maide
then a Countesse, for all her youth and beautie.   80

    Le. True sir, yet of her is the old Count so iealous that he will
suffer no man to come at her, yet I will find a meanes, that two of vs
will haue accesse to her, tho before his face, which shal so heate his
ielous humor til he be start mad: but *Colenet* go you first to louely
Martia, for tis too soone for the old Lord and his faire yong Lady   85
to rise.

    Col. Adue Monseur *Blanuel.*

    Blan. Adue good Monsieur *Colinet.*   *Exit Col.*

    Le. Monseur *Blanuel* your kindnes in this wil bind me much to you.

    Blan. Monseur *Lemot* your kindnes in this will bind me much to   90
you. /

    Le. I pray you do not say so sir.   [A4]

    Blan. I pray you do not say so sir.

    Le. Wilt please you to go in?

    Blan. Wilt please you to go in?   95

    Le. I will follow you.

    Blan. I will follow you.

    Le. It shall be yours.

    Blan. It shall be yours.

    Le. Kind Monsieur *Blanuel.*   100

    Blan. Kind Monsier *Lemot.*   *Exeunt.*

[I.iii]

Enter Foyes, and Martia, and Besha.

    Foyes. Come on faire daughter fall to your worke of mind, and
make your body fit to imbrace the body of this Gentlemans, tis art:
happy are they say I.

---

65 *Morens*] *Shepherd; Moris* ‖ **72** SD *Aside to Lemot.*] *Parrott* ‖ **74** SD *Aside.*] *Parrott* | *Catalian;—*]
Cat.∧ ‖ **83** her, tho] *Shepherd;* ∼∧ ∼, ‖ **84** start] *stet* (*See Textual Note*) ‖ **94** in?] ∼. ‖ **95** in?]
∼. ‖ **101** SD *Exeunt*] *Parrott subs.; Exit* ‖ I.iii] ‖

Labes. I protest sir you speake the best that euer I heard.

Foyes. I pray sir take acquaintance of my daughter.   5

Labes. I do desire you of more acquaintance.

Foyes. [*To Martia.*] Why dost not thou say yea, and I the same of you?

Mar. That euery body sayes.

Foyes. O you would be singular.   10

Mar. Single indeede.

Foyes. Single indeede that's a prety toy,
Your betters dame bear double, and so shall you.

Labes. Exceeding prety, did you marke it forsooth?

Mar. What should I marke forsooth?   15

Labes. Your bearing double, which equificate is and hath a fit illu-
sion to a horse that beares double, for your good father meanes you
shall indure your single life no longer, not in worse sense then bearing
double forsooth.

Mar. I crie you mercy, you know both belike.   20

Labes. Knowlege forsooth is like a horse and you, that can beare
double: it nourisheth both Bee and Spider, the Bee honnisuckle, the
Spider poyson, I am that Bee.

Mar. I thought so by your stinging witte.

Labes. Lady I am a Bee without a sting, no way hurting any, but   25
good to all, and before all, to your sweete selfe. /

Foyes. Afore God daughter, thou art not worthy to heare him   [A4ᵛ]
speake: but who comes here?

Enter Colinet.

Col. God saue you sir.

Foyes. You are welcome sir for ought that I know yet.   30

Col. I hope I shall be so still sir.

Foyes. What is your busines sir, and then Ile tell you?

Col. Mary thus sir, the Countesse *Morene* intreats your faire daughter to beare her company this fore-noone.

Foyes. This forenoone sir, doth my Lord or Lady send for her I   35
pray?

Col. My Lady I assure you.

Foyes. My Lady you assure me; very wel sir, yet that house is full
of gallant Gentlemen, dangerous thornes to pricke yong maides I can
tell you.   40

Col. There are none but honest and honourable Gentlemen.

Foyes. Al is one sir for that, Ile trust my daughter with any man,
but no man with my daughter, only your selfe Monser *Besha,* whom I
wil intreat to be her gardian, and to bring her home againe.

---

7 SD *To Martia.*] ‖ **12-13** Single . . . toy, / Your . . . you. /] *stet* ‖ **12** that's] thats ‖ **21** horse
and you,] *Parrott;* ∼, ∼ ∼∧ ‖ **28** SD *Enter Colinet.*] *flush right* ‖ **38** me;] *Shepherd;* ∼, ‖

Col. I will waite vpon her, and it please you.   45

Foyes. No sir, your weight vpon her wil not be so good: here Monser *Besha* I deliuer my daughter vnto you a perfect maide, and so I
pray you looke well vnto her.

Col. Farewell Monser *Foyes.*

Labes. I warrant Ile looke vnto her wel enough. Mistris will it   50
please you to preambulate?

Mar. With all my heart.   *Exeunt.*

[I.iv]

Enter the puritane.

Flo. What haue I done? put on too many clothes; the day is hote,
and I am hoter clad then might suffice health; my conscience telles me
that I haue offended, and Ile put them off; that will aske time that
might be better spent, one sin will draw another quickly so, see how
the diuell tempts: but what's here? iewels? how should these come   5
here?

Enter Laberuele. /

Lab. Good morrow louely wife, what hast thou there?   [B1]

Flo. Iewels my Lord which here I strangely found.

Lab. That's strange indeede, what, where none comes
But when your selfe is here? surely the heauens   10
Haue rained thee iewels for thy holy life,
And vsing thy olde husbande louingly,
Or else doe Fairies haunt this holy greene,
As euermore mine auncesters haue thought.

Flo. Fairies were but in times of ignorance, not since the true pure 15
light hath beene reuealed; and that they come from heauen I scarce
beleeue: for iewels are vaine things, much gold is giuen for such fan-
tastical and fruitlesse iewels, and therfore heauen I know wil not maintain the vse of vanitie; surely I feare I haue much sinned to stoupe
and take them vp, bowing my bodie to an idle worke, the strength   20
that I haue had to this verie deed might haue beene vsed to take a
poore soule vp in the hie way.

Lab. You are too curious wife, behold your iewels:
What, me thinks there's posies written on them.

                                                      Then hee reades.
            Dispaire not of children,   25
               Loue with the longest,
            When man is at the weakest,
               God is at the strongest.

---

51 preambulate?] ∼. ‖ [I.iv] ‖ 1 clothes;] ∼, ‖ 2 health;] ∼, ‖ 3 off;] ∼, ‖ 5 what's] whats ‖
9 That's] Thats ‖ 16 reuealed;] ∼, ‖ 17 much] *Q(c)*; more *Q(u)* ‖ 19 vanitie;] ∼, ‖ 23-24
You ... them.] *so lined by P* ‖ 24 What,] whatΛ │ there's] thers *Q(u)*; theres *Q(c)* │ posies]
Q(c); poises *Q(u)* │ SD *hee*] *Q(c)*; *shee Q(u)*; *SD in margin* ‖ 24-25 them. Dispaire] *Q(c)*; them,
dispaire *Q(u)* ‖ 28 God] god ‖ 28-29 strongest. Wonderfull] *Q(c)*; strongest; wonderfull *Q(u)* ‖

72

Wonderfull rare and wittie, nay diuine,
Why this is heauenly comfort for thee wife,   30
What is this other?
           God will reward her a thousand folde
           That takes what age can, and not what age would.
The best that euer I heard, no mortall braine
I thinke did euer vtter such conceit   35
For good plaine matter, and for honest rime.
   Flo. Vaine Poetry, I pray you burne them sir.
   Lab. You are to blame wife, heauen hath sent you them
To decke your self withall, like to your self,
Not to go thus like a milk-maid,   40
Why there is difference in all estats
By al religion.
   Flo.   There is no difference.
   Lab. I prethee wife be of another mind,
And weare these iewels and a veluet hood.
   Flo. A veluet hood! O vaine diuelish deuise! a toy made with a   45
superfluous flap, which being cut off, my head were still as warme.
Diogenes did cast away his dish, because his hand would serue to helpe
him drinke; surely these heathens / shall rise vp against vs.   [B1ᵛ]
   Lab. Sure wife I thinke thy keeping alwaies close, making thee melancholy, is the cause we haue no children, and therefore if thou wilt,   50
be mery, and keepe companie a gods name.
   Flo. Sure my lord, if I thought I shold be rid of this same banishment of barrennes, and vse our marriage to the end it was made, which
was for procreation, I should sinne, if by my keeping house I should
neglect the lawful means to be a fruitful mother, and therfore if it   55
please you ile vse resort.
   Lab. [*Aside.*] God's my passion what haue I done? who woulde
haue thought her purenesse would yeeld so soone to courses of tempta-
tions? — nay harke you wife, I am not sure that going abroad will
cause fruitfulnesse in you; that you know none knowes but God   60
himselfe.
   Flo. I know my lord tis true, but the lawfull means must still be vsed.
   Lab. Yea, the lawfull meanes indeed must still — but now I remember, that lawfull meanes is not abroad.
   Flo. Well, well, Ile keepe the house still.   65
   Lab. Nay, heark you lady, I would not haue you thinke — mary, I
must tel you this, if you shuld change the maner of your life, the world
would think you changed religion too.
   Flo. Tis true, I will not go.

33-34 would. The] *Q(c)*; would, the *Q(u)* ‖ **38-42** You . . . religion.] *so lined by P* ‖ **45** hood!]
Q(c); ~, *Q(u)* ‖ **46** off, my head] *Q(c)*; ~ₐ ~ ~, *Q(u)* ‖ **47** would] *Q(c)*; will *Q(u)* | helpe]
Q(u); help *Q(c)* ‖ **48** drinke;] ~, ‖ **52-53** banishment] *stet* (*See Textual Note*) ‖ **56** resort.] ~ₐ
‖ **57** SD *Aside.*] *Parrott* | God's] Gods ‖ **58-59** temptations?—] ~?ₐ ‖ **60** you;] ~, ‖ **63** still—]
~, ‖ **63-64** remember,] ~ₐ ‖ **66** thinke—] ~, ‖

Lab. Nay, if you haue a fancie.   70

Flo. Yea a fancie, but that's no matter.

Lab. Indeed fancies are not for iudicial and religious women.

Enter Catalian like a scholer.

Cat. God saue your lordship, and you most religious lady.

Lab. Sir you may say God saue vs well indeed

That thus are thrust vpon in priuate walkes.   75

Cat. A slender thrust sir, where I toucht you not.

Lab. Well sir what is you busines?

Cat. Why sir, I haue a message to my ladie from Monsier *du Barto.*

Lab. To your lady, wel sir, speake your mind to your lady. /

Flo. You are very welcome sir, and I pray how doth he?   [B2] 80

Cat. In health Madam, thanks be to God, commending his dutie to
your ladiship, and hath sent you a message which I would desire your
honour to heare in priuate.

Flo. My ladiship, and my honor, they be words which I must haue
you leaue, they be ydle woordes, and you shal answere for them truly: 85
my dutye to you, or I desire you, were a great deale better, then, my
ladiship, or my honour.

Cat. I thanke you for your christian admonition.

Flo. Nay thanke God for me: Come I will heare your message with
all my heart, and you are very welcome sir.   90

Lab. [*Aside.*] With all my heart, and you are very welcome sir, and
go and talke with a yong lustie fellow able to make a mans haire stand
vpright on his head; what puritie is there in this trow you? Ha, what
wench of the facultie could haue beene more forward? Well sir, I will
know your message. — You sir, you sir, what sayes the holy man sir?   95
come tell true, for by heauen or hell I will haue it out.

Cat. Why you shall sir, if you be so desirous.

Lab. Nay sir, I am more then so desirous: come sir, study not for a
new deuice now.

Cat. Not I my lord, this is both new and old. I am a scholer, and   100
being spiritually inclined by your ladies most godly life, I am to professe the ministerie, and to become her chaplaine, to which end monsier *du Barto* hath commended me.

Lab. Her chaplaine in the diuels name, fit to be vickar of hell.

Flo. My good head, what are you afraid of? he comes with a godly   105
and neighborly sute: what, think you his words or his looks can tempt
me? haue you so litle faith? if euery word he spake were a serpent, as
suttle as that which tempted *Eue,* he cannot tempt me I warrant you.

Lab. Wel answered for him lady by my faith: wel hark you Ile

---

71 that's] thats ‖ 78 Monsier] *italic* ‖ 80 he?] ∼. ‖ 91 SD *Aside.*] *Parrott* ‖ 93 head;] ∼, | Ha]
ha ‖ 95 message.—You] message, you | sir?] ∼, ‖ 100 old.] ∼, ‖ 102-3 monsier *du Barto*]
monsier du Barte ‖ 106 what,] ∼∧ ‖

keepe your chaplaines place yonder for a while, and at length put in   110
one my self:

Enter Lemot.

what more yet? Gods my passion whom do I see, the very imp of desolation, the minion of our / King, whome no man sees to enter his   [B2ᵛ]
house but hee lockes vp, his wife, his children, and his maides, for
where hee goes hee carries his house vppon his head like a snaile: 115
now sir I hope your busines is to me.

Le. No sir, I must craue a word with my ladie.

Lab. These words are intollerable, and she shal hear no more.

Le. She must heare me speake.

Lab. Must she sir, haue you brought the kings warrant for it?   120

Le. I haue brought that which is aboue Kings.

Lab. Why euery man for her sake is a puritan. The Diuill I thinke
wil shortly turne Puritan, or the Puritan wil turne Diuell.

Flo. What haue you brought sir?

Le. Mary this Madam, you know we ought to proue one anothers   125
constancie, and I am come in all chast and honourable sort to proue
your constancie.

Flo. You are verie welcome sir, and I will abide your proofe: it is
my dutie to abide your proofe.

Lab. You'le bide his proofe, it is your dutie to bide his proofe, how   130
the diuell will you bide his proofe?

Flo. My good head, no other wise then before your face in all honorable and religious sort; I tell you I am constant to you, and he comes
to trie whether I be so or no, which I must indure; begin your proofe
sir.   135

Le. Nay Madam, not in your husbands hearing, thogh in his
sight, for there no woman wil shewe shee is tempted from her constancie, though she be a little: withdraw your selfe sweete ladie.

[*They withdraw.*]

Lab. Well I will see though I do not heare, women may be courted
without offence, so they resist the courtier.   140

Le. Deare and most beautifull ladie, of all the sweet honest and
honorable meanes to proue the puritie of a ladies constancy, kisses are
the strongest; I will therefore be bold to begin my proofe with a kisse.

Flo. No sir, no kissing. /

Le. No kissing Madam? how shall I proue you then sufficiently, not [B3]   145
vsing the most sufficient proofe? to flatter your selfe by affection of
spirit, when it is not perfitly tried, is sin.

Flo. You say well sir, that which is truth is truth.

Le. Then do you wel Lady and yeeld to the truth.

---

111 SD *Enter Lemot.*] *Shepherd; in margin* ‖ **112-13** desolation] *stet* (*See Textual Note*) ‖ **114** lockes]
Shepherd; lookes ‖ **118** more.] ∼∧ ‖ **133** sort;] ∼, | to you] *Q(c);* o you *Q(u)* ‖ **134** must indure;]
tmust ∼, *Q(u);* ∼ ∼, *Q(c)* ‖ **136** thogh] *Q(c);* thou *Q(u)* ‖ **137** sight,] ∼∧ | there no] there
is no (*See Textual Note*) ‖ **138** SD *They withdraw.*] *Parrott* ‖ **140** courtier] *Q(c);* Cortier *Q(u)* ‖
141 all] *Q(u);* al *Q(c)* | the] *Q(c);* he *Q(u)* ‖ **143** strongest;] ∼, ‖ **146** proofe?] *Q(c);* ∼∧ *Q(u)* ‖

Flo. By your leaue sir, my husband sees, peraduenture it may breed   150
an offence to him.

Le. How can it breed an offence to your husband to see your constancie perfectly tried?

Flo. You are an odde man I see, but first I pray tel me how kissing
is the best proofe of chast Ladies.   155

Le. To giue you a reason for that, you must giue me leaue to be
obscure and Philosophicall.

Flo. I pray you be, I loue Philosophie well.

Le. Then thus Madam: euery kisse is made as the voice is by imagination and appetite, and as both those are presented to the eare in   160
the voyce, so are they to the silent spirites in our kisses.

Flo. To what spirit meane you?

Le. To the spirites of our bloud.

Flo. What if it doe?

Le. Why then my imagination, and mine appetite working vpon   165
your eares in my voyce, and vpon your spirites in my kisses, pearcing
therein the more deeply, they giue the stronger assault against your
constancie.

Flo. Why then to say, proue my constancy, is as much as to say,
kisse me.   170

Le. Most true rare Ladie.

Flo. Then prooue my constancie.

Le. Beleeue me Madam, you gather exceeding wittily vpon it.   [*Kisses her.*]

Lab. O my forehead, my very heart akes at a blowe! what dost thou
meane wife? thou wilt loose thy fame, discredite thy religion, and dis-   175
honour me for euer.

Flo. Away sir, I wil abide no more of your proofe, nor endure any
more of your triall. /

Le. O she dares not, she dares not, I am as glad I haue tride your   [B3ᵛ]
puritie as may be: you the most constant Lady in *France*? I know an   180
hundred Ladies in this towne that wil dance, reuill all night amongst
gallants, and in the morning goe to bed to her husband as cleere a
woman as if she were new christned, kisse him, imbrace him, and say,
no, no husband, thou art the man, and he takes her for the woman.

Flo. And all this can I doe.   185

Lab. Take heede of it wife.

Flo. Feare not my good heade, I warrant you for him.

Le. Nay Madam, triumph not before the victorie, howe can you
conquer that, against which you neuer striue, or striue against that

---

153 tried?] ∼. ‖ **159** Madam:] *Q(c)*; ∼, *Q(u)* ‖ **167** more deeply] *Q(c)*; most deepely *Q(u)* ‖
171 Most] most ‖ true] *Q(c)*; ∼, *Q(u)* ‖ **173** SD *Kisses her.*] *Parrott* ‖ **174** blowe!] ∼, ‖ **180**
France] roman ‖ **189** striue against] *Q(c)*; ∼ ahainst *Q(u)* ‖

which neuer incounters you? To liue idle in this walke, to inioy this   190
companie, to weare this habite, and haue no more delights then those
will affoorde you, is to make vertue an idle huswife, and to hide her-
selfe [in] slouthfull cobwebbes that still should be adorned with actions
of victorie: no Madam, if you wil worthilly prooue your constancie to
your husband, you must put on rich apparrell, fare daintily, heare mu-   195
sique, reade Sonetes, be continually courted, kisse, daunce, feast, reuell
all night amongst gallants, then if you come to bed to your husband
with a cleere minde, and a cleere body, then are your vertues *ipsissima;*
then haue you passed the ful test of experiment, and you shall haue an
hundred gallants fight thus farre in bloud for the defence of your   200
reputation.

Lab. O vanitie of vanities!

Flo. O husband this is perfect tryall indeede.

Lab. And you wil try all this now, wil you not?

Flo. Yea my good head, for it is written, we must passe to perfec-   205
tion through al temptation, *Abacuke* the fourth.

Lab. Abacucke, cucke me no cuckes, in a doores I saye, theeues,
Puritanes, murderers, in a doores I / say.   *Exeunt Laberuele and Florila.* [B4]

Le. So now is he start mad yfaith: but sirra, as this is an old Lorde
iealous of his yong wife, so is antient Countesse *Moren* iealous of her   210
yong husband; weele thither to haue some sport yfaith.   *Exeunt.*

[I.v]

Enter Besha hanging vpon Martia sleeue, and the Lord Moren comes to them.

Mor. I prethee *Besha* keepe a little off;
Hang not vpon her shoulders thus for shame.

Labes. My Lord, *Pardon a moy,* I must not let her talk alone with
any one, for her father gaue me charge.

Mor. O you are a goodly charger for a Goose.   5

Labes. A Goose, you are a Gander to call me Goose, I am a christian Gentleman as well as you.

Mor. Well sirra get you hence, or by my troth Ile haue thee taken
out in a blanket, tossed from forth our hearing.

Labes. In a blanket? what, do you make a puppie of me? by skies   10
and stones I will go and tell your Lady.   *Exit.*

Mor. Nay but *Besha.*

Mar. Nay he will tell my Lorde.

---

190 you?] ∼∧ | To] *Q(c);* to *Q(u)* | idle] *Q(c);* ∼, *Q(u)* | walke,] *Q(c);* ∼∧ *Q(u)* ‖ **191**
companie,] *Q(c);* ∼∧ *Q(u)* | habite,] *Q(c);* ∼? *Q(u)* ‖ **193** in] *Shepherd* ‖ **194** worthilly] *Parrott,*
Brereton conj.; vnworthilly ‖ **196** Sonetes,] ∼∧ ‖ **205** head,] *Q(c);* ∼∧ *Q(u)* ‖ **208** SD *Exeunt*
. . . Florila] Parrott subs.; Exet Q(u); Exit Q(c) ‖ **211** husband;] ∼, | SD *Exeunt] Exit* ‖ I.v] ‖
1, 5 *Mor.] Parrott; Mar.* ‖ **8** *Mor.] Shepherd; Mar.* ‖ **10** what,] ∼∧ | me?] ∼, ‖

Enter the Countesse Moren and Besha.

Coun. Why how now my Lord; what, thought you I was dead, that
you are wooing of another thus, or are you laying plots to worke my   15
death?

Mor. Why neither sweete bird, what need you moue these questions
vnto me, whome you know loues you aboue all the women in the
world?

Coun. How he can flatter now he hath made a fault.   20

Labes. He can do little, and he cannot cogge.

Mor. Out you asse.

Coun. Wel, come tell me what you did intreat.

Mor. Nothing by heauen sweete bird I sweare, but to intreat her
loue — /   25

Coun. But to intreat her loue?   [B4ᵛ]

Mor. Nay heare me out.

Coun. Nay here you are out, you are out too much me thinkes, and
put me in —

Mor. And put you in?   30

Coun. In a faire taking sir I meane.

Mor. O you may see what hastie taking is, you women euermore
scramble for our woordes, and neuer take them mannerly from our
mouths.

Coun. Come tell me what you did intreat.   35

Mor. I did intreat her loue to *Colinet.*

Coun. To *Colinet?* O he is your deare cousen, and your kinde heart
yfaith is neuer well but when you are doing good for euery man:
speake, do you loue me?

Mor. Yfaith sweete bird.   40

Coun. Best of all others?

Mor. Best of all others.

Coun. That's my good bird yfaith.

Labes. O mistris, will you loue me so?

Mar. No by my troth will I not.   45

Labes. No by my troth will I not: Why that's well said, I could
neuer get her to flatter me yet.

Enter Lemot, Blanuel, and Catalian, and Colinet.

Le. Good morrow my good Lord, and these passing louely Ladies.

Coun. So now we shall haue all maner of flattering with Monsieur
Lemot.   50

---

14 Lord; what,] ~, ~∧ ‖ **19** world?] *Q(c)*; ~. *Q(u)* ‖ **25** loue—] ~. ‖ **26** loue?] ~. ‖ **29**
in—] ~. ‖ **32** euermore] *Q(c)*; euer more *Q(u)* ‖ **41** others?] ~. ‖ **42** others.] ~? ‖ **43** That's]
Thats ‖ **45** *Mar.*] *Shepherd; Mor.* ‖ **46** not:] *Q(c)*; ~? *Q(u)* | that's] thats | said,] *Q(c)*; ~∧
Q(u) ‖ **49** *Coun.*] *Parrott, Brereton conj.; Cat.* ‖

Le. You are all manner of waies deceiued Madam, for I am so farre from flattering you, that I do not a whit praise you.

Coun. Why do you call vs passing louely then?

Le. Because you are passing from your louelines.

Mar. Madam we shall not haue one mot of Monsieur *Lemot,* but it shal be as it were a mote to drown al our conceit in admiration.   55

Le. See what a mote her quick eye can spie in mine, be / fore she lookes in it.   [C1]

Mar. So mote I thee, thine answer is as good as mought be.

Le. Here's a poore name run out of breath quickly.   60

Coun. Why Monsieur *Lemot,* your name is runne out of breath at euery word you speake.

Le. That's because my name signifies word.

Mar. Wel hit, Monsieur *verbum.*

Le. What, are you good at latine Lady?   65

Mar. No sir, but I know what *verbum* is.

Le. Why tis greenebum, *ver* is greene, and you know what bum is, I am sure of that.

Mar. No sir, tis a verbe, and I can decline you.

Le. That you can Ile be sworne.   70

Mar. What can I do?

Le. Decline me, or take me a hole lower, as the prouerbe is.

Mar. Nay sir, I meane plaine Gramatical declination.

Le. Well, let's heare your schollership, and decline me.

Mar. I will sir, *moto, motas.*   75

Labes. O excellent! she hath cald him asse in latine.

Le. Well sir, forward.

Mar. Nay there's enough to trie both our scholerships.

Le. Moto, motas, nay faith forward to *motaui,* or *motandi.*

Mar. Nay sir, Ile leaue when I am well.   80

Coun. Why Monsieur *Lemot,* your name being in word general, is in nini, or in hammer, or in cock, or in buzzard.

Le. Or in wagtaile, or in woodcocke, or in dotteril, or in dizard.

Mar. Or in clotte, or in head, or in cow, or in baby.

Le. Or in maukin, or in trash, or in pape, or in Lady.   85

Coun. Or in deed in euery thing.

Le. Why then tis in Thing.

Mar. Then good Monsier *Thing,* there let it rest.

Le. Then aboue all things I must haue a woorde with you. /

60 Here's] Heres ‖ 61 *Coun.] Parrott; Co.* ‖ 63 That's] Thats ‖ 65 What,] ∼∧ ‖ 73 declination.] ∼∧ ‖ 78 there's] theres | scholerships.] ∼∧ ‖ 81, 86 *Coun.] Parrott; Co.* ‖ 88 *Thing*] roman ‖

Labes. Hands off sir, she is not for your mowing. [C1ᵛ] 90

Le. She is for your mocking.

Labes. And she mocke me, Ile tell her father.

Le. That's a good child, thou smellest of the mother, and she was a foole I warrant you.

Labes. Meddle with me, but doe not meddle with my mother. 95

Le. That's a good child; [*To Martia.*] come, I must needes haue a word with you.

Labes. You shall do none of your needs with her sir.

Cat. Why what will you do?

Labes. What will I doe? you shall see what Ile do. *Then he* 100 *offereth to draw.*

Blan. Go to you asse, offer to draw here, and weele draw thee out of the house by the heeles.

Labes. What, three against one? now was euer proper hard fauord Gentleman so abused? Go to, Mistris *Martia,* I see you well enough, 105 are you not ashamed to stand talking alone with such a one as hee?

Le. How sir? with such a one as I sir?

Labes. Yea sir, with such a one as you sir.

Le. Why, what am I?

Labes. What are you sir? why I know you well enough. 110

Le. Sirra tel me what you know me for, or else by heauen Ile make thee; better thou hadst neuer knowne how to speake.

Labes. Why sir, if you wil needes know, I know you for an honorable gentleman and the Kings minion, and were it not to you, there's nere a gentleman in Paris should haue had her out of my hands. 115

Mar. Nay, hee's as tall a Gentleman of his hands as any is in Paris.

Col. There's a fauour for you sir.

Le. But I can get no fauour for you sir.

Blan. I pray my Lord intreat for your cossen *Colinet.*

Mor. Alas man, I dare not for my wife. / 120

Cat. Why my Lord she thinkes it is for nothing, but to speake for [C2] your cosen.

Mor. I pray you birde, giue me leaue to speake for my cosen.

Coun. I am content for him.

Mor. Then one woorde with you more, curteous ladie *Martia.* 125

Labes. Not, and you were my father.

Mor. Gentlemen, for God sake thrust this asse out of the doores.

Le. Nay, birladye he'le runne home and tell her father.

---

93 That's] Thats ‖ **96** That's] Thats | child;] ∼, | SD *To Martia.*] ‖ **100** SD *Then ... draw.*] *Shepherd; in margin* ‖ **105** to,] *Shepherd;* ∼∧ ‖ **111** tel me] ∼ ∼, ‖ **112** thee;] ∼∧ ‖ **114** there's] theres ‖ **116** hee's] hees ‖ **117** There's] Theres ‖

Cat. Well, go to her, I warrant he shall not trouble you;   [*To Labesha.*]
(kind gentleman) how we dote on thee: — imbrace him gentlemen.   130
    Blan. O sweete *Besha* how we honour thee.
    Col. Nay Gentlemen, looke what a pearcing eye hee hath.
    Labes. An eie? I haue an eie and it were a pole-cat.
    Cat. Nay, looke what a nose he hath.
    Labes. My nose is nete crimson.   135
    Blan. Nay, looke what a handsome man he is. O Nature, Nature,
Thou neuer madest man of so pure a feature.
    Labes. Truly truly Gentlemen, I do not deserue this kindnesse.
    Cat. O Lorde sir, you are too modest, come shall we walke?
    Labes. Whither? to the alehouse?   140
    Le. Hearke you Madam, haue you no more care of the right of your
husband, then to let him talke thus affectionately with another?
    Coun. Why he speakes not for himselfe, but for his cosen *Colinet.*
    Le. God's my life, he telles you so? nay and these excuses may serue,
I haue done. /   145
    Coun. By the masse now I obserue him, he lookes very suspitiously   [C2ᵛ]
indeede, nere trust me if his lookes, and his iesture doe not plainely
shewe himselfe to sweare, by this light I do loue thee.
    Le. Burlady Madam you gesse shrewdly indeede, but hearke you
Madam, I pray let not me be the author of discord beteene my good   150
Lord and you.
    Coun. No no Monsieur *Lemot,* I were blinde if I could not see this.
Ile slit her nose by *Iesus.*   [*Starting for Martia.*]
    Mor. How now what's the matter?
    Coun. What's the matter? if I could come at your Mistris, she   155
should know what's the matter.
    Mor. My Mistris?
    Coun. Yea your Mistris, O here's faire dissimulation. [*To Martia.*]
O ye impudent gossip, do I send for you to my house to make you my
companion, and do you vse me thus? little dost thou know what tis   160
to loue a man truly, for if thou didst, thou wouldst be ashamed to
wrong me so.
    Mar. You wrong me Madam to say I wrong you.
    Coun. Go to, get you out of my house.
    Mar. I am gone Madam.   165
    Mor. Well, come in sweete bird and Ile perswade thee, ther's no
harme done.
    Coun. Well, we shall heare your perswasions.

                              [*Exeunt Moren and Countess.*]

129 you;] ∼∧ | SD *To Labesha.] Parrott* ‖ **132** *Col.] Co.* ‖ **136** *Blan.*] stet (*See Textual Note*) | is.]
∼, ‖ **143-45** *Coun.* . . . done.] ∼. . . . ∼. Enter Lemot *SD in margin* (*See Textual Note*) ‖ **144**
God's my life, . . . so?] Gods my life? . . . so, | serue,] ∼∧ ‖ **152-53** this. Ile] this, ile ‖ **153** *Iesus.*]
Iesus∧ | SD *Starting for Martia.] Parrott subs.* ‖ **154** *Mor.] Shepherd; Me.* | what's] whats ‖ **155**
What's] Whats ‖ **156** what's] whats ‖ **158** here's] heres | dissimulation.] *Shepherd;* ∼, | SD
To Martia.] Parrott ‖ **168** SD *Exeunt . . . Countess.] Parrott* ‖

Le. Well God knowes, and I can partly gesse what he must do to
perswade her: well, take your faire charge, faire and manly Lord   170
Monsieur *Labesha*.

Col. One word with you more faire ladie.

Le. Not a word, no man on paine of death, not a word, he comes
vpon my rapiers point, that comes within fortie foote on her.

Labes. Thankes good *Lemot*, and thankes gentlemen all, and her   175
father shal thanke you.   [*Exeunt Labesha and Martia.*]

Col. Much good do it you sir: come Gentlemen, lets go wait vpon
the king, and see the humour of the young lord *Dowsecer.* /

Le. Excuse me to the King, and tell him I will meet him there: [C3]
                                        [*Exeunt Colinet, Catalian, and Blanuel.*]
so this is but the beginning of sport betweene this fine lord and his old   180
lady: but this wench *Martia* hath happy starres raigned at the disposition of her beautie, for the King him selfe doth mightily dote on
her. Now to my Puritane, and see if I can make vp my full proofe of
her.   [*Exit.*]

[II.i]

Enter the puritane in her best attyre.

Flo. Now am I vp and ready, ready? why?
Because my cloathes once on, that call we ready:
But readinesse I hope hath reference
To some fit action for our seuerall state:
For when I am attyred thus Countesse-like,   5
Tis not to worke, for that befittes me not,
Tis on some pleasure, whose chiefe obiect is
One mans content, and hee my husbande is,
But what need I thus to be attyred,
For that he would be pleased with meaner weed?   10
Besides I take no pleasure thus to please him:
I am content, because it is my duty
To keep to him, and not to seeke no further:
But if that pleasure be a thing that makes
The time seeme short, if it do laughter cause,   15
If it procure the tongue but hartily
To say, I thanke you, I haue no such thing,
Nor can the godliest woman in the worlde,
Against her nature please her sense, or soule.
She may say, this I will, or this I will not,   20
But what shall she reape hereby? comfort in
An other world, if she will stay till then.

176 SD *Exeunt . . . Martia.*] *Parrott* ‖ 177 *Col.*] *Parrott; C* ‖ 178 *Dowsecer*] Dowseger ‖ 179 SD
Exeunt . . . Blanuel.] *Parrott* ‖ 184 SD *Exit.*] *Parrott* ‖ II.i] ‖ 1-87 Now . . . one] *so lined by P* ‖
2 Because] because ‖ 11 Besides] besides ‖ 19 soule.] ∼, ‖ 20 She] she | not,] ∼. ‖

Enter her husband behind her.

Lab. Yea mary sir now I must looke about,
Now if her desolate proouer come againe,
Shal I admit him to make farther triall?   25
Ile haue a Dialogue betweene my selfe
And manly reason to that speciall end:
Reason, shall I indure a desolate man to come
And court my wife, and proue her constancie?
Reason: To court and proue her you may beare my lord,   30
For perfite things are not the worse for triall;
Gold will not turne to drosse for deepest triall:
Before God a comfortable saying:
Thanks gentle reason, Ile trouble you no more. /
God saue sweet wife, look vp, thy tempter comes.   [C3ᵛ] 35
Flo. Let him my lord, I hope I am more blest
Then to relent in thought of lewde suggestion.
Lab. But if by frailtie you should yeeld in thought,
What will you do?
Flo.   Then shall you keepe me close,
And neuer let me see man but your selfe;   40
If not, then boldly may I go abroade.
Lab. But how shall I know whether you yeeld, or no?
Flo. Heare vs your selfe, my lord.
Lab.   Tut, that were grosse,
For no woman will yeeld in her husbands hearing.
Flo. Then to assure you if I yeelde or no,   45
Marke but these signes: as hee is proouing me,
If I doe yeelde, you shall perceyue my face
Blush and looke pale, and put on heauie lookes.
If I resist I will triumph, and smile,
And when I hold but vp my finger,   50
Stop his vaine lips, or thrust him on the breast,
Then is he ouerthrowne both horse and foote.
Lab. Why, this doth satisfie me mightily:

[Enter Lemot.]

See hee is come.
Le. Honor to my good lord, and his faire yong ladie.   55
Lab. Nowe Monsieur *Sathan,* you are come to tempt
And prooue at full the spirit of my wife.
Le. I am my lord, but vainly I suppose.

---

27 reason] *Shepherd;* ∼: | end:] *Shepherd;* ∼∧ ‖ **29** constancie?] ∼: ‖ **30** Reason: To] reason,
to ‖ **40** selfe;] ∼, ‖ **42** how] ∼, ‖ **53** SD *Enter Lemot.] Parrott* ‖ **56** *Sathan*] roman ‖

Lab. You see she dares put on this braue attire
Fit with the fashion, which you think serues much   60
To lead a woman into light desires.
    Le. My lord I see it: and the sight thereof
Doth halfe dismay me to make further proofe.
    Lab. Nay prooue her, proue her sir, and spare not:
What, doth the wittie minion of our King   65
Thinke any dame in *France* will say him nay?
But proue her, proue her, sir and spare not.
    Le. Well sir, though halfe discouraged in my comming,
Yet Ile go forward: ladie, by your leaue.   [*He withdraws with Florila.*]
    Flo. Nowe sir, your cunning in a Ladyes proofe. /   70
    Le. Madam, in prouing you I find no proofe   [C4]
Against your piercing glauncings,
But swear I am shot thorow with your loue.
    Flo. I do beleeue you: who will sweare he loues,
To get the thing he loues not? if he loue,   75
What needs more perfite triall?
    Le.   Most true rare ladie.
    Flo. Then are we fitly met, I loue you too.
    Le. Exceeding excellent.
    Flo. Nay, I knowe you will applaude mee in this course,
But to let common circumstaunces passe,   80
Let vs be familiar.
    Le. Deare Life, you rauish my conceit with ioy.
    Lab. [*Aside.*] I long to see the signes that she will make.
    Flo. I told my husband I would make these signes:
If I resisted, first hold vp my finger,   85
As if I said, yfaith sir you are gone,
But it shall say, yfayth sir, we are one.
    Lab. [*Aside.*] Nowe shee triumphes, and pointes to heauen I
warrant you.
    Flo. Then must I seeme as if I woulde heare no more and stoppe   90
your vaine lips: go cruell lippes, you haue bewitcht me, go.
    Lab. [*Aside.*] Now she stops in
His scorned wordes, and rates him for his paines.
    Flo. And when I thrust you thus against the breast,
Then are you ouerthrowne both horse and foote.   95
    Lab. [*Aside.*] Now is he ouerthrowne both horse and foote.
    Flo. Away vaine man, haue I not answered you?

---

65 What,] *Parrott;* ~∧ ‖ **66** *France*] roman ‖ **67** But] but | sir] *Parrott;* see ‖ **69** SD *He . . . Florila.*]
Parrott ‖ **70** Ladyes proofe] Ladyesproofe ‖ **83** SD *Aside.*] *Parrott* ‖ **88** SD *Aside.*] *Parrott* ‖ **90**
more] moret ‖ **91** lips:] ~, ‖ **92** SD *Aside.*] *Parrott* ‖ **92-136** Now . . . come.] *so lined by P* ‖ **96**
SD *Aside.*] *Parrott* ‖

Le. Madam, I yeeld and sweare, I neuer saw
So constant, nor so vertuous a ladie.

    Lab. [*To Lemot.*] Now speake I pray, and speake but truly,   100
Haue you not got a wrong sow by the eare?

    Le. My lord, my labor is not altogether lost,
For now I find that which I neuer thought.

    Lab. Ah, sirrah, is the edge of your steele wit
Rebated then against her Adamant? /   105

    Le. It is my Lord, yet one word more faire ladie.   [C4ᵛ]

    Lab. Faine would he haue it do, and it will not be: harke you
wife, what signe will you make mee nowe if you relent not?

    Flo. Lend him my handkercher to wipe his lips of their last
disgrace.   110

    Lab. Excellent good, go forward, sir I pray.

    Flo. [*To Lemot.*] An other signe yfaith, loue, is required.

    Le. Let him haue signes inowe, my heauenly loue;
Then knowe there is a priuate meeting
This day at *Verones* ordinarie,   115
Where if you will do me the grace to come,
And bring the beauteous *Martia* with you,
I wil prouide a faire and priuate roome,
Where you shal be vnseene of any man,
Onely of me, and of the King himselfe,   120
Whom I will cause to honour your repaire
With his high presence,
And there with Musicke and quicke reuellings
You may reuiue your spirits so long time dulled.

    Flo. Ile send for *Martia* then, and meete you there,   125
And tell my husband, I wil locke my selfe
In my close walke till supper-time:
We pray sir, wipe your lips of the disgrace
They tooke in their last labour.

    Le. Mary the diuell was neuer so dispited.   130

    Lab. Nay stay, sir.

    Le. No, no, my Lord, you haue the constantst wife
That euer — wel, Ile say no more.   *Exit.*

    Lab. Neuer was minion so disminioned,
Come constancie, come my girle, Ile leaue thee loose   135
To twentie of them yfaith.   *Then he sighes.*

    Flo.   Come my good head, come.   *Exeunt.*

---

100 SD *To Lemot.*] *Parrott* ‖ 104 Ah,] A∧ ‖ 111 sir] *Parrott*; see ‖ 112 SD *To Lemot.*] *Parrott* |
loue,] *Parrott*; ~∧ ‖ 113 loue;] ~, ‖ 115 *Verones*] roman ‖ 127 close] *Parrott*; choise ‖ 131 sir]
Parrott; see ‖ 133 euer—] ~: ‖ 136 SD *Then he sighes.*] *Parrott*; *in margin* | SD *Exeunt*] *Exit* ‖

[II.ii]

Enter the King and all the lords, with the Trumpets.

King. Why sound these Trumpets, in the Diuelles name?

Cat. To shew the King comes.

King. To shew the King comes?

Go hang the Trumpetters, they mocke me boldly,

And euery other thing that / makes me knowne,　　　　　　　　[D1] 5

Not telling what I am, but what I seem,

A King of clouts, a scarcrow, full of cobwebs,

Spiders and earewigs, that sets Iackdawes long tongue

In my bosome, and vpon my head,

And such are all the affections of loue　　　　　　　　　　　10

Swarming in me, without commaund or reason.

Le. Howe nowe my liege! what, quackemyred in Philosophie, bounde with loues whipcorde, and quite robbed of reason: and Ile giue you a receyte for this presently.

King. Peace *Lemot,* they say the yong lord *Dowsecer*　　15

Is rarely learned, and nothing lunatike

As men suppose,

But hateth companie, and worldly trash.

The iudgement and the iust contempt of them,

Haue in reason arguments that breake affection　　　　　　20

(As the most sacred Poets write) and still the roughest wind:

And his rare humour come we now to heare.

Le. Yea, but hearke you my liege, Ile tell you a better humour then that; here presently will be your faire loue *Martia,* to see his humour, and from thence faire countesse *Florula* and she will go vnto *Verones*　　25 ordinarie, where none but you and I, and Count *Moren,* will be most merry.

King. Why Count *Moren* I hope dares not aduenture into any womans companie, but his wiues.

Le. Yes, as I will worke, my liege, and then let me alone to keepe　　30 him there till his wife comes.

King. That will be royall sport: see where all comes: welcome faire lords and ladies.

Enter Laberuele, Labesha, and all the rest.

Lab. My liege you are welcome to my poore house.

Le. [*Presenting Labesha.*] I pray, my liege know this Gentleman　　35 especially, he is a Gentleman borne I can tell you.

King. With all my heart: what might I call your name?

Labes. Monsieur *Labesha, siniora defoulasa.*

II.ii] ‖ **1** Trumpets,] ∼∧ | name?] ∼. ‖ **2** *Cat.*] *Shepherd; C. (See Textual Note)* ‖ **3-11** To . . . reason.] *so lined by P* ‖ **12** what,] ∼∧ ‖ **15-22** Peace . . . heare.] *so lined by P* ‖ **15** Dowsecer] *Dowseger* ‖ **18** trash.] ∼, ‖ **19** The] *the* ‖ **24** that;] ∼, ‖ **25** *Florula*] ∼, | *Verones*] *roman* ‖ **35** SD *Presenting Labesha.*] *Parrott subs.* ‖ **38** Monsieur] *italic* ‖

King. Defoulasa? an il sounding barony of my word: but to the purpose. Lord Laberuell, we are come to see the hu / mour of your [D1ᵛ] 40 rare sonne, which by some meanes I pray let vs pertake.

Lab. Your highnes shal too vnworthily pertake the sight which I with griefe and teares daily behold, seeing in him the end of my poore house.

King. You know not that (my lord); your wife is yong, and he   45 perhaps hereafter may be mooued to more societie.

Lab. Would to God hee would, that wee might do to your crowne of *France,* more worthy and more acceptable seruice.

King. Thanks good my lord, see where he appeeres.

Enter Lauele with a picture, and a paire of large hose, and a codpeece, and a sword.

King. Say *Lauel,* where is your friend the yong lord *Dowsecer?*   50

La. I looke my liege he will be here anone, but then I must intreat your Maiestie and all the rest, to stand vnseen, for he as yet will brooke no companie.

King. We will stand close *Lauele,* but wherefore bring you this apparell, that picture, and that sword?   55

La. To put him by the sight of them in mind of their braue states that vse them, or at the least of the true vse they should be put vnto.

King. Indeede the sence doth still stir vp the soule, and though these obiects do not worke, yet it is very probable in time she may; at least, we shal discerne his humor of them.   60

Le. See where he comes contemplating, stand close.

Enter Dowsecer.

[*Dow.*] *Quid ei potest videri magnum in rebus humanis cui aeternitas omnis totiusque nota sit mundi magnitudo.*
What can seeme strange to him on earthly things
To whom the whole course of eternitie,   65
And the round compasse of the world is knowne?
A speech diuine, but yet I maruaile much
How it should spring from thee, *Marke Cicero*
That sold for glory the sweet peece of life,
And made a torment of rich natures work,   70
Wearing thy self by watchful candel light,
When all the Smithes and Weauers were at rest,
And yet was gallant / ere the day bird sung   [D2]
To haue a troope of clyents at thy gates,
Armed with religious suplications,   75
Such as wold make sterne *Minos* laugh to reade:

39 *Defoulasa?*] ~, | barony] *Parrott;* barrendrie *Q(u);* barendrie *Q(c)* | but] *Q(c);* bur *Q(u)* ‖ **40** purpose. Lord] ~, lord ‖ **45** lord);] lord)∧ ‖ **48** *France*] roman ‖ **57** or at] *Shepherd;* or that at ‖ **59** may;] ~, ‖ **62** *Dow.*] *Parrott* ‖ **62-63** *Quid . . . magnitudo.*] *Parrott; Quid Dei potes videri magnum in rebus humanis quae aeterni omnes* to thy *ousque notas sic omnibus magna tutor,* (*See Textual Note*) ‖ **67** A] a ‖ **70** made] *Shepherd;* make ‖

Look on our lawyers billes, not one containes
Virtue or honest drifts; but snares, snares, snares;
For acorns now [no more] are in request,
But [when] the okes poore fruite did nourish men,   80
Men were like okes of body, tough, and strong;
Men were like Gyants then, but Pigmies now,
Yet full of villanies as their skinne can hold.
   Le. How like you this humor my liege?
   King. This is no humour, this is but perfit iudgement.   85
   Coun. Is this a frensie?
   Mar.   O were al men such,
Men were no men but gods: this earth a heauen.
   Dow. [*Noticing the sword.*] See see the shamelesse world,
That dares present her mortall enemie
With these grose ensignes of her lenity,   90
Yron and steele, vncharitable stuffe,
Good spittle-founders, enemies to whole skinnes,
As if there were not waies enow to die
By natural and casuall accidents,
Diseases, surfeits, braue carowses, old aquavitae, and too base wines,   95
And thousands more; hence with this art of murder.
[*Noticing the hose and codpiece.*] But here is goodly geare, the soule
of man,
For tis his better part; take away this,
And take away their merites, and their spirites.
Scarce dare they come in any publike view,   100
Without this countenance giuer,
And some dares not come, because they haue it too;
For they may sing, in written books they find it.
What is it then the fashion, or the cost?
The cost doth much, but yet the fashion more,   105
For let it be but meane, so in the fashion,
And tis most gentleman like, is it so?
Make a hand in the margent, and burne the booke,
A large hose and a codpeece makes a man;
A codpece, nay indeed but hose must down: 110
Well for your gentle forgers of men,
And for you come to rest me into fashion,
Ile weare you thus, and sit vpon the matter. [*He sits on the hose and codpiece.*]
   Lab. And [so] he doth despise our purposes.

77-83 Look ... hold.] *so lined by P* ‖ **78** snares, snares, snares] *Parrott*; he cares, he cares, he cares
(*See Textual Note*) ‖ **79** no more] *Parrott* ‖ **80** when] *Parrott* ‖ **81** strong;] *Parrott*; ∼∧ ‖ **88** SD
Noticing the sword.] *Parrott subs.* ‖ **88-113** See ... matter.] *so lined by P* ‖ **95** wines] wiues ‖ **96**
more;] ∼∧ ‖ **97** SD *Noticing . . . codpiece.*] *Parrott subs.* ‖ **98** part;] ∼, ‖ **99** spirites.] ∼, ‖ **100**
Scarce] scarce ‖ **102** too;] ∼, ‖ **103** it.] ∼, ‖ **104** What] what | cost?] ∼, ‖ **105** The] the | much]
Parrott; match ‖ **108** Make] make ‖ **109** hose] *Parrott*; house | man;] *Parrott*; ∼∧ ‖ **110** hose]
Parrott; house ‖ **113** SD *He . . . codpiece.*] ‖ **114** Lab.] *Parrott*; *La.* | so] *Parrott* (*See Textual Note*) ‖

Cat. Beare with him yet my Lorde, hee is not resolued. /   115
La. I would not haue my friend mocke worthy men,   [D2ᵛ]
For the vaine pride of some that are not so.
  Dow. I do not here deride difference of states,
No not in shew, but wish that such as want shew
Might not be scorned with ignorant Turkish pride,   120
Beeing pompous in apparel, and in mind:
Nor would I haue with imitated shapes
Menne make their natiue land, the land of apes,
Liuing like strangers when they be at home,
And so perhaps beare strange hearts to their home,   125
Nor looke a snuffe like a piannets taile,
For nothing but their curls and formall lockes,
When like to creame boules all their vertues swim
In their set faces, all their in parts then
Fit to serue pesants or make curdes for dawes: 130
[*Noticing the picture.*] But what a stocke am I thus to neglect
This figure of mans comfort, this rare peece?
  Lab. Heauens grant that make him more humane, and sotiable.
  King. Nay hee's more humane then all we are.
  Lab. I feare he will be too sharp to that sweete sex.   135
  Dow. She is very faire, I thinke that she be painted;
And if she be, sir, she might aske of mee,
How many is there of our sexe that are not?
Tis a sharpe question: marry and I thinke
They haue small skill; if they were all of painting,   140
Twere safer dealing with them, and indeed
Were their minds strong enough to guide their bodies,
Their beuteous deeds shoulde match with their heauenly lookes,
Twere necessarie they should weare them,
And would they vouchsafe it, euen I   145
Would ioy in their societie.
  Mar. And who would not die with such a man?
  Dow. But to admire them as our gallants do,
O what an eie she hath, O dainty hand,
Rare foote and legge, and leaue the minde respectles,   150
This is a plague, that in both men and women
Make much pollution of our earthly beeing:
Well I will practice yet to court this peece.
  Lab. O happie man, now haue I hope in her.
  King. Me thinkes I could indure him daies and nights.   155

---

116 *La.*] *By preserving the prefix La., Q apparently intends Labervele* ‖ **127** curls] *Parrott, Brereton conj.*;
tailes ‖ **131** SD *Noticing the picture.*] *Parrott subs.* | But] but ‖ **132** comfort,] ∼∧ ‖ **133** *Lab.*] *Parrott*;
La. ‖ **134** hee's] hees ‖ **135** *Lab.*] *Parrott*; *La.* ‖ **136-46** *She . . . societie.*] *so lined by P* ‖ **137** be,]
Shepherd; ∼∧ ‖ **139** Tis] tis ‖ **140** skill;] ∼, ‖ **149** O what] *stet* ‖

Dow. [*Pretending to court the picture.*] Well sir, now thus must I
do sir, ere it come to / women; now sir a plague vpon it, tis so ridic- [D3]
ulous I can no further: what poore asse was it that set this in my way?
now if my father should be the man: Gods precious coles tis he.

    Lab. Good sonne go forward in this gentle humor, 160
Obserue this picture, it presents a maide
Of noble birth and excellent of parts,
Whom for our house and honor sake, I wish
Thou wouldst confesse to marrie.

    Dow. To marrie father? why we shall haue children. 165

    Lab. Why that's the ende of marriage, and the ioye of men.

    Dow. O how you are deceiued, you haue but me,
And what a trouble am I to your ioy?
But father, if you long to haue some fruite of me,
See father I will creepe into this stuborne earth 170
And mix my flesh with it, and they shall breede grasse,
To fat oxen, asses and such like,
And when they in the grasse the spring conuerts
Into beasts nourishment,
Then comes the fruite of this my body forth; 175
Then may you well say,
Seeing my race is so profitably increased,
That good fat oxe, and that same large eard asse
Are my sonne sonnes, that caulfe with a white face
Is his faire daughter, with which, when your fields 180
Are richly filled, then will my race content you,
But for the ioyes of children, tush tis gone,
Children will not deserue, nor parents take it:
Wealth is the onely father and the child,
And but in wealth no man hath any ioy. 185

    Lab. Some course deare sonne take for thy honor sake.

    Dow. Then father here's a most excellent course.

    Lab. This is some comfort yet.

    Dow. If you will strait be gone and leaue me here,
Ile stand as quietlye as anye lambe, 190
And trouble none of you.

    Lab.   An haplesse man.

    Le. How like you this humour yet my liege?

    King. As of a holy fury, not a frensie.

    Mor. See see my liege, he hath seene vs sure.

    King. Nay looke how he viewes *Martia* and makes him fine. / 195

    Le. Yea my liege, and she as I haue wel obserued, hath vttered [D3ᵛ]
many kind conceits of him.

---

156 SD *Pretending . . . picture.*] || **160-64** Good . . . marrie.] *so lined by P* || **167-85** O . . . ioy.] *so
lined by P* || **169** But] but || **173** in] *stet* (*See Textual Note*) || **187** here's] heres || **189-91** If . . . you.]
so lined by P || **191** you.] ∼∧ || **196** haue] *Greg conj.*; hope || **197** him] *Greg conj.*; hers ||

King. Well Ile be gone, and when shee comes to *Verones* ordinarie,
Ile haue her taken to my custodie.
   Le. Ile stay my liege, and see the euent of this.   200
   King. Do so *Lemot.*   *Exit the king.*
   Dow. What haue I seene? howe am I burnt to dust
With a new Sun, and made a nouell Phoenix?
Is she a woman that obiects this sight,
Able to worke the chaos of the world   205
Into gestion? O diuine aspect,
The excellent disposer of the mind
Shines in thy beautie, and thou hast not chaunged
My soule to sense, but sense vnto my soule,
And I desire thy pure societie,   210
But euen as angels do, to angels flie.   *Exit.*
   Mar. Flie soule and follow him.
   Lab. I maruaile much at my sonnes sodaine straunge behauiour.
   Le. Beare with him yet my Lord, tis but his humour: come, what,
shall we go to *Verones* ordinarie?   215
   Labes. Yea for Gods sake, for I am passing hungry.
   Mor. Yea, come Monsieur *Lemot,* will you walke?
   Coun. What, will you go?
   Mor. Yea sweet bird, I haue promised so.
   Coun. Go to, you shall not go and leaue me alone.   220
   Mor. For one meale gentle bird: *Veron* inuites vs to buy some
iewels he hath brought of late from *Italie*: Ile buy the best, and bring
it thee, so thou wilt let me go.
   Coun. Well said flattering *Fabian,* but tel me then what ladies will
be there?   225
   Mor. Ladies? why none.
   Le. No ladies vse to come to ordinaries, Madam.
   Coun. Go to bird, tell me now the very truth.
   Mor. None, of mine honour bird, you neuer heard that ladies came
to ordinaries.   230
   Coun. O that's because I should not go with you.
   Mor. Why tis not fit you should.
   Coun. Well heark you bird, of my word you shall not go, / vnlesse   [D4]
you will sweare to me, you will neither court nor kisse a dame in any
sort, till you come home againe.   235
   Mor. Why I sweare I will not.
   Coun. Go to, by this kisse.
   Mor. Yea, by this kisse.
   Foyes. Martia, learne by this when you are a wife.

---

198 *Verones*] *roman throughout scene* ‖ **202-11** What . . . flie.] *so lined by P* ‖ **214**
what,] ∼∧ ‖ **229** None,] ∼∧ ‖ **231** that's] thats ‖ **232, 236, 238** *Mor.*] *Parrott; Mar.* ‖

Labes. I like the kissing well. 240

Flo. My lord Ile leaue you; your sonne *Dowsecer* hath made me melancholy with his humour, and Ile go locke my selfe in my close walke till supper time.

Lab. What, and not dine to day?

Flo. No my good head: come *Martia,* you and I will fast togither. 245

Mar. With all my heart Madam. *Exeunt.*

Lab. Well Gentlemen Ile go see my sonne. *Exit.*

Foyes. Birlady Gentlemen Ile go home to dinner.

Labes. Home to dinner? birlord but you shall not, you shall go with vs to the ordinarie, where you shall meete Gentlemen of so good 250 carriage, and passing complements, it will do your hart good to see them, why you neuer saw the best sort of Gentlemen if not at ordinaries.

Foyes. I promise you that's rare, my lord; and Monsieur *Lemot,* Ile meet you there presently. 255

Le. Weele expect your comming. *Exeunt all.*

[III.i]

Enter Verone with his Napkin vpon his shoulder, and his man Iaques with another, and his sonne bringing in cloth and napkins.

Ver. Come on my maisters, shadow these tables with their white vailes, accomplish the court Cupboord, waite diligently to day for my credite and your owne, that if the meate should chance to be raw, yet your behauiors being neither rude nor raw, may excuse it, or if the meate should chaunce to be tough, be you tender ouer them in your 5 attendance, that the one may beare with the other. /

Iaq. Faith some of them bee so hard to please, finding fault with [D4ᵛ] your cheere, and discommending your wine, saying, they fare better at *Valeres* for halfe the mony.

Boy. Besides, if there be any cheboules in your napkins, they say 10 your nose or ours haue dropt on them, and then they throw them about the house.

Ver. But these bee small faultes, you may beare with them, young Gentlemen and wilde heades will be doing.

Enter the Maide.

Maid. Come, whose wit was it to couer in this roome, in the name 15 of God I trow?

Boy. Why I hope this roome is as faire as the other.

Maid. In your foolish opinion: you might haue tolde a wise body so, and kept your selfe a foole still.

---

241 you;] ~, ‖ 246 SD *Exeunt*] *Exit* ‖ 254 that's rare, my lord;] *Shepherd*; thats ~, ~ ~, ‖ III.i] ‖ 9 *Valeres*] *Shepherd*; Verones ‖ 15-16 in the name of God I trow?] *Parrott*; name in the of God I trowee. ‖

Boy. I cry you mercie, how bitter you are in your prouerbs.   20
Maid. So bitter I am sir.
Ver. [*Aside.*] O sweet *Iaquena* I dare not say I loue thee.
Iaq. Must you controule vs you proud baggage you?
Maid. Baggage? you are a knaue to call me baggage.
Iaq. A knaue? my maister shall know that.   25
Ver. [*Aside.*] I will not see them.
Iaq. Maister, here is your Maid vses her selfe so sawsily, that one
house shall not hold vs two long, God willing.
Ver. Come hither huswife. [*Aside to Maid.*] Pardon mee sweete
Iaquena, I must make an angry face outwardly, though I smile in-   30
wardly.
Maid. Say what you will to me sir.
Ver. O you are a fine Gossip, can I not keepe honest seruants in my
house, but you must controule them? you must be their mistres?
Maid. Why I did but take vp the cloth, because my mistresse would   35
haue the dinner in an other roome, and hee called me baggage. /
Iaq. You called me knaue and foole, I thanke you small bones.   [E1]
Maid. Go to, go to, she were wise enough would talke with you.
Boy. Go thy waies for the prowdest harlotrie that euer came in our
house.   [*Exit Maid.*]
Ver. Let her alone boy, I haue scoold her I warant thee; she shall
not be my maide long, if I can helpe it.
Boy. No, I thinke so sir; but what, shal I take vppe the cloath?
Ver. No, let the cloth lie, hither theile com first, I am sure of it,
then If they will dine in the other roome, they shal.   45

Enter Rowle.

Row. Good morrow my host, is no body come yet?
Ver. Your worship is the first sir.
Row. I was inuited by my cosen *Colinet,* to see your iewells.
Ver. I thanke his worship and yours.
Row. Here's a prettie place for an ordinarie, I am very sory I haue   50
not vsed to come to ordinaries.
Ver. I hope we shall haue your company hereafter.
Row. You are very like to.

Enter Berger.

Ber. Good morrow my host, good morrow good Monsieur *Rowle.*
Row. Good morrow to you sir.   55
Ber. What, are we two the first? giue's the cardes here; come, this
gentleman and I wil go to cardes while dinner be ready.
Row. No truly I cannot play at cardes.

---

22 SD *Aside.*] *Parrott* | *Iaquena*] *Parrott; Sateena* ‖ **26** SD *Aside.*] *Parrott* ‖ **29** SD *Aside to Maid.*]
Parrott ‖ **30** *Iaquena*] *Parrott; Iacenan* ‖ **34** mistres?] ∼. ‖ **40** SD *Exit Maid.*] ‖ **41** thee;] ∼, ‖ **43**
sir;] ∼, ‖ **45** SD *Rowle.*] *Rowl.* ‖ **50** Here's] *Heres* ‖ **53** to] *Greg;* so ‖ **55** sir.] ∼, ‖ **56** What,]
∼∧ | cardes here;] *Parrott subs.;* ∼, ∼∧ ‖

Ber. How! not play, O for shame say not so, how can a yong gentleman spend his time but in play, and in courting his Mistris: come vse   60
this, least youth take too much of the other.

    Row. Faith I cannot play, and yet I care not so much / to venture   [E1ᵛ]
two or three crownes with you.

    Ber. O I thought what I shuld find of you, I pray God I haue not
met with my match.   65

    Row. No trust me sir, I cannot play.

    Ber. Hearke you my host, haue you a pipe of good Tabacco?

    Ver. The best in the towne: boy drie a leafe.

    Boy. [*Aside.*] There's none in the house sir.

    Ver. [*Aside.*] Drie a docke leafe.   [*Boy exits and returns with pipe.*]

    Ber. My host, do you know Monsieur *Blanuel*?

    Ver. Yea passing well sir.

    Ber. Why, he was taken learning trickes at old *Lucilas* house, the
muster mistris of all the smocktearers in *Paris,* and both the bawde and
the pander were carried to the dungeon.   75

    Ver. There was dungeon vpon dungeon, but call you her the
muster-mistris of al the smocktearers in *Paris?*

    Ber. Yea, for she hath them all trained vp afore her.

Enter Blanuel.

    Blan. Good morow my host, good morow gentlemen al.

    Ver. Good morow Monsieur *Blanuel,* I am glad of your quicke   80
deliuery.

    Blan. Deliuery? what, didst thou thinke I was with child?

    Ver. Yea of a dungeon.

    Blan. Why, how knew you that?

    Row. Why *Berger* told vs.   85

    Blan. Berger who told you of it?

    Ber. One that I heard, by the lord.

    Blan. O excellent, you are still playing the wagge.

Enter Lemot and Moren.

    Le. Good morrow Gentlemen all, good morrow good Monsieur
Rowle.   90

    Row. At your seruice.

    Le. I pray my lord, look what a pretty falling band he hath, tis
[as] pretty fantasticall, as I haue seen, made with good iudgement,
great shew, and but little cost. /

    Mor. And so it is I promise you, who made it I pray?   [E2] 95

    Row. I know not yfaith, I bought it by chance.

    Le. It is a very pretty one, make much of it.

---

69 SD *Aside.*] *Parrott* | There's] Theres ‖ **70** SD *Aside.*] *Parrott* | SD *Boy . . . pipe.*] ‖ **73** house,]
∼∧ ‖ **74** *Paris*] *roman throughout scene* ‖ **82** Deliuery? what,] *Shepherd*; ∼, ∼∧ ‖ **92** lord,] ∼∧
‖ **92-93** tis as pretty] as *om.* ‖ **93** seen, made] *Parrott*; ∼∧ ∼, ‖ **94** little] *Parrott*; tittle ‖

Enter Catalian sweating.

Cat. Boy, I prethee call for a course napkin. [*Exit Boy.*] Good
morrow Gentlemen, I would you had bin at the tenniscourt, you
should haue seene me a beat Monsieur *Besan,* and I gaue him fifteene   100
and all his faults.

Le. Thou didst more for him, then euer God wil do for thee.

Cat. Iaques, I prethee fill me a cup of canary, three parts water.

[*Exit Iaques.*]

Le. You shall haue all water and if it please you.

Enter Maide.

Maid. Who cald for a course napkin?   105

Cat. Marry I, sweete heart, do you take the paines to bring it
your selfe? haue at you by my hosts leaue.   [*He kisses her.*]

Maid. Away sir, fie for shame.

Cat. Hearke you my host, you must marry this young wench, you
do her mighty wrong els.   110

Ver. O sir, you are a merry man.   [*Exit Verone.*]

Enter Foyes and Labesha.

Foyes. Good morrow gentlemen, you see I am as good as my word.

Mor. You are sir, and I am very glad of it.

Le. You are welcome Monsieur *Foyes*: [*To Labesha.*] but you
are not, no not you.   115

Labes. No, welcome that Gentleman, tis no matter for me.

Le. How sir? no matter for you? by this rush I am angry with
you, as if al our loues protested vnto you were dissembled; no matter
for you?

Labes. Nay sweet *Lemot* be not angry, I did but iest, as I am   120
a Gentleman. /

Le. Yea but there's a difference of iesting, you wrong all our   [E2ᵛ]
affections in so doing.

Labes. Faith and troth I did not, and I hope sirs you take it not so.

All. No matter for me, twas very vnkindly sayd, I must needs say so.   125

Labes. You see how they loue me.

Foyes. I do sir, and I am very glad of it.

Labes. And I hope *Lemot,* you are not angry with me stil.

Le. No faith, I am not so very a foole to be angry with one that
cares not for me.   130

Labes. Do not I care for you? nay then —   [*He begins to cry.*]

Cat. What, dost thou cry?

Labes. Nay I do not cry, but my stomacke waters to thinke that
you should take it so heauily; if I do not wish that I were cut into

98 SD *Exit Boy.*] ‖ **103** *Iaques*] roman ǀ water.] ∼∧ ǀ SD *Exit Iaques.*] ‖ **107** selfe?] ∼, ǀ SD *He
kisses her.*] *Parrott subs.* ‖ **111** SD *Exit Verone.*] ‖ **114** SD *To Labesha.*] ‖ **116** *Labes.*] *Be.* ‖ **117**
for you?] *Greg conj.*; to ∼, ‖ **118** dissembled;] ∼, ‖ **120** *Labes.*] *Be.* ‖ **122** there's] theres ‖ **124**
Labes.] *Be.* ‖ **126** *Labes.*] *Parrott*; *La.* ‖ **128** *Labes.*] *Be,* ‖ **131** *Labes.*] *Be.* ǀ then—] ∼. ǀ SD *He
. . . cry.*] *Parrott subs.* ‖ **134** heauily;] ∼, ‖

three peeces, and that these peeces were turned into three blacke   135
puddings, and that these three blacke puddings were turned into three
of the fairest Ladies in the land for your sake, I would I were hanged;
whata diuel can you haue more then my poore heart?

Cat. Well harke you *Lemot,* in good faith you are too blame to
put him to this vnkindnes, I prethee be friends with him.   140

Le. Well, I am content to put vp this vnkindnesse for this once,
but while you liue take heede of: no matter for me.

Labes. Why is it such a hainous word?

Le. O the hainousest word in the world.

Labes. Wel, Ile neuer speake it more, as I am a gentleman.   145

Le. No I pray do not.

Foyes. My lord, will your lordship go to cards?

Mor. Yea with you Monsieur *Foyes.*

Row. Lemot, will you play?

Le. Pardon good Monsieur *Rowle,* if I had any disposition to   150
gaming, your company should draw me before any mans here. /

Foyes. Labesha, what, will you play?   [E3]

Labes. Play, yea with all my heart, I pray lend me three pence.

Row. Ile play no more.

Cat. Why, haue you wonne or lost?   155

Row. Faith I haue lost two or three crownes.

Cat. Well to him againe, Ile be your halfe.

Le. [*Aside.*] Sirrah *Catalian,* while they are playing at cardes, thou
and I will haue some excellent sport: sirrah, dost thou know that
same Gentleman there?   [*Indicating Rowley.*]

Cat. No yfaith, what is he?

Le. A very fine gull, and a neat reueller, one that's heire to a great
liuing, yet his father keepes him so short, that his shirts will scant couer
the bottom of his belly, for all his gay outside; but the linings be very
foule and sweatie, yea and perhappes lowsie, with dispising the vaine   165
shiftes of the world.

Cat. But he hath gotten good store of money now me thinks.

Le. Yea, and I wonder of it; some ancient seruing man of his
fathers, that hath gotten fortie shillings in fiftie years vpon his great
good husbandrie, he swearing monstrous othes to pay him againe, and   170
besides to doe him a good turne (when God shall heare his prayer
for his father) hath lent it him I warrant you, but howsoeuer, we
must speake him faire.

Cat. O what else!

137 hanged;] ∼, ‖ 143, 145 *Labes.*] *Be.* ‖ 148 *Mor.*] *Parrott; Lor.* ‖ 151 gaming,] ∼∧ ‖ 152 what,] *Parrott;* ∼∧ ‖ 153 *Labes.*] *Lab.* ‖ 158 SD *Aside.*] *Parrott* | Sirrah] ∼, ‖ 160 SD *Indicating Rowley.*] ‖ 162 that's] thats ‖ 164 outside;] ∼, ‖ 168 it;] ∼, ‖

Le. God saue, sweete Monsieur *Rowle,* what, loose or win, loose or   175
win?

Row. Faith sir saue my selfe, and loose my money.

Le. There's a prouerbe hit dead in the necke like a Cony; why
hearke thee *Catalian,* I could haue told thee before what he would
haue said.   180

Cat. I do not thinke so.

Le. No? thou seest heer's a fine plumpe of gallants, such as thinke
their wits singular, and their selues rarely accom / plished, yet to   [E3ᵛ]
shew thee how brittle their wittes be, I will speake to them seuerally,
and I will tell thee before what they shall answer me.   185

Cat. That's excellent, lets see that yfaith.

Le. Whatsoeuer I say to Monsieur *Rowlee,* he shall say, O sir,
you may see an ill weed growes apace.

Cat. Come, lets see.

Le. Now Monsieur *Rowlee,* me thinks you are exceedingly growne   190
since your comming to *Paris.*

Row. O sir, you may see an ill weed growes a pace.

Cat. [*Aside.*] This is excellent, forward sir I pray.

Le. [*Aside.*] What soere I say to *Labesha,* he shall answer me,
blacke will beare no other hue, and that same olde Iustice, as greedie   195
of a stale prouerbe, he shall come in the necke of that and say, Blacke
is a pearle in a womans eye.

Cat. [*Aside.*] Yea, much yfayth.

Le. [*Aside.*] Looke thee, here [he] comes hither. — *Labesha,*
Catalian and I haue beene talking of thy complexion, and I say, that   200
all the faire ladies in *France* would haue beene in loue with thee, but
that thou art so blacke.

Labes. O sir blacke will beare no other hue.

Foyes. O sir blacke is a pearle in a womans eye.

Le. You say true sir, you say true sir; [*Aside.*] sirrah *Catalian,*   205
whatsoere I say to *Berger* that is so busie at Cardes, he shall answer
me, sblood, I do not meane to die as long as I can see one aliue.

Cat. [*Aside.*] Come let vs see you.

Le. Why *Berger,* I thought thou hadst beene dead, I haue not heard
thee chide all this while.   210

Ber. Sblood, I do not meane to die, as long as I can see one aliue.

Cat. [*Aside.*] Why but hearke you *Lemot,* I hope you cannot make
this lord answer so roundly.

---

175 saue,] ∼∧ | what,] ∼∧ ‖ **178** There's] Theres | Cony;] ∼, ‖ **182** No?] ∼, | heer's] heers
‖ **186** That's] Thats ‖ **193, 194** SD *Aside.*] *Parrott* ‖ **198, 199** SD *Aside.*] *Parrott* ‖ **199** he] *Shepherd*
‖ **199-200** hither.— *Labesha, Catalian*] *Shepherd;* ∼∧ ∼, ∼, ‖ **201** *France*] roman ‖ **205** sir;] ∼,
‖ **205, 208, 212** SD *Aside.*] *Parrott* ‖

Le. [*Aside.*] O, as right as any of them all, and he shall aunswere
mee with an olde Latine Prouerbe, that is, *vsus promptum facit.* /   215
Cat. [*Aside.*] Once more lets see.   [E4]
Le. My lord, your lordship could not play at this game verie latelie,
and nowe me thinkes you are growne exceeding perfite.
Mor. O sir, you may see, *vsus promptum facit.*

Enter Iaques.

Iaq. Monsieur *Lemot,* here is a Gentleman and two Gentlewomen   220
do desire to speake with you.
Le. What, are they come? *Iaques,* conuey them into the inwarde
Parlour by the inwarde roome, and there is a brace of Crownes for
thy labour, but let no bodie know of their being here.
Iaq. I warrant you sir.   [*Exit Iaques.*]
Le. [*Aside.*] See where they come: — welcome my good lord and
ladies, Ile come to you presently: so, now the sport begins; I shall
starte the disguised King plaguilie, nay I shall put the ladie that loues
me in a monstrous fright, when her husband comes and finds her here.

[*Enter Boy.*]

Boy. [*To Lemot.*] The Gentleman, and the two Gentlewomen de-   230
sires your companie.
Le. Ile come to them presently.

The boy speakes in Foies his ear.

Foyes. Gentlemen, Ile go speake with one, and come to you
presently.
Le. My lord, I would speake a worde with your lordship, if it were   235
not for interrupting your game.
Mor. No, I haue done *Lemot.*
Le. My lord there must a couple of ladies dine with vs to day.
Mor. Ladies? God's my life I must be gone.
Le. Why hearke you my Lorde, I knewe not of their comming   240
I protest to your Lordship, and woulde you haue mee turne such
faire Ladies as these are away?
Mor. Yea but hearke you *Lemot,* did not you heare mee sweare
to my Wife, that I woulde not tarie, if there / were any women?   [E4ᵛ]
I wonder you would suffer any to come there.   245
Le. Why you swore but by a kisse, and kisses are no holie things,
you know that.
Mor. Why but hearke you *Lemot,* indeed I would be very loath to
do any thing, that if my wife should know it, should displease her.
Le. Nay then you are to obsequious; hearke you, let me intreate   250
you, and Ile tell you in secrete, you shall haue no worse company then
the Kings.

214, 216 SD *Aside.*] *Parrott* ‖ 215, 219 *promptum*] *promptus* ‖ 222 What,] ∼∧ ‖ 225 SD *Exit*
Iaques.] *Parrott* ‖ 226 SD *Aside.*] | come:—]∼:∧ ‖ 227 begins;] ∼, ‖ 229 SD *Enter Boy.*] *Parrott* ‖
230 SD *To Lemot.*] ‖ 232 SD *The . . . ear.*] *Shepherd*; in margin | SD ear.] ∼∧ ‖ 237 *Mor.*] *Lord*
throughout remainder of scene ‖ 239 God's] Gods ‖ 244 women?] ∼, ‖ 250 obsequious;] ∼, ‖

Mor. Why will the King be there?

Le. Yea, though disguised.

Mor. Who are the ladies?   255

Le. The flowers of Paris, I can tell you, faire countesse *Florila,* and the ladie *Martia.*

Enter Iaques.

Iaq. Monsieur *Lemot,* the gentleman and the two Gentlewomen desire your companie.

Le. Ile come to them straight: but *Iaques* come hither I prethee,   260
go to *Labesha,* and tell him that the Countesse *Florila,* and the ladie *Martia* be here at thy maisters house: and if it come in question hereafter, denie that thou tolde him any such thing.

Iaq. What, is this all? Sblood Ile denie it, and forsweare it too.

Le. My Lorde, Ile goe and see the roome be neate and fine, and   265
come to you presently.

Mor. Yea but hearke you *Lemot,* I prethee take such order that they be not knowne of any women in the house.

Le. O how shuld they? [*Aside.*] now to his wife go [I] yfaith!   *Exit.*

Iaq. Hearke you, Monsieur *Labesha,* I pray let me speak a worde   270
with you.

Labes. With all my heart; I pray looke to my stake, there's three pence vnder the Candlesticke.

Iaq. I pray sir, do you know the Countesse *Florila,* and the ladie *Martia?* /   275

Labes. Do I know the ladie *Martia?* I knew her before she was   [F1]
borne, why do you aske me?

Iaq. Why, they are both here at my masters house.

Labes. What, is Mistris *Martia* at an ordinarie?

Iaq. Yea that she is.   280

Labes. By skies and stones Ile go and tel her father   *Exit.*

[III.ii]

Enter Lemot and the Countesse.

Coun. What, you are out of breath me thinks Monsieur *Lemot?*

Le. It is no matter Madam, it is spent in your seruice, that beare your age with your honesty, better then an hundred of these nise gallants, and indeed it is a shame for your husband, that contrary to his oath made to you before dinner, he shoud be now at the ordinary   5
with that light huswife *Martia,* which I could not chuse but come and tell you; for indeede it is a shame that your motherly care should be so slightly regarded.

Coun. Out on the strumpet; and accurst, and miserable dame.

---

257 SD *Iaques.*] *Iaque.* ‖ **269** they?] *Shepherd;* ∼∧ | SD *Aside.*] *Parrott* | I] *Parrott* ‖ **272** heart;]
Shepherd; ∼, | there's] theres ‖ **274** sir] *Parrott;* see ‖ III.ii ‖ **1** What,] *Shepherd;* ∼∧ ‖ **9** the
strumpet;] thee ∼∧ ‖

Le. Well, there they are, nothing els: [*Aside.*] now to her husband 10
go I.   *Exit.*
   Coun. Nothing els quoth you, can there be more?
O wicked man, would he play false,
That would so simply vow, and sweare his faith,
And would not let me be displeased a minute,   15
But he would sigh, and weepe til I were pleased?
I haue a knife within that's rasor sharp,
And I wil lay an yron in the fire,
Making it burning hot to mark the strumpet,
But t'will bee colde too ere I can come thither;   20
Doe something wretched woman, staies thou here?   *Exit.*

[III.iii]

Enter Lemot.

   Le. My lorde, the roome is neate and fine, wilt please you go in?

[Enter Verone.]

   Ver. Gentlemen, your dinner is ready.
   All. And we are ready for it.
   Le. Iaquis, shut the doores; let no body come in.   *Exeunt omnes. /*

[IV.i]

Enter Laberuele, Foyes, Labesha, and the Countesse.   [F1ᵛ]

   Lab. Where be these puritanes, these murderers, let me come in
here?
   Foyes. Where is the strumpet?
   Coun. Where is this harlot? let vs come in here.
   Lab. What shall we do? the streets do wonder at vs,   5
And we do make our shame knowne to the world,
Let vs go, and complaine vs to the King.
   Foyes. Come *Labesha,* will you go?
   Labes. No no I scorne to go; no King shal heare my plaint,
I will in silence liue a man forlorne,   10
Mad, and melancholy, as a cat,
And neuer more weare hat band on my hat.   *[Exeunt.]*

Enter Moren, and Martia.

   Mor. What dost thou meane? thou must not hang on me.

10 are, nothing els: . . . now] *Shepherd;* ~: ~ ~∧ . . . ~, | SD *Aside.*] *Parrott* ‖ **12-21** Nothing
. . . here?] *so lined by P* ‖ **16** pleased?] ~, ‖ **17** that's] thats ‖ **20** thither;] ~, ‖ III.iii] ‖ 1 SD
Enter Verone.] *Parrott* ‖ **4** doores;] ~∧ ‖ IV.i] ‖ **1** *Lab.*] *Parrott; La.* ‖ **4** Where] where | harlot?]
~, ‖ **5** *Lab.*] *Parrott; La.* ‖ **5-7** What . . . King.] *so lined by P* ‖ **9** *Labes.*] *Parrott; La.* ‖ **9-12** No
. . . hat.] *so lined by P* ‖ **10** silence] *Shepherd;* silent ‖ **12** And] *Q(c);* an *Q(u)* | SD *Exeunt.*]
Parrott ‖

Mar. O good lord *Moren,* haue me home with you,
You may excuse all to my father for me.   15

Enter Lemot.

Le. O my lord, be not so rude to leaue her now.
Mor. Alas man, and if my wife should see it, I were vndone.

                                    [*Exeunt Moren and Martia.*]

Enter the King and another.

King. Pursue them sirs, and taking *Martia* from him,
Conuay her presently to *Valeres* house.   [*Exeunt King and another.*]

Enter the Puritane to Lemot.

[*Flo.*] What vilain was it that hath vttered this?   20
Le. Why twas euen I; I thanke you for your gentle tearmes, you
giue me vilain at the first. I wonder where's this old doter; what, doth
he thinke we feare him?
Flo. O monstrous man, what, wouldst thou haue him take vs? /
Le. Would I? quoth you; yea by my troth would I, I know he is [F2] 25
but gone to cal the constable, or to raise the streets.
Flo. What meanes the man trow? is he mad?
Le. No, no, I know what I do, I doe it of purpose, I long to see him
come and raile at you, to call you harlot, and to spurne you too. O
you'l loue me a great deale the better; and yet let him come, and if   30
he touch but one thread of you, Ile make that thread his poyson.
Flo. I know not what to say.
Le. Speake, do you loue me?
Flo. Yea surely do I.
Le. Why then haue not I reason that loue you so dearely as I do,   35
to make you hatefull in his sight, that I might more freely enioy you?
Flo. Why let vs be gon my kind *Lemot,* and not be wondered at in
the open streets.
Le. Ile go with you through fire, through death, throgh hell,
Come giue me your hand, my owne deare heart,   40
This hand that I adore and reuerence,
And loath to haue it touch an olde mans bosome,
O let me sweetely kisse it. *He bites.*
Flo. Out on thee wretch, he hath bit me to the bone,
O barbarous Canibal, now I perceiue   45
Thou wilt make me a mocking stocke to all the world.
Le. Come, come, leaue your passions, they cannot mooue mee, my
father and my mother died both in a day, and I rung mee a peale for
them, and they were no sooner brought to the church and laide in

---

14-15 O . . . me.] *so lined by* P ‖ **17** Mor.] *Parrott;* Lor. | SD Exeunt . . . Martia.] *Parrott* ‖ **18-19**
Pursue . . . house.] *so lined by* P ‖ **19** SD Exeunt . . . another.] *Parrott* | SD Enter . . . Lemot.] *follows
succeeding line* | SD the] tbe ‖ **20** Flo.] *Parrott* | this?] ∼. ‖ **21** I;] ∼, ‖ **22** first.] ∼, | where's]
wheres | doter; what,] ∼, ∼∧ ‖ **23** him?] ∼. ‖ **25** I?] ∼∧ | you;] he, Q*(u);* you, Q*(c)* ‖ **29**
too.] ∼, ‖ **30** better;] ∼, ‖ **34** Yea surely do I] Q*(c);* I shew I do Q*(u)* ‖ **35** do,] Q*(c);* ∼∧
Q*(u)* ‖ **36** you?] ∼. ‖ **39-56** Ile . . . go.] *so lined by* P ‖ **40** your hand] your owne hand ‖ **42**
it] ∼, ‖ **43** O] *stet* | it. He bites] it; he bites ‖ **45** O] *stet* ‖

their graues, but I fetcht me two or three fine capers aloft, and took   50
my leaue of them, as men do of their mistresses at the ending of a
galiard; *Beso las manos.*

Flo. O brutish nature, how accurst was I
Euer to indure the sound of this damned voice?

Le. Well, and you do not like my humor, I can be but sory for it,   55
I bit you for good will, and if you accept it, so, if no, go. /

Flo. Vilain, thou didst it in contempt of me.   [F2ᵛ]

Le. Well, and you take it so, so be it: harke you Madam, your
wisest course is, euen to become puritane againe; put off this vaine
attire, and say, I haue despised all: thanks my God; good husband,   60
I do loue thee in the Lord, and he (good man) will thinke all this
you haue done, was but to shew thou couldest gouerne the world,
and hide thee as a rainebow doth a storme: my dainty wench, go go,
what, shall the flattering words of a vaine man make you forget your
dutie to your husband? away, repent, amend your life, you haue   65
discredited your religion for euer.

Flo. Well wretch, for this foule shame thou puttest on me,
The curse of all affection light on thee.   *Exit.*

Le. Go *Abacuck,* go, why this is excellent, I shal shortly become
a schoolemaster, to whom men will put their wiues, to practise; well   70
now wil I go set the Queene vpon the King, and tell her where he is
close with his wench: and he that mends my humor, take the spurres:
sit fast, for by heauen, ile iurke the horse you ride on.   [*Exit.*]

[IV.ii]

Enter my host, Catalian, Blanuel, Berger, Iaquis, Maide, and Boy.

Ver. Well Gentlemen, I am vtterly vndone without your good
helpes; it is reported that I receiued certaine ladies or gentlewomen
into my house: now here's my man, my maid, and my boy, now if
you saw any, speak boldly before these Gentlemen.

Iaq. I saw none sir.   5

Maid. Nor I, by my maidenhead.

Boy. Nor I, as I am a man.

Cat. Wel my host, weele go answere for your house at this time, but
if at other times you haue had wenches, and would not let vs know it,
we are the lesse beholding to you.   10

Exeunt al, but my host and the Gentlemen.

Ber. Peraduenture the more beholding to him, but I laye my life
Lemot hath deuised some ieast, he gaue / vs the slip before dinner.   [F3]

Cat. Well Gentlemen, since we are so fitly mette, Ile tell you an excellent subiect for a fit of myrth, and if it bee well handled.

50 aloft] *Q(c)*; a loft *Q(u)* ‖ 52 *Beso las manos*] *Parrott; Besilus manus Q(u); Besilos manus Q(c)*
‖ 59 againe;] ∼, ‖ 60 God;] ∼, ‖ 64 what,] *Shepherd;* ∼∧ ‖ 67 wretch] *Shepherd;* wench ‖ 73
SD *Exit.*] *Parrott* ‖ IV.ii] ‖ 1 *Ver.*] *Host throughout scene* ‖ 2 helpes;] ∼, ‖ 3 now here's] *Shepherd;*
no heres ‖ 10 SD *Gentlemen*] *Parrott; Gentleman* ‖

Ber. Why, what is it?   15

Cat. Why man, *Labesha* is grown maruelous malecontent, vpon some amorous disposition of his mistres, and you know he loues a mease of cream, and a spice-cake with his heart, and I am sure he hath not dined to day, and he hath taken on him the humour of the yong lord *Dowsecer,* and we will set a mease of creame, a spice-cake,   20 and a spoone, as the armour, picture, and apparell was set in the way of *Dowsecer,* which I doubt not but will woorke a rare cure vpon his melancholie.

Ver. Why, this is excellent, Ile go fetch the creame.

Cat. And I the cake.   25

Ber. And I the spoone.   *Exeunt, and come in againe.*

Cat. See where hee comes as like the lord *Dowsecer* as may be, nowe you shall heare him begin with some Latin sentence that hee hath remembred euer since hee read his Accidence.

Enter Labesha.

Labes. Fælix quem faciunt aliena pericula cautum. O sillie state   30 of things, for things they be that cause this sillie state: and what is a thing? a bable, a toy, that stands men in small stead: *He spies the creame.* but what haue we here? what vanities haue we here?

Ver. He is strongly tempted, the lord strengthen him; see what a vaine he hath.   35

Labes. O cruell fortune, and dost thou spit thy spite at my poore life? but O sowre creame; what, thinkest thou that I loue thee still? no, no, faire and sweete is my mistries; if thou haddest strawberries and sugar in thee — but it may bee thou art set with stale cake to choke me: well taste it, and trie it, spoonefull by spoonefull: bitterer   40 and bitterer still, but O sowre creame, wert thou an Onion — since Fortune set thee / for mee, I will eate thee, and I will deuour thee   [F3ᵛ] in spite of Fortunes spite, Choake I, or burst I; mistres for thy sake, To end my life eate I this creame and cake.

Cat. So he hath done, his Melancholy is well eased I warrant you.   45

Ver. [*Advancing.*] God's my life Gentlemen, who hath beene at this creame?

Labes. Creame, had you creame? where is your creame? Ile spend my penny at your creame.

Cat. Why, did not you eate this creame?   50

Labes. Talke not to me of creame, for such vaine meate I do despise as food; my stomack dies
Drowned in the cream boules of my mistres eyes.   [*He starts to leave.*]

Cat. Nay stay *Labesha.*

Labes.   No not I, not I.   [*Exit.*]

---

32 thing?] ∼, ‖ 32-33 SD *He . . . creame.*] *Shepherd; in margin* ‖ 34 him;] ∼, ‖ 37 life?] ∼: | creame; what,] ∼∧ ∼∧ ‖ 38 mistries;] ∼, ‖ 39 thee—] ∼: ‖ 41 Onion—] ∼, ‖ 43 burst I;] ∼ ∼, ‖ 46 SD *Advancing.*] *Parrott* | God's] Gods ‖ 52 food;] ∼, ‖ 53 SD *He . . . leave.*] ‖ 54 SD *Exit.*] *Parrott* ‖

Ver. O he is ashamed yfayth: but I will tell thee howe thou shalt   55
make him mad indeed, say his mistres for loue of him hath drowned
her selfe.

Cat. Sblood, that will make him hang himselfe.   *Exeunt omnes.*

[IV.iii]

Enter the Queene, Lemot, and all the rest of the lordes,
and the Countesse: Lemots arme
in a scarffe.

Le. [*Aside.*] Haue at them yfayth with a lame counterfeite humor: —
Ake on rude arme, I care not for thy paine,
I got it nobly in the kings defence,
And in the gardiance of my faire Queenes right.

Queen. O tell me sweet *Lemot,* how fares the king?   5
Or what my right was that thou didst defend?

Le. That you shall know when other things are told.

Lab. Keepe not the Queene too long without her longing.

Foyes. No, for I tell you it is a daungerous thing.

Coun. Little care cruell men how women long.   10

Le. What, would you haue me then put poyson in my breath,
And burne the eares of my attentiue Queene? /

Queen. Tell me; what ere it be, Ile beare it all.   [F4]

Le. Beare with my rudenesse then in telling it,
For alas you see I can but act it with the left hande,   15
This is my gesture now.

Queen.   Tis well enough.

Le. Yea well enough you say,
This recompence haue I for all my woundes:
Then thus,
The King inamoured of an other ladie   20
Compares your face to hers, and saies that yours
Is fat and flat, and that your neather lip
Was passing big.

Queen.   O wicked man,
Doth he so sodainlie condemne my beautie,
That when he married me he thought diuine: 25
For euer blasted be that strumpets face,
As all my hopes are blasted, that did change them.

Le. Nay Madam, though he saide your face was fat,
And flat, and so forth, yet he liked it best,
And said, a perfect beautie should be so.   30

IV.iii] ‖ SD *Queene*] *Q(c); Qeene Q(u)* ‖ 1 SD *Aside.*] *Parrott* | Haue] haue | humor:—] ~:∧
‖ **5** sweet] *Q(c);* swaet *Q(u)* ‖ **6** Or] or | my] *Parrott;* his ‖ **11-30** What . . . so.] *so lined by P* ‖
11 What,] ~∧ ‖ **12** Queene?] ~. ‖ **13** me;] ~∧ (*See Textual Note*) ‖ **14** Beare] beare ‖ **15**
hande,] *Q(c);* ~∧ *Q(u)* ‖ **19** thus,] ~∧ ‖

Lab. O did he so! why that was right euen as it should be.

Foyes. You see now Madam, howe much too hastie you were in
your griefes.

Queen. If he did so esteeme of me indeed,
Happie am I.   35

Coun. So may your highnesse be that hath so good a husband,
but hell hath no plague to such an one as I.

Le. Indeed Madam, you haue a bad husband: truly then did the
king growe mightily in loue with the other ladie,
And swore, no king could more inriched be,   40
Then to inioy so faire a dame as shee.

Queen. O monstrous man, and acurst most miserable dame!

Le. But saies the king I do inioy as faire,
And though I loue [her] in al honored sort,
Yet Ile not wrong my wife for al the world.   45

Foyes. This proues his constancie as firme as brasse.

Queen. It doth, it doth: O pardon me my lord,
That I mistake thy royall meaning so.

Coun. In heauen your highnesse liues, but I in hell.

Le. But when he vewd her radient eyes againe,   50
Blinde was hee strooken with her feruent beames:
And now good / King he gropes about in corners   [F4ᵛ]
Voide of the chearefull light should guide vs all.

Queen. O dismall newes; what, is my soueraigne blind?

Le. Blind as a Beetle madam, that a while   55
Houering aloft, at last in cowsheds falls.

Lab. Could her eyes blind him?

Le. Eyes or what it was I know not,
But blind I am sure he is as any stone.

Queen. Come bring me to my Prince, my lord, that I may leade   60
him, none aliue but I may haue the honour to direct his feete.

Le. How lead him madam? why hee can go as right as you, or any
here, and is not blind of eyesight.

Queen. Of what then?

Le. Of reason.   65

Queen. Why thou saidest he wanted his cheerfull light.

Le. Of reason still I meant, whose light you knowe
Should cheerefully guide a worthie King,
For he doth loue her, and hath forced her,
Into a priuate roome where now they are.   70

Queen. What mocking chaunges is there in thy wordes!
Fond man, thou murtherest me with these exclaimes.

34-35 If . . . I.] *so lined by P* ‖ **42** Queen.] *Cat.* ‖ **44** her] *Shepherd* (*See Textual Note*) ‖ **45** world.]
∼∧ ‖ **54** newes; what,] ∼, ∼∧ ‖ **56** cowsheds] *stet* (*See Textual Note*) | falls] *Shepherd*; fall ‖
58-59 Eyes . . . stone.] *so lined by P* ‖ **60** Prince, my lord,] ∼∧ ∼ ∼∧ ‖ **67-70** Of . . . are.]
so lined by P ‖ **71** wordes!] ∼∧ ‖

Le. Why madam tis your fault, you cut mee off before my words
be halfe done.

 Queen. Forth and vnlade the poyson of thy tongue.   75
 Le. Another lord did loue this curious ladie,
Who hearing that the King had forced her,
As she was walking with another Earle,
Ran straightwaies mad for her, and with a friend
Of his, and two or three blacke ruffians more,   80
Brake desperately vpon the person of the King,
Swearing to take from him, in traiterous fashion,
The instrument of procreation:
With them I fought a while, and got this wound,
But being vnable to resist so many,   85
Came straight to you to fetch you to his ayde.
 Lab. Why raised you not the streetes?
 Le.   That I forbore,
Because I would not haue the / world, to see   [G1]
What a disgrace my liege was subiect to,
Being with a woman in so meane a house.   90
 Foyes. Whose daughter was it that he forst I pray?
 Le. Your daughter sir.
 Lab. Whose sonne was [it] that ranne so mad for her?
 Le. Your sonne my Lord.
 Lab. O Gods, and fiends forbid.   95
 Coun. I pray sir, from whom did he take the Ladie?
 Le. From your good Lord.
 Coun. O Lord I beseech thee no.
 Le. Tis all too true, come follow the Queen and I,
Where I shall leade you.   100
 Queen. O wretched Queene! what would they take from him?
 Le. The instrument of procreation.   *[Exeunt omnes.]*

[V.i]

Enter Moren.

 Mor. Now was there euer man so much accurst, that when his
minde misgaue him, such a man was haplesse, to keep him company?
yet who would keep him company but I? O vilde *Lemot*, my wife
and I are bound to curse thee while we liue, but chiefely I. Well:
seeke her, or seek her not; find her, or find her not, I were as good see   5
how hell opens, as looke vpon her.

76-86 Another . . . ayde.] *so lined by P* ‖ 87-90 That . . . house.] *so lined by P* ‖ 93 it] *Shepherd* ‖
101 Queene!] ∼, ‖ 102 procreation] *Q(c)*; procrearion *Q(u)* | SD *Exeunt omnes.] Parrott* ‖ V.i]
‖ 2 haplesse,] *Q(c)*; ∼∧ *Q(u)* | company?] *Q(c)*; ∼, *Q(u)* ‖ 3 I?] *Shepherd*; ∼, | *Lemot,*] ∼∧
‖ 4 I. Well:] I, well: *Q(c)*; I, well, *Q(u)* ‖

Enter Catalian, and Berger behind him.

Cat. We haue [him] yfaith, stop thou him there, and I wil meet him here.

Mor. Well, I will venture once to seek her.

Ber. God's Life, my Lord, come you this way? why your wife   10
runnes ranging like as if she were mad, swearing to slit your nose if
she can catch you.   *Exit.*

Mor. What shal I do at the sight of her and hern?

Cat. Gods precious my Lord, come you this way? your wife comes
ranging with a troope of dames, like *Bacchus* drunken froes, iust as   15
you go; shift for your selfe my Lord.

Mor. Stay good *Catalian.*

Cat. No not I my Lord.   *Exit.* /

Enter Iaques.   [G1ᵛ]

Mor. How now *Iaques,* what's the newes?

Iaq. None but good my Lord.   20

Mor. Why, hast not seene my wife run round about the streets?

Iaq. Not I my Lorde, I come to you from my maister, who would
pray you to speake to *Lemot,* that *Lemot* might speake to the King,
that my masters lottery for his iewells may go forward; he hath made
the rarest deuice that euer you heard; we haue *Fortune* in it, and she   25
our maide plaies; and I, and my fellow carrie two torches, and our boy
goes before and speakes a speech, tis very fine yfaith sir.

Mor. Sirra in this thou maiest highly pleasure me, let me haue thy
place to beare a torch, that I may look on my wife, and she not see
me, for if I come into her sight abruptly, I were better be hanged.   30

Iaq. O sir you shall, or any thing that I can do, Ile send for your
wife to.

Mor. I prethee do.   *Exeunt both.*

[V.ii]

Enter the Queene, and all that were in before.

Le. This is the house
Where the mad Lord did vow to do the deed,
Draw all your swoords couragious gentlemen,
Ile bring you there where you shall honor win,
But I can tell you, you must breake your shinne.   5

Cat. Who will not breake his necke to saue his King?
Set forward *Lemot.*

---

7 haue him] *Shepherd;* him *om.* ‖ **10** God's Life] Gods Lord | way?] ∼, | why] *Q(c);* ∼: *Q(u)*
‖ **13** at] *Q(c);* om. *Q(u)* | hern?] ∼. ‖ **14** way?] ∼, ‖ **15** froes] *Parrott;* foes ‖ **16** go;] ∼, ‖ **18**
SD *Enter Iaques.] Parrott; follows succeeding line* ‖ **19** Iaques] *roman* | what's] whats ‖ **21** Why,]
Shepherd; ∼∧ | streets?] ∼. ‖ **24** forward;] ∼, ‖ **25** heard;] ∼, | *Fortune*] fortune ‖ **26** plaies;]
∼, ‖ **V.ii**] ‖ **1-13** This . . . gone.] *so lined by P* ‖ **6** Cat.] Ca. | King?] ∼: ‖

Le. Yea, much good can I do with a wounded arme, Ile go and call more helpe.

Queen. Others shall go, nay we will raise the streets,   10
Better dishonor, then destroy the King.

Le. [*Aside.*] Sbloud I know not how to excuse my villany, I would faine be gone.

Enter Dowsecer, and his friend.

Dow. Ile geld the adulterous goate, and take from him
The instrument, that plaies him such sweete musicke. /   15

Le. [*Aside.*] O rare, this makes my fiction true: now ile stay.   [G2]

Queen. Arrest these faithlesse traitrous gentlemen.

Dow. What is the reason that you call vs traitours?

Le. Nay, why do you attempt such violence against the person of the King?   20

Dow. Against the King? why this is strange to me.

Enter the King, and Martia.

King. How now my masters? what, weapons drawne,
Come you to murder me?

Queen.   How fares my Lord?

King. How fare I? well; [*To Lemot.*] but you yfaith shall get me speak for you another time; — he got me here to wooe a curious   25
Lady, and she temptes him; say what I can, offer what state I will in your behalfe *Lemot*, she will not yeeld.

Le. Yfaith my liege, what a hard heart hath she; [*Aside to the King.*] well hearke you, I am content your wit shall saue your honesty for this once.   30

King. [*Aside.*] Peace, a plague on you, peace; [*To the Queen.*] but wherefore asked you how I did?

Queen. Because I feared that you were hurte my Lord.

King. Hurt, how I pray?

Le. Why hurt, Madam? [*Aside.*] I am well againe.   [*He removes the scarf.*]

Queen. Do you aske? why he told me *Dowsecer* and this his friend, threatned to take away —

King. To take away, what should they take away?

Le. Name it Madam.

Queen. Nay, I pray name it you.   40

Le. Why then, thus it was my liege, I told her *Dowsecer*, and this his friende threatned to take away, and if they could, the instrument of procreation, and what was that now, but *Martia*? beeing a fayre woman, is not shee the instrument of procreation, as all women are?

---

12 SD *Aside.*] *Parrott* ‖ 16 *Le.*] *Parrott*; *La.* | SD *Aside.*] *Parrott* ‖ 19 *Le.*] *Parrott*; *La.* ‖ 21 King?] ~, ‖ 22-23 How . . . me?] *so lined by P* ‖ 22 masters? what,] ~, ~? ‖ 23 me?] ~. ‖ 24 well;] ~, | SD *To Lemot.*] *Parrott* ‖ 25 time;—] ~;∧ ‖ 26 him;] *Parrott*; ~, | offer] *Parrott*; ouer ‖ 28 she;] ~, ‖ 28-29 SD *Aside . . . King.*] *Parrott* ‖ 31 SD *Aside.*] *Parrott* | SD *To the Queen.*] ‖ 35 Why hurt, Madam?] *Shepherd*; ~, ~∧ ~, | SD *Aside.*] *Parrott* | SD *He . . . scarf.*] ‖ 37 away—] ~. ‖ 38 away?] ~. ‖ 42 could,] ~∧ ‖ 43 *Martia*?] *Shepherd*; ~∧ ‖ 44 are?] ~. ‖

Queen. O wicked man. / 45

Le. Go to, go to, you are one of those fiddles too yfaith. [G2ᵛ]

King. Well pardon my minion, that hath frayd you thus,

Twas but to make you mery in the end.

Queen. I ioy it endes so well, my gracious Lord.

Foyes. But say my gracious Lord, is no harme done, 50

Betweene my louing daughter, and your grace?

King. No, of my honor and my soule *Foyes.*

Dow. The fire of loue which she hath kindled in me

Being greater then my heate of vanity,

Hath quite expelled [it]. 55

King. Come *Dowsecer*, receiue with your lost wittes your loue,

thought lost; I know youle yeeld, my lord, and you her father.

Both. Most ioyfully my Liege.

King. And for her part I know her disposition well enough.

Le. What, will you haue her? 60

Dow. Yea mary will I.

Le. Ile go and tell *Labesha* presently.

Enter Iaquis, and my Host.

Iaq. Monsieur *Lemot*, I pray let me speake with you, I come to you

from the Lord *Moren,* who would desire you to speake to the King for

my masters lottery, and he hath my place to beare a torch, for bare 65

faced hee dares not look vpon his wife, for his life.

Le. O excellent, Ile further thy masters lottery and it be but for

this iest only; harke you my liege, here's the poore man hath bin at

great charges for the preparation of a lottery, and he hath made the

rarest deuice, that I know you wil take great pleasure in it; I pray let 70

him present it before you at *Verones* house.

King. With all my heart, can you be ready so soone?

Ver. Presently and if it like your grace.

King. But hearke you *Lemot*, how shall we do for euery mans posie.

Le. Will you all trust me with the making of them? 75

All. With all our hearts.

Le. Why then Ile go to make the poses and bring *Labesha* to the

lottery presently. / [*Exit.*]

Enter Florila like a Puritan. [G3]

Flo. Surely the world is full of vanitie,

A woman must take heed she do not heare 80

A lewd man speake, for euery woman cannot

When shee is tempted, when the wicked fiend

50-55 But . . . it.] *so lined by* P ‖ 55 it] ‖ 57 thought] though (*See Textual Note*) | lord,] ∼∧ ‖
58 Liege] Lord ‖ 61 mary] *Q(c)*; marry *Q(u)* ‖ 68 only;] ∼, | here's] heres ‖ 70 it;] ∼, ‖ 71
Verones] Shepherd; Valeres (*See Textual Note*) ‖ 72 With] Whith ‖ 73 Ver.] *Host throughout scene*
‖ 78 SD *Exit.*] Parrott ‖ 79-88 Surely . . . any.] *so lined by* P ‖

Gets her into his snares, escape like me,
For graces measure is not so filled vp,
Nor so prest downe in euery one as me, 85
But yet I promise you a little more —
Well, Ile go seeke my head, who shal take me in
The gates of his kind armes vntoucht of any.
 King. What, Madam are you so pure now?
 Flo. Yea, would not you be pure?
 King.   No puritane. 90
 Flo. You must be then a diuell, I can tell you.
 Lab. O wife where hast thou beene?
 Flo. Where did I tell you I would be, I pray?
 Lab. In thy close walke thou saidst.
 Flo.   And was I not?
 Lab. Truly I know not, I neither looked nor knocked, for *Labesha* 95
told me that you, and faire *Martia* were at *Verones* ordinarie.
 King. *Labesha?* my lord you are a wise man to beleeue a fool.
 Flo. Well my good head, for my part I forgiue you:
But surely you do much offend to be
Suspicious: where there is no trust, there is no loue, 100
And where there is no loue twixt man and wife,
There's no good dealing surely: for as men
Should euer loue their wiues, so should they euer trust them,
For what loue is there where there is no trust?
 King. She tels you true, my lord. 105
 Lab. Shee doth my liege; and deare wife pardon this
And I will neuer be suspicious more.
 Flo. Why I say, I do.

     Enter Lemot, leading Labesha in a halter.

 Le. Looke you my liege, I haue done simple seruice amongest you,
here is one had hanged himselfe for loue, thinking his Mistresse had 110
done so for him: well, see your Mistresse liues.
 Labes. And doth my Mistresse liue? /
 King. Shee doth, O noble knight, but not your Mistresse now.   [G3ᵛ]
 Labes. Sblood, but she shall for me, or for no body else.   [*Drawing.*]
 Le. How now, what, a traitor? draw vpon the King? 115
 Labes. Yea, or vpon any woman here in a good cause.
 King. Well sweete *Besha* let her marry *Dowsecer,* Ile get thee a wife
worth fifteene of her, wilt thou haue one that cares not for thee?
 Labes. Not I by the Lord, I scorne her, Ile haue her better if I can
get her. 120

---

83 snares,] ∼∧ ‖ 86 more—] ∼: ‖ 87 Well] well ‖ 89 What,] ∼∧ ‖ 93 Where] where | be,] ∼∧ | pray?] ∼. ‖ 96 *Verones*] roman ‖ 98-107 Well . . . more.] *so lined by P* ‖ 102 There's] theres ‖ 110 himselfe] *Q(c);* himseife *Q(u)* ‖ 114 SD *Drawing.*] *Parrott* ‖ 115 what, a traitor?] ∼∧ ∼ ∼, | King?] ∼. ‖

King. Why that's well said.

Le. What Madam, are you turned puritan againe?

Flo. When was I other, pray?

Le. Marie Ile tell you when, when you went to the Ordinarie, and
when you made false signes to your husband, which I could tell him all.　　125

Flo. Cursed be he that maketh debate twixt man and wife.

Le. O rare scripturian! you haue sealed vp my lips. A hall, a hall,
the pageant of the Butterie.

> *Enter two with torches, the one of them Moren, then my host and*
> *his son, then his maid drest like Queene Fortune,*
> *with two pots in her hands.*

King. What is he?

Le. This is *Verones* sonne, my liege.　　130

King. What shall he do?

Cat. Speak some speach that his father hath made for him.

Queen. Why, is he good at speeches?

Cat. O he is rare at speaches.

Boy.　　　　　　Faire ladies most tender,　　135
　　　　　　　　And nobles most slender,
　　　　　　　　And gentles whose wits be scarce —

King. My host, why do you call vs nobles most slender?

Ver. And it shall please your Grace, to be slender is to be proper,
and therfore where my boy saies nobles most slender, it is as much [as]　　140
to say, fine and proper nobles.

Le. Yea, but why do you call vs gentles whose wits are scarce? /

Ver. To be scarce, is to be rare: and therefore whereas he sayes　　[G4]
Gentles whose wits be scarce, is as much as to say, Gentles whose wits
be rare.　　145

Le. Well, forwards trunchman.

Boy.　　　　　　Faire ladies most tender,
　　　　　　　　And nobles most slender,
　　　　　　　　And gentles whose wittes bee scarce,
　　　　　　　　Queene *Fortune* doth come　　150
　　　　　　　　With her trumpe, and her drumme,
　　　　　　　　As it may appeare by my voice —

Labes. Come hither, are you a schoolemaister, where was *Fortune*
Queene, of what countrey or kingdome?

Ver. Wy sir, *Fortune* was Queene ouer all the world.　　155

Labes. That's a lie, there's none that euer conquered all the world,
but maister *Alisander,* I am sure of that.

---

121 that's] thats ‖ 123 *Flo.*] *Elo.* ‖ 127 lips. A] lips, a ‖ 128 SD *then his*] *tben his* ‖ 130 *Verones*]
roman ‖ 132 him.] ∼∧ ‖ 133 Why,] *Shepherd;* ∼∧ ‖ 137 scarce—] ∼. ‖ 140-41 as to] as *om.* ‖
142 scarce?] ∼. ‖ 143 whereas] where as ‖ 146 trunchman] *stet* (*See Textual Note*) ‖ 150 *Fortune*]
roman throughout scene ‖ 152 voice—] ∼. ‖ 156 That's] Thats | there's] theres ‖

Le. O rare Monsieur *Labesha,* who would haue thought hee could haue found so rare a fault in the speach?

Ver. Ile alter it if it please your grace. 160

King. No, tis very well.

Boy. Father I must begin againe they interrupt me so.

Ver. I beseech your grace giue the boy leaue to begin again.

King. With all my heart, tis so good we cannot heare it too oft.

Boy.   Faire ladies most tender, 165
    And nobles most slender,
    And gentles whose wittes are scarce,
    Queene *Fortune* doth come
    With her Fife, and her Drum,
    As it doth appeare by my voice, 170
    Here is Fortune good,
    Not il by the rood,
    And this naught but good shall do you, [sir,]
    Dealing the lots
    Out of our pots, 175
    And so good Fortune to you sir.

Le. Looke you my liege, how hee that caries the torch trembles extreamly.

King. I warrant tis with care to carie his torch well.

Le. Nay there is something else in the wind: why my host, what 180
meanes thy man *Iaques* to tremble so?

Ver. Hold still thou knaue; what, art thou afraid to looke vpon the goodly presence of a king: hold vp for shame.

Le. [*Aside.*] Alas poore man, he thinks tis *Iaques* his man: poore
lord, how much is he bound to suffer for his wife? / 185

King. Hearke you mine host, what goodly person is that? is it *For-* [G4ᵛ]
tune her selfe?

Ver. Ile tell your Maiestie in secrete who it is, it is my maide *Iaquena.*

King. I promise you she becomes her state rarely. 190

Le. Well my liege, you were all content that I should make your
poses: well here they be: euery one giue Master *Verone* his fiue
crownes.

King. There's mine and the Queenes.

Lab. Their's ours. 195

Dow. And there is mine and *Martias.*

Le. Come *Labesha* thy money.

Labes. You must lend me some, for my boy is runne away with my
purse.

---

159 speach?] ∼. ‖ **172** Not] *Parrott*; but ‖ **173** sir,] *Parrott* ‖ **182** knaue; what,] ∼, ∼ʌ ‖ **184**
SD *Aside.*] *Parrott* ‖ **192** be: euery one] ∼ʌ ∼ ∼: ‖ **194** There's] Theres ‖ **195** *Lab.*] *Parrott*;
Labesh. | Their's ours.] Theirs ∼ʌ ‖

Le. Thy boy? I neuer knew any that thou hadst.   200

Labes. Had not I a boy three or foure yeares ago, and he ran away?

Le. And neuer since he went thou hadst not a peny: but stand by,
Ile excuse you. But sirrah *Catalian,* thou shalt stand on one side and
reade the prises, and I will stand on the other and read the Poses.

Cat. Content *Lemot.*   205

Le. Come on Queene *Fortune,* tell euery man his posie; this is orderly, the King and Queene are first.

King. Come let vs see what goodly poses you haue giuen vs.

Le. This is your Maiesties: At the fairest, so it bee not *Martia.*

King. A plague vpon you, you are still playing the villain with me.   210

Le. This is the Queenes, Obey the Queene: and she speakes it to
her husband, or to *Fortune,* which she will.

Cat. A prise: your Maiesties is the summe of foure shillings in gold.

King. Why how can that be? there is no such coyne.

Ver. Here is the worth of it, if it please your grace.   [*Offering gold.*] /

Queen. Well, what's for me?   [H1]

Cat. A heart of gold.

Queen. A goodly iewell.

Le. Count *Laberuele* and *Florila.*

Lab. What's my posie sir I pray?   220

Le. Mary this my Lord,

      Of all fortunes friends, that hath ioy in this life,

      He is most happy that puts a sure trust in his wife.

Lab. A very good one sir, I thanke you for it.

Flo. What's mine I pray?   225

Le. Mary this Madam,

      Good fortune be thou my good fortune bringer,

      And make me amends for my poore bitten finger.

Lab. Who bit your finger wife?

Flo. No body; tis [a] vaine posie.   230

Cat. Blanke for my lord *Laberuele*; for his wife a posie, a paire of
holy beades with a crucifix.

Flo. O bommination Idole, Ile none of them.

King. Keepe them thy self *Veron,* she will not haue them.

Le. Dowsecer and *Martia,* I haue fitted your lordship for a posie.   235

Dow. Why what is it?

Le. Ante omnia vna.

Mar. And what is mine sir?

Le. A serious one I warrant you: Change for the better.

---

201 foure] *Q(c)*; four *Q(u)* | he] *Q(c)*; hee *Q(u)* | away?] ~. ‖ **202** peny:] ~, ‖ **206** posie;]
~, ‖ **209** Maiesties:] ~, ‖ **210** villain] *Shepherd*; villaines ‖ **213** gold.] ~∧ ‖ **214** be?] ~, ‖ **215**
SD *Offering gold.*] ‖ **216** what's] whats ‖ **220** What's] Whats ‖ **222-23** Of . . . life, / He . . .
wife. /] *stet* ‖ **225** What's] Whats ‖ **227-28** Good . . . bringer, / And . . . finger. /] *stet* ‖ **230**
a] *Parrott* ‖ **231** *Laberuele*;] ~, | a paire] *Q*; a a paire *Q(r)* ‖ **234** *Veron*] roman ‖ **235** *Martia,*] ~
∧ | posie.] *Q(c)*; ~∧ *Q(u)* ‖ **239** you: Change] ~, change *Q(u), Q(r)*; ~∧ change: *Q(c)* ‖

Mar. That's not amisse.   240

Cat. A prize: *Dowsecer* hath a caduceus or *Mercuries* rod of gold, set with Iacinths and Emeralds.

Dow. What is for *Martia*?

Cat. Martia hath the two serpents heades set with Diamonds.

Le. What my host *Verone*?   245

King. What? is he in for his owne iewells?

Le. O what els my liege? tis our bountie, and his posie is
　　　　　To tel you the truth in words plaine and mild,
　　　　　Verone loues his maide, and she is great with child. /

King. What, Queene *Fortune* with child, shall we haue yong for-   [H1ᵛ]
tunes my host?

Ver. I am abused, and if it please your Maiestie.

Maid. Ile play no more.

Le. No faith you need not now, you haue plaid your bellie full
alreadie.   255

Ver. Stand still good *Iaquena,* they do but ieast.

Maid. Yea, but I like no such ieasting.

Le. Come great Queene *Fortune,* let see your posies. [*To the Countess.*] What, madam, alas, your ladiship is one of the last.

Coun. What is my posie sir I pray?   260

Le. Marie Madam your posie is made in maner and forme of an
Eccho, as if you were seeking your husbande; and *Fortune* should be
the Eccho, and this you say: where is my husband hid so long vnmaskt? maskt, sayes the Eccho: but in what place sweete *Fortune*?
let me heare: heare, sayes the Eccho.   265

King. There you lie Eccho, for if he were here we must needes see
him.

Le. Indeed sweete King, there me thinkes the Eccho must needes
lie: if hee were here wee must needes see him; tis one of them that
caries the torches: no that cannot be neither, and yet by the Masse   270
here's *Iaques*; why my host, did not you tell me that *Iaques* should be
a torchbearer? who is this? [*Revealing Moren.*] God's my life, my
lord!

Mor. [*Trying to leave.*] And you be Gentlemen let me go.

Coun. Nay come your way, you may be well enough ashamed to   275
shew your face that is a periured wretch; did not you sweare, if there
were any wenches at the ordinarie, you would straight come home?

King. Why, who tolde you Madam, there were any there?

---

240 That's] Thats ‖ 241 prize] *Q(r)*; price *Q* | *Dowsecer*] *Q(c)*; ∼, *Q(u)* | caduceus] *Parrott*;
cats eyes ‖ 246 iewells?] ∼. ‖ 247 liege?] ∼, ‖ 248 tel you the] *Q(c)*; tell youthe *Q(u)* ‖ 248-
49 mild, / *Verone* loues] *Q(c)*; mild, *Verone* loues / *Q(u)* ‖ 250 What,] ∼∧ ‖ 258-59 posies.
... What,] *Parrott*; ∼, ... what∧ | SD *To the Countess.*] ‖ 262 husbande;] ∼, ‖ 263 say:]
Q(c); ∼, *Q(u)* ‖ 263-64 vnmaskt? maskt,] ∼, ∼, *Q(c)*; ∼, ∼? *Q(c)* ‖ 265 heare,] here∧
Q(u); ∼∧ *Q(c)* ‖ 269 lie:] ∼, | him;] ∼, | tis one] *Q(c)*; one *Q(u)* ‖ 270 torches:] *Q(c)*; ∼,
Q(u) ‖ 271 here's *Iaques*;] heres ∼, ‖ 272 torchbearer?] torch bearer: *Q(u)*; ∼: *Q(c)* | SD
Revealing Moren.] *Parrott subs.* | God's] Gods ‖ 273 lord!] ∼. ‖ 274 SD *Trying to leave.*] ‖ 276
wretch;] ∼, ‖ 277 would] yould | home?] ∼. ‖

Coun. He that will stand to it, *Lemot* my liege.

    Le. Who I stand to it? alas, I tolde you in kindnesse, and good will,   280
because I would not haue you companie long from your husband. /

    Mor. Why loe you bird, how much you are deceiued.   [H2]

    Coun. Why wherefore were you afraid to be seene?

    Mor. Who I afraid? alas I bore a torch to grace this honorable
presence, for nothing els sweete bird.   285

    King. Thanks good *Moren,* see lady with what wrong
You haue pursued your most inamored lord:
But come, now al are friends, now is this day
Spent with vnhurtfull motiues of delight,
And ouerioyes more my senses at the night: 290
And now for *Dowsecer,* if all will follow my deuise,
His beauteous loue and he shal married be,
And here I solemnly inuite you all
Home to my court, where with feastes wee will crowne
This myrthfull day, and vow it to renowne.   295

Finis.

280 it?] ~, ‖ **287** haue pursued] *Q(c)*; hane persued, *Q(u)* ‖ **288** come,] ~∧ ‖ **289** vnhurtfull]
Q(r); an hurtfull *Q* ‖ **290** ouerioyes] ouer ioyes ‖ **291-93** if . . . all] *so lined by P* ‖

HISTORICAL COLLATION

[Editions collated: Shepherd (=*S*, in *The Works of George Chapman: Plays*, 1875, pp. 23-45); Parrott (=*P*, in *The Plays and Poems of George Chapman: The Comedies* [1914], pp. 45-98). The siglum *Q* identifies the quarto of 1599, with *Q(c)* and *Q(u)* distinguishing corrected and uncorrected states of that text, and *Q(r)* a resetting of the half-sheet H. In addition, emendations proposed by K. Deighton, *The Old Dramatists: Conjectural Readings* (Westminster, 1896); J. Brereton, "Notes on the Text of Chapman's Plays," *MLR*, III (1907), 56-68; and W.W. Greg, ed., *An Humorous Day's Mirth, 1599* (Malone Society Reprints, 1938) are also recorded. Although Greg reprints the Q text, he includes a "List of Doubtful, Irregular, and Variant Readings" with suggested emendations. Only substantive and semi-substantive variants are recorded; obvious errors are not recorded. Lemmata are taken from the present text. Where lemma represents the reading of Q copy-text, omission of siglum indicates agreement with lemma.]

I.i

I.i] *om. Q, S; Scene I P, G*
1 throwt] through *S*; throughout *or* thwart *G conj.*
11 By] *Brereton conj.*; to *Q, S, P, G*
   the] *om. S*
16 al for] all careful for *P*
17 Tis] *P*; is *Q, S, G*
27 iewell;] ~∧ *Q, G*; ~, *S, P*
28 enough] *P*; in nought *Q, S, G*
29 Dispaire] *Q(c)*; tis spare, *Q(u), G*; 'Tis-/ Despair∧ *S*
32 the] *S*; *om. Q, P, G*
33 knowing;] *S, P*; ~∧ *Q*; ~: *G*
   that] *om. G conj.*

I.ii

I.ii] *om. Q, S; Scene II P, G*
55 cariages] carriage *S*
56 cariages] carriage *S*
62 louely] *P, Deighton conj.*; loue, by *Q, S, G*
65 *Morens*] *S, P, G*; *Moris Q*
68 he] him *G*
72 SD *Aside to Lemot.*] *P*; *om. Q, S, G*
74 SD *Aside.*] *P*; *om. Q, S, G*
83 her, tho] *S, P*; ~∧ ~, *Q, G*
84 start] stark *S, Deighton conj.*
101 SD *Exeunt.*] *Exit. Q, S, G*; *Exit* Lemot *with* Blanuel *P*

I.iii

I.iii] *om. Q, S; Scene III P, G*
2 Gentlemans] Gentleman *S, G conj.*
7 SD *To Martia.*] *om. Q, S, P, G*
16 equificate] equivocate *S, P, G conj.*
16-17 illusion] allusion *S, P, G conj.*
21 horse and you,] *P;* ~, ~ ~∧ *Q, S, G*
38 me;] *S, P;* ~, *Q, G*

I.iv

I.iv] *om. Q, S; Scene IV P, G*
17 much] *Q(c);* more *Q(u), G*
24 SD *Then hee reades.*] *S, P; in margin Q, G*
   SD *hee*] *Q(c);* shee *Q(u)*
46 off, my head] *Q(c);* ~∧ ~ ~, *Q(u), G*
47 would] *Q(c);* will *Q(u), G*
52-53 banishment] punishment *S, P, Brereton conj.*
57 SD *Aside.*] *P; om. Q, S, G*
91 SD *Aside.*] *P; om. Q, S, G*
95 You sir, you sir] you sir *S*
111 SD *Enter Lemot.*] *S, P; in margin Q, G*
114 lockes] *S, P, G;* lookes *Q*
133 to you] *Q(c);* o you *Q(u)*
136 thogh] *Q(c);* thou *Q(u)*
137 there no] there is no *Q, S, P, G*
138 SD *They withdraw.*] *P; om. Q, S, G*
141 the] *Q(c);* he *Q(u)*
146 proofe?] *Q(c);* ~∧ *Q(u), G*
167 more] *Q(c);* most *Q(u), G*
173 SD *Kisses her.*] *P; om. Q, S, G*
193 in] *S, P, G; om. Q*
194 worthilly] *P, G, Brereton conj.;* vnworthilly *Q, S*
208 SD *Exeunt . . . Florila*] *Exit Q, S, G; Exit with* Florilla *P*
209 start] stark *S*
211 SD *Exeunt*] *Exit Q, S, G; Exit with* Catalian *P*

I.v

I.v] *om. Q, S; Scene V P, G*
1 *Mor.*] *P, G; Mar. Q, S*
5 *Mor.*] *P, G; Mar. Q, S*
8 *Mor.*] *S, P, G; Mar. Q*
45 *Mar.*] *S, P, G; Mor. Q*
49 *Coun.*] *P, G, Brereton conj.; Cat. Q, S*
61 *Coun.*] *P; Co. Q, S, G*
81 *Coun.*] *P; Co. Q, S, G*
86 *Coun.*] *P; Co. Q, S, G*
96 SD *To Martia.*] *om. Q, S, P, G*

100 SD *Then . . . draw.*] S, P; *in margin* Q, G
105 to,] S, P; ~∧ Q, G
112 thee;] ~∧ Q, S, P, G
114 to] *om.* G *conj.*
129 you;] ~∧ Q; ~. S, P; ~: G
 SD *To Labesha.*] P; *om.* Q, S, G
132 *Col.*] Co. Q, G; Ca. S; Cat. P
135 nete] net S
136 *Blan.*] Ca. S; Cat. P
143 Why . . . Colinet.] P, G; ~ . . . ~. *Enter Lemot* Q, S; *in margin* Q
153 SD *Starting for Martia.*] *om.* Q, S, G; *Running at* Moren P
154 *Mor.*] S, P, G; Me. Q
158 dissimulation.] S, P; ~, Q, G
 SD *To Martia.*] P; *om.* Q, S, G
168 SD *Exeunt . . . Countess.*] P; *om.* Q, S, G
170 Lord] *om.* S
172 *Col.*] Mo. S
176 SD *Exeunt . . . Martia.*] P; *om.* Q, S, G
177 *Col.*] P; C. Q, G; Mo. S
179 SD *Exeunt . . . Blanuel.*] P; *om.* Q, S, G
184 SD *Exit.*] P; *om.* Q, S, G

II.i

II.i] *om.* Q, S; *Scene VI* P, G
24 desolate] dissolute S, G
27 reason] S, P, G; ~: Q
 end:] S, P, G; ~∧ Q
28 desolate] dissolute S, G
50 but] *om.* S
53 SD *Enter Lemot.*] P; *om.* Q, S, G
65 What,] P; ~∧ Q, S, G
67 sir] P, G; *see* Q, S
69 SD *He . . . Florila.*] P; *om.* Q, S, G
73 thorow] through S; thorough P
77 are we] we are S, P
83 SD *Aside.*] P; *om.* Q, S, G
88 SD *Aside.*] P; *om.* Q, S, G
92 SD *Aside.*] P; *om.* Q, S, G
96 SD *Aside.*] P; *om.* Q, S, G
100 SD *To Lemot.*] P; *om.* Q, S, G
111 sir] P, G; *see* Q, S
112 SD *To Lemot.*] P; *om.* Q, S, G
 loue, is required] P, G; loue∧ is required Q; love∧ is requited S
127 close] P; choise Q, S, G
131 sir] P, G; *see* Q, S
136 SD *Then he sighes.*] P; *in margin* Q, G; *follows* come *in next speech by Florila* S
 SD *Exeunt*] Exit Q, S, G; *Exit with* Labervele P

II.ii

II.ii] *om. Q, S; Scene VII P, G*
2 *Cat.*] *S; C. Q; Col. P;* Colinet or Catalian *G*
12 quackemyred] quagmired *S, P*
18 trash.] ∼, *Q, S, G;* ∼; *P*
35 SD *Presenting Labesha.*] *om. Q, S, G; introducing* Labesha *follows especially P*
38 *siniora*] *Signor S;* Seigneur *P*
39 barony] *P;* barrendrie *Q(u), G;* barendrie *Q(c), S*
40 purpose. Lord] ∼, ∼ *Q, G;* ∼∧ ∼ *S;* ∼; ∼ *P*
49 SD *and a paire . . . and a codpeece*] *a paire . . . a codpiece S, P*
50 your friend] your young friend *S, P*
57 or at] *S, P, G;* or that at *Q*
59 may;] ∼, *Q, G;* ∼ — *S, P*
62 *Dow.*] *P, G; om. Q, S*
62-63 *Quid . . . magnitudo.*] *P, G; Quid Dei potes videri magnum in rebus humanis quae aeterni omnes to thy ousque notas sic omnibus magna tutor, Q, S*
70 made] *S, P;* make *Q, G*
78 snares, snares, snares] *P;* he cares, he cares, he cares *Q, S, G*
79 no more] *P; om. Q, S, G*
80 when] *P; om. Q, S, G*
81 strong;] *P, G;* ∼∧ *Q, S*
88 SD *Noticing the sword.*] *om. Q, S, G; seeing the sword P*
90 lenity] levity *P*
95 wines] wiues *Q, S, P, G*
97 SD *Noticing . . . codpiece.*] *om. Q, S, G; Seeing the hose and codpiece P*
105 much] *P, G;* match *Q, S*
109 hose] *P, G;* house *Q, S*
   man;] *P, G;* ∼∧ *Q, S*
110 but hose] *P, G;* but house *Q;* but the house *S*
111 your] you *P*
112 rest] *S, P do not modernize to wrest*
113 Ile] *om. S*
   SD *He . . . codpiece.*] *om. Q, S, P, G*
114 *Lab.*] *P, G; La. Q, S*
   so] *P; om. Q, S, G*
116 *La.*] *By preserving the prefix La., Q, S apparently assign this to Labervele*
127 curls] *P, Brereton conj.;* tailes *Q, S, G*
131 SD *Noticing the picture.*] *om. Q, S, G; Seeing the picture P*
133 *Lab.*] *P, G; La. Q, S*
135 *Lab.*] *P; La. Q, S; Lavele G conj.*
137 be,] *S, P;* ∼∧ *Q, G*
152 Make] Makes *S*
156 SD *Pretending . . . picture.*] *om. Q, S, P, G*
164 confesse] consent *P*
191 An] Ah *P*
196 haue] *G conj.;* hope *Q, S, P*

197 him] *G conj.*; hers *Q, S*; her *P, Brereton conj.*
206 gestion] digestion *P*
209 sense vnto my soule] my sense unto soul *S*
232 *Mor.*] *P, G; Mar. Q, S*
236 *Mor.*] *P, G; Mar. Q, S*
238 *Mor.*] *P, G; Mar. Q, S*
246 SD *Exeunt*] *Exit Q, S, G; Exit* Florilla *with* Martia *P*
249 *Labes.*] *La. S*
254 lord;] *S, P;* ~, *Q, G*

III.i

III.i] *om. Q, S; Scene VIII P, G*
9 *Valeres*] *S, P;* Verones *Q, G*
15-16 in the name of God I trow] *P, G;* name in the of God I trowee *Q;* in the
     name of God, I trow ye *S*
20 *Boy.*] *Fo. S*
    you mercie] for mercy *S*
22 SD *Aside.*] *P; om. Q, S, G*
    Iaquena] *P, G; Sateena Q, S*
26 SD *Aside.*] *P; om. Q, S, G*
29 SD *Aside to Maid.*] *P; om. Q, S, G*
30 *Iaquena*] *P, G; Iacenan Q, S*
40 SD *Exit Maid.*] *om. Q, S, P, G*
53 to] *G;* so *Q, S, P*
54 *Rowle*] *regularly spelled Rowl S*
56 cardes here;] ~, ~∧ *Q, G;* ~. ~, *S;* ~ ~, *P*
64 what] that *S*
69 SD *Aside.*] *P; om. Q, S, G*
70 SD *Aside.*] *P; om. Q, S, G*
    SD *Boy . . . pipe.*] *om. Q, S, G; Exit* Boy *P*
82 Deliuery? what,] *S, P;* ~, ~∧ *Q, G*
92-93 tis as pretty] as *om. Q, S, P, G*
93 seen, made] *P;* ~∧ ~, *Q, S, G*
94 little] *S, P;* tittle *Q, G*
98 SD *Exit Boy.*] *om. Q, S, P, G*
103 SD *Exit Iaques.*] *om. Q, S, P, G*
107 SD *He kisses her.*] *P; om. Q, S, G*
111 SD *Exit Verone.*] *om. Q, S, P, G*
114 SD *To Labesha.*] *om. Q, S, P, G*
116 for] to *S, G conj.*
125 vnkindly] kindly *S*
126 *Labes.*] *P; La. Q, S, G*
131 SD *He . . . cry.*] *P; om. Q, S, G*
148 *Mor.*] *P, G; Lor. Q, S*
152 what,] *P;* ~∧ *Q, S, G*
153 *Labes.*] *Lab. Q, P, G; La. S*
158 SD *Aside.*] *P; om. Q, S, G*

160 SD *Indicating Rowley.*] *om.* Q, S, P, G
183 their selues] themselves S
193 SD *Aside.*] P; *om.* Q, S, G
194 SD *Aside.*] P; *om.* Q, S, G
198 SD *Aside.*] P; *om.* Q, S, G
199 SD *Aside.*] P; *om.* Q, S, G
    here he comes hither.] P; here comes hither∧ Q, G; he comes hither. S
200 *Catalian*] S, P, G; ∼, Q
202 that] *om.* S
205 SD *Aside.*] P; *om.* Q, S, G
208 SD *Aside.*] P; *om.* Q, S, G
212 SD *Aside.*] P; *om.* Q, S, G
214 SD *Aside.*] P; *om.* Q, S, G
215 *promptum*] *promptus* Q, S, G; *promptos* P
216 SD *Aside.*] P; *om.* Q, S, G
219 *promptum*] *promptus* Q, S, G; *promptos* P
225 SD *Exit Iaques.*] P; *om.* Q, S, G
226 SD *Aside.*] *om.* Q, S, P, G
229 SD *Enter Boy.*] P; *om.* Q, S, G
230 SD *To Lemot.*] *om.* Q, S, P, G
230-31 desires] desire S, P
232 SD *The . . . ear.*] S, P; *in margin* Q, G
    SD *his*] *om.* S
237 *Mor.*] *Throughout remainder of scene the* Q, S *prefix is* Lord
269 they?] S, P, G; ∼∧ Q
    SD *Aside.*] P; *om.* Q, S, G
    wife go I] P, G; wife go Q; wife; go, S
    yfaith] faith G; 'faith P
272 heart;] S; ∼, Q, G; ∼! P
274 sir] P, G; see Q, S

III.ii

III.ii] *om.* Q, S; *Scene IX* P, G
1 What,] S, P; ∼∧ Q, G
10 are, nothing els: . . . now] S, P; ∼: ∼ ∼∧ . . . ∼, Q, G
    SD *Aside.*] P; *om.* Q, S, G

III.iii

III.iii] *om.* Q, S; *Scene X* P, G
1 SD *Enter Verone.*] P; *om.* Q, S, G
3 *All.*] *Le.* S; *Labes.* P

IV.i

IV.i] *om.* Q, S; *Scene XI* P, G
1 *Lab.*] P, G; *La.* Q, S
5 *Lab.*] P, G; *La.* Q, S
9 *Labes.*] P, G; *La.* Q, S
10 silence] S, P, G; silent Q

121

12 And] *Q(c)*; an *Q(u)*
  SD *Exeunt.*] *P*; *om. Q, S, G*
17 *Mor.*] *P, G*; *Lor. Q*; *Lord. S*
  SD *Exeunt . . . Martia.*] *P*; *om. Q, S, G*
19 *Valeres*] Verone's *S*
  SD *Exeunt . . . another.*] *P*; *om. Q, S, G*
  SD *Enter . . . Lemot.*] *follows succeeding line Q, G*
20 *Flo.*] *P, G*; *om. Q*; *Pu. S*
22 doter; what,] ∼, ∼∧ *Q, G*; ∼? ∼, *S, P*
25 you] *Q(c)*; he *Q(u)*
34 Yea surely do I] *Q(c)*; I shew I do *Q(u)*
40 your hand] your owne hand *Q, S, P, G*
52 *Beso las manos*] *P*; *Besilus manus Q(u)*; *Besilos manus Q(c), G*; *Besilas manos S*
64 what,] *S, P*; ∼∧ *Q, G*
67 wretch] *S, P, G*; wench *Q*
68 affection] affliction *G conj.*
73 SD *Exit.*] *P*; *om. Q, S, G*

IV.ii

IV.ii] *om. Q, S*; *Scene XII P, G*
1 *Ver.*] *throughout this scene the Q, S, G prefix is Host*
3 now here's] *S, P*; no heres *Q, G*
10 SD *Gentlemen*] *P, G*; *Gentleman Q, S*
14 if] *om. S*
32-33 SD *He . . . creame.*] *S, P*; *in margin Q, G*
34 *Ver.*] ∼. *Aside P*
37 creame; what,] ∼∧ ∼∧ *Q, G*; ∼, ∼∧ *S, P*
43 burst I;] ∼ ∼, *Q, S, P, G*
45 *Cat.*] ∼. *Aside P*
46 SD *Advancing.*] *P*; *om. Q, S, G*
53 SD *He . . . leave.*] *om. Q, S, P, G*
54 SD *Exit.*] *P*; *om. Q, S, G*

IV.iii

IV.iii] *om. Q, S*; *Scene XIII P, G*
1 SD *Aside.*] *P*; *om. Q, S, G*
6 my] *P*; his *Q, S, G*
13 me;] ∼∧ *Q, P, G*; ∼, *S*
42 *Queen.*] *Cat. Q*; *Ca. S*; *Count. P, G conj.*
44 her] *S, P*; *om. Q, G*
56 falls] *S, P*; fall *Q, G*
93 it] *S, P*; *om. Q, G*
102 SD *Exeunt omnes.*] *P*; *om. Q, S, G*

V.i

V.i] *om. Q, S*; *Scene XIV P, G*
3 I?] *S, P*; ∼, *Q, G*
  vilde] vile *S*

7 haue him] *S*, *P*; him *om. Q*, *G*
  and] *om. P*
10 Life] Lord *Q*, *S*, *P*, *G*
11 ranging] raging *S*, *P*
13 do at the] *Q(c)*; do the *Q(u)*
15 ranging] raging *S*, *P*
  froes] *P*; foes *Q*, *S*, *G*
18 SD *Enter Iaques.*] *follows next line Q*, *S*, *G*
21 Why,] *S*, *P*; ∼∧ *Q*, *G*

V.ii

V.ii] *om. Q*, *S*, *P*; *Scene XV G*
6 *Cat.*] *Ca. Q*, *S*; *Count. P*, *G conj.*
12 SD *Aside.*] *P*; *om. Q*, *S*, *G*
13 SD *friend.*] *friend Lavel. P*
16 *Le.*] *P*, *G*; *La. Q*, *S*
  SD *Aside.*] *P*; *om. Q*, *S*, *G*
19 *Le.*] *S*, *P*; *La. Q*, *G*
24 SD *To Lemot.*] *P*; *om. Q*, *S*, *G*
26 him;] *P*; ∼, *Q*, *S*, *G*
  offer] *P*; ouer *Q*, *S*, *G*
27 behalfe] ∼. *S*
28-29 SD *Aside . . . King.*] *P*; *om. Q*, *S*, *G*
31 SD *Aside.*] *P*; *om. Q*, *S*, *G*
  SD *To the Queen.*] *om. Q*, *S*, *P*, *G*
35 Why hurt, Madam?] *S*, *P*; ∼, ∼∧ ∼, *Q*, *G*
  SD *Aside.*] *P*; *om. Q*, *S*, *G*
  SD *He . . . scarf.*] *om. Q*, *S*, *P*, *G*
39 *Le.*] *La. S*
43 *Martia?*] *S*, *P*; ∼∧ *Q*, *G*
55 it] *om. Q*, *S*, *P*, *G*
57 thought] though *Q*, *S*, *P*, *G*
58 Liege] Lord *Q*, *S*, *P*, *G*
71 *Verones*] *S*, *P*, *G*; *Valeres Q*
73 *Ver.*] *throughout scene the Q*, *S*, *G prefix is Host*
78 SD *Exit.*] *P*; *om. Q*, *S*, *G*
91 be then] then be *S*
114 SD *Drawing.*] *P*; *om. Q*, *S*, *G*
115 what, a traitor?] ∼∧ ∼ ∼, *Q*, *G*; ∼, ∼ ∼! *S*, *P*
119 I by] ∼; ∼ *S*, *P*
133 Why,] *S*, *P*; ∼∧ *Q*, *G*
140 where] when *S*
140-41 much as to] as *om. Q*, *S*, *P*, *G*
152 voice—] ∼. *Q*, *S*, *G*; verse. *P*
170 voice] verse *P*
172 Not] *P*; but *Q*, *S*, *G*
173 sir] *P*; *om. Q*, *S*, *G*

184 SD *Aside.*] *P*; *om. Q, S, G*
192 be: euery one] ∼∧ ∼ ∼: *Q, S, G*; ∼. ∼ ∼∧ *P*
195 *Lab.*] *P*; *Labesh. Q*; *La. S*; *Laber. G*
210 villain] *S*; villaines *Q, P, G*
215 SD *Offering gold.*] *om. Q, S, P, G*
230 a] *P*; *om. Q, S, G*
231 a paire] *Q*; a a paire *Q(r)*
239 you: Change] ∼∧ ∼: *Q, G*; ∼, ∼∧ *Q(r)*; ∼. ∼: *S, P*
241 prize] *Q(r)*; price *Q*
    caduceus] *P*; cats eyes *Q, S, G*
252 *Ver.*] *S, P*; *Host. Q, G*
256 *Ver.*] *S, P*; *Host. Q, G*
258-59 posies. What,] *P*; ∼, ∼∧ *Q, G*; ∼; ∼, *S*
        SD *To the Countess.*] *om. Q, S, P, G*
268-69 there . . . him] *all om. except* me thinkes *S*
269 tis] *Q(c)*; *om. Q(u)*
272 SD *Revealing Moren.*] *om. Q, S, G*; *unmasking* Moren *P*
274 SD *Trying to leave.*] *om. Q, S, P, G*
277 would] you'ld *G conj.*
289 vnhurtfull] *Q(r)*; an hurtfull *Q*
290 ouerioyes] o'er joys *S*

PRESS-VARIANTS

[Copies collated: BM (British Museum C. 34. c. 14); Bodl (Bodleian Library); CLUC (William A. Clark Library, the University of California at Los Angeles); CSmH (Huntington Library); CtY (Yale University Library); DFo (Folger Shakespeare Library, wants A1); Dyce (Victoria and Albert Museum); GWU (Glasgow University Library); King's (King's College Library, Cambridge; wants C1 and sheets E and H); MH (Harvard University Library)]

Sheet A (inner forme)

Corrected: MH
Uncorrected: BM, Bodl, CLUC, CSmH, CtY, DFo, Dyce, GWU, King's
Sig. A2
    I.i.29 dispaire] tis spare

Sheet B (outer forme)

First State Corrected: BM
Uncorrected: Bodl, DFo, King's, MH
Sig. B1
    I.iv.24 posies] poises
        SD *hee*] *shee*
Sig. B2^v
    I.iv.132 in] ịn

        133 to you] o you
        134 must] tmust
        136 *Le.*] *Lem.*
            thogh] thou
        141 al the] all he
Second State Corrected: CLUC, CSmH, CtY, Dyce, GWU
Sig. B1
    I.iv.17 much] more
        18 &] and
        24 thers] theres
        24-25 thẽ. Dispaire] thẽ, dispaire
        28-29 strongest. Wonderfull] strongest; wonderfull
        33 &] and
        33-34 would. The] would, the
        45 hood!] hood,
        46 off, my head] off∧ my head,
        47 would] will
            help] helpe

Sig. B2^v

I.iv.140 courtier] Cortier

Sig. B3

I.iv.146 proofe?] proofe∧

159 Madam:] Madam,

167 more deeply] most deepely

171 true] true,

Sig. B4^v

I.v.32 euermore] euer more

46 not:] not?

said,] said∧

Sheet B (inner forme)

Corrected: BM, Bodl, CLUC, CSmH, CtY, DFo, Dyce, GWU, MH
Uncorrected: King's

Sig. B2

I.iv.96 haue] h aue

Sig. B3^v

I.iv.189 striue against] striue ahainst

190 To] to

idle] idle,

walke,] walke∧

191 companie,] companie∧

habite,] habite?

205 head,] head∧

Sig. B4

I.iv.208 SD *Exit.*] *Exet.*

I.v.19 world?] world.

Sheet D (outer forme)

Corrected: BM, Bodl, CSmH, DFo, King's, MH
Uncorrected: CLUC, CtY, Dyce, GWU

Sig. D1

II.ii.39 barendrie] barrendrie

but] bur

Sig. D4^v

III.i.20 in] !n

Sheet F (inner forme)

Corrected: BM, Bodl, CLUC, CSmH, CtY, Dyce, GWU, King's
Uncorrected: DFo, MH

Sig. F1^v

IV.i.12 and] an

Sig. F2

IV.i.25 you] he

34 Yea surely do I] I shew I do

35 do,] do∧

50 aloft] a loft

52 *Besilos*] *Besilus*

Sig. F3v
IV.iii SD *Queene*] *Qeene*
5 sweet] swaet
Sig. F4
IV.iii.15 hande,] hande‸
27 blasted] bl asted

Sheet F (outer forme)

Corrected: BM, Bodl, CLUC, CSmH, CtY, Dyce, GWU, King's
Uncorrected: DFo, MH
Sig. F4v
IV.iii.88 the] th$_{e}$
catchword world] worl$_{d}$

[Professor Akihiro Yamada's discovery of a proof-sheet, bound into the Bute copy of Q, provides us with a previously unknown, uncorrected state of the outer forme of sheet G. See his "A Proof-Sheet in *An Humorous Day's Mirth* (1599), Printed by Valentine Simmes, "*The Library*, Fifth Series, XXI (June, 1966), 155-57. I record here the variants that identify the two states.]

Sheet G (outer forme)

Sig. G1
IV.iii.102 procreation] procrearion
V.i.2 haplesse,] haplesse‸
company?] company,
3 *Lemot*,] *Lemot*‸
4 I, well:] I, well,
10 why] why:
13 do at the] do the
14 way, your] *an inked space quad after the comma was adjusted*
Sig. G2v
V.ii.61 mary] marry
Sig. G3
V.ii.78 SD *Florila*] *Flo rila*
98 part] pert
110 himselfe] himseife
186 mine] miue
201 foure] four
he] hee

[Professor Yamada's "Bibliographical Studies of George Chapman's *An Humorous Day's Mirth* (1599)," in *Shakespeare Studies* (The Shakespeare Society of Japan, 1966-67), V, 119-49, which appeared after my collations were essentially complete, describes an uncorrected state of the half-sheet H preserved in the Eton copy. I had not examined this copy and was therefore unaware of this variant. So far as I have discovered, it exists only in the Eton copy. I am happy to call attention to Professor Yamada's valuable article.]

Sheet H (outer forme)

Sig. H1

V.ii.235 posie.] posi e
239 you change:] you, change
241 *Dowsecer*] *Dowsecer*,
248 tel you the] tell youthe
248-49 mild,/ *Verone* loues] mild, *Verone* loues/

Sheet H (inner forme)

Sig. H1ᵛ

V.ii.263 say:] say,
264 maskt?] maskt,
265 heare sayes] here sayes
269 tis one of thē] one of them
270 torches:] torches,
272 torchbearer] torch bearer

Sig. H2

V.ii.287 haue pursued] hane persued,

TEXTUAL NOTES

I.ii

84 start] Although "start" seems rarely to have occurred as an adverb, Chapman, by coupling it with "mad," exploits one of its usual meanings as a noun, i.e., a sudden humor, a fit of passion or madness. See also I.iv.209.

I.iv

52-53 banishment] Shepherd and Parrott, heeding Deighton, emend to "punishment." But I take "banishment," in the sense of isolation from grace, to be particularly appropriate to Florila's Puritan speech, that smacks of casuistry and refers to sin and to the "lawful means."

112-13 desolation] Labervele twice refers to Lemot as desolate (II.i.24, 28). Deighton, dismissing both instances as "obvious misprints," would emend to "dissolute." But Labervele's further designation of Lemot as "the very imp of desolation" strongly implies the quarto's accuracy.

137 there no] Shepherd and Parrott follow Q, thus distorting Lemot's meaning; "there" is here used adverbially, not as an expletive. For confirmation see II.i.44.

I.v

136 *Blan.*] Parrott, for no evident reason, assigns this speech to Catalian, as he does that beginning with l. 132. But since Blanuel is involved in the gulling of Labesha, I see no reason to emend Q.

143-45 *Coun. . . . done.*] The marginal direction *"Enter Lemot,"* incorrectly printed opposite these lines in Q, was originally incorporated in the skeleton during imposition of inner B. In transferring the skeleton to inner C, the compositor failed to remove the direction.

II.ii

2 *Cat.*] Since "all the lords" have just entered with the King, the equivocal speech head in Q (i.e., *C.*) could designate either Colinet or Catalian. Parrott, perhaps correctly, chooses Colinet. But since, of the two, only Catalian speaks during the rest of this scene, I assign this speech to him.

62-63 *Quid . . . magnitudo*] The errors in Q indicate an inexpert compositor, not Chapman's intention to suggest Dowsecer's bad Latin or imperfect recollection. My restoration of the text, which agrees with Parrott's, derives from an edition of the *Tusculan Disputations* contemporaneous with the play, i.e., *M.*

Tvlli Ciceronis Tvscvlanarvm Qvaestionvm sev Dispvtationvm (London, 1599).

78 snares . . . snares] Errors riddle this passage, which Parrott has corrected with imagination and skill. His emendation to "snares" satisfies the requirements of meaning and meter and, on the whole, seems the likeliest possibility. The Q reading, though not absolutely unacceptable, poses a serious problem in meaning.

114 so] The corrupt state of the Q text at this point renders it suspect. And both sense and meter support Parrott's emendation. Labervele's "And so he doth despise our purposes" refers, of course, to Dowsecer's scornful gesture which accompanies his remark, "Ile weare you thus, and sit vpon the matter"; clearly, the "so" serves to indicate the relationship of Labervele's remark to Dowsecer's action.

173 in] In his "Notes on George Chapman's Plays," *MLR*, XXXIII (April, 1938), 248, George G. Loane explains this passage: "Clearly 'in' is a verb, as in *Bussy D'Ambois*, iii.2.259, and the line means 'when men bring in the grass which . . .'."

IV.iii

13 me;] The ambiguously placed phrase "what ere it be," like the similar one in V.ii.119, makes complete certainty impossible here. Parrott reads the phrase as modifying "tell"; I think it more likely that the queen, impatient at Lemot's equivocation, would use the abrupt imperative, followed by the explanatory "what ere it be, Ile beare it all."

44 her] Both meter and meaning confirm Shepherd's emendation. "Her" refers, of course, not to the queen, but to "the other ladie" of Lemot's preceding speech; its presence thus enhances Lemot's jest, which depends upon a convincing account of the king's vacillation.

56 cowsheds] Deighton conjectures "cowsherds," the more conventional spelling.

V.ii

57 thought] Shepherd and Parrott follow Q; but the context of the speech corroborates my emendation. The king alludes, of course, to the recent episode in which Dowsecer thought that Martia had been stolen from him.

71 Verones] Apparently Shepherd and Parrott correctly emend Q; since this scene opens near Verone's house, the "device" must occur there also. Other, similar confusions occur in Q.

146 trunchman] Deighton would emend to "truchman," the more usual spelling.

The Gentleman Usher

edited by Robert Ornstein

❖

TEXTUAL INTRODUCTION

The Gentleman Usher was entered for Valentine Simmes as "Vincentio and Margaret" in the *Stationers' Register* on November 26, <u>1605.</u> It exists in a single seventeenth-century edition, a quarto (hereafter Q), printed in 1606 by V[alentine] S[immes] for Thomas Thorpe. The title page mentions no theater or acting company (see Greg, *Bibliography*, pp. 353-54), nor is there other record of performance. But two fairly elaborate masques in Acts I and II suggest that Chapman may have written *The Gentleman Usher,* as he did other plays of the period, for the Children of the Chapel. Apart from an apparent reference to *Sir Gyles Goosecap* (II.i.81), a play generally supposed to have been written about 1601, no internal evidence points to a date of composition. Fleay conjectures the Christmas season of 1601-02, Wallace the summer of 1601. Parrott suggests that the play was probably written late in 1602; Chambers thinks that 1602 is plausible but also accepts the possibility of 1604.

The problem of textual provenance proves difficult to solve. Q may well have derived from fair copy, although it is doubtful that the manuscript was, as Parrott theorizes, a prompt copy. Several stage directions, some of which occur in Latin, seem to be authorial. For example, in Act II, the directions supply picturesque details of the costuming of the actors in the masque, but, as we might expect in an author's draft, provide exits and entrances only for the speaking actors. Similarly, entrances are missing for Margaret (III.ii) and for Bassiolo in the last scene. Also the direction at the beginning of Act IV, *"Enter Pogio running in, and knocking at Cynanches doore,"* would seem more literary than theatrical, especially since no entrance is provided for Cynanche in this scene. But while there are such leisurely authorial directions as *"Vin. & St. have all this while talked togither a prettie way,"* there are also directions terse enough to satisfy a prompter, such as *"a great bumbasted legge"*; *"he studies"*; *"he reads"*; *"he rends it."* It is possible, therefore, that Q was printed from a fair copy of Chapman's play which had been marked by the prompter, and from which the prompt copy was made.

On the other hand, some evidence implying that the printer's copy may not have been as fair as I have suggested deserves notice. Confusions do sometimes occur in the speech-prefixes; and twice, in uncorrected sheets, "Superintendent" appears for "Usher."[1] Such mistakes, though explainable on other grounds, might well derive from the author's working draft. Mention of Ancilla among the characters who enter at V.ii. raises yet another question. Chapman, with his penchant for Latin stage directions, may simply have indicated here the presence among the other characters of an attendant maid. But if not, then Ancilla is a mute of the sort that do sometimes characterize working papers. The puzzling stage direction at the start of Act III, *"Medice after the song, whispers alone with his seruant"* may, of course, refer to the final song of the masque. But since that entertainment was formally concluded in the previous act, the direction here could refer to a song sung on stage but not present in an early draft of the text. And finally, the widespread confusion of verse and prose throughout the play is surely consistent with an assumption that the printer worked from less than fair copy.

On the whole the printing is, for a dramatic text of the period, reasonably careful. Palpable misreadings of the manuscript occur infrequently; and, though two dozen or so obvious compositor's errors escape correction, they rarely cause serious trouble. What seem to be two gross errors were corrected by stop-press revision: a stage direction was added at III.ii.276, and an omitted line, "Lead sir I pray," restored at V.ii.79. But this second emendation, though I adopt it, is somewhat suspect: first, because it was inserted after the couplet which would normally close the scene; second, because it is superfluous; and third, because its deferential tone sharply contrasts with that of Strozza's preceding lines and with his attitude toward Pogio, whom he addresses. Although one hesitates to suggest that the proof corrector gratuitously added a line, it is possible that this addition and, likewise, the previously mentioned alterations of "Superintendent" to "Usher" (II.i.154,162), are sophistications of the text by a corrector rather than corrections of a compositor's mistakes.

The heaviest revision — and that which is textually most significant — is found in both formes of H and in outer I; in these two adjacent sheets occurred nearly three-fourths of the known stop-press revision of Q. Here the corrector added two new stage directions, made semi-substantive spelling and punctuation alterations, modified meter (i.e., by correcting "louest" to "lou'st"), and, interestingly enough, effected numerous non-substantive orthographic changes that imply a tendency to modernize (e.g., he emended "doe" to "do," "sweete" to "sweet," "worke" to "work," "sonnes" to "sons," "arrand" to "errant," and "heade" to "head").[2] The heavy clustering of these revisions in two sheets suggests the intrusion at this point of a new corrector. And since several of the

---

[1] E.g., speech-prefixes are omitted at I.ii.11 and II.ii.36 and confused at IV.iv.25 (*Lass.* for *Med.*); "Superintendent," revised to "Usher," occurs in the uncorrected state of II.i.154, 162.

[2] After my collations were complete, I learned that Professor Akihiro Yamada of Shinshu University, Japan, had found an uncorrected state of H inner in the Eton College Library copy, which I was unable to examine. Professor Yamada also found a unique uncorrected state of E inner in the Ashley 374 British Museum copy, which I also did not examine. I have included Professor Yamada's collations of these copies in my table of press-variants, and I am happy to acknowledge my indebtedness to his valuable article "Bibliographical Studies of George Chapman's *The Gentleman Usher* (1606), Printed by Valentine Simmes," *Shakespeare Studies,* II (1963), 82-113.

changes reflect his unusual thoroughness and perhaps imply for him more than customary authority, one is tempted to hypothesize for his revisions authorial provenance. The fact that Chapman did sometimes read proof surely strengthens this assumption; in the early pages of the *Memorable Masque* (sigs. a1^v-a2) he complains of inconveniences caused by the printer's "neuer sending me a proofe" until work had progressed beyond the point at which Chapman had planned to make important corrections.

Even though a study of punctuation and spelling yields no pattern varying from sheet to sheet that would indicate the activity of more than one compositor,[3] other evidence that copy was cast off by formes for two workmen proves compelling. The running titles, for example, reveal that two skeletons were employed in printing the play, each one used for both inner and outer formes of a single sheet and regularly alternated with the other, so that one set of running titles appears in sheets A, C, E, G, and I; the other in sheets B, D, F, and H. Half-sheet K uses the titles from the outer forme of H. Since such use of one skeleton for both formes of a single sheet when two skeletons were available would represent highly inefficient procedure for a single workman composing *seriatim,* one assumes that copy was cast off, probably for two compositors. And a typographical oddity corroborates this supposition, implying that the workmen set by formes, not *seriatim.* Because of the extensive use of the names "Bassiolo" and "Lasso" in the text and speech heads, the supply of ſ type, at least in one printer's case, was evidently strained. Occasionally on the outer formes, the speech head *Bass.* is set as *Baſ.*, but there are no gross signs on these formes of a shortage of ſ type. On the inner formes of B, D, E, F, and G, however, the compositor ran short of the ſ type recurrently and set the double s in speech heads and text as ſs. This peculiarity, which occasionally occurs in inner formes where I detect no sign of type shortage, never appears in the text or speech heads of the outer formes, though it does turn up once in a catchword on D3. Such evidence would seem to imply two compositors, each working from his own case of type, one setting all inner, the other all outer formes.

Once alerted to the possibility of two compositors at work in this fashion, we find corroborating evidence of differing compositorial habits in inner and outer formes. For example, only on inner formes (e.g., F, H, and I) do we find long dashes connecting the end of a line to the stage direction *Exit.* One suspects this to be no true mark of punctuation but a scribal convention (cf. the manuscript of *The Second Maiden's Tragedy*), usually ignored by compositors, which the printer at work on these inner formes occasionally included in his text. In addition, some persuasive evidence suggests that the compositor of the inner formes, though less skilled than his fellow in reading manuscript, made fewer "mechanical" mistakes. Textual cruxes implying misreadings of the manuscript tend to occur on the inner formes; but if one notes among my emendations those instances in which typographical errors have been corrected (omitting such mistakes as failure to capitalize at the start of a verse line) and adds the similar corrections that were made by the proofreader, he finds that nearly twice as

---

[3] Indeed, the idiosyncratic spelling "haz" for "has," occurring in both inner and outer formes and in several sheets, possibly suggests one compositor.

many typographical mistakes (as differentiated from misreadings of the manuscript) occurred during work on the outer as on the inner formes.

Distinctions between the two workmen may be further sharpened by those speech head confusions mentioned earlier. Though foul copy, as we recognized, could for any printer increase the likelihood of such mistakes, the occurrence of all these errors on the inner formes corroborates our assumption that the compositor at work here tended somewhat more than did his fellow to misread. Furthermore, one of the errors, because we can guess how it came about, particularly supports our theory of cast-off copy. Although the assumed omission of the prefix *Lass.* at I.ii.11 remains equivocal,[4] the printing of *Lass.* for *Med.* at IV.iv.25 represents a certain error. Not only is it corrected in ink by the same seventeenth-century hand in both the Folger and Huntington copies, but, even more to the point, the context clearly establishes that the speaker is Medice, not Lasso; indeed, just twenty-four lines earlier the stage direction which opens the scene indicates that Lasso, to whom the compositor gives the speech, is not even on stage. The fact to note at the moment, of course, is that the direction appears on G3 (i.e., in an outer forme) which presumably the compositor of G3^v, because this page belongs to the inner forme, did not see. But, of course, he did see the speech heads for Lasso in the following scene (i.e., in IV.v.), which fell to him.

Our evidence seems, then, to warrant an assumption that Q was set from cast-off copy. And although we find no gross signs of crowding or spacing out (probably because much of the text is verse), we do note three additional bits of corroborative evidence which, though subtle, deserve mention: the erroneous catchword on A2 is correctly set on A2^v; D3^v contains an extra line; and, at the bottom of E4, the text is patently crowded.

Casting off by formes, one assumes, was undertaken to facilitate simultaneous work by two compositors, a supposition supported by evidence from the formes. For example, several irregularities in the type clearly indicate that the running titles of G inner were directly transferred to I outer. Similarly, an irregularity that first appears in the title of F reappears in both formes of H and in half-sheet K. Clearly, therefore, inner and outer formes were imposed together, as we should expect if the two compositors worked simultaneously on the text.

The regularity with which one skeleton was used for both formes of a single sheet indicates the following order of imposition: X outer, Y inner, X inner (printed with the skeleton from X outer), Y outer (printed with the skeleton from Y inner), Z outer, and so on. That is to say, we must assume that in every other sheet, the outer formes were regularly set before the inner formes, while in the alternating sheets, the inner formes were set before the outers. Since irregularities in the running titles evidence that the outer formes of G and I were set before the inner formes, and the inner forme of H was set before the outer forme, we can hypothesize that on sheets A, C, E, G, and I the outer formes were set first, and that inner formes were set first on sheets B, D, F, H,

---

[4] Shepherd, first among editors to detect a crux at this point, suggested that the speech head *Lass.* is missing; Parrott thought Shepherd's emendation likely, though he did not adopt it. But the presence of other speech head errors on inner formes strongly supports Shepherd's emendation, which I have adopted.

and possibly K. If the compositors began work as soon as the first sheets were cast off, it would be logical that, to avoid conflicts over manuscript copy, one would begin setting A outer while the other began with B inner; and this procedure would continue throughout.

The Gentleman Usher was edited by Shepherd, and by Parrott, in his Belles-Lettres edition of *"All Fooles" and "The Gentleman Usher,"* and again in his edition of *The Comedies.* My indebtedness to these editions is recorded in the textual apparatus. Significant variant readings in Shepherd and Parrott are noted in the historical collation.

I wish also to thank my friend and former colleague Allan Holaday for the many hours he generously spent editing my manuscript of *The Gentleman Usher*. His comprehensive knowledge of the Chapman quartos helped to shape my textual introduction. I am grateful also to Michael Kiernan, whose meticulous and dedicated assistance contributed much to the accuracy of my text and apparatus, and to the comprehensiveness of my historical collations. I am indebted too to my friend and former colleague Gwynne Evans, who from the beginning of my work on Chapman gave freely of his wisdom, good counsel, and encouragement.

THE

GENTLEMAN
USHER.

By
GEORGE CHAPMAN.

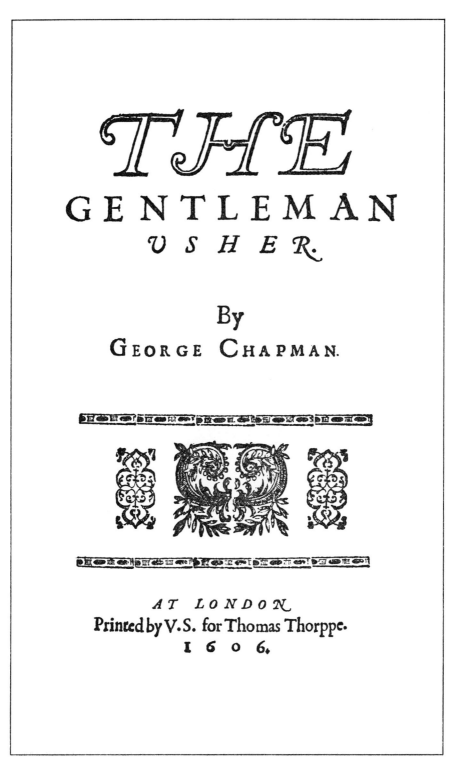

AT LONDON
Printed by V.S. for Thomas Thorppe.
1 6 0 6.

DRAMATIS PERSONAE

[Duke Alphonso
Prince Vincentio, his son
Medice, his favorite
Strozza, a Lord
Pogio, his nephew
Earl Lasso, an old Lord
Bassiolo, gentleman usher to Lasso
Fungus, a servant of Lasso
Benevenius, a doctor
Sarpego, a pedant
Iulio, a courtier
A servant of Medice

Cynanche, wife of Strozza
Corteza, sister of Lasso
Margaret, daughter of Lasso
Ancilla]

Attendants, servants, huntsmen, guards, two pages, maids
Figures in the Masques
 Enchanter, Spirits, Sylvanus, A Nymph, Broom-man, Rush-man,
 Broom-maid, Rush-maid, a man-bug, a woman-bug.

THE GENTLEMAN VSHER

ACTVS PRIMVS, SCAENA PRIMA.

Enter Strozza, Cynanche, and Pogio.

Stro. Haste nephew, what, a sluggard? Fie for shame,　　　　[A2]
Shal he that was our morning Cock, turn Owle,
And locke out day light from his drowsie eies?

Pog. Pray pardon mee for once, lord vnkle, for Ile bee sworne, I
had such a dreame this morning: me thought one came with a com-　　5
mission to take a Sorrell curtoll, that was stolne from him, wheresoeuer
hee could find him. And because I feared he would lay claime to my
sorrell curtoll in my stable I ran to the Smith to haue him set on his
mane againe, and his taile presently, that the Commision-man might
not thinke him a curtoll. And when the Smith would not doe it, I fell　　10
a beating of him, so that I could not wake for my life til I was reuenged on him.

Cyn. This is your old valure nephew, that will fight sleeping as well
as waking.

Pog. Slud Aunt, what if my dreame had beene true (as it might　　15
haue beene for any thing I knew) there's neuer a smith in Italie, shall
make an Asse of me in my sleepe, if I can chuse.

Stro. Well said, my furious nephew: but I see
You quite forget that we must rowse to day
The sharp-tuskt Bore: and blaze our huntsmanship　　20
Before the duke.

Pog. Forget Lord vncle? I hope not; you thinke belike / my wittes　　[A2ᵛ]
are as brittle as a Beetle, or as skittish as your Barbarie Mare: one
cannot crie wehie, but straight shee cries tihi.

Stro. Well ghest coosen *Hysteron Proteron*.　　25

Pog. But which way will the dukes grace hunt to day?

Stro. Toward Count *Lassos* house his Grace will hunt,
Where he will visit his late honourd mistresse.

---

21 Before] before ‖ 26 day?] *Q(c)*; ∼. *Q(u)* ‖

Pog. Who, Ladie *Margaret,* that deare yong dame?
Will his antiquitie, never leave his iniquitie?   30
   Cyn. Why how now nephew? turnd Parnassus lately?
   Pog. Nassus? I know not: but I would I had all the dukes liuing
for her sake, Ide make him a poore duke ifaith.
   Stro. No doubt of that, if thou hadst all his liuing.
   Pog. I would not stand dreaming of the matter as I do now.   35
   Cyn. Why how doe you dreame nephew?
   Pog. Mary all last night me thought I was tying her shoostring.
   Stro. What all night tying her shoostring?
   Pog. I that I was, and yet I tied it not neither; for as I was tying it,
the string broke me thought, and then me thought, hauing but one   40
poynt at my hose, me thought, I gaue her that to tie her shoo withall.
   Cyn. A poynt of much kindnesse I assure you.
   Pog. Wherevpon, in the verie nicke me thought the Count came
rushing in, and I ranne rushing out, with my heeles about my hose for
haste.   45
   Stro. So; will you leaue your dreaming, and dispatch?
   Pog. Mum, not a worde more, Ile goe before, and ouertake you
presently.   *Exit.*
   Cyn. My Lord I fancie not these hunting sports,
When the bold game you follow turnes againe,   50
And stares you in the face: let me behold
A cast of Faulcons on their merry wings,
Daring the stooped prey, that shifting flies:
Or let me view the fearefull Hare or Hinde,
Tosst like a musicke point with harmonie   55
Of well mouthed hounds. This is a sport for Princes,
The other rude; Boares yeeld fit game for Boores.
   Stro. Thy timorous spirit blinds thy iudgement, wife,
Those are most royall sports that most approue /
The huntsmans prowesse, and his hardie minde.   [A3] 60
   Cyn. My Lord, I know too well your vertuous spirit,
Take heede for Gods loue if you rowse the Bore,
You come not neere him, but discharge aloofe
Your wounding Pistoll, or well aymed Dart.
   Stro. I Mary wife this counsaile rightly flowes   65
Out of thy bosome, pray thee take lesse care,
Let Ladies at their tables iudge of Bores,
Lords in the field: And so farewell sweete loue;
Faile not to meete me at Earle *Lassos* house.
   Cyn. Pray pardon me for that: you know I loue not   70

---

35 now.] *Q(c);* ∼; *Q(u)* ‖ **43** Wherevpon] *Q(u);* Whervpon *Q(c)* | Count] *Q(c);* count *Q(u)*
‖ **51** face: let] ∼; ∼ *Q(u);* facel: et *Q(c)* ‖ **53** prey,] *Q(c);* ∼; *Q(u)* ‖ **57** rude;] *Parrott;* ∼∧
‖ **64** Dart.] *Q(c);* dart *Q(u)* ‖

These solemne meetings.
   Stro.   You must needes, for once
Constraine your disposition; and indeede
I would acquaint you more with Ladie *Margaret*;
For speciall reason.
   Cyn.   Very good, my Lord.
Then I must needes go fit me for that presence.   75
   Stro. I pray thee doe, farewell.   *Exit Cyn.*
                Here comes my friend.

          Enter Vincentio.

Good day my Lord; why does your grace confront
So cleare a morning with so clowdie lookes?
   Vin. Ask'st thou my griefes, that knowst my desprate loue
Curbd by my fathers sterne riualitie: 80
Must not I mourne that know not whether yet
I shall enioy a stepdame or a wife?
   Stro. A wife prince, neuer doubt it; your deserts
And youthfull graces haue engag'd so farre,
The beauteous *Margaret,* that she is your owne.   85
   Vin. O but the eie of watchfull iealousie
Robs my desires of meanes t'inioy her fauour.
   Stro. Despaire not: there are meanes enow for you,
Suborne some seruant of some good respect,
Thats neere your choice, who though she needs no wooing,   90
May yet imagine you are to begin,
Your strange yong love sute, and so speake for you,
Beare your kind letters, and get safe accesse.
All which when he shall do; you neede not feare
His trustie secrecie, because he dares not /   95
Reueale escapes, whereof himselfe is Author;   [A3ᵛ]
Whom you may best attempt, she must reueale;
For if she loues you, she already knowes,
And in an instant can resolue you that.
   Vin. And so she will, I doubt not: would to heauen   100
I had fit time, euen now to know her minde:
This counsaile feedes my heart with much sweet hope.
   Stro. Pursue it then; t'will not be hard t'effect:
The Duke haz none for him, but *Medice*
That fustian Lord, who in his buckram face,   105
Bewraies, in my conceit, a map of basenesse.
   Vin. I, theres a parcell of vnconstrued stuffe,
That unknowne Minion raisde to honours height,

---

72 your] *Q(c);* yonr *Q(u)* ‖ **75** go fit me for] gofitme for *Q(u);* go fit me for. *Q(c)* ‖ **79** desprate] *Q(c);* desperate *Q(u)* ‖ **80** Curbd . . . riualitie:] *Q(c);* curbd . . . ∼? *Q(u)* ‖ **89** seruant of] *Q(c);* seruantof *Q(u)* ‖ **93** accesse.] *Q(c);* ∼, *Q(u)* ‖ **96** Author;] ∼, ‖

Without the helpe of Vertue, or of Art,
Or (to say true) of any honest part: 110
O how he shames my father! he goes like
A Princes foote-man, in old fashioned silkes,
And most times, in his hose and dublet onely,
So miserable, that his owne few men
Doe beg by vertue of his liuerie;   115
For he giues none for any seruice done him,
Or any honour, any least reward.
   Stro. Tis pittie such should live about a Prince:
I would haue such a noble counterfet, nailde
Vpon the Pillory, and after, whipt   120
For his adultery with nobilitie.
   Vin. Faith I would faine disgrace him by all meanes,
As enemy to his base-bred ignorance,
That being a great Lord, cannot write nor reade.
   Stro. For that, wee'le follow the blinde side of him,   125
And make it sometimes subiect of our mirth.

Enter Pogio poste.

   Vin. See, what newes with your Nephew *Pogio*?
   Stro. None good I warrant you.
   Pog. Where should I finde my Lord Vnckle?
   Stro. Whats the huge haste with you?   130
   Pog. O ho, you will hunt to day.
   Stro. I hope I will. /
   Pog. But you may hap to hop without your hope: for the truth is,   [A4]
Kilbucke is runne mad.
   Stro. Whats this?   135
   Pog. Nay, t'is true sir: and *Kilbucke* being runne mad, bit *Ring-*
wood so by the left buttocke, you might haue turnd your nose in it.
   Vin. Out Asse.
   Pog. By heauen you might my Lord: d'ee thinke I lie?
   Vin. Zwoundes, might I? lets blanket him my Lord: a blanket   140
heere.
   Pog. Nay, good my Lord *Vincentio,* by this rush I tell you for good
will: and *Venus* your brache there, runnes so prowd, that your Hunts-
man cannot take her downe for his life.
   Stro. Take her vp foole, thou wouldst say.   145
   Pog. Why sir, he would soone take her downe, and he could take
her vp I warrant her.
   Vin. Well said, hammer, hammer.
   Pog. Nay, good, now lets alone, and theres your horse, Gray Strozza

---

110 of any] *Shepherd;* nay of ‖ 111 he shames] *Shepherd;* she ∼ ‖ 121 nobilitie.] ∼, ‖ 148 said,
hammer] ∼, ham mer ‖ 149 good,] ∼∧ ‖

too haz the staggers, and haz strooke bay-Bettrice, your Barbary mare   150
so, that shee goes halting a this fashion, most filthily.

    Stro. What poison blisters thy vnhappy tongue
Euermore braying forth vnhappy newes,
Our hunting sport is at the best my Lord:
How shall I satisfie the Duke your father,   155
Defrauding him of his expected sport?
See, see, he comes.

           Enter Alphonso, Medice, Sarpego, with attendants.

    Alp.   Is this the copie
Of the speech you wrote, Signieur *Sarpego*?
    Sar. It is a blaze of wit poeticall,
Reade it, braue Duke, with eyes pathetical.   160
    Alp. We will peruse it strait: well met *Vincentio*,
And good Lord *Strozza*, we commend you both
For your attendance: but you must conceiue,
Tis no true hunting we intend to day,
But an inducement to a certaine shew,   165
Wherewith we will present our beauteous loue,
And therein we bespeake your company. /
    Vin. We both are ready to attend your Highnesse.   [A4ᵛ]
    Alp. See then, heere is a Poeme that requires
Your worthy censures; offerd if it like   170
To furnish our intended amorous shew:
Reade it *Vincentio*.
    Vin.   Pardon me my Lord,
Lord *Medices* reading, will expresse it better.
    Med. My patience can digest your scoffes my Lord,
I care not to proclaime it to the world: 175
I can nor write, nor reade; and what of that?
I can both see and heare, as well as you.
    Alp. Still are your wits at warre: heere, read this poeme.
    Vin. The red fac'd Sunne hath firkt the flundering shades,
And cast bright ammell on *Auroraes* brow.   180
    Alp. High words and strange: Reade on *Vincentio*.
    Vin. The busky groues that gag-tooth'd boares do shrowd
With cringle crangle hornes do ring alowd.
    Pog. My Lord, my Lord, I have a speech heere worth ten of this,
and yet Ile mend it too.   185
    Alp. How likes *Vincentio*?
    Vin.   It is strangely good,
No inkehorne euer did bring forth the like,
Could these braue prancing words with Actions spurre,

157-58 Is . . . *Sarpego*?] Is . . . wrote, / Signieur *Sarpego*? ‖ **166** beauteous] *Shepherd*; beateous ‖ **173** better.] ∼; ‖ **179** the flundering] *Q(c)*; theflundering *Q(u)* ‖ **181** High . . . *Vincentio*.] High . . . strange: / Reade . . . *Vincentio*. ‖

Be ridden throughly, and managed right,
T'would fright the audience, and perhaps delight. 190
   Sarp. Doubt you of action sir?
   Vin.   I, for such stuffe.
   Sarp. Then know my Lord, I can both act and teach
To any words; when I in *Padua* schoolde it,
I plaid in one of *Plautus* Comedies,
Namely, *Curculio,* where his part I acted, 195
Proiecting from the poore summe of foure lines,
Forty faire actions.
   Alp.   Lets see that I pray.
   Sarp. Your Highnesse shall commaund, but pardon me,
If in my actions heate, entering
In post post haste I chaunce to take vp / 200
Some of your honord heels.   [B1]
   Pog.   Y'ad best leaue out
That action for a thing that I know sir.
   Sarp. Then shal you see what I can do without it.
                           [*Sarp. puts on parasite's dress.*]
   Alp. See see, he hath his furniture and all.
   Sarp. You must imagine, Lords, I bring good newes, 205
Whereof being princely prowd I scowre the streete
And over-tumble every man I meete.   *Exit Sarp.*
   Pog. Beshrew my heart if he take vp my heeles.

                 Enter Sarp.
   *Sarp. Date viam mihi Noti atque Ignoti dum ego hic officium meum
Facio: fugite omnes abite et de via decedite,* 210
Ne quem in cursu aut capite aut cubito aut pectore offendam aut genu.
   Alp. Thankes good *Seigneur Sarpego.*
How like you Lords, this stirring action?
   Stro. In a cold morning it were good my Lord,
But something harshe upon repletion. 215
   Sarp. Sir I have ventred, being enioynde to eate
Three schollers commons, and yet drewe it neate.
   Pog. Come sir, you meddle in too many matters; let vs I pray tend
on our owne shew at my lord *Lassos.*
   Sarp. Doing obeisance then to euery lord 220
I now consorte you sir euen *toto corde.*   *Exit Sarp. and Pog.*
   Med. My lord, away with these scholastique wits,
Lay the inuention of your speech on me,

198-200 Your . . . vp] Your . . . commaund, / But . . . heate / entering . . . vp] *Q* (if . . . in)
|| **199** heate,] ∼∧ || **201** heels.] ∼; || **201-2** Some . . . sir.] *Parrott*; Some . . . heels; / Y'ad
. . . sir. *Q* (that) || **203** SD *Sarp.* . . . *dress.*] *Parrott*[1] *subs.* || **209-11** *Date* . . . *genu.*] *Parrott*; *Date
viam mihi Noti, atq Ignoti. / Dum ego, hîc, officium meum facio. / Fugite omnes atq abite, & de via
secedite, ne quem / in cursu; aut capite, aut pectore / offendam, aut genu.* ||

And the performance too; ile play my parte,
That you shall say, Nature yeelds more then Art.   225
   Alp. Bee't so resolu'd; vnartificiall truth
An vnfaind passion can descipher best.
   Vin. But t'wil be hard my lord, for one vnlearnd.
   Med. Vnlearnd? I cry you mercie sir; vnlearnd?
   Vin. I meane, vntaught my lord, to make a speech,   230
As a pretended Actor, without close,
More gratious then your doublet and your hose.
   Alp. What, think you sonne we meane t'expresse a speech
Of speciall weight without a like attire?   *[Alp. puts rich robes on Med.]*
   Vin. Excuse me then my lord; so stands it well.   235
   Stro. Haz brought them rarely in, to pageant him.
   Med. What, thinke you lord, we thinke not of attire? /
Can we not make vs ready at this age?   *[B1ᵛ]*
   Stro. Alas my lord, your wit must pardon his.
   Vin. I hope it will, his wit is pittyfull.   240
   Stro. I pray stand by my Lord; y'are troublesome.
   Vin. To none but you; am I to you my Lord?
   Med. Not vnto mee.
   Vin.   Why then you wrong me *Strozza.*
   Med. Nay, fall not out my Lords.
   Stro.   May I not know
What your speech is my Liege?
   Alp.   None but my selfe,   245
And the Lord *Medice.*
   Med.   No, pray my Lord
Let none partake with vs.
   Alp.   No be assur'd,
But for another cause; *[Aside to Strozza.]* a word Lord *Strozza,*
I tell you true, I feare Lord *Medice*
Will scarce discharge the speach effectually: 250
As we goe therefore, ile explaine to you
My whole intent; that you may second him
If need and his debilitie require.
   Stro. Thanks for this grace my Liege.   *Vincentio ouerheares.*
   Med.   My Lord; your sonne.
   Alp. Why how now sonne? forbeare; yet tis no matter,   255
Wee talke of other businesse *Medice*;
And come, we will prepare vs to our shew.
   Stro. Vin. [Aside.] Which as we can, weele cast to ouerthrow.   *Exeunt.*

---

225 That] that ‖ 234 SD *Alp. . . . Med.*] *Parrott* ‖ 237 What, . . . lord,] ∼; . . . ∼; ‖ 245-46
What . . . Lord] What . . . Liege? / None . . . *Medice.* / No . . . Lord ‖ 248 SD *Aside to Strozza.*]
Parrott² ‖ 255 matter,] ∼∧ ‖ 256 *Medice*;] ∼∧ ‖ 258 SD *Aside.*] *Parrott* ‖

[I.ii]

Enter Lasso, Bassiolo, Sarpego, two Pages, Bassiolo bare before.

Bass. Stand by there, make place.

Lass. Saie now *Bassiolo*; you on whom relies
The generall disposition of my house,
In this our preparation for the Duke,
Are all our officers at large instructed,   5
For fit discharge of their peculiar places?

Bass. At large my lord instructed.

Lass. Are all our chambers hung? Thinke you our house
Amplie capacious to lodge all the traine? /

Bass. Amply capacious: I am passing glad.   [B2] 10

[*Lass.*] And now then to our mirth and musicall shew,
Which after supper we intend t'indure,
Welcomes cheefe dainties: for choice cates at home,
Euer attend on Princes; mirth abroad:
Are all parts perfect?

Sarp.   One I know there is.   15

Lass. And that is yours.

Sarp.   Well guest in earnest Lord,
I neede not *erubescere*, to take
So much vpon me: That my backe will beare.

Bass. Nay, he will be perfection it selfe,
For wording well, and dexterous action too.   20

Lass. And will these waggish pages, hit their songs?

Two Pag. Re mi fa sol la?

Lass. O they are practising; good boyes, well done;
But where is *Pogio?* there y'are ouershot,
To lay a capitall part upon his braine,   25
Whose absence tells me plainely hee'le neglect him.

Bass. O no my Lord, he dreames of nothing else,
And giues it out in wagers, hee'le excell;
And see, (I told your Lordship) he is come.

Enter Pogio.

Pog. How now my Lord, have you borrowed a Suite for me? Seig-   30
neur *Bassiolo*, can all say, are all things ready? the Duke is hard by,
and little thinks that Ile be an Actor ifaith, I keepe all close my Lord.

Lass. O, tis well done, call all the Ladies in,
Sister and daughter, come, for Gods sake come,
Prepare your courtliest carriage for the Duke.   35

I.ii] *Parrott* ‖ SD *Lasso, Bassiolo*] *Parrott; Lasso, Corteza, Margaret, Bassiolo* ‖ **4** preparation . . .
Duke,] ∼, . . . ∼∧ ‖ **9** Amplie] amplie ‖ **11** *Lass.*] *Shepherd*; *om. Q* (*reads* Amply . . . perfect?
ll. 10-15 as single speech by Bass.) ‖ **14** abroad:] ∼, ‖ **15** perfect?] ∼. ‖ **22** *Two*] 2 ‖ **24** ouershot,]
∼. ‖ **29** Lordship] Lo: ‖ **30** Suite . . . me?] Snite . . . ∼: ‖

Enter Corteza, Margaret, and maids.

Cort. And Neece, in any case remember this,
Praise the old man, and when you see him first,
Looke me on none but him, smiling and louingly:
And then, when he comes neere, make beisance low,
With both your hands thus mouing, which not onely   40
Is as t'were courtly, and most comely too,
But speakes (as who should say) come hither Duke;
And yet saies nothing, but you may denie.
　　Lass. Well taught sister. /
　　Mar.　　　　　　　　I, and to much end: [B2ᵛ]
I am exceeding fond to humour him.   45
　　Lass. Harke, does he come with musicke? what, and bound?
An amorous deuice: daughter, obserue.

*Enter Enchanter, with spirits singing; after them, Medice,
like Syluanus, next the Duke bound, Vincentio,
Strozza, with others.*

　　Vin. [*Aside to Strozza.*] Now lets gull *Medice,* I doe not doubt,
But this attire put on, will put him out.
　　Stro. [*Aside to Vincentio.*] Weele doe our best to that end, therefore   50
marke.
　　En. Lady, or Princesse, both your choice commands,
These spirits and I, all seruants of your beautie,
Present this royall captiue to your mercie.
　　Mar. Captiue to mee a subiect?
　　Vin.　　　　　　　　　I, faire Nimph;   55
And how the worthy mystery befell
Syluanus heere, this woodden god, can tell.
　　Alp. Now my Lord.
　　Vin.　　　　　　Now is the time man, speake.
　　Med. Peace.
　　Alp.　　　Peace *Vincentio.*
　　Vin.　　　　　　　　　Swonds my Lord,
Shall I stand by and suffer him to shame you?   60
My Lord *Medice?*
　　Stro.　　　Will you not speake my Lord?
　　Med. How can I?
　　Vin.　　　　　But you must speake in earnest:
Would not your Highnesse haue him speake my Lord?

---

35 SD *Corteza, Margaret,*] ∼∧, *Margarite,* ‖ **48** SD *Aside tο Strozza.*] *Parrott* ‖ **50** SD *Aside to
Vincentio.*] *Parrott* ‖ **55** subiect?] ∼. ‖ **57** god,] ∼∧ ‖ **58** Now is] Nowcis ‖ **59** Peace *Vincentio*]
Pea e ∼ ‖

Med. Yes, and I will speake, and perhaps speake so,
As you shall neuer mend : I can I know.   65
   Vin. Doe then my good Lord.
   Alp.   *Medice,* forth.
   Med. Goddesse, faire goddesse, for no lesse, no lesse —
   Alp. No lesse, no lesse? no more, no more : [*to Strozza.*] speake you.
   Med. Swounds they haue put me out.
   Vin.   Laugh you faire goddesse?
This nobleman disdaines to be your foole.   70
   Alp. Vincentio, peace.
   Vin. Swounds my Lord, it is as good a shew :
Pray speake Lord *Strozza.* /
   Stro.   Honourable dame —   [B3]
   Vin. Take heede you be not out I pray my Lord.
   Stro. I pray forbeare my Lord *Vincentio* :   75
How this destressed Prince came thus inthralde,
I must relate with words of height and wonder :
His Grace this morning visiting the woods,
And straying farre, to finde game for the Chase,
At last, out of a mirtle groue he rowsde   80
A vast and dreadfull Boare, so sterne and fierce,
As if the Feend fell Crueltie her selfe
Had come to fright the woods in that strange shape.
   Alp. Excellent good.
   Vin. [*Aside.*]   Too good, a plague on him.
   Stro. The princely *Sauage* being thus on foote,   85
Tearing the earth vp with his thundering hoofe,
And with th'enragde Ætna of his breath,
Firing the ayre, and scorching all the woods,
Horror held all vs Huntsmen from pursuit,
Onely the Duke incenst with our cold feare,   90
Incouragde like a second *Hercules.*
   Vin. [*to Strozza.*] Zwounds, too good man.
   Stro. [*to Vin.*]   Pray thee let me alone : —
And like the English signe of great Saint *George* —
   Vin. [*Aside.*] Plague of that *Simile.*
   Stro. Gaue valorous example, and like fire,   95
Hunted the monster close, and chargde so fierce,
That he inforc'd him (as our sence conceiu'd)
To leape for soile into a cristall spring,
Where on the suddaine strangely vanishing,

---

67 goddesse, . . . lesse—] goddesle, . . . ∼. ‖ **68** SD *to Strozza.*] *Parrott*[2] ‖ **69** you] *Shepherd;*
your | goddesse?] ∼, ‖ **73** dame—] ∼. ‖ **84** SD *Aside.*] *Parrott*[1] | good,] ∼∧ ‖ **87** th'enragde]
the'nragde | breath,] ∼. ‖ **92** SD *to Strozza.*] | SD *to Vin.*] | alone : —] ∼: ∧ ‖ **93** *George*—]
∼. ‖ **94** SD *Aside.*] *Parrott*[1]‖

Nimph-like for him, out of the waues arose   100
Your sacred figure like *Diana* armde,
And (as in purpose of the beasts reuenge)
Dischargde an arrow through his Highnesse breast,
Whence yet no wound or any blood appearde:
With which, the angry shadow left the light: 105
And this Enchanter with his power of spirits,
Brake from a caue, scattering enchanted sounds,
That strooke vs sencelesse, while in these strange bands,
These cruell spirits thus inchainde his armes, /
And led him captiue to your heauenly eyes,   [B3ᵛ] 110
Th'intent whereof on their report relies.
   En. Bright Nimph, that Boare figur'd your crueltie,
Charged by loue, defended by your beautie.
This amorous Huntsman heere, we thus inthral'd,
As the attendants on your Graces charmes,   115
And brought him hither by your bounteous hands,
To be releast, or liue in endlesse bands.
   Lass. Daughter, release the Duke: alas my Liege,
What meant your Highnesse to indure this wrong?
   Cort. Enlarge him Neece, come dame, it must be so.   120
   Mar. What Madam, shall I arrogate so much?
   Lass. His Highnesse pleasure is to grace you so.
   Alp. Performe it then sweete loue, it is a deede
Worthy the office of your honor'd hand.
   Mar. Too worthie I confesse my Lord for me,   125
If it were serious: but it is in sport,
And women are fit Actors for such pageants.
   Alp. Thanks gracious loue; why made you strange of this?
I rest no lesse your captiue then before,
For me untying, you have tied me more.   130
Thanks *Strozza* for your speech, [*to Med.*] no thanks to you.
   Med. No, thanke your sonne my Lord.
   Lass.   T'was very well,
Exceeding well performed on euery part,
How say you *Bassiolo?*
   Bass.   Rare I protest my Lord,
   Cort. O, my Lord *Medice* became it rarely,   135
Me thought I likde his manlie being out;
It becomes Noblemen to doe nothing well.
   Lass. Now then wil't please your Grace to grace our house,
And still vouchsafe our seruice further honour?

---

113 Charged] *Parrott²* (*Bradley conj.*); Chared ‖ 131 SD *to Med.*] *Parrott* ‖ 134 *Bassiolo*] Bassialo
‖ 139 honour?] ∼. ‖

Alp. Leade vs my Lord, we will your daughter leade.   140
Exeunt. Manent Vin. and Stro.
Vin. You do not leade, but drag her leaden steps.
Stro. How did you like my speech?
Vin.   O fie vpon't,
Your Rhetoricke was too fine.
Stro.   Nothing at all:
I hope saint *Georges* signe was grosse enough: /
But (to be serious) as these warnings passe,   [B4] 145
Watch you your father, Ile watch *Medice,*
That in your loue-suit, we may shun suspect:
To which end, with your next occasion, vrge
Your loue to name the person she will choose,
By whose meanes you may safely write or meete.   150
  Vin. Thats our cheefe businesse: and see, heere she comes.

Enter Margaret in haste.

  Mar. My Lord, I onely come to say, y'are welcome,
And so must say, farewell.
  Vin.   One word I pray.
  Mar. Whats that?
  Vin.   You needes must presently deuise,
What person trusted chiefely with your guard,   155
You thinke is aptest for me to corrupt,
In making him a meane for our safe meeting?
  Mar. My fathers *Vsher,* none so fit,
If you can worke him well: and so farewell,
With thanks my good Lord *Strozza* for your speech.   *Exit.*
  Stro. I thanke you for your patience, mocking Lady.
  Vin. O what a fellow haz she pickt vs out?
One that I would haue choosde past all the rest,
For his close stockings onely.
  Stro.   And why not
For the most constant fashion of his hat?   165
  Vin. Nay then, if nothing must be left vnspoke,
For his strict forme, thus still to weare his cloke.
  Stro. Well sir, he is your owne, I make no doubt:
For to these outward figures of his minde,
He hath two inward swallowing properties   170
Of any gudgeons; servile Auarice,
And ouerweening thought of his owne worth,
Ready to snatch at euery shade of glory:
And therefore, till you can directlie boord him,

---

140 SD *Exeunt . . . Stro.*] *Parrott (subs.); Exit.* ‖ **142-43** How . . . all:] *Parrott;* How . . . speech?
/ O . . . fine. / Nothing . . . all: Q (your) ‖ **164** not] ~? ‖

Waft him aloofe with hats, and other fauours,   175
Still as you meete him.
   Vin.   Well, let me alone,
He that is one mans slaue, is free from none.   *Exeunt.*

Finis Actus Primi. /

ACTVS SECVNDVS SCAENA PRIMA   [B4ᵛ]

Enter Medice, Corteza, a Page with a cuppe of Secke, Strozza following close.
   Med. Come Lady, sit you heere: Page, fill some Sacke,
[*Aside.*] I am to worke vpon this aged Dame,
To gleane from her, if there be any cause
(In louing others) of her Neeces coines
To the most gratious loue suite of the Duke: —   5
Heere noble Lady, this is healthfull drinke
After our supper.
   Cort.   O, tis that my Lorde,
That of all drinkes keeps life and soule in me.
   Med. Heere, fill it Page, for this my worthy loue:
O how I could imbrace this good olde widdow.   10
   Cort. Now lord, when you do thus, you make me thinke
Of my sweete husband; for he was as like you;
Eene the same words, and fashion: the same eies,
Manly, and cholerike, eene as you are iust,
And eene as kinde as you for all the world.   15
   Med. O my sweete widdow, thou dost make me prowd.
   Cort. Nay, I am too old for you.
   Med.   Too old, thats nothing,
Come pledge me wench, for I am drie againe,
And strait will charge your widdowhood fresh ifaith:
Why thats well done.
   Cort.   Now fie on't, heeres a draught.   20
   Med. O, it will warme your blood: if you should sip,
Twould make you heart-burnd.
   Cort.   Faith and so they say:
Yet I must tell you, since I plide this geere,
I have beene hanted with a horson paine heere,
And euery moone almost with a shrewd feuer,   25
And yet I cannot leaue it: for thanke God,
I neuer was more sound of winde and limbe.

SD *Corteza,*] ∼∧ ‖ **2** SD *Aside.*] *Parrott* ‖ **5** Duke:—] ∼: ∧ ‖

Enter Strozza.

Looke you, I warrant you I haue a leg,

She shows a great bumbasted legge. /
[C1]

Holds out as hansomly.

   Med.   Beshrew my life,

But tis a legge indeed, a goodly limbe.   30

   Stro. [*Aside.*] This is most excellent.

   Med.   O that your Neece

Were of as milde a spirit as your selfe.

   Cort. Alas Lord *Medice,* would you have a girle,

As well seene in behauiour as I?

Ah shees a fond yong thing, and growne so prowde,   35

The wind must blow at west stil, or sheele be angry.

   Med. Masse so me thinke; how coy shees to the duke?

I lay my life she haz some yonger love.

   Cort. Faith like enough.

   Med.   Gods me, who should it bee?

   Cort. If it be any; *Page,* a little Sacke,   40

If it be any: harke now; if it be,

I know not, by this Sacke, but if it be,

Marke what I say, my Lord; I drinke tee first.

   Med. Well said good widdow, much good do thy heart,

So; now what if it be?

   Cort.   Well, if it be;   45

To come to that I said, for so I said,

If it be any, tis the Shrewde yong Prince,

For eies can speake, and eies can vnderstand,

And I haue markt her eies; yet by this cup,

Which I will onely kisse —

   Stro. [*Aside.*]   O noble Crone,   50

Now such a huddle and kettle neuer was.

   Cort. I neuer yet have seene; not yet I say,

But I will marke her after for your sake.

   Med. And doe I pray; for it is passing like;

And there is *Strozza,* a slie Counsailor   55

To the yong boy: O I would giue a limbe,

To have their knauerie limm'd and painted out.

They stand vpon their wits and paper-learning:

Giue me a fellow with a naturall wit,

That can make wit of no wit; and wade through   60

28 SD *She . . . legge.*] *Parrott²*; *A great bumbasted legge.* ‖ 30 a legge] *Q(c)*; al egge *Q(u)* ‖ 31 SD *Aside.*] *Parrott* ‖ 50 kisse—] ~. | SD *Aside.*] *Parrott* ‖

Great things with nothing, when their wits sticke fast,
O they be scuruie Lords. /
    Cort.   Faith so they be,   [C1ᵛ]
Your Lordship still is of my mind in all,
And eene so was my husband.
    Med.   Gods my life,
Strozza hath Evesdropt here, and over-heard vs.   65
    Stro. [*Aside.*] They have descried me; — what, Lord *Medice,*
Courting the lustie widow?
    Med.   I, and why not?
Perhaps one does as much for you at home.
    Stro. What, cholericke man? and toward wedlocke too?
    Cort. And if he be my Lord; he may do woorse.   70
    Stro. If he be not; madame, he may do better.

       Enter Bassiolo with seruants with Rushes, and a Carpet.

    Bass. My Lords, and Madame, the Dukes grace intreates you
T'attend his new-made Dutchesse for this night,
Into his presence.
    Stro.   We are readie sir.   *Exeunt Cort. Med. Stro. and Page.*
    Bass. Come strew this roome afresh; spread here this carpet,   75
Nay quickly man, I pray thee; this way foole,
Lay me it smoothe, and Euen; looke if he will;
This way a little more: a little there.
Hast thou no forecast? slood me thinks a man
Should not of meere necessitie be an Asse.   80
Looke how he strowes here too: Come sir Giles Goosecap,
I must do all my selfe, lay me vm thus:
In fine smoothe threaues, looke you sir, thus in threaues.
Perhaps some tender Ladie will squat here,
And if some standing Rush should chance to pricke her,   85
Shee'd squeak and spoile the songs that must be sung.

           Enter Vin. and Stroz.

    Stro. See where he is; now to him, and prepare
Your familiaritie.
    Vin.   Saue you master *Bassiolo,*
I pray a word sir; but I feare I let you.
    Bass. No my good Lord, no let.   90
    Vin. I thanke you sir. Nay pray be couerd;
O I crie you mercie, you must be bare.

---

66 SD *Aside.*] *Parrott*[1] | me;—] ~; ∧ | what,] ~∧ ‖ **71** madame,] ~. ‖ **74** SD *Exeunt . . . Page.*]
Parrott; *Exeunt* ‖ **86** SD *Enter . . . Stroz.*] *Parrott*; *after Strozza's speech ll. 87-88* ‖ **91-92** I . . .
bare.] I . . . sir. / Nay . . . mercie, / You . . . bare. Q (you) ‖

  Bass. Euer to you my Lord.

  Vin.   Nay, not to me sir, /

But to the faire right of your worshipfull place.   [C2]

  Stro. [*Aside.*] A shame of both your worships.   [*Exit.*]

  Bass.   What meanes your Lordship?

  Vin. Onely to doe you right sir, and my selfe ease.

And what sir, will there be some shew to night?

  Bass. A slender presentation of some musick

And some thing else my Lord.

  Vin.   T'is passing good sir,

Ile not be ouer bold t'aske the particulars.   100

  Bass. Yes, if your Lordship please.

  Vin.   O no good sir,

But I did wonder much; for as me thought

I saw your hands at work.

  Bass.   Or else my Lord

Our busines would be but badly done.

  Vin. How vertuous is a worthy mans example?   105

Who is this throne for pray?

  Bass.   For my Lords daughter,

Whom the duke makes to represent his dutches.

  Vin. T'will be exceeding fit; and all this roome

Is passing wel preparde; a man would sweare,

That all presentments in it would be rare.   110

  Bass. [*to servants.*] Nay, see if thou canst lay vm thus in threaues.

  Vin. In threaues dee call it?

  Bass.   I my Lord in threaues.

  Vin. A pretty terme:

Well sir I thanke you highly for this kindnesse,

And pray you alwayes make as bold with me   115

For kindnesse more then this, if more may bee.

  Bass. O my Lord this is nothing.

  Vin.   Sir, tis much.

And now ile leaue you sir; I know y'are busie.

  Bass. Faith sir a little.

  Vin.   I commend me tee Sir.   *Exit Vin.*

  Bass. A courteous prince beleeve it; I am sory   120

I was no bolder with him; what a phrase

He usde at parting! I commend me tee.

Ile ha't yfaith.

93 Lord.] ∼, ‖ 95 SD *Aside.*] *Parrott* | SD *Exit.*] *Parrott*[1] *subs.; om.* ‖ 111 SD *to servants.*] ‖ 119 a little] alittle ‖ 123 ha't] *Shepherd*; h'ate | yfaith. . . . drest.] ∼; . . . ∼? ‖

Enter Sarpego halfe drest. /

Sarp. Good master Vsher, will you dictate to me,   [C2ᵛ]
Which is the part precedent of this night-cap,   125
And which posterior? I do *ignorare*
How I should weare it.
    Bass.   Why sir, this I take it
Is the precedent part; I, so it is.
    Sarp. And is all well sir thinke you?
    Bass.   Passing well.

Enter Pogio, and Fungus.

    Pog. Why sir come on; the Vsher shal be iudge: 130
See master Vsher: this same *Fungus* here,
Your Lords retainer, whom I hope you rule,
Would weare this better Ierkin for the Rush-man,
When I doe play the Broome-man; and speake first.
    Fun. Why sir, I borrowed it, and I will weare it.   135
    Pog. What sir, in spite of your Lords gentleman Vsher?
    Fun. No spite sir, but you have changde twice already,
And now woulde ha't againe.
    Pog.   Why thats all one sir,
Gentillitie must be fantasticall.
    Bass. I pray thee *Fungus* let master *Pogio* weare it.   140
    Fun. And what shall I weare then?
    Pog.   Why here is one,
That was a Rush-mans Ierkin; and I pray,
Wer't not absurd then, a Broome-man should weare it?
    Fun. Foe, theres a reason, I will keepe it sir.
    Pog. Well sir! then do your office maister Vsher,   145
Make him put off his Ierkin; you may plucke
His coate over his eares, much more his Ierkin.
    Bass. Fungus y'ad best be rulde.
    Fun.   Best sir! I care not.
    Pog. No sir? I hope you are my Lords retainer.
I neede not care a pudding for your Lord: 150
But spare not, keepe it, for perhaps Ile play
My part as well in this, as you in that.
    Bass. Well said, master *Pogio*; [*to Fungus.*] my Lord shall know it.

136 Vsher?] ∼: ‖ **140** thee] *Q(c)*; the *Q(u)* ‖ **141-43** Why . . . it?] *Parrott; as prose* (that . . . wer't) ‖ **142** Ierkin;] ∼, ‖ **143** then,] ∼; ‖ **145** sir!] ∼; ‖ **148** sir!] *Q(c)*; ∼, *Q(u)* ‖ **152** that.] ∼, ‖ **153** SD *to Fungus.*] *Parrott* ‖

Enter Corteza, with the Broom-wench, and Rush-wench in their petticotes,
clokes ouer them, with hats ouer their head-tyres.

Cort. Looke master *Superintendent,* are these wags wel drest?
I haue beene so in labour with vm truly. /   155
Bass. Y'aue had a verie good deliuerance, Ladie: [C3]
[*Aside.*] How I did take her at her labour there,
I vse to gird these Ladies so sometimes.
Enter Lasso, with Syluan, and a Nymph, a man Bugge, and a woman-Bug.
    1. I pray my Lord, must not I weare this haire?
Lass. I pray thee aske my Vsher; Come, dispatch,   160
The duke is readie: are you readie there?
    2. See master *Superintendent*: must he weare this haire?
    1. Bug. Pray master Vsher, where must I come in?
    2. Am not I well for a *Bug,* master *Vsher?*
Bass. What stirre is with these boyes here, God forgiue me,   165
If t'were not for the credite on't, I'de see
Your apish trash afire, ere I'de indure this.
    1. But pray good master Vsher.
Bass.   Hence ye Brats,
You stand vpon your tyre; but for your action
Which you must vse in singing of your songs,   170
Exceeding dexterously and full of life,
I hope youle then stand like a sort of blocks,
Without due motion of your hands, and heads,
And wresting your whole bodies to your words,
Looke too't, y'are best; and in; Go; All go in.   175
    Pog. Come in my masters; lets be out anon.
                                        Exeunt manent Lass. and Bass.
Lass. What, are all furnisht well?
Bass.   All well my Lord.
Lass. More lights then here, and let lowd musicke sound.
Bass. Sound Musicke.
                                                            Exeunt.

[II.ii]

Enter Vincentio, Strozza bare, Margaret, Corteza, and
Cynanche bearing her traine. After her the duke
whispering with Medice, Lasso with Bassiolo, &c.

Alp. Aduaunce your selfe, faire Dutchesse to this Throne,
As we have long since raisde you to our heart,
Better *decorum* neuer was beheld,
Then twixt this state and you: And as all eyes

---

154 *Superintendent,*] *Q(u)*; Vsher, *Q(c)* ‖ 157 SD *Aside.*] *Parrott* ‖ 158 SD *woman-Bug.*] *Parrott;*
woman. ‖ 159 Lord,] *Q(c)*; ~∧ *Q(u)* ‖ 162 *Superintendent:*] *Q(u)*; Vsher; *Q(c)* ‖ 168 *1.*] ~∧ ‖
175 go in.] ~ ~: ‖ 176 SD *Exeunt . . . Bass.*] *Parrott (subs.); Exeunt.* ‖

Now fixt on your bright Graces thinke it fit,   5
So frame your fauour to continue it. /
    Mar. My Lord; but to obey your earnest will,   [C3ᵛ]
And not make serious scruple of a toy,
I scarce durst haue presumde this minuts height.
    Lass. Vsher, cause other musicke; begin your shew.   10
    Bass. Sound Consort; warne the Pedant to be readie.
    Cort. Madam, I thinke you'le see a prettie shew.
    Cyn. I can expect no lesse in such a presence.
    Alp. Lo what attention and state beautie breedes,
Whose mouing silence no shrill herauld needes.   15

Enter Sarpego.

Sarp.	Lords of high degree,
	And Ladies of low courtesie,
	I the Pedant here,
	Whom some call schoolmaistere,
	Because I can speake best, 20
	Approch before the rest.
Vin.	A verie good reason.
Sarp.	But there are others comming,
	Without maske or mumming:
	For they are not ashamed, 25
	If need be, to be named,
	Nor will they hide their faces,
	In any place or places;
	For though they seeme to come,
	Loded with Rush, and Broome: 30
	The Broomeman you must know,
	Is seigneur *Pogio,*
	Nephew, as shall appeare,
	To my Lord *Strozza* here.
Stro.	O Lord, I thanke you sir, you grace me much. 35
[*Sarp.*]	And to this noble dame,
	Whome I with finger name.
Vin.	A plague of that fooles finger.
Sarp.	And women will ensue,
	Which I must tell you true, 40
	No women are indeed,
	But Pages made for need,
	To fill vp womens places. /
	By vertue of their faces, [C4]

---

15 mouing] *Shepherd;* moning ‖ **36** *Sarp.*] *Shepherd (subs.)* ‖

And other hidden graces.   45
A hall, a hall; whist, stil, be mum,
For now with siluer song they come.

Enter Pogio, Fungus, with the song, Broome-maid, and
Rush-maid. After which, Pogio.

Pog. Heroes, and Heroines, of gallant straine,
Let not these Broomes, motes in your eies remaine,
For in the Moone, theres one beares with'red bushes: 50
But we (deare wights) do beare greene broomes, green rushes,
Whereof these verdant herbals cleeped Broome,
Do pierce and enter euerie Ladies roome,
And to proue them high borne, and no base trash,
Water with which your phisnomies you wash,   55
Is but a Broome. And more truth to deliuer,
Grim *Hercules* swept a stable with a riuer,
The wind that sweepes fowle clowds out of the ayre,
And for you Ladies makes the Welkin faire,
Is but a Broome: and O Dan *Titan* bright,   60
Most clearkly calld the Scauenger of night,
What art thou, but a verie broome of gold?
For all this world not to be cride nor sold;
Philosophy, that passion sweepes from thought,
Is the soules Broome, and by all braue wits sought,   65
Now if Philosophers but Broomemen are,
Each Broomeman then is a Philosopher.
And so we come (gracing your gratious Graces)
To sweepe Cares cobwebs from your cleanly faces.
    Alp. Thanks good master Broomeman.
    Fun.   For me Rushman then,   70
To make Rush ruffle in a verse of ten,
A Rush which now your heeles doe lie on here —
    Vin. Crie mercie sir.
    Fun. Was whilome vsed for a pungent speare,
In that odde battaile, neuer fought but twice   75
(As *Homer* sings) betwixt the frogs and mice, /
Rushes make True-loue knots; Rushes make rings,   [C4ᵛ]
Your Rush maugre the beard of winter springs.
And when with gentle, amorous, laysie lims,
Each Lord with his faire Ladie sweetly swims   80
On these coole Rushes; they may with these bables,
Cradles for children make; children for cradles.
And lest some Momus here might now crie push,
Saying our pageant is not woorth a Rush,
Bundles of Rushes, lo, we bring along,   85
To picke his teeth that bites them with his tongue.

---

47 SD *song,*] ∼∧ ‖ **70** Broomeman.] ∼, ‖ **72** here—] ∼. ‖

Stro. See, see, thats Lord *Medice*.
 Vin.   Gods me, my Lord,
Haz hee pickt you out, picking of your teeth?
 Med. What picke you out of that?
 Stro.   Not such stale stuffe
As you picke from your teeth.
 Alp.   Leave this warre with Rushes,   90
Good master pedant; pray forth with your shew.
 Sarp.   Lo thus farre then (braue duke) you see,
     Meere entertainement; Now our glee
     Shall march forth in Moralitie:
     And this queint Dutchesse here shall see,   95
     The fault of virgine Nicetie,
     First wooed with Rurall courtesie;
     Disburthen them; praunce on this ground,
     And make your *Exit* with your Round.

Pogio and Fungus dance with Broom-maid and Rush-maid and exeunt.
     Well haue they daunc'd as it is meet,   100
     Both with their nimble heades and feet.

    Enter Sylvan and Nymph.
     Now, as our country girls held off,
     And rudely did their lovers scoff;
     Our Nymph likewise shall onely glaunce
     By your faire eies, and looke askaunce   105
     Vpon her feral friend that wooes her,
     Who is in plaine field forc'd to loose her.
         Exeunt Sylvan and Nymph.
     And after them, to conclude all,
     The purlue of our Pastorall.
     A female bug, and eke her friend,   110
     Shall onely come and sing, and end. /

    Enter Bugs, sing, and exeunt.   [D1]
     Thus Lady and Dutchesse we conclude,
     Faire Virgins must not be too rude:
     For though the rurall wilde and antike,
     Abusde their loues as they were frantike;   115
     Yet take you in your Iuory clutches,
     This noble Duke, and be his Dutches.
     Thus thanking all for their *tacete*,
     I void the roome, and cry *valete*.   *Exit.*

---

92 duke)] *Q(c)*; ~∧ *Q(u)* ‖ **97** courtesie;] ~, ‖ **99** SD *Pogio . . . exeunt.*] *Parrott; Exeunt.* ‖ **101**
SD *Enter . . . Nymph.*] om. *Q (See Textual Note)* ‖ **102-7** Now . . . her.] *enclosed by large single
bracket* ‖ **105** askaunce] *Q(c)*; a skaunce *Q(u)* ‖ **106** feral] *Parrott*[2] *(Bradley conj.)*; female ‖ **107**
SD *Exeunt . . . Nymph.*] ‖ **110** female] *Q(c)*; Femall *Q(u)* ‖ **111** SD *Enter . . . exeunt.*] *Bugs
song.* ‖ **112** Thus] *Q catchword*; This *Q text* ‖

Alp. Generally well, and pleasingly performed. 120
Mar. Now I resigne this borrowed maiesty,
Which sate vnseemely on my worthlesse head,
With humble service to your Highnesse hands.
Alp. Well you became it Lady, and I know
All heere could wish it might be euer so. 125
 Stro. [*Aside.*] Heeres one saies nay to that.
 Vin. [*Aside to Strozza.*]   Plague on you, peace.
Lass. Now let it please your Highnesse to accept
A homely banquet, to close these rude sports.
 Alp. I thanke your Lordship much.
 Bass.   Bring lights, make place.

   Enter Pogio in his cloke and broome-mans attire.

 Pog. How d'ee my Lord? 130
Alp. O master broomeman, you did passing well.
Vin. A, you mad slaue you! you are a tickling Actor.
Pog. I was not out like my Lord *Medice.*
How did you like me Aunt?
 Cyn.   O rarely, rarely.
 Stro. O thou hast done a worke of memory, 135
And raisde our house vp higher by a story.
 Vin. Friend how conceit you my young mother heere?
 Cyn. Fitter for you my Lord, than for your father.
 Vin. No more of that sweete friend, those are bugs words. *Exeunt.*

   Finis Actus Secundi.

   ACTVS TERTII SCAENA PRIMA

  Medice after the song, whispers alone with his seruant.
 Med. Thou art my trusty seruant, and thou knowst, /
I haue beene euer bountifull Lord to thee, [D1ᵛ]
As still I will be: be thou thankfull then,
And doe me now a seruice of import.
 Ser. Any my Lord in compasse of my life. 5
 Med. To morrow then the Duke intends to hunt,
Where *Strozza* my despightfull enemie,
Will giue attendance busie in the chase,
Wherein (as if by chance, when others shoote

At the wilde Boare) do thou discharge at him, 10
And with an arrow, cleaue his canckerd heart.
  Ser. I will not faile my Lord.
  Med.   Be secret then.
And thou to me shalt be the dear'st of men.   *Exeunt.*

[III.ii]

Enter Vincentio, and Bassiolo.

  Vin. [*Aside.*] Now Vanitie and Policie inrich me
With some ridiculous fortune on this Vsher. —
Wheres Master Vsher?
  Bass.   Now I come my Lord.
  Vin. Besides, good sir, your shew did shew so well.
  Bass. Did it in deede my Lord?
  Vin.   O sir, beleeue it; 5
Twas the best fashiond and well orderd thing
That euer eye beheld: and there withall,
The fit attendance by the seruants usde,
The gentle guise in seruing euery guest,
In other entertainements; euery thing 10
About your house so sortfully disposde,
That euen as in a turne-spit calld a Iacke,
One vice assists another; the great wheeles   ⚹
Turning but softly, make the lesse to whirre
About their businesse; euery different part 15
Concurring to one commendable end:
So, and in such conformance, with rare grace,
Were all things orderd in your good lordes house.
  Bass. The most fit *simile* that euer was.
  Vin. But shall I tell you plainely my conceit, 20
Touching the man that I thinke causde this order?
  Bass. I good my Lord.
  Vin.   You note my *simile.*
  Bass. Drawne from the turne-spit.
  Vin.   I see you haue me,
Euen as in that queint engine you haue seene,
A little man in shreds stand at the winder, / 25
And seemes to put all things in act about him,   [D2]
Lifting and pulling with a mightie stirre,

III.ii] *Parrott* ‖ 1 SD *Aside.*] *Parrott* ‖ 2 Vsher.—] ∼. ∧ ‖ 4 well.] ∼, ‖

Yet addes no force to it, nor nothing does:
So, though your Lord be a braue Gentleman
(And seemes to do this busines), he does nothing;   30
Some man about him was the festiuall robe,
That made him shew so glorious and diuine.
   Bass. I cannot tell my Lord, yet I should know
If any such there were.
   Vin.   Should know quoth you;
I warrant you know: well, some there be   35
Shall haue the fortune to haue such rare men,
(Like braue beasts to their Armes) support their state,
When others of as high a worth and breede,
Are made the wastefull food of them they feede:
What state hath your Lord made you for your seruice?   40
   Bass. He haz beene my good Lord, for I can spend
Some fifteene hundred crownes in lands a yeare,
Which I have gotten since I seru'd him first.
   Vin. No more then fifteene hundred crownes a yeare?
   Bass. It is so much as makes me liue my Lord,   45
Like a poore Gentleman.
   Vin.   Nay, tis prettie well:
But certainely my nature does esteeme
Nothing enough for vertue; and had I
The Duke my fathers meanes, all should be spent,
To keepe braue men about me: but good sir,   50
Accept this simple iewell at my hands,
Till I can worke perswasion of my friendship,
With worthier arguments.
   Bass.   No, good my Lord,
I can by no meanes merite the free bounties
You have bestowed besides.
   Vin.   Nay, be not strange,   55
But doe your selfe right, and be all one man
In all your actions, doe not thinke but some
Haue extraordinarie spirits like your selfe,
And wil not stand in their societie, /
On birth and riches, but on worth and vertue,   [D2ᵛ] 60
With whom there is no nicenesse, nor respect
Of others common friendship; be he poore
Or basely borne, so he be rich in soule,
And noble in degrees of qualities,
He shall be my friend sooner then a King.   65
   Bass. Tis a most kingly iudgement in your lordship.

---

30 (And . . . busines)] *Parrott; in Q parentheses are on preceding line* (though . . . Gentleman) |
And . . . nothing;] And . . . busines, / He . . . nothing; ‖ **33-34** I . . . were] *Shepherd; as prose*
(if) ‖ **53** No,] ∼∧ ‖ **60** riches,] ∼: ‖ **66** lordship.] ∼, ‖

Vin. Faith sir I know not, but tis my vaine humour.

Bass. O, tis an honour in a Nobleman.

Vin. Y'aue some lords now so politike and prowd,
They skorne to give good lookes to worthy men.   70

    Bass. O fie upon vm; by that light my lord,
I am but seruant to a Nobleman,
But if I would not skorne such puppet lords,
Would I weare breathlesse.

Vin.   You sir? so you may,
For they will cogge so when they wish to vse men,   75
With, pray be coverd sir, I beseech you sit,
Whoe's there? waite of Master Vsher to the doore.
O, these be godly gudgeons: where's the deedes?
The perfect Nobleman?

    Bass.   O good my Lord —

Vin. Away, away, ere I would flatter so,   80
I would eate rushes like lord *Medice.*

    Bass. Well, wel my Lord, would there were more such Princes.

Vin. Alas, twere pitty sir, they would be gulld
Out of their very skinnes.

    Bass.   Why, how?
Are you my lord?

Vin.   Who I? I care not: 85
If I be guld where I professe plaine love,
T'will be their faults you know.

    Bass.   O t'were their shames.

Vin. Well, take my iewell, you shall not be strange,
I loue not manie words.

    Bass.   My lord, I thanke you,
I am of few words too.

Vin.   Tis friendlie said,   ⋆ 90
You proue your selfe a friend, and I would haue you
Aduance your thoughts, and lay about for state, /
Worthy your vertues: be the Mineon   [D3]
Of some great King or Duke: theres *Medice,*
The Minion of my Father: O the Father!   95
What difference is there? but I cannot flatter;
A word to wise men.

    Bass.   I perceiue your Lordship.

Vin. Your Lordship? talke you now like a friend?
Is this plaine kindnesse?

    Bass.   Is it not my Lord?

---

79 Lord—] ∼. ‖ **81** *Medice*] *Medici* ‖ **84-85** Out . . . not:] Out . . . skinnes. / Why . . . lord? /
Who . . . not: *Q* (are) ‖ **84** Why, how?] ∼∧ ∼∧ ‖ **85** I?] ∼, ‖ **89-90** My . . . too.] *Parrott; as*
prose ‖ **90** of few] offew ‖ **94** *Medice*] *Medici* ‖ **96** flatter;] ∼∧ ‖

Vin. A palpable flattring figure for men common:　　　　　100
A my word I should thinke, if twere another,
He meant to gull mee.
　　Bass.　　　　　　Why tis but your due.
　　Vin. Tis but my due: if youle be still a stranger:
But as I wish to choose you for my friend,
As I intend when God shall call my father,　　　　　105
To doe I can tell what: but let that passe,
Thus tis not fit; let my friend be familiar,
Use not my Lordship, nor yet call me Lord,
Nor my whole name *Vincentio*; but *Vince,*
As they call Iacke or Will, tis now in vse,　　　　　110
Twixt men of no equallity or kindnesse.
　　Bass. I shall be quickely bold enough my Lord.
　　Vin. Nay, see how still you vse that coy terme, Lord,
What argues this, but that you shunne my friendship?
　　Bass. Nay, pray say not so.
　　Vin.　　　　　　Who should not say so?　　　　　115
Will you afford me now no name at all?
　　Bass. What should I call you?
　　Vin.　　　　　　Nay, then tis no matter.
But I told you *Vince.*
　　Bass.　　　　Why then my sweete *Vince.*
　　Vin. Whie so then; and yet still there is a fault,
In vsing these kind words, without kinde deedes:　　　　　120
Pray thee imbrace me too.
　　Bass.　　　　　Why then sweete *Vince.*
　　Vin. Why now I thank you, sblood shall friends be strange?
Where there is plainenesse, there is euer truth:
And I will still be plaine since I am true:
Come let vs lie a little, I am wearie. /　　　　　125
　　Bass. And so am I, I sweare since yesterday.　　　　　[D3ᵛ]
　　Vin. You may sir by my faith; and sirra, hark thee,
What lordship wouldst thou wish to haue ifaith,
When my old father dies?
　　Bass.　　　　Who I? alas.
　　Vin. O not you? well sir, you shall haue none,　　　　　130
You are as coy a peece as your Lords daughter.
　　Bass. Who, my mistris?
　　Vin.　　　　　Indeede, is she your Mistris?
　　Bass. I faith sweet *Vince,* since she was three yeare old.

---

108 my] *Parrott*; me ‖ 109 *Vince*] *vince* ‖ 113 Lord,] ∼∧ ‖ 130 you?] ∼, ‖

Vin. And are we not two friends?

Bass.   Who doubts of that?

Vin. And are not two friends one?

Bass.   Euen man and wife.   135

Vin. Then what to you she is, to me she should be.

Bass. Why *Vince,* thou wouldst not haue her?

Vin.   O not I:

I doe not fancie any thing like you.

   Bass. Nay but I pray thee tell me.

   Vin. You do not meane to marry her your self?   140

   Bass. Not I by heauen.

   Vin.   Take heede now, do not gull me.

   Bass. No by that candle.

   Vin.   Then will I be plaine.

Thinke you she dotes not too much on my father?

   Bass. O yes, no doubt on't.

   Vin.   Nay, I pray you speake.

   Bass. You seely man you, she cannot abide him.   145

   Vin. Why sweete friend pardon me, alas I knew not.

   Bass. But I doe note you are in some things simple,

And wrong your selfe too much.

   Vin.   Thanke you good friend,

For your playne dealing, I doe meane, so well.

   Bass. But who saw euer summer mixt with winter?   150

There must be equall yeares where firme loue is.

Could we two loue so well so soddainely

Were we not some thing equaller in yeares,

Than he and shee are?

   Vin.   I cry ye mercy sir,

I know we could not, but yet be not too bitter, /   155

Considering loue is fearefull. And sweete friend,   [D4]

I haue a letter t'intreate her kindnesse

Which if you would conuay —

   Bass.   I, if I would sir?

   Vin. Why fayth, deare friend, I would not die requitelesse.

   Bass. Would you not so sir? by heauen a little thing   160

Would make me boxe you: Which if you would conuaie?

Why not I pray? Which (friend) thou shalt conuaie.

   Vin. Which friend, you shall then.

   Bass.   Well friend, and I will then.

   Vin. And vse some kind perswasiue words for me?

---

135 two] *Shepherd;* too ‖ **137-38** O . . . you.] *Parrott; one line* ‖ **149** meane,] *Parrott;* ∼∧ ‖ **153** yeares,] ∼. ‖ **154-55** I . . . bitter,] *Shepherd; one line* ‖ **158** conuay—] ∼. ‖ **160-62** Would . . . conuaie.] Would . . . sir? / By . . . you, / Which . . . pray? / Which . . . conuaie. *Q* (would . . . why) ‖

Bass. The best I sweare that my poore toung can forge.   165
   Vin. I, wel said, poore toung: O tis rich in meekenesse;
You are not knowne to speake well? You haue wonne
Direction of the Earle and all his house,
The fauour of his daughter, and all Dames
That euer I sawe, come within your sight,   170
With a poore tongue? A plague a your sweete lippes.
   Bass. Well, we will doe our best: And faith my *Vince*,
She shall haue an vnweldie and dull soule,
If she be nothing moou'd with my poore tongue,
Call it no better; Be it what it will.   175
   Vin. Well said ifaith; Now if I doe not thinke
Tis possible, besides her bare receipt
Of that my Letter, with thy friendly tongue,
To get an answere of it, neuer trust me.
   Bass. An answer man? Sbloud make no doubt of that.   180
   Vin. By heauen I thinke so; now a plague of Nature,
That she giues all to some, and none to others.
   Bass. [*Aside.*] How I endeare him to me ! — Come *Vince*, rise,
Next time I see her, I will giue her this:
Which when she sees, sheele thinke it wondrous strange   185
Love should goe by descent, and make the sonne
Follow the father in his amorous steppes.
   Vin. She needes must thinke it strange, that neuer yet saw I durst
speake to her, or had scarce hir sight.
   Bass. Well *Vince*, I sweare thou shalt both see and kisse her. /   190
   Vin. Sweares my deere friend? by what?   [D4ᵛ]
   Bass.   Euen by our friendship.
   Vin. O sacred oath! which, how long will you keepe?
   Bass. While there be bees in *Hybla,* or white swannes
In bright *Meander*; while the banks of *Po*
Shall beare braue lillies; or Italian dames   195
Be called the Bone robes of the world.
   Vin. Tis elegantly said: and when I faile,
Let there be found in *Hybla* hiues no bees;
Let no swannes swimme in bright *Meander* streame,
Nor lillies spring vpon the banks of *Po,*   200
Nor let one fat Italian dame be found,
But leane and brawn-falne; I, and scarsly sound.
   Bass. It is enough, but lets imbrace withal.
   Vin. With all my hart.
   Bass.   So, now farewell sweet *Vince*.   *Exit.*

---

183 SD *Aside.*] *Parrott* | me!—] ∼!∧ ‖ **198** Let] Ler ‖ **203** withal] with all ‖

Vin. Farewell my worthie friend, I thinke I haue him.   205

Enter Bassiolo.

Bass. [*Aside.*] I had forgot the parting phrase he taught me —
I commend me t'ee sir.   *Exit instant.*
Vin.   At your wisht seruice sir:
O fine friend, he had forgot the phrase:
How serious apish soules are in vaine forme:
Well, he is mine, and he being trusted most   210
With my deare loue, may often worke our meeting,
And being thus ingagde, dare not reueale.

Enter Pogio in haste, Strozza following.

Pog. Horse, horse, horse, my lord, horse, your father is going a
hunting.

Vin. My Lord horse? you asse you, d'ee call my Lord horse?   215

Stro. Nay, he speakes huddles still, lets slit his tongue.

Pog. Nay good vnkle now, sbloud, what captious marchants you be;
so the Duke tooke me vp euen now: my lord vnckle heere, and my
old lord *Lasso,* by heauen y'are all too witty for me, I am the veriest
foole on you all, Ile be sworne.   220

Vin. Therein thou art worth vs all, for thou knowst thy selfe.

Stro. But your wisedom was in a pretty taking last night; was it not
I pray?

Pog. O, for taking my drink a little? ifaith my Lord, for that you
shall haue the best sport presently with Madam *Corteza,* / that euer [E1] 225
was; I haue made her so drunke, that she does nothing but kisse my
Lord *Medice.* See shee comes riding the Duke, shees passing well
mounted, beleeue it.

Enter Alphonso, Corteza, Cynanche, Margaret, Bassiolo
first, two women attendants, and hunts-men, Lasso.

Alp. Good wench forbeare.

Cort. My Lord, you must put forth your selfe among Ladies, I war-   230
rant you haue much in you, if you would shew it; see, a cheeke a twentie; the bodie of a *George,* a good legge still; still a good calfe, and not
flabby, nor hanging I warrant you; a brawne of a thumbe here, and
t'were a pulld partridge; Neece *Meg,* thou shalt haue the sweetest bedfellow on him, that ever call'd Ladie husband; trie him you shame-   235
fac'd bable you, trie him.

Mar. Good Madame be rulde.

Cort. What a nice thing it is, my Lord, you must set foorth this

---

206 SD *Aside.*] *Parrott* | me—] ∼, ‖ **211** loue] *Shepherd*; ioue ‖ **226** that she] thar she ‖ **227-28**
See . . . it.] *on separate line* ‖ **228** SD *Cynanche, Margaret, Bassiolo*] *Parrott; Cynanche, Bassiolo* ‖
233 flabby] *Shepherd*; slabby ‖

gere, and kisse her; yfaith you must; get you togither and be naught
awhile, get you together.   240

   Alp. Now what a merrie harmlesse dame it is!

   Cort. My Lord *Medice*, you are a right noble man, and wil do a
woman right in a wrong matter and neede be; pray do you giue the
duke ensample upon me; you come a wooing to me now; I accept it.

   Lass. What meane you sister?   245

   Cort. Pray my Lord away; consider me as I am, a woman.

   Pog. [*Aside.*] Lord how I haue whittld her?

   Cort. You come a wooing to me now; pray thee Duke marke my
Lord *Medice*; and do you marke me virgin; Stand you aside, my Lord,
all, and you; giue place; now my Lord *Medice*; put case I be strange   250
a little, yet you, like a man, put me to it. Come kisse me my Lord, be
not ashamde.

   Med. Not I Madame, I come not a wooing to you.

   Cort. Tis no matter my Lord, make as though you did, and come
kisse me; I won't be strange a whit.   255

   Lass. Fie sister, y'are too blame; pray will you goe to your chamber?

   Cort. Why, harke you brother.

   Lass. Whats the matter?

   Cort. Dee thinke I am drunke? /

   Lass. I thinke so truly.   [E1ᵛ] 260

   Cort. But are you sure I am drunke?

   Lass. Else I would not thinke so.

   Cort. But, I would be glad to be sure on't.

   Lass. I assure you then.

   Cort. Why then say nothing; and Ile begone.   265
God b'w'y' lord duke, Ile come againe anone.   *Exit.*

   Lass. I hope your Grace will pardon her my liege,
For tis most strange; shees as discreete a dame
As any in these countries, and as sober,
But for this onely humour of the cup.   270

   Alp. Tis good my Lord sometimes:
Come, to our hunting; now tis time I thinke.

   Omn. The verie best time of the day, my Lord.

   Alp. Then my Lord, I will take my leaue till night,
Reseruing thanks for all my entertainment,   275
Till I returne; in meane time, louely dame,   *Vin. and St. have all this*
                                                          while talked togither a prettie
                                                            way.

Remember the high state you last presented,
And thinke it was not a mere festiuall shew,

239 naught] naughts ‖ **247** SD *Aside.*] *Parrott* ‖ **251** you, . . . man,] ∼∧ . . . ∼∧ ‖ **256** chamber?]
∼. ‖ **265-66** Why . . . anone.] *Shepherd*; Why . . . duke / Ile . . . anone. ‖ **265** begone.] ∼∧ ‖
266 b'w'y'] *Parrott*²; bwy | lord duke,] ∼, ∼∧ ‖ **271** sometimes:] *Q(c)*; sometimes; Soune and
my Lords, *Q(u)* ‖ **273** *Omn.*] ∼∧ ‖ **276** I returne] *Q(c)*; Ireturne *Q(u)* ‖

But an essentiall type of that you are
In full consent of all my faculties.   280
[*to Lasso.*] And harke you good my Lord.
  Vin. [*to Strozza.*]   See now, they whisper
Some priuate order, (I dare lay my life)
For a forc'd marriage t'wixt my loue and father,
I therefore must make sure: [*to others.*] And noble friends,
Ile leaue you all, when I haue brought you forth,   285
And seene you in the chase. [*to Strozza.*] Meane-while obserue
In all the time this solemne hunting lasts,
My father and his minion *Medice,*
And note, if you can gather any signe,
That they haue mist me, and suspect my being,   290
If which fall out, send home my Page before.
  Stro. I will not faile my Lord.   *Medice whispers with 1.*
                             Huntsman all this while.
  Med.   Now take thy time.
  Hunt. I warrant you my Lord, he shall not scape me.
  Alp. Now my deere Mistresse, till our sports intended
End with my absence, I will take my leaue. /   295
  Lass. Bassiolo, attend on my daughter.   [E2]
        Exeunt manent Vin., Mar., Bass., Cyn. and women attendants.
  Bass. I will my Lord.
  Vin. [*Aside.*] Now will the sport beginne; I think my loue
Will handle him, as well as I haue doone.   *Exit.*
  Cyn. Madam, I take my leaue, and humblie thanke you.   300
  Mar. Welcome good madam; mayds wait on my Lady.
                   Exeunt Cyn. and attendants.
  Bass. So mistris, this is fit.
  Mar.   Fit sir, why so?
  Bass. Why so? I haue most fortunate newes for you.
  Mar. For me sir? I beseech you what are they?
  Bass. Merit and Fortune, for you both agree;   305
Merit what you haue, and haue what you merit.
  Mar. Lord with what Rhetorike you prepare your newes!
  Bass. I need not; for the plaine contents they beare
Vttred in any words, deserue their welcome,
And yet I hope the words will serue the turne.   310
  Mar. What, in a letter?
  Bass.   Why not?
  Mar.   Whence is it?

---

281 SD *to Lasso.*] | SD *to Strozza.*] ‖ **284** SD *to others.*] | And] and ‖ **286** chase. Meane-while]
∼; mean-while | SD *to Strozza.*] ‖ **295** End] end ‖ **296** SD *Exeunt . . . attendants.*] *Parrott (subs.*);
Exeunt ‖ **298** SD *Aside.*] *Parrott* ‖ **301** SD *Exeunt . . . attendants.*] *Exit.* ‖

Bass. From one that will not shame it with his name.
And that is Lord *Vincentio*.
    Mar.   King of Heaven!
Is the man madde?
    Bass.   Mad Madam, why?
    Mar. O heauen, I muse a man of your importance,   315
Will offer to bring me a letter thus?
    Bass. Why, why good Mistresse, are you hurt in that?
Your answer may be what you will your selfe.
    Mar. I, but you should not doe it: Gods my life,
You shall answer it.
    Bass.   Nay, you must answer it.   320
    Mar. I answer it! are you the man I trusted?
And will betray me to a stranger thus?
    Bass. Thats nothing, dame, all friends were strangers first.
    Mar. Now was there euer woman overseene so,
In a wise mans discretion?   325
    Bass. Your braine is shallow, come, receiue this letter.
    Mar. How dare you say so? when you know so well
How much I am engaged to the duke? /
    Bass. The duke? a proper match: a graue olde gentman: [E2ᵛ]
Haz beard at will; and would, in my conceyt,   330
Make a most excellent patterne for a potter,
To haue his picture stampt on a Iugge,
To keepe ale-knights in memorie of sobrietie.
Heere gentle madam, take it.
    Mar.   Take it sir?
Am I common taker of loue letters?   335
    Bass. Common? why when receiu'd you one before?
    Mar. Come, tis no matter; I had thought your care
Of my bestowing, would not tempt me thus
To one I know not; but it is because
You know I dote so much on your direction.   340
    Bass. On my direction?
    Mar.   No sir, not on yours.
    Bass. Well mistris, if you will take my aduice
At any time, then take this letter now.
    Mar. Tis strange, I woonder the coy gentleman,
That seeing me so oft, would neuer speake,   345
Is on the sodaine so far wrapt to write.
    Bass. It shewd his iudgement, that he would not speake
Knowing with what strict and iealous eie

---

331 patterne . . . potter,] ∼, . . . ∼∧ ‖ 332 Iugge,] Iug ge. ‖ 339 not] Not ‖

He should be noted; holde, if you loue your selfe;
Now will you take this letter? pray be rulde. 350
    Mar. Come, you haue such another plaguie toung,
And yet yfayth I will not.
    Bass.   Lord of heauen,
What, did it burne your hands? holde, hold, I pray,
And let the words within it fire your heart.
    Mar. I woonder how the deuill, he found you out 355
To be his spokesman, — O the duke would thanke you,
If he knew how you vrgde me for his sonne.
    Bass. [*Aside.*] The duke? I haue fretted her, euen
To the liver, and had much adoe
To make her take it, but I knew t'was sure; 360
For he that cannot turne and winde a woman
Like silke about his finger, is no man,
Ile make her answer't too. /
    Mar.   O here's good stuffe. [E3]
Hold, pray take it for your paines to bring it.
    Bass. Ladie you erre in my reward a little, 365
Which must be a kind answere to this letter.
    Mar. Nay then yfaith, t'were best you brought a Priest;
And then your client; and then keepe the doore.
Gods me I neuer knew so rude a man.
    Bass. Wel, you shall answer; Ile fetch pen and paper. *Exit.*
    Mar. Poore Vsher, how wert thou wrought to this brake?
Men worke on one another for we women,
Nay each man on himselfe; and all in one
Say; No man is content that lies alone.
Here comes our gulled Squire.

                  [*Re-enter Bassiolo.*]
    Bass.   Here Mistresse, write. 375
    Mar. What should I write?
    Bass.   An answer to this letter.
    Mar. Why sir, I see no cause of answer in it,
But if you needs will shew how much you rule me,
Sit downe; and answer it, as you please your selfe,
Here is your paper, lay it faire afore you. 380
    Bass. Lady, content, Ile be your Secretorie.
    Mar. [*Aside.*] I fit him in this taske; he thinkes his penne
The Shaft of *Cupid,* in an amorous letter.

---

358 SD *Aside.*] *Parrott* ǁ **358-59** The . . . adoe] The . . . her, / Euen . . . adoe ǁ **375** SD *Re-enter Bassiolo.*] *Parrott*[1] ǁ **382** SD *Aside.*] *Parrott* ǁ

Bass. Is heere no great worth of your answer say you?
Beleeue it, tis exceedingly well writ.   385
   Mar. So much the more vnfit for me to answere,
And therefore let your Stile and it contend.
   Bass. Well, you shall see I will not be farre short,
Although (indeede) I cannot write so well
When one is by, as when I am alone.   390
   Mar. O, a good Scribe must write, though twenty talke,
And he talke to them too.
   Bass.   Well, you shall see.
   Mar. [*Aside.*] A proper peece of Scribeship theres no doubt;
Some words, pickt out of Proclamations,
Or great mens Speeches; or well-selling Pamphlets: 395
See how he rubbes his temples: I beleeue
His Muse lies in the back-part of his braine, /
Which thicke and grosse, is hard to be brought forward —   [E3ᵛ]
What? is it loath to come?
   Bass.   No, not a whit:
Pray hold your peace a little.
   Mar. [*Aside.*]   He sweates, with bringing   400
On his heauie stile; Ile plie him still,
Till he sweate all his wit out. What man, not yet?
   Bass. Swoons, yowle not extort it from a man,
How do you like the worde Endeare?
   Mar. O fie vpon't.   405
   Bass. Nay, then I see your iudgement: what say you to condole?
   Mar. Worse and worse.
   Bass. O braue! I should make a sweete answer, if I should use no
words but of your admittance.
   Mar. Well sir, write what you please.   410
   Bass. Is modell a good word with you?
   Mar. Put them togither I pray.
   Bass. So I will I warrant you.
   Mar. [*Aside.*] See, see, see, now it comes powring downe.
   Bass. I hope youle take no exceptions to beleeue it.   415
   Mar. Out vpon't, that phrase is so runne out of breath in trifles,
that we shall haue no beleefe at all in earnest shortly. Beleeue it tis a
prettie feather; beleeue it a daintie Rush; beleeue it an excellent
Cocks-combe.
   Bass. So, so, so, your exceptions sort very collaterally.   420
   Mar. Collaterally? theres a fine word now; wrest in that if you can
by any meanes.

---

392 And] and ‖ **393** SD *Aside.*] *Parrott* ‖ **398** forward—] ∼, ‖ **400** SD *Aside.*] *Parrott* ‖ **400-402**
He . . . yet?] He . . . stile, / Ile . . . out, / What . . . yet? Q (on . . . till) ‖ **401** stile;] ∼, ‖ **402**
out.] ∼, ‖ **414** SD *Aside.*] *Parrott* ‖

Bass. [*Aside.*] I thought she would like the very worst of them all. —
How thinke you? do not I write, and heare, and talke too now?

Mar. By my soule, if you can tell what you write now, you write   425
verie readily.

Bass. That you shall see straight.

Mar. But do you not write that you speake now?

Bass. O yes, doe you not see how I write it? I can not write when
any bodie is by me, I.   430

Mar. Gods my life, stay man; youle make it too long.

Bass. Nay, if I can not tell what belongs to the length of a Ladies
device yfaith. /

Mar. But I will not have it so long.   [E4]

Bass. If I cannot fit you?   435

Mar. O me; how it comes vpon him? pre-thee be short.

Bass. Wel, now I haue done, and now I wil reade it; your Lordships motive accommodating my thoughts, with the very model of my
hearts mature consideration: it shall not be out of my Element to ne-
gotiate with you in this amorous duello; wherein I will condole with   440
you, that our proiect cannot be so collaterally made, as our endeared
hearts may verie well seeme to insinuate.

Mar. No more: no more; fie vpon this.

Bass. Fie vpon this? hees accurst that haz to doe with these vn-
sound women, of iudgement: if this be not good yfaith.   445

Mar. But tis so good, t'will not be thought to come from a womans
braine.

Bass. Thats another matter.

Mar. Come, I will write my selfe.

Bass. A Gods name Lady: and yet I will not loose this I warrant   450
you; I know for what Ladie this will serue as fit; now we shall have a
sweete peece of inditement.

Mar. How spell you foolish?

Bass. F,oo,l,i,sh; [*Aside.*] she will presume t'endite that cannot spel.

Mar. How spell you Vsher?   455

Bass. Sblood, you put not in those words togither, do you?

Mar. No, not togither.

Bass. What is betwixt I pray?

Mar. Asse the.

Bass. Asse the? betwixt foolish, and Vsher, Gods my life, foolish   460
Asse the Vsher?

Mar. Nay then you are so iealous of your wit: now reade all I
haue written I pray.

---

423 SD *Aside.*] | all.—How] ∼, how ‖ **436** pre-thee] pre thee ‖ **448** matter.] ∼∧ ‖ **454** i,] ∼.
| SD *Aside.*] *Parrott* ‖ **460-61** Asse . . . Vsher?] Asse . . . Vsher, / Gods . . . Vsher? ‖

Bass. I am not so foolish as the Vsher would make me: O so foolish as the Usher would make me? Wherein would I make you foolish?   465

Mar. Why sir, in willing me to beleeue he lov'd me so wel, being so
meere a stranger.

Bass. O, is't so? you may say so indeed.

Mar. Cry mercie sir, and I will write so too; and yet my hand is so
vile. Pray thee sit thee downe and write as I bid thee. /   470

Bass. With all my heart Lady, what shall I write now?   [E4ᵛ]

Mar. You shall write this sir, I am not so foolish to thinke you loue
me, being so meere a stranger.

Bass. So meere a stranger!

Mar. And yet I know, loue works strangely.   475

Bass. Loue workes strangely.

Mar. And therefore take heed, by whom you speake for loue.

Bass. Speake for loue.

Mar. For he may speake for himselfe.

Bass. May speake for himselfe.   480

Mar. Not that I desire it —

Bass. Desire it.

Mar. But if he do; you may speede, I confesse.

Bass. Speede I confesse.

Mar. But let that passe, I do not loue to discourage any bodie.   485

Bass. Discourage any bodie.

Mar. Do you, or he, picke out what you can; and so farewell.

Bass. And so fare well. Is this all?

Mar. I, and he may thanke your Syrens tongue that it is so much.

Bass. A proper Letter if you marke it.   490

Mar. Well sir, though it be not so proper as the writer; yet tis as
proper as the inditer; Euerie woman cannot be a gentleman Vsher;
they that cannot go before, must come behind.

Bass. Well Ladie, this I will carrie instantly, I commend me tee
Ladie.   *Exit.*

Mar. Pittifull Vsher, what a prettie sleight,
Goes to the working vp of euerie thing?
What sweet varietie serues a womans wit?
We make men sue to vs for that we wish.
Poore men; hold out a while; and do not sue,   500
And spite of Custome we will sue to you.   *Exit.*

Finis Actus tertij.

<hr>

469 too;] ∼, ‖ **470** vile.] ∼, ‖ **481** it—] ∼, ‖

ACTVS QVARTI,   SCAENA PRIMA

Enter Pogio running in, and knocking at Cynanches doore.

Pog. O God, how wearie I am? Aunt, Madam, *Cynanche,* Aunt? /

[*Enter Cynanche.*]

Cyn. How now?   [F1]

Pog. O God, Aunt: O God Aunt: O God.

Cyn. What bad newes brings this man? where is my Lord?

Pog. O Aunt, my Vnkle, hees shot.

Cyn.   Shot, ay me!   5
how is he shot?

Pog.   Why with a forked shaft
As he was hunting, full in his left side.

Cyn. O me accurst, where is hee? bring me, where?

Pog. Comming with Doctor *Benevenius,*
Ile leaue you, and goe tell my Lord *Vincentio.*   *Exit.*

*Enter Benevenius with others, bringing in Strozza with
an arrow in his side.*

Cyn. See the sad sight, I dare not yeeld to griefe,
But force faind patience to recomfort him:
My Lord, what chance is this: how fares your lordship?

Stro. Wounded, and faint with anguish, let me rest.

Ben. A chaire.

Cyn.   O Doctor, ist a deadly hurt?   15

Ben. I hope not Madam, though not free from danger.

Cyn. Why plucke you not the arrow from his side?

Ben. We cannot Lady, the forckt head so fast
Stickes in the bottome of his sollide ribbe.

Stro. No meane then Doctor rests there to educe it?   20

Ben. This onely, my good Lord, to give your wound
A greater orifice, and in sunder break
The pierced ribbe; which being so neere the midriffe,
And opening to the region of the heart,
Will be exceeding dangerous to your life.   25

Stro. I will not see my bosome mangled so,
Nor sternely be anatomizde aliue,
Ile rather perish with it sticking still.

Cyn. O no; sweete doctor thinke vpon some help.

---

1 SD *Enter Cynanche.*] *Parrott* ‖ **7** side.] *Q(c);* ∼? *Q(u)* ‖ **9** *Benevenius*] *Beniuemus (See Textual
Note)* ‖ **10** SD *Benevenius*] *Beniuemus* ‖

Ben. I tolde you all that can be thought in Arte,   30
Which since your Lordship will not yeelde to vse,
Our last hope rests in Natures secret aide,
Whose power at length may happily expell it.
    Stro. Must we attend at deaths abhorred doore, /
The torturing delaies of slauish Nature?   [F1ᵛ] 35
My life is in mine owne powers to dissolue:
And why not then the paines that plague my life?
Rise furies, and this furie of my bane,
Assaile and conquer; what men madnesse call
(That hath no eye to sense, but frees the soule,   40
Exempt of hope, and feare with instant fate)
Is manliest reason; manliest reason then,
Resolue and rid me of this brutish life,
Hasten the cowardly protracted cure
Of all diseases: King of Phisitians, death,   45
Ile dig thee from this Mine of miserie.
    Cyn. O hold my Lord, this is no christian part,
Nor yet skarce manly, when your mankinde foe,
Imperious death shall make your grones his trumpets
To summon resignation of lifes Fort,   50
To flie without resistance; you must force
A countermine of Fortitude, more deepe
Than this poore Mine of paines, to blow him vp,
And spight of him liue victor, though subdu'd:
Patience in torment, is a valure more   55
Than euer crownd *Th'Alcmenean* Conquerour.
    Stro. Rage is the vent of torment, let me rise.
    Cyn. Men doe but crie, that rage in miseries,
And scarcely beaten children, become cries:
Paines are like womens clamors, which the lesse   60
They find mens patience stirred, the more they cease.
Of this tis said, afflictions bring to God,
Because they make vs like him, drinking vp
Ioyes that deforme vs with the lusts of sense,
And turne our generall being into soule,   65
Whose actions simply formed and applied,
Draw all our bodies frailties from respect.
    Stro. Away with this vnmedcinable balme
Of worded breath; forbeare friends, let me rest,

39 call] ∼: ‖

I sweare I will be bands vnto my selfe. 70
 Ben. That will become your lordship best indeed.
 Stro. Ile breake away, and leape into the Sea. /
Or from some Turret cast me hedlong downe, [F2]
To shiuer this fraile carkasse into dust.
 Cyn. O my deare Lord, what vnlike words are these, 75
To the late fruits of your religious Noblesse?
 Stro. Leaue me fond woman.
 Cyn.   Ile be hewne from hence
Before I leaue you; helpe me gentle Doctor.
 Ben. Haue patience good my Lord.
 Stro.   Then leade me in,
Cut off the timber of this cursed Shaft, 80
And let the fork'd pile canker to my heart.
 Cyn. Deare Lord, resolue on humble sufferance.
 Stro. I will not heare thee, woman, be content.
 Cyn. O neuer shall my counsailes cease to knocke
At thy impatient eares, till they flie in 85
And salue with Christian patience, Pagan sinne.   *Exeunt.*

[IV.ii]

Enter Vincentio with a letter in his hand, Bassiolo.

 Bass. This is her letter sir, you now shall see
How seely a thing tis in respect of mine,
And what a simple woman she haz prou'd,
To refuse mine for hers; I pray looke heere.
 Vin. Soft sir, I know not, I being her sworn seruant, 5
If I may put vp these disgracefull words,
Giuen of my Mistris, without touch of honour.
 Bass. Disgracefull words; I protest I speake not
To disgrace her, but to grace my selfe.
 Vin. Nay then sir, if it be to grace your selfe, 10
I am content; but otherwise you know,
I was to take exceptions to a King.
 Bass. Nay, y'are ith right for that; but reade I pray,
If there be not more choice words in that letter,
Than in any three of *Guevaras* golden epistles, 15
I am a very asse. How thinke you *Vince?*

IV.ii] *Parrott* ‖ **1** letter] lettter ‖ **13-16** Nay . . . *Vince?*] *Parrott; as prose* (if . . . than) ‖

Vin. By heauen no lesse sir, it is the best thing;   *he rends it.*
Gods what a beast am I.
    Bass.   It is no matter,
I can set it together againe.
    Vin. Pardon me sir, I protest I was rauisht: 20
But was it possible she should preferre hers
Before this? /
    Bass.   O sir, she cride fie vpon this.   [F2ᵛ]
    Vin. Well, I must say nothing, loue is blind
You know, and can finde no fault in his beloued.
    Bass. Nay, thats most certaine.
    Vin.   Gee't me: Ile haue this letter.   25
    Bass. No good *Vince,* tis not worth it.
    Vin.   Ile ha't
Ifaith, heeres enough in it to serue for my letters
As long as I live; Ile keepe it to breede on as twere:
But I much wonder you could make her write.
    Bass. Indeede there were some words belongd to that.   30
    Vin. How strong an influence works in well plac'd words,
And yet there must be a prepared loue,
To give those words so mighty a command,
Or twere impossible they should moue so much:
And will you tell me true?
    Bass.   In any thing.   35
    Vin. Does not this Lady loue you?
    Bass. Love me? why yes; I thinke she does not hate me.
    Vin. Nay but ifaith, does she not loue you dearely?
    Bass. No I protest.
    Vin. Nor haue you neuer kist her?   40
    Bass. Kist her, thats nothing.
    Vin. But you know my meaning:
Haue you not beene, as one would say, afore me?
    Bass. Not I, I sweare.
    Vin.   O, y'are too true to tell.
    Bass. Nay be my troth, she haz, I must confesse,   45
Vsde me with good respect, and nobly still,
But for such matters —
    Vin. [*Aside.*]   Verie little more,
Would make him take her maidenhead vpon him: —

---

18 It] *Shepherd*; Is ‖ **20-22** Pardon . . . this?] *as prose* (but . . . before) ‖ **23-24** Well . . . beloued.]
as prose (you) ‖ **26-28** Ile . . . twere:] *as prose* (ifaith . . . as) ‖ **47** matters—] ∼. | SD *Aside.*]
Parrott ‖ **48** him:—] ∼: ∧ ‖

Well friend, I rest yet in a little doubt,
This was not hers.
 Bass.   T'was by the light that shines,   50
And Ile goe fetch her to you to confirme it.
 Vin. O passing friend.
 Bass. But when she comes, in any case be bold,
And come vpon her with some pleasing thing,
To shew y'are pleasde: how euer she behaues her, /   55
As for example; if she turne her backe,   [F3]
Vse you that action you would doe before,
And court her thus; Lady, your backe part
Is as faire to me, as is your fore part.
 Vin. T'will be most pleasing.
 Bass.   I, for if you loue   60
One part above another, tis a signe
You like not all alike, and the worst part
About your Mistris, you must thinke as faire,
As sweete, and daintie, as the very best,
So much, for so much, and considering too,   65
Each seuerall limbe and member in his kinde.
 Vin. As a man should.
 Bass.   True, will you thinke of this?
 Vin. I hope I shall.
 Bass.   But if she chance to laugh,
You must not lose your countenance but deuise
Some speech to shew you pleasde, euen being laugh'd at.   70
 Vin. I, but what speech?
 Bass. Gods pretious man! do something of your selfe?
But Ile deuise a speech.   *he studies.*
 Vin. [*Aside.*]   Inspire him folly.
 Bass. Or tis no matter, be but bold enough,
And laugh when she laughs, and it is enough: 75
Ile fetch her to you.   *Exit.*
 Vin. Now was there ever such a demilance,
To beare a man so cleare through thicke and thinne?

        Enter Bassiolo.

 Bass. Or harke you sir, if she should steale a laughter
Vnder her fanne, thus you may say, sweete Lady,   80
If you will laugh and lie downe, I am pleasde.
 Vin. And so I were by heauen; how know you that?

58-59 And . . . fore part.] *Shepherd*; *as prose* (Is) ‖ **73** SD *Aside.*] *Parrott*

179

Bass. Slid man, Ile hit your very thoughts in these things.
Vin. Fetch her sweete friend, Ile hit your words I warrant.
Bass. Be bold then *Vince,* and presse her to it hard,   85
A shamefac'd man, is of all women barr'd.   *Exit.*
 Vin. How easly worthlesse men take worth vpon them,
And being ouer credulous of their owne worths,
Doe vnderprize as much the worth of others. /
The foole is rich, and absurd riches thinks   [F3ᵛ] 90
All merit is rung out, where his purse chinks.

    Enter Bassiolo and Margaret.

 Bass. My Lord, with much intreaty heeres my Lady.
Nay Maddam, looke not backe: why *Vince* I say?
 Mar. [*Aside.*] *Vince?* O monstrous ieast!
 Bass.   To her for shame.
 Vin. Lady, your backe part is as sweete to me   95
As all your fore part.
 Bass. [*Aside.*] He miss'd a little: he said
Her back part was sweet, when he should haue said faire;
But see, she laughs most fitly, to bring in the tother: —
Vince, to her againe, she laughs.
 Vin.   Laugh you faire Dame?
If you will laugh and lie downe, I am pleasde.   100
 Mar. What villanous stuffe is heere?
 Bass. Sweete Mistris of meere grace imbolden now
The kind young Prince heere, it is onely loue
Vpon my protestation, that thus daunts
His most Heroicke spirit: so a while   105
Ile leaue you close together; *Vince* I say —   *Exit.*
 Mar. O horrible hearing, does he call you *Vince?*
 Vin. O I, what else? and I made him imbrace me,
Knitting a most familiar league of friendship.
 Mar. But wherefore did you court me so absurdly?   110
 Vin. Gods me, he taught me, I spake out of him.
 Mar. O fie vpon't, could you for pitty make him
Such a poore creature? twas abuse enough
To make him take on him such sawcie friendship;
And yet his place is great; for hees not onely   115
My fathers Vsher, but the worlds beside,
Because he goes before it all in folly.
 Vin. Well, in these homely wiles, must our loues maske,
Since power denies him his apparant right.

84 warrant.] ∼, ‖ **94** SD *Aside.*] *Parrott* ‖ **96** SD *Aside.*] *Parrott* ‖ **96-99** He ... laughs.] He ... when / He ... fitly, / To ... laughs. Q (her ... but ... to) ‖ **98** tother:—] ∼:∧ ‖ **106** say—] ∼ *long dash connecting to Exit.* ‖

180

Mar. But is there no meane to dissolue that power,   120
And to preuent all further wrong to us,
Which it may worke, by forcing Mariage rites,
Betwixt me and the Duke?
   Vin.   No meane but one, /
And that is closely to be maried first,   [F4]
Which I perceiue not how we can performe: 125
For at my fathers comming backe from hunting,
I feare your father and himselfe resolue,
To barre my interest with his present nuptialls.
   Mar. That shall they neuer doe; may not we now
Our contract make, and marie before heauen?   130
Are not the lawes of God and Nature, more
Than formall lawes of men? are outward rites,
More vertuous then the very substance is
Of holy nuptialls solemnizde within?
Or shall lawes made to curbe the common world,   135
That would not be contain'd in forme without them,
Hurt them that are a law vnto themselves?
My princely loue, tis not a Priest shall let vs:
But since th'eternall acts of our pure soules,
Knit vs with God, the soule of all the world,   140
He shall be Priest to vs; and with such rites
As we can heere deuise, we will expresse,
And strongly ratifie our hearts true vowes,
Which no externall violence shall dissolue.
   Vin. This is our onely meane t'enioy each other: 145
And, my deare life, I will deuise a forme
To execute the substance of our mindes,
In honor'd nuptialls. First then hide your face
With this your spotlesse white and virgin vaile:
Now this my skarfe Ile knit about your arme,   150
As you shall knit this other end on mine,
And as I knit it, heere I vow by Heauen,
By the most sweete imaginarie ioyes,
Of vntride nuptialls; by loues ushering fire,
Fore-melting beautie, and loues flame it selfe,   155
As this is soft and pliant to your arme
In a circumferent flexure, so will I
Be tender of your welfare and your will,
As of mine owne, as of my life and soule,

155 selfe,] ∼. ‖

In all things, and for euer; onelie you   160
Shall haue this care in fulnesse, onely you /
Of all dames shall be mine, and onely you   [F4ᵛ]
Ile court, commend and ioy in, till I die.
    Mar. With like conceit on your arme this I tie,
And heere in sight of heauen, by it I sweare,   165
By my loue to you, which commands my life,
By the deare price of such a constant husband,
As you have vowed to be: and by the ioy
I shall imbrace by all meanes to requite you:
Ile be as apt to gouerne as this silke,   170
As priuate as my face is to this vaile,
And as farre from offence, as this from blacknesse:
I will be courted of no man but you,
In, and for you, shall be my ioyes and woes:
If you be sicke, I will be sicke, though well: 175
If you be well, I will be well, though sicke:
Your selfe alone my compleat world shall be,
Euen from this houre, to all eternity.
  *   *Vin.* It is inough and binds as much as marriage.

              Enter Bassiolo.

    Bass. Ile see in what plight my poore louer stands,   180
Gods me! a beckons me to have me gone,
It seems hees entred into some good vaine:
Ile hence, loue cureth when he vents his paine.   *Exit.*
    Vin. Now my sweet life, we both remember well
What we have vow'd shall all be kept entire   185
Maugre our fathers wraths, danger and death:
And to confirme this, shall we spend our breath?
Be well advisde, for yet your choice shall be
In all things as before, as large and free.
    Mar. What I have vow'd, Ile keepe euen past my death.   190
    Vin. And I: and now in token I dissolue
Your virgin state, I take this snowie vaile,
From your much fairer face, and claime the dues
Of sacred nuptialls: and now fairest heauen,
As thou art infinitely raisde from earth,   195
Diffrent and opposite, so blesse this match,
As farre remou'd from Customes popular sects,
And as vnstaind with her abhorr'd respects.

---

174 you,] *Q(u)*; ∼∧ *Q(c)* ‖ **177** alone] *Q(c)*; ∼, *Q(u)* ‖ **191** I:] *Q(c)*; ∼, *Q(u)* ‖ **196** Diffrent]
Q(c); different *Q(u)* ‖

Enter Bassiolo.

Bass. Mistris, away, *Pogio* runnes vp and downe, /
Calling for Lord *Vincentio*; come away,   [G1] 200
For hitherward he bends his clamorous haste.
   Mar. Remember loue.   *Exit Mar. and Bassiolo.*
   Vin.   Or else forget me heauen.
Why am I sought for by this *Pogio?*
The Asse is great with child of some ill newes,
His mouth is never fill'd with other sound.   205

Enter Pogio.

   Pog. Where is my Lord *Vincentio,* where is my Lord?
   Vin. Here he is Asse, what an exclaiming keep'st thou?
   Pog. Slood, my Lord, I haue followed you vp and downe like a
Tantalus pig, till I have worne out my hose here abouts, Ile be sworne,
and yet you call me Asse still; But I can tell you passing ill newes my   210
Lord.
   Vin. I know that well sir, thou neuer bringst other; whats your
newes now, I pray?
   Pog. O Lord, my Lord vncle is shot in the side with an arrow.
   Vin. Plagues take thy tongue, is he in any danger?   215
   Pog. O danger; I, he haz lien speechlesse this two houres, and talkes
so idlely.
   Vin. Accursed newes, where is he, bring me to him.
   Pog. Yet, do you lead, and Ile guide you to him.   *Exeunt.*

[IV.iii]

Enter Strozza; brought in a Chaire, Cynanche,
with others.

   Cyn. How fares it now with my deare Lord and husband?
   Stro. Come neere me wife, I fare the better farre
For the sweete foode of thy diuine advice,
Let no man value at a little price
A vertuous womans counsaile, her wing'd spirit   5
Is featherd oftentimes with heauenly words;
And (like her beautie) rauishing, and pure.
The weaker bodie, still the stronger soule,
When good endeuours do her powers applie,

216-17 O . . . idlely.] O . . . houres, / And . . . idlely ‖ IV.iii] *Parrott* ‖ SD *Cynanche, with*
others.] Parrott; Cynanche, Benenemus, with others. ‖ **4** price] ∼. ‖

Her loue drawes neerest mans felicitie;   10
O what a treasure is a vertuous wife,
Discreet and louing; Not one gift on earth,
Makes a mans life so highly bound to heauen;
She giues him double forces, to endure
And to enjoy; by being one with him, /   15
Feeling his ioies and Griefes with equall sence;   [G1ᵛ]
And like the twins *Hypocrates* reports:
If he fetch sighes, she drawes her breath as short:
If he lament, she melts her selfe in teares:
If he be glad, she triumphs; if he stirre,   20
She moou's his way; in all things his sweete Ape:
And is in alterations passing strange,
Himselfe diuinely varied without change:
Gold is right pretious; but his price infects
With pride and auarice; *Aucthority* lifts   25
Hats from mens heades; and bowes the strongest knees,
Yet cannot bend in rule the weakest hearts;
Musicke delights but one sence, nor choice meats;
One quickly fades, the other stirre to sinne;
But a true wife, both sence and soule delights,   30
And mixeth not her good with any ill;
Her vertues (ruling hearts) all powres command;
All Store without her, leaues a man but poore;
And with her, Pouertie is exceeding Store;
No time is tedious with her, her true woorth   35
Makes a true husband thinke, his armes enfold
(With her alone) a compleate worlde of gold.
    Cyn. I wish (deare loue) I could deserue as much,
As your most kind conceipt hath well exprest:
But when my best is done, I see you wounded;   40
And neither can recure nor ease your pains.
    Stro. Cynanche, thy aduise hath made me well;
My free submission to the hand of heauen
Makes it redeeme me from the rage of paine.
For though I know the malice of my wound   45
Shootes still the same distemper through my vaines,
Yet the Iudiciall patience I embrace,
(In which my minde spreads her impassiue powres
Through all my suffring parts;) expels their frailetie;

---

10 felicitie;] ∼, ‖ **12** louing;] ∼, ‖ **22** alterations] *Shepherd*; alteratious | strange,] ∼. ‖ **28** sence, nor . . . meats;] ∼; Nor . . . ∼∧ (*See Textual Note*) ‖ **36** enfold] ∼; ‖

And rendering vp their whole life to my soule,   50
Leaues me nought else but soule; and so like her,
Free from the passions of my fuming blood.
    Cyn. Would God you were so; and that too much payne /
Were not the reason, you felt sence of none.   [G2]
    Stro. Thinkst thou me mad *Cynanche*? for mad men,   55
By paynes vngouernd, have no sence of payne.
But I, I tell you am quite contrary,
Easde with well gouerning my submitted payne.
Be cheerd then wife; and looke not for, in mee,
The manners of a common wounded man.   60
Humilitie hath raisde me to the starres;
In which (as in a sort of Cristall Globes)
I sit and see things hidde from humane sight.
I, euen the very accidents to come
Are present with my knowledge; the seuenth day   65
The arrow head will fall out of my side.
The seauenth day wife, the forked head will out.
    Cyn. Would God it would my Lord, and leaue you wel.
    Stro. Yes, the seuenth day, I am assurd it will:
And I shall liue, I know it; I thanke heaven,   70
I knowe it well; and ile teach my phisition,
To build his cures heereafter vpon heauen
More then on earthly medcines; for I knowe
Many thinges showne me from the op'ned skies,
That passe all arts. Now my phisition   75
Is comming to me, he makes friendly haste;
And I will well requite his care of mee.
    Cyn. How knowe you he is comming?
    Stro.   Passing well;
And that my deare friend lord *Vincentio*
Will presently come see me too; ile stay   80
(My good phisition) till my true friend come.
    Cyn. [*Aside.*] Ay me, his talke is idle; and I feare,
Foretells his reasonable Soule now leaues him.
    Stro. Bring my Physition in, hee's at the doore.
    Cyn. Alas, theres no Physition.
    Stro.   But I know it;   85
See, he is come.

53 payne] ∼. ‖ **72** cures] *Parrott*; cares ‖ **78-79** Passing . . . *Vincentio*] *Shepherd*; *one line* (and) ‖ **82** SD *Aside.*] *Parrott* ‖

Enter Beneuenius.

Ben.   How fares my worthy Lord?

Stro. Good Doctor, I endure no paine at all,
And the seauenth day, the arrowes head will out.

    Ben. Why should it fall out the seuenth day my Lord? /

    Stro. I know it; the seuenth day it will not faile.   [G2ᵛ] 90

    Ben. I wish it may my Lord.

    Stro.   Yes, t'will be so,
You come with purpose to take present leaue,
But you shall stay a while; my Lord *Vincentio*
Would see you faine, and now is comming hither.

    Ben. How knowes your Lordship? haue you sent for him?   95

    Stro. No, but t'is very true; hee's now hard by,
And will not hinder your affaires a whit.

    Ben. [*Aside.*] How want of rest distempers his light braine? —
Brings my Lord any traine?

    Stro.   None but himselfe.
My nephew *Pogio* now hath left his Grace.   100
Good Doctor go, and bring him by his hand,
(Which he will giue you) to my longing eyes.

    Ben. Tis strange, if this be true.   *Exit.*

    Cyn.   The Prince I thinke,
Yet knowes not of your hurt.

Enter Vincentio holding the Doctors hand.

    Stro.   Yes wife, too well,
See he is come; welcome my princely friend: 105
I haue beene shot my Lord, but the seuenth day
The arrowes head will fall out of my side,
And I shall liue.

    Vin.   I do not feare your life,
But, Doctor, is it your opinion,
That the seuenth day the arrow head will out?   110

    Stro. No, t'is not his opinion, t'is my knowledge:
For I doe know it well; and I do wish
Euen for your onely sake, my noble Lord,
This were the seuenth day; and I now were well,
That I might be some strength to your hard state,   115
For you haue many perils to endure:
Great is your danger; great; your vniust ill
Is passing foule and mortall; would to God
My wound were something well, I might be with you,

---

86 SD *Beneuenius*] *Beneuemius* Q(c); *Beneuemisu* Q(u) ‖ **94** hither.] ∼: ‖ **98** SD *Aside.*] *Parrott* ‖ braine?—] ∼?∧ ‖ **102** eyes.] ∼, ‖

Nay do not whisper; I know what I say,   120
Too well for you, my Lord; I wonder heauen /
Will let such violence threat an innocent life.   [G3]
    Vin. What ere it be, deare friend, so you be well,
I will endure it all; your wounded state
Is all the daunger I feare towards me.   125
    Stro. Nay, mine is nothing; For the seuenth day
This arrow head will out, and I shall liue,
And so shall you, I thinke; but verie hardly.
It will be hardly, you will scape indeed.
    Vin. Be as will be; pray heauen your prophecie   130
Be happily accomplished in your selfe,
And nothing then can come amisse to me.
    Stro. What sayes my Doctor? thinks he I say true?
    Ben. If your good Lordship could but rest a while,
I would hope well.
    Stro.   Yes, I shall rest I know,   135
If that will helpe your iudgement.
    Ben.   Yes, it will,
And good my Lord, lets helpe you in to trie.
    Stro. You please me much, I shall sleepe instantly.   *Exeunt.*

[IV.iv]

Enter Alphonso, and Medice.

    Alp. Why should the humorous boy forsake the chace?
As if he tooke aduantage of my absence,
To some act that my presence would offend.
    Med. I warrant you my Lord, t'is to that end:
And I beleeue he wrongs you in your loue.   5
Children presuming on their parents kindnesse,
Care not what vnkind actions they commit
Against their quiet: and were I as you,
I would affright my sonne from these bold parts,
And father him as I found his deserts.   10
    Alp. I sweare I will: and can I proue he aymes
At any interruption in my loue,
Ile interrupt his life.
    Med.   We soone shall see,
For I haue made Madam *Corteza* search

IV.iv] *Parrott* ‖

With pick-locks, all the Ladies Cabynets   15
About Earle *Lassos* house; and if there be
Traffique of loue, twixt any one of them, /
And your suspected sonne; t'will soone appeare,   [G3ᵛ]
In some signe of their amorous marchandise;
See where she comes, loded with Iems and papers.   20

Enter Cort.

   Cort. See here, my Lord, I have rob'd all their Caskets,
Know you this Ring? this Carquanet? this Chaine?
Will any of these letters serue your turne?
   Alp. I know not these things; but come: let me reade
Some of these letters.
   Med.   Madam, in this deed   25
You deserue highly of my Lord the Duke.
   Cort. Nay my Lord *Medice,* I thinke I told you
I could do prettie well in these affaires:
O these yong Girles engrosse vp all the loue
From us, (poore Beldams;) but I hold my hand,   30
Ile ferret all the Cunni-holes of their kindnesse
Ere I haue done with them.
   Alp.   Passion of death!
See, see, Lord *Medice,* my trait'rous sonne,
Hath long ioyde in the fauours of my loue:
Woe to the wombe that bore him: and my care   35
To bring him vp to this accursed houre,
In which all cares possesse my wretched life.
   Med. What father, would beleeue he had a sonne
So full of trecherie to his innocent state?
And yet my Lord, this letter shewes no meeting,   40
But a desire to meete.
   Cort.   Yes, yes, my Lord,
I doe suspect they meete; and I beleeue
I know well where too; I beleeue I doe;
And therefore tell me; does no creature know,
That you have left the chase thus suddenly?   45
And are come hither? haue you not beene seene
By any of these Louers?
   Alp.   Not by any.
   Cort. Come then, come follow me; I am perswaded
I shall go neare to shew you their kind hants.

20 SD *Enter*] ∼. ‖ **25** Some] some | *Med.*] *MS correction in DFo, CSmH copies of Q; Lass.* ‖ **49** hants] *Parrott conj.*; hands ‖

Their confidence, that you are still a hunting,   50
Will make your amorous sonne that stole from thence, /
Bold in his loue-sports; Come, come, a fresh chace,   [G4]
I hold this pickelocke, you shall hunt at view.
What, do they thinke to scape? An old wiues eye
Is a blew Cristall full of sorcerie.   55
    Alp. If this be true, the traitrous boy shall die.   *Exeunt.*

[IV.v]

Enter Lasso, Margaret, Bassiolo going before.

    Lass. Tell me I pray you, what strange hopes they are
That feed your coy conceits against the Duke,
And are prefer'd before th'assured greatnes
His highnesse graciously would make your fortunes?
    Mar. I haue small hopes, my Lord; but a desire   5
To make my nuptiall choice of one I loue,
And as I would be loath t'impaire my state;
So I affect not honours that exceed it.
    Lass. O you are verie temp'rate in your choice,
Pleading a iudgement past your sexe, and yeares.   10
But I beleeue some fancie will be found,
The forge of these gay Gloses: if it be,
I shall decipher what close traitor tis
That is your Agent in your secret plots —
    Bass. [*Aside.*] Swoones.   15
    Lass. And him for whom you plot; and on you all
I will reuenge thy disobedience,
With such seuere correction, as shall fright
All such deluders from the like attempts:
But chiefly he shall smart that is your factor.   20
    Bass. [*Aside.*] O me, accurst!
    Lass.   Meane time Ile cut
Your poore craft short yfaith.
    Mar.   Poore craft indeede,
That I, or any others, vse for me.
    Lass. Well Dame, if it be nothing but the iarre
Of your vnfitted fancie, that procures   25
Your wilfull coynesse to my Lord the Duke,
No doubt but Time, and Iudgement will conforme it

54 What,] ∼∧ ‖ **IV.v]** ‖ **14** plots—] ∼. ‖ **15** SD *Aside.*] *Parrott* ‖ **21** SD *Aside.*] *Parrott* ‖ **23** others, vse] ∼∧ ∼, ‖

To such obedience, as so great desert
Proposde to your acceptance doth require.
To which end doe you counsaile her *Bassiolo.* /   30
And let me see Maid gainst the Duks returne,   [G4ᵛ]
Another tincture set vpon your lookes
Then heretofore; For be assur'd, at last
Thou shalt consent, or else incurre my curse:
Aduise her, you *Bassiolo.*   *Exit.*
    Bass.   I, my good Lord;   35
[*Aside.*] Gods pittie, what an errant Asse was I,
To entertaine the Princes craftie friendship?
Slood, I halfe suspect, the villaine guld me.
    Mar. Our squire I thinke is startl'd.
    Bass.   Nay Ladie it is true,
And you must frame your fancie to the Duke,   40
For I protest I will not be corrupted,
For all the friends and fortunes in the world,
To gull my Lord that trusts me.
    Mar.   O sir, now,
Y'are true too late.
    Bass.   No Ladie, not a whit,
Slood, and you thinke to make an Asse of me,   45
May chance to rise betimes; I know't, I know.
    Mar. Out seruile coward, shall a light suspect,
That hath no slendrest proofe of what we do,
Infringe the weightie faith that thou hast sworne,
To thy deare friend the Prince that dotes on thee?   50
And will in peeces cut thee for thy falshood.
    Bass. I care not; Ile not hazard my estate,
For any Prince on earth: and Ile disclose
The complot to your father, if you yeeld not
To his obedience.
    Mar.   Doe if thou dar'st,   55
Even for thy scrapt up liuing, and thy life,
Ile tell my father then, how thou didst wooe me
To loue the yong Prince; and didst force me too,
To take his Letters; I was well enclin'd,
I will be sworne before, to loue the Duke,   60
But thy vile railing at him, made me hate him.
    Bass. I raile at him?
    Mar.   I marie did you sir, /
And said he was a patterne for a Potter,   [H1]

---

30 *Bassiolo*] *Bassio lo* ‖ 33 assur'd,] ∼∧ ‖ 36 SD *Aside.*] *Parrott* ‖ 38 me.] ∼; ‖ 46 know't,] ∼∧
(*See Textual Note*) ‖ 50 thee?] ∼; ‖ 51 falshood.] ∼; ‖

Fit t'haue his picture stampt on a stone Iugge,
To keepe *Ale-knights* in memorie of Sobriety.   65
    Bass. Sh'as a plaguie memory.
    Mar. I could haue lou'd him else; nay, I did loue him,
Though I dissembled it, to bring him on,
And I by this time might have beene a Dutchesse;
And now I thinke on't better: for reuenge,   70
Ile haue the Duke, and he shall haue thy head,
For thy false wit within it, to his loue.
Now goe and tell my Father, pray be gone.
    Bass. Why and I will goe.
    Mar. Goe, for Gods sake goe, are you heere yet?   75
    Bass. Well, now I am resolu'd.
    Mar. Tis brauely done, farewell: but do you heare sir?
Take this with you besides; the young Prince keepes
A certaine letter you had writ for me,
(Endearing, and Condoling, and Mature)   80
And if you should denie things, that I hope
Will stop your impudent mouth: but goe your waies,
If you can answer all this, why tis well.
    Bass. Well Lady, if you will assure me heere,
You will refraine to meete with the young Prince,   85
I will say nothing.
    Mar.   Good sir, say your worst,
For I will meete him, and that presently.
    Bass. Then be content I pray, and leaue me out,
And meete heereafter as you can your selues.
    Mar. No, no sir, no, tis you must fetch him to me,   90
And you shal fetch him, or Ile do your arrand.
    Bass. [*Aside.*] Swounds what a spight is this, I will resolue
T'endure the worst; tis but my foolish feare,
The plot will be discouerd: O the gods!
Tis the best sport to play with these young dames; —   95
I have dissembl'd, Mistris, all this while
Haue I not made you in a pretty taking?
    Mar. O tis most good; thus you may play on me;
You cannot be content to make me loue   /
A man I hated till you spake for him,   [H1ᵛ] 100
With such inchanting speeches, as no friend
Could possibly resist: but you must vse
Your villanous wit, to driue me from my wits:

64 Iugge,] *Q(c)*; iugge, *Q(u)* ‖ **65** Sobriety] *Q(c)*; sobriety *Q(u)* ‖ **66** Sh'as] *Q(c)*; S'has *Q(u)* ‖ **69** time] *Q(c)*; ~, *Q(u)* ‖ **91** arrand] *Q(c)*; errant *Q(u)* ‖ **92** SD *Aside.*] *Parrott* ‖ **94** gods!] *Q(c)*; ~, *Q(u)* ‖ **95** dames;—] ~;∧ ‖

A plague of that bewitching tongue of yours;
Would I had neuer heard your scuruie words.   105
   Bass. Pardon deare Dame, Ile make amends ifaith,
Thinke you that Ile play false with my deare *Vince?*
I swore that sooner *Hybla* should want bees,
And *Italy* bone robes, then I faith;
And so they shall.   110
Come, you shall meete, and double meete, in spight
Of all your foes, and Dukes that dare maintaine them,
A plague of all old doters, I disdaine them.
   Mar. Said like a friend; O let me combe the cokscombe.   *Exeunt.*

Finis Actus Quarti.

ACTVS QVINTI SCÆNA PRIMA

Enter Alphonso, Medice, Lasso, Corteza aboue.

   Cort. Heere is the place will doe the deede ifaith;
This Duke will shew thee how youth puts downe age,
I, and perhaps how youth does put downe youth.
   Alp. If I shall see my loue in any sort
Preuented, or abusde, th'abuser dies.   5
   Lass. I hope there is no such intent my Liege,
For sad as death should I be to behold it.
   Med. You must not be too confident my Lord,
Or in your daughter, or in them that guard her.
The Prince is politike, and enuies his Father: 10
And though not for himselfe, nor any good
Intended to your daughter, yet because
He knowes t'would kill his father, he would seeke her.
   Cort. Whist, whist, they come.

Enter Bassiolo, Vincentio, and Margaret.

   Bass.   Come, meete me boldly, come,
And let them come from hunting when they dare. /   15
   Vin. Haz the best spirit.   [H2]
   Bass.   Spirit? what a plague,
Shall a man feare Capriches? [*To Margaret.*] you forsooth
Must haue your loue come t'ee, and when he comes,
Then you grow shamefac'd, and he must not touch you:

---

109 I faith;] *Parrott;* ~; ~∧ *Q(c);* ~, ~∧ *Q(u) (See Textual Note)* ‖ **113** them.] ~: ‖ V.i.
SD *Corteza*] *Cortezza* ‖ **17** SD *To Margaret.*] ‖

But fie, my Father comes, and foe, my Aunt,   20
O t'is a wittie hearing, ist not thinke you?
   Vin. Nay, pray thee doe not mocke her gentle friend.
   Bass. Nay, you are euen as wise a wooer too,
If she turne from you, you euen let her turne,
And say; you do not loue to force a Lady.   25
T'is too much rudenesse; gosh hat, what's a Lady?
Must she not be touch'd? what, is she copper thinke you?
And will not bide the touch-stone? kisse her *Vince,*
And thou doost love me, kisse her.
   Vin.   Lady, now
I were too simple if I should not offer.   30
   Mar. O God sir, pray away, this man talks idlely.
   Bass. How shay by that; now by that candle there,
Were I as *Vince* is, I would handle you
In ruftie tuftie wise, in your right kinde.
   Mar. [*Aside.*] O, you haue made him a sweete beagle, ha'y not?   35
   Vin. [*Aside.*] T'is the most true beleeuer in himselfe:
Of all that sect of follie faith's his fault.
   Bass. So, to her *Vince,* I give thee leaue my lad,
         Sweete were the words my mistris spake,
           When teares fell from her eyes.   *He lies down by them.*
Thus, as the Lyon lies before his den,
Guarding his whelps, and streakes his carelesse limbs,
And when the Panther, Foxe, or Wolfe comes neere,
He neuer daines to rise, to fright them hence,
But onely puts forth one of his sterne pawes,   45
And keepes his deare whelps safe, as in a hutch,
So I present his person, and keepe mine.
Foxes, goe by, I put my terror forth.   *Cant.*
        Let all the world say what they can,
          Her bargaine best she makes,   50
        That hath the wit to choose a man,
          To pay for that he takes.
               Belle Piu. &c. iterum cant. /
Dispatch sweete whelps the bug, the Duke comes strait: [H2ᵛ]
O tis a grave old louer that same Duke,
And chooses Minions rarely, if you marke him.   55
The noble *Medice,* that man, that Bobbadilla,
That foolish knaue, that hose and dublet stinckard.

26 gosh hat] *stet (See Textual Note)* || **32** shay by] *stet (See Textual Note)* || **34** ruftie] *Q(c)*; ~, *Q(u)* || **35** SD *Aside.*] *Parrott* || **36** SD *Aside.*] *Parrott* | T'is ... himselfe:] *Q(c)*; T's ... ~, *Q(u)* || **37** follie] *Q(c)*; ~; *Q(u)* || **39-40** Sweete ... eyes.] *Shepherd; one line* || **40** SD *He ... them.*] *Q(c); om. Q(u)* || **48** Foxes,] *Q(c)*; ~∧ *Q(u)* | forth.] ~, || **49-52** Let ... takes.] *Parrott; as dialogue* || **53** strait:] *Q(c)*; ~, *Q(u)* ||

Med. Swounds my Lord, rise, lets indure no more.
    Alp. A little, pray my Lord, for I beleeue
We shall discouer very notable knauery.   60
    Lass. Alas how I am greeu'd and sham'd in this.
    Cort. Neuer care you Lord brother, theres no harme done.
    Bass. But that sweet Creature, my good Lords sister,
Madam *Corteza,* she, the noblest Dame
That euer any veine of honour bled;   65
There were a wife now, for my Lord the Duke
Had he the grace to choose her, but indeede,
To speake her true praise, I must vse some study.
    Cort. Now truly brother, I did euer thinke
This man the honestest man that ere you kept.   70
    Lass. So sister, so, because he praises you.
    Cort. Nay sir, but you shall heare him further yet.
    Bass. Were not her head sometimes a little light,
And so vnapt for matter of much weight,
She were the fittest, and the worthiest Dame   75
To leape a window, and to breake her necke,
That euer was.
    Cort.   Gods pitty, arrant knaue,
I euer thought him a dissembling varlot.
    Bass. Well, now my hearts be warie, for by this,
I feare the Duke is comming; Ile go watch,   80
And give you warning: I commend me t'ee.   *Exit.*
    Vin. O fine phrase.
    Mar.   And very timely vsde.
    Vin. What now sweete life, shall we resolue vpon?
We neuer shall inioy each other heere.
    Mar. Direct you then my Lord, what we shall doe,   85
For I am at your will, and will indure
With you, the cruellst absence, from the state
We both were borne too, that can be supposde. /
    Vin. That would extreamely greeue me; could my selfe   [H3]
Onely indure the ill, our hardest fates   90
May lay on both of vs, I would not care;
But to behold thy sufferance, I should die.
    Mar. How can your Lordship wrong my loue so much,
To thinke the more woe I sustaine for you,
Breedes not the more my comfort? I alas   95
Haue no meane else, to make my merit euen
In any measure, with your eminent worth.

---

63 sweet Creature,] *Q(c);* sweete creature *Q(u)* ‖ 64 *Corteza*] *Cortezza* ‖ 70 honestest] *Q(c);*
honest *Q(u)* ‖ 82 phrase.] ∼, ‖ 83 *Vin.*] *Q(c); Vnn Q(u)* ‖ 89 me;] ∼, ‖ 90 fates] ∼, ‖ 91 vs,
. . . care;] ∼; . . . ∼, ‖ 97 eminent] eniment ‖

Enter Bassiolo.

Bass. [*Aside.*] Now must I exercise my timorous louers,
Like fresh arm'd souldiers, with some false alarms,
To make them yare and warie of their foe   100
The boistrous bearded Duke: Ile rush vpon them
With a most hideous cry, — the Duke, the Duke, the Duke,
Ha, ha, ha, wo ho, come againe I say,
The Duke's not come ifaith.
    Vin.   Gods precious man,
What did you meane to put vs in this feare?   105
    Bass. O sir, to make you looke about the more;
Nay, we must teach you more of this I tell you:
What, can you be too safe sir? what I say,
Must you be pamperd in your vanities?
[*Aside.*] Ah, I do domineere and rule the rost.   *Exit.*
    Mar. Was ever such an Ingle? would to God,
(If twere not for our selues) my father saw him.
    Lass. Minion, you haue your praier, and my curse,
For your good Huswiferie.
    Med.   What saies your Highnesse?
Can you indure these iniuries any more?   115
    Alp. No more, no more, aduise me what is best,
To be the penance of my gracelesse sonne?
    Med. My Lord, no meane but death or banishment,
Can be fit penance for him: if you meane
T'inioy the pleasure of your loue your selfe.   120
    Cort. Giue him plaine death my Lord, and then y'are sure.
    Alp. Death or his banishment, he shall indure,
For wreake of that ioyes exile I sustaine.
Come, call our Gard, and apprehend him strait.   *Exeunt. /*
    Vin. I haue some Iewells then my dearest life,   [H3ᵛ] 125
Which with what euer we can get beside,
Shall be our meanes, and we will make escape.

Enter Bassiolo running.

    Bass. Sblood, the Duke and all come now in earnest;
The Duke, by heauen, the Duke.
    Vin.   Nay, then ifaith
Your ieast is too too stale.
    Bass.   Gods pretious,   130
By these ten bones, and by this hat and heart,
The Duke and all comes, see, we are cast away.   [*Exeunt Vin. and Bass.*]

---

98 SD *Aside.*] *Parrott* ‖ **101** Duke:] *Q(c)*; ∼, *Q(u)* ‖ **102** cry,—] ∼,∧ ‖ **110** SD *Aside.*] *Parrott* | do domineere] *Q(c)*; doe dominere *Q(u)* ‖ **111** Ingle?] *Q(c)*; ∼, *Q(u)* ‖ **114** Huswiferie] *Q(c)*; huswiferie *Q(u)* ‖ **124** Gard] *Q(c)*; guard *Q(u)* ‖ **129** heauen,] *Q(c)*; ∼∧ *Q(u)* ‖ **132** SD *Exeunt . . . Bass.*] *Exeunt.* ‖

Enter Alphonso, Medice, Lasso, Cortezza, and Iulio.

Alp. Lay hands vpon them all, pursue, pursue.

Lass. Stay thou vngracious girle.

Alp.   Lord *Medice,*
Leade you our Guard, and see you apprehend   135
The treacherous boy, nor let him scape with life,
Vnlesse he yeelde to his externall exile.

Med. Tis princely said my Lord.   *Exit.*

Lass.   And take my Vsher.

Mar. Let me goe into exile with my Lord,
I will not liue, if I be left behinde.   140

Lass. Impudent Damzell, wouldst thou follow him?

Mar. He is my husband, whom else should I follow?

Lass. Wretch, thou speakest treason to my Lord the Duke.

Alp. Yet loue me Lady, and I pardon all.

Mar. I haue a husband, and must loue none else.   145

Alp. Dispightfull Dame, Ile dis-inherit him,
And thy good Father heere shall cast off thee,
And both shall feede on ayre, or starue, and die.

Mar. If this be iustice, let it be our doomes:
If free and spotlesse loue in equall yeares,   150
With honours vnimpaired deserve such ends,
Let vs approue what iustice is in friends.

Lass. You shall I sweare: sister, take you her close
Into your chamber, locke her fast alone,
And let her stirre nor speake with any one.   155

Cort. She shall not brother: come Neece, come with me. /

Mar. Heauen save my loue, and I will suffer gladly. *Exeunt Cor. Mar.* [H4]

Alp. Haste *Iulio,* follow thou my sons pursuit,
And will Lord *Medice* not to hurt nor touch him,
But either banish him, or bring him backe: 160
Charge him to vse no violence to his life.

Iulio. I will my Lord.   *Exit Iulio.*

Alp.   O Nature! how alas
Art thou and Reason thy true guide opposde?
More bane thou tak'st, to guide Sense, led amisse,
Then being guided, Reason gives thee blisse.   *Exeunt.*

---

137 externall exile] *stet* (*See Textual Note*) ‖ **139** exile . . . Lord,] *Q(c)*; ∼, . . . ∼∧ *Q(u)* ‖
148 starue,] *Q(c)*; etarue *Q(u)* ‖ **157** SD *Exeunt Cor. Mar.*] *Q(c)*; *Ex. Co. Ma. Q(u)* ‖ **158** sons]
Q(c); sonnes *Q(u)* ‖

[V.ii]

Enter Cynanche, Beneuenius, Ancilla, Strozza hauing the
Arrow head.

Stro. Now see good Doctor, t'was no frantike fancie,
That made my tongue presage this head should fall
Out of my wounded side the seuenth day;
But an inspired rapture of my minde,
Submitted and conioynde in patience,   5
To my Creator, in whom I fore-saw
(Like to an Angell) this diuine event.

   Ben. So is it plaine, and happily approu'd,
In a right christian president, confirming
What a most sacred medcine Patience is,   10
That with the high thirst of our soules cleare fire
Exhausts corporeall humour; and all paine,
Casting our flesh off, while we it retaine.

   Cyn. Make some religious vow then my deare Lord,
And keepe it in the proper memorie,   15
Of so Celestiall and free a grace.

   Stro. Sweete wife, thou restest my good Angell still,
Suggesting by all meanes, these ghostly counsailes.
Thou weariest not thy husbands patient eares,
With motions for new fashions in attire,   20
For change of Iewells, pastimes, and nice cates,
Nor studiest eminence, and the higher place
Amongst thy consorts, like all other Dames:
But knowing more worthy obiects appertaine
To euery woman that desires t'inioy   25
A blessed life in mariage: thou contemn'st /
Those common pleasures, and pursu'st the rare,   [H4ᵛ]
Vsing thy husband in those vertuous gifts:
For which, thou first didst choose him, and thereby
Cloy'st not with him, but lou'st him endlesly.   30
In reuerence of thy motion then, and zeale
To that most soueraigne power, that was my cure,
I make a vow to goe on foote to *Rome,*
And offer humbly in S. *Peters* Temple,

V.ii] *Parrott* ‖ **2** head] *Q(c)*; heade *Q(u)* ‖ **10** medcine] *Q(c)*; Medicine *Q(u)* ‖ **11** soules] ∼,
‖ **27** pursu'st] *Q(c)*; pursuest *Q(u)* ‖ **28** vertuous gifts:] *stet* (*See Textual Note*) ‖ **29** thereby]
Q(c); ∼, *Q(u)* ‖ **30** lou'st] *Q(c)*; louest *Q(u)* ‖ **32** cure,] *Q(u)*; ∼. *Q(c)* ‖

This fatall Arrow head: which work, let none iudge   35
A superstitious Rite, but a right vse,
Proper to this peculiar instrument,
Which visiblie resignde to memorie,
Through euery eye that sees, will stirre the soule
To Gratitude and Progresse, in the vse   40
Of my tried patience, which in my powers ending,
Would shut th'example out of future liues:
"No act is superstitious, that applies
"All power to God, deuoting hearts, through eyes.
    Ben. Spoke with the true tongue of a Nobleman: 45
But now are all these excitations toyes,
And Honor fats his braine with other ioyes.
I know your true friend, Prince *Vincentio,*
Will triumph in this excellent effect
Of your late prophecie.
    Stro.   O, my deare friends name   50
Presents my thoughts, with a most mortall danger,
To his right innocent life: a monstrous fact
Is now effected on him.
    Cyn.   Where? or how?
    Stro. I doe not well those circumstances know,
But am assur'd, the substance is too true.   55
Come reuerend Doctor, let vs harken out
Where the young Prince remaines, and beare with you
Medcines t'allay his danger: if by wounds,
Beare pretious Balsome, or some soueraigne iuyce;
If by fell poison, some choice *Antidote,*   60
If by blacke witchcraft, our good spirits and prayers
Shall exorcise the diuelish wrath of hell, /
Out of his princely bosome.   [I1]
                    Enter Pogio running.
    Pog.   Where? where? where?
Where's my Lord vncle, my Lord my vncle?
    Stro. Here's the ill tydings-bringer; what newes now,   65
With thy vnhappie presence?
    Pog.   O my Lord, my Lord *Vincentio,*
Is almost kild by my Lord *Medice.*
    Stro. See Doctor, see, if my presage be true.
And well I know if he haue hurt the Prince,
T'is trecherously done, or with much helpe.   70

35 Arrow . . . work] *Q(c)*; arrow . . . worke *Q(u)* ‖ 36 Rite,] *Q(c)*; rite *Q(u)* ‖ 42 liues:] *Q(u)*;
∼. *Q(c)* ‖ 43 "No] *Q(c) second state*; ∧∼ *Q(u) second state* ‖ 44 "All] *Q(c) second state*; ∧∼
Q(u) second state ‖ 46 excitations] *Q(c)*; ∼, *Q(u)* ‖ 47 Honor] *Q(c)*; honour *Q(u)* ‖ 48 *Vincentio,*]
Q(u); ∼∧ *Q(c)* ‖ 50 O,] *Q(c)*; ∼∧ *Q(u)* ‖ 53 Where?] *Q(c)*; where *Q(u)* ‖ 56 out] *Q(c)*; ∼,
Q(u) ‖ 57 remaines, . . . you] *Q(c)*; ∼∧ . . . ∼, *Q(u)* ‖ 58 *Medcines* . . . danger:] *Q(c)*; Med-
icines . . . ∼, *Q(u)* ‖ 63-64 Where? . . . vncle?] *Parrott*; *as prose* (where's) ‖ 66 With] with ‖
66-67 O . . . *Medice.*] *Parrott*; *one line* (is) ‖

Pog. Nay sure he had no helpe, but all the Dukes Guard; and they
set vpon him indeed; and after he had defended himselfe, dee see?
he drew, and hauing as good as wounded the Lord *Medice* almost, he
strake at him, and missd him, dee marke?

   Stro. What tale is here? where is this mischiefe done?   75

   Pog. At Monks-well, my Lord, Ile guide you to him presently.

   Stro. I doubt it not; fooles are best guides to ill,
And mischiefes readie way lies open still.
Lead sir I pray.   *Exeunt.*

[V.iii]

Enter Corteza, and Margaret aboue.

   Cort. Quiet your selfe, Nece; though your loue be slaine,
You have another that's woorth two of him.

   Mar. It is not possible; it cannot be
That heauen should suffer such impietie.

   Cort. T'is true, I sweare neece.

   Mar.   O most vniust truth!   5
Ile cast my selfe downe headlong from this Tower,
And force an instant passage for my soule,
To seeke the wandring spirit of my Lord.

   Cort. Will you do so Neece? That I hope you will not,
And yet there was a Maid in Saint *Marks* streete,   10
For such a matter did so; and her clothes
Flew vp about her so, as she had no harme:
And grace of God your clothes may flie vp too,
And save you harmlesse; for your cause and hers
Are ene as like as can be.

   Mar.   I would not scape;   15
And certainly I thinke the death is easie.

   Cort. O t'is the easiest death that euer was,
Looke Neece, it is so farre hence to the ground. /
You shoulde bee quite dead, long before you felt it.   [I1ᵛ]
Yet do not leape Neece.

   Mar.   I will kill my selfe   20
With running on some sworde; or drinke strong poison;
Which death is easiest I would faine endure.

   Cort. Sure *Cleopatra* was of the same minde,
And did so; she was honord euer since,
Yet do not you so Neece.   25

---

71 sure] *Q(c);* ∼, *Q(u)* ‖ **72** himselfe] him-/selfe ‖ **78** still.] *Q(c);* ∼. *Exeunt. Q(u)* ‖ **79** Lead
. . . pray.] *Q(c);* *om. Q(u)* ‖ V.iii] *Parrott* ‖ **12** harme:] *Q(c);* ∼. *Q(u)* ‖

Mar. Wretch that I am; my heart is softe and faint;
And trembles at the verie thought of death,
Though thoughts ten-folde more greeuous do torment it;
Ile feele death by degrees; and first deforme
This my accursed face with vglie wounds,   30
That was the first cause of my deare loues death.
   Cort. That were a cruell deed; yet *Adelasia*;
In *Pettis Pallace of Petit* pleasure,
For all the worlde, with such a knife as this
Cut off her cheeks, and nose, and was commended   35
More then all Dames that kept their faces whole;
O do not cut it.
   Mar.   Fie on my faint heart,
It will not giue my hand the wished strength;
Beholde the iust plague of a sensuall life,
That to preserue it selfe in Reasons spight,   40
And shunne deaths horror, feels it ten times more.
Vnworthy women, why doe men adore
Our fading Beauties, when their worthiest liues,
Being lost for vs, we dare not die for them?
Hence haplesse Ornaments that adorn'd this head: 45
Disorder euer these enticing curles
And leave my beautie like a wildernesse,
That neuer mans eie more may dare t'inuade.
   Cort. Ile tell you Neece; and yet I will not tell you,
A thing that I desire to haue you doe.   50
But I will tell you onely what you might doe,
Cause I would pleasure you in all I cud.
I haue an Ointment heere, which we Dames vse,
To take off haire when it does growe too lowe /
Vpon our foreheads, and that for a neede,   [I2] 55
If you should rub it hard vpon your face,
Would blister it, and make it looke most vildely.
   Mar. O giue me that Aunt.
   Cort. Giue it you virgin? that were well indeede:
Shall I be thought to tempt you to such matters?   60
   Mar. None (of my faith) shall know it: gentle Aunt,
Bestow it on me, and Ile ever loue you.
   Cort. Gods pitty, but you shall not spoile your face.
   Mar. I will not then indeede.
   Cort.   Why then Neece take it:

46 enticing curles] *Shepherd*; entring carles ‖ **58** giue] Giue ‖

But you shall sweare you will not.

   Mar.   No, I sweare.   65

   Cort. What, doe you force it from me? Gods my deare,

Will you mis-vse your face so? what, all ouer?

Nay, if you be so desp'rate, Ile be gone.   *Exit.*

   Mar. Fade haplesse beautie, turne the ugliest face

That euer *Aethiop,* or affrightfull fiend   70

Shew'd in th'amaz'd eye of prophan'd light:

See pretious Love, if thou be yet in ayre,

And canst breake darknesse, and the strongest Towres,

With thy dissolued intellectuall powres,

See a worse torment suffered for thy death,   75

Then if it had extended his blacke force,

In seuen-fold horror to my hated life.

Smart pretious ointment, smart, and to my braine

Sweate thy enuenom'd furie, make my eyes

Burne with thy sulphre, like the lakes of hell,   80

That feare of me may shiuer him to dust,

That eate his owne childe with the jawes of lust.   *Exit.*

[V.iv]

Enter Alphonso, Lasso, and others.

   Alp. I wonder how farre they pursu'd my Sonne,

That no returne of him or them appears,

I feare some haplesse accident is chanc'd,

That makes the newes so loath to pierce mine eares.

   Lass. High heauen vouchsafe no such effect succeede   5

Those wretched causes that from my house flow,

But that in harmelesse loue all acts may end.

Enter Corteza. /

   Cort. What shall I do? Alas I cannot rule   [12ᵛ]

My desparate Neece, all her sweete face is spoylde,

And I dare keepe her prisoner no more: 10

See, see, she comes frantike and all vndrest.

Enter Marg.

   Mar. [*Removing her mask*] Tyrant! behold how thou hast vsde thy loue,

See, theefe to Nature, thou hast kil'd and rob'd,

---

68 gone.] ∼∧ *long dash connecting to Exit.* ‖ **70** That] *Shepherd*; The ‖ **72** yet] *Parrott*; it ‖ **82**
lust.] ∼∧ *long dash connecting to Exeunt.* | *Exit.*] *Parrott*; *Exeunt.* ‖ V.iv] *Parrott* ‖ **7** SD *Corteza*]
Cortezza ‖ **10** more:] *Q(c)*; ∼; *Q(u)* ‖ **12** SD *Removing her mask*] | Tyrant!] *Q(c)*; ∼, *Q(u)* ‖

Kil'd what my selfe kill'd, rob'd what makes thee poore.
Beautie (a Louers treasure) thou hast lost   15
Where none can find it; all a poor Maides dowre
Thou hast forc'd from me: all my ioy and hope.
No man will loue me more; all Dames excell me,
This ougly thing is now no more a face,
Nor any vile forme in all Earth resembled,   20
But thy fowle tyrannie; for which all the paines
Two faithfull Louers feele, that thus are parted,
All ioyes they might haue felt, turne all to paines;
All a yong virgin thinks she does endure,
To loose her loue and beautie; on thy heart   25
Be heapt and prest downe till thy soule depart.

Enter Iulio.

  Iul. Haste Liege, your sonne is daungerously hurt.
Lord *Medice* contemning your commaund,
By me deliuered, as your Highnesse will'd,
Set on him with your Guard; who strooke him downe;   30
And then the coward Lord, with mortall wounds,
And slauish insolencie, plow'd vp his soft breast;
Which barbarous fact, in part is laid on you,
For first enioyning it, and fowle exclaimes
In pittie of your sonne, your subiects breathe   35
Gainst your vnnaturall furie; amongst whom
The good Lord *Strozza* desparately raues,
And vengeance for his friends iniustice craues.
See where he comes burning in zeale of friendship.

  Enter Strozza, Vincentio, brought in a chaire, Beneuenius,
  Pogio, Cynanche, with a guard, Strozza before and Medice.

  Stro. Where is the tyrant? let me strike his eyes   40
Into his braine, with horror of an obiect.
See Pagan *Nero*; see how thou hast ript
Thy better bosome; rooted vp that flowre, /
From whence thy now spent life should spring anew,   [13]
And in him kild, (that would haue bred thee fresh)   45
Thy mother and thy father.
  Vin.   Good friend cease.
  Stro. What hag with child of Monster, would haue nurst
Such a prodigous longing? But a father
Would rather eate the brawne out of his armes

14 poore.] *Q(c)*; ∼, *Q(u)* ‖ **15** lost] *Q(c)*; ∼, *Q(u)* ‖ **16** Maides dowre] ∼ ∼: *Q(c)*; Maide ∼ *Q(u)* ‖ **17** me: . . . hope.] *Q(c)*; ∼; . . . ∼, *Q(u)* ‖ **26** heapt . . . *Iulio.*] *Q(c)*; ∼, . . . *Inlio. Q(u)* ‖ **27** hurt.] *Q(c)*; ∼, *Q(u)* ‖ **29** deliuered,] *Q(c)*; ∼∧ *Q(u)* ‖ **37** desparately] *Q(u)*; desp'rately *Q(c)* ‖ **39** SD *Enter Strozza*] ∼ Srozza (*in Q proper names in SD in roman*) ‖

Then glut the mad worme of his wilde desires 50
With his deare issues entrailes.
    Vin.   Honourd friend;
He is my father, and he is my Prince,
In both whose rights he may commaund my life.
    Stro. What is a father? turne his entrailes gulfs
To swallow children, when they haue begot them? 55
And whats a Prince? Had all beene vertuous men,
There neuer had beene Prince vpon the earth,
And so no subiect; all men had been Princes:
A vertuous man is subiect to no Prince,
But to his soule and honour; which are lawes, 60
That carrie Fire and Sword within themselues
Neuer corrupted, never out of rule;
What is there in a Prince? That his least lusts
Are valued at the liues of other men,
When common faults in him should prodigies be, 65
And his grosse dotage rather loath'd then sooth'd.
    Alp. How thicke and heavily my plagues descend!
Not giuing my mazde powres a time to speake:
Poure more rebuke vpon me worthie Lord,
For I have guilt and patience for them all: 70
Yet know, deare sonne, I did forbid thy harme:
This Gentleman can witnes, whom I sent
With all command of haste to interdict
This forward man in mischiefe; not to touch thee:
Did I not *Iulio*? utter nought but truth. 75
    Iul. All your guard heard, my Lord, I gaue your charge,
With lowd and violent itterations.
After all which, Lord *Medice* cowardly hurt him.
    The Guard. He did my Princely Lord. /
    Alp.   Beleeue then sonne, [I3ᵛ]
And know me pierst as deeply with thy wounds: 80
And pardon vertuous Ladie that haue lost
The dearest treasure proper to your sexe.
Ay me, it seemes by my vnhappie meanes!
O would to God, I could with present cure
Of these vnnaturall wounds; and moning right 85
Of this abused beautie, ioyne you both,
(As last I left you) in eternall nuptials.

---

59 man] *Q(c)*; ∼, *Q(u)* ‖ **63** least] *Q(c)*; lest *Q(u)* ‖ **68** mazde ... speake:] *Q(c)*; Mazde ... ∼? *Q(u)* ‖

   Vin. My Lord, I know the malice of this man,
Not your vnkinde consent hath vsde vs thus.
And since I make no doubt I shall suruiue   90
These fatall dangers; and your grace is pleasde,
To giue free course to my vnwounded loue;
T'is not this outward beauties ruthfull losse,
Can any thought discourage my desires:
And therefore, deare life, doe not wrong me so,   95
To thinke my loue the shadow of your beautie,
I wooe your vertues, which as I am sure
No accident can alter or empaire;
So, be you certaine nought can change my loue.
   Mar. I know your honourable minde my Lord,   100
And will not do it that vnworthie wrong,
To let it spend her forces in contending
(Spite of your sence) to loue me thus deformed:
Loue must haue outward obiects to delight him,
Else his content will be too graue and sowre.   105
It is inough for me my Lord, you loue,
And that my beauties sacrifice redeemde
My sad feare of your slaughter. You first lou'd me
Closely for beautie; which being with'red thus,
Your loue must fade; when the most needfull rights   110
Of Fate, and Nature, haue dissolu'd your life,
And that your loue must needs be all in soule,
Then will we meete againe: and then (deare Loue)
Loue me againe; for then will beautie be
Of no respect with loues eternitie.   115
   Vin. Nor is it now; I wooed your beautie first /
But as a louer: now as a deare husband,   [I4]
That title and your vertues binde me euer.
   Mar. Alas, that title is of little force
To stirre vp mens affections: when wiues want   120
Outward excitements, husbands loues grow skant.
   Ben. Assist me Heauen, and Art; [*to Mar.*] giue me your Maske,
Open thou little store-house of great Nature,
Vse an Elixar drawne through seuen yeares fire,
That, like *Medeas* Cauldron, can repaire   125
The vgliest losse of liuing temp'rature:
And for this princely paire of vertuous Turtles,
Be lauish of thy pretious influence.

---

120 affections] *Shepherd*; affectious ‖ **122** Art;] ∼, | SD *to Mar.*] ‖ **128** influence.] ∼∧ ‖

Lady, t'attone your honourable strife,
And take all let from your loues tender eyes,   130
Let me for euer hide this staine of Beauty,
With this recureful Maske; heere be it fix'd
With painelesse operation; of it selfe,
(Your beauty hauing brook'd three daies eclips)
Like a dissolued clowd it shall fall off,   135
And your faire lookes regaine their freshest raies:
So shall your Princely friend, (if heauen consent)
In twice your sufferd date renue recure,
Let me then haue the honor to conioyne
Your hands, conformed to your constant hearts.   140
    Alp. Graue *Beneuenius*, honorable Doctor,
On whose most soueraigne *Aesculapian* hand,
Fame with her richest miracles attends,
Be fortunate, as euer heeretofore,
That we may quite thee both with gold and honour,   145
And by thy happy meanes, haue powre to make
My Sonne, and his much iniur'd loue amends,
Whose well proportion'd choice we now applaud,
And blesse all those that euer further'd it.
Where is your discreete Vsher my good Lord,   150
The speciall furtherer of this equall match?
    Iulio. Brought after by a couple of your Guard.
    Alp. Let him be fetch'd, that we may doe him grace.
    Pog. Ile fetch him my Lord: away, you must not go: O here / he   [14ᵛ]
comes; [*Enter Bassiolo guarded.*] O master Vsher, I am sorie for you, 155
you must presently be chopt in peeces.
    Bass. Wo to that wicked Prince that ere I saw him.
    Pog. Come, come, I gull you master Vsher, you are like to be the
Dukes Minion man; dee thinke I would haue beene seene in your com-
panie, and you had beene out of fauour? Here's my friend maister   160
Vsher, my Lord.
    Alp. Giue me your hand friend, pardon vs I pray,
We much haue wrong'd your worth, as one that knew
The fitnesse of this match aboue our selues.
    Bass. Sir, I did all things for the best, I sweare,   165
And you must thinke I would not have beene gul'd,
I know what's fit sir; as I hope you know now:
Sweete *Vince,* how far'st thou, be of honourd cheere.

---

130 eyes,] ∼. ‖ **152** *Iulio.*] ∼∧ ‖ **154** he] He ‖ **155** SD *Enter . . . guarded.*] *Parrott* ‖ **163-64**
We . . . selues.] *Shepherd; as prose* ‖ **167** now:] *Q(c)*; ∼, *Q(u)* ‖

Lass. *Vince* does he call him? O Foole, dost thou call
The Prince *Vince,* like his equall?
 Bass.   O my Lord, ahlas   170
You know not what haz past twixt vs two;
Here in thy bosome I will lie sweete *Vince,*
And die if thou die; I protest by heauen.
 Lass. I know not what this meanes.
 Alp.   Nor I my Lord:
But sure he saw the fitnes of the match,   175
With freer and more noble eies then we.
 Pog. Why I saw that as well as he, my Lord; I knew t'was a foolish
match betwixt you two; did not you thinke so, my Lord *Vincentio?*
Lord vncle, did not I say at first of the Duke; will his Antiquitie neuer
leave his Iniquitie?   180
 Stro. Go to, too much of this; but aske this Lord,
If he did like it.
 Pog.   Who, my Lord *Medice?*
 Stro. Lord *Stinkard,* Man, his name is; aske him Lord *Stinkard,*
did you like the match? say.
 Pog. My Lord *Stinkard,* did you like the match betwixt the Duke, 185
and my Ladie *Margaret?*
 Med. Presumptuous Sicophant, I will haue thy life.
 Alp. Vnworthie Lord, put up: thirst'st thou more blood?
Thy life is fitt'st to be call'd in question, /
For thy most murthrous cowardise on my sonne;   [K1] 190
Thy forwardnesse to euery cruelty
Calls thy pretended Noblesse in suspect.
 Stro. Noblesse my Lord? set by your princely fauour,
That gaue the lustre to his painted state;
Who euer view'd him but with deepe contempt,   195
As reading vilenesse in his very lookes?
And if he proue not sonne of some base drudge,
Trim'd vp by Fortune, being dispos'd to ieast
And dally with your state, then that good Angell,
That by diuine relation spake in me,   200
Fore-telling these foule dangers to your sonne,
And without notice brought this reuerend man
To rescue him from death, now failes my tongue,
And Ile confesse, I doe him open wrong.

---

170 ahlas] Ahlas ‖ **177** he,] *Q(u)*; ∼∧ *Q(c)* ‖ **178** so,] *Q(u)*; ∼∧ *Q(c)* ‖ **183** *Stinkard,* Man]
Shepherd; ∼∧ *Man* ‖ **187** Presumptuous] Presumptuons ‖ **194** state;] ∼, ‖ **203** death,] ∼: ‖

Med. And so thou doost; and I returne all note   205
Of infamy or basenesse on thy throte:
Damne me my Lord, if I be not a Lord.
   Stro. My Liege, with all desert, euen now you said
His life was duely forfet, for the death
Which in these barbarous wounds he sought your sonne;   210
Vouchsafe me then his life, in my friends right,
For many waies I know he merits death;
Which, (if you grant) will instantly appeare,
And that I feele with some rare miracle.
   Alp. His life is thine Lord *Strozza,* giue him death.   215
   Med. What my Lord, will your grace cast away an innocent life?
   Stro. Villaine thou liest, thou guiltie art of death
A hundred waies, which now Ile execute.
   Med. Recall your word my Lord.
   Alp.   Not for the world.
   Stro. O my deare Liege, but that my spirit prophetike   220
Hath inward feeling of such sinnes in him,
As aske the forfait of his life and soule,
I would, before I tooke his life, give leaue
To his confession, and his penitence:
O, he would tell you most notorious wonders, /   225
Of his most impious state; but life and soule   [K1ᵛ]
Must suffer for it in him, and my hand
Forbidden is from heauen to let him liue,
Till by confession he may have forgiuenesse.
Die therefore monster.
   Vin.   O be not so vncharitable sweete friend,   230
Let him confesse his sinnes, and aske heauen pardon.
   Stro. He must not Princely friend, it is heauens iustice
To plague his life and soule, and heer's heauens iustice.
   Med. O saue my life my Lord.
   Lass.   Hold good Lord *Strozza,*
Let him confesse the sinnes that heauen hath told you,   235
And aske forgiueness.
   Med.   Let me good my Lord,
And Ile confesse what you accuse me of;
Wonders indeede, and full of damn'd deserts.

215 giue] Giue ‖ **216** will] Will ‖ **228** heauen] *Q(c)*; ∼, *Q(u)* ‖ **234** *Strozza,*] *Q(c)*; ∼. *Q(u)* ‖

Stro. I know it, and I must not let thee liue
To aske forgivenesse.
   Alp.   But you shall my Lord,   240
Or I will take his life out of your hand.
   Stro. A little then I am content my Liege:
Is thy name *Medice?*
   Med.   No my Noble Lord,
My true name is *Mendice.*
   Stro.   *Mendice?* see,
At first a Mighty scandall done to Honour.   245
Of what countrie art thou?
   Med.   Of no Country, I,
But borne upon the Seas, my mother passing
Twixt *Zant* and *Venice.*
   Stro. Where wert thou christned?
   Med.   I was never christned,
But being brought vp with beggars, call'd *Mendice.* 250
   Alp. Strange, and vnspeakeable.
   Stro.   How cam'st thou then
To beare that port thou didst, entring this Court?
   Med. My lord, when I was young being able limb'd,
A Captaine of the Gipsies entertain'd me,
And many yeares I liu'd a loose life with them: 255
At last I was so fauor'd, that they made me
The King of Gipsies; and being told my fortune
By an old Sorceresse, that I should be great /
In some great Princes loue, I tooke the treasure [K2]
Which all our company of Gipsies had   260
In many yeares, by seuerall stealths collected,
And leauing them in warres, I liu'd abroad,
With no lesse shew then now: and my last wrong
I did to Noblesse, was in this high Court.
   Alp. Neuer was heard so strange a counterfet. 265
   Stro. Didst thou not cause me to be shot in hunting?
   Med. I did my Lord, for which, for heauens loue pardon.
   Stro. Now let him liue my Lord, his bloods least drop
Would staine your Court, more then the Sea could cleanse:
His soule's too foule to expiate with death.   270
   Alp. Hence then, be euer banish'd from my rule,
And liue a monster, loath'd of all the world.

---

246 Country,] *Q(c);* ∼∧ *Q(u)* ‖ **251** Strange,] *Q(c);* ∼∧ *Q(u)* ‖ **256** fauor'd,] *Q(c);* ∼∧
Q(u) ‖ **269** cleanse] *Q(c);* clense *Q(u)* ‖ **270** foule] *Q(c);* fowle *Q(u)* ‖

Pog. Ile get boyes and baite him out a'th Court my Lord.

Alp. Doe so I pray thee, rid me of his sight.

Pog. Come on my Lord *Stinckerd,* Ile play Fox, Fox, come out of   275
thy hole with you ifaith.

Med. Ile runne and hide me from the sight of heauen.

Pog. Fox, Fox, goe out of thy hole; a two leg'd Fox, a two leg'd Fox.

                                        Exit with Pages beating Medice.

Bene. Neuer was such an accident disclosde.

Alp. Let vs forget it honourable friends,   280
And satisfie all wrongs with my sonnes right,
In solemne mariage of his loue and him.

Vin. I humbly thanke your Highnesse; honor'd Doctor,
The Balsome you infusde into my wounds,
Hath easde me much, and giuen me sodaine strength   285
Enough t'assure all danger is exempt,
That any way may let the generall ioy,
My Princely Father speakes of in our nuptialls.

Alp. Which my deere Sonne shall with thy full recure
Be celebrate in greater Maiesty,   290
Than euer grac'd our greatest Ancestrie.
Then take thy loue, which heauen with all ioyes blesse,
And make yee both mirrors of happinesse.

FINIS.

278 Fox, a] ∼, A ‖ 283 Highnesse;] ∼∧ ‖

HISTORICAL COLLATION

[Editions collated: Shepherd (=S, in *The Works of George Chapman: Plays*, 1875, pp. 78-112); Parrott (=*P*¹, "*All Fooles*" *and* "*The Gentleman Usher*," 1907, pp. 146-280); Parrott (=*P*², in *The Plays and Poems of George Chapman: The Comedies* [1914], pp. 235-305; *P*=agreement of both Parrott editions). Only substantive and semi-substantive variants are recorded; obvious errors are not recorded. Lemmata are taken from the present text. Where lemma represents the reading of Q copy-text, omission of siglum indicates agreement with lemma.]

I.i

SD] *Before the House of Strozza* P
6 stolne] stolen *S, P*² (*not hereafter recorded*)
13 valure] valour *S, P*²
24 wehie] wehee *P*²
    tihi] tehee *P*²
25 ghest] guessed *S, P*
57 rude; Boares] *P* (*Daniel conj.*); ~∧ ~ *Q, S*
61 vertuous] venturous *Daniel conj.* (*in P*)
76 Here . . . friend.] *after SD Enter Vincentio. S, P*²
79 desprate] *Q(c)*; desperate *Q(u), S*
110 of any] *S, P*; nay of *Q*
111 he shames] *S, P*; she ~ *Q*
113 dublet] doubtlet *P*²
126 SD *poste.*] *poste-haste. P*
131 O ho] Oh, oh *S*
139 d'ee] d'ye (*not hereafter recorded*)
149 alone, and] ~. *to Strozza* And *P*¹
151 a] o' *P*² (*not hereafter recorded*)
153 newes,] ~? *S, P*
158 Signieur] Signor *S, P*² (*not hereafter recorded*)
178 warre: heere] war. *To Vincentio* Here *P*
179, 182 *Vin.*] *Vin. reads P*
189 throughly] thoroughly *S*
203 SD *Sarp. . . . . dress.*] *P*¹; *Sarpego puts on his parasite's costume P*²; *om. Q, S*
208 SD *Enter Sarp.*] *Re-enter Sarpego as Curculio P*¹; *Enter Sarpego running about the stage P*²
209 *Sarp.*] *Sar. running wildly about the stage P*¹
216 ventred] ventured *S*; ventur'd *P*²
234 SD *Alp. . . . . Med.*] *P*; *om. Q, S*

236 *Stro.*] ∼. *aside P*[1]
239 *Stro.*] ∼. *to Alphonso P*[1]
241 *Stro.*] ∼. *to Medice P*
242 *Vin.*] *Med. P*
243 *Med.*] *Vin. P*
    Vin.] *Med. P*
244 *Med.*] *Vin. P*
248 SD *Aside to Strozza.*] *P*[2]; *om. Q, S, P*[1]
254 SD *Vincentio ouerheares.*] *Vincentio overheares them. P*[1]
257 shew.] ∼. *Exeunt. S;* ∼. *Exeunt Alphonso, Medice, and attendants. P*
258 SD *Aside.*] *P; om. Q, S, P*

I.ii

I.ii] *P; om. Q, S*
SD] *A Room in the House of Lord Lasso. P*
SD *Lasso, Bassiolo*] *P; Lasso, Corteza, Margaret, Bassiolo Q, S*
SD *before.*] *before the rest. P*[1]
11 *Lass.*] *S; om. Q, P (read* Amply . . . perfect?, *ll. 10-15, as single speech by Bass.)*
12 t'indure] t'induce *Bradley conj. (in P)*
22 *Two Pag.*] 2 *Pag. Q;* 2nd *Page S; Both Pages P*
30 Suite] *S, P;* Snite *Q*
42 (as . . . say)] (as . . . Duke;) *P*
48 SD *Aside to Strozza.*] *P; om. Q, S*
50 SD *Aside to Vincentio.*] *P; om. Q, S*
67 no lesse—] ∼ ∼— *Medice is at a loss P*[1]; ∼ ∼— *Medice hesitates P*[2]
68 *Alp.*] ∼. *to Strozza. P*[1]
    speake you.] *to Strozza P*[2]
69 you] *S, P;* your *Q*
84 SD *Aside.*] *P*[1]; *om. Q, S, P*[2]
87 th'enragde] *P;* the'nragde *Q;* the enraged *S*
92 SD *to Strozza.*] *om. Q, S, P*[2]; *aside. P*[1]
    SD *to Vin.*] *om. Q, S, P*[2]; *aside. P*[1]
94 SD *Aside.*] *P*[1]; *om. Q, S, P*[2]
97 inforc'd] inforced *S;* enforc'd *P*[2]
108 strooke] struck *S*
113 Charged] *P*[2] *(Bradley conj.);* Chased *S;* Chared *Q, P*[1]
127 pageants.] ∼. *She unbinds Alphonso. P*
131 SD *to Med.*] *P; om. Q, S*
140 SD *Exeunt . . . Stro.*] *Exeunt all but Vincentio and Strozza. P; Exit. Q, S*

II.i

SD] *A Room in the House of Lasso. P*
SD *Strozza . . . close.*] *om. P (see l. 27)*
2 SD *Aside.*] *P; om. Q, S*
6 Heere] *To Corteza* ∼ *P*[1]
10 O] *Aside* ∼ *P*[1]

14 cholerike,] ~∧ S
  are] ~, P
19 ifaith:] ~: *She drinks* P
27 SD *Enter Strozza.*] *Enter Strozza close. Corteza thrusts out a great bumbasted legge.*
  P¹; *Enter Strozza behind.* P²
28 SD *She . . . legge.*] P²; *A great bumbasted legge.* Q, S, P¹
31 SD *Aside.*] P; om. Q, S
37 thinke] thinks P
44 do] do't P
50 kisse—] ~— *She drinks again.* P¹; ~— *She drinks* P²
  SD *Aside.*] P; om. Q, S
64 *Med.* Gods] ~. *spying Strozza* ~ P
66 *Aside.*] P¹; om. Q, S, P²
  me;— what] ~. *Coming forward* ~ P¹; ~. *Advancing* ~ P²
74 SD *Exeunt . . . Page.*] P; *Exeunt.* Q, S
82 vm] 'em S, P²
86 SD *Enter . . . Stroz.*] P; *after Strozza's speech 11. 87-88* Q, S
94 place.] ~. *Vincentio uncovers.* P
95 SD *Aside.*] P; om. Q, S
  SD *Exit.*] *Exit Strozza.* P¹; *Exit Strozza (after Bassiolo's speech)* P²; om. Q, S
100 t'aske] to ask S
111 SD *to servants.*] om. Q, S, P
  threaues.] ~. *Giving Vincentio a bundle of rushes.* P¹
123 ha't] S, P²; h'ate Q, P¹
144 Foe] Foh S, P²
153 SD *to Fungus.*] P; om. Q, S
154 *Superintendent*,] Q(u); Vsher, Q(c), S, P
157 SD *Aside.*] P; om. Q, S
158 SD *woman-Bug.*] P; *woman.* Q, S
162 *Superintendent*:] Q(u); *Vsher*; Q(c), S, P
176 SD *Exeunt . . . Bass.*] *Exeunt all but Lasso and Bassiolo.* P; *Exeunt.* Q, S
179 SD *Exeunt.*] *Exeunt Lasso and Bassiolo.* P¹

II.ii

II.ii] om. Q, S, P
15 mouing] S, P; moning Q
36 *Sarp.*] S, P; om. Q
37 name.] ~. *Pointing to Cynanche.* P
47 SD *Rush-maid. After*] ~, *Sylvan, a Nymph, and two Bugs.* ~ P
  SD *Pogio.*] *Pogio speaks* P¹
49 Broomes,] ~∧ S, P
72 here—] ~— *Pointing to Vincentio.* P
85 bring] hung S
99 SD *Pogio . . . exeunt.*] P; *Exeunt.* Q, S
101 SD *Enter . . . Nymph.*] om. Q, S, P
106 feral] P² (*Bradley conj.*); female Q, S, P¹

107 SD *Exeunt . . . Nymph.*] *om.* Q, S, P
111 SD *Enter . . . exeunt.*] *Bugs song.* Q, S, P
112 Thus] Q (*catchword*); This_∧ Q (*text*); This, S
119 SD *Exit.*] *Exit Sarpego, Nymph, Sylvan and the two Bugs.* P
121 borrowed] borrow'd S
126 SD *Aside.*] P; *om.* Q, S
     SD *Aside to Strozza.*] P; *om.* Q, S

III.i

SD] *A Room in the House of Lasso.* P
13 SD *Exeunt.*] *Exeunt Medice and Servant.* P¹

III.ii

III.ii] P; *om.* Q, S
SD *Bassiolo.*] *Bassiolo severally.* P
1 SD *Aside.*] P; *om.* Q, S
29 though . . . Gentleman] P; (~ . . . ~) Q, S
30 (And . . . busines)] P; _∧~ . . . ~_∧ Q, S
35 you] ~, you S
55 bestowed] bestow'd S
78 godly] goodly P² (*Deighton conj.*)
78-79 where's . . . Nobleman?] whereas the deed's the perfect nobleman.
     Deighton conj. (*in* P²)
93 Mineon] minion S, P²
100 flattring] flattering S; flatt'ring P²
103 youle] you S, P²
108 my] P; me Q, S
121 *Vince.*] ~. *He embraces Vincentio.* P
126 yesterday.] ~. *They lie down together.* P
135 two] S, P; too Q
145 seely] silly S
183 SD *Aside.*] P; *om.* Q, S
     Bass. How] ~. *rising, aside* ~ P
188 neuer] ne'er S
196 Bone robes] Bonarobbas S; bona-robas P²
205 SD *Enter*] *Re-enter* P¹
206 SD *Aside.*] P; *om.* Q, S
207 SD *instant.*] *instanter* P
211 loue] S, P; ioue Q
216 huddles] riddles S
228 SD *Corteza,*] *Cortezza leaning on the Duke* P
     SD *Cynanche,*] *Cynanche, Margaret* P
233 flabby] S, P; slabby Q
239 naught] naughts Q, S, P
247 SD *Aside.*] P; *om.* Q, S
     whittld] whittled P²; wittolled S

249-50 Lord, all] lords all *P*
250 all, and] and$_\wedge$ all *S*
253 *Med.*] Ma. *S*
255 won't] wont *S*
266 b'w'y'] *P²*; b'w'y *S*; bwy *Q, P¹*
276 SD *Vin. . . . way.*] after Lord *l. 281 S, P*
281 SD *To Lasso.*] om. *Q, S, P*
    Lord.] ∼. *He whispers to Lasso. P*
    SD *to Strozza.*] *aside to Strozza and Cynanche P* (*entire speech* See . . . before.
    ll. 281-91 is aside); om. *Q, S*
284 SD *to others.*] om. *Q, S, P*
286 SD *to Strozza.*] om. *Q, S, P*
293 *Hunt.*] *1st Hunt. P*
296 SD *Exeunt . . . attendants.*] *Exeunt Alphonso, Lasso, Medice, Strozza, Huntsmen,*
    and attendants. P; *Exeunt Q, S*
298 SD *Aside.*] *P*; om. *Q, S*
301 SD *Exeunt . . . attendants.*] *Exit Cynanche. P*; *Exit. Q, S* (*after l. 300*)
310 turne.] ∼. *He offers Margaret the letter. P¹*
311 letter?] ∼? *Offers her a letter. P²*
329 gentman] gentleman *S, P²*
332 Iugge] stone jug *S*
335 I common] I a common *S, P*
350 rulde.] ∼. *He puts the letter into her hands. P¹*; ∼. *Gives her the letter. P²*
352 not.] ∼. *She drops the letter. P¹*; ∼. *Drops the letter. P²*
354 heart.] ∼. *He gives her the letter again. P¹*; ∼. *Gives her the letter again. P²*
357 sonne.] ∼. *She reads the letter. P¹*; ∼. *Reads the letter. P²*
358 SD *Aside.*] *P*; om. *Q, S*
364 it.] ∼. *She returns him the letter. P¹*; ∼. *Returning the letter. P²*
375 SD *Re-enter Bassiolo.*] *P¹*; om. *Q, S, P²*
381 Secretorie.] ∼. *He sits down to write. P*
382 SD *Aside.*] *P*; om. *Q, S*
392 see.] ∼. *He writes. P*
393 SD *Aside.*] *P*; om. *Q, S*
400 SD *Aside.*] *P*; om. *Q, S*
414 SD *Aside.*] *P*; om. *Q, S*
423 SD *Aside.*] om. *Q, S, P*
437 it;] ∼: *Reads P¹*
449 selfe.] ∼. *She sits down to write. P*
451 you; I] ∼; *folding up the letter.* ∼ *P¹*; ∼; *Folding up his letter.* ∼ *P²*
454 SD *Aside.*] *P*; om. *Q, S*
459 Asse the] As the *S, P²*
464 *Bass.* I] ∼. *reads* ∼ *P*
469 too; and] ∼. *She begins to write, but stops.* And *P*
474 *Bass.* So] ∼. *writing* ∼ *P*
490 *Bass.* A] ∼. *looking over the letter.* ∼ *P*

IV.i

SD] *Before the House of Strozza. P*
1 SD *Enter Cynanche.*] *P*; *om. Q, S*
8 me, where?] ~∧ ~. *S*
48 mankinde] unkind *S*
61 stirred] stirr'd *S*

IV.ii

IV.ii] *P*; *om. Q, S*
SD] *A Room in the House of Lasso. P*
SD *hand,*] ~, *and P*[1]
13 ith] i'th' *S, P*[2]
27 Ifaith, heeres] i'faith. *Taking Bassiolo's letter.* Here's *P*
45 be] by *S, P*[2]
47 SD *Aside.*] *P*; *om. Q, S*
50 hers.] ~. *Pointing to Margaret's letter. P*[1]
73 SD *Aside.*] *P*; *om. Q, S*
78 SD *Enter*] *Re-enter P*[1]
87 easly] easily *S*
94 SD *Aside.*] *P*; *om. Q, S*
 shame.] ~. *As Vincentio approaches, Margaret turns her back upon him. P*[1]
96 SD *Aside.*] *P*; *om. Q, S*
118 loues] love *P conj.*
182 entred] enter'd *S, P*[2]
196 Diffrent] *Q(c)*; Different *Q(u), S, P*
217 idlely] idly *S, P*

IV.iii

IV.iii] *P*; *om. Q, S*
SD] *A Room in the House of Strozza. P*
SD *Cynanche, with*] *P*; *Cynanche, Benenemus, with Q, S (Benevemus)*
22 alterations] *S, P*; alteratious *Q*
29 stirre] stirs *P*[2]
49 suffring] suffering *S*
72 cures] *P*; cares *Q, S*
73 medcines] medicines *S*
74 op'ned] open'd *S, P*[2]
81 (My . . . phisition)] ∧~ . . . ~∧ *S, P*[2]
82 SD *Aside.*] *P*; *om. Q, S*
98 SD *Aside.*] *P*; *om. Q, S*
131 accomplished] accomplish'd *S*

IV.iv

IV.iv] *P*; *om. Q, S*
SD] *A Room in the House of Lasso. P*
25 *Med.*] *MS correction in copies DFo and CSmH of Q, P; Lass. Q, S*
31 Cunni-holes] coney-holes *S*; cony-holes *P*[2]
33 trait'rous] traitorous *S*
49 hants] *P conj.*; hands *Q, S, P*
56 traitrous] traitorous *S*

IV.v

IV.v] *om. Q, S, P*
3 th'assured] the assured *S, P*[1]
9 temp'rate] temperate *S*
15 SD *Aside.*] *P; om. Q, S*
21 SD *Aside.*] *P; om. Q, S*
36 SD *Aside.*] *P; om. Q, S*
38 Slood] Sblood *S*
45 Slood] Sblood *S*
48 slendrest] slenderest *S*
55 dar'st] darest *S*
64 Fit t'haue] To have *S*
76 resolu'd.] ∼. *Going P*
92 SD *Aside.*] *P; om. Q, S*
109 bone robes] bonarobbas *S*; bona-robas *P*[2]
    then I faith;] *P*; ∼∧ ∼; ∼∧ *Q(c)*; ∼∧ ∼, ∼∧ *Q(u)*; ∼— i'faith *S*
114 the] thy *P*[2] (*P*[1] *conj.*)

V.i

SD] *A Room, with a Gallery, in the House of Lasso. P*[1]; *A Room in the House of Lasso P*[2]
14 come.] ∼. *They crouch in upper stage. P*[1]
    SD *Enter*] ∼ *below P*[1]
17 SD *To Margaret.*] *om. Q, S, P*
20 fie, . . . comes,] *in quotes S, P*
    foe . . . Aunt,] *in quotes S, P*
26 gosh hat] God save't *S*
27 copper] fine copper *S*
30 offer.] ∼. *He kisses her. P*
31 idlely] idly *S, P*[2]
32 shay by] say ye *S*
35 SD *Aside.*] *P; om. Q, S*
    ha'y not] ha' y'not *S, P*
36 SD *Aside.*] *P; om. Q, S*
48, 52 SD *Cant.*] *Cantat P*
56 Bobbadilla] Bobbadilia *P*[2]
97 SD *Enter*] *Re-enter P*
98 SD *Aside.*] *P; om. Q, S*
102 Duke,] ∼! *Vincentio and Margaret run out. P*
104 ifaith.] ∼. *Re-enter Vincentio and Margaret. P*[1]; ∼. *Enter Vincentio and Margaret P*[2]
110 SD *Aside.*] *P; om. Q, S*
124 SD *Exeunt.*] *Exeunt Alphonso, Medice, Lasso, and Corteza P*
132 SD *Exeunt . . . Bass.*] *Exeunt Bassiolo and Vincentio. P; Exeunt. Q, S*
    SD *Lasso,*] *Lasso who seizes Margaret, P*[1]
137 externall] eternal *S, P*
151 vnimpaired] unimpair'd *S*
164 tak'st] takest *S*
165 thee] the *S*

V.ii

V.ii] *P*; *om. Q, S*
SD] *A Room in the House of Strozza. P*
8 approu'd] approved *S*
9 president] precedent *S, P²*
10 medcine] *Q(c)*; medicine *Q(u), S*
27 pursu'st] *Q(c)*; pursuest *Q(u), S*
30 lou'st] *Q(c)*; louest *Q(u), S*
34 S.] Saint *P*
43 "No] *Q(c) second state;* ∧~ *Q(u), P*
44 "All] *Q(c) second state;* ∧~ *Q(u), P*
58 *Medcines*] *Q(c)*; *Medicines Q(u), S*
65 ill tydings-bringer] ~-~∧ ~ *S, P²*

V.iii

V.iii] *P*; *om. Q, S*
SD] *Corteza's Chamber, a Tower-room in Lasso's House. P¹*; *Cortezza's Chamber P²*
8 wandring] wandering *S*
36 whole;] ~. *Margaret seizes the knife and offers to cut her face. P*
46 enticing curles] *S, P*; entring carles *Q*
57 vildely] vilely *S*
65 sweare.] ~. *She seizes the box and rubs her face with the ointment. P*
68 desp'rate] desperate *S*
70 That] *S, P*; The *Q*
71 th'amaz'd] th'amazed *S, P¹*
72 yet] *P*; it *Q, S*
75 suffered] suffer'd *S*
82 *Exit.*] *P*; *Exeunt. Q, S*

V.iv

V.iv] *P*; *om. Q, S*
SD] *A Room in Lasso's House. P*
12 SD *Removing her mask*] *om. Q, S, P*
20 resembled] resembles *S*
25 loose] lose *S, P²*
30 strooke] struck *S*
32 insolencie] insolence *S*
37 desparately] *Q(u)*; desp'rately *Q(c), P*
39 SD *Strozza before*] *om. P*
85 moning right] moving sight *Daniel conj. (in P)*
103 deformed] deform'd *S*
109 with'red] wither'd *S, P²*
116 wooed] woo'd *S*
122 Heauen, and Art;] ~; ~ ~, *P¹, S*; ~∧ ~ ~! *P²*
    SD *to Mar.*] *om. Q, S, P*
126 temp'rature] temperature *S*
132 Maske; heere] maske. *Putting a mask on Margaret's face.* Heere *P*
154 Lord: away] lord; *detaining Julio.* ~∧ *P¹*
155 SD *Enter . . . guarded.*] *P*; *om. Q, S*

217

156 chopt] chopped *S*, *P*²
159 Minion man;] ∼, ∼∧ *S*, *P*
168 far'st] farest *S*
171 past twixt] passed twixt *P*¹ *conj.*; pass'd betwixt *S*
183 *Stinkard,* Man] *S*, *P*; *Stinkard*∧ *Man Q*
187 life.] ∼. *He draws on Pogio. P*¹ ∼! *Draws P*²
189 fitt'st] fittest *S*
190 murthrous] murtherous *S*
205 doost] dost *S*, *P*²
221 of] if *P*¹
233 iustice.] ∼. *He draws. P*¹; ∼. *Draws P*²
249 (twice) christned] christen'd *S*, *P*²
251 cam'st] camest *S*
252 that] the *S*
      entring] entering *S*
278 (twice) leg'd] legged *S*, *P*²

PRESS-VARIANTS

[Copies collated: BM (British Museum, Ashley 374, collated by A. Yamada), CSmH (Huntington Library), CtY (Yale University), DFo (Folger Shakespeare Library), DLC (Library of Congress), Eton (Eton College, collated by A. Yamada), IU (University of Illinois), MB (Boston Public Library), MH (Harvard University), MWiWc (Chapin Collection of Williams College), TxU (University of Texas), Worc (Worcester College, Oxford)]

Sheet A (outer forme)

Corrected: BM, CSmH, CtY, DFo, Eton, IU, MB, MH, MWiWc, Worc
Uncorrected: DLC, TxU

Sig. A2ᵛ

    I.i.26 day?] day.

        35 now.] now;

        43 Whervpon] Wherevpon

          Count] count

        51 facel:et] face; let

        53 prey,] prey;

        57 Boares] Boares,

Sig. A3

    I.i.64 Dart] dart

        72 your] yonr

        75 go fit me for.] gofitme for∧

        79 desprate] desperate

        80 Curbd] curbd

          riualitie:] riualitie?

        89 seruant of] seruantof

        93 accesse.] accesse,

Sig. A4ᵛ

    I.i.179 the flundering] theflundering

Sheet C (outer forme)

Corrected: BM, CSmH, CtY, DFo, DLC, Eton, IU, MB, MH, MWiWc, TxU
Uncorrected: Worc

Sig. C

    II.i.30 a legge] al egge

Sig. C2ᵛ

    II.i.140 thee] the

        148 sir!] sir,

        154 Vsher] *Superintendent*

Sig. C3
    II.i.159 Lord,] Lord∧
        162 Vsher;] *Superintendent*:
        169 tyre;] tyres∧
Sig. C4ᵛ
    II.ii.92 duke)] duke∧
        105 askaunce] a skaunce
        110 female] Femall

Sheet E (inner forme)

Corrected: CSmH, DFo, Eton, IU, MB, MWiWc, Worc
Corrected but catchword dropped out: CtY, DLC, MH, TxU
Uncorrected: BM

Sig. E1ᵛ
    III.ii.271 sometimes:] sometimes; Soune and my Lords,
        276 I returne] Ireturne
        catchword *Lass.*] *om.*

Sheet F (outer forme)

Corrected: BM, CSmH, CtY, DFo, DLC, Eton, IU, MB, MWiWc, TxU
Uncorrected: MH, Worc

Sig. F1
    IV.i.7 side.] side?
Sig. F4ᵛ
    IV.ii.174 you] you,
        177 alone] alone,
        191 I:] I,
        196 Diffrent] different

Sheet G (inner forme)

Corrected: BM, CSmH, CtY, DFo, DLC, Eton, IU, MB, MWiWc, TxU, Worc
Uncorrected: MH

Sig. G2
    IV.iii.86 SD *Beneuemius*] *Beneuemisu*

Sheet H (outer forme)

First State Corrected: BM, DFo, DLC, Eton, MB, MH, MWiWc, Worc
Uncorrected: CtY

Sig. H1
    IV.v.64 Iugge] iugge
        65 Sobriety] sobriety
        66 Sh'as] S'has
        69 time] time,
        91 arrand] errant
        94 gods!] gods,

Sig. H2ᵛ
    V.i.53 strait:] strait,
        63 sweet] sweete
          Creature] creature
        70 honestest] honest
        83 *Vin.*] *Vnn.*
Sig. H3
    V.i.99 arm'd] arm'd
        101 Duke:] Duke,
        110 do] doe
          domineere] dominere
        111 Ingle?] Ingle,
        114 Huswiferie] huswiferie
        124 Gard] guard
Sig. H4ᵛ
    V.ii.27 pursu'st] pursuest
        28 gifts] guifts
        29 thereby] thereby,
        30 lou'st] louest
        32 cure.] cure,
        35 Arrow] arrow
          work] worke
        36 Rite] rite
        42 liues.] liues:
        46 excitations] excitations,
        47 Honor] honour
        48 *Vincentio*] *Vincentio,*
        50 O,] O∧
        53 Where] where
        56 out] out,
        57 remaines,] remaines∧
          you] you,
        58 *Medcines*] *Medicines*
          danger:] danger,
    Second State Corrected: CSmH, IU, TxU
Sig. H4ᵛ
    V.ii.43 "No] No
        44 "All] All

Sheet H (inner forme)

    Corrected: BM, CSmH, CtY, DFo, DLC, IU, MB, MH, MWiWc, TxU,
          Worc
    Uncorrected: Eton
Sig. H1ᵛ
    IV.v.109 I;] I,

Sig. H2
    V.i.34 ruftie] ruftie,
       36 T'is] T's
         himselfe:] himselfe,
       37 follie] follie;
       40 *He lies down/ by them.*] *om.*
       48 Foxes,] Foxes

Sig. H3ᵛ
    V.i.129 heauen,] heauen
      139 exile] exile,
        Lord,] Lord∧
      148 starue,] etarue

Sig. H4
    V.i.157 *Exeunt Cor. Mar.*] *Ex. Co. Ma.*
      158 sons] sonnes
    V.ii.2 head] heade
      10 medcine] Medicine

Sheet I (outer forme)
Corrected: BM, CSmH, CtY, DFo, DLC, Eton, IU, MB, MWiWc, TxU,
      Worc
Uncorrected: MH

Sig. I1
    V.ii.71 sure] sure,
      78 still.] still. *Exeunt.*
      79 Lead sir I pray. *Exeunt.*] *om.*
    V.iii.5 *Cort.* . . . truth! (*on one line*)] *Cort.* . . . neece./ *Mar.* . . . truth!
      Ma.] *Mar.*
      9 *Cort.*] *Cort;*
      12 harme:] harme.

Sig. I2ᵛ
    V.iv.10 more:] more;
      12 Tyrant!] Tyrant,
      14 poore.] poore,
      15 lost] lost,
      16 Maides dowre:] Maide dowre∧
      17 me:] me;
        hope.] hope,
      26 heapt] heapt,
        SD *Iulio*] *Inlio*
      27 hurt.] hurt,
      29 deliuered,] deliuered∧
      37 desp'rately] desparately

Sig. I3
    V.iv.59 man] man,
      63 least] lest
      68 mazde] Mazde
        speake:] speake?

Sig. I4ᵛ

    V.iv.167 now:] now,
         177 he] he,
         178 so] so,

Sheet K (inner forme)

    Corrected: BM, CSmH, CtY, DFo, DLC, Eton, IU, MB, MH, MWiWc,
        Worc
    Uncorrected: TxU

Sig. K1ᵛ

    V.iv.228 heauen] heauen,
         234 *Strozza*,] *Strozza*.
         246 Country,] Country∧
         251 Strange,] Strange∧
         256 fauor'd,] fauor'd∧

Sig. K2

    V.iv.269 cleanse] clense
         270 foule] fowle

TEXTUAL NOTES

II.ii

101 SD *Enter . . . Nymph.*] Since the masque is divided into three dramatic episodes, as is partly indicated by the brackets in the text, I have provided separate entrances and exits (at lines 101, 107, and 111) to match the action as described in Sarpego's lines. Parrott has Sylvan, Nymph, and Bugs enter with Pogio and Fungus.

IV.i

9 *Benevenius.*] Although Parrott follows Shepherd in naming the doctor "Benevemus," "Benevemus" apparently derives from a compositor's misreading of "m" for "ni." The doctor's name appears in four different forms in the play: "Benivemus" (twice), "Benenemus," "Benevemius," and "Benevenius" (twice). In the two instances where the name appears in the text, the meter of the line calls for "Benevenius."

IV.iii

28 sence, nor . . . meats;] This difficult line apparently means: Music like choice meats delights but one sense; one [music] quickly fades, the other [choice meats] stir to sin. Parrott's emendation of "stirre" to "stirs" is unnecessary.

IV.v

46 I know't] Q's reading "I know't I know" is puzzling. Possibly the manuscript read "I know what I know."

109 I faith;] Parrott's emendation, which I adopt, makes sense, but I think it likely from the shortness of the following line that some part of the original text has been omitted here; the verse otherwise conforms well to the normal pentameter pattern. Possibly relevant also is the fact that the corrector emended at this point, changing "I, faith" to "I; faith."

V.i

26 gosh hat,] The *NED* records "gods hat" in contemporary usage, although "gosh" as a corruption of "gods" is not noted until the eighteenth century. I would agree with Parrott that Bassiolo's tongue in this scene has been somewhat thickened with wine. See following note.

32 shay by] Shepherd's emendation "say ye" does not seem very likely. The boisterous and completely indecorous behavior of Bassiolo in this scene supports Parrott's suggestion that Bassiolo "has fortified himself with Dutch courage" (p. 768).

137 externall exile.] Parrott follows Shepherd in emending "externall" to "eternal." While the emendation is a likely one, it is not absolutely necessary for the meaning of the line, because "exile" for the Elizabethans did not necessarily mean banishment to a foreign country. Like Falstaff one could be banished or exiled from the court. In *Sir Thomas More* (IV.v.31) we find "We are exilde the courte."

V.ii

28 vertuous gifts:] I have retained the colon, which appears in both uncorrected and corrected states of this line, because I think the "vertuous gifts" are Cynanche's, not Strozza's, unless Strozza is something of a prig. "For which" in the next line would seem to refer to the whole conduct of married life referred to in the preceding ten lines.

All Fooles

edited by G. Blakemore Evans

❖

TEXTUAL INTRODUCTION

Chapman's *All Fooles* exists in a single seventeenth-century edition, a quarto printed for Thomas Thorpe in 1605 (hereafter referred to as Q). Although no printer's name appears on the title page, the printer was George Eld.[1]

According to the title page *All Fooles* had been presented at the Blackfriars and "lately before his Maiestie." Records show that the "Boyes of the Chapell" (i.e., the Blackfriars company) performed the play at court on 1 January 1605[2] and we may presume that it was being acted at the Blackfriars in 1604. Whether *All Fooles* is the same play as *The World Runs a' Wheels,* which Chapman completed in 1599 for the Admiral's company, is a question raised by an ambiguous entry in Henslowe's *Diary.* In the last of four entries in Henslowe (2 July 1599) relating to this otherwise lost play, reference is made to Chapman's "Boocke called the world Rones a whelles & now all foolles but the foolle."[3] Greg thinks the reference is to two plays and that the second play is some form of the play we now know as *All Fooles.*[4] Chambers, on the other hand, believes that reference is made to only one play, that is, that "the world Rones a whelles" is "now" to be called "all foolles but the foolle."[5] "The world goes (or runs) on wheels" is, of course, proverbial (see Tilley, W893) and means that life (or things in general) is going smoothly, a title that is not in any way applicable to *All Fooles,* at least as we now have it, nor does the expression occur anywhere in the dialogue. However, one piece of evidence which suggests a date before 1600 appears in the play itself. In IV.i.299-320, the Notary reads an instrument of divorce drawn up for Cornelio that con-

[1] W. W. Greg, *A Bibliography of the English Printed Drama to the Restoration,* I (London, 1939), 346-47. Greg gives a full descriptive collation of Q. The identification of George Eld as the printer (first pointed out to T. M. Parrott by Sidney Lee; see Parrott's edition in the Belles-Lettres Series, Boston, 1907, p. xlvii), originally made on the basis of the ornaments in Q, is substantiated by the identification of two of the compositors in Q with the two compositors in Eld's printing of the 1609 quarto of *Troilus and Cressida.* See the later discussion of this identification.

[2] E. K. Chambers, *The Elizabethan Stage* (Oxford, 1923), IV, 171.

[3] W. W. Greg, *Henslowe's Diary,* Pt. i (London, 1904), p. 109.

[4] Greg, *Henslowe's Diary,* Pt. ii (1908), p. 203.

[5] Chambers, III, 252.

cludes "giuen the 17. of Nouember 1500. and so forth." On the whole Greg's interpretation of the Henslowe entry seems the more probable, though whether the play we now call *All Fooles* represents a later reworking of the play referred to in 1599 must, I think, remain an open question.

Q is on the whole a good text, most of the difficulties in it, apart from a certain amount of mislineation, arising, I believe, from compositorial errors. Nothing in the format of Q suggests prompt-copy provenance. Indeed, it seems likely, from the evidence of certain characteristic spellings and the sporadic use of Latin stage directions, that the copy-text for Q was Chapman's own fair copy, or at least a transcript of that manuscript.

Q was set by three compositors:[6] Compositor A, sheets A, B, E, F; Compositor B, sheets C, D, I, ?K; and Compositor C, sheets G, H. The work of Compositor A is clearly distinguished from that of Compositor B by the regular use of 'me,' 'she,' 'he,' for B's 'mee,' 'shee,' 'hee,' by 'vm' for B's 'am' (='em), by 'alas' for B's 'ahlas,' and by a preponderance of final '-y' forms for B's final '-ie' forms (also by a fondness for medial 'y' for B's medial 'i'). Compositor B also usually uses a period after his signature notations. A comparison of B's part of Q with the 1609 quarto of *Troilus and Cressida,* a volume also printed by George Eld, shows that B was probably one of the compositors who set that text (there also called Compositor B).[7] The spelling preferences of Compositor C are not so obvious, partly because he shares characteristics of both A and B. On the whole, however, he favors final '-y' forms, uses a colon to punctuate abbreviated proper names, and alone employs the speech-prefix *Rinal.* (for *Rinaldo*) and the spelling *Marc-Antonio* (or *Marc-Ant:*). C also usually sets 38 lines to the page as against A's and B's 36 lines. There is, I think, no doubt that Compositor C is the same person as Compositor A in the *Troilus and Cressida* quarto.

If we use Compositor C as a kind of control, it would appear that Compositor B followed his copy more closely than Compositor A. Compositor A regularly reads 'vm' for B's 'am' and 'alas' for B's 'ahlas,' but C uses both 'ahlas' and 'alas' and 'am' for A's 'vm.' Since both 'ahlas' and 'am' are quite

[6] After my own work on this play was essentially completed, Professor Akihiro Yamada of Shinshu University kindly sent me an offprint of his article in *Shakespeare Studies,* III (1964), 73-99, entitled "Bibliographical Studies of George Chapman's *All Fools* (1605), Printed by George Eld." The article is valuable and deserves consultation by all students of Chapman's text. Professor Yamada reports several press corrections which I had missed, especially those in sheets C and D. These I have gratefully incorporated in my list of press-variants. On certain matters my conclusions about Q differ from those of Professor Yamada. He believes that Q was set by the method known as cast-off copy; I see no persuasive evidence of this, except perhaps in the stint of Compositor C. He divides the composition among four compositors (Compositor A: sheets A, B, K; Compositor B: sheets C, D, I; Compositor C: sheets E, F; Compositor D: sheets G, H); I do not think that the spelling evidence, set forth at considerable length by Professor Yamada, warrants postulating more than three compositors. He suggests the use of five sets of running titles, agreeing with my distribution except that he assigns separate sets to sheets F and H. Since the running title *All Fooles* is short and difficult to work with, Professor Yamada may well be right in his judgment on this point.

[7] See the compositor study of *Troilus and Cressida* by Philip Williams in "Shakespeare's *Troilus and Cressida:* The Relationship of Quarto and Folio," *SB,* III (1950-51), 131-43, and Alice Walker, New Cambridge *Troilus and Cressida* (1957), pp. 122-34.

unusual spelling forms[8] and occur in Chapman's works set by other printers (*Widow's Tears, Gentleman Usher, Monsieur D'Olive, Sir Gyles Goosecap, The Iliads*), we may argue, convincingly, I think, that these were Chapman's own spelling forms, and that when they appear in a printed text the likelihood is great that such a text was printed from Chapman's autograph (or, at least, a transcript directly from autograph).

In noting the increased number of lines per page in sheets G and H, Greg also observes that the typefont used in these two sheets "seems to be different."[9] I cannot see any significant difference, but Greg's eye was sharp and trained and I hestitate to disagree with his years of experience on such a matter.

Q was printed with probably three sets of running titles: set I in sheets B, G, H; set II in sheets C, D, I; and set III in sheets E, F.[10] Since the same set, with one or two slight irregularities, was used on both the inner and outer formes of the same sheet, it is probable that Q was printed on a single press.

The seventeen copies here collated show an above average amount of press correction. Press-variants appear in sheets A (inner, three states), B (outer and inner), C (outer, two states, and inner), D (inner), E (outer and inner), G (outer and inner), H (outer), I (inner), K (inner). None of the corrections, except 'vnusering' (corrected) for 'vnnurishing' (uncorrected), sig. B2^v and '*are* ( ) *welcome*' (corrected) for '*are welcome*' (uncorrected), sig. K1^v, suggests either an author's correction or necessary consultation of copy.

Three character names pose a problem for the editor. 'Bellanora,' which occurs on sigs. E3^v and H4, also appears as 'Bellonora' on sigs. A2^v (the list of actors) and C2. Thus Compositor A uses both forms, Compositor B uses 'Bellonora,' and Compositor C uses 'Bellanora'; there is, therefore, independent witness for both forms. I have, like Shepherd and Parrott, arbitrarily adopted 'Bellanora' as the more likely form. The confusion may well be Chapman's own. 'Marc. Antonio' occurs in several forms: 'Marc. Antonio' (sigs. B3^v, I2^v); 'Marcantonio' (sigs. B3^v, C4^v); 'Marc Antonio' (sig. F1^v); 'Marc-Antonio' (sigs. G2, G2^v, G4^v); and 'Mar. Antonio' (sig. A2^v). Again the spellings cut across Compositors A and B; only Compositor C is consistent. I have adopted 'Marc. Antonio,' as do Reed and all later editors. The third name which causes confusion is 'Dariotto.' It occurs as 'Dariotto' (sigs. D4, D4^v, E1, E2, F3^v, F4, I1, I3, I3^v); 'Darioto' (sigs. F4^v, G1, H1, H3^v, H4, H4^v); 'Doriotto' (sigs. D3^v, D4, D4^v). Since Compositors A and B generally agree on 'Dariotto' I have, like all earlier editors, adopted this form. The forms 'Rinaldo' and 'Rynaldo' appear in the work of all three compositors. I have allowed the variant forms to stand as they occur in the text.

Two copies of Q require special comment. One of the two University of Texas copies (designated as TxU[1]) contains a unique leaf, inserted following sig. A2. On the recto of this leaf (unsigned, verso blank) is a dedicatory

---

[8] The form 'am' occurs in the bad quarto of Shakespeare's *Henry V* (1600; printed by Thomas Creed), IV.iii.124. It also occurs in John Day's *Law Tricks* (1608; printed by Edward Allde) several times, together with one example of 'ahlas.'

[9] Greg, *Bibliography*, I, 346.

[10] See note 6, above.

sonnet addressed to Sir Thomas Walsingham. The problem raised by this unique leaf is one of authenticity. John Payne Collier, whose unsavory reputation for forgery is all too well known, first called attention to a copy containing this leaf and reprinted the sonnet in his edition of *All Fooles* in volume four of his 1825 edition of Dodsley's *Select Collection of Old Plays.* The copy dropped from sight and when T. M. Parrott came to do his edition of the play for the Belles-Lettres Series in 1905 no trace of it was to be found. He wrote to T. J. Wise on 15 November of that year asking Wise if he could give him any information about the missing copy.[11] Some further correspondence between the two men followed,[12] in which Wise seems to have helped Parrott to trace Collier's copy of *All Fooles* from the Ouvry sale (1882) into the hands of a dealer called Robson, who in turn had sold it to an "unknown purchaser." Here the matter rested until suddenly, on 20 October 1907, Wise, in a letter to J. H. Wrenn, the Chicago book collector, announced that he had discovered the missing Collier copy, dedication intact, among a collection of plays he had just bought from a Mr. Hadlow.[13] In this same letter he comments: "A moment's inspection satisfied me that the leaf was a forgery." Wise then communicated a full statement of his position to Parrott, who published Wise's letter in *The Athenaeum* (1908, i, 788-89).

Wise is quite categorical in denouncing the dedication leaf as a Collier forgery. There is, perhaps, a certain nice irony here. But his evidence does not strike me as entirely convincing, since he bases his case exclusively on the fact that the dedication leaf was originally slightly smaller than those in the rest of the volume and has been re-margined. He also suggests that Collier, by placing the inserted leaf after the title page (unsigned, actually sig. A2) and the first signed leaf (sig. A3) and destroying the blank first leaf (signed A) of the gathering, was attempting to mislead the unwary into thinking that the inserted leaf was a part of the original first sheet and later cancelled. If this were Collier's intention I do not see why he did not have his "forged" leaf actually signed as A2 when he was about it. Either way, any careful examination of the volume would have revealed that the dedication leaf was never part of the first sheet.

The smaller size of the dedication leaf does not seem to me a decisive argument for forgery. The leaf would presumably have been "sized" in some way before insertion (at whatever date) and since this particular copy was intended, one may suppose, for Walsingham himself, an over-trimmed leaf may have been tipped-in to a specially bound presentation copy after sewing or binding. This is just one of several hypotheses which might be suggested to explain the discrepency in size.

W. W. Greg also feels, though he does not say why, that Wise dismissed the dedication leaf as a forgery "on insufficient grounds" and suggests that the

[11] Fannie E. Ratchford, ed., *Letters of Thomas J. Wise to John Henry Wrenn* (New York, 1944), pp. 428-29 (T. M. Parrott to T. J. Wise).
[12] Ratchford, *Letters,* pp. 450-51.
[13] Ratchford, *Letters,* pp. 485-86. Miss Ratchford kindly informs me that there is not "a whit of evidence to confirm the provenance Wise gave Parrott" (private letter, 2 February 1962) so far as this copy is concerned.

leaf "may very likely come from some other book of the time."[14] Curiously enough, this was Wise's first suggestion to Parrott before his recovery of Collier's copy.[15] Unfortunately, no such book has been found and it now seems unlikely that it ever will be, since the recent definitive bibliography[16] of all such dedications by Franklin Williams failed to turn it up.

Another approach to the problem of the dedication leaf has been suggested to me by Miss Fannie Ratchford. Miss Ratchford believes that not Collier but Wise is responsible for forging the suspect leaf in the Texas copy, that what we actually have is not one forgery, but probably two. According to this theory Collier either discovered a copy of Q containing a genuine dedicatory leaf, or he forged the dedication sonnet himself, had twelve copies set in modern type but Jacobean spelling and distributed to his friends, and printed a modernized text of the sonnet in his 1825 edition of the play. Later, when Parrott began creating interest in the "lost" Collier copy, Wise decided to capitalize on the situation, had the dedication leaf forged from one of Collier's old-spelling copies, and inserted it into a copy of the play which he had at hand. Then, since Parrott would naturally be on the lookout for evidences of forgery, considering the supposed Collier provenance, he did not dare to claim it as anything but a Collier forgery. This is an ingenious theory and I agree with Miss Ratchford that if we are looking for a forger in the case, the quality of the inserted leaf is more like the work of Wise than Collier. Everything considered, however, I am inclined to question the basic assumption of forgery, at least so far as Collier is concerned. Greg's questioning of Wise's summary dismissal of the leaf as a forgery has already been noticed. Parrott, who originally accepted Wise's opinion and banished the sonnet to his notes, later changed his mind and considered the sonnet genuine, though he believed that it must have been specially printed for Chapman in connection with some later comedy, *May Day* (1611) or *Widow's Tears* (1612).[17] As his reason for dissociating the sonnet from *All Fooles* (1605) Parrott cites Chapman's dedication of the Byron plays to Walsingham and his son in 1608, in which he writes: "Sir, though I know, you euer stood little affected to these vnprofitable rites of Dedication; (which disposition in you, hath made me hetherto dispence with your right in my other impressions), yet, least the world may repute it a neglect in me, of so ancient and worthy a friend; (hauing heard your approbation of these in their presentment) I could not but prescribe them with your name." From this statement Parrott argues that Chapman had never before dedicated to Walsingham and that the *All Fooles* sonnet dedication must therefore have been properly intended for some later comedy. Parrott's argument here seems at least open to question, inasmuch as the *All Fooles* sonnet was in the nature of a private address, while the dedication to the Byron

[14] Greg, *Bibliography*, I, 346-47. See also his autograph note, dated 26 November 1936 in the British Museum copy (C. 34. c. 10).
[15] T. M. Parrott, ed., *"All Fooles" and "The Gentleman Usher"* (Belles-Lettres Series, Boston, 1907), p. 141.
[16] Franklin B. Williams, *Index of Dedications and Commendatory Verses in English Books Before 1641* (London, 1962).
[17] Phyllis B. Bartlett, ed., *The Poems of George Chapman* (New York, 1941), pp. 470-71.

plays is a public declaration, "least the world may repute it a neglect in me." Nor is the specially printed dedicatory sonnet unique in Chapman's work. Miss Phyllis Bartlett, in her edition of Chapman's poems, points out that three extra dedicatory sonnets are to be found in a few copies of Chapman's *Iliads* (1611). She also inclines to the view that the sonnet is genuine and calls attention to a striking parallel between the second line of the sonnet ("The least allow'd birth of my shaken braine") and the opening line of the "Corollarium ad Principem" in *The Teares of Peace* ("Thus shooke I this abortiue from my Braine").[18]

The other copy of Q which deserves special notice is one of the two Yale copies (here designated as CtY²). It contains Thomas Dring's advertising label (after 1649) pasted on the verso of sig. A2 and again on sig. K1ᵛ. Greg does not list a copy of *All Fooles* with this label.[19]

A list of the edited texts of *All Fooles* which have been collated for the present edition will be found in the headnote to the Historical Collation.[20]

[18] Bartlett, pp. 470-71.

[19] Greg, *Bibliography,* III (1957), 1155.

[20] I regret that the Regents Series edition (1968), ed. Frank Manley, appeared too late for inclusion. Mr. Manley records three press-variants not noted by either Mr. Yamada or myself: I.i.1 (sig. A4, inner forme) subiect (uncorrected), subiects (corrected); I.i.342 (sig. C1, outer forme) wine (uncorrected), mine (corrected); V.ii.52 (sig. I1, outer forme) *petibus* (uncorrected), *potibus* (corrected). The second of these ("wine" corrected to "mine") is a definite variant. The uncorrected "wine" occurs in only one of the seventeen copies I have collated (CtY¹). The correction "mine" must represent a "First State Corrected" and thus makes what I have described as "First State Corrected" and "Second State Corrected" into "Second" and "Third" respectively. The other two variants are, I believe, in a different category. On sig. A4 (inner forme) all copies I have examined read "subiects," but the final "s" prints very faintly in the "Uncorrected" and "First State Corrected" states. When the changes were being made for the "Second State Corrected," the "s" was presumably adjusted (or replaced) and thereafter prints clearly. On sig. I1 (outer forme) what Mr. Manley reads as an *"e"* in *"potibus"* is, I think, only an *"o"* which in some copies has printed so unclearly that it looks like an *"e."*

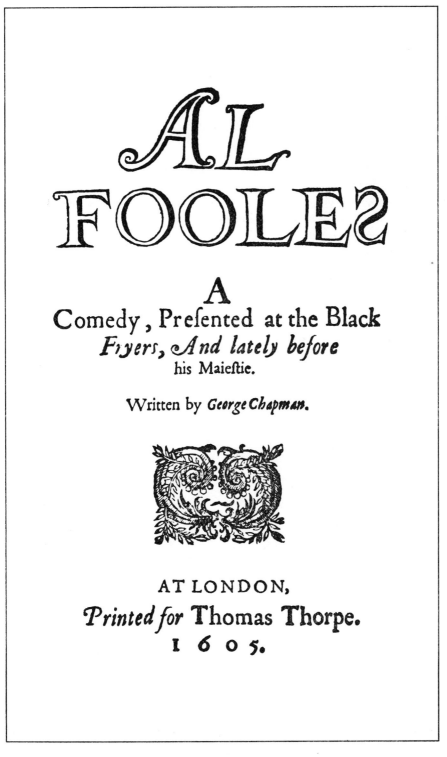

AL
FOOLES

A
Comedy, Prefented at the Black
Fryers, And lately before
his Maieftie.

Written by *George Chapman*.

AT LONDON,
Printed for Thomas Thorpe.
1 6 0 5.

Gostanzo. ⎫
Mar. Antonio. ⎬ Knights.

Valerio, sonne to Gostanzo.

Fortunio, elder sonne to Marc. Antonio.

Rynaldo, the younger.

Dariotto. ⎫
Claudio. ⎬ Courtiers.

Cornelio, A start-vp Gentleman.

Curio, a Page.

Kyte, a Scriuener.

Fraunces Pock, a Surgeon.

[Drawer.]

Gazetta, wife to Cor:

Bellanora, daughter to Gostanzo.

Gratiana, Stolne wife to Valerio.

To my long lou'd and Honourable
friend Sir Thomas Walsingham
Knight.

Should I expose to euery common eye,
    The least allow'd birth of my shaken braine;
And not entitle it perticulerly
    To your acceptance, I were wurse then vaine.
And though I am most loth to passe your sight   5
    with any such light marke of vanitie,
Being markt with Age for Aimes of greater weight,
    and drownd in darke Death-vshering melancholy,
Yet least by others stealth it be imprest,
    without my pasport, patcht with others wit,   10
Of two enforst ills I elect the least;
    and so desire your loue will censure it;
        Though my old fortune keepe me still obscure,
        The light shall still bewray my ould loue sure.

Prologus. [A3]

The fortune of a Stage (like Fortunes selfe)
Amazeth greatest iudgements: And none knowes
The hidden causes of those strange effects,
That rise from this Hell, or fall from this Heauen:
    Who can shew cause, why your wits, that in-ayme   5
At higher Obiects, scorne to compose Playes;
(Though we are sure they could, would they vouchsafe it?)
Should (without meanes to make) iudge better farre,
Then those that make, and yet yee see they can;
For without your applause, wretched is he   10
That vndertakes the Stage, and he's more blest,
That with your glorious fauours can contest.
    Who can shew cause, why th'ancient Comick vaine
Of Eupolis *and* Cratinus *(now reuiu'd,*

Subiect to personall application) 15

Should be exploded by some bitter splenes?

Yet merely Comicall, and harmelesse iestes

(Though nere so witty) be esteem'd but toyes,

If voide of th'other satyrismes sauce?

   Who can shew cause why quick Venerian iestes, 20

Should sometimes rauish? sometimes fall farre short,

Of the iust length and pleasure of your eares?

When our pure Dames, thinke them much less obscene, /

Then those that winne your Panegyrick splene? [A3ᵛ]

But our poore doomes (alas) you know are nothing; 25

To your inspired censure, euer we

Must needs submit, and there's the mistery.

   Great are the giftes giuen to vnited heades,

To gifts, attyre, to faire attyre, the stage

Helps much, for if our other audience see 30

You on the stage depart before we end,

Our wits goe with you all, and we are fooles;

So Fortune gouernes in these stage euents,

That merit beares least sway in most contents.

Auriculas Asini quis non habet? 35

How we shall then appeare, we must referre

To Magicke of your doomes, that neuer erre. /

---

27 *mistery*] Q(u); *misery* Q(c) *(See Textual Note)* ‖

ALL FOOLES.

Actus primi.   Scæna prima.

Enter Rynaldo, Fortunio, Valerio.

Rin. Can one selfe cause, in subiects so alike
As you two are, produce effects so vnlike?
One like the Turtle, all in mournefull straines,
Wailing his fortunes? Th'other like the Larke
Mounting the sky in shrill and cheerefull notes,   5
Chaunting his ioyes aspir'd, and both for loue:
In one, loue rayseth by his violent heate,
Moyst vapours from the heart into the eyes,
From whence they drowne his brest in dayly showers;
In th'other, his diuided power infuseth   10
Onely a temperate and most kindly warmth,
That giues life to those fruites of wit and vertue,
Which the vnkinde hand of an vnciuile father,
Had almost nipt in the delightsome blossome.
  For. O brother loue rewards our seruices   15
With a most partiall and iniurious hand,
If you consider well our different fortunes:
Valerio loues, and ioyes the dame he loues:
I loue, and neuer can enioy the sight
Of her I loue, so farre from conquering   20
In my desires assault, that I can come
To lay no battry to the Fort I seeke;
All passages to it, so strongly kept,
By straite guard of her Father.
  Rin.   I dare sweare,
If iust desert in loue measur'd reward,   25
Your fortune should exceede *Valerios* farre:
For I am witnes (being your Bedfellow)
Both to the dayly and the nightly seruice, /
You doe vnto the deity of loue,   [A4ᵛ]

1 alike] a like ‖ 2 effects] *Q(c)*; effect *Q(u)* ‖ 3 straines] *Q(c)*; steaines *Q(u)* ‖ 5 notes,] *Q(c)*;
~: *Q(u)* ‖ 6 loue:] *Q(c)*; ~? *Q(u)* ‖

237

In vowes, sighes, teares, and solitary watches; 30
He neuer serues him with such sacrifice,
Yet hath his Bowe and shaftes at his commaund:
Loues seruice is much like our humorous Lords;
Where Minions carry more then Seruitors,
The bolde and carelesse seruant still obtaines: 35
The modest and respectiue, nothing gaines;
You neuer see your loue, vnlesse in dreames,
He, *Hymen* puts in whole possession:
What different starres raign'd when your loues were borne,
He forc't to weare the Willow, you the horne? 40
But brother, are you not asham'd to make
Your selfe a slaue to the base Lord of loue,
Begot of Fancy, and of Beauty borne?
And what is Beauty? a meere Quintessence,
Whose life is not in being, but in seeming; 45
And therefore is not to all eyes the same,
But like a cousoning picture, which one way
Shewes like a Crowe, another like a Swanne:
And vpon what ground is this Beauty drawne?
Vpon a Woman, a most brittle creature, 50
And would to God (for my part) that were all.
   For. But tell me brother, did you neuer loue?
   Rin. You know I did, and was belou'd againe,
And that of such a Dame, as all men deem'd
Honour'd, and made me happy in her fauours; 55
Exceeding faire she was not; and yet faire
In that she neuer studyed to be fayrer
Then Nature made her; Beauty cost her nothing,
Her vertues were so rare, they would haue made
An *Æthyop* beautifull: At least, so thought 60
By such as stood aloofe, and did obserue her
With credulous eyes: But what they were indeed
Ile spare to blaze, because I lou'd her once,
Onely I found her such, as for her sake /
I vow eternall warres against their whole sexe, [B1] 65
Inconstant shuttle-cocks, louing fooles, and iesters,
Men rich in durt and tytles, sooner woone
With the most vile, then the most vertuous:
Found true to none: if one amongst whole hundreds

---

30 watches;] ∼, ‖ **55** fauours;] ∼, ‖ **66** iesters,] *Parrott*; ∼; ‖ **67** durt and tytles,] *Collier*; ∼, ∼ ∼∧ ‖

238

Chance to be chaste, she is so proude withall,   70
Wayward and rude, that one of vnchaste life,
Is oftentimes approu'd, a worthier wife:
Vndressed, sluttish, nasty, to their husbands,
Spung'd vp, adorn'd, and painted to their louers:
All day in cesselesse vprore with their housholdes,   75
If all the night their husbands haue not pleas'd them:
Like hounds, most kinde, being beaten and abus'd,
Like wolues, most cruell, being kindelyest vs'd.
    For. Fye, thou profan'st the deity of their sexe.
    Rin. Brother I read, that *Ægipt* heretofore,   80
Had Temples of the richest frame on earth;
Much like this goodly edifice of women,
With Alablaster pillers were those Temples,
Vphelde and beautified, and so are women:
Most curiously glaz'd, and so are women;   85
Cunningly painted too, and so are women;
In out-side wondrous heauenly, so are women:
But when a stranger view'd those phanes within,
In stead of Gods and Goddesses, he should finde
A painted fowle, a fury, or a serpent,   90
And such celestiall inner parts haue women.
    Val. Rynaldo, the poore Foxe that lost his tayle,
Perswaded others also to loose theirs:
Thy selfe, for one perhaps that for desert
Or some defect in thy attempts refus'd thee,   95
Reuil'st the whole sexe, beauty, loue and all:
I tell thee, Loue, is Natures second sunne,
Causing a spring of vertues where he shines,
And as without the Sunne, the Worlds great eye,
All colours, beauties, both of Arte and Nature, /   100
Are giuen in vaine to men, so without loue   [B1ᵛ]
All beauties bred in women are in vaine;
All vertues borne in men lye buried,
For loue informes them as the Sunne doth colours,
And as the Sunne reflecting his warme beames   105
Against the earth, begets all fruites and flowers:
So loue, fayre shining in the inward man,
Brings foorth in him the honourable fruites
Of valour, wit, vertue, and haughty thoughts,

76 them:] ∼, ‖ **81** richest] *Reed*; riches ‖ **97** sunne] *Shepherd*; sonne ‖

Braue resolution, and diuine discourse: 110
O tis the Paradice, the heauen of earth,
And didst thou know the comfort of two hearts,
In one delicious harmony vnited?
As to ioy one ioy, and thinke both one thought,
Liue both one life, and therein double life: 115
To see their soules met at an enter-view
In their bright eyes, at parle in their lippes,
Their language kisses: And t'obserue the rest,
Touches, embraces, and each circumstance
Of all loues most vnmatched ceremonies: 120
Thou wouldst abhorre thy tongue for blasphemy,
O who can comprehend how sweet loue tastes,
But he that hath been present at his feastes?
 Rin. Are you in that vaine too *Valerio?*
Twere fitter you should be about your charge,   125
How Plow and Cart goes forward: I haue knowne
Your ioyes were all imployde in husbandry,
Your study was how many loades of hay
A meadow of so many acres yeelded;
How many Oxen such a close would fat?   130
And is your rurall seruice now conuerted
From *Pan* to *Cupid?* and from beastes to women?
O if your father knew this, what a lecture
Of bitter castigation he would read you?
 Val. My father? why my father? does he thinke 135
To rob me of my selfe? I hope I know /
I am a Gentleman; though his couetous humour   [B2]
And education hath transform'd me Bayly,
And made me ouerseer of his pastures,
Ile be my selfe, in spight of husbandry.   140

Enter Gratiana.

And see bright heauen here comes my husbandry, *Amplectitur eam.*
Here shall my cattle graze, here *Nectar* drinke,
Here will I hedge and ditch, here hide my treasure,
O poore *Fortunio,* how wouldst thou tryumph,
If thou enioy'dst this happines with my Sister?   145
 For. I were in heauen if once twere come to that.
 Rin. And me thinkes tis my heauen that I am past it:
And should the wretched Macheuilian,

---

126 forward] (?) fo.ward ‖ **137** Gentleman;] $\sim$, ‖ **147** it:] $\sim$, ‖

The couetous knight your father see this sight
Lusty *Valerio?*
   Val.   Sfoote Sir if he should,   150
He shall perceiue ere long my skill extends
To something more, then sweaty husbandry.
   Rin. Ile beare thee witnes, thou canst skill of dice,
Cards, tennis, wenching, dauncing, and what not?
And this is something more then husbandry: 155
Th'art knowne in Ordinaries, and *Tabacco* shops,
Trusted in Tauernes and in vaulting houses,
And this is something more then husbandry:
Yet all this while, thy father apprehends thee
For the most tame and thriftie Groome in *Europe.*   160
   For. Well, he hath venter'd on a mariage
Would quite vndoe him, did his father know it.
   Rin. Know it? alas Sir where can he bestow
This poore Gentlewoman he hath made his wife,
But his inquisitiue father will heare of it?   165
Who, like the dragon to th'esperean fruite,
Is to his haunts? Slight hence, the olde knight comes.

          Intrat Gostanzo. Omnes aufugiunt.

   Gost. Rynaldo.
   Rin.   Whose that calles? what Sir *Gostanzo?*
How fares your Knighthood Sir? /
   Gost.   Say who was that   [B2ᵛ]
Shrunke at my entry here? was't not your brother?   170
   Rin. He shrunke not sir, his busines call'd him hence.
   Gost. And was it not my sonne that went out with him?
   Rin. I saw not him, I was in serious speech
About a secret busines with my brother.
   Gost. Sure twas my sonne, what made he here? I sent him   175
About affaires to be dispacht in hast.
   Rin. Well sir, lest silence breed vniust suspect,
Ile tell a secret I am sworne to keep,
And craue your honoured assistance in it.
   Gost. What ist *Rynaldo?*
   Rin.   This sir, twas your sonne.   180
   Gost. And what yong gentlewoman grac'st their company?
   Rin. Thereon depends the secret I must vtter:
That gentlewoman hath my brother maryed.

---

150 *Valerio?*] *Q(c)*; ∼. *Q(u)* ‖ **162** it.] *Q(u)*; ∼? *Q(c)* *(See Textual Note)* ‖ **167** Slight] slight
| SD *Intrat . . . aufugiunt.*] *Intrat Gostanzo. (after Rynaldo., l. 168*; *Omnes aufugiunt. (after Gostanzo?,*
l. 168) ‖

Gost. Maryed? what is she?

Rin.   Faith sir, a gentlewoman:

But her vnusering dowry must be tolde   185

Out of her beauty.

Gost.   Is it true *Rynaldo*?

And does your father vnderstand so much?

    Rin. That was the motion sir, I was entreating

Your sonne to make to him, because I know

He is well spoken, and may much preuaile   190

In satisfying my father, who much loues him,

Both for his wisedome and his husbandry.

    Gost. Indeede he's one can tell his tale I tell you,

And for his husbandry —

    Rin.   O sir, had you heard,

What thrifty discipline he gaue my brother,   195

For making choyce without my fathers knowledge,

And without riches, you would haue admyr'd him.

    Gost. Nay, nay, I know him well, but what was it?

    Rin. That in the choyce of wiues men must respect

The chiefe wife, riches, that in euery course /   200

A mans chiefe Load-starre should shine out of riches,   [B3]

Loue nothing hartely in this world but riches;

Cast off all friends, all studies, all delights,

All honesty, and religion for riches:

And many such, which wisedome sure he learn'd   205

Of his experient father; yet my brother,

So soothes his rash affection, and presumes

So highly on my fathers gentle nature,

That he's resolu'd to bring her home to him,

And like enough he will.

    Gost.   And like enough   210

Your silly father too, will put it vp,

An honest knight, but much too much indulgent

To his presuming children.

    Rin.   What a difference

Doth interpose it selfe, twixt him and you?

Had your sonne vs'd you thus?

    Gost.   My sonne? alas   215

I hope to bring him vp in other fashion,

Followes my husbandry, sets early foote

---

185 vnusering] *Q(c)*; vnnurishing *Q(u)* (*See Textual Note*) ‖ **194** husbandry—] ∼. ‖ **210** enough] ∼. ‖

Into the world; he comes not at the citty,
Nor knowes the citty Artes.
    Rin.   But dice and wenching.   *Auersus.*
    Gost. Acquaints himselfe with no delight but getting,   220
A perfect patterne of sobriety,
Temperance and husbandry to all my housholde,
And what's his company I pray? not wenches.
    Rin. Wenches? I durst be sworne he neuer smelt
A wenches breath yet, but me thinkes twere fit   225
You sought him out a wife.
    Gost.   A wife *Rynaldo?*
He dares not looke a woman in the face.
    Rin. Sfoote holde him to one, your sonne such a sheep?
    Gost. Tis strange in earnest.
    Rin. Well sir, though for my thriftlesse brothers sake,   230
I little care how my wrong'd father takes it,
Yet for my fathers quiet, if your selfe /
Would joyne hands with your wise and toward Sonne,   [B3ᵛ]
I should deserue it some way.
    Gost.   Good *Rynaldo,*
I loue you and your father, but this matter   235
Is not for me to deale in: And tis needlesse,
You say your brother is resolu'd, presuming
Your father will allow it.
                   Enter Marc. Antonio.
    Rin.   See my father:
Since you are resolute not to moue him Sir,
In any case conceale the secret   *Abscondit se.*
By way of an attonement, let me pray
You will.
    Gost. Vpon mine honour.
    Rin.   Thankes Sir.
    Mar. God saue thee honourable Knight *Gostanzo.*
    Gost. Friend *Marc. Antonio?* welcome, and I thinke
I haue good newes to welcome you withall.   245
    Rin. He cannot holde.
    Mar.   What newes I pray you Sir?
    Gost. You haue a forward, valiant eldest Sonne,
But wherein is his forwardnes, and valour?
    Mar. I know not wherein you intend him so.

224-26 Wenches . . . wife.] *Shepherd*; Wenches . . . breath / Yet . . . wife. Q (a . . . you) ‖ **224** be sworne] besworne ‖ **227** looke] lookee ‖ **233** wise] *Shepherd*; wife ‖ **238** SD *Marc. Antonio.*] *Marcantonio.* ‖ **238-42** See . . . will.] See . . . Sir, / In . . . secret / By . . . will. Q (since . . . you) ‖ **238** father:] ∼, ‖ **240** SD *se.*] ∼, *(set in as if part of l. 240 in Q)* ‖ **241** attonement,] ∼∧ ‖

Gost. Forward before, valiant behinde, his duety,   250
That he hath dar'd before your due consent
To take a wife.
    Mar.   A wife sir? what is she?
    Gost. One that is rich enough, her hayre pure Amber,
Her forehead mother of pearle, her faire eyes
Two wealthy diamants: her lips, mines of Rubies: 255
Her teeth, are orient pearle; her necke, pure Iuory.
    Mar. Iest not good Sir, in an affayre so serious,
I loue my sonne, and if his youth reward me
With his contempt of my consent in mariage:
Tis to be fear'd that his presumption buildes not   260
Of his good choyce, that will beare out it selfe,
And being bad, the newes is worse then bad.
    Gost. What call you bad? is it bad to be poore?
    Mar. The world accounts it so; but if my sonne /
Haue in her birth and vertues helde his choice,   [B4] 265
Without disparagement, the fault is lesse.
    Gost. Sits the winde there? blowes there so calme a gale
From a contemned and deserued anger?
Are you so easie to be disobay'd?
    Mar. What should I doe? if my enamour'd sonne   270
Haue been so forward; I assure my selfe
He did it more to satisfie his loue,
Then to incense my hate, or to neglect me.
    Gost. A passing kinde construction; suffer this,
You ope him doores to any villany,   275
He'le dare to sell, to pawne, runne euer ryot,
Despise your loue in all, and laugh at you:
And that knights competency you have gotten
With care and labour, he with lust and idlenesse
Will bring into the stypend of a begger;   280
All to maintaine a wanton whirly-gig,
Worth nothing more then she brings on her back,
Yet all your wealth too little for that back:
By heauen I pitty your declining state,
For be assur'd your sonne hath set his foote,   285
In the right path-way to consumption:
Vp to the heart in loue; and for that loue,
Nothing can be too deare his loue desires:
And how insatiate and vnlymited,

264 sonne] *Reed*; soone ‖ 279 labour,] ∼; ‖

Is the ambition and the beggerly pride 290
Of a dame hoysed from a beggers state,
To a state competent and plentifull,
You cannot be so simple not to know.
   Mar. I must confesse the mischiefe: But alas
Where is in me the power of remedy? 295
   Gost. Where? in your iust displeasure: cast him off,
Receiue him not, let him endure the vse
Of their enforced kindnesse that must trust him
For meate and money, for apparrell, house,
And euery thing belongs to that estate, / 300
Which he must learne with want of misery, [B4ᵛ]
Since pleasure and a full estate hath blinded
His dissolute desires.
   Mar.   What should I doe?
If I should banish him my house and sight,
What desperate resolution might it breed? 305
To runne into the warres, and there to liue
In want of competencie: and perhaps
Taste th'vnrecouerable losse of his chiefe limbes,
Which while he hath in peace, at home with me,
May with his spirit, ransome his estate 310
From any losse his mariage can procure.
   Gost. Ist true? No let him runne into the warre,
And lose what limbes he can: better one branch
Be lopt away, then all the whole tree should perish:
And for his wants, better young want then olde; 315
You have a younger sonne at *Padoa,*
I like his learning well, make him your heire,
And let your other walke: let him buy wit
Att's owne charge, not at's fathers, if you loose him,
You loose no more then that was lost before, 320
If you recouer him, you finde a sonne.
   Mar. I cannot part with him.
   Gost.   If it be so,
And that your loue to him be so extreame,
In needfull daungers, euer chuse the least:
If he should be in minde to passe the Seas, 325
Your sonne *Rynaldo* (who tolde me all this)
Will tell me that, and so we shall preuent it:
If by no sterne course you will venture that,

312 No] *Collier;* Ne ‖ 315 olde;] ∼, ‖ 322-23 If . . . extreame,] *Reed; one line* Q (and) ‖

Let him come home to me with his faire wife:
And if you chaunce to see him, shake him vp,   330
As if your wrath were hard to be reflected,
That he may feare hereafter to offend
In other dissolute courses: At my house
With my aduice and my sonnes good example,
Who shall serue as a glasse for him to see /   335
His faults, and mend them to his president: [C1]
I make no doubt but of a dissolut Sonne
And disobedient, to send him home
Both dutifull and thriftie.
    Mar.   O *Gostanzo!*
Could you do this, you should preserue your selfe,   340
A perfect friend of mee, and mee a Sonne.
    Gost. Remember you your part, and feare not mine:
Rate him, reuile him, and renounce him too:
Speake, can you doo't man?
    Mar.   Ile do all I can.   *Exit Mar.*
    Gost. Ahlas good man, how Nature ouer-wayes him.   345

              Rynaldo comes foorth.

    Rin. God saue you Sir.
    Gost.   *Rynaldo,* All the Newes
You told mee as a secret, I perceiue
Is passing common; for your Father knowes it,
The first thing he related, was the Marriage.
    Rin. And was extreamly moou'd?
    Gost.   Beyond all measure: 350
But I did all I could to quench his furie:
Told him how easie t'was for a young man
To runne that Amorous course: and though his choyce
Were nothing rich, yet shee was gentlie borne,
Well quallified and beautifull: But hee still   355
Was quite relentles, and would needes renounce him.
    Rin. My brother knowes it well, and is resolud
To trayle a Pyke in Field, rather then bide
The more feard push of my vext Fathers furie.
    Gost. Indeed that's one way: but are no more meanes   360
Left to his fine wits, then t'incence his Father
With a more violent rage, and to redeeme
A great offence with greater?
    Rin.   So I told him:
But to a desperat minde all breath is lost.

---

339 thriftie.] ∼, ‖ **342** mine] *Q(c)*; wine *Q(u)* ‖ **364** lost.] ∼, ‖

Gost. Go to, let him be wise, and vse his friendes, /   365
Amongst whom, Ile be formost to his Father: [C1ᵛ]
Without this desperate errour he intends
Ioynd to the other, Ile not doubt to make him
Easie returne into his Fathers fauour:
So he submit himselfe, as duetie bindes him: 370
For Fathers will be knowne to be them selues,
And often when their angers are not deepe,
Will paint an outward Rage vpon their lookes.
   Rin. All this I told him Sir; but what sayes hee?
I know my Father will not be reclaymde,   375
Heele thinke that if he wincke at this offence,
T'will open doores to any villanie:
Ile dare to sell, to pawne, and run all ryot,
To laugh at all his patience, and consume
All he hath purchast to an honord purpose,   380
In maintenance of a wanton Whirligigg,
Worth nothing more then she weares on her backe.
   Gost. [*Aside.*] The very words I vsd t'incense his Father. —
But good *Rinaldo* let him be aduisde:
How would his Father grieue, should he be maynd,   385
Or quite miscarie in the ruthles warre?
   Rin. I told him so; but better farr (sayd hee)
One branch should vtterly be lopt away,
Then the whole Tree of all his race should perish:
And for his wants, better yong want, then eld.   390
   Gost. [*Aside.*] By heauen the same words still I vsde t'his Father.
Why comes this about? — Well, good *Rinaldo,*
If hee dare not indure his Fathers lookes,
Let him and his faire wife come home to me,
Till I haue quallified his Fathers passion,   395
He shall be kindly welcome, and be sure
Of all the intercession I can vse.
   Rin. I thanke you sir, Ile try what I can doe,
Although I feare me I shall striue in vaine.
   Gost. Well, try him, try him.   *Exit.*
   Rin.   Thanks sir, so I will. /   400
See, this olde politique dissembling Knight,   [C2]
Now he perceiues my Father so affectionate,
And that my brother may hereafter liue
By him and his, with equall vse of either,

368 other,] ∼; ‖ 378 sell,] ∼∧ ‖ 379 patience,] (?) ∼; ‖ 381 wanton] wenton ‖ 383 SD *Aside.*]
Collier | Father.—] ∼, ‖ 384 *Rinaldo*] *Rinoldo* ‖ 391 SD *Aside.*] *Collier* ‖

He will put on a face of hollowe friendship.   405
But this will proue an excellent ground to sowe
The seede of mirth amongst vs; Ile go seeke
Valerio and my brother, and tell them
Such newes of their affaires, as they'le admire.   *Exit.*

[I.ii]

Enter Gazetta, Bellanora, Gratiana.

    Gaz. How happie are your fortunes aboue mine?
Both still being woode and courted: still so feeding
On the delightes of loue, that still you finde
An appetite to more; where I am cloyde,
And being bound to loue sportes, care not for them.   5
    Bell. That is your fault *Gazetta,* we haue Loues
And wish continuall company with them
In honour'd marriage rites, which you enioy.
But seld or neuer can we get a looke
Of those we loue, *Fortunio* my deare choyce   10
Dare not be knowne to loue me, nor come neere
My Fathers house, where I as in a prison
Consume my lost dayes, and the tedious nights,
My Father guarding me for one I hate;
And *Gratiana* here my brothers loue,   15
Ioyes him by so much stelth, that vehement feare
Drinkes vp the sweetnesse of their stolne delightes:
Where you enioye a husband, and may freely
Performe all obsequies you desire to loue.
    Gaz. Indeede I haue a husband, and his loue   20
Is more then I desire, being vainely ielouse:
Extreames, though contrarie, haue the like effects,
Extreame heate mortifies like extreame colde: /
Extreame loue breedes sacietie as well   [C2ᵛ]
As extreame Hatred: and too violent rigour,   25
Tempts Chastetie as much, as too much Licence:
There's no mans eye fixt on mee but doth pierce
My Husbandes soule: If any aske my wel-fare?
Hee straight doubts Treason practis'd to his bed:
Fancies but to himselfe all likelihoods   30
Of my wrong to him, and layes all on mee

I.ii] *Parrott* ‖ SD *Bellanora*] *Bellonora* ‖ **14** hate;] ∼∧ ‖ **20** haue] hane ‖ **23** Extreame] *Reed;*
Extreames ‖

For certaine trueths; yet seekes he with his best,
To put Disguise on all his Ielosie,
Fearing perhaps, least it may teach me that,
Which otherwise I should not dreame vpon: 35
Yet liues he still abrode, at great expence,
Turns merely Gallant from his Farmers state,
Vses all Games and recreations:
Runnes Races with the Gallants of the Court,
Feastes them at home, and entertaines them costly,   40
And then vpbraydes mee with their companie:

     Enter Cornelio.

See see, wee shalbe troubl'd with him now.
 Cor. Now Ladyes, what plots haue we now in hand?
They say, when onely one Dame is alone,
Shee plots some mischiefe; but if three together,   45
They plot three hundred: Wife, the Ayre is sharpe,
Y'ad best to take the house least you take cold.
 Gaz. Ahlas this time of yeere yeeldes no such danger.
 Cor. Goe, in I say; a friend of yours attends you.
 Gaz. Hee is of your bringing, and may stay.   50
 Cor. Nay stand not chopping Logicke; in I pray.
 Gaz. Yee see, Gentlewomen, what my happines is,
These humors raigne in mariage; humors, humors. *Exit, he followeth.*
 Gra. Now by my Sooth I am no fortune teller,
And would be loth to prooue so; yet pronounce   55
This at aduenture, that t'were indecorum
This Heffer should want hornes.
 Bell.   Fie on this Loue, /
I rather wish to want, then purchase so.   [C3]
 Gra. In deede such Loue is like a Smokie fire
In a cold morning; though the Fire be cheerefull,   60
Yet is the Smoke so sowre and combersome,
T'were better lose the Fire, then finde the Smoke:
Such an attendant then as Smoke to Fire,
Is Ielosie to Loue: Better want both,
Then haue both.

    Enter Valerio and Fortunio.

 Val.   Come *Fortunio,* now take hold   65
On this occasion, as my selfe on this:
One couple more would make a Barly-breake.

---

42 see, wee] *Q(c)*; see wee, wee *Q(u)* ‖ **48** danger.] ∼, ‖ **52** Gentlewomen] Gentle women ‖

Gra. I feare *Valerio,* wee shall breake too soone,
Your Fathers Ielosie, Spy-all, will displease vs.
    Val. Well Wench, the daye will come his Argus eyes   70
Will shut, and thou shalt open: Sfoote, I thinke
Dame *Natures* memorie begins to fayle her:
If I write but my Name in Mercers Bookes,
I am as sure to haue at sixe months end
A Rascole at my elbow with his Mace,   75
As I am sure my Father's not farre hence:
My Father yet hath ought *Dame Nature* debt
These threescore yeeres and ten, yet cals not on him:
But if shee turne her Debt-booke ouer once,
And finding him her debtor, do but send   80
Her Sergeant *Iohn Death* to arrest his body,
Our Soules shall rest Wench then, and the free Light
Shall triumph in our faces; where now Night,
In imitation of my Fathers frownes,
Lowres at our meeting:

Enter Rinald.

                See where the Scholler comes.   85
    Rin. Downe on your knees; poore louers reuerence learning.
    For. I pray thee why *Rinaldo?*
    Rin.   Marke what cause /
Flowes from my depth of knowledge to your loues,   [C3ᵛ]
To make you kneele and blesse me while you liue.
    Val. I pray thee good Scholard giue vs cause.   90
    Rin. Marke then, erect your eares: you know what horror
Would flye on your loue from your fathers frownes,
If he should know it. And your sister here,
(My brothers sweete hart) knowes aswell what rage
Would sease his powers for her, if he should knowe   95
My brother woo'd her, or that she lou'd him:
Is not this true? speake all.
    Omn.   All this is true.
    Rin. It is as true that now you meete by stelth
In depth of midnight, kissing out at grates,
Clime ouer walles. And all this Ile reforme.   100
    Val. By Logicke?
    Rin.   Well sir, you shall haue all meanes
To liue in one house, eate and drinke together,
Meete and kisse your fils.
    Val.   All this by learning?

---

68 *Gra.*] *Parrott; For.* ‖ **69** Ielosie,] *Reed;* ∼∧ ‖ **76** Father's] Fathers ‖ **82** and] And ‖ **86** learning.] ∼∧ ‖ **90** Scholard] *Reed;* Scholards ‖ **96** him:] ∼, ‖ **100** reforme] *Q(c)*; adforme *Q(u)* ‖
101 Logicke?] ∼. ‖

Rin. I, and your frowning father know all this.

Val. I marry, small learning may proue that. 105

Rin. Nay he shall know it, and desire it too,
Welcome my Brother to him, and your wife,
Entreating both to come and dwell with him.
Is not this strange?

For.　　　　I, too strange to be true.

Rin. Tis in this head shall worke it: Therefore heare; 110
Brother this Lady you must call your wife,
For I haue tolde her sweet harts Father here
That she is your wife; and because my Father
(Who now beleeues it) must be quieted
Before you see him, you must liue a while 115
As husband to her, in his Fathers house.
Valerio here's a simple meane for you
To lye at racke and manger with your wedlocke,
And brother, for your selfe to meete as freely /
With this your long desir'd and barred loue. [C4] 120

For. You make vs wonder.

Rin.　　　　　　Peace, be ruld by mee,
And you shall see to what a perfect shape
Ile bring this rude Plott, which blind Chaunce (the Ape
Of Counsaile and aduice) hath brought foorth blind.
Valerio, can your heat of loue forbeare 125
Before your Father, and allow my Brother
To vse some kindnes to your wife before him?

Val. I, before him, I do not greatlie care,
Nor anie where in deed; my Sister heere
Shall be my spie: if shee will wrong her selfe, 130
And giue her right to my wife, I am pleasd.

For. My dearest life I know, will neuer feare
Anie such will or thought in all my powers:
When I court her then, thinke I thinke tis thee:
When I embrace her, hold thee in mine Armes: 135
Come, let vs practise gainst wee see your Father.

Val. Soft Sir, I hope you need not do it yet,
Let mee take this time.

Rin.　　　　　Come, you must not touch her.

Val. No not before my Father?

Rin.　　　　　　　No nor now,
Because you are so soone to practise it; 140
For I must bring them to him presentlie.

---

109 I,] ∼∧ ‖ **113** wife] *Q(c)*; wifs *Q(u)* ‖ **118** wedlocke,] ∼∧ ‖ **128** I,] ∼∧ ‖

Take her *Fortunio*; goe, hence man and wife,
Wee will attend you rarely with fixt faces.
Valerio keepe your countenaunce, and conseaue
Your Father in your forged sheepishnes,   145
Who thinks thou dar'st not looke vpon a Wench,
Nor knowest at which end to begin to kisse her.   *Exeunt.*

Finis Actus Primi. /

Actus secundi. Scæna prima.   [C4ᵛ]

Gostanzo, Marc. Antonio.

Gost. It is your owne too simple lenitie,
And doting indulgence showne to him still
That thus hath taught your Sonne to be no Sonne,
As you haue vs'd him, therefore so you haue him:
Durst my Sonne thus turne rebell to his dutie,   5
Steale vp a match vnshuting his estate
Without all knowledge of or friend or father;
And to make that good with a worse offence
Resolue to runne beyond Sea to the warres?
Durst my Sonne serue me thus? well, I haue stayd him,   10
Though much against my disposition,
And this howre I haue set for his repayre,
With his young mistresse and concealed wife,
And in my house here they shall soiourne both
Till your blacke angers storme be ouer-blowne.   15
Mar. My angers storme? Ah poore *Fortunio,*
One gentle word from thee would soone resolue
The storme of my rage to a showre of teares.
Gost. In that vaine still? well *Marc. Antonio,*
Our olde acquaintance and long neighbourhood   20
Ties my affection to you, and the good
Of your whole house; in kinde regard whereof
I haue aduisde you for your credite sake,
And for the tender welfare of your sonne,
To frowne on him a little; if you do not   25
But at first parle take him to your fauour,
I protest vtterly to renownce all care
Of you and yours, and all your amities.
They say hee's wretched that out of himselfe

144 countenaunce] conntenaunce ‖ **147** SD *Primi*] *Parrott*; *Prima* ‖ II.i secundi.] secundi, ‖
SD *Marc. Antonio*] *Marcantonio* ‖ **4** him:] *Q(c)*; ~, *Q(u)* ‖ **9** Resolue] resolue *Q(c)*; Adsolue
Q(u) | warres?] ~. ‖ **10** thus?] *Q(c)*; ~, *Q(u)* ‖ **19** *Marc. Antonio*] *Marcantonio* ‖ **20** Our] Gur ‖

252

Cannot draw counsell to his propper weale, 30
But hee's thrice wretched that has neither counsell
Within himselfe, nor apprehension /
Of counsaile for his owne good, from another. [D1]
    Mar. Well, I will arme my selfe against this weaknes
The best I can; I long to see this *Hellene* 35
That hath enchaunted my young *Paris* thus,
And's like to set all our poore *Troye* on fire.

Enter Valerio with a Page.
Marc. retyres himselfe.

    Gost. Here comes my Sonne; withdraw, take vp your stand,
You shall heare odds betwixt your Sonne and mine.
    Val. Tell him I can not doo't: Shall I be made 40
A foolish Nouice, my Purse set a broch
By euerie cheating come you seauen? to lend
My Money and be laught at? tell him plaine
I professe Husbandrie, and will not play
The Prodigall like him, gainst my profession. 45
    Gost. [*Aside to Mar.*] Here's a Sonne.
    Mar. [*Aside to Gost.*]   An admirable sparke.
    Pag. Well sir, Ile tell him so.   *Exit Page.*
    Val.   Sfoote, let him lead
A better Husbands life, and liue not idlely,
Spending his time, his coyne, and selfe on Wenches.
    Gost. Why what's the matter Sonne? 50
    Val. Cry mercie Sir; why there comes messengers
For this and that braue Gallant: and such Gallants,
As I protest I saw but through a Grate.
    Gost. And what's this Message?
    Val.   Faith Sir, hee's disappoynted
Of payments; and disfurnisht of meanes present: 55
If I would do him the kind office therefore
To trust him but some seuen-night with the keeping
Of fourtie Crownes for mee, hee deepely sweares
As hee's a Gentleman, to discharge his trust,
And that I shall eternally endeare him 60
To my wisht seruice, he protestes and contestes. /
    Gost. Good words *Valerio*; but thou art too wise [D1ᵛ]
To be deceiu'd by breath: Ile turne thee loose
To the most cunning Cheater of them all.

---

30 weale] *Q(c)*; veale *Q(u)* ‖ **37** *Troye*] *Reed*; *Trope* | SD *himselfe.*] ∼, ‖ **46** SD *Aside to Mar.*]
Parrott[1] | SD *Aside to Gost.*] *Parrott*[1] ‖

Val. Sfoote, Hee's not ashamde besides to charge mee   65
With a late Promise: I must yeeld in deed,
I did (to shift him with some contentment)
Make such a friuall promise.
    Gost.   I, well done,
Promises are no Fetters: with that tongue
Thy promise past, vnpromise it againe.   70
Wherefore has Man a Tongue, of powre to speake,
But to speake still to his owne priuate purpose?
Beastes vtter but one sound; but Men haue change
Of speach and Reason, euen by Nature giuen them:
Now to say one thing, and an other now,   75
As best may serue their profitable endes.
    Mar. [*Aside.*] Ber-Ladie sound instructions to a Sonne.
    Val. Nay Sir, he makes his claime by debt of friendship.
    Gost. Tush, Friendship's but a Terme boy: the fond world
Like to a doting Mother glases ouer   80
Her Childrens imperfections with fine tearmes:
What she calls Frindship and true humane kindnes,
Is onely want of true Experience:
Honestie is but a defect of Witt,
Respect but meere Rusticitie and Clownerie.   85
    Mar. [*Aside.*] Better and better. Soft, here comes my Sonne.

        Enter Fortunio, Rinaldo, and Gratiana.

    Rin. [*Aside.*] *Fortunio,* keepe your countenance: — See sir here
The poore young married couple, which you pleasd
To send for to your house.
    Gost.   *Fortunio* welcome,
And in that welcome I imploy your wiues,   90
Who I am sure you count your second selfe.   *He kisses her.* /
    For. Sir, your right noble fauours do exceede   [D2]
All powre of worthy gratitude by words,
That in your care supplie my Fathers place.
    Gost. Fortunio, I can not chuse but loue you,   95
Being Sonne to him who long time I haue lou'd:
From whose iust anger, my house shall protect you,
Till I haue made a calme way to your meetings.
    For. I little thought Sir, that my Fathers loue
Would take so ill, so sleight a fault as this.   100
    Gost. Call you it sleight? Nay though his spirit take it
In higher manner then for your lou'd sake,

77 SD *Aside.*] *Collier* ‖ **81** tearmes:] *Q(c);* ∼. *Q(u)* ‖ **86** SD *Aside.*] *Collier* | SD *Fortunio*] *Fortunion*
‖ **87** SD *Aside.*] *Parrott* ‖

I would haue wisht him; yet I make a doubt,
Had my Sonne done the like, if my affection
Would not haue turnd to more spleene, then your Fathers: 105
And yet I quallifie him, all I can,
And doubt not but that time and my perswasion,
Will worke out your excuse: since youth and loue
Were th'vnresisted orgaines to seduce you:
But you must give him leaue, for Fathers must   110
Be wonne by penitence and submission,
And not by force or opposition.
    For. Ahlas Sir, what aduise you mee to doe?
I know my Father to be highly moou'd,
And am not able to endure the breath   115
Of his exprest displeasure, whose hote flames
I thinke my absence soonest would haue quencht.
    Gost. True Sir, as fire with oyle, or else like them
That quench the fire with pulling downe the house:
You shall remaine here in my house conceal'd   120
Till I haue wonne your Father to conceiue
Kinder opinion of your ouersight.
Valerio entertaine *Fortunio*
And his faire wife, and giue them conduct in.
    Val. Y'are welcome sir.
    Gost.   What sirha is that all?   125
No entertainment to the Gentlewoman? /
    Val. Forsooth y'are welcome by my Fathers leaue.   [D2ᵛ]
    Gost. What no more complement? kisse her you sheepes-head,
Why when? Go go Sir, call your Sister hither.   *Exit Val.*
Ladie, youle pardon our grosse bringing vp?   130
Wee dwell farre off from Court you may perceiue:
The sight of such a blazing Starre as you,
Dazles my rude Sonnes witts.
    Gra.   Not so good Sir,
The better husband, the more courtlie euer.
    Rin. In deed a Courtier makes his lipps go farre,   135
As he doth all things else.

Enter Valerio, Bell.

    Gost.   Daughter reciue
This Gentlewoman home, and vse her kindly.   *She kisses her.*
    Bell. My Father bids you kindly welcome Lady,
And therefore you must needes come well to mee.

---

109 orgaines] *Reed*; organies ‖ **117** thinke] thiuke ‖ **119** house:] ∼, ‖ **128** What . . . sheepes-head,] *Shepherd*; What . . . complement? / Kisse . . . sheepes-head, ‖ **136** SD *Valerio*] *Volerio* ‖ **137** SD *her.*] ∼∧ ‖

Gra. Thanke you for-soth.
Gost.   Goe Dame, conduct am in.   140
                         Exeunt Rinaldo, Fortunio, Bell. Grat.
Ah errant Sheepes-head, hast thou liu'd thus long,
And dar'st not looke a Woman in the face?
Though I desire especially to see
My Sonne a Husband, shall I therefore haue him
Turne absolute Cullion? Lets see, kisse thy hand.   145
Thou kisse thy hand? thou wip'st thy mouth by th'masse.
Fie on thee Clowne; They say the world's growne finer,
But I for my part, neuer saw Young men
Worse fashin'd and brought vp then now adayes.
Sfoote, when my selfe was young, was not I kept   150
As farre from Court as you? I thinke I was:
And yet my Father on a time inuited
The Dutchesse of his house; I beeing then
About some fiue and twentie yeares of age, /
Was thought the onelie man to entertaine her: [D3] 155
I had my Conge; plant my selfe of one legg,
Draw backe the tother with a deepe fetcht honor:
Then with a Bell regard aduant mine eye
With boldnes on her verie visnomie.
Your Dauncers all were counterfets to mee: 160
And for discourse in my faire Mistresse presence,
I did not as you barraine Gallants doe,
Fill my discourses vp drinking *Tobacco*;
But on the present furnisht euer more
With tales and practisde speeches; as some times,   165
What ist a clocke? What stuff's this Petticoate?
What cost the making? What the Frindge and all?
And what she had vnder her Petticoate?
And such like wittie complements: and for need,
I could haue written as good Prose and Verse,   170
As the most beggerlie Poet of am all,
Either *Accrostique, Exordion,*
Epithalamions, Satyres, Epigrams,
Sonnets in Doozens, or your *Quatorzaines,*
In any Rime *Masculine, Feminine,*   175
Or *Sdruciolla,* or *cooplets, Blancke Verse*:
Y'are but bench-whistlers now a dayes to them
That were in our times: well, about your Husbandrie,
Go, for I'fayth th'art fit for nothing else.   *Exit Val. prodit Mar.*

---

140 conduct am] conduct-am ‖ 144 shall] Shall ‖ 148 Young men] Youngmen ‖ 165 times,]
~∧ ‖ 172 *Accrostique*] accrostique ‖ 172-76 *Exordion . . . cooplets*] *italics throughout in Q* ‖ 173
Epithalamions] *Epithalamious* ‖ 174 *Quatorzaines*] *Shepherd*; *Qutorzanies* ‖ 176 *Sdruciolla*] *Shepherd*;
Sdrnciolla | *Blancke Verse*:] Blancke Verse, ‖

Mar. Ber-Ladie you haue plaide the Courtier rarelie.   180
Gost. But did you euer see so blanck a Foole,
When he should kisse a Wench, as my Sonne is?
Mar. Ahlas tis but a little bashfulnes,
You let him keepe no companie, nor allow him
Monie to spend at Fence and Dauncing-scholes,   185
Y'are too seueere y'faith.
Gost.   And you too supple.
Well Sir, for your sake I haue staide your Sonne
From flying to the warres: now see you rate him,
To staie him yet from more expencefull courses, /
Wherein your lenitie will encourage him.   [D3ᵛ] 190
Mar. Let me alone, I thank you for this kindnes.   *Exeunt.*

Enter Valerio and Rinaldo.

Rin. So, are they gone? Now tell me braue *Valerio*
Haue I not wonne the wreath from all your wits,
Brought thee t'enioy the most desired presence
Of thy deare loue at home? and with one labour   195
My brother t'enioy thy sister, where
It had beene her vndooing t'haue him seene,
And make thy father craue what he abhorres:
T'entreate my brother home t'enioy his daughter,
Commaund thee kisse thy wench, chide for not kissing,   200
And worke all this out of a Macheuil,
A miserable Politician?
I thinke the like was neuer plaid before!
Val. Indeede I must commend thy wit of force,
And yet I know not whose deserues most praise   205
Or thine, or my wit: thine for plotting well,
Mine, that durst vndertake and carrie it
With such true forme.
Rin.   Well, th'euening crownes the daie,
Perseuer to the end, my wit hath put
Blinde Fortunne in a string into your hand,   210
Vse it discreetlie, keepe it from your Father,
Or you may bid all your good daies good night.
Val. Let me alone boy.
Rin.   Well sir, now to varie
The pleasures of our wits, thou knowst *Valerio*
Here is the new turnd Gentlemans faire wife,   215
That keepes thy wife and sister companie;

206 Or] Of ‖

257

With whome the amorous Courtier *Dariotto*
Is farre in loue, and of whome her sowre husband
Is passing ielous, puts on Eagles eies
To prie into her carriage. Shall wee see /   220
If he be now from home, and visite her?   [D4]

        Enter Gazetta sowing, Cornelio following.

See, see, the prisoner comes.
   Val.   But soft Sir, see
Her ielous Iaylor followes at her heeles:
Come, we will watch some fitter time to boord her,
And in the meane time seeke out our mad crue.   225
My spirit longs to swagger.
   Rin.   Goe too youth,
Walke not too boldly; if the Sergeants meete you,
You may haue swaggering worke your bellie full.
   Val. No better Copesmates,   *Gazetta sits and singes sowing.*
Ile go seeke am out with this light in my hand,   230
The slaues grow proud with seeking out of vs.   *Exeunt.*
   Cor. A prettie worke, I pray what flowers are these?
   Gaz. The Pancie this.
   Cor.   O that's for louers thoughtes.
What's that, a Columbine?
   Gaz. No, that thankles Flower fitts not my Garden.   235
   Cor. Hum? yet it may mine:
This were a prettie present for some friend,
Some gallant Courtier, as for *Dariotto,*
One that adores you in his soule I know.
   Gaz. Mee? why mee more then your selfe I pray?   240
   Cor. O yes, hee adores you, and adhornes mee:
Yfaith deale plainelie; Doe not his kisses relish
Much better then such Pessants as I am?
   Gaz. Whose kisses?
   Cor.   *Dariottoes*; does he not
The thing you wot on? /
   Gaz.   What thing good Lord?   [D4ᵛ] 245
   Cor. Why Lady, lie with you?
   Gaz.   Lie with mee?
   Cor. I with you.
   Gaz.   You with mee indeed.

---

217 *Dariotto*] *Doriotto* ‖ **221** her?] ∼. ‖ **226-27** *Goe . . . you,*] *Shepherd; one line Q* (walke) ‖ **227** boldly; . . . you,] *Reed;* ∼, . . . ∼; ‖ **229** SD *Gazetta*] *Gazetto* ‖ **233** that's] thats ‖ **234** What's] Whats ‖ **236** Hum] Him ‖ **237** prettie] pretrie ‖ **238** *Dariotto*] *Doriotto* ‖ **242** plainelie;] ∼, ‖ **244** *Dariottoes*] *Doriottoes* | not] ∼? ‖

Cor. Nay I am told that he lies with you too,
And that he is the onely Whore-maister
About the Cittie.
    Gaz.   Yf he be so onely,   250
Tis a good hearing that there are no more.
    Cor. Well Mistresse well, I will not be abusde,
Thinke not you daunce in Netts; for though you do not
Make brode profession of your loue to him,
Yet do I vnderstand your darkest language,   255
Your treads ath'toe, your secret iogges and wringes:
Your entercourse of glaunces: euery tittle
Of your close Amorous rites I vnderstand,
They speake as loud to mee, as if you said,
My dearest *Dariotto,* I am thine.   260
    Gaz. Iesus what moodes are these? did euer Husband
Follow his Wife with Ielosie so vniust?
That once I lou'd you, you your selfe will sweare.
And if I did, where did you lose my Loue?
In deed this strange and vndeserued vsage,   265
Hath powre to shake a heart were nere so setled:
But I protest all your vnkindnes, neuer
Had strength to make me wrong you, but in thought.
    Cor. No, not with *Dariotto*?
    Gaz.   No by heauen.
    Cor. No Letters past, nor no designes for meeting?   270
    Gaz. No by my hope of heauen.
    Cor.   Well, no time past,
Goe goe; goe in and sow.
    Gaz.   Well, bee it so.   *Exit Gaz.*
    Cor. Suspition is (they say) the first degree
Of deepest wisedome: and how euer others /
Inueygh against this mood of Ielousy,   [E1] 275
For my part I suppose it the best curb,
To check the ranging appetites that raigne
In this weake sexe: my neighbours poynt at me
For this my ielousy; but should I doe
As most of them doe; let my wife fly out   280
To feasts and reuels, and inuite home Gallants,
Play *Menelaus,* giue them time and place,

269 *Dariotto*] *Doriotto* ‖

While I sit like a well-taught wayting-woman,
Turning her eyes vpon some worke or picture,
Read in a Booke, or take a fayned nap,   285
While her kind Lady takes one to her lap?
No, let me still be poynted at, and thought
A ielouse Asse, and not a wittally Knaue.
I haue a shew of Courtyers haunt my house,
In shew my friends, and for my profit too: 290
But I perceiue vm, and will mock their aymes,
With looking to their marke, I warrant vm:
I am content to ride abroad with them,
To reuell, dice, and fit their other sports;
But by their leaues ile haue a vigilant eye   295
To the mayne chaunce still. See my braue Comrades.

*Enter Dariotto and Page, Claudio and Valerio: Valerio putting
vp his Sword.*

  Dar. Well, wag, well, wilt thou still deceiue thy father,
And being so simple a poore soule before him,
Turne swaggerer in all companies besides?
    Clau. Hadst thou bin rested, all would haue come forth.   300
    Val. Soft, sir, there lyes the poynt; I do not doubt,
But t'haue my pennyworths of these Rascals one day:
Ile smoke the buzzing Hornets from their nests,
Or else ile make their lether Ierkins stay.
The whorson hungry Horse-flyes; Foot, a man   305
Cannot so soone, for want of Almanacks,
Forget his day but three or foure bare moneths, /
But strait he sees a sort of Corporals,   [E1ᵛ]
To lye in Ambuscado to surprize him.
    Dar. Well, thou hadst happy fortune to escape vm.   310
    Val. But they thought theirs was happier to scape me.
I walking in the place, where mens law suites
Are heard and pleaded, not so much as dreaming
Of any such encounter, steps me forth
Their valiant fore-man, with the word, I rest you.   315
I made no more adoe, but layd these pawes
Close on his shoulders, tumbling him to earth;
And there sate he on his *posteriors,*
Like a Baboone; and turning me about,
I strayt espyed the whole troope issuing on me.   320
I stept me backe, and drawing my olde friend heere,

296 SD *and Page*] *Parrott* ‖ **308** sees] *Reed*; fees *Q* ‖

Made to the midst of them, and all vnable
T'endure the shock, all rudely fell in rout,
And downe the stayres they ranne with such a fury,
As meeting with a troope of Lawyers there,   325
Man'd by their Clyents: some with ten, some with twenty,
Some fiue, some three; he that had least, had one:
Vpon the stayres they bore them downe afore them:
But such a rattling then was there amongst them
Of rauisht Declarations, Replications,   330
Reioynders and Petitions; all their bookes
And writings torne and trod on, and some lost,
That the poore Lawyers comming to the Barre,
Could say nought to the matter, but instead,
Were fayne to rayle and talke besides their bookes   335
Without all order.
    Clau.   Fayth, that same vayne of rayling
Became now most applausiue; your best Poet,
Is he that rayles grossest.
    Dar.   True, and your best foole
Is your broad rayling foole.
    Val.   And why not, sir?
For by the gods, to tell the naked trueth, /   340
What obiects see men in this world, but such   [E2]
As would yeeld matter to a rayling humour?
When he that last yere carryed after one
An empty Buckram bag, now fills a Coach,
And crowds the Senate with such troops of Clyents,   345
And seruile followers, as would put a mad spleene
Into a Pigeon.
    Dar.   Come, pray leaue these crosse capers,
Let's make some better vse of precious time.
See, here's *Cornelio*: come, Lad, shall we to dice?
    Cor. Any thing I.
    Clau.   Well sayd, how does thy wife?   350
    Cor. In health, God saue her.
    Val.   But where is she, man?
    Cor. Abroad about her businesse.
    Val.   Why, not at home?
Foot, my masters, take her to the Court,
And this rare Lad her husband: and doest heare?

336-38 Fayth . . . grossest.] Fayth . . . became / Now . . . is / He . . . grossest. *Q* (is) ‖

Play me no more the miserable Farmer,   355
But be aduisde by friends, sell all ith countrey,
Be a flat Courtier, follow some great man,
Or bring thy wife there, and sheele make thee great.
    Cor. What, to the Court? then take me for a Gull.
    Val. Nay, neuer shun it to be cald a Gull: 360
For I see all the world is but a Gull:
One man Gull to another in all kinds:
A Marchant to a Courtyer is a Gull:
A Clyent to a Lawyer is a Gull:
A marryed man to a Bacheler, a Gull: 365
A Bacheler to a Cuckold is a Gull:
All to a Poet, or a Poet to himselfe.
    Cor. [*Aside.*] Hark *Dariotto,* shall we gull this Guller?
    Dar. [*Aside.*] He gulls his father, man, we cannot gull him.
    Cor. [*Aside.*] Let me alone. — Of all mens wits aliue,   370
I most admyre *Valerioes,* that hath stolne,
By his meere industry, and that by spurts, /
Such qualities, as no wit else can match,   [E2ᵛ]
With plodding at perfection euery houre;
Which, if his father knew eche gift he has,   375
Were like enough to make him giue all from him:
I meane besides his dycing and his wenching,
He has stolne languages, th'Italian, Spanish,
And some spice of the French, besides his dauncing,
Singing, playing on choyce Instruments: 380
These has he got, almost against the hayre.
    Clau. But hast thou stolne all these, *Valerio*?
    Val. Toyes, toyes, a pox; and yet they be such toyes,
As euery Gentleman would not be without.
    Cor. Vayne glory makes yee iudge vm lyte yfayth.   385
    Dar. Afore heauen I was much deceyu'd in him:
But hee's the man indeed that hides his gifts,
And sets them not to sale in euery presence.
I would haue sworne, his soule were far from musike;
And that all his choyce musike was to heare   390
His fat beastes bellow.
    Cor.   Sir, your ignorance
Shall eftsoone be confuted. Prythee *Val,*
Take thy *Theorbo* for my sake a little.
    Val. By heauen, this moneth I toucht not a *Theorbo.*

368, 369, 370 SD *Aside.*] *Parrott* ‖ **385** Vayne] *Q(c)*; Vay ne *Q(u)* ‖ **385** vm] *Parrott*[1]; on ‖

Cor. Toucht a *Theorbo*? marke the very word.   395
Sirra, goe fetch.   *Exit Page.*
  Val. If you will haue it, I must needs confesse,
I am no husband of my qualityes.

                   He vntrusses and capers.

  Cor. See what a Caper there was!
Clau.   See agayne.
  Cor. The best that euer; and how it becomes him!   400
  Dar. O that his father saw these qualityes!

             Enter a Page with an Instrument.

  Cor. Nay, that's the very wonder of his wit,
To carry all without his fathers knowledge.
  Dar. Why, we might tell him now. /
  Cor.   No but we could not,   [E3]
Although we think we could: his wit doth charme vs.   405
Come sweet *Val,* touch and sing.
  Dar.   Foote, will you heare
The worst voyce in Italy?

                     Enter Rinaldo.

  Cor.   O God, sir.   *He sings.*
Courtiers, how like you this?
  Dar.   Beleeue it excellent.
  Cor. Is it not naturall?
  Val.   If my father heard me,
Foot, hee'd renounce me for his naturall sonne.   410
  Dar. By heauen, *Valerio,* and I were thy father,
And lou'd good qualities as I doe my life,
Ide disinherit thee: for I neuer heard
Dog howle with worse grace.
  Cor.   Go to, Signeur Courtier,
You deale not courtly now to be so playne,   415
Nor nobly, to discourage a young Gentleman,
In vertuous qualityes, that has but stolne vm.
  Clau. Call you this touching a *Theorbo*?
Omn.   Ha, ha, ha.

               Exeunt all but Val. and Rin.

  Val. How now, what's heere?
  Rin.   Zoones, a plot layd to gull thee.
Could thy wit thinke the voyce was worth the hearing?   420
This was the Courtiers and the Cuckolds proiect.

407-8 O God ... this?] *Parrott; one line* Q ‖ **418** Ha] ha ‖ **420** the voyce] *better perhaps read* thy voyce *as in Shepherd* ‖

Val. And ist eene so? tis very well, Mast Courtier,
And Dan Cornuto, ile cry quit with both:
And first, ile cast a iarre betwixt them both,
With firing the poore cuckolds ielousy.   425
I haue a tale will make him madde,
And turne his wife diuorced loose amongst vs.
But first let's home, and entertayne my wife.
O father, pardon, I was borne to gull thee.   *Exeunt.*

Finis Actus secundi. /

ACTVS III. SCENA I.   [E3ᵛ]

*Enter Fortunio, Bellanora, Gratiana, Gostanzo
following closely.*

For. How happy am I, that by this sweet meanes
I gayne accesse to your most loued sight,
And therewithall to vtter my full loue,
Which but for vent would burne my entrayles vp!
    Gost. [*Aside.*] Byth masse they talke too softly.
    Bell.   Little thinks   5
The austere mind my thrifty father beares,
That I am vowd to you, and so am bound
From him: who for more riches he would force
On my disliking fancy.
    For.   Tis no fault,
With iust deeds to defraud an iniury.   10
    Gost. [*Aside.*] My daughter is perswading him to yeeld
In dutifull submission to his father.

Enter Valerio.

    Val. Do I not dreame? do I behold this sight
With waking eyes? or from the Iuory gate
Hath *Morpheus* sent a vision to delude me?   15
Ist possible that I a mortall man,
Should shrine within mine armes so bright a Goddesse,
The fayre *Gratiana,* beautyes little world!
    Gost. [*Aside.*] What haue we heere?
    Val. My dearest Myne of Gold,   20
All this that thy white armes enfold,
Account it as thine owne free-hold.

422-25 And . . . ielousy.] *Collier; as prose Q* (& . . . with) ‖ **422** Mast] mast ‖ **5, 11, 19** SD *Aside.*]
Parrott ‖

Gost. [*Aside.*] Gods my deare soule, what sudden change is here!
I smell how this geare will fall out yfayth.
    Val. Fortunio, sister; come, let's to the garden.   *Exeunt.*
    Gost. Sits the wind there yfayth? see what example
Will worke vpon the dullest appetite.
My sonne last day so bashfull, that he durst not
Looke on a wench, now courts her; and byrlady, /
Will make his friend *Fortunio* weare his head   [E4] 30
Of the right moderne fashion. What *Rinaldo.*

             Enter Rin.

    Rin. I feare I interrupt your priuacy.
    Gost. Welcome, *Rinaldo,* would't had bin your hap
To come a little sooner, that you might
Haue seene a handsome sight: but let that passe,   35
The short is, that your sister *Gratiana*
Shall stay no longer here.
    Rin.   No longer, sir?
Repent you then so soone your fauour to her,
And to my brother?
    Gost.   Not so, good *Rinaldo;*
But to preuent a mischiefe that I see   40
Hangs ouer your abused brothers head.
In briefe, my sonne has learn'd but too much courtship.
It was my chaunce euen now to cast mine eye
Into a place whereto your sister entred:
My metamorphosde sonne: I must conceale   45
What I saw there: but to be playne, I saw
More then I would see: I had thought to make
My house a kind receypt for your kind brother;
But ide be loth his wife should find more kindnesse,
Then she had cause to like of.
    Rin.   What's the matter?   50
Perhaps a little complement or so.
    Gost. Wel, sir, such complement perhaps may cost
Marryed *Fortunio* the setting on:
Nor can I keepe my knowledge; He that lately
Before my face I could not get to looke   55
Vpon your sister; by this light, now kist her,
Embrac't and courted with as good a grace,
As any Courtyer could: and I can tell you

23 SD *Aside.*] *Parrott*[2] ‖

(Not to disgrace her) I perceyu'd the Dame
Was as far forward as himselfe, byth masse.   60
   Rin. You should haue schoold him for't.
   Gost.   No, Ile not see't: /
For shame once found, is lost; Ile haue him thinke   [E4ᵛ]
That my opinion of him is the same
That it was euer; it will be a meane,
To bridle this fresh humour bred in him.   65
   Rin. Let me then schoole him; foot, ile rattle him vp.
   Gost. No, no, *Rinaldo,* th'onely remedy,
Is to remoue the cause; carry the obiect
From his late tempted eyes.
   Rin.   Alas, sir, whither?
You know, my father is incenst so much,   70
Heele not receyue her.
   Gost.   Place her with some friend
But for a time, till I reclayme your father:
Meane time your brother shall remaine with me.
   To himself. Rin. The care's the lesse then, he has still his longing,
To be with this Gulls daughter.
   Gost.   What resolue you?   75
I am resolu'd she lodges here no more:
My friends sonne shall not be abusde by mine.
   Rin. Troth, sir, ile tell you what a sudden toy
Comes in my head; what think you if I brought her
Home to my fathers house?
   Gost.   I mary, sir;   80
Would he receyue her?
   Rin.   Nay, you heare not all:
I meane, with vse of some deuice or other.
   Gost. As how, *Rinaldo?*
   Rin.   Mary sir, to say,
She is your sonnes wife, maryed past your knowledge.
   Gost. I doubt, last day he saw her, and will know her   85
To be *Fortunioes* wife.
   Rin.   Nay, as for that
I wil pretend she was euen then your sonnes wife,
But faynde by me to be *Fortunioes,*
Onely to try how he would take the matter.

78-80 Troth ... house?] *Reed; as prose* Q (comes ... home) ‖ **86** To] to ‖

Gost. 'Fore heauen 'twere pretty. /
Rin.   Would it not doe well?   [F1] 90
Gost. Exceeding well in sadnesse.
Rin.   Nay, good sir,
Tell me vnfaynedly, do ye lik't indeed.
Gost. The best that ere I heard.
Rin.   And do you thinke
Heele swallow downe the Gudgion?
Gost.   A my life
It were a grosse gob would not downe with him,   95
An honest knight, but simple, not acquainted
With the fine slights and policies of the world,
As I my selfe am.
Rin.   Ile go fetch her strait:
And this iest thriue, 'twill make vs princely sport:
But you must keepe our counsell, second all,   100
Which to make likely, you must needs sometimes
Giue your sonne leaue (as if you knew it not)
To steale and see her at my fathers house.
Gost. I, but see you then that you keepe good gard
Ouer his forward new begun affections: 105
For by the Lord, heele teach your brother else,
To sing the Cuckooes note: spirit will breake out,
Though neuer so supprest and pinioned.
Rin. Especially your sonnes: what would he be,
If you should not restrayne him by good counsell?   110
Gost. Ile haue an eye on him, I warrant thee.
Ile in and warne the Gentlewoman to make ready.
Rin. Wel, sir, and ile not be long after you.   *Exit Gost.*
Heauen, heauen, I see these Politicians
(Out of blind Fortunes hands) are our most fooles.   115
Tis she that giues the lustre to their wits,
Still plodding at traditionall deuices:
But take vm out of them to present actions,
A man may grope and tickle vm like a Trowt,
And take vm from their close deere holes, as fat   120
As a Phisician; and as giddy-headed, /
As if by myracle heauen had taken from them,   [F1ᵛ]
Euen that which commonly belongs to fooles.

110 counsell] connsell ‖ 122 by] *Reed*; be ‖

Well, now let's note what black ball of debate,
Valerioes wit hath cast betwixt *Cornelio*, 125
And the inamoured Courtyer; I beleeue
His wife and he will part: his ielousy
Hath euer watcht occasion of diuorce,
And now *Valerioes* villany will present it.
See, here comes the twyn-Courtier his companion. 130

Enter Claud.

Clau. Rinaldo, well encountred.
Rin. Why? what newes?
Clau. Most sudden and infortunate, *Rinaldo*:
Cornelio is incenst so 'gainst his wife,
That no man can procure her quiet with him.
I haue assayd him, and made *Marc. Antonio*, 135
With all his gentle Rethorike second me,
Yet all I feare me will be cast away.
See, see, they come: ioyne thy wit, good *Rinaldo*,
And helpe to pacify his yellow fury.
Rin. With all my heart, I consecrate my wit 140
To the wisht comfort of distressed Ladies.

Enter Cornelio, Marc. Ant. Valerio, Page.

Cor. Will any man assure me of her good behauiour?
Val. Who can assure a ielous spirit? you may be afrayd of the
shaddow of your eares, and imagine them to be hornes: if you will
assure your selfe, appoynt keepers to watch her. 145
Cor. And who shall watch the keepers?
Mar. To be sure of that, be you her keeper.
Val. Well sayd, and share the hornes your selfe:
For that's the keepers fee.
Cor. But say I am gone out of town, and must trust others; how 150
shall I know if those I trust be trusty to me?
Rin. Mary, sir, by a singular instinct, giuen naturally to all you
maryed men, that if your wiues play legerdeheele, though you bee a
hundred miles off, yet you shall be sure instantly to find it in your
forheads. / 155
Cor. Sound doctrine I warrant you: I am resolu'd ifaith. [F2]
Pag. Then giue me leaue to speak, sir, that hath all this while bene
silent: I haue heard you with extreme patience, now therefore pricke
vp your eares, and vouchsafe me audience.

135 *Marc.*] ~∧ ‖ **141** SD *Marc.*] ~∧ ‖

Clau. Good boy, a mine honour. 160

Cor. Pray what are you, sir?

Pag. I am here, for default of better, of counsel with the fayre *Gazetta,* and though her selfe had bene best able to defend her selfe, if she had bin here, and would haue pleasd to put forth the Buckler, which Nature hath giuen all women, I meane her tongue. 165

Val. Excellent good boy.

Pag. Yet since she either vouchsafes it not, or thinks her innocence a sufficient shield against your ielous accusations, I wil presume to vndertake the defence of that absent and honorable Lady, whose sworne Knight I am; and in her of all that name (for Lady is growne 170 a common name to their whole sex) which sex I haue euer loued from my youth, and shall neuer cease to loue, till I want wit to admire.

Mar. An excellent spoken boy.

Val. Giue eare, *Cornelio,* heere is a yong *Mercurio* sent to perswade thee. 175

Cor. Well, sir, let him say on.

Pag. It is a heauy case, to see how this light sex is tumbled and tost from post to piller, vnder the vnsauory breath of euery humourous Peasant: *Gazetta,* you sayd, is vnchaste, disloyall, and I wot not what; Alas, is it her fault? is shee not a woman? did she not suck it (as 180 others of her sex doe) from her mothers brest? and will you condemne that, as her fault, which is her Nature? Alas, sir, you must consider, a woman is an vnfinisht Creature, deliuered hastyly to the world, before Nature had set to that Seale which should haue made them perfect. Faultes they haue (no doubt) but are wee free? Turne your eye into 185 your selfe (good Signeur *Cornelio*) and weygh your owne imperfec-tions with hers: If shee be wanton abroad, are / not you wanting [F2ᵛ] at home? if she be amorous, are not you ielous? If she be high set, are not you taken downe? If she be a Courtizan, are not you a Cuckold? 190

Cor. Out you rogue.

Rin. On with thy speech, boy.

Mar. You doe not well, *Cornelio,* to discourage the bashfull youth.

Clau. Forth, boy, I warrant thee.

Pag. But if our owne imperfections will not teach vs to beare with 195 theirs; yet let their vertues perswade vs: let vs indure their bad qualities for their good; allow the prickle for the Rose; the bracke for the Veluet; the paring for the cheese, and so forth: if you say they range abroad, consider it is nothing but to auoyd idlenesse at home:

their nature is still to be doing: keepe vm a doing at home; let them 200
practise one good quality or other, either sowing, singing, playing,
chiding, dauncing or so, and these will put such idle toyes out of their
heads into yours: but if you cannot find them variety of businesse
within dores, yet at least imitate the ancient wise Citizens of this City,
who vsed carefully to prouide their wiues gardens neere the towne, 205
to plant, to graft in, as occasion serued, onely to keepe vm from
idlenesse.

Val. Euerlasting good boy.

Cor. I perceyue your knauery, sir, and will yet haue patience.

Rin. Forth, my braue *Curio.* 210

Pag. As to her vnquietnesse (which some haue rudely tearm'd
shrewishnesse) though the fault be in her, yet the cause is in you.
What so calme as the sea of it own nature? Arte was neuer able to
equall it: your dycing tables, nor your bowling alleys are not com-
parable to it; yet if a blast of wind do but crosse it, not so turbulent 215
and violent an element in the world: So (nature in lieu of womens
scarcity of wit, hauing indued them with a large portion of will) if
they may (without impeach) inioy their willes, no quieter creatures
vnder heauen: but if the breath of their husbands / mouthes once [F3]
crosse their wils, nothing more tempestuous. Why then, sir, should 220
you husbands crosse your wiues wils thus, considering the law allowes
them no wils at all at their deaths, because it intended they should
haue their willes while they liued?

Val. Answere him but that, *Cornelio.*

Cor. All shall not serue her turne, I am thinking of other matters. 225

Mar. Thou hast halfe wonne him, Wag; ply him yet a little further.

Pag. Now (sir) for these Cuckooish songs of yours, of Cuckolds,
hornes, grafting, and such like; what are they, but meere imaginary
toyes, bred out of your owne heads, as your owne, and so by tradition
deliuered from man to man, like Scar-crowes, to terrify fooles from 230
this earthly paradice of wedlock, coyn'd at first by some spent Poets,
superannated Bachelers, or some that were scarce men of their hands;
who, like the Foxe, hauing lost his taile, would perswade others to
lose theirs for company? Agayne, for your Cuckold, what is it but
a meere fiction? shew me any such creature in nature; if there be, I 235
could neuer see it, neyther could I euer find any sensible difference
betwixt a Cuckold and a Christen creature. To conclude, let Poets
coyne, or fooles credit what they list; for mine owne part, I am cleere
of this opinion, that your Cuckold is a meere *Chymæra,* and that there

210 *Curio*] Curio ‖

are no Cuckoldes in the world, but those that haue wiues: and so I   240
will leaue them.

Cor. Tis excellent good, sir; I do take you, sir, d'ye see? to be,
as it were bastard to the sawcy Courtier, that would haue me father
more of your fraternity, d'ye see? and so are instructed (as we heare)
to second that villayne with your toung, which he has acted with his   245
Tenure piece, d'ye see?

Pag. No such matter, a my credit, sir.

Cor. Wel, sir, be as be may, I scorn to set my head against yours,
d'ye see? when in the meane time I will fircke your / father, whether   [F3ᵛ]
you see or no.   *Exit drawing his rapier.*

Rin. Gods my life, *Cornelio.*   *Exit.*

Val. Haue at your father ifaith, boy, if he can find him.

Mar. See, he comes here, he has mist him.

Enter Dariot.

Dar. How now, my hearts, what, not a wench amongst you?
Tis a signe y'are not in the grace of wenches,   255
That they will let you be thus long alone.

Val. Well, *Dariotto,* glory not too much,
That for thy briske attyre and lips perfumde,
Thou playest the Stallyon euer where thou com'st;
And like the husband of the flocke, runn'st through   260
The whole towne heard, and no mans bed secure:
No womans honour vnattempted by thee.
Thinke not to be thus fortunate for euer:
But in thy amorous conquests at the last
Some wound will slice your mazer: *Mars* himselfe   265
Fell into *Vulcans* snare, and so may you.

Dar. Alas, alas, fayth I haue but the name:
I loue to court and wynne; and the consent,
Without the act obtayn'd, is all I seeke.
I loue the victory that drawes no bloud.   270

Clau. O, tis a high desert in any man
To be a secret Lecher; I know some,
That (like thy selfe) are true in nothing else.

Mar. And, me thinks, it is nothing, if not told;
At least the ioy is neuer full before.   275

Val. Well, *Dariotto,* th'hadst as good confesse,
The Sunne shines broad vpon your practises:
Vulcan will wake and intercept you one day.

277 practises:] ∼. (*? possible colon*) ‖

Dar. Why, the more ielous knaue and coxcombe he.
What, shall the shaking of his bed a little   280
Put him in motion? It becomes him not;
Let him be duld and stald, and then be quiet.
The way to draw my costome to his house,
Is to be mad and ielous; tis the sauce
That whets my appetite. /
    Val.   Or any mans: [F4] 285
Sine periculo friget lusus.
They that are ielous, vse it still of purpose
To draw you to their houses.
    Dar.   I, by heauen,
I am of that opinion. Who would steale
Out of a common Orchard? Let me gayne   290
My loue with labour, and inioy't with feare,
Or I am gone.

Enter Rinaldo.

    Rin.   What, *Dariotto* here?
Foot, dar'st thou come neere *Cornelioes* house?
    Dar. Why? is the Bull run mad? what ayles he, trow?
    Rin. I know not what he ayles; but I would wish you   295
To keepe out of the reach of his sharpe hornes:
For by this hand heele gore you.
    Dar.   And why me,
More then thy selfe, or these two other whelps?
You all haue basted him as well as I.
I wonder what's the cause.
    Rin.   Nay, that he knowes,   300
And sweares withall, that wheresoere he meets you,
Heele marke you for a marker of mens wiues.
    Val. Pray heauen he be not ielous by some tales
That haue bin told him lately: did you neuer
Attempt his wife? hath no Loues Harbenger,   305
No looks, no letters past twixt you and her?
    Dar. For lookes I cannot answere; I bestow them
At large, and carelesly, much like the Sunne:
If any be so foolish to apply them
To any priuate fancy of their owne,   310
(As many doe) it's not my fault, thou knowest.
    Val. Well, *Dariotto,* this set face of thine
(If thou be guilty of offence to him)

<hr>

307 lookes] *Shepherd;* looke ‖

Comes out of very want of wit and feeling
What danger haunts thee: for *Cornelio*   315
Is a tall man, I tell you; and 'twere best /
You shund his sight awhile, till we might get   [F4ᵛ]
His patience, or his pardon: for past doubt
Thou dyest if he but see thee.

Enter Cornelio.

Rin.   Foot, he comes.
Dar. Is this the Cockatrice that kils with sight?   320
How doest thou boy? ha?
Cor.   Well.
Dar.   What, lingring still
About this paltry towne? hadst thou bin rulde
By my aduice, thou hadst by this time bene
A gallant Courtyer, and at least a Knight:
I would haue got thee dubd by this time certayne.   325
    Cor. And why then did you not your selfe that honour?
    Dar. Tush, tis more honour still to make a Knight,
Then tis to be a Knight: to make a Cuckold,
Then tis to be a Cuckold.
    Cor.   Y'are a villayne.
    Dar. God shield man: villayne?
    Cor.   I, ile proue thee one.   330
    Dar. What, wilt thou proue a villayne? By this light
Thou deceyu'st me then.
    Cor.   Well, sir, thus I proue it.   *Drawes.*
    Omn. Hold, hold, rayse the streets.
    Clau.   *Cornelio.*
    Rin. Hold, *Dariotto,* hold.
    Val.   What, art thou hurt?
    Dar. A scratch, a scratch.
    Val.   Goe sirra, fetch a Surgeon.   [*Exit Page.*]
    Cor. Youle set a badge on the ielous fooles head, sir;
Now set a Coxcombe on your owne.
    Val. What's the cause of these warres, *Dariotto?*
    Dar. Foot, I know not.
    Cor.   Well, sir, know and spare not;
I will presently bee diuorst, and then take her amongst ye.   340
    Rin. Diuorst? nay good *Cornelio.*
    Cor.   By this sword
I will, the world shall not disswade me.   *Exit. /*

331-32 What . . . then.] What . . . villayne? / By . . . then. Q (thou) ‖ **334** *Dariotto*] *Darioto* ‖
335 SD *Exit Page.*] *Parrott* ‖ **338** *Dariotto*] *Darioto* ‖ **339-42** Foot . . . me.] Foot . . . not. / *Cor.*
Well . . . bee / diuorst . . . ye. / *Rin.* Diuorst . . . *Cornelio.* / *Cor.* By . . . disswade / me. ‖

Val. Why this has bin your fault now *Dariotto,*   [G1]
You youths haue fashions when you haue obtein'd
A Ladies fauour, straight your hat must weare it,   345
Like a Iacke-daw that when he lights vpon
A dainty morsell, kaas and makes his brags,
And then some kite doth scoope it from him straight,
Where if he fed without his dawish noise,
He might fare better, and haue lesse disturbance: 350
Forbeare it in this case; and when you proue,
Victorious ouer faire *Gazettas* Forte,
Doe not for pittie sound your trumpe for ioy,
But keepe your valour close, and 'tis your honour.

Enter Page and Pock.

Poc. God saue you Signior *Dariotto.*   355
Dar. I know you not Sir, your name I pray?
Poc. My name is *Pock* Sir; a practitioner in Surgery.
Dar. *Pock* the Surgeon, y'are welcome Sir, I know a Doctor of your
name maister *Pocke.*
Poc. My name has made many Doctors Sir.   360
Rin. Indeede tis a worshipfull name.
Val. Mary is it, and of an auncient discent.
Poc. Faith Sir I could fetch my pedigree far, if I were so dispos'd.
Rin. Out of France at least.
Poc. And if I stood on my armes as others doe —   365
Dar. No doe not *Pock,* let others stand a their armes, and thou a thy
legs as long as thou canst.
Poc. Though I liue by my bare practise, yet I could shew good
cardes for my Gentilitie.
Val. Tush thou canst not shake off thy gentry *Pock,* tis bred i'th   370
bone; but to the maine *Pock,* what thinkest thou of this gentlemans
wound, *Pock,* canst thou cure it *Pock?*
Poc. The incision is not deepe, nor the Orifice exorbitant, the Peri-
cranion is not dislocated, I warrant his life for forty crownes, without
perishing of any ioynt.   375
Dar. Faith Pock, tis a ioynt I would be loath to loose, for the best
ioynt of Mutton in Italy.
Rin. Would such a scratch as this hazard a mans head?
Poc. I Byr-lady Sir, I haue knowen some haue lost there / heads   [G1ᵛ]
for a lesse matter I can tell you, therefore sir you must keepe good   380
dyet: if you please to come home to my house till you be perfectly
cur'd, I shall haue the more care on you.
Val. That's your onely course to haue it well quickly.

---

343 *Dariotto*] *Darioto* ‖ 344 obtein'd] *Reed*; obtei'nd ‖ 345 straight] *Q(c)*; straght *Q(u)* ‖ 354
'tis] ti's ‖ 355 *Dariotto.*] *Darioto,* ‖ 357 Surgery.] ~, ‖ 365 doe—] ~, ‖ 366 others] *Reed*; other
(*Reed's emendation accepted because of* others *in l. 365*) ‖ 372 *Pock?*] ~. ‖ 378 hazard] *Reed*; hazards
‖ 383 That's] Thats ‖

274

Poc. By what time would he haue it well sir?

Dar. A very necessary question, canst thou limit the time?   385

Poc. O sir, cures are like causes in law, which may be lengthned or shortned at the discretion of the Lawyer, he can either keepe it greene with replications or reioinders, or sometimes skinne it faire a'th outside for fashion sake, but so he may be sure 'twill breake out againe by a writt of error, and then has he his suite new to begin, but I will cou-   390
enant with you, that by such a time Ile make your head as sound as a Bell, I will bring it to suppuration, and after I will make it coagulate and growe to a perfect *Cycatrice,* and all within these ten dayes, so you keepe a good dyet.

Dar. Well come Pock, weele talke farther on't within, it drawes   395
neere dinner time; what's a clock boye?

Pag. By your clock sir it should be almost one, for your head rung noone some halfe houre agoe.

Dar. Ist true sir?

Val. Away let him alone, though he came in at the window he sets   400
the gates of your honor open I can tell you.

Dar. Come in *Pock,* come, apply; and for this deede
Ile giue the Knaue a wound shall neuer bleed:
So sir I thinke this knock rings lowd acquittance,
For my ridiculouse —   *Exeunt all but Rinal. and Valer.*

Rin. Well sir to turne our heads to salue your licence:
Since you haue vsd the matter so vnwisely,
That now your father has discern'd your humor,
In your too carelesse vsage in his house,
Your wife must come from his house to *Antonios,*   410
And he, to entertaine her must be tould
She is not wife to his sonne, but to you:
Which newes will make his simple wit triumphe
Ouer your father; and your father thinking
He still is guld, will still account him simple: 415
Come sir, prepare your villanous witt to faine /
A kinde submission to your fathers fury,   [G2]
And we shall see what harty policie,
He will discouer, in his fained Anger,
To blinde *Antonios* eyes, and make him thinke,   420
He thinkes her hartely to be your wife.

Val. O I will gull him rarely with my wench,
Lowe kneeling at my heeles before his furie,
And iniury shalbe salu'd with iniurie.   *[Exeunt.]*

Finis Actus 3.

384 sir?] ∼. ‖ 385 time?] ∼. ‖ 405 ridiculouse—] *Reed;* ∼. ‖ 406 licence:] ∼, ‖ 424 SD *Exeunt.*] ‖

ACTVS 4. SCENA 1.

Marc. Ant: Gostanzo.

Mar. You see how too much wisdome euermore,
Out-shootes the truth: you were so forwards still,
To taxe my ignorance, my greene experience
In these gray haires, for giuing such aduantage,
To my sonnes spirit, that he durst vndertake   5
A secret match, so farre short of his woorth:
Your sonne so seasoned with obedience,
Euen from his youth, that all his actions relish
Nothing but dutie, and your angers feare:
What shall I say to you, if it fall out   10
That this most precious sonne of yours, has plaide
A part as bad as this, and as rebellious:
Nay more has grosely guld your witt withall?
What if my sonne has vndergone the blame
That appertain'd to yours? and that this wench   15
With which my sonne is charg'd, may call you father:
Shall I then say you want experience?
Y'are greene, y'are credulous; easie to be blinded.
    Gost. Ha, ha, ha, good *Marc. Antonio,* when't comes to that;
Laugh at me, call me foole, proclaime me so,   20
Let all the world take knowledge I am an Asse.
    Mar. O the good God of Gods,
How blinde is Pride? what Eagles we are still,
In matters that belong to other men?
What Beetles in our owne? I tell you Knight,   25
It is confest to be as I haue tould you; /
And *Gratiana,* is by young *Rinaldo,*   [G2ᵛ]
And your white sonne, brought to me as his wife:
How thinke you now Sir?
    Gost.   Euen iust as before,
And haue more cause to thinke honest *Credulity,*   30
Is a true Loadstone to draw on *Decrepity*:
You haue a hart to open to imbrace,
All that your eare receiues: alas good man,
All this is but a plot for entertainment
Within your house, for your poore sonnes yong wife   35
My house without huge danger cannot holde.

SD *Marc. Ant:*] *Marc-Ant:* ‖ **9** feare:] ∼, ‖ **13** withall?] ∼. ‖ **19** *Marc. Antonio*] *Marc-Antonio* ‖ **19-20** when't . . . so,] *one line* Q (When't . . . laugh) ‖ **30** *Credulity,*] Q(c); ∼: Q(u) ‖ **31** *Decrepity:*] Q(c); ∼, Q(u) ‖ **36** holde.] ∼: ‖

Mar. Ist possible, what danger Sir I pray?

Gost. Ile tell you Sir, twas time to take her thence:

My sonne that last day you saw could not frame,

His lookes to entertaine her, now bir-lady   40

Is grone a Courtier: for my selfe vnseene,

Saw when he courted her, imbrac't and kist her,

And I can tell you left not much vndone,

That was the proper office of your sonne.

   Mar. What world is this?

   Gost.   I tolde this to *Rinaldo,*   45

Aduising him to fetch her from my house,

And his yong wit not knowing where to lodge her

Vnlesse with you: and saw that could not be,

Without some wyle: I presently suggested

This queint deuise, to say she was my sonnes: 50

And all this plot, good *Marc. Antonio,*

Flow'd from this fount, onely to blinde your eyes.

   Mar. Out of how sweete a dreame haue you awak't me?

By heauen, I durst haue laid my part in heauen

All had bin true; it was so liuely handled,   55

And drawne with such a seeming face of trueth:

Your sonne had cast a perfect vaile of griefe

Ouer his face, for his so rash offence,

To seale his loue with act of marriage,

Before his father had subscrib'd his choyce: 60

My sonne (my circumstance lessening the fact)

Intreating me to breake the matter to you, /

And ioyning my effectuall perswasions,   [G3]

With your sonnes penitent submission,

Appease your fury; I at first assented,   65

And now expect their comming to that purpose.

   Gost. T'was well, t'was well, seeme to beleeue it still,

Let Art end what Credulitie began:

When they come, suite your words and lookes to theirs,

Second my sad Sonnes fain'd submission,   70

And see in all points how my braine will answere,

His disguisde griefe, with a set countenance

Of rage and choller; now obserue and learne

To schoole your sonne by me.

---

51 *Marc. Antonio*] *Marc-Antonio* ‖ **52** your] *Reed*; our ‖ **68** began:] ∼, ‖

Intrant Rynaldo, Val: Grat:

Mar.   On with your maske;
Here come the other maskers sir.
    Rin.   Come on I say,   75
Your Father with submission wilbe calm'd;
Come on; downe a your knees.
    Gost.   Villaine durst thou
Presume to gull thy Father? doost thou not
Tremble to see my bent and cloudy browes
Ready to thunder on thy gracelesse head,   80
And with the bolt of my displeasure cut
The thred of all my liuing from thy life,
For taking thus a beggar to thy wife?
    Val. Father, if that part I haue in your blood,
If teares, which so aboundantly distill   85
Out of my inward eyes: and for a neede,
Can drowne these outward ([*aside to Rinaldo*] lend me thy hand-kercher)
And being indeed as many drops of blood,
Issuing from the Creator of my hart,
Be able to beget so much compassion,   90
Not on my life, but on this louely Dame,
Whom I hold dearer —
    Gost.   Out vpon thee villaine.
    Mar. Nay good *Gostanzo*, thinke you are a Father.
    Gost. I will not heare a word; out, out vpon thee:
Wed without my aduise, my loue, my knowledge,   95
I, and a begger too, a trull, a blowse?
    Rin. [*Aside to Gost.*] You thought not so last day, when you offerd her
A twelue months boord for one nights lodging with her. /
    Gost. [*Aside to Rin.*] Goe too, no more of that, peace good *Rinaldo*,   [G3ᵛ]
It is a fault that onely she and you know.   100
    Rin. [*Aside to Gost.*] Well sir, go on I pray.
    Gost.   Haue I fond wretch,
With vtmost care and labour brought thee vp,
Euer instructing thee, omitting neuer
The office of a kinde and carefull Father,
To make thee wise and vertuous like thy father: 105
And hast thou in one acte euerted all?
Proclaim'd thy selfe to all the world a foole?
To wedde a begger?
    Val.   Father, say not so.

---

74 SD *Rynaldo,*] ∼∧ ‖ 74-77 On . . . knees.] *Collier;* On . . . sir, / *Rinal.* Come . . . say, / Your
. . . knees: *Q* (here . . . come on;) ‖ 75 sir.] ∼, ‖ 77 knees.] ∼: ‖ 87 SD *aside to Rinaldo*] *Parrott*
‖ 92 dearer—] *Reed;* ∼? ‖ 97, 101 SD *Aside to Gost.*] *Parrott* ‖ 99 SD *Aside to Rin.*] *Parrott* ‖
101 *Rin.*] *Rein.* ‖ 108 so.] ∼, ‖

Gost. Nay shees thy owne, here, rise foole, take her to thee,
Liue with her still, I know thou countst thy selfe   110
Happy in soule, onely in winning her:
Be happy still, heere, take her hand, enioy her,
Would not a sonne hazard his Fathers wrath,
His reputation in the world? his birth-right,
To haue but such a messe of broth as this?   115
     Mar. Be not so violent, I pray you good *Gostanzo,*
Take truce with passion, licence your sad sonne,
To speake in his excuse.
     Gost.   What? what excuse?
Can any orator in this case excuse him?
What can he say? what can be said of any?   120
     Val. Ahlas sir, heare me, all that I can say
In my excuse, is but to shew loues warrant.
     Gost. [*Aside.*] Notable wagge.
     Val.   I know I haue committed
A great impiety, not to mooue you first
Before the dame, I meant to make my wife.   125
Consider what I am, yet young, and greene,
Beholde what she is, is there not in her,
I, in her very eye, a power to conquer,
Euen age it selfe and wisdome? Call to minde
Sweete Father, what your selfe being young haue bin,   130
Thinke what you may be, for I doe not thinke
The world so farre spent with you, but you may /
Looke back on such a beauty, and I hope   [G4]
To see you young againe, and to liue long
With young affections, wisdome makes a man   135
Liue young for euer: and where is this wisdome
If not in you? ahlas I know not what
Rests in your wisedome to subdue affections,
But I protest it wrought with me so strongly,
That I had quite bin drownd in seas of teares   140
Had I not taken hold in happy time
Of this sweete hand; my hart had beene consum'de
T'a heape of Ashes with the flames of loue,
Had it not sweetly bin asswag'd and cool'd,
With the moist kisses of these sugred lippes.   145
     Gost. [*Aside to Mar.*] O puisant wag, what huge large thongs he cuts
Out of his friend *Fortunios* stretching leather.

---

109 *Gost.* Nay] *Q(c)*; Nay *Q(u)* ‖ **112** hand,] ∼∧ ‖ **123** SD *Aside.*] *Parrott* ‖ **125** wife.] ∼∧ ‖
127 her,] ∼∧ ‖ **129** wisdome? Call] ∼, call ‖ **134** againe, and] *comma uncertain* ‖ **142** hand;]
∼, ‖ **146** SD *Aside to Mar.*] *Parrott* ‖

Mar. [*Aside.*] He knows he does it but to blinde my eyes.
Gost. [*Aside.*] O excellent, these men will put vp any thing.
Val. Had I not had her, I had lost my life,   150
Which life indeed I would haue lost before
I had displeasd you, had I not receau'd it
From such a kinde, a wise, and honour'd Father.
Gost. [*Aside.*] Notable Boy.
Val.   Yet doe I here renounce
Loue, life and all, rather then one houre longer   155
Indure to haue your loue eclipsed from me.
Gra. O I can hold no longer, if thy words
Be vs'd in earnest my *Valerio,*
Thou woundst my hart, but I know tis in iest.
Gost. [*Aside.*] No ile be sworne she has her lyripoope too.   160
Gra. Didst thou not sweare to loue me, spight of Father,
And all the world? That nought should seuer vs
But death it selfe?
Val.   I did, but if my father
Will haue his sonne foresworne, vpon his soule,
The blood of my black periurie shall lye,   165
For I will seeke his fauour though I dye.
Gost. No, no, liue still my sonne, thou well shalt know,
I haue a fathers hart, come ioyne your hands,
Still keepe thy vowes, and liue together still, /
Till cruell death set foote betwixt you both.   [G4ᵛ] 170
Val. O speake you this in earnest?
Gost.   I by heauen.
Val. And neuer to recall it?
Gost.   Not till death.
Rin. Excellent sir, you haue done like your selfe:
What would you more *Valerio*?
Val.   Worshipfull Father.
Rin. Come sir, come you in, and celebrate your ioyes.   175
                              Exeunt all saue the old men.
Gost. O *Marc. Antonio,*
Had I not armd you with an expectation,
Would not this make you pawne your very soule,
The wench had bin my sonnes wife?
Mar.   Yes by heauen:
A knauerie thus effected might deceiue   180
A wiser man then I, for I ahlas,

148, 149 SD *Aside.*] *Parrott* ‖ **151** before] ∼, ‖ **154** SD *Aside.*] *Parrott* ‖ **159** tis] *Reed*; tist ‖ **160** SD *Aside.*] *Parrott* ‖ **161-63** Didst . . . selfe?] *Collier*; Didst . . . world / That . . . selfe. *Q* (&) ‖ **176** *Marc. Antonio*] *Marc-Antonio* ‖ **181** ahlas] ah las ‖

Am noe good polititian, plaine beleeuing
Simple honesty, is my policy still.
    Gost. The visible markes of folly, honesty,
And quick Credulitie his yonger brother.   185
I tell you *Marc. Antonio* there is mutch
In that young boy my Sonne.
    Mar.   Not much honesty,
If I may speake without offence to his father.
    Gost. O God you cannot please me better sir,
H'as honesty enough to serue his turne,   190
The lesse honesty euer the more wit,
But goe you home, and vse your daughter kindly,
Meane time Ile schoole your sonne: and do you still
Dissemble what you know, keepe off your sonne,
The wench at home must still be my sonnes wife,   195
Remember that, and be you blinded still.
    Mar. You must remember too, to let your sonne
Vse his accustom'd visitations,
Onely to blinde my eyes.
    Gost.   He shall not faile:
But still take you heede, haue a vigilant eye,   200
On that slie childe of mine, for by this light,
Heele be too bould with your sonnes forhead els. /
    Mar. Well sir let me alone, Ile beare a braine.   *Exeunt.* [H1]

                Enter Valerio, Rynaldo.

    Val. Come they are gone.
    Rin.   Gone, they were farre gone heere.
    Val. Guld I my father, or guld he himselfe?   205
Thou toldst him *Gratiana* was my wife,
I haue confest it, he has pardoned it.
    Rin. Nothing more true, enow can witnesse it.
And therefore when he comes to learne the truth,
(As certainly for all these slie disguises,   210
Time will strip Truth into her nakednesse)
Thou hast good plea against him to confesse,
The honor'd Action, and to claime his pardon.
    Val. Tis true, for all was done he deeply swore
Out of his hart.
    Rin.   He has much faith the whiles,   215
That swore a thing, so quite against his hart.

184-85 The . . . brother.] *Collier; one line* Q (and) ‖ **186** *Marc. Antonio*] *Marc-Antonio* ‖ **187-88** Not . . . father.] *Collier; one line* Q (if) ‖ **198** accustom'd] *Q(c)*; accustomm'd *Q(u)* ‖ **216** hart.] ∼: ‖

Val. Why this is pollicie.

Rin.   Well see you repaire,
To *Gratiana* daily, and enioy her
In her true kinde; and now we must expect
The resolute, and ridiculous diuorce,   220
Cornelio hath sued against his wedlock.

Val. I thinke it be not so; the Asse dotes on her.

Rin. It is too true, and thou shalt answere it,
For setting such debate twixt man and wife:
See, we shall see the solemne maner of it.   225

Enter Cor: Dariotto, Claud. Notarie, Page, Gazetta,
Bell: Gratiana.

Bell. Good Signior *Cornelio* let vs poore Gentlewomen intreate you
to forbeare.

Cor. Talke no more to me, Ile not be made Cuckold in my owne
house: Notarie read me the diuorce.

Gaz. My deare *Cornelio,* examine the cause better before you con-   230
demne me.

Cor. Sing to me no more Syren, for I will heare thee no more, I
will take no compassion on thee.

Pag. Good Signior *Cornelio* be not too mankinde against / your   [H1ᵛ]
wife, say y'are a cuckold (as the best that is may be so at a time) will   235
you make a trumpet of your owne hornes?

Cor. Goe too sir, y'are a rascall, ile giue you a fee for pleading for
her one day. *Notary* doe you your office.

Val. Goe too Signior, looke better to your wife, and be better ad-
uised, before you grow to this extremitie.   240

Cor. Extremity? go too, I deale but too mercifully with her: If I
should vse extremitie with her I might hang her, and her copesmate
my drudge here. How say you M. *Notary,* might I not doe it by law?

Not. Not hang am, but you may bring them both to a white sheete.

Cor. Nay by the masse they haue had too much of the sheete   245
already.

Not. And besides you may set capitall letters on their foreheads.

Cor. What's that to the capitall letter that's written in mine? I say
for all your law, maister *Notary* that I may hang am. May I not hang
him that robs me of mine honour, as well as he that robs me of my   250
horse?

Not. No sir your horse is a chattell.

Cor. Soe is honour, a man may buy it with his peny, and if I may

225 SD *Dariotto, . . . Gazetta,*] *Darioto. . . . Gazetta.* ‖ **238** day.] ∼, ‖ **239** Signior,] ∼∧ ‖ **241**
her:] ∼, ‖ **243** here. How] ∼, how ‖ **247** foreheads] fore- / heads ‖ **248** that's] thats | mine?]
Reed; minde, ‖ **249** am. May] ∼, may ‖

hang a man for stealing my horse (as I say) much more for robbing
mee of my honour; for why? if my horse be stolne, it may bee my   255
owne fault; for why? eyther the stable is not strong enough, or the
pasture not well fenc't, or watcht, or so foorth: But for your wife
that keepes the stable of your honour: Let her be lockt in a brazen
towre, let *Argus* himselfe keepe her, yet can you neuer bee secure of
your honour, for why? she can runne through all with her serpent   260
nodle: besides you may hang a locke vpon your horse, and so can you
not vpon your wife.

Rin. But I pray you Sir what are the presumptions on which you
would build this diuorce?

Cornelio. Presumption enough Sir, for besides their entercourse, or   265
commerce of glances that past betwixt this cockrill-drone, and her, at
my table the last Sunday night at supper, their winckes, their beckes
(due gard) / their treads a'the toe (as by heauen I sweare she trode [H2]
once vpon my toe instead of his) this is chiefly to be noted, the same
night she would needs lie alone; and the same night her dog barkt, did 270
not you heare him *Valerio?*

Val. And vnderstand him too, Ile be sworne of a booke.

Cornelio. Why very good, if these be not manifest presumptions
now, let the world be iudge: Therefore without more ceremony,
Maister *Notarie* plucke out your Instrument.   275

Not. I will sir, if there be no remedie.

Cor. Haue you made it strong in law Maister *Notary*? haue you put
in words enough?

Not. I hope so sir, it has taken me a whole skinne of Parchment you
see.   280

Cor. Very good, and is Egresse and Regresse in?

Not. Ile warrant you sir, it is *forma Iuris.*

Cor. Is there no hoale to be found in the Ortography?

Not. None in the world sir.

Cor. You haue written *Sunt* with an *S* haue you not?   285

Not. Yes that I haue.

Cor. You haue done the better for quietnesse sake: and are none
of the Autenticall dashes ouer the head left out? if there be Maister
Notary an error will lye on't.

Not. Not for a dashe ouer head sir I warrant you, if I should ouer- 290
see; I haue seene that tryed in *Butiro et Caseo,* in *Butler* and *Casons*
case, *Decimo sexto* of Duke *Anonimo.*

Rin. Y'aue gotten a learned Notarie *Signior Cornelio.*

267-68 beckes (due gard)] ∼, due gard, ‖ **269** this] This ‖ **283** Ortography?] ∼. ‖ **289** on't]
Parrott (Gilchrist conj.); out ‖ **290-91** ouer- / see] ouersee ‖ **291** *et*] *&* ‖

Cor. Hees a shroad fellow indeed, I had as leeue haue his head in
a matter of fellony, or Treason, as any Notary in *Florence.* Read out   295
Maister *Notary,* harken you mistresse, Gentlemen marke I beseech you.

Omn. We will all marke you sir, I warrant you.

Not. I thinke it would be something tedious to read all, and therfore
Gentlemen the summe is this: That you *Signior Cornelio* Gentleman,
for diuers and sundry waighty and mature considerations, you espe-   300
cially mouing, specifying all the particulars of your wiues enormities
in a scedule hereunto annexed, / the transcript whereof is in your   [H2ᵛ]
owne tenure, custodie, occupation, and keeping: That for these the
afore said premises, I say, you renounce, disclaime and discharge
Gazetta from being your leeful, or your lawfull wife: And that you   305
eftsoones deuide, disioyne, seperate, remoue, and finally eloigne, sequester, and diuorce her, from your bed and your boord; That you
forbid her all accesse, repaire, egresse or regresse to your person, or
persons, mansion or mansions, dwellings, habitations, remainenances
or abodes, or to any shop, sellar, Sollar, easements chamber, dormer,   310
and so forth, now in the tenure, custody, occupation or keeping of the
said *Cornelio;* notwithstanding all former contracts, couenants, bar-
gaines, conditions, agreements, compacts, promises, vowes, affiances,
assurances, bonds, billes, indentures, pole-deedes, deeds of guift, defes-
ances, feoffments, endowments, vowchers, double vowchers, priuie   315
entries, actions, declarations, explications, reioinders, surreioinders,
rights, interests, demands, claymes, or titles whatsoeuer, heretofore
betwixt the one and the other party, or parties, being had, made, past,
couenanted and agreed, from the beginning of the world, till the day
of the date hereof, giuen the 17. of Nouember 1500. and so forth.   320
Here Sir you must set to your hand.

Cor. What els maister *Notary?* I am resolute ifaith.

Gaz. Sweete husband forbeare.

Cor. Auoyde, I charge thee in name of this diuorce: Thou mightst
haue lookt to it in time, yet this I will doe for thee; if thou canst spie   325
out any other man that thou wouldest cuckolde, thou shalt haue my
letter to him: I can do no more: more Inke maister *Notary,* I wright
my name at large.

Not. Here is more Sir.

Cor. Ah asse that thou could not know thy happinesse till thou hadst   330
lost it. How now? my nose bleed? shall I write in blood? what onely
three drops? Sfoote thi's Ominous: I will not set my hand toot now
certaine. Maister *Notary* I like not this abodement: I will deferre the

295 *Florence.* Read] ∼, read ‖ **303** custodie] cuffodie ‖ **313** compacts, promises,] ∼. / Promises,
(*second line indented Q*) ‖ **320-21** forth. Here] ∼, here ‖ **322** *Notary?*] Notary, ‖ **330** Ah asse]
read perhaps Ahlasse (*cf. IV.i.181*) ‖ **331** it. How] ∼, how ‖ **332** Ominous] *Reed;* Omninous ‖
333 certaine. Maister] *Parrott;* ∼, maister ‖

284

setting too of my hand till the next court day: keepe the diuorce I
pray you, and the woman in your house together.   335

    Omn. Burne the diuorce, burne the diuorce.

    Cor. Not so Sir, it shall not serue her turne. M. *Notary,* keep /
it at your perill, and gentlemen you may be gone a Gods name, what   [H3]
haue you to doe to flocke about me thus? I am neither *Howlet,* nor
Cuckooe: gentlewomen for gods sake medle with your owne cases, it   340
is not fit you should haunt these publike assembles.

    Omn. Well, farewell *Cornelio.*

    Val. Vse the gentlewoman kindely maister *Notary.*

    [*Not.*] As mine owne wife, I assure you Sir.   *Exeunt.*

    Clau. Signior *Cornelio* I cannot but in kindenes tell you that *Valerio*   345
by counsaile of *Rinaldo* hath whispered all this iealosie into your eares,
not that he knew any iust cause in your wife, but only to be reuengd on
you, for the gull, you put vpon him, when you drew him with his glory
to touch the *Theorbo.*

    Cor. May I beleeue this?   350

    Clau. As I am a gentleman: and if this accident of your nose had
not falne out, I would haue told you this before you set too your hand.

    Cor. It may well be, yet haue I cause enough
To perfect my diuorce, but it shall rest,
Till I conclude it with a Counterbuffe,   355
Giuen to these noble rascals: *Claudio* thankes:
What comes of this, watch but my braine a little,
And yee shall see, if like two partes in me,
I leaue not both these gullers wits Imbrierd,
Now I perceiue well where the wilde winde sits: 360
Here's Gull for Gull and wits at warre with wits.   *Exeunt.*

ACTVS QVINTI: SCENA PRIMA.

Rinaldo solus.

Fortune the great commandresse of the world,   ✗
Hath diuers wayes to aduance her followers:
To some she giues honour without deseruing,
To other some deseruing without honour,
Some wit, some wealth: and some wit without wealth: 5
Some wealth without wit, some, nor wit nor wealth
But good smocke-faces: or some qualities,

---

337 turne.] *Shepherd;* ∼∧ ‖ **342** Well] well ‖ **343** *Notary.*] ∼, ‖ **344** *Not.* As] *Shepherd (Collier*
conj.); As ‖ **345** *Valerio*] *Balerio* ‖ **356** Giuen] giuen ‖ **360** sits:] ∼, ‖ **361** Here's] Heres | SD
Exeunt.] (Exeunt. ‖ ACTVS] AGTVS ‖

By nature without iudgement, with the which
They liue in sensuall acceptation, /
And make show onely, without touche of substance;　　　　[H3ᵛ] 10
✦✦ My fortune is to winne renowne by Gulling,
Gostanzo, Dariotto, and *Cornelio:*
All which suppose in all their different kindes,
Their witts entyre, and in themselues no piece,
All at one blow, my helmet yet vnbruisde,　　　　　　　　15
I haue vnhorst, laid flat on earth for Guls;
Now in what taking poore *Cornelio* is,
Betwixt his large diuorce, and no diuorce,
I long to see, and what he will resolue:
I lay my life he cannot chew his meate,　　　　　　　　20
And lookes much like an Ape had swallowed pilles,
And all this comes of bootelesse iealousie:
And see where bootlesse iealousie appeares.

　　　　　　　　　Enter Cornel.

Ile bourd him straight; how now *Cornelio?*
Are you resolu'd on the diuorce or no?　　　　　　　　25
　　Cor. What's that to you? looke to your owne affaires,
The time requires it; are not you engag'd
In some bonds forfeit for *Valerio?*
　　Rin. Yes, what of that?
　　Corn. 　　　　　　　Why so am I my selfe,
And both our dangers great, he is arrested　　　　　　30
On a recognizance, by a vsuring slaue.
　　Rin. Arrested? I am sorry with my hart,
It is a matter may import me much:
May not our bayle suffize to free him thinke you?
　　Cor. I thinke it may, but I must not be seene in't,　　35
Nor would I wish you, for we both are parties,
And liker farre to bring our selues in trouble,
Then beare him out: I haue already made
Meanes to the officers to sequester him
In priuate for a time, till some in secret　　　　　　　40
Might make his Father vnderstand his state,
Who would perhaps take present order for him,
Rather then suffer him t'endure the shame
Of his imprisonment; Now, would you but goe
And breake the matter closely to his Father,　　　　　45

8 By] by ‖ **12** *Dariotto*] *Darioto* ‖ **15** blow,] ∼; ‖ **33** much:] ∼, ‖

(As you can wisely doo't) and bring him to him, /
This were the onely way to saue his credit,   [H4]
And to keepe off a shrowd blow from our selues.
    Rin. I know his Father will be moou'd past measure.
    Cor. Nay if you stand on such nice ceremonies,   50
Farewell our substance: Extreame diseases   k
Aske extreame remedies, better he should storme
Some little time, then we be beate for euer
Vnder the horred shelter of a prison.
    Rin. Where is the place?
    Cor.   Tis at the Halfe Moone Tauerne,   55
Hast, for the matter will abide no staye.
    Rin. Heauen send my speed be equall with my hast.   *Exit.*
    Cor. Goe shallow scholler, you that make all Guls,
You that can out-see cleere-ey'd ieolousie,
Yet make this slight a Milstone, where your braine   60
Sticks in the midst amazd: This Gull to him
And to his fellow Guller, shall become
More bitter then their baiting of my humour:
Heere at this Tauerne shall *Gostanzo* finde,
Fortunio, Dariotto, Claudio,   65
And amongst them, the ringleader his sonne,
His husband, and his Saint *Valerio,*
That knowes not of what fashion Dice are made,
Nor euer yet lookt towards a red Lettice,
(Thinkes his blinde Sire) at drinking and at Dice,   70
With all their wenches, and at full discouer
His owne grose folly, and his sonnes distempers,
And both shall know (although I be no scholler)
Yet I haue thus much Latin, as to say
Iam sumus ergo pares.   *Exit.*

[V.ii]

    Enter Valerio, Fortunio, Claudio, Page, Grat: Gazetta,
      Bellanora. A Drawer or two, setting a Table.

    Val. Set me the Table heere, we will shift roomes,
To see if Fortune will shift chances with vs:
Sit Ladies, sit, *Fortunio* place thy wench, /
And *Claudio* place you *Dariottos* mistresse,   [H4ᵛ]

---

54 prison.] ∼, ‖ **55** Halfe] halfe ‖ **65** *Fortunio, Dariotto*] *Fortuuio, Darioto* ‖ **66** sonne,] ∼∧ ‖ **71**
With all] Withall ‖ V.ii] *Parrott* ‖ **4** *Dariottos*] *Dariotos* ‖

I wonder where that neate spruce slaue becomes: 5
I thinke he was some Barbers sonne by th'masse,
Tis such a picked fellow, not a haire
About his whole Bulke, but it stands in print,
Each Pinne hath his due place, not any point,
But hath his perfect tie, fashion, and grace,   10
A thing whose soule is specially imployde
In knowing where best Gloues, best Stockings, Wasecotes,
Curiously wrought are solde; sacks Milleners shops
For all new tyres and fashions, and can tell yee
What new deuices of all sorts there are: 15
And that there is not in the whole *Rialto,*
But one new-fashion'd Wast-cote, or one Night-cap,
One paire of Gloues, pretty or well perfum'd,
And from a paire of Gloues of halfe a crowne,
To twenty crownes, will to a very scute   20
Smell out the price: and for these womanly parts
He is esteem'd a witty Gentleman.
    For. See where he comes.

Enter Dariotto.

    Dar.   God saue you louely Ladies.
    Val. I, well said louely *Paris,* your wall eye,
Must euer first be gloting on mens wiues,   25
You thinke to come vpon vs, being halfe drunke,
And so to part the freshest man amongst vs,
But you shall ouer-take vs, Ile be sworne.
    Dar. Tush man where are your dice? lets fall to them.
    Clau. We haue bin at am. Drawer, call for more.   30
    Val. First lets haue Wine, Dice haue no perfect edge,
Without the liquid whetstone of the Sirrope.
    For. True, and to welcome *Dariotto's* latenes,
He shall (vnpledg'd) carouze one crowned cup
To all these Ladies health.
    Dar.   I am well pleasd.   35
    Val. Come on, let vs varie our sweete time
With sundry excercises. Boy? Tabacco.
And Drawer, you must get vs musique too,
Call's in a cleanly noyse, the slaues grow lowzy. /
    Drawer. You shall haue such as we can get you sir.   *Exit.* [I1]
    Dar. Let's haue some Dice: I pray thee, they are clenly.

---

20 crownes,] ∼: ‖ **23** SD *Dariotto*] *Darioto* ‖ **24** I,] ∼∧ ‖ **30** am.] ∼, ‖ **33** *Dariotto's*] *Darioto's* ‖
37 excercises.] ∼, ‖ **39** Call's] Calls ‖

Val. Page, let mee see that Leafe?

Pag.   It is not Leafe Sir,

Tis pudding cane *Tabacco.*

Val.   But I meane,

Your Linstock sir, what leafe is that I pray?

   Pag. I pray you see sir, for I cannot read.   45

   Val. Sfoote a rancke stincking Satyre: this had been

Enough to haue poysned euerie man of vs.

   Dar. And now you speake of that, my Boy once lighted

A pipe of Cane *Tabacco* with a peece

Of a vild Ballad, and Ile sweare I had   50

A singing in my head a whole weeke after.

   Val. Well, th'old verse is, *A potibus incipe io-c-um.*

Enter Drawer with Wine and a Cupp.

   Val. Drawer, fill out this Gentlemans Carowse,

And harden him for our societie.

   Dar. Well Ladies heere is to your honourd healths.   55

   For. What *Dariotto,* without hat or knee?

   Val. Well said *Fortunio,* O y'are a rare Courtier,

Your knee good Signior, I beseech your knee.

   Dar. Nay pray you, lets take it by degrees *Valerio;*

On our feete first, for this will bring's too soone   60

Vpon our knees.

   Val.   Sir, there are no degrees

Of order in a Tauerne, heere you must,

I chargd yee, runne all a head: Slight, Courtier, downe;

I hope you are no Elephant, you haue Ioynts?

   Dar. Well Sir, heere's to the Ladies on my knees.   65

   Val. Ile be their pledge.

Enter, behind, Gostanzo and Rinaldo.

Fort.   Not yet *Valerio,*

This hee must drinke vnpledgd.

   Val. Hee shall not, I will giue him this aduantage.

   Gost. How now? what's heere? are these the Officers?

   Rin. Slight, I would all were well.

Enter, behind, Cornelio.

Val.   Heere is his pledge: 70

Heere's to our common friend *Cornelioes* health. /

   Dar. Health to *Gazetta,* Poyson to her husband.   *He kneeles.* [I1ᵛ]

---

42 let] Let ‖ **42-44** It . . . pray?] *Parrott*; It . . . *Tabacco:* / *Val.* But . . . pray *Q* (your) ‖ **43**
Tabacco.] ∼: ‖ **44** pray?] ∼∧ ‖ **59-61** Nay . . . knees.] *as prose Q* (on . . . vpon) ‖ **61-63** Sir
. . . downe;] Sir . . . Tauerne, / Heere . . . head, / Slight . . . downe; *Q* (of) ‖ **63** yee,] ∼∧ ‖
66 SD *behind*] *Parrott* ‖ **69** what's] whats ‖ **70** SD *behind*] *Parrott* ‖ **72** *Dar.*] *Parrott*; *Clau.* ‖

289

Cor. Excellent Guestes: these are my dayly Guestes.
Val. Drawer make euen th'impartiall skales of Iustice,
Giue it to *Claudio,* and from him fill round.   75
Come *Dariotto,* sett mee, let the rest
Come in when they haue done the Ladyes right.
    Gost. Sett mee, doe you know what belongs to setting?
    Rin. What a dull slaue was I to be thus gull'd.
    Cor. Why *Rinald,* what meant you to intrap your friend,   80
And bring his Father to this spectacle?
You are a friend in deed.
    Rin.   Tis verie good Sir,
Perhaps my friend, or I, before wee part,
May make euen with you.
    For.   Come, lets sett him round.
    Val. Doe so: at all. A plague vpon these Dice.   85
Another health, sfoote I shall haue no lucke,
Till I be druncke: come on, heere's to the comfort,
The Caualier my Father should take in mee,
If he now saw mee, and would do me right.
    For. Ile pledge it, and his health *Valerio.*   90
    Gost. Heere's a good Husband.
    Rin.   I pray you haue patience Sir.
    Val. Now haue at all, an't were a thousand pound.
    Gost. [*Advancing.*] Hold Sir, I barr the Dice.
    Val.   What Sir, are you there?
Fill's a fresh pottle, by this light, Sir Knight,
You shall do right.

                Enter Marc. Ant.
    Gost.   O thou vngratious villaine.   95
    [*Val.*] Come, come, wee shall haue you now thunder foorth
Some of your thriftie sentences, as grauely:
For as much *Valerius* as euery thing has time, and a Pudding has two:
yet ought not satisfaction to swerue so much from defalcation of well
dispos'd people, as that indemnitie should preiudice what securitie   100
doth insinuate: a tryall yet once againe. /
    Mar. Heere's a good sight, y'are well encountred sir,   [I2]
Did not I tell you you'd oreshoote your selfe
With too much wisedome?
    Val.   Sir, your wisest do so.
Fill the old man some wine.
    Gost.   Heere's a good Infant.   105

---

76 the rest] *Parrott;* mee rest, ‖ **93** SD *Advancing.*] *Parrott* ‖ **95** villaine.] ∼, ‖ **96** *Val.* Come] *Shepherd;* Come ‖ **104** wisedome?] ∼. ‖

Mar. Why Sir: Ahlas Ile wager with your wisedome,
His consorts drew him to it, for of him selfe
He is both vertuous, bashfull, innocent:
Comes not at Cittie: knowes no Cittie Art,
But plies your Husbandrie; dares not view a Wench.   110
    Val. Father, hee comes vpon you.
    Gost.   Heere's a Sonne.
    Mar. Whose wife is *Gratiana* now I pray?
    Gost. Sing your old song no more, your braine's too short
To reach into these pollicies.
    Mar.   Tis true,
Mine eye's soone blinded: and your selfe would say so,   115
If you knew all: Where lodg'd your Sonne last night?
Doe you know that with all your pollicie?
    Gost. Youle say he lodg'd with you, and did not I
Foretell you: all this must for cullour sake
Be brought about, onely to blinde your eyes?   120
    Mar. By heauen I chaunc't this morne, I know not why,
To passe by *Gratianas* bed-chamber,
And whom saw I fast by her naked side,
But your *Valerio*?
    Gost.   Had you not warning giuen?
Did not I bidd you watch my Courtier well,   125
Or hee would set a Crest a your Sonnes head?
    Mar. That was not all, for by them on a stoole,
My Sonne sate laughing, to see you so gull'd.
    Gost. Tis too too plaine.
    Mar.   Why Sir, do you suspect it
The more for that?
    Gost.   Suspect it? is there any   130
So grosse a wittoll, as if t'were his wife, /
Would sit by her so tamelie?   [12ᵛ]
    Mar.   Why not Sir,
To blind my eyes?
    Gost.   Well Sir, I was deceiu'd,
But I shall make it prooue a deare deceipt
To the deceiuer.
    Rin.   Nay Sir, lets not haue   135
A new infliction, set on an old fault:
Hee did confesse his fault vpon his knees,
You pardned it, and swore twas from your hart.

---

115 eye's] eyes ‖ 121 why,] ∼∧ ‖ 128 gull'd.] ∼, ‖ 129-30 Why . . . that?] *Collier; one line* Q
(the) ‖ 132-33 Why . . . eyes?] *Collier; one line* Q ‖ 135 To] to ‖

Gost. Swore; a great peece of worke, the wretch shall know
I haue a Daughter heere to giue my land too,   140
Ile giue my Daughter all: the prodigall
Shall not haue one poore House to hide his head in.
   For. I humblie thanke you Sir, and vow all duetie
My life can yeelde you.
   Gost.   Why are you so thankfull?
   For. For giuing to your Daughter all your Lands,   145
Who is my Wife, and so you gaue them mee.
   Gost. Better, and better.
   For.   Pray Sir be not moou'd,
You drew mee kindlie to your house, and gaue mee
Accesse to woe your Daughter, whom I lou'd:
And since (by honord mariage) made my wife.   150
   Gost. Now all my Choller flie out in your witts:
Good trickes of Youth y'faith, no *Indecorum*,
Knights sonne, Knights daughter; *Marc. Antonio*
Giue mee your hand: There is no remedie,
Mariage is euer made by Destenie.   155
   Rin. Scilence my Maisters, now heere all are pleas'd,
Onelie but *Cornelio*: who lackes but perswasion
To reconcile himselfe to his faire wife:
Good Sir will you (of all men our best speaker)
Perswade him to receiue her into grace?   160
   Gost. That I will gladlie, and he shalbe rul'd. Good *Cornelio*: I
haue heard of your wayward Ielosie, and I must tell you plaine as a
friend, y'are an Asse: you must pardon me, I knew your Father. /
   Rin. Then you must pardon him, indeed Sir.   [I3]
   Gost. Vnderstand mee: put case *Dariotto* lou'd your wife, whereby 165
you would seeme to refuse her; would you desire to haue such a Wife
as no man could loue but your selfe?
   Mar. Answere but that *Cornelio*.
   Gost. Vnderstand mee: Say *Dariotto* hath kist your wife, or per-
form'de other offices of that nature, whereby they did conuerse to-   170
geather at bedd and at boord, as friendes may seeme to doe:
   Mar. Marke but the now vnderstand mee.
   Gost. Yet if there come no proofes, but that her actions were clean-
lie, or indiscreete priuate, why t'was a signe of modestie: and will
you blow the Horne your selfe, when you may keepe it to your selfe?   175
Goe to, you are a Foole, vnderstand mee?
   Val. Doe vnderstand him *Cornelio*.

---

154 hand:] ~, ‖ **161** rul'd. Good] *Shepherd*; ~∧ good ‖ **174** indiscreete] *stet (See Textual Note)* ‖ **175** the] rhe ‖

Gost. Nay *Cornelio* I tell you againe, I knew your Father; Hee was a wise Gentleman, and so was your Mother: mee thinkes I see her yet, a lustie stoute Woman, bore great Children, you were the verie skun-   180
drell of am all; but let that passe: As for your Mother, shee was wise, a most flippant tongue she had, and could set out her Taile with as good grace as any shee in *Florence,* come cut and long-tayle; and she was honest enough too: But yet by your leaue she would tickle *Dob*
now and then, as well as the best on am; By *Ioue* it's true *Cornelio,*   185
I speake it not to flatter you: your Father knew it well enough, and would he do as you do, thinke you? set Rascalles to vndermine her, or looke to her water, (as they say)? No, when he saw twas but her humour (for his owne quietnesse sake) hee made a Backe-doore to his house for conuenience, gott a Bell to his fore doore, and had an odd   190
fashion in ringing, by which shee and her Mayde knew him; and would stand talking to his next neighbour to prolong time, that all thinges might be ridde clenly out a the way before he came, for the credite of his Wife: This was wisedome now, for a mans owne quiet. /
Mar. Heere was a man *Cornelio.*   [I3ᵛ] 195
Gost. What I say? Young men thinke old men are fooles; but old men know young men are fooles.
Cor. Why harke you, you two Knights; Doe you thinke I will for-
sake *Gazetta*?
Gost. And will you not?   200
Cor. Why theer's your wisedome; why did I make shew of Diuorce thinke you?
Mar. Pray you why Sir?
Cor. Onelie to bridle her stout stomack: and how did I draw on the cullour for my diuorce? I did traine the Woodcocke *Dariotto* into   205
the net, drew him to my house, gaue him opportunitie with my wife (as you say my Father dealt with his wiues friendes) onely to traine him in: let him alone with my wife in her bed-chamber; and some-
times founde him a bedd with her, and went my way backe againe softlie, onelie to draw him into the Pitte.   210
Gost. This was well handled in deed *Cornelio.*
Mar. I marrie Sir, now I commend your wisedome.
Cor. Why, if I had been so minded as you thinke, I could haue flung his Pantable downe the staires, or doone him some other dis-
grace: but I winckt at it, and drew on the good foole more and more,   215
onelie to bring him within my compasse.
Gost. Why, this was pollicie in graine.
Cor. And now shal the world see I am as wise as my father.

---

178 *Cornelio*] *Cornalio* ‖ **182** tongue] tongne ‖ **187** do, thinke] ∼∧ ∼ ‖

Val. Is't come to this? then will I make a speech in praise of this reconcilement, including therein the praise and honor of the most   220 fashionable and autenticall *HORNE*: stande close Gentles, and be silent.

He gets into a chaire.

   Gost. Come on, lets heare his wit in this potable humour.

Valerio.

The course of the world (like the life of man) is said to be deuided into seuerall ages: As wee into Infancie, Childhood, Youth, and so   225 forward to Old-age: So the World into the Golden age, the Siluer, the Brasse, the / Iron, the Leaden, the Wooden; and now into this   [I4] present age, which wee tearme the *Horned age*: not that but former ages haue inioyde this benefite as well as our times; but that in ours it is more common, and neuerthelesse pretious. It is said, that in the   230 Golden age of the world, the vse of Gold was not then knowne: an argument of the simplicitie of that age; least therefore succeeding ages should hereafter impute the same fault to vs, which wee lay vpon the first age; that wee liuing in the Horned age of the world, should not vnderstand the vse, the vertue, the honour, and the very royaltie of   235 the Horne; I will in briefe sound the prayses thereof, that they who are alreadie in possession of it, may beare their heades aloft, as beeing proud of such loftie acowtrementes: And they that are but in possibil- itie, may be rauisht with a desire to be in possession.

   A Trophey so honorable, and vnmatchably powerfull, that it is able   240 to raise any man from a Beggar to an Emperours fellow, a Dukes fel- low, a Noble-mans fellow, Aldermans fellow; so glorious, that it de- serues to be worne (by most opinions) in the most conspicuous place about a man: For what worthier Crest can you beare then the Horne? which if it might be seene with our mortall eyes, what a wonderfull   245 spectacle would there be? and how highly they would rauish the beholders? But their substaunce is incorporall, not falling vnder sence, nor mixt of the grosse concretion of Elementes, but a quintessence beyond them; a spirituall essence inuisible, and euerlasting.

   And this hath been the cause that many men haue called their bee-   250 ing in question, whether there be such a thing in *rerum natura,* or not; because they are not to be seene: as though nothing were that were not to be seene? Who euer saw the Winde? yet what wonderfull effectes are seene of it? It driues the cloudes, yet no man sees it: It rockes the House, beares downe Trees, Castles, Steeples, yet who sees   255 it? In like sort does your Horne, it swelles the Forehead, yet none sees it: it rockes the Cradle, yet none sees it: so that you / plainely per-   [I4v] ceiue Sence, is no Iudge of Essence. The Moone to any mans sence,

---

232 age;] ∼, ‖ **238** acowtrementes] *Q(c);* a cowtrementes *Q(u)* ‖

seemes to be Horned; yet who knowes not the Moone to be euer per-
fectly round: So likewise your Heades seeme euer to be round, when   260
in deed they are oftentimes Horned: for their originall, it is vnsearch-
able: Naturall they are not; for there is [no] Beast borne with Hornes,
more then with Teeth: Created they were not, for *Ex nihilo nihil fit;*
Then will you aske mee, How came they into the world? I know not;
but I am sure Women brought them into this part of the world, how-   265
soeuer some Doctors are of opinion that they came in with the Diuell:
and not vnlike; for, as the Diuell brought Sinne into the worlde; but
the Woman brought it to the Man: so it may very well be that the
Diuell brought Hornes into the world; but the Woman brought them
to the man.   270

For their power it is generall ouer the world, no Nation so barba-
rous, no Countrey so proude, but doth equall homage to the Horne.
Europa when shee was carried through the Sea by the *Saturnian* Bull,
was said (for feare of falling) to haue held by the Horne: and what
is this but a plaine shewing to vs, that all *Europe,* which tooke name   275
from that *Europa,* should likewise hold by the Horne: So that I say,
it is vniuersall ouer the face of the world, general ouer the face of
Europe, and common ouer the face of this Countrey. What Cittie,
what Towne, what Village, what Streete? nay what House can quit
it selfe of this prerogatiue? I haue read that the Lion once made a   280
Proclamation through all the Forrest, that all Horned Beastes should
depart foorthwith vpon paine of death: If this Proclamation should
be made through our Forrest, Lord what pressing, what running, what
flying, would there be euen from all the parts of it? he that had but
a bunch of Flesh in his head would away: and some foolishly feare-   285
full, would imagine the shadow of his Eares to be Hornes: Ahlas how
desart would this Forrest be left? /

To conclude: for there force it is irreuitable, for were they not   [K1]
irreuitable, then might eyther propernesse of person secure a man, or
wisedome preuent am; or greatnesse exempt, or riches redeeme them,   290
but present experience hath taught vs, that in this case, all these
stand in no steade: for we see the properst men take part of them, the
best wits cannot auoide them (for then should Poets be no cuckolds)
nor can money redeeme them, for then would rich-men fine for their
hornes, as they do for offices: But this is held for a maxime, that there   295
are more rich cuckolds then poore; lastly for continuance of the horne
it is vndeterminable till death: Neither doe they determine with the
wiues death, (howsoeuer ignorant writers holde opinion they doe);
For as when a knight dies, his Ladie still retaines the title of Ladie;

---

262 is no Beast] *Parrott*; is Beast ‖ **270** man.] ∼, ‖ **275** *Europe*] *Reed*; *Europa* ‖ **285-86** feare-
/ full] fearefull ‖ **288** conclude:] ∼∧ (To conclude *not indented in* Q) ‖ **296** poore;] ∼, ‖ **298**
doe);] ∼)∧ ‖

when a company is cast yet the Captaine still retaines the title of Cap-   300
taine; So though the wife die by whom this title came to her husband,
yet by the curtesie of the City, he shalbe a cuckold during life, let all
ignorant asses prate what they list.

    Gost. Notable wag, come sir shake hands with him,
In whose high honour you haue made this speech.   305
    Mar. And you sir come, ioyne hands, y'are one amongst them.
    Gost. Very well done, now take your seuerall wiues,
And spred like wilde-geese, though you now grow tame:
Liue merily together and agree,
Hornes cannot be kept off with iealousie.   310

FINIS. /

EPILOGUE.   [K1ᵛ]

Since all our labours are as you can like,
We all submit to you; nor dare presume,
To thinke ther's any reall worth in them:
Sometimes feastes please the Cookes, and not the guestes,
Sometimes the guestes, and curious Cookes contemne them: 5
Our dishes we intirely dedicate
To our kinde guestes, but since yee differ so,
Some to like onely mirth without taxations,
Some to count such workes trifles, and such like,
We can but bring you meate, and set you stooles,   10
And to our best cheere say, you all are (   ) welcome.

---

305 speech.] ∼: ‖ **306** amongst] amogst ‖ Epilogue **5** *them:*] ∼, ‖ **11** *are* (   ) *welcome*]
Q(c); are welcome Q(u) ‖

HISTORICAL COLLATION

[Editions collated: Reed (= *R*, in *A Select Collection of Old Plays*, 2nd. ed., 1780, IV, 116-98); Collier (= *C*, in *A Select Collection of Old Plays*, 3rd. ed., 1825, IV, 109-81); Shepherd (= *S*, in *The Works of George Chapman: Plays*, 1875, pp. 46-77); Phelps (= *Ph*, *George Chapman* in *The Mermaid Series* [1895], pp. 34-119); Parrott (= *P¹*, *"All Fooles" and "The Gentleman Usher,"* 1907, pp. 1-116); Parrott (= *P²*, in *The Plays and Poems of George Chapman: The Comedies* [1914], pp. 100-162; *P*= agreement of both Parrott editions). Only substantive and semi-substantive variants are recorded; obvious errors are not recorded. Lemmata are taken from the present text. Where lemma represents the reading of Q copy-text, omission of siglum indicates agreement with lemma.]

Prologus

4 *or . . . Heauen*] from this Heauen fall *Brereton conj.*
5 *wits, that*] ∼_∧ ∼, *P¹*; ∼, ∼, *P²*
  in-ayme] in aim *R, C, S, Ph, P*
6 *Obiects*] object *Ph*
14-15 (*now . . . Subiect*] now . . . (*Subject C*
20 *Venerian*] Venerean *C*
25-26 *nothing; To . . . censure,*] ∼_∧ ∼ . . . ∼; *S, Ph*
27 *mistery*] *Q(u)*; misery *Q(c), R, S, Ph, P, C*
31 *end,*] ∼; *S, Ph*
32 *wits*] wit *C*
33 *euents,*] ∼; *S, Ph, P²*

I.i

SD] *A Street in Florence. P*
2 effects] *Q(c)*; effect *Q(u), R, C, S, Ph, P*
22 battry] battery *R, C, S, Ph*; batt'ry *P*
33 Lords] lords' *P²*
66 iesters,] *P*; iesters; *Q, R, C, S, Ph*
67 durt and tytles,] *C, P*; ∼, ∼ ∼_∧ *Q, R, S, Ph*
79 profan'st] profanest *S, Ph*
81 richest] *R, C, S, Ph, P*; riches *Q*
83 Alablaster] alabaster *R, C, S, Ph*
96 Reuil'st] Revilest *S, Ph*
97 sunne] *S, Ph, P²*; sonne *Q, R, C, P¹*
113 vnited?] ∼, *R, C, S, Ph, P*
117 parle] parley *R, C, S, Ph, P²*
118 t'obserue] to observe *S, Ph*

138 Bayly] bailiff *R, C*; bailie *P²*

141 SD *Amplectitur eam.*] *Embraces her. R, C*

146 that.] ∼∧ *R*

150 *Valerio?*] *Q(c)*, *S, Ph, P*: ∼. *Q(u)*; ∼ — *R, C*

161 venter'd] ventur'd *R, C, P*; ventured *S, Ph*

162 it.] *Q(u), R, C, S, Ph, P*; it? *Q(c)*

164 hath] has R, C

166 th'esperean] th' Hesperean *R, C*; th' Hesperian *S, Ph, P²*

167 SD *Intrat Gostanzo. Omnes aufugiunt.*] *Enter* Gostanzo. *R, C*

169 Sir?] sir? *All go out except* Rynaldo. *R, C*

185 vnusering] *Q(c)*; vnnurishing *Q(u), R, C, S, Ph, P*

206 experient] experienc'd *R*

209 resolu'd] resolved *C, S, Ph*

214 you?] ∼! *R, C, P*; ∼, *S, Ph*

215 sonne? alas] son, alas! *S, Ph*; son? Alas! *P*

219 SD *Auersus.*] *Aside. R, C*

233 wise] *S, Ph, P*; wife *Q, R, C*

242 Sir.] sir. *Hides himself. C*

246 holde.] hold. *Aside. C*

255 diamants] diamonds *R, C*

264 sonne] *R, C, S, Ph, P*; soone *Q*

275 ope] ope' *R*

312 No] Ne *Q, R, P¹*; no *C*; No, *S, Ph*; Nay, *P²*

316 *Padoa*] Padua *S, Ph, P²*

378 sell,] *R, C, S, Ph, P*; ∼∧ *Q*

383 SD *Aside.*] *C, P*; *om. Q, R, S, Ph*

385 maynd] maim'd *R, C, S, Ph, P²*

390 eld] old *R, C, S, Ph*

391 SD *Aside.*] *C, P*; *om. Q, R, S, Ph*

　　 t'his] to his *S, Ph*

392 comes] how ∼ *S*

I.ii

I.ii] *P*

SD] *Before the House of Cornelio. P*

5 loue sportes] love-sports *R, C, S, Ph, P²*

7 continuall] continued *C*

9 seld] seldom *R*

17 stolne] stolen *R, S, Ph* (*not hereafter recorded*)

23 Extreame] *R, C, S, Ph, P*; Extreames *Q*

24 sacietie] satiety *R, C, S, Ph, P*

49 Goe, in] Go in, *R, C, S, Ph, P*

68 *Gra.*] *P*; *For. Q, R, C, S, Ph*

69 Ielosie, Spy-all] *R, C*; ∼∧ ∼ *Q*; jealous spy-all *S, Ph*; jealous espial *P*; jealous spial *Bradley conj.* (*in P*)

　　 displease] disperse *Bradley conj.* (*in P*)

77 ought] owed *R, C*

85 Lowres] Lours *R*, *C*; Lowers *S*, *Ph*, *P²*
90 Scholard] *P*; Scholards *Q*; scholar *R*, *C*, *S*, *Ph*
94 sweete hart] sweet-heart *R*, *C*; sweetheart *S*, *Ph*, *P²*
112 sweet harts] sweet-heart's *R*, *C*; sweetheart's *S*, *Ph*, *P²*
139 Father?] father. *S*, *Ph*; father! *P*
144 conseaue] conceive *R*, *C*, *S*, *Ph*; conferme *Bradley conj. (in P²)*, *P¹*; confirm
    P²; conserve *P.A. Daniel conj. (in P)*
146 dar'st] darest *S*, *Ph*
147 knowest] know'st *S*, *Ph*

II.i

SD] *A Street in Florence, before the House of Gostanzo. P¹*; *Before the house of* Gostanzo
    P²
6 vnshuting] unsuiting *R*, *C*, *S*, *P²*
7 or friend] a friend *S*, *Ph*
9 Resolue] resolue *Q(c)*; Adsolue *Q(u)*, *R*, *C*, *S*, *Ph*
23 credite] credit's *S*, *Ph*
26 parle] parley *R*, *C*, *S*, *Ph*, *P²*
37 *Troye*] *P¹*; *Troy R*, *C*, *S*, *Ph*, *P²*; *Trope Q*
    SD *Marc. . . . himselfe.] after l. 39 P*
42 come you seauen] come-you-seven *R*, *C*, *S*, *Ph*, *P²*
46 SD *Aside to Mar.*] *P¹*; *aside P²*; *om. Q*, *R*, *C*, *S*, *Ph*
    SD *Aside to Gost.*] *P¹*; *aside P²*; *om. Q*, *R*, *C*, *S*, *Ph*
51 comes] come *R*, *C*
68 friuall] frival *R*, *C*; frivall *S*, *Ph*; frivol *P²*
70 past] pass'd *P²*
77 SD *Aside.*] *C*, *P*; *om. Q*, *R*, *S*, *Ph*
80 glases] glosses *R*, *C*; glozes *S*, *Ph*; glazes *P²*
82 humane] human *P²*
86 SD *Aside.*] *C*, *P*; *om. Q*, *R*, *S*, *Ph*
87 SD *Aside.*] *P*; *om. Q*, *R*, *C*, *S*, *Ph*
90 imploy] employ *R*, *C*; imply *S*, *Ph*, *P²*
91 Who] Whom *R*, *C*
134 courtlie] courtlier *P¹*
140 conduct am] conduct-am *Q*, *P¹*; conduct 'em *R*, *C*, *S*, *Ph*, *P²*
142 dar'st] darest *S*, *Ph*
146 wip'st] wipest *S*, *Ph*
148 Young men] *R*, *C*, *S*, *Ph*, *P*; Youngmen *Q*
149 brought vp] brought-up *S*
153 of his] to ~ *R*, *C*
157 the tother] ~ other *R*, *C*; t'other *S*, *Ph*
165 some times] sometime *C*
168 had] *om. Ph*
171 am] 'em *R*, *C*, *S*, *Ph*, *P²* (*not hereafter recorded*)
172 *Exordion*] *Exordium P²*
174 *Quatorzaines*] *S*, *Ph*, *P*; *Quatorzanies Q*, *R*, *C*
176 *Sdruciolla*] *S*, *Ph*, *P*; *Sdrnciolla Q*, *R*; *Sdruciola C*

179 SD *Exit. . . . Mar.*] *Exit* Valerio. Marc. Antonio *appears.* R, C
194 desired] desir'd R, C
196 t'enioy] to enjoy S, Ph
198 make] made P
201 worke] workt P¹; work'd P²
    Macheuil] Machiavel C, S, Ph, P²
206 Or] Of Q, R, C, S, Ph, P
208 th'euening] the evening S, Ph
209 Perseuer] Persevere S
212 good night] good-night S, Ph, P²
226 too] to R, C, S, Ph, P²
227 boldly; . . . you,] R, C, S, Ph, P; ∼, . . . ∼; Q
229 SD *Gazetta . . . sowing.*] *after l. 231* P¹
231 *Exeunt.*] ∼∧ [Valerio *and* Rinaldo] P
236 Hum] Him Q, S, Ph; Hem R, C, P
256 ath'toe] o'th'toe P²
289 shew] crew P²; sort *Brereton conj.* (*in* P²)
291, 292 vm] 'em R, C, S, Ph, P² (*not hereafter recorded*)
296 SD *and Page,*] P; *om.* Q, R, C, S, Ph
301 poynt;] ∼, S, Ph
302 day:] ∼, S, Ph
308 sees] R, C, S, Ph, P; fees Q
318 sate] sat R, C
326 with twenty] twenty R, C, S, Ph
335 besides] beside C, Ph
336-37 rayling Became] railing has become *C conj.*; railing is become S
368 SD *Aside.*] P; *om.* Q, R, C, S, Ph
369 SD *Aside.*] P; *om.* Q, R, C, S, Ph
370 SD *Aside.*] P; *om.* Q, R, C, S, Ph
385 vm lyte] P¹; on lyte Q; on lite R, C; 'em light *C conj.*; on't light S; on light Ph; 'em lite P²
397 needs] need Ph
406 *Dar.*] *Val.* P
414 Signeur] Signior R, C; Signor S, Ph, P² (*not hereafter recorded*)
420 the voyce] thy ∼ S, Ph, P
422 Mast] mast Q; master R, C, S, Ph; ∼. P¹; Master P²

III.i

SD] *A Street in Florence, before the House of* Gostanzo. P¹; *Before the house of* Gostanzo P²
5 SD *Aside.*] P; *om.* Q, R, C, S, Ph
11 SD *Aside.*] P; *om.* Q, R, C, S, Ph
19 SD *Aside.*] P; *om.* Q, R, C, S, Ph
23 SD *Aside.*] P²; *om.* Q, R, C, S, Ph P¹
60 byth] by the S, Ph
94 A] Aye, R, C; O' P²
97 slights] flights C
105 new begun] ∼-∼ R, C, S, Ph, P²

120 fat] far *R*; pat *Deighton conj. (in P²)*
122 by] *R, C, S, Ph, P*; be *Q*
126 inamoured] enamour'd *S, Ph, P²*
131 encountred] encountered *R, C*; encounter'd *S, Ph, P²*
160 a] o' *P²*
164 pleasd] pleased *R, C, S, Ph, P²*
166 Excellent good boy] ∼ ∼, ∼ *R, C*; ∼, ∼ ∼ *Ph*
170 of all] all of *C conj.*
177 tumbled] tŭbled *Q*; troubled *R, C*
200 vm] them *R, C*; 'em *S, Ph, P²*
206 vm] them *R*; 'em *C, S, Ph, P²*
213 it] its *R, C, S, Ph*
232 superannated] superannuated *R, C, S, Ph*
237 Christen] christian *R, C, S*; Christian *Ph*; christen *P*
245 villayne] villainie *P¹ conj.*; villainy *P²*
247 a] o' *P²*
259 playest . . . com'st] play'st . . . com'st *R, C*; play'st . . . comest *S, Ph*
267 fayth] i'faith *S*
282 stald] stall'd *R, C, S, Ph*
293 dar'st] darest *S, Ph*
300 cause.] ∼, *P*
307 lookes] *S, P*; looke *Q, R, C, Ph*
321 lingring] lingering *R, C, S, Ph, P²*
332 deceyu'st] deceivest *R, C, S, Ph*
335 SD *Exit Page.] P*; *om. Q, R, C, S, Ph*
349 Where] When *S, Ph*
366 others stand a] *S, Ph, P¹*; other stand a *Q*; others stand on *R, C*; others
    stand o' *P²*
    a thy] on ∼ *R, C*; o' ∼ *P²*
378 hazard] *R, C, S, Ph, P*; hazards *Q*
387 shortned] shortened *R, C, S, Ph, P²*
388 a'th] o'th' *P²*
396 a] o' *S, Ph, P²*
404 So] *Val.* ∼ *P*
405 ridiculouse—] *R, C, S, Ph, P*; ∼. *Q*

IV.i

SD] *A Street in Florence, before the House of Gostanzo P¹*; *Before the House of* Gostanzo
    P²
2 forwards] forward *C, S*
7 seasoned] season'd *S, Ph*
52 your] *R, C, P*; our *Q, S, Ph*
77 a] on *R, C*; o' *P²*
87 SD *aside to Rinaldo] P*; *om. Q, R, C, S, Ph*
89 Creator] crater *C conj., S*
97 SD *Aside to Gost.] P*; *om. Q, R, C, S, Ph*

99 SD *Aside to Rin.*] P; *om.* Q, R, C, S, Ph
101 SD *Aside to Gost.*] P; *om.* Q, R, C, S, Ph
123 SD *Aside.*] P; *om.* Q, R, C, S, Ph
138 Rests] Rest R, C
145 sugred] sugar'd R, C, S, Ph, P²
146 SD *Aside to Mar.*] P; *om.* Q, R, C, S, Ph
148 SD *Aside.*] P; *om.* Q, R, C, S, Ph
149 SD *Aside.*] P; *om.* Q, R, C, S, Ph
152 displeasd . . . receau'd] displeased . . . receiv'd R, C; displeased . . . received
    S, Ph
154 SD *Aside.*] P; *om.* Q, R, C, S, Ph
160 SD *Aside.*] P; *om.* Q, R, C, S, Ph
161 loue me] love S, Ph
167 still my] ∼, ∼ S, Ph, P
207 pardoned] pardon'd S, Ph, P²
234 mankinde] unkind S
248 in] on C
    mine?] R, C, S, Ph, P²; minde, Q; minde? P¹
257 fenc't] fenced R, C, S, Ph, P²
264 would] will Ph
266 cockrill-drone] cockeril-∼ R, C; cockerel-∼ P²
267 table the last] table last S, Ph
267-68 beckes (due gard)] ∼, ∼ ∼, Q; becks, ∼ guard. R, C, Ph; becks, ∼ ∼,
    S; ∼, —∼ ∼!— P¹; becks—Dieu garde!— P²
268 a'] o' P²
289 on't] *Gilchrist conj.* (*in* C), P; out Q, R, C, S, Ph
291 *et*] & Q, P¹; and R, C, S, Ph, P²
294 shroad] shrewd R, C, S, Ph, P²
    leeue] leave R, C; lieve S, Ph; lief P²
295 Notary] Notary's R, C
299-300 *Cornelio* Gentleman, for] Cornelio, for S
309 remainenances] remainnances R, C; remainences S, Ph; remanences P²
310 easements chamber] ∼, ∼ C; easements' ∼ S, Ph; easement's ∼ P²
326 wouldest] wouldst Ph
330 could] couldst R, C, S, Ph
332 thi's] this is R, C; 'tis S, Ph; this's P²
333 certaine. Maister *Notary*] ∼, maister ∼ Q; certain; master ∼, R, C; certain,
    master ∼, S, Ph; ∼. ∼ ∼, P
337 turne. M.] S, Ph, P; ∼_∧ ∼. Q; turn, master R, C
338 be gone . . . name:] ∼ ∼ . . . ∼, Q; ∼ ∼ . . . ∼; R, C; begone; . . . ∼ S;
    begone . . . ∼; Ph; ∼ ∼, . . . ∼; P¹; begone; . . . ∼, P²
    a] o' P²
339 *Howlet*] owlet S
341 assembles] assemblies S, Ph, P²
344 *Not.* As] C *conj.*, S, Ph, P; As Q, R, C
345 *Valerio*] C, S, Ph, P; *Balerio* Q; Bellonora R

347 reuengd] revenged *R, C, S, Ph, P*²
358 like . . . me] like two harts in May *conj. anon.* (*in P*²); like two fast in ice
   Brereton conj. (*in P*²)

V.i

SD] *A Street in Florence. P*
11-12 Gulling, . . . *Cornelio*:] gulling . . . ∼: *R, C*; gulling . . . ∼; *S, Ph*; gulling
   . . . ∼, *P*
14 no piece] one ∼ *P conj.*
21 swallowed] swallow'd *C, S, Ph*
24 bourd] board *S, Ph, P*²
48 shrowd] shrewd *R, C, S, Ph, P*²
55 Halfe Moone] Half-Moon *R, C*
60 slight a Milstone] ∼ ∼ mill-stone *R, C*; ∼ ∼ milestone *S, Ph*; sleight ∼
   millstone *Brereton conj., P*²
61 amazd] amazed *R, C, S, Ph*
69 Lettice] lattice *Ph*

V.ii

23 SD *Enter Dariotto.*] *after l. 22 S, Ph, P*²
27 amongst] among *S, Ph, P*²
41 Dice: . . . thee,] dice; . . . thee *S, Ph*; dice, . . . thee: *P*¹; dice, . . . thee; *P*²
46 Satyre] satire *R, C, P*²; Satyr *S, Ph*
47 poysned] poisoned *R, C*; poison'd *S, Ph, P*²
50 vild] vile *R, C, S, Ph*
52 SD *a Cupp*] *four cups R*
63 chargd] charge *S, Ph, P*
   a head] ahead *S, Ph, P*²
66 SD *behind*] *om. Q, R, C, S, Ph; follows Rinaldo in P*
70 SD *behind*] *om. Q, R, C, S, Ph; follows Cornelio in P*
72 *Dar.*] *P; Clau. Q, R, C, S, Ph*
76 the] *P*; me *Q, R, C, S, Ph*
80 *Rinald*] *Rinaldo C, S, Ph*
92 an't were] and 'twere *S, Ph*
   pound] pounds *S, Ph*
93 SD *Advancing.*] *P; om. Q, R, C, S, Ph*
94 pottle] bottle *Ph*
96 *Val.* Come] *S, Ph, P*; Come *Q, R, C*
98-101 For . . . insinuate:] "∼ . . . ∼;" *S, Ph, P*
98 time] fine *or* term *Daniel conj.* (*in P*)
99-100 well dispos'd] ∼-∼ *R, C*; ∼-disposed *S, Ph, P*²
101 a tryall] at all *Daniel conj.* (*in P*²)
102 encountred] encountered *R, C*; encounter'd *S, Ph, P*²
109 at Cittie] o'th'city *C conj.*
115 eye's] *S, Ph, P*; eyes *Q, R, C*
126 a] o' *C, P*²
150 honord] honored *R, C*
157 Onelie but *Cornelio*] Only *Cornelio R, C, S, Ph*

172 now ... mee.] "~ ... me." *S, Ph, P*
174 indiscreete] in discreet *P*
185 it's] 'tis *R, C*
193 a] of *R*; o' *C, P*²
232 age;] *P*; ~, *Q, S, Ph*; ~. *R, C*
262 there is no Beast] *P*; there is Beast *Q, R, C, Ph*; where is beast *C conj., S*
275 *Europe] R, C, Ph, P*; *Europa Q, S*
288 conclude:] *R, C, S, Ph, P*; ~∧ *Q*
288, 289 irreuitable] irrenitable *P*; inevitable *Brereton conj. (in P*²)
292 properst] properest *R, C, S, Ph, P*²
    of them, the] of, the *R*
298-99 doe); For] ~)∧ ~ *Q*; do. For *R, C*; do, for *S, Ph, P*²; do); for *P*¹

Epilogue

9 *such like*] ~-~ *S, Ph*; suchlike *P*²
11 *are* (   ) *welcome] Q(c), R, C, P*; *are welcome Q(u), S*; are—welcome *Ph*

PRESS-VARIANTS

[Copies collated: BM (British Museum C. 34. c. 10), Bodl (Bodleian Library Malone 240[6]), CLUC (W. A. Clark Library), CSmH (Huntington Library), CtY¹ (Yale University Library), CtY² (Yale University Library, with Thomas Dring's advertising slip on sig. A2ᵛ), DFo (Folger Shakespeare Library), DLC (Library of Congress), Dyce (Victoria and Albert Museum 2030. 16. c. 2), EHU (Edinburgh University Library), MB (Boston Public Library), MH (Harvard University Library), NN (New York Public Library), NNP (Pierpont Morgan Library), TxU¹ (University of Texas Library C366.605a), TxU² (University of Texas Library C366.605a, copy 2), Worc (Worcester College Library, Oxford)]

Sheet A (inner forme)

First State Corrected: Bodl, EHU
Uncorrected: DLC, Dyce, MH, NNP (See Introduction, p. 232, note 20)
Sig. A4
    Actus] *Actu*s
    Second State Corrected: CLUC, CSmH, CtY¹
Sig. A4
    I.i.3 straines] steaines
        5 notes,] notes:
        6 loue:] loue?
    Third State Corrected: BM, CtY², DFo, MB, NN, TxU¹, TxU², Worc
Sig. A2 (title page)
    Comedy] Comody
Sig. A3ᵛ (Prologue)
    27 *misery*] *mistery*
Sig. A4
    I.i.2 effects] effect

Sheet B (outer forme)

Corrected: CSmH, CtY¹, CtY², DFo, EHU, MB, MH, NN, NNP, TxU¹, TxU², Worc
Uncorrected: BM, Bodl, CLUC, DLC, Dyce
Sig. B2ᵛ
    I.i.185 vnusering] vnnurishing

Sheet B (inner forme)

Corrected: CtY¹, DFo, EHU, MB, MH, NN, NNP, TxU¹
Uncorrected: BM, Bodl, CLUC, CSmH, CtY², DLC, Dyce, TxU², Worc

305

Sig. B2

    I.i.150 *Valerio?*] *Valerio.*

      163 it?] it.

Sheet C (outer forme)

First State Corrected: BM, CLUC, DLC, Dyce, DFo, EHU, MB, MH, NNP,
                TxU[1]

Uncorrected: CtY[1], TxU[2] (See Introduction, p. 232, note 20)

Sig. C4[v]

    II.i.4 haue him:] haue him,

      10 thus?] thus?,

Second State Corrected: Bodl, CSmH, CtY[2], NN, Worc

Sig. C2[v]

    I.ii.42 See see, wee] See see wee, wee

Sig. C4[v]

    II.i.9 resolue] Adsolue

      30 weale] veale

Sheet C (inner forme)

Corrected: BM, Bodl, CLUC, CSmH, CtY[1], CtY[2], DFo, DLC, Dyce, EHU,
          MB, MH, NN, NNP, TxU[1], Worc

Uncorrected: TxU[2]

Sig. C2

    I.ii.12 I] *I*

Sig. C3[v]

    I.ii.100 reforme] adforme

      113 wife] wifs

    (catchword) With] Will

Sheet D (inner forme)

Corrected: BM, Bodl, CLUC, CSmH, CtY[2], DFo, DLC, Dyce, EHU, MB,
          MH, NN, NNP, TxU[1], TxU[2], Worc

Uncorrected: CtY[1]

Sig. D1[v]

    II.i.81 tearmes:] tearmes.

Sheet E (outer forme)

Corrected: BM, Bodl, CLUC, CSmH, CtY[1], CtY[2], DFo, DLC, Dyce, EHU,
          MB, MH, NNP, TxU[1], TxU[2], Worc

Uncorrected: NN

Sig. E2[v]

    II.i.385 Vayne] Vay ne

Sheet E (inner forme)

Corrected: CLUC, CSmH, CtY[2], MB, NN, NNP, TxU[2], Worc

Uncorrected: BM, Bodl, CtY[1], DFo, DLC, Dyce, EHU, MH, TxU[1]

Sig. E4

    (catchword) For] Fo

Sheet G (outer forme)

Corrected: BM, CLUC, CSmH, CtY¹, CtY², DLC, Dyce, EHU, MH, NN,
NNP, TxU¹, TxU², Worc

Uncorrected: Bodl, DFo, MB

Sig. G1

III.i.345 straight] straght

Sig. G2ᵛ

IV.i.30 *Credulity,*] *Credulity*:
31 *Decrepity*:] *Decrepity,*

Sig. G3

(signature) G3] H3

Sig. G4ᵛ

IV.i.198 accustom'd] accustomm'd

Sheet G (inner forme)

Corrected: BM, CLUC, CtY¹, CtY², DLC, Dyce, EHU, MH, NN, NNP,
TxU¹, TxU², Worc

Uncorrected: Bodl, CSmH, DFo, MB

Sig. G3ᵛ

IV.i.109 *Gost.* Nay] Nay

Sheet H (outer forme)

Corrected: BM, Bodl, CSmH, CtY¹, CtY², DFo, DLC, Dyce, EHU, MB,
MH, NN, NNP, TxU¹, TxU², Worc

Uncorrected: CLUC

Sig. H4ᵛ

(running title) *All*] *All*

Sheet I (inner forme)

Corrected: BM, Bodl, CLUC, DLC, Dyce, MB, MH, NNP, TxU¹, TxU²

Uncorrected: CSmH, CtY¹, CtY², DFo, EHU, NN, Worc

Sig. I4

V.ii.238 acowtrementes] a cowtrementes

Sheet K (inner forme)

Corrected: BM, Bodl, CLUC, CtY¹, DFo, DLC, MB, MH, NNP, TxU¹

Uncorrected: CSmH, CtY², Dyce, EHU, NN, TxU², Worc

Sig. K1ᵛ (Epilogue)

11 *are* (   ) *welcome*] *are welcome*

TEXTUAL NOTES

Dramatis Personae

10 Kyte, A Scriuener.] This character, otherwise unnamed, is called a Notary in the text, stage directions, and speech-prefixes. The name Kyte does not appear in the play. It is possible that the appearance of the name in the list of actors reflects some earlier stage in the composition of the play. See the Textual Introduction.

Prologus

27 *mistery*] This is the reading of the uncorrected state of sheet A (inner forme). The corrected reading (third state of correction) is *"misery"*, a reading adopted only by Collier. That the uncorrected *"mistery"* is actually correct is shown through its context with lines 20-22, the "mystery" being why *"quick Venerian iestes, / Should sometimes rauish? sometimes fall farre short."* The press-corrector did not understand the relation between lines 20-22 and line 27 and produced a reading which makes an obvious kind of sense in its immediate context.

I.i

162 did his father know it.] I have retained here what I consider the uncorrected reading, reversing the correction order suggested by Professor Yamada. The question mark after *"Valerio"* in line 150 above is certainly correct and represents a press correction of the original period. In the present passage the press-corrector mistook the conditional clause "did . . . it." for an independent question and thus wrongly changed the period after "it" to a question mark. Lines 163-65 clearly support this interpretation.

185 vnusering dowry] This is the reading of what I have arbitrarily distinguished as the corrected state of sheet B (outer forme). The uncorrected state reads "vnnurishing dowry" and is followed by all earlier editors. Yamada reverses my order and considers "vnusering" to be the uncorrected state. Since there is no other proof-correction in the outer forme of sheet B, there is no further determining evidence to establish the order. Whichever order is chosen, there is no doubt, I think, that "vnusering" is right. An "vnusering dowry" is one giving no return or increase and fits the context perfectly. The *NED* records a single use of "vnusering" by Middleton in 1622. "vnnurishing" is a comparatively weak reading and must represent either a misreading of the manuscript or a press-corrector's attempt to emend a word he did not understand; in the second case "vnusering" would have to be considered as the uncorrected state.

I.ii

69 Your Fathers Ielosie, Spy-all,] The principal textual crux. Various emendations have been suggested (see the Historical Collation); that adopted here (Reed's), by placing a comma after "Ielosie," makes "Spy-all" an appositive. I have preferred it because I suspect that "Spy-all" may have been a term used in connection with the game of barley-brake, referring to the couple "in hell" (here, however, with reference to Gostanzo), who according to Sidney (*Arcadia,* ed. A. Feuillerat, II,220) "Must strive with waiting foot, and watching eye / To catch of them [the other two couples], and them to hell to beare." Such an interpretation, which continues the explicit references to the game of barley-brake in the two preceding lines, sets Gostanzo in the position of the couple in "hell" whose business it was to make the other couples "break" up to avoid capture.

V.ii

174 or indiscreete priuate] Parrott emends to "or in discreet private," but the Q reading makes good sense, i.e., 'or (if) indiscreet (then at least) private.'

May Day

edited by Robert F. Welsh

❖

TEXTUAL INTRODUCTION

The only known seventeenth-century edition of *May Day* is a quarto of 1611[1] (hereafter designated Q) in which I find remarkably clear evidence of the work of two compositors. For example, in some passages of Q the length of the quads which follow the speech-prefixes is varied in such a way that initial capitals for each verse produce a straight line down the page; in other passages the quads are of fixed length, so that no such alignment results. Furthermore, the distribution of variant spellings in Q confirms the evidence from the speech heads: for example, the forms "Mistris" and "Lieftenant" appear only in nonaligned passages; the ampersand appears frequently as a substitute for "and" in the text, but, with one exception, only in nonaligned passages. Thus, the combined evidence of alignment and variant spellings permits the following unusually precise identification of the work stints of the two compositors:[2] Compositor X (aligned work) — A2-D1, D4^v(lines 15-33)-E3(1-20), F3^v(12-33)-G1(1-9), G3-H3(1-27), I2^v(12-37)-K3; Compositor Y — D1^v-D4^v (lines 1-14), E3(21-31)-F3^v(1-11), G1(10-36)-G2^v, H3(28-33)-I2^v(1-11), K3^v-K4^v. The location of errors and proof corrections in Q indicates Compositor X's superior skill; although Y set less than forty per cent of Q, more

---

[1] For bibliographical description, see Greg, *Bibliography,* No. 297. The title page gives the date of printing and the publisher's name, John Browne, but not that of the printer. Greg's conjecture that William Stansby was the printer, based primarily on the evidence of the title page device (McKerrow, No. 252) can be confirmed by the following additional evidence: both the head-ornament used on sig. A2 of *May-Day* and the ornamental *S* which appears three times in Q appear also in a book of 1611 bearing Stansby's imprint (*STC* 745); and the ornamental *W* which appears on sig. A2 of Q appears in *STC* 23200 of 1611, which also bears Stansby's imprint.

[2] Only two details of the assignments made here remain in doubt. Lines 1-14 of sig. D4^v and lines 1-11 of sig. F3^v do not contain conclusive evidence either of alignment or of distinctive spellings. Each of these passages concludes a scene set by Compositor Y; and immediately below each is the beginning of a new scene and the work of Compositor X. I conjecture Y as the compositor of both passages because of slight misalignment in both, and because elsewhere in Q (sigs. E3, H3) a compositor change occurred mid-page at the point of a scene division.

than eighty per cent of the literal errors appear in his work;[3] and thirty-three of the thirty-seven proof corrections in Q also occur in his stint. This latter fact is a clear indication of concern in the shop to check Compositor Y's work carefully and of relative confidence in the accuracy of Compositor X. This evidence provides a basis for my treatment of doubtful readings in Q. Compositor X's work is generally free from error, and I treat it conservatively in doubtful cases (e.g., see note to II.iv.281). Compositor Y's work is far less reliable, and I am therefore willing at doubtful points to emend it, particularly to remove errors of the sort to which Compositor Y was prone. These particularly include the following: errors of omission (e.g., at III.iii.123); confusion of proper sequence (II.iv.85); errors due to the influence of proximate forms (II.iv.158); and errors resulting from problems of justification (III.iii.123).

Evidence from the head lines (the play's title heads each page) provides a basis for conjecturing how the composition and printing of Q proceeded. For imposition of sheets A-C, Compositor X, working alone, used two skeletons for each sheet. These reappear in the formes of sheet D, the first sheet that contains work by Compositor Y. But someone assembled a third skeleton to impose E inner, and it, along with both of the other two, was used in sheets F-G. This change to three-skeleton work in the sheet following Compositor Y's entrance is clear evidence that at least in sheets E-G the two compositors cast off their copy and set type simultaneously rather than in turn. Evidence of recurring identifiable type pieces suggests that composition of these sheets was by formes, inner first.[4] Thus Compositor X worked on E1^v-E2 while Compositor Y worked on E3^v-E4, and so on through the formes of the three sheets. (As my chart of work stints shows, the work of both compositors appears in every forme of sheets E-G.) The three skeletons used in sheets E-G were broken up after the printing of sheet G and head lines from all three used to form two new skeletons, one of which imposed H inner, the other H outer and *both* formes of sheet I. This evidence suggests that the rate of composition dropped sharply in sheet I and, in turn, that the two compositors might have changed their method of composition. But since both workmen continued to divide the copy between them as they had in earlier sheets, the explanation for the slowdown probably lies in the fact that sheet I contains considerably more type than any of the preceding sheets; recognizing that by crowding they could fit the text into ten sheets (it ends below the middle of sig. K4^v), the compositors added two extra lines to each page in sheet I and used a measure 8 mm. longer

[3] Of the thirty-seven unquestionable literal errors in Q (involving letters, not punctuation), thirty appear in the work of Compositor Y.

[4] Five identifiable pieces from sheet D (inner) appear on sig. E3, while no identifiable pieces from sheet D appear in E inner; two identifiable pieces from E inner appear on sig. F1 and three on sig. F3, while pieces from E outer first reappear in sheet G. (The extraordinary spacing of the last three lines on sig. D3 suggests that sheet D also was composed by formes, inner first.)

In recent years Professors Robert K. Turner, Jr. and J. R. Brown have studied a number of seventeenth-century quartos divided between two compositors in roughly the same way as is *May Day* and found that in them also the two compositors set type simultaneously and composed by formes rather than seriatim. See *Studies in Bibliography*, XII (1959), 198-203 and XV (1962), 57-69.

than that employed earlier. Whether other developments also retarded composition remains uncertain. I have been unable satisfactorily to identify recurring type pieces in sheets H-K, but I find other evidence of composition by formes in sheet H. A verse section of IV.iii. set by Compositor Y extends from the middle of sig. H4 to the middle of sig. H4ᵛ. The portion on sig. H4, which is twenty-two lines of verse when properly set, occurs as nineteen lines of prose in Q; the remainder of the scene on sig. H4ᵛ is set as verse. The important fact here is that in sheet I no apparent change occurs in either the general quality of the text or in the accuracy of either compositor's work. Another irregularity in the printing process which also seems to lack textual import occurred in sheet K; the two skeletons used to impose the formes were newly assembled and incorporated head lines from several previous skeletons.

Convincing evidence indicates that printer's copy for Q was a manuscript which preserved the text in a final and fairly accurate state. The play as we have it is a coherent whole in which are neatly interwoven several threads of a complex plot; it is, in general, quite free from the confusions and inconsistencies that one associates with foul papers.[5] Further, clear evidence (cited earlier) that the compositors were able to cast off copy as they set the text, almost all of which is in prose, suggests a manuscript generally free from cancellations, interlinear revisions, marginal additions, and the like. But whether it originally served as theater promptbook and whether it was a holograph or a scribal transcript remain, for lack of conclusive evidence, unanswered questions. The stage directions in Q supply only an equivocal answer to the first of these questions;[6] and I find insufficient evidence of any kind to justify even a guess as to whether the manuscript was a holograph or a transcript thereof.[7]

My general treatment of the thirty-seven proof corrections in Q reflects an assumption that they derive from a proofreader's judgment rather than the manuscript. This hypothesis rests on two facts. First, at least two of the corrections can be shown to have such provenance: the Q(c) form at

---

[5] The speech-prefixes are consistent in form throughout Q. The one "loose end" in the text which seems to suggest a manuscript in less than final form is the *etc.* which ends a speech at IV.ii.73. The confusions at V.i.123 and 234 are the only ones in Q not readily explained as compositorial (usually Y's) errors.

[6] For a lengthy discussion of Q's stage directions, see Professor Akihiro Yamada's "Bibliographical Studies of George Chapman's *May-Day* (1611), Printed by William Stansby," *Journal of the Faculty of Liberal Arts and Science,* Shinshu University, No. 15 (December, 1965), 13-34. Professor Yamada concludes that the manuscript could not possibly have served as a promptbook, but the evidence does not seem to support such a conclusion. There is, indeed, some indication that the manuscript was in a pre-promptbook state: four of the directions are in Latin, and there are three instances of the Latin speech-prefix *Amb.*; several of the directions have a descriptive character, and one (at V.i.80) provides for the entrance of *another woman* who is unknown; six necessary exit directions and entrance directions for two characters are missing. But on the whole the directions regulate the stage business quite well, and there is one strong piece of evidence, the note in the margin at I.ii.1-2, *A purse of twenty pound in gold,* suggesting that the manuscript might have been used in the theater.

[7] Given our present, very limited knowledge of Chapman's distinctive habits, the only evidence in Q suggesting a holograph are the two forms *am* (for *'em*), one of which appears in the work of each compositor.

III.i.12,13 (E inner) introduces an error into an obviously correct Q(u) reading; and the Q(u) form at II.iv.41 (D inner) is a distinctive Chapman form which the proofreader altered to a more conventional form. Second, none of the corrections can be shown to derive from the manuscript; typically, most of them involve either punctuation or obvious literal corrections and could have originated either in a reader's judgment or in consultation of the manuscript.[8] In accordance with this hypothesis, I treat the proof corrections as edited readings and adopt them only when they represent both necessary and logical corrections.

In Q, the play is divided into five acts and further subdivided into unnumbered scenes, the divisions marked by full-width rules across the page. Six of these rules appear not at points where the scene changes, but where two or more characters enter and give the action a fresh direction.[9] Thus Q is in a sense the authority for scene division in the play, though several of its demarkations indicate developments other than scene changes. In this edition I divide the play into scenes in accordance with modern standards and assign specific credit for any given division only to the edition which is both divided and numbered as is this one.

The dash is used twice in Q, once to indicate a change of addressee and once to indicate the end of an aside (in mid-speech). I introduce the dash at other points to perform those two functions and to indicate incomplete (interrupted) speeches.

Editions of *May Day* (other than Q) cited in the footnotes to the text and in textual notes are those of C. W. Dilke (in *Old English Plays,* IV, 1814), R. H. Shepherd (*The Works of George Chapman: Plays,* 1875), and T. M. Parrott (*The Plays and Poems of George Chapman: The Comedies,* [1914]).

[8] The enigmatic Q(c) form at II.iv.168 presents a special problem; see note.
[9] The six divisions in Q which by modern standards are not scene divisions appear immediately before the entrance directions at II.iv.206, III.i.22, III.iii.158, IV.ii.24, IV.iii.53, and V.i.101.

MAY-DAY.

A vvitty Comedie,

diuers times acted at the
Blacke Fryers.

VVritten by GEORGE CHAPMAN.

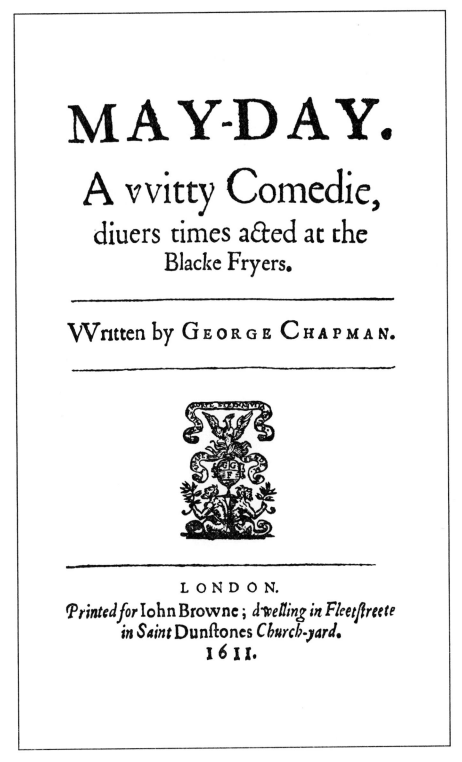

LONDON.

Printed for Iohn Browne; *dwelling in Fleetstreete*
in Saint Dunstones *Church-yard.*
1611.

DRAMATIS PERSONAE

[Lorenzo

Lodovico (Lodowick), his nephew

Giacono

Honorio

Aurelio, his son

Angelo, Aurelio's servant

Quintiliano

Fannio, his page

Innocentio

Leonoro

Lionell, his page, the disguised Theagine

Gasparo

Giovenelli

Cuthbert Barber (Cutbeard)

A Tailor

His son

A Drawer

A Messenger

AEmilia, Lorenzo's daughter

Francischina, Quintiliano's wife

Lucretia, the disguised Lucretio

Temperance, servant to Lucretia

Another woman]

MAY-DAY.

Actus prima, Scæna prima.

Chorus Iuuenum cantantes et saltantes.　　　*Exeunt saltan.*

Interim, Intrat Lorenzo, Papers in his hand.

Lor. Well done my lusty bloods, Well done. Fit, fit obseruance for
this May-morning; Not the May-Moneth alone, they take when it
comes; Nor the first weeke of that Moneth; Nor the first day; but the
first minute of the first houre, of the first day. Loose no time bloods,
loose no time; though the Sunne goe to bedde neuer so much before　　5
you, yet be you vp before him; call the golden sluggard from the siluer
armes of his Lady, to light you into yours; when your old father *Ianu-*
ary here in one of his last dayes, thrusts his fore-head into the depth of
Mayes fragrant bosome, What may you *Aprilles* performe then? O
what may you doe? Well yet will I say thus much for my selfe, where-　　10
soeuer the affections of youth are, there must needs be the instruments,
and where the instruments are, there must of necessity be the faculties;
What am I short of them then? A sound old man, ably constituted,
holsomly dyeted, that tooke his *May* / temperately at their ages, and　　[A2ᵛ]
continued his owne; why should he not continue their ages in his　　15
owne? By the Masse I feele nothing that stands against it, and therefore sweet *May* I salute thee with the yongest: I haue loue to employ
thee in, as well as the prowdest yong princock, and so haue at you
Mistris *Francischina*: haue at you Mistris *Franke*: I'le sprede my
nets for you yfaith, though they be my very purse nets, wherein what　　20
heart will not willingly lye panting?

(Enter Angelo.)

Ang. How now? Gods my life, I wonder what made this *May-*
morning so cold, and now I see 'tis this *Ianuary* that intrudes into it;
what paper is that he holds in hand trow we?

Lor. Here haue I put her face in rime, but I feare my old vaine will　　25
not stretch to her contentment.
O haire, no haire but beames stolne from the Sunne.

Ang. Out vpon her, if it be shee that I thinke, shee has a Fox red
cranion.

---

7 yours;] ∼, ‖ 9 bosome,] ∼: ‖ 19 *Francischina*] *Frances China* ‖ 22 wonder] *stet* ‖ 24 trow we]
stet ‖ 27 O . . . Sunne.] *Dilke; as prose* ‖ 29 cranion.] ∼; ‖

Lor. A forehead that disdaines the name of faire.   30
Ang. And reason, for 'tis a fowle one.
Lor. A matchlesse eye.
Ang. True, her eyes be not matches.
Lor. A cheeke, vermillion red.
Ang. Painted I warrant you.   35
Lor. A farre commanding mouth.
Ang. It stretches to her eares in deede.
Lor. A nose made out of waxe.
Ang. A red nose, in sincerity.
   Lor. This could I send, but person, person does it: A good pres-   40
ence, to beare out a good wit; a good face, a prety Court legge, and a
deft dapper personage, no superfluous dimensions, but fluent in com-
petence; for it is not *Hector* but *Paris,* not the full armefull, but the
sweet handfull that Ladies delight in.
   Ang. O notable old whyniard.   45
   Lor. Such a size of humanity now, and braine enough / in it, it is   [A3]
not in the strength of a woman to withstand; well shee may hold out a
parlee or two, for 'tis a weake fort that obeyes at the first or second
summons; if shee resist the third shee is discharg'd, though shee yeeld
in future: for then it appeares it was no fault of hers, but the man   50
that would take no deniall. What rests now? meanes for accesse:
True. O an honest Baude were worth gold now.
   Ang. A plague vpon him, I had thought to haue appear'd to him,
but now if I doe, he will take me for the man he talks on: I will therefore post by his dull eye-sight, as in hast of businesse.   55
   Lor. What, Signior *Angelo?* soft I command you.
   Ang. Gods precious, what meane you Sir?
   Lor. I would be loth to be out-runne I assure you Sir: was I able to
stay you?
   Ang. Your ability stood too stiffe Sir, beshrow me else.   60
   Lor. O most offencelesse fault; I would thou would'st blaze my
imperfection to one thou know'st, yfaith.
   Ang. Well Sir another time tell me where shee is, and Ile doe so
much for you *gratis.* Good morrow Sir.
   Lor. Nay stay good *Angelo.*   65
   Ang. My businesse sayes nay Sir, you haue made me stay to my
paine Sir, I thanke you.
   Lor. Not a whit man I warrant thee.

49 summons;] ∼, ‖ **50** hers,] ∼: ‖ **56** What,] ∼∧ ‖ **61** fault;] ∼, ‖ **63** time] ∼, ‖

Ang. Goe to then; briefly, to whom shall I commend your imperfections, will you tell me if I name her?   70

Lor. That I will, yfaith Boy.

Ang. Is not her haire, no haire, but beames stolne from the Sunne?

Lor. Blacke, blacke as an Ouzell.

Ang. A fore-head that disdaines the name of faire.

Lor. Away Witch, away.   75

Ang. A matchlesse eye.

Lor. Nay fie, fie, fie. I see th'art a very Deuill *Angelo.* And in earnest, I iested, when I said my desire of thy friendship touch'd my selfe,
for it concernes a friend of mine iust / of my standing.   [A3ᵛ]

Ang. To whom then would he be remembred that I can sollicite?   80

Lor. To sweet Mistris *Francischina*: with whom I heare thou art
ready to lye downe, thou art so great with her.

Ang. I am as great as a neare Kinseman may be with her Sir, not
otherwise.

Lor. A good consanguinity: and good *Angelo,* to her wilt thou   85
deliuer from my friend, in all secrecy, these poore brace of bracelets?

Ang. Perhaps I will Sir, when I know what the Gentleman and
his intent is.

Lor. Neuer examine that, man; I would not trouble you with carry-
ing too much at once to her, only tell her, such a man will resolue her,   90
naming me: and I doe not greatly care if I take the paines to come
to her, so I stay not long, and be let in priuily: and so without making
many wordes, here they be, put them vp closely I beseech thee, and
deliuer them as closely.

Ang. Well Sir, I loue no contention with friends, and therefore   95
pocket many things, that otherwise I would not: but I pray Sir licence
me a question. Doe not I know this Gentleman that offers my Cozen
this kindnesse?

Lor. Neuer saw'st him in thy life, at least neuer knew'st him; but
for his bounty sake to all his well willers, if this message be friendly   100
discharged, I may chance put a deare friend of him into your bosome,
Sir, and make you profitably acquainted.

Ang. But I pray you Sir, is he not a well elderly Gentleman?

Lor. Wide, wide; as yong as day, I protest to thee.

Ang. I know he is yong too, but that is in ability of body, but is   105
he not a prety little squat Gentleman, as you shall see amongst a
thousand?

69 then;] ∼, ‖ **75** away.] ∼: ‖ **81** *Francischina*] *Franciscina* ‖ **84** otherwise.] ∼: ‖ **89** that,] ∼∧ ‖
91 care] ∼, ‖ **93** wordes,] ∼: ‖ **101** bosome,] ∼: ‖

Lor. Still from the cushion, still, tall and high, like a Cedar. /

Ang. I know he is tall also, but it is in his minde Sir, and it is   [A4]
not *Hector* but *Paris,* not thy full armefull, but the sweet handfull   110
that a Lady delights to dandle.

Lor. Now the good Deuill take thee, if there be any such in hell;
I beseech thee —

Ang. Well, well Signior *Lorenzo,* yfaith the litle Squire is thought
to be as parlous a peece of flesh, for a peece of flesh, as any hunts the   115
hole pale of *Venus* I protest t'ee.

Lor. I cannot containe my selfe, yfaith Boy, if the Wenches come
in my walke, I giue 'em that they come for, I dally not with 'hem.

Ang. I know you doe not Sir, [*Aside*] his dallying dayes be done.

Lor. It is my infirmity, and I cannot doe withall, to die for't.   120

Ang. I beleeue you Sir.

Lor. There are certaine enuious old fellowes, my neighbours,
that say, I am one vnwieldy and stiffe: *Angelo,* didst euer heare any
wench complaine of my stiffenesse?

Ang. Neuer in my life: your old neighbours measure you by   125
themselues.

Lor. Why ther's the matter then.

Ang. But yfaith Sir: doe you euer hope to winne your purpose at
my losing hands, knowing her (as all the world does) a woman of that
approued lowlynesse of life, and so generally tryed?   130

Lor. As for that take thou no care, shee's a woman, is shee not?

Ang. Sure I doe take her to haue the flesh and blood of a woman.

Lor. Then good enough, or then bad enough, this token shall be
my Gentleman Vsher to prepare my accesse, and then let me alone
with her.   135

Ang. I, marry Sir, I thinke you would be alone with her; Well Sir,
I will doe my best, but if your Gentleman Vsher should not get entrance for you now, it would be a griefe / to me.   [A4ᵛ]

(*Enter Gasparo an old Clowne.*)

Lor. Feare it not man: Gifts and gold, take the strong'st hold;
Away, here comes a snudge that must be my sonne in law: I would   140
be loth he should suspect these tricks of youth in me, for feare he
feare my daughter will trot after me.

Ang. Fare you well Sir.   *Exit.*

Gasp. Godge you God morrow Sir, godge you God morrow.

Lor. God morrow neighbour *Gasparo*: I haue talk't with my   145
daughter, whom I doe yet finde a greene yong plant, and therefore

---

108 Cedar] *Cedar* ‖ **110** thy] *stet* ‖ **112-13** hell; I] *Shepherd*; hell, hell I (*See Textual Note*) ‖ **113**
thee—] *Shepherd*; ∼. ‖ **115** parlous] *Parrott*; parlesse ‖ **119** SD *Aside*] *Dilke* ‖ **127** then.] ∼? ‖
136 I,] ∼∧ ‖ **144** Godge . . . morrow.] *stet* (*See Textual Note*) ‖

vnapt to beare such ripe fruit, I thinke I might haue said rotten, as
your selfe: But shee is at my disposition, and shall be at yours in
the end, here's my hand, and with my hand take hers.

Gasp. Nay by my faith Sir, you must giue me leaue to shake her   150
portion by the hand first.

Lor. It is ready told for you Sir, come home when you will and
receiue it, *(Enter AEmilia.)* and see, yonder shee comes; away, shee
cannot yet abide you, because shee feares shee can abide you too well.

Gasp. Well, I will come for her portion Sir, and till then, God take   155
you to his mercy.   *Exit.*

Lor. Adiew my good sonne in law. — Ile not interrupt her, let
her meditate a my late motion.   *Exit.*

AEm. 'Tis strange to see the impiety of parents,
Both priuiledgd by custome, and profest;   160
The holy institution of heauen,
Ordeyning marriage for proportiond minds,
For our chiefe humane comforts, and t'encrease
The loued images of God in men,
Is now peruerted to th'increase of wealth;   165
We must bring riches forth, and like the Cuckoe
Hatch others egges; Ioyne house to house, in choices
Fit timber-logs and stones, not men and women:

(Enter Aurelio.)

Ay me, here's one I must shunne, woude embrace.   *Exit. /*

Aur. O stay and heare me speake or see me dye.   *[Falls prostrate.]* [B1]

(Enter Lodouico and Giacono.)

Lod. How now? what haue we here? what a loathsome creature
man is, being drunke: Is it not pitty to see a man of good hope, a
toward Scholler, writes a theame well, scannes a verse very well, and
likely in time to make a proper man, a good legge, specially in a
boote, valiant, well spoken, and in a word, what not? and yet all   175
this ouerthrowne as you see, drownd, quite drownd in a quarte pott.

Giac. O these same wicked healths, breede monstrous diseases.

Lod. Aurelio, speake man, *Aurelio?*

Giac. Pray heauen all be well.

Lod. O speake, if any sparke of speech remaine.   180
It is thy deare *AEmilia* that calles.

Aur. Well, well, it becomes not a friend to touch the deadly wounds
of his friend with a smiling countenance.

---

155 portion] *Dilke*; potion ‖ **157** law.—] ∼, ‖ **160** profest;] ∼, ‖ **161** heauen,] ∼; ‖ **163**
comforts,] ∼; ‖ **164** men,] ∼: ‖ **170** SD *Falls prostrate.] Parrott subs. (after Dilke)* ‖ **172** is,] ∼∧ ‖

Lod. Touch thee? sblood I could finde in my heart to beate thee; vp in a fooles name, vp: what a Scene of foppery haue we here? 185

Aur. Prethee haue done.

Lod. Vp Cuckoe, *Cupids* bird, or by this light Ile fetch thy father to thee.

Aur. Good *Lodouico,* if thou lou'st me, leaue me; thou com'st to counsaile me from that, which is ioynd with my soule in eternity: I 190 must and will doe what I doe.

Lod. Doe so then, and I protest thou shalt neuer licke thy lips after my Kinsewoman, while thou liu'st: I had thought to haue spoken for thee, if thou hadst taken a manly course with her: but to fold vp thy selfe like an Vrchine, and lye a caluing to bring forth a 195 husband: I am asham'd to thinke on't: sblood I haue heard of wenches that haue been wonne with singing and dancing, and some with riding, but neuer heard of any that was wonne with tumbling in my life.

Aur. If thou knew'st how vaine thou seem'st. / 200

Lod. I doe it of purpose, to shew how vaine I hold thy disease, [B1ᵛ] S'hart art thou the first that has shot at a wenches heart and mist it? must that shot that mist her wound thee? let her shake her heeles in a shrowes name: were shee my Cozen a thousand times, and if I were as thee, I would make her shake her heeles too, afore I would shake 205 mine thus.

Aur. O vanity, vanity.

Lod. S'death, if any wench should offer to keepe possession of my heart against my will, I'de fire her out with Sacke and Suger, or smoke her out with Tobacko, like a hornet, or purge for her, for loue 210 is but a humor: one way or other I would vent her, thats infallible.

Aur. For shame hold thy tongue, me thinks thy wit should feele how stale are these loue stormes, and with what generall priuiledge loue pierses the worthiest. Seeke to help thy friend, not mocke him.

Lod. Marry, seeke to helpe thy selfe then, in a halters name, doe 215 not lie in a ditch, and say God helpe me, vse the lawfull tooles he hath lent thee. Vp I say, I will bring thee to her.

Aur. Shee'll not endure me.

Lod. Shee shall endure thee doe the worst thou canst to her, I and endure thee till thou canst not endure her; But then thou must vse 220 thy selfe like a man, and a wise man; how deepe soeuer shee is in thy thoughts, carry not the prints of it in thy lookes; be bold and carelesse, and stand not sauntring a farre of, as I haue seene you, like a Dogge

---

in a firmetypot, that licks his chops and wags his taile, and faine would
lay his lips to it, but he feares tis too hot for him: thats the only way   225
to make her too hot for thee. He that holds religious and sacred
thought of a woman, he that beares so reuerend a respect to her, that
he will not touch her but with a kist hand and a timorous heart; he
that adores her like his Goddesse: Let him be sure shee will shunne
him like her slaue. Alas good soules, women of themselues are tract-   230
able and tactable enough, and would returne *Quid* for / *Quod* still,   [B2]
but we are they that spoile 'em, and we shall answere for't another
day. We are they that put a kind of wanton Melancholie into 'em,
that makes 'em thinke their noses bigger then their faces, greater then
the Sunne in brightnesse; and where as Nature made 'em but halfe   235
fooles, we make 'em all foole. And this is our palpable flattery of
them, where they had rather haue plaine dealing. Well, in conclusion,
Ile to her instantly, and if I doe not bring her to thee, or at the least
some speciall fauour from her, as a feather from her fanne, or a string
from her shoo, to weare in thy hat, and so forth, then neuer trust my   240
skill in poultry whilst thou liu'st againe.   *Exeunt.*

[I.ii]

Enter Quintiliano, Innocentio, Fransischina,
Angelo, and Fannio.

Fran. Thou shalt not to the warres, or if thou do'st Ile beare thee
company, deare *Quint.* doe not offer to forsake me.

Quint. Hands off wife, hang not vpon me thus; how can I maintaine thee but by vsing my valour? and how can I vse that, but in action and employment? goe in, play at cardes with your Cozen *Angelo*   5
here, and let it suffise I loue thee.

Ang. Come sweet Cozen, doe not cloy your husband with your loue
so, especially to hinder his preferment; who shall the Duke haue to
employ in these Marshall necessities if not Captaine *Quintiliano*? he
beares an honorable minde, and tis pitty but he should haue employ-   10
ment. Let him get a company now, and he will be able to maintaine
you like a Duches hereafter.

Innoc. Well said Signior *Angelo*, gossaue me you speake like a
true Cozen indeede, does he not *Quint*?

Quint. He does so, and I thanke him; yet see how the foole puts   15
finger ith' eye still.

---

241 SD *Exeunt.*] *Parrott subs.*; *Exit.* ‖ I.ii] *Shepherd* ‖ **1-2** Thou . . . me.] *Q has marginal note:*
A purse of / twenty / pound in / gold. ‖ **9** *Quintiliano?*] ∼, ‖

Ang. Ile cheere her vp, I warrant you Captaine; come / Cuze,   [B2ᵛ]
lets in to tables.

Innoc. Farewell sweet Mistris.

Fran. Farewell my good seruant.   20

Ang. [*Aside to Fran.*] Now take away thy hand, and show thou
didst laugh all this while; good Lord who would not marry to haue
so kinde a wife make much on him?   *Exit with Fran.*

Quint. After Boy, giue your attendance.

Fann. Could you not spare me money for mine hostesse, where   25
you put me to boarde? y'are a whole fortnight in arrerages.

Quint. Attend I say, the hostes of the Lyon has a legge like a
Gyant, want for nothing Boy, so shee score truly.

Fann. Faith Sir, shee has chaulk't vp twenty shillings already, and
sweares shee will chaulke no more.   30

Quint. Then let her choke, and choke thou with her: S'blood
hobby horse, and she had chaulkt vp twenty pounds, I hope the world
knowes I am able to pay it with a wet finger.

Fann. Alas Sir, I thinke y'are able, but the world does not know it.

Quint. Then the worlds an ignorant Sir, and you are an innocent,   35
vanish Boy, away.

Fann. [*Aside.*] I hope he will foist some money for my score, out
of this gull here.   *Exit.*

Innoc. 'Tis a plaguy good wagge *Quint.* ist not?

Quint. Ile make him a good one 'ere I ha done with him; but this   40
same louing foole my wife now, will neuer leaue weeping, till I make
her beleeue I will not haue a company. Who would be combred with
these soft hearted creatures, that are euer in extreames, either too
kinde, or too vnkind?

Innoc. Saue me, 'tis true, 'tis a hard thing must please 'em, in   45
sadnesse.

Quint. Damne me, if I doe not pitty her with my heart; plague on
her kindnesse, she has halfe perswaded me to take no company.

Innoc. Nay sweet *Quint:* then how shall I be a Lieftenant? /

Quint. Well, and my promise were not past to thee, I am a villaine   [B3] 50
if all the world should part *Franke* and me; thinke I loue thee therefore, and will doe thee credit: It will cost me a great deale a this
same foolish money to buy me drum and ensigne, and furnish me
throughly, but the best is I know my credit.

Innoc. Sfut *Quint*, wee'll want no money, man, Ile make my row   55
of houses flie first.

Quint. Let 'em walke, let 'em walke; Candle rents: if the warres
hold, or a plague come to the towne, theill be worth nothing.

---

21 SD *Aside to Fran.*] *Dilke subs.* ‖ **23** SD *Exit with Fran.*] *Dilke subs.; Exit.* ‖ **37** SD *Aside.*] *Dilke*
‖ **45** 'em,] ∼∧ ‖ **55** money,] ∼∧ ‖

Innoc. True, or while I am beyond Sea, some sleepy wench may set fire ith bed-straw.　　　　　　　　　　　　　　　　　　　60

Quint. Right, or there may come an earthquake, and ouerturne 'em.

Innoc. Iust, or there may be coniuring, and the winde may downe with 'em.

Quint. Or some crafty petty-fogger may finde a hole in the title, a thousand casualties belongs to 'em.　　　　　　　　　　　65

Innoc. Nay, they shall walke, thats certaine, Ile turne 'em into money.

Quint. Thats thy most husbandly course yfaith Boy, thou maist haue twenty ith' hundred for thy life, Ile be thy man for two hundred.

Innoc. Wilt yfaith *Quint*? gossaue me tis done.　　　　　70

Quint. For your life, not otherwise.

Innoc. Well, I desire no more, so you'll remember me for my Lieftenantship.

Quint. Remember thee? 'tis thine owne already Boy, a hundred pounds shall not buy it from thee; giue me thy hand, I doe here create　75 thee Lieftenant *Innocentio.*

Innoc. If you haue a company Captaine.

Quint. If I haue: damne me if such another word doe not make me put thee out ath' place againe; if I haue a company, Sfut, let the Duke deny me one, I would twere come to that once, that employment　80 should goe with the vnde- / seruer, while men of seruice sit at home,　[B3ᵛ] and feede their anger with the blood of red lattices. Let the Duke denie me to day, Ile renounce him to morrow. Ile to the enimy point blanke, I'me a villaine else.

Innoc. And I by heauen I sweare.　　　　　　　　　　85

Quint. Well if that day come, it will proue a hot day with some body.

Innoc. But Captaine, did not you say that you would enter me at an Ordinary, that I might learne to conuerse?

Quint. When thou wilt Lieftenant; No better time then now, for　90 now th'art in good clothes, which is the most materiall point for thy entrance there.

Innoc. I but how should I behaue my selfe?

Quint. Marry Sir, when you come first in, you shall see a crew of Gallants of all sorts.　　　　　　　　　　　　　　95

Innoc. Nay Captaine if I come first in I shall see no body.

Quint. Tush man, you must not doe so; if you haue good clothes and will be noted let am all come in afore you, and then as I said shall you see a lusty crew of Gallants, some Gentlemen, some none; but

70 Wilt] Wil't ‖ **84** else.] ∼: ‖ **95** sorts.] ∼: ‖ **97** so;] ∼, ‖

thats all one: he that beares himselfe like a Gentleman, is worthy   100
to haue beene borne a Gentleman: some aged haue beards, and some
haue none, some haue money, and some haue none, yet all must
haue meate: Now will all these I say at your first entrance wonder
at you, as at some strange Owle, Examine your person, and obserue
your bearing for a time. Doe you then ath' tother side seeme to   105
neglect their obseruance as fast, let your countenance be proofe
against all eyes, not yeelding or confessing in it any inward defect. In
a word be impudent enough, for thats your chiefe vertue of society.

Innoc. Is that? faith and I neede not learne that, I haue that by
nature I thanke God.   110

Quint. So much the better, for nature is farre aboue Art, or iudgement. Now for your behauiour; let it be free and negligent, not
clogg'd with ceremony or obseruance, giue / no man honour, but   [B4]
vpon equall termes; for looke how much thou giu'st any man aboue
that, so much thou tak'st from thy selfe: he that will once giue the   115
wall, shall quickly be thrust into the kennell: measure not thy carriage
by any mans eye, thy speech by no mans eare, but be resolute and confident in doing and saying, and this is the grace of a right Gentleman
as thou art.

Innoc. Sfut, that I am I hope, I am sure my father has beene twise   120
Warden on's company.

Quint. Thats not a peare matter man, ther's no prescription for
Gentility, but good clothes and impudence: for your place, take it
as it fals, but so as you thinke no place to good for you; fall too with
ceremony whatsoeuer the company be: and as neere as you can, when   125
they are in their Mutton, be thou in thy Wood-cocke, it showes resolution. Talke any thing, thou car'st not what, so it be without offence,
and as neere as thou canst without sence.

Innoc. Let me alone for that Captaine I warrant you.

Quint. If you chance to tell a lye, you must binde it with some   130
oath, as By this bread, for breads a binder you know.

Innoc. True.

Quint. And yet take heede you sweare by no mans bread but your
owne, for that may breede a quarrell: aboue all things you must carry
no coales.   135

Innoc. By heauen not I, Ile freeze to death first.

Quint. Well Sir, one point more I must remember you of. After
dinner there will be play, and if you would be counted compleate,
you must venture amongst them; for otherwise, theill take you for a
Scholler or a Poet, and so fall into contempt of you: for there is no   140

---

104 Owle,] ∼: ‖ **124** with] *stet (See Textual Note)* ‖ **131** By] by ‖

vertue can scape the accompt of basenesse if it get money, but gaming
and law; yet must you not loose much money at once, for that argues
little wit at all times.

Innoc. As gossaue me, and thats my fault; for if I be in once, I   145
shall loose all I haue about me.

Quint. Is true, Lieftenant? birlady Sir Ile be your mode- / rator,   [B4ᵛ]
therefore let me see how much money haue you about you?

Innoc. Not much, some twenty marke or twenty pound in gold.

Quint. 'Tis too much to loose by my faith, Lieftenant; giue me
your purse Sir; hold yee, heers two brace of Angels, you shall venture   150
that for fashion sake, Ile keepe the rest for you, till you haue done play.

Innoc. That will be all one, for when thats lost I shall neuer leaue
till I get the rest from you: for I know thou wilt let me haue it if
I aske it.

Quint. Not a penny by this gold.   155

Innoc. Prethee doe not then, as gossaue me and you do —

Quint. And I doe, hang me; Come lets to the Duke.   *Exeunt.*

Finis Actus Primi.

Actus Secundi, Scaena prima.

Enter Lucretia and Temperance, seuerall wayes.

Temp. Nay Mistris, pray eene goe in againe, for I haue some
inward newes for you.

Lucr. What are those pray?

Temp. Tis no matter Mistris till you come in, but make much a
time in the meane time, good fortune thrusts her selfe vpon you in the   5
likenesse of a fine yong Gentleman, hold vp your apron and receiue
him while you may, a Gods name.

Lucr. How say by that? y'are a very wise counsailer.

Temp. Well Mistris, when I was a Maide, and that's a good while
agoe I can tell you.   10

Lucr. I thinke very well. /

Temp. You were but a little one then I wisse.   [C1]

Lucr. Nor you neither I beleeue.

Temp. Faith it's one of the furthest things I can remember.

Lucr. But what when you were a Maide?   15

Temp. Marry Mistris I tooke my time, I warrant you. And ther's
Signior *Leonoro* now, the very flower of Venice, and one that loues
you deerely I ensure you.

---

146 Is] *stet* ‖ **150** Sir;] ~, ‖ **156** do—] ~: ‖ **3** pray?] ~. ‖

Lucr. God forgiue him if he doe, for Ile be sworne I neuer deseru'd
his loue, nor neuer will while I liue.   20

Temp. Why then, what say to Signior *Collatine?* ther's a dainty
peece of Venzon for you, and a feruent louer indeed.

Lucr. He? I dare say, he knowes not what wood loues shafts are
made of, his Signiory woud think it the deepest disparagement could
be done to him, to say that euer he spent sigh for any Dame in Italy.   25

Temp. Well, you haue a whole browne dozen a suters at least, I
am sure; take your choice amongst 'em all; if you loue not all, yet you
may loue three or foure on 'em to be doing withall.

Lucr. To be doing withall? loue three or foure?

Temp. Why not, so you loue 'em moderately. What, must that   30
strange made peece *Theagines* that you cry out vpon so often, haue
all from other, and yet [you] know not where he is?

Lucr. [*Aside.*] O my *Theagine,* not *Theagines,*
Thy loue hath turn'd me woman like thy selfe,
Shall thy sight neuer turne me man againe?   35
Come lets to the Minster, God heare my prayers as I intend to stop
mine eares against all my suters.

Temp. Well Mistris, yet peraduenture, they may make you open
afore the Priest haue a penny for you.   *Exeunt.* /

[II.ii]

Enter Lodouico and AEmilia.   [C1ᵛ]

Lod. Heer's a coyle to make wit and women friends: come hither
wench, let me haue thee single; now sit thee downe, and heare good
counsaile next thy heart, and God giue thee grace to lay it to thy heart.

AEm. Fie Cozen, will this wilde tongue of yours neuer receiue the
bridle?   5

Lod. Yes, thou shalt now see me stroke my beard, and speake
sententiously: thou tell'st me thy little father is in hand with a great
rich marriage for thee, and would haue thee commit matrimony with
old *Gasparo,* art thou willing with it?

AEm. I rather wish my selfe marryed to a thousand deaths.   10

Lod. Then I perceiue thou know'st him not; did he neuer wooe
thee?

AEm. I protest, I neuer chang'd three words with him in my
life; he hath once or twice woo'de my father for me, but neuer me.

Lod. Why thats the reason thou lou'st him not, because thou tak'st   15
in none of his valiant breath to enflame thee, nor vouchsaf'st his

---

27 all;] ∼, ‖ **30** What,] ∼∧ ‖ **32** you] *Dilke* ‖ **33** SD *Aside.*] *Dilke* ‖ **33-35** O . . . againe?]
Shepherd; as prose (thy . . . shall) ‖ **35** againe?] ∼. ‖ II.ii] *Shepherd* ‖

knowledge; Ile tell thee what he is, an old saplesse trunke, fit to make
touch-wood of, hollow, and bald like a blasted Oke, on whose top
Rauens sit and croke the portents of funerals; one that noints his nose
with clowted creame, and Pomatum. His breath smels like the butt   20
end of a shoo-makers horne. A leprous scaly hide like an Elephant.
The sonne of a Sow-gelder, that came to towne (as I haue heard thy
father himselfe say) in a tottred russet cote, high shooes, and yet his
hose torne aboue 'em; A long pike-staffe in his necke (and a tord in
his teeth) and a wallet on his right shoulder; and now the cullion   25
hath with / *Nouerint vniuersi* eaten vp some hundred Gentlemen,   [C2]
he must needs rise a Gentleman as 'twere out of their Ashes, or disparage a Gentlewoman, to make himselfe a Gentleman, at least by the
wiues side.

    AEm. The wurse my fortune to be entangled with such a winding   30
bramble.

    Lod. Entangl'd? Nay if I thought twould euer come to that, I'de
hire some shag-ragge or other for halfe a chickeene to cut's throat, only
to saue thy hands from doing it; for I know thou wouldst poison him
within one moneth; loue thee he will neuer, and that must be thy hap-   35
pinesse: for if he doe, looke to be coop't vp like a prisoner condemn'd
to execution, scarce suffred to take the aire, so much as at a window,
or waited on continually by an old beldame, not to keepe thee
company, but to keepe thee from company: thy pocket searcht, thy
cabinets ransackt for letters: euer in opposition, vnlesse (like the   40
Moone) once a Moneth in coniunction; wealth thou maist haue indeede, but enioy it as in a dreame, for when thou wak'st thou shalt
finde nothing in thy hand; (*Gasparo crosses*) and (to keepe my tale
in goodness) see how all the ill that can be spoken of him is exprest
in his presence.   45

    AEm. O ougly, and monstrous spectacle.

    Lod. Now tell me whether thou wouldst make choice of him or a
yong gallant in prime of his choicenesse; one that for birth, person,
and good parts, might meritoriously marry a Countesse; and one to
whom his soule is not so deere as thy selfe. (*Enter Aurelio*) For all   50
the world such another as he that comes here now: marke him well,
see whether *Gasparo* and he be not a little different. *Exit AEmilia.*
How now? Sownds, *Aurelio?* stay beast, wilt thou make such a blest
opportunity curse thee? Ile fetch her out to thee.   *Exit Lod.*

    Aur. Wretch that I am, how shee lothes me? if I abide her, I shall   55
consume in the lightnings of her anger.   *Exit Aure.*

---

18 of,] ∼∧ ‖ **20** Pomatum] *Pomatum* ‖ **25** shoulder;] ∼, ‖ **26** Gentlemen,] ∼: ‖ **36** prisoner]
∼, ‖ **38** beldame,] ∼: ‖ **43** SD (*Gasparo crosses*)] *Dilke subs.*; (*Enter Gasparo*) ‖ **53** Sownds,] ∼∧ ‖

(*Enter Lodouico with AEmilia.*) /

Lod. [*Aside.*] Here's a life indeede; what's he gone? passion of   [C2ᵛ]
death, what a babe 'tis? I could finde in my heart to ierke him, but
temper me friendship, no remedy now; now wit turne his defects
to perfection. — Why Cuze hee's quite out of sight. By my life I com-   60
mend him; why this is done like thy selfe *Aurelio*, were shee the
Queene of loue and woude runne from thee, flie thou from her; why
now I loue thee, for I see th'art worthy of my loue, thou carriest a
respect to thine owne worth, and wilt expresse it with spirit; I dare
say, thou look'st to haue had him fall on his knees, and ador'd thee,   65
or begge his life at thy hands: or else turn'd Queene *Dido, And*
pierce his tender heart with sword full sharpe; no, faith wench, the
case is altered, loue made *Hercules* spin, but it made him rage after:
there must goe time to the bridling of euery passion; I hope my friend
will not loue a wench against her will; if shee woude haue met his   70
kindnesse halfe way, so: if shee skit and recoile, he shootes her off
warily, and away he goes: I, marry Sir, this was a Gentlemanly part
indeede. Farewell Cuze, be thou free in thy choice too, and take a
better and thou canst a Gods name.   *Exiturus.*

AEm. Nay deere Cuze, a word.   75

Lod. A word? what's the matter? I must needs after him, and clap
him ath' backe, this spirit must be cherisht.

AEm. Alas what would you wish me to doe?

Lod. Why, nothing.

AEm. Would you counsaile me to marry him against my fathers   80
will?

Lod. Not for the world, leaue him, leaue him, leaue him: you
see hee's resolu'd, hee'll take no harme an you, neuer feare to embrew
your hands with his liuer I warrant you.

AEm. Come you are such an other.   85

Lod. This same riches with a husband, is the only thing in the
world, I protest; good *Gasparo*, I am sorry I haue abused thee yfaith,
for my Cozens sake; how prettily the wretch came crawling by with
his crooked knees euen now: / I haue seene a yong Gentlewoman,   [C3]
liue as merry a life with an old man, as with the proudest yong vpstart   90
on'em all: farewell Cuze, I am glad th'art so wise yfaith.

AEm. If you goe, I die: fie on this affection, it rageth with sup-
pression. Good Cuze, I am no longer able to continue it, I
loue *Aurelio* better then it is possible for him to loue me.

---

57 SD *Aside.*] *Dilke* ‖ **60** perfection.—] ∼. ‖ **61** *Aurelio*] *Dilke; Aurelia* ‖ **66-67** *And . . . sharpe*]
italics Dilke; and . . . sharpe ‖ **67** no,] ∼∧ ‖ **70** will;] ∼, ‖ **72** I,] ∼∧ ‖

Lod. Away, away, and could not this haue beene done at first, 95
without all these superfluous disgracings? O this same vnhearty nicenesse of women, is good for nothing but to keepe their huswife hands
still occupied in this warp of dissembling. Well wench redeeme thy
fault, and write a kinde letter to him presently, before this resolution
of his take too deepe roote in him. 100

AEm. Nay sweet Cuze, make me not so immodest, to write so
sodainly, let me haue a little time to thinke vpon't.

Lod. Thinke me on nothing till you write: thinke as you write,
and then you shall be sure to write as you thinke. Women doe best
when they least thinke on't. 105

AEm. But rather then write I will meete him at your pleasure.

Lod. Meete him? dost thou thinke that I shall euer draw him againe
to meete thee, that rush't from thee euen now with so iust a
displeasure?

AEm. Nay good Cuze, vrge not my offence so bitterly, our next 110
meeting shall pay the forfeit of all faults.

Lod. Well th'art my pretty Cuze, and Ile doe my best to bring him
to thee againe; if I cannot, I shall be sorry yfaith, thou wr't so iniuri-
ously strange to him. But where shall this interview be now?

AEm. There is the mischiefe, and we shall hardly auoide it, my 115
father plies my haunts so closely: and vses meanes by our maide to
entrap vs, so that this Tarrasse at our backe gate is the only place
we may safely meete at: from whence I can stand and talke to you.
But sweet Cuze you shall / sweare, to keepe this my kindnesse from [C3ᵛ]
Aurelio, and not intimate by any meanes that I am any thing ac- 120
quainted with his comming.

Lod. Slife, do'st thinke I am an Asse? to what end should I tell
him? hee and Ile come wandring that way to take the aire, or so, and
Ile discouer thee.

AEm. By meere chance as t'were. 125

Lod. By chance, by chance, and you shall at no hand see him at
first, when I bring him, for all this kindnesse you beare him.

AEm. By no meanes Cuze.

Lod. Very good: And if you endure any conference with him, let
it be very little; and as neere as you can, turne to your former strange- 130
nesse in any case.

AEm. If doe not Cuze, trust me not.

Lod. Or if you thinke good, you may flirt away againe as soone as
you see him, and neuer let your late fault be any warning t'ee.

---

96 disgracings] *Q(c)*; disgracing *Q(u)* ‖ **98-100** Well . . . him.] *as separate paragraph* ‖ **113**
againe;] ∼, ‖ **114** now?] ∼. ‖ **117** Tarrasse] *Tarrasse* ‖ **127** him,] ∼∧ ‖

AEm. I will doe all this, I warrant thee Cuze. 135

Lod. Will you so Cozen foole? canst thou be brought to that silly humour againe by any perswasions? by Gods Lord, and you be strange againe, more then needs must, for a temperat modesty, Ile break's necke downe from thee, but he shall doe as he did to thee.

AEm. Now, fie vpon you Cuze, what a foole doe you make me? 140

Lod. Well Dame, leaue your superfluous nicety in earnest, and within this houre I will bring him to this Tarrasse.

AEm. But good Cuze if you chance to see my chamber window open, that is vpon the Tarrasse, doe not let him come in at it in any case. 145

Lod. Sblood how can he? can he come ouer the wall think'st?

AEm. O Sir, you men haue knot deuices with ladders of ropes to scale such walles at your pleasure, and abuse vs poore wenches. /

Lod. Now a plague of your simplicity, would you discourage him [C4] with prompting him? well Dame, Ile prouide for you. 150

AEm. As you loue me Cuze, no wordes of any kindnesse from me to him.

Lod. Goe to, no more adoe. *Exit Lodouico and AEmilia.*

[II.iii]

Enter Leonoro, Lionell and Temperance.

Temp. God yee God morrow Sir, truly I haue not heard a sweeter breath then your Page has.

Leo. I am glad you like him Mistris *Temperance.*

Temp. And how d'ee Sir?

Leo. That I must know of you Lady, my welfare depends wholly 5 vpon your good speede.

Temp. How say Sir? and by my soule I was comming to you in the morning when your yong man came to me; I pray let him put on, vnlesse it be for your pleasure.

Leo. He is yong, and can endure the cold well enough bare-headed. 10

Temp. A pretty sweet child 'tis I promise you.

Leo. But what good newes Mistris *Temperance,* will your Mistris be wonne to our kinde meeting?

Temp. Faith Ile tell you Sir, I tooke her in a good moode this morning, and broke with her againe about you, and shee was very pleasant 15 as shee will be many times.

Leo. Very well, and is there any hope of speede?

Temp. No by my troth Gentleman, none in the world, an obstacle

147 knot] not (*See Textual Note*) ‖ **151** any] *Parrott*; my (*See Textual Note*) ‖ II.iii] *Shepherd* ‖ SD *Leonoro,*] ∼∧ ‖ **4** d'ee] dee ‖

332

yong thing it is, as euer I broke withall in my life: I haue broke with
a hundred in my dayes, tho I say it, yet neuer met her comparison.   20

   Leo. Are all my hopes come to this, Mistris *Temperance*?

   Temp. Nay 'tis no matter Sir, this is the first time that e- / uer I   [C4ᵛ]
spake to any in these matters, and it shall be the last God willing.

   Leo. And euen now shee had broke with a hundred and a hundred.

   Temp. But doe you loue her Sir indeede?   25

   Leo. Do'st thou make a question of that?

   Temp. Pardon me I pray Sir, I meane d'ee loue her as a Gentleman ought to doe, that is, to consummate matrimony with her as
they say?

   Leo. Thats no matter to you Mistris *Temperance*, doe you procure   30
our meeting, and let my fauour be at her hands as I can enforce it.

   Temp. You say like an honest Gentleman; a woman can haue no
more: and faith Sir I wish you well, and euery day after dinner my
Mistris vses to go to her chaire or else lie down vpon her bedde, to
take a nappe or so, to auoide idlenesse as many good huswifes do, you   35
know, and then doe I sit by her and sew, or so: and when I see her
fast a-sleepe, Lord doe I thinke to my selfe, (as you know we waiting
women haue many light thoughts in our heads) Now if I were a man,
and should beare my Mistris an ill will, what might I doe to her now.

   Leo. Indeede then you haue very good opportunity.   40

   Temp. The best that may be, for shee sleepes like a sucking Pigge,
you may jogge her a hundred times, and shee'll stirre no more then
one of your stones, here.

   Leo. And could you put a friend in your place thinke you?

   Temp. Nay birlady Sir, backe with that legge, for if any thing   45
come on't but well, all the burthen will lye vpon me.

   Leo. Why what can come of it? only that by this meanes I may
solicite her loue my selfe.

   Temp. I but who knowes if the Deuill (God blesse vs) should be
great w'ee, how you would vse her?   50

   Leo. What, do'st thou take me for a beast, to force her that I would
make my wife? /

   Temp. Beast Sir; Nay ther's no beastlinesse in it neither, for a   [D1]
man will shew like a man in those cases: and besides, you may marre
the bedde, which euery body will see that comes in; and that I would   55
not for the best gowne I shall weare this twelue Moneth.

   Leo. Well, to put thee out of that feare, it shall be worth such a
gowne to thee.

---

19 withall] *Dilke*; with all ‖ **21** this,] ∼∧ ‖ **27** d'ee] dee ‖ **33** after] ter ‖ **50** w'ee] wee' ‖ **51**
What,] ∼∧ ‖

Temp. I thanke you for that Sir, but thats all one, and thus Sir, my old Master *Honorio,* at two a clocke will be at Tilting, and then will his sonne Signior *Aurelio,* and his man *Angelo,* be abroad; at which houre if you will be at the backe gate, and muffle your selfe handsomely, you may linger there till I call you. 60

Leo. I, marry Sir, so I may be there long enough.

Temp. Nay, but two a clocke, now; now is my houre Sir. 65

Leo. Very well, and till then farewell.

Temp. Boye, to you hartily.

Lio. [Aside.] Boy to him indeede if he knew all. *Exeunt.*

[II.iv]

Enter Lodouico and Aurelio.

Lod. I haue prouided thee a ladder of ropes, therefore resolue to meete her, goe wash thy face, and prepare thy selfe to die, Ile goe make ready the ladder.

Aur. But when is the happy houre of our meeting?

Lod. Marry Sir, thats something vncertaine, for it depends wholly 5 vpon her fathers absence, and when that will be God knowes: but I doubt not it will happen once within this twelue-Moneth.

Aur. Sownds a twelue-Moneth.

Lod. Nay harke you, you are all vpon the spurre now, but how many louers haue seru'd seauen twelue-Moneths prenticeships, for the free- 10 dome of their Mistris fauours? notwithstanding, to shorten your tor-ments, your man *An- / gelo* must be the meane, to draw the lapwing [D1ᵛ] her father from his nest, by this deuice that I tell you.

(Enter Angelo.)

Ang. I did euer dreame that once in my life good fortune would warme her cold hand in my naked bosome. And that once is now 15 come; Ile lay hold vpon't, yfaith; I haue you my little squire, I haue you vpon mine Anueill, vpon which I will mallet you and worke you; coyning crownes, chickeens, bracelets, and what not out of you, for procuring you the deere gullage of my sweete heart mistresse *Fran-cischina.* 20

Aur. I am glad it rests in my kinde seruant *Angelo. — Angelo,* well met, it lies in thee now, make me no more thy master, but thy friend, and for euer happy in thy friendship.

Ang. In what part of me does that lie Sir, that I may pull it out, for you presently? 25

---

64 I,] ∼∧ | Sir] *stet* ‖ **65** now;] *Parrott;* ∼, ‖ **67** Boye,] ∼∧ ‖ **68** Lio.] Leo. *(See Textual Note)* | SD *Aside.*] ‖ II.iv] *Shepherd* ‖ **11** notwithstanding,] ∼∧ ‖ **13** SD *Angelo.*)] *Q(c);* ∼. ∧ *Q(u)* ‖ **16** come;] ∼, ‖ **18** chickeens] chickins | you,] ∼; ‖ **21** *Angelo.*—] ∼.∧ ‖

Aur. My friend *Lodouico* heere hath told me, what thou reuealedst to him to day, touching his vncle *Lorenzo,* and his louesute to *Francischina.*

Ang. Slight I told it him in secret sir.

Lod. And so did I tell it him *Angelo,* I am a Iew else.   30

Ang. It may well be sir, but what of that?

Lod. This, *Angelo,* he would haue thee procure my olde vnckles absence from home this afternoone, by making him meete or pretending his meeting with his mistresse and thy sweete heart, *Francischina.*

Aur. Which if thou do'st *Angelo,* be sure of reward to thy wishes.   35

Ang. What talke you of reward sir? to the louing and dutifull seruant, 'tis a greater encouragement to his seruice to heare his master say, God a mercy *Angelo,* spie out *Angelo,* Ile thinke of thy paines one day *Angelo,* then all your base rewards and preferments: yet not to hinder your hand sir, I will extend mine to his seruice presently, and   40 get your old vncle (*Signior Lorenzo*) out of the waies long enough I warrant you.

Lod. Tis honestly said, which when thou hast performed, enforce vs.

Exeunt. /

Ang. I will not faile sir. — I was resolu'd to make him away afore   [D2]
they spake to me, in procuring his accesse to *Francischina,* for what is   45
his presence at her house, but his absence at his ownes? and thus shall
I with one trewell daube two walles; (*Enter Francisc.*) see how fitly
shee meetes me. I will stand close heere as if it were in my shop of
good fortune, and in respect of all ornaments I can help her to, I will
out of the fulnesse of my ioy, put her out of her studie and encounter   50
her thus; [*holds vp bracelets*] D'ee lacke gentlewoman, d'ee lacke:
very fayre new gownes, kirtles, petticots, wrought smocks, bracelets,
d'ee lacke gentlewoman, d'ee lacke?

Fran. What means my loue by these strange salutations?

Ang. Pre thee aske me no questions; hold, take these bracelets, put   55
vp this purse of gold quickly, and if thou wilt haue any of these things
I haue cried to thee, speake and tis performed.

Fran. From whose treasury comes all this, I pre thee?

Ang. Lorenzo, Lorenzo, a gentleman of much antiquitie, and one
that for his loue hath burn'd hundreds of hearts to powder; yet now it   60
fals out, that his tree of life is scorch't and blasted with the flames of
thy beauty, readie to wither eternally, vnlesse it be speedily comforted
with the sweete drops of thy nose.

Fran. Gods my life, is that old squire so amorous?

---

32 This,] ∼∧ ‖ **34** mistresse] ∼, | heart,] ∼∧ ‖ **41** waies] *Q(u)*; waie *Q(c)* (*See Textual Note*) ‖ **43** enforce] *stet* (*See Textual Note*) | vs.] ∼∧ ‖ **44** sir.—] ∼, ‖ **47** walles;] ∼, ‖ **51** SD *holds vp bracelets*] *Q has marginal note: Hold vp the / bracelets.* ‖ **55** hold,] ∼∧ ‖ **56** things] ∼, ‖

Ang. You wrong him to terme him old, he can draw his bow, ride   65
his horse, vse his sword, and traile his pike vnder Loues colours, as
well as euer he did.

Fran. I beleeue that easily.

Ang. Well, go thy waies in and prepare to entertaine him now thy
husband is from home, only with good words, and best kindnesses,   70
making him put all into deeds till his treasury be deedlesse.

Fran. You speake as if I had nothing to respect but his entertainment, when you know how close and timely it must be put in execution, considering with what enuious eyes my neighbours suruey mee. /

Ang. Think'st thou, I consider not all this? he shall come in dis- [D2ᵛ] 75
guis'd, wench, and do thou deuise for our mirth, what ridiculous disguise he shall come in, and he shall assume it.

Fran. What, a magnifico of the Citie, and one of the Senate, thinkest thou he will not see into that inconuenience?

Ang. No more then no Senator, for in this case, my assurance is   80
that *Cupid* will take the scarfe from his owne eyes, and hoodwinke the
old buzzard, while two other true turtles enioy their happinesse: get
thee in I beseech thee loue, tell thy gold, and say thy prayers. (*Enter
Lorenzo.*) Now for a farre fetch't deuice to fetch ouer my loue-squire.
Exit Fran. I see him within eare-shot. — Well, beauty may inflame   85
others, riches may tempt others; but for mee, mine eares and mine eyes
are proofe against all the Syrens, and Venusses, in all the seas of the
world; beauty is a whore, riches a baud, and Ile trust none an you.

Lor. What ailes poore *Angelo*?

Ang. Nay mistresse *Franke,* if you proue disloyall once, farewell all   90
constancy in women.

Lor. How now man? what's the matter?

Ang. O Sir are you so neare? I shall trust your experience in women
the better while I liue.

Lor. I pre thee why so?   95

Ang. Say true Sir, did you neuer sollicite your loue-sute to fayre
mistresse *Francischina*?

Lor. Neuer I protest *Angelo*.

Ang. Vpon my life 'tis a strange thing; I would haue sworne all
Italy could not so sodainly haue fastned a fauour vpon her, I look't   100
for a siege of Troy at least, to surprize the turrets of her continence;
but to yeeld at the first sight of her assaylants colours, and before any
Cannon was mounted afore her, 'tis one of the loosest parts of a
modest woman that euer I heard of.

---

78 What,] ∼∧ ‖ **84** loue-squire.] *Q(c)*; ∼, *Q(u)* ‖ **85** eare-shot.—] ∼; | Well, beauty may]
Parrott (after Dilke); well may beauty (*See Textual Note*) ‖ **86** eyes] ∼, ‖ **100** Italy] ∼, ‖

Lor. How saist thou? did not I tell thee as much? beware of an old 105
cock while you liue, he can tell when to strike I warrant you. /

Ang. Women and fethers? now fie on that affinity. [D3]

Lor. Alas *Angelo,* a feeble generation, soone ouercome God knowes,
the honester minde, the sooner ouercome.

Ang. Gods my life, what light huswife would yeeld at first to a 110
stranger? and yet does this whirligig stand vpon termes of honour
forsooth, tenders her reputation as the Apple of her eye; she has a
ielous and a cutting husband, enuious neighbours, and will die many
deathes rather then by any friends open accesse to her, be whip't naked
with the tongues of scandall and slander; and a whole sanctuary of 115
such ceremonies.

Lor. O she does worthily in that *Angelo,* and like a woman of honour, thou hast painted her perfection in her faults thou find'st, and
tickil'st me with her appetite.

Ang. And to auoid all sight of your entrance, you must needs come 120
in some disguise she sayes; so much she tenders your high credit in the
Citie and her owne reputation, forsooth.

Lor. How, come in some disguise?

Ang. A toy, a very toy which runnes in her head with such curious
feete Sir, because if there be any resemblances of your person seene to 125
enter her house, your whole substantiall selfe will be called in question;
any other man she saies, might better aduenture with the least thing
chang'd about 'em then you with all; as if you were the onely noted
mutton-monger in all the Citie.

Lor. Well *Angelo,* heauen forgiue vs the sinnes of our youth. 130

Ang. That's true Sir, but for a paltry disguise, being a magnifico,
she shall goe snicke vp.

Lor. Soft good *Angelo,* soft, let's think on't a little: what disguise
would serue the turne saies shee?

Ang. Faith, I know not what disguise shee would haue for you: 135
shee would haue you come like a Calfe with a white face, I thinke,
shee talkes of Tinkers, / pedlers, porters, chimney-sweepers, fooles [D3ᵛ]
and Physitians, such as haue free egresse and regresse into mens houses
without suspicion.

Lor. Out vpon 'em, would she haue me vndergoe the shame and 140
hazard of one of those abiects?

Ang. Yfaith I told her so, a squire of that worship, one of the Senate, a graue Iusticer, a man of wealth, a magnifico?

106 cock] *Dilke*; colt (*See Textual Note*) ‖ **111** stranger?] ∼, ‖ **112** forsooth,] ∼? ‖ **115** slander;]
Q(c); ∼, *Q(u)* ‖ **119** tickil'st] *Q(c)*; ticki'st *Q(u)* ‖ **120** auoid] *Q(c)*; auod *Q(u)* ‖ **122** Citie]
Q(u); ∼, *Q(c)* ‖ **130** *Lor.*] *Dilke*; *Ang.* ‖

Lor. And yet by my troth, for the safegard of her honour, I would doe much; me thinks a Friers weede were nothing.   145

Ang. Out vppon't, that disguise is worne thread bare vpon euery stage, and so much villany committed vnder that habit, that 'tis growne as suspicious as the vilest. If you will hearken to any, take such a transformance, as you may be sure will keepe you from discouery: for though it be the stale refuge of miserable Poets, by change of a hat or a   150 cloake, to alter the whole state of a Comedie, so as the father must not know his owne child forsooth, nor the wife her husband, yet you must not thinke they doe in earnest to carry it away so: for say you were stuffed into a motley coate, crowded in the case of a base Violl, or buttond vp in a cloak-bag, euen to your chinne, yet if I see your face,   155 I am able to say this is signior *Lorenzo,* and therefore vnlesse your disguise be such that your face may beare as great a part in it as the rest, the rest is nothing.

Lor. Good reason, in faith *Angelo*; and what, shall I then smurch my face like a chimney sweeper, and weare the rest of his smokinesse?   160

Ang. Ile tell you sir, if you be so mad to condescend to the humour of a foolish woman, by consideration that *Ioue* for his loue tooke on him the shape of a Bull, which is farre worse then a chimney sweeper, I can fit you rarely.

Lor. As how I pre thee?   165

Ang. There is one little *Snaile* you know, an old chimney sweeper.

Lor. What, hee that sings, Maids in your smocks, hold / open your   [D4]
locks? flues?

Ang. The very same sir, whose person (I borrowing his weeds) you will so liuely resemble, that himselfe in person cannot detect you.   170

Lor. But is that a fit resemblance to please a louer *Angelo*?

Ang. For that sir, she is prouided: for you shall no sooner enter but off goes your rustie skabberd, sweete water is readie to scoure your filthy face, milk, and a bath of fernebraks for your fustie bodie, a chamber perfum'd, a wrought shirt, night cap, and her husbands   175 gowne, a banquet of Oyster pyes, Potatoes, Skirret rootes, Eringos, and diuers other whetstones of venery.

Lor. O let me hugge thee *Angelo.*

Ang. A bed as soft as her hayre, sheets as delicate as her skinne, and as sweete as her breath, pillowes imitating her breasts, and her breasts   180 to boote, Hypocras in her cups, and Nectar in her lips, Ah, the gods haue bene beasts for lesse felicitie.

Lor. No more good *Angelo*, no more, how shall I requite the happinesse thou wilt bring me too? haste any mind of marriage?

---

147 habit,] ∼; ‖ **153** in] *Dilke*; it (*See Textual Note*) ‖ **166** *Snaile*] *Dilke*; snaile ‖ **168** locks?] ∼, | flues?] fluds. *Q(u)*; fludgs. *Q(c)* (*See Textual Note*) ‖ **169** weeds] *Parrott* (*Dilke conj.*); words (*See Textual Note*) ‖ **176** Oyster] *Dilke*; Oysters | Eringos] *Q(c)*; Eringes *Q(u)* ‖

Ang. Not much sir, but an extraordinary wife might tempt me.   185

Lor. By my troth and she were not promist, thou shouldest haue my
daughter: but come lets to our disguise, in which I long to be singing.

Ang. Ile folow you presently. *Exit Lor.* Signior *Lodouico.*

           (*Enter Lodouico and Giouenelle.*)

Lod. How now *Angelo?*

Ang. Why sir, I am prouiding meanes to leade your old vncle out   190
ath' way, as you will'd me, by drawing him into the way of *Quin-*
tilianoes wife, my sweet heart; and so make roome for him by *Quin-*
tilianoes roome: you that lead him any way, must needes seeke him
out and employ him to some tauerne. /

Lod. He will be with me presently *Angelo,* and here's a freshman   [D4ᵛ]
come from Padua, whom I will powder with his acquaintance, and so
make him an excellent morsell to rellish his carouses.

Ang. Goe to Sir, by this light you'll be complain'd on, there cannot
be a foole within twenty mile of your head, but you engrosse him for
your owne mirth: Noble-mens tables cannot be seru'd for you.   200

Lod. Sfut, Ile complaine of them man, they hunt me out and hang
vpon me, so that I cannot be ridde on 'em; but they shall get some
body else to laugh at, or Ile turne 'em ouer to our Poets, and make all
the world laugh at 'em.

Ang. Well Sir, here comes your man, make him sure from his wife,   205
and I'le make the tother sure with her.   *Exit.*

Enter Quintiliano reading a bill, Innocentio, Fannio, Taylor, Taylors sonne.

Lod. See Signior *Giouanelle,* here comes the famous Captaine you
would so faine bee acquainted withall; be acquainted with him at your
perill: Ile defend you from his swaggering humor, but take heede of
his cheating.   210

Giou. I warrant you Sir, I haue not beene matriculated at the Vni-
uersity, to be meretriculated by him: salted there to be colted here.

Lod. Very well Sir, lets heare him.

Quint. I haue examin'd the particulars of your bill Master *Taylor,*
and I finde them true Orthographie, thy payment shall be correspon-   215
dent: marry I will set no day, because I am loth to breake.

Tay. Alas Sir, pray let this be the day: consider my charge, I haue
many children, and this my poore child here whom I haue brought vp
at schoole, must loose all I haue bestowed on him hitherto, if I pay not
his Master presently / the quartridge I owe him.   [E1] 220

Quint. Foole, do'st thou delight to heare thy sonne begge in Latin?
pose him Lieftenant.

---

188 SD *Exit Lor.*] *Dilke; Exit.* ‖ **192** heart;] ∼, ‖ **202** 'em;] ∼, ‖ **206** SD *Enter . . . sonne.*]
Dilke subs.; Enter Quintiliano, Innocentio, Fannio, Taylor, Taylors sonne, he Reades a bill. ‖ **215**
Orthographie] *Orthographie* ‖ **221** Foole,] ∼∧ | Latin?] ∼, ‖

Innoc. How make you this in Latin boy? My father is an honest Taylor.

Boy. That will hardly be done in true Latin Sir.   225

Innoc. No? why so Sir?

Boy. Because it is false English sir.

Quint. An excellent Boy.

Innoc. Why is it false English?

Boy. Marry sir, as *bona Mulier* is said to be false Latin, because   230
though *bona* be good, *Mulier* is naught; so to say My father is an honest Taylor, is false English; for though my father be honest, yet the
Taylor is a theefe.

Quint. Beleeue it a rare shred, not of home-spunne cloth vpon my
life: Taylor, goe, send the schoole-master to me at night and Ile pay   235
him.

Tay. Thanke you good Captaine, and if you doe not pay him at
night, my wife will come to you her selfe, that's certaine, and you know
what a tongue shee has.

Quint. Like the sting of a Scorpion, shee nailes mine eares to the   240
pillory with it, in the shame and torment shee does me. Goe, I will
voide this Bill and auoide her.

Tay. I thanke you sir.   *Exit cum filio.*

Quint. Lieftenant, is not this a braue gullery? The slaue has a
pretty wife, and shee will neuer haue me pay him, because shee may   245
euer come to my chamber, as shee sayes, to raile at me, and then shee
goes home and tels her husband shee has tickled me yfaith.

Innoc. By my life, a rare jest.

Quint. Thou maist see this Boy is no shred of a Taylor, is he not
right of my looke and spirit?   250

Innoc. Right as a line, yfaith.

Lod. And will agree in the halter.—Saue you Captaine *Quintiliano.*

Quint. And do'st thou liue my noble *Lodouico?* Boy, take / my   [E1ᵛ]
cloake. — When shal's haue a rouse, ha? my Lieftenant and I were
drunke last night, with drinking health on our knees to thee.   255

Giou. Why, would not your legs beare you Sir?

Quint. How many miles to midsommer? S'blood, whose foole are
you? are not you the tassell of a Gander?

Giou. No indeede not I Sir: I am your poore friend Sir glad to see
you in health.   260

Quint. Health? S'fut, how meane you that? d'ee thinke I came
lately out ath' powdering Tubbe?

Giou. Gossaue mee Sir 'twas the furthest part of my thought.

---

231 My] my ‖ **237-38** him at night,] *Shepherd;* ∼, ∼ ∼∧ ‖ **241** Goe,] ∼∧ ‖ **254** cloake.—
When] ∼, when | shal's] shals ‖ **261** d'ee] dee ‖

Quint. Why y'are not angry, are you?

Lod. No, nor you shall not be. 265

Quint. S'blood, I hope I may and I will.

Lod. Be and you dare Sir.

Quint. Dare?

Lod. I, dare.

Quint. Plague on thee, th'art the mad'st *Lodouico* in the world, 270
s'fut doe thou stabbe me, and th'ast a minde too't, or bid me stabbe
my selfe; is this thy friend? do'st thou loue *Lodouico*?

Giou. With my heart I protest Sir.

Quint. S'heart, a lyes in's throate that does not; and whence com'st
thou wagge, ha? 275

Giou. Euen new arriued from Padua Sir to see fashions.

Quint. Giue me thy hand, th'art welcome; and for thy fashions,
thou shalt first drinke and wench it: to which end we will carouse a
little, some sixe or seauen miles hence, and euery man carry his wench.

Innoc. But where shall we haue them Captaine? 280

Quint. Haue 'em Lieftenant? if we haue 'em not. My Valentine
shall be one, and shee shall take a neighbour or two with her to see
their nurst childes or so; wee'll want for no wenches I warrant thee.

(*Enter Cuthbert Barber.*) /

Lod. But who comes here? [E2]

Quint. O tis my Barber. 285

Lod. S'blood how thy trades men haunt thee.

Quint. Alas they that liue by men, must haunt 'em.

Cut. God saue you Sir.

Quint. How now *Cutberd*, what newes out of Barbary?

Cut. Sir, I would borrow a word with you in priuate. 290

Quint. Be briefe then *Cutbeard*, thou look'st leane me thinks, I
thinke th'art newly marryed.

Cut. I am indeede Sir.

Quint. I thought so, keepe on thy hat man, twill be the lesse perceiu'd; what, is not my Taylor and you friends yet? I will haue you 295
friends thats certaine, Ile maintaine you both else.

Cut. I know no enmity betwixt vs Sir, you know Captaine I come
about another matter.

Quint. Why but *Cutbeard*, are not you neighbours? your trades
Cosen german, the Taylor and the Barber? does not the Taylor sow? 300
doest not thou Barber reape? and doe they not both band themselues
against the common enemy of mankinde, the louse? are you not both

---

272 selfe;] ∼, ‖ **281** not. My] *Q(u)*; ∼, my *Q(c)* (*See Textual Note*) ‖ **287** 'em.] ∼, ‖ **294-95**
perceiu'd;] ∼, ‖

honest men alike? is not he an arrant knaue? you next dore to a knaue, because next dore to him?

Cut. Alas Sir, all this is to no purpose, there are certaine odde   305
crownes betwixt vs you know.

Quint. True *Cutbeard*, wilt thou lend me as many moe to make 'em euen Boy?

Cut. Faith Sir, they haue hung long enough a conscience.

Quint. Cut 'em downe then *Cutbeard*, it belongs to thy profession if   310
they hang too long.

Cut. Well Sir if this be all, Ile come by 'em as I can; and you had any honesty —

Giou. S'blood honesty you knaue? doe you taxe any Gentleman in this company for his honesty?   315

Cut. Blame me not sir, I am vndone by him, and yet / I am still of   [E2ᵛ]
as good credit in my Parish as he too.

Quint. S'blood Rascall, as good credit as I?

Lod. Nay pre thee Captaine forbeare.

Innoc. Good Captaine be gone.   320

Quint. Let me alone; Ile not strike him by this hand; why hearke yee Rogue: put your credit in ballance with mine? do'st thou keepe this company? here's Signior *Lodouico*, one of the *Clarissimi*, a man of worship: here's a Gentleman of Padua, a man of rare parts, an excellent scholler, a fine Ciceronian.   325

Cut. Well sir.

Quint. And here's my Lieftenant, I hope thou know'st the Worship-full man his father with the blew beard, and all these are my com-panions; and dare you, a barbarous slaue, a squirting companion, com-pare with me? but here's the point; now behold and see: Signior   330
Giouenelle, lend me foure or fiue pounds, let it be fiue pounds, if you haue so much about you.

Giou. Here's my purse sir, I thinke there be iust so much in't.

Quint. Very good, now *Cutbeard*, are you a slanderous cut-throat or no? will thy credit doe this now? without scrip or scrowle. But   335
thou wilt thinke this is done for a colour now; doe you not lend it me simply?

Giou. What a question's that?

Quint. For how long?

Giou. At your pleasure Captaine.   340

Quint. Why so, here you poling Rascall, here's two crownes out of this money: now I hope wilt beleeue 'tis mine, now the property is altered.

---

312 can;] ∼, ‖ 313 honesty—] ∼. ‖ 321 hand;] ∼, ‖ 329 you,] ∼∧ ‖

Cut. Why you might a done this before then.

Quint. No *Cutbeard,* I haue beene burnd ith' hand for that, Ile pay   345
n'ere a knaue an yee all money, but in the presence of such honest
Gentlemen that can witnesse it; of my conscience I haue paid it thee
halfe a dozen times; goe to sir be gone. /

Cut. Fare yee well sir.   [*Exit.*] [E3]

Quint. Thanke you Signior *Giouenelle;* though y'are sure of this   350
money againe at my hands, yet take heede how this same *Lodouico* get
it from you, he's a great sharker; but th'ast no more money about thee
hast thou?

Giou. Not a doit, by this candle.

Quint. All the better, for hee'd cheat thee on't, if thou had'st euer   355
so much, therefore when thou com'st to Padua, ply thy booke and take
good courses, and 'tis not this againe shall serue thy turne at my
handes, I sweare to thee.

Giou. Thanke you good Captaine.

Quint. Signior *Lodouico,* adiew.   360

Lod. Not so sir, we will not part yet, a carouse or two me thinks is
very necessary betwixt vs.

Quint. With all my heart Boy, into the Emperours head here.

Lod. Content.   *Exeunt.*

Actus secundi Finis.

Actus Tertius.

Lodouico, Angelo.

Ang. Say Sir, haue you plaid the man and hous'd the Captaine?

Lod. I haue hous'd and lodg'd him in the Emperours head Tauerne,
and there I haue left him glorified with his two guls, so that presume
of what thou wilt at his house, for he is out of the way by this time
both waies.   5

Ang. T'is very well handled sir, and presume you and your friend
my master *Aurelio* of what may satisfie you at your / vncles, for he is   [E3ᵛ]
now going out of the way, and out of himselfe also: I haue so be-
smeard him with a chimney sweepers resemblance, as neuer was poore
Snaile, whose counterfaite he triumphes in, neuer thinking I haue   10
daubd his face sufficient, but is at his glasse as curiously busied to
beautifie his face (for as of Moo'rs so of chimney sweepers, the blackest
is most beautifull) as any Lady to paint her lips.

---

347 Gentlemen] *Shepherd*; Gentleman ‖ 349 SD *Exit.*] *Parrott* ‖ 10 *Snaile*] Snaile *Q(c)*; snaile
Q(u) ‖ 12 sweepers,] *Q(u)*; ~) *Q(c)* ‖ 13 beautifull)] *Q(u)*; ~∧ *Q(c)* | lips] *Q(c)*; lipst *Q(u)* ‖

Lod. Thou art a notable villaine.

Ang. I am the fitter for your imployment Sir: stand close I beseech   15
you, and when I bring him into the streets, encounter and bayte him
in stead of *Snayle,* but in any case let none else know it.

Lod. Not for the world.

Ang. If you should tell it to one, so you charge him to say nothing,
'twere nothing, and so if one by one to it play holy water frog with   20
twentie, you know any secret is kept sufficiently; and in this, we shall
haue the better sport at a Beare baiting, fare ye well Sir.   [*Exit.*]

Enter Honorio and Gasparo.

Hon. Signior *Lodouico* good euen to you.

Lod. The like to Signior *Honorio,* and harke you Sir, I must be
bound with my vncle *Lorenzo,* and tell you a pleasant secrete of him,   25
so in no sort you will vtter it.

Hon. In no sort as I am a Gentleman.

Lod. Why Sir hee is to walke the streets presently in the likenesse of
Snayle the chimney sweeper, and with his crie.

Hon. What, is hee Sir? to what end I beseech you Sir wil hee dis-   30
figure himselfe so?

Lod. Yfaith Sir I take it for some matter of pollicy, that concernes
towne gouernment.

Hon. Towne-bull gouernment, do you not meane so Sir?

Lod. O no Sir, but for the generall businesse of the Citie I take it. /   35

Hon. Well sir well we will not examine it too farre, but gesse at it.   [E4]

Lod. So sir when he comes forth do you take one corner to encounter him as I will doe another, and taking him for *Snayle,* Imagine
hee went about stealing of Citie venison, (though he do not,) and
make what sport you thinke good with him, alwaies prouided it be   40
cleanly, and that he may still thinke he goes inuisible.

Hon. I warrant yee Signior *Lodouico,* and thanke you hartily for
this good cause of our honest recreation.

Lod. Scarce honest neither sir, but much good do it you, as it is.

Hon. O that my sonne, your friend *Aurelio,* were heere to helpe to   45
candy this ieast a little.

Lod. Alas sir, his sicke stomacke can abide no sweete meates, hee's
all for Aye me, wee'll make the Ieast rellish well enough I warrant
you: *Lorenzo* my vncle an old Senator, one that has read *Marcus
Aurelius, Gesta Romanorum,* the *Mirror of Magistrates, &c.* to be led   50
by the nose like a blind Beare that has read nothing. Let any man
reade how hee deserues to be bayted.

18 world] *Q(c);* worl *Q(u)* ‖ **20** one by one to] *Q(c);* one to by one *Q(u)* ‖ **22** SD *Exit.*] *Dilke*
‖ **30** What,] ∼∧ ‖ **35** *Lod.*] *Lon.* ‖ **38** Imagine] *Q(u);* imagine *Q(c)* ‖ **44** neither] *Q(c);* nerther
Q(u) | is.] ∼, ‖ **48** Aye] aye ‖ **51** any] *Dilke;* my (*See Textual Note*) ‖

Hon. 'Tis a pretty wonder yfaith Signior *Lodouico.*

Lod. Slife, 'twere a good deed, to get boyes to pinne cards at his backe, hang squibs at his tayle, ring him through the towne with   55
basons, besnowball him with rotten egges, and make him asham'de of
the Commission before hee seale it.   [*Exit.*]

Gasp. What saies Signior *Lodouico,* I beseech you sir? me thinkes
his pleasant disposition should intend some waggerie.

Hon. I will tell you Signior *Gasparo,* but in any case you must say   60
nothing.

Gasp. In no case will I say any thing sir.

Hon. Then this is the case: Signior *Lorenzo* (your probable father
in law) in the case of *Snayle* the chimney sweeper, will straight tread
the streets for his pleasure. /   65

Gasp. For his pleasure?   [*E4ᵛ*]

Hon. For his pleasure sir, say it be so, wonder not, but ieast at it,
consider what pleasure the world sayes he is most giuen to, and helpe
baite him hereafter, but in any case cleanly, and say nothing.

Gasp. O monstrous, I conceiue you, my father in law; will his   70
daughter haue his tricks thinke you?

Hon. Faith for that you must euen take fortune *de la pace,* kisse
the Paxe, and be patient like your other neighbours. So, here stand I,
[*stands aside*] chose you another place.

Gasp. O me, what if a man should call him to sweepe a chimney in   75
earnest, what would he doe? Ile put him too't a my credit, and here
will I stand.   [*stands aside*]

(*Enter Lorenzo with his glasse in his hand, and Angelo with a pot of painting.*)

Ang. How now sir, are you well yet thinke you?

Lor. A little more here good *Angelo.*

Ang. Very well sir, you shall haue enough.   80

Lor. It will be the most perfect disguise that euer was imitated.

Ang. Ile warrant you that yfaith sir; ya're fitted beyonde the forehead for a right counterfaite; It is well now sir?

Lor. Yet a little more heere *Angelo,* and then master Painter let
Michael Angelo himselfe amend thee.   85

Ang. For a perfect naturall face, I care not if all the world explaine it.

Lor. So now take this glasse, and giue me my furniture, and haue at
your smoaky chimney.

---

57 SD *Exit.*] *Dilke* ‖ **63** case:] *Q(c);* ∼∧ *Q(u)* ‖ **64** case] *Q(c);* ∼: *Q(u)* ‖ **70** law;] ∼, ‖ **72**
de la pace] stet (*See Textual Note*) ‖ **74, 77** SD *stands aside*] *Parrott subs.* ‖

Ang. Haue at your smoakie chimney Mistresse *Franke*: heere sir   90
take vp your occupation, and downe with *Snayle* for a chimney
sweeper.

Lor. Away, see if the coast be cleare.

Ang. I will sir.

Lor. Take good view, looke about to the doores and windowes.   95

Ang. Not a dogge at a doore, not a cat at a window. / Appeare in   [F1]
your likenesse, and not with your quality.

Lor. Chimney sweepe; worke for chimney sweepe; wil't do sirha?

Ang. Admirably.

Lor. Does my sute become me?   100

Ang. Become you sir? would to heauen mistresse *Franke* could
bring you to the wearing of it alwaies.

Lor. Ile forth yfaith then;

           Maids in your smocks,

           Set open your locks,   105

             Downe, downe, downe:

           Let chimney sweeper in:

           And he will sweepe your chimneys cleane,

             Hey derry, derry, downe.

How do'st like my crie, ha?   110

Ang. Out of all crie, I forbid *Snayle* himselfe to creepe beyond you.

Lor. As God helpe, I begin to be proud on't: Chimney sweepe.

Ang. Gods pitty, who comes yonder?

Lor. My nephew *Lodowicke*; Gods me, Ile start backe againe.

Ang. Nay ther's no starting now, hee'll see you go into your house   115
then; fall into your note; stand to *Snayles* person and I warrant you.   *Exit Ang.*

              (*Enter Lodouico.*)

Lor. Chimney sweepe.

Lod. How now *Snayle*, how do'st thou?

Lor. Thanke your good worship.

Lod. Me thinkes thy song is more hearty then 'twas wont to be, and   120
thou look'st much better.

Lor. Thanke God and good friends sir; and a merry heart that pro-
longs life. Chimney sweepe.

Lod. Nay good *Snayle*, lets talke a little, you know *Rose* mine vncle
Lorenzoes maide *Snayle*!   125

Lor. That I do well sir.

Lod. She complaines of you *Snayle*, and sayes, y'are the bawdiest
old knaue in venery. /

98 sweepe; wil't] ∼, wilt ‖ **100** me?] *Q(c)*; ∼. *Q(u)* ‖ **103-5** Ile . . . locks,] *Dilke*; *as prose* ‖
110 How . . . ha?] *set as part of song* ‖ **125** *Lorenzoes*] *Lorensoes* ‖

346

Lor. Alas sir, she wrongs me: I am not fedde thereafter, let her [F1ᵛ]
looke for that commendation in her richer customers. 130

Lod. Who are they *Snayle*? I hope you doe not meane mine vncle
her Master; hee's mine vncle and I loue him well, and I know the old
lickspiggot will be nibling a little when he can come too't: but I must
needs say he will do no hurt, hee's as gentle as an Adder that has his
teeth taken out. 135

Lor. Y'are a merry Gentleman sir; and I haue hastie labour in
hand, I must craue pardon. (*Enter Honorio.*) Chimney sweepe.

Hon. What, old *Snayle*? how do'st thou and thy chimneyes?

Lod. Marry sir I was asking him questions about one of them.

Hon. What, Signior *Lodouico*? what one is that I pray? 140

Lod. Mine vncle *Lorenzos* maide *Rose* sir, and hee will needs perswade me, her old master keepes her for his owne saddle.

Hon. Her old master? I dare sweare they wrong him that say so;
his very age would make him asham'd to be ouertaken with those
goatish licences. 145

Lod. True sir, and his great authority in the Citie, that should
whippe such vnseasonable letchers about the wals of it.

Hon. Why, y'are ith' right sir, and now you talke of your vncle, I
heard say Captaine *Quintiliano* cheated him yesterday of fiue pounds,
as hee did a yong Gentleman of Padua this morning of as much more. 150

Lod. Faith sir he drew such a kinde of tooth from him indeede.

Hon. Is it possible he should be so wrought vpon by him? Now
certaine I haue euer held him a most wise Gentleman.

Lod. An arrant Rooke by this light; a capable cheating / stocke; a [F2]
man may carry him vp and downe by the eares like a pipkin. 155

Hon. But do you thinke he will let the Captaine passe so?

Lod. Why alas, what should he doe to him sir? the pasture is so
bare with him, that a goose cannot graze vpon't.

Hon. Marry sir then would I watch him a time when he were
abroad, and take out my penniworthes of his wife; if hee drew a tooth 160
from me, I would draw another from her.

Lor. Well, God be with your worships: chimney sweeper, [*Aside.*]
I thought I should neuer haue bene ridde of them — (*Enter Gasparo*)
Chimney sweepe.

Gasp. What old *Snayle,* do'st thou crie chimney sweepe still? why 165
they say thou art turnd mightie rich of late.

Lor. I would they said true sir?

138, 140 What,] ∼∧ ‖ **160** wife;] ∼, ‖ **162** *Lor.*] *Dilke*; *Lod.* | SD *Aside.*] *Dilke* ‖

Gasp. Yes by the masse, by the same token, that those riches make thy old name for venery encrease vpon thee.

Lor. Foolish tales sir, foolish tales. 170

Gasp. Yes by the masse, *Snayle,* but they be told for such certaine tales, that if thou hast a daughter to marrie with tenne thousand crownes, I would see her pithole, afore I would deale with her, for feare she should trot through her fathers trumperies.

Lor. Alas sir your worship knowes, I haue neither daughter nor 175 riches, Idle talke sir, Idle talke: chimney sweepe.

Gasp. Nay stay *Snayle,* and come into my house, thou shalt earne some money of mee, I haue a chimney to sweepe for thee.

Lor. I thanke your worship, I will waite vpon you next morning early sir: but now I haue promi'st to sweepe another mans chimney 180 in truth.

Gasp. But good *Snayle* take mine in the way.

Lod. What, does he crie chimney sweepe, and refuse to sweepe 'em?

Lor. No master, alas you know I liue by it, and now I / crie as I go [F2ᵛ] to worke that I haue promi'st, that I may get more against other 185 times: what would ye haue me do tro'e?

Hon. Alas poore *Snayle*; farewell good *Snayle,* farewell.

Lor. Lord keepe your good worship. — [*Aside.*] And a very vengeance, I beseech the blacke father of vengeance. [*Exit.*]

Lod. Poore vncle, he begins to be melancholy, has lost his song 190 among's.

Gasp. Was neuer such man touch't with such ouersight?

Hon. Beare with age, Signior *Gasparo,* beare with age, and let vs all tender his credite as we haue vow'd, and be silent; he little thought to haue beene thus betrayed as he is; and where secrecy is assur'd, it 195 beares with many bad actions in the very best I can tell you, and so good Signior *Lodouico* adew, and I heartily thanke you.

Lod. Adue good Signior *Honorio.*

Gasp. Adue to you likewise sir.   *Exeunt Gasparo and Honorio.*

Lod. Likewise to you sir. — Alas poore vncle, I haue monstrously 200 abused him; and yet maruellous worthie, for he disparageth the whole bloud of vs; and I wish all such old sheepebiters might alwaies dippe their fingers in such sauce to their mutton; but thus will he presently bee safe; for by this hee is neere his sweete hearts house, where he is like to be entertain'd with worse cheere then we made him. *Quintil-* 205 *liano* is now carousing in the Emperours head, while his owne head buddes hornes to carouse in; and in the meane time will my amorous friend and I, make both their absences shooing hornes to draw on the presence of *AEmilia.*   *Exit. /*

---

182 good] goodd ‖ **183** What,] ∼∧ ‖ **186** tro'e] troe (*See Textual Note*) ‖ **188** SD *Aside.*] *Dilke* ‖
189 SD *Exit.*] *Dilke* ‖ **191** among's.] ∼∧ ‖ **200** sir.—] ∼. ‖

[III.ii]

Enter Lorenzo and Angelo. (Francisc. aboue.)   [F3]

Ang. What sayes your worship now? Do you not walke inuisible, all
your ancient acquaintance, your owne nephew to talke with you and
neuer discouer you?

Lor. But *Angelo,* a villanous feare shooke me the whiles I sweare,   5
for still I was afraid my tongue would haue likt away the soote of my
face, and bewrayed me; but *Snayle,* hitherto thy rustie shell has pro-
tected me: perseuer till I haue yonder house a my head, hold in thy
hornes, till they looke out of *Quintillianoes* forehead: for an old man
to make a yong man cuckold, is one of *Hercules* labours.

Ang. [*Aside.*] That was the cleansing of other mens stables.   10

Lor. To make youth rampant in age, and age passant in youth, to
take a man downe at his owne weapon; to call backe time in one, and
thrust him headlong vpon another.

Ang. Now your worship is Oracle to your owne miracles; how you
shine in this smoaky cloud? which you make the golden net to em-   15
brace *Venus;* y'aue past the pikes yfaith, and all the Iayes of the loue-
god swarme in yonder house, to salute your recouery.

Lor. Wel *Angelo,* I tell thee, now we are past the danger, I would
not for 40 crowns but haue heard, what I haue heard.

Ang. True sir, now you know what the world thinks on you; 'tis not   20
possible for a great man, that shines alwaies in his greatnesse, to know
himselfe; but O twice yong *Leander,* see where your *Hero* stands with
torch of her beauty to direct you to her tower, aduance your sweet
note, and vpon her.

Lor. Chimney sweepe, worke for chimney sweepe.   25

Fran. Come in chimney sweeper.

Lor. O *Angelo.*

Ang. Why now sir thine *Angelo* is your good Angell; enter and
prosper, and when you are in the mid'st of your happinesse, thinke of
him that prefer'd you.   *Exit Lorenzo.* /

Fran. *Angelo,* giue him not too much time with me, for feare of the   [F3ᵛ]
worst, but goe presently to the backe gate, and vse my husbands
knocke, then will I presently thrust him into my cole-house: and there
shall the old flesh-monger fast for his iniquity.   *Exit.*

Ang. Well said mine owne *Franke* yfaith, we shall trim him betwixt   35
vs, I for the most slouenly case in the towne; shee, for the most sluttish
place in the house: Neuer was old horse-man so notoriously ridden;
well, I will presently knocke him into the cole-house, and then haste
to *Lodouico,* to know when he shall be releast.   *Exit.*

III.ii] *Shepherd* ‖ SD *Francisc.*] *Dilke subs.*; *Francisco* ‖ **10** SD *Aside.*] ‖ **16** *Venus;*] ∼, | Iayes]
Iayles (*See Textual Note*) ‖ **20** you;] *Dilke*; ∼, ‖

[III.iii]

Enter Lodouico with a ladder of ropes, Aurelio,
(AEmilia aboue.)

Lod. Here's thy ladder, and ther's thy gallowes, thy Mistris is thy
hangman, and must take thee downe: This is the Tarrasse where thy
sweet heart tarries; what wouldst thou call it in Rime?

Aur. Celestiall spheare, wherein more beauty shines —

Lod. Roome for a passion.   5

Aur. Then on Dardanian Ida, where the pride
Of heauens selected beauties striu'd for prize.

Lod. Nay you shall know, we haue watred our houses in Helicon.
I cannot abide this talking and vndoing Poetry, leaue your mellifluous
numbers: yonder's a sight will steale all reason from your rime I can   10
tell you; downe of your knees you slaue, adore. Now lets heare you
inuocate; O the suple hammes of a louer, goe to, doe not, stand vp
close, for she must not see you yet, though she know you are here.

AEm. Cozen *Lodowicke?*

Lod. Who cals *Lodowicke?*   15

AEm. What tempest hath cast you on this sollitary shore? Is the
party come?

Lod. The party? now a plague of your modesty, are / your lips too   [F4]
nice to name *Aurelio?*

AEm. Well, is he come then?   20

Lod. He, which he? s'fut name your man with a mischiefe to you,
I vnderstand you not.

AEm. Was there euer such a wild-braine? *Aurelio.*

Lod. Aurelio? Lord how loth you are to let any sound of him come
out an you, you hold him so deare within; Ile present her with a sight,   25
will startle her nicety a little better; hold you, fasten the end of this
ladder I pray.

AEm. Now Iesus blesse vs, why cosen, are you mad?

Lod. Goe to you spirit of a feather, be not so soft hearted, leaue
your nicety, or by this hemp Ile so hamper thy affections in the halter   30
of thy louers absence, making it vp in a gordian knot of forgetfulnesse,
that no *Alexander* of thy allurements, with all the swordes of thy sweet
words, shall euer cut in peeces.

AEm. Lord, how you roule in your rope-ripe termes.

Lod. Goe to, tell me, will you fasten the ladder or no?   35

AEm. I know not what I should say t'ee: I will fasten it, so only
your selfe will come vp.

III.iii] *Shepherd* ‖ **4** shines—] ∼. ‖ **8** houses] *stet (See Textual Note)* ‖ **12** inuocate;] ∼, ‖ **25**
within;] ∼, ‖

Lod. Only my selfe will come vp then.

AEm. Nay sweet Cuze, sweare it.

Lod. If I should sweare thou wouldst curse me: take my word in 40
a halters name, and make the ladder as fast to the Tarrasse, as thou
would'st be to *Aurelio*.

AEm. Nay see if he doe not make me giue ouer againe?

Lod. Was there euer such a blew kitling? fasten it now, or by
heauen thou do'st loose me for euer. 45

AEm. Well sir, remember your word; I will fasten it, but yfaith
Cuze, is not the Gentleman, and his parting choller parted yet?

Lod. Yfaith with much adoe.

AEm. Nay, nay, choose him; I shall liue, if they be not: and if
I liue till his choller kill me, I shall liue till he leaue louing me, and 50
that will be a good while first.

Lod. Lord, Lord, who has enform'd you of such a- / morous fer- [F4ᵛ]
uency in him: are you so confident in his kindnesse?

AEm. Nay by my troth, tis but a carelesse confidency neither, which
alwaies last longer then that which is timorous: well Cuze, here I 55
haue fastned it for your pleasure; but alas, the feare of my fathers
comming does so distract me, that I scarce know what I doe or say.

Lod. Your father? do'st thinke we would venture all this preparation, and not make him safe?

AEm. But are you sure he is safe? 60

Lod. Am I sure this is *Aurelio*? looke vpon him wench, is it not
thy loue? thy life? come sir, mount.

AEm. O cosen *Lodwicke,* doe you thus cosen and betray me?

Lod. Cuze, Cuze, thou hast acted thy dissembling part long enough,
in the most modest iudgement, and passing naturally, giue ouer with 65
thy credit then, vnmaske thy loue, let her appeere in her natiue
simplicity, striue to conceale her no longer from thy loue, for I must
needs tell thee he knowes all.

AEm. What does he know?

Lod. Why all that thou told'st me, that thou lou'st him more then 70
he can loue thee, that thou hast set vp thy resolution, in despight of
friends or foes, weales or woes, to let him possesse thee wholly, and
that thou didst wooe me to bring him hither to thee: All this he
knowes; that it was thy deuice to prepare this ladder, and in a word,
all the speech that past betwixt thee and me he knowes, I told him 75
euery word truly and faithfully Gods my Iudge.

AEm. Now was there euer such an immodest creature?

Lod. *Via* with all vaine modesty, leaue this colouring, and strip

78 *Via*] ∼, ‖

351

thy loue starke naked, this time is too precious to spend vainly; mount
I say.   80

Aur. Modell of heauenly beauty —

Lod. Sownds, wilt thou melt into rime a the tother side? shall
we haue lines? change thy stile for a ladder, this / will bring thee   [G1]
to Parnassus, vp I say.

Aur. Vnworthy I t'approach the furthest step   85
To that felicity that shines in her.

Lod. O spurblinde affection, I haue seene a fellow, to a worse
end ascend a ladder with a better will, and yet this is in the way of
marriage, and they say, marriage and hanging haue both one constel-
lation. To approue the which old saying, see if a new ladder make   90
'em not agree.

AEm. Peace, some bodie comes.

Lod. That you heard, was but a mouse. — So boy I warrant thee.

Aur. O sacred goddesse, what soe're thou art
That in meere pitty to preserue a soule   95
From vndeseru'd destruction, hast vouchsaf't
To take *AEmiliaes* shape —

Lod. What a poeticall sheepe is this? S'life, will you stand riming
there vpon a stage, to be an eye-marke to all that passe? is there not a
chamber by? withdraw I say for shame, haue you no shame in you?   100
heere will come some bodie presently I lay my life on't.

Aur. Deare mistresse, to auoid that likely danger,
Vouchsafe me onely priuate conference,
And 'tis the fulnes of my present hopes.   *Exeunt Aur. and AEm.*

Lod. Aurelio, Occasion is bald, take her by the forelock; so, so.   105
In *Hymens* name get you together, heere will I stand Sentinell. —
This is the backe gate to *Honorios* house, which shall be *Aurelios,*
if God giue him grace to weepe for his fathers death in time. And
in this garden, if I could see the chaste *Lucresse,* or the affable mistresse *Temperance,* I might (thus wrapt in my cloake) steale a   110
little courtship through the chinke of a pale. But indeed I thinke
it safer to sit closer, and so to cloud the sunne of my visnomy, that no
eye discerne it. (*He sits downe, and muffles himselfe in his cloake.*)
So be it, thats my resolution. Now to my contemplation: this is no
Pandarisme, is it? / No, for there is neither money nor credit   [G1ᵛ]
propos'd or expected, and besides there is no vnlawfull act intended,
no not this same *lasciua actio animi* I thinke for his part, much lesse
hers: go to, let me do my kinswoman and her sex right, sit at rest with
me then reputation, and conscience, fall asleepe with the world; but

81 beauty—] ∼. ‖ 85-86 Vnworthy . . . her] *Dilke; as prose* (to) ‖ 93 mouse.—So] ∼,∧ so ‖
97 shape—] ∼. ‖ 104 SD *Exeunt Aur. and AEm.*] *Parrott subs.; Exeunt* ‖ 106 Sentinell.—] ∼. ‖
112 sunne] *Dilke;* summe ‖ 114 it,] *Q(c);* ∼∧ *Q(u)* | contemplation:] ∼, ‖ 117 *animi*] ∼: ‖
118 kinswoman] ∼, ‖ 119 world;] ∼, ‖

this same idle attendance is the spite of it, Idlenesse is accounted with   120
other men a sinne, to me 'tis a penance, I was begot in a stirring
season, for now hath my soule a thousand fancies in an instant, as
what [a] wench dreams on when she lies on her backe: when one
hen layes an egge and another sits it, whether that hen shall mother
that chicken? If my bull leape your cow, is not the calfe yours? yes   125
no doubt, for *AEdificium cedit solo* saies the Lawyer: and then to
close all comes in a sentence, *Non omnia possumus omnes*: for some
are borne to riches, others to verses, some to be bachelers, others to
be cuckolds, some to get crownes, and others to spend'm, some to get
children, and others to keepe 'em: and all this is but idlenesse,   130
would to God I had some scuruy poeme about me to laugh at,
(*Enter Temperance.*) but marke, yonders a motion to be seene.

   Temp. Yonder he sits yfaith, well done true loue, good Signior
Leonoro, he keepes promise the best, he does not see me yet.

   Lod. 'Tis the stai'd Madam *Temperance,* a pretty pinnace she has   135
bene in her daies, and in her nights too, for her burthen, and reasonable good vnder sayle, and see she hath discoured a sayle, see, see,
she hales him in, ha? tis this way to the rewards, slight 'tis this way:
[*Exit Temp.*] I hope the baud knowes not me, and yet I know not,
she may be a witch, for a whore she was before I knew her, a baud I   140
haue knowne her any time this dozen yeares, the next step to honour
then is a witch, because of Nature, for where the whore ends, the baud
begins, and the corruption of a baud, is the generation of a witch.
And *Pythagoras* holds opinion, that a witch turnes to a wild Cat,
as an old Ostler turnes to an ambling nagge.   145

      (*Enter Leonoro muffled in his cloake with Lyonell.* /

   Leo. This is the backe gate, where *Temperance* should meete me   [G2]
at this howre.

   Lio. I wonder she fayles, for I see her not.

   Leo. Why sits that fellow there tro'e? come let's houer here abouts,
'twill not be long er'e we encounter.   *Exit with Lio.*

   Lod. So, now this riddle is expounded, this baud tooke me for
this aduenturer whom (twentie to one) she attended, to waft him into
Lucretias chamber, what a beast was I, not to apprehend this aduantage; thus muffled as I am, she could not haue perceiued mee
till I had bene in, And I might safely haue staid a while without   155
endangering my louers: (*Enter Temperance stealing along the stage.*)
S'light she takes me still for her first man.

   Temp. Come, come, gingerly for Gods sake, gingerly.   *Exeunt.*

---

123 a wench] *Dilke*; wench | backe:] ∼, ‖ **139** SD *Exit Temp.*] *Parrott (after Dilke)* ‖ **149** tro'e]
troe | abouts,] ∼∧ ‖ **150** SD *Exit . . . Lio.*] *Parrott*; *Exit.* ‖ **153-54** aduantage;] ∼, ‖

Enter Leonoro and Lyonell.

Leo. See *Lyonell,* yet she is not come, and the priuy attendant is
gone.   160

Lio. I wonder what it was.

Leo. I feare me some other clyent of hers, whom she preferres before me; come, we must not linger here too long together, wee'll
enter on this backside, to the Emperours head, where we will stay
a little, and then make the last triall of this bauds honesty.   165

(*Enter Quintiliano, Giouenelli, and Fannio in their doublet and hose.*)

Quint. Come Ancient, lets leaue our company a little, and ayre
our selues in this backside. — Who goes there?

Leo. A friend.

Quint. The word.

Leo. God saue you Captaine *Quintiliano.*   170

Quint. Shote him Ancient, a spie, the word's the Emperours head,
and thither you shall go sir.

Leo. Pardon me good Captaine.

Giou. Come, be not retrograde to our desires.

Leo. I attend a friend of mine. /   175

Quint. Th'ast attended him already, I am witnesse too't; deni't and   [G2ᵛ]
he dare, whatsoe're he bee, and he shall attend thee another while, and
he will: Th'art as good a man as he, and he be the Duke himselfe, for
a *Clarissimo*; entertaine him Ancient, bid the *Clarissimo* welcome, Ile
call a drawer, and wee'll haue some wine in this Arbor.   *Exit.*

Giou. Y'are very welcome Signior *Clarissimo,* desire you more acquaintance sir.

Leo. My name is *Leonoro* sir, and indeed I scarce know you.

Giou. No sir, and you know me, you must know as much as I know,
for *Scientia* and *Scientificus* is all one; but that's all one; in truth sir,   185
you shall not spend a penny here, I had money, I thanke God euen
now, and peraduenture shall haue againe e're we part, I haue sent to
a friend of mine.

(*Enter Quintilliano and a drawer with a cup of wine and a towell.*)

Quint. Here honourable *Clarissimo,* I drinke to thee.

Leo. Thanke you good Captaine.   190

Quint. S'fut, winesucker, what haue you fild vs heere, baldredash?
taste *Leonoro.*

Leo. Me thinks 'tis sacke.

---

163 me;] ∼, ‖ **176** too't;] ∼, ‖ **179** the *Clarissimo*] ∼ ∼, ‖ **185** one; in] ∼, ∼ ‖

Giou. Let vs taste sir; 'tis claret, but it has beene fetch't againe
with *Aqua vitae.*   195

Quint. S'light me thinks t'as taken salt water, who drew this wine
you rogue?

Draw. My fellow *Sam* drew it sir, the wine's a good neat wine, but
you loue a pleasanter grape, I'le fit your pallate sir.   (*He stands close.*)

Quint. Is this thy boy *Leonoro?*   200

Leo. For fault of a better sir.

Quint. Afore heauen 'tis a sweete fac't child, me thinks he should
show well in womans attire: *And hee tooke her by the lilly white
hand, and he laid her vpon a bed.* Ile helpe thee to three crownes a
weeke for him, and she can act well. Ha'st euer practis'd, my pretty   205
Ganimede?

Lio. No, nor neuer meane sir.

Giou. Meane sir? No marry Captaine, there will neuer / be meane   [G3]
in his practise I warrant him.

Quint. O finely taken; Sirha *Clarissimo,* this fellow was an arrant   210
Asse this fore-noone, afore he came to be an Antient.

Leo. But where's your Lieftenant, Captaine?

Quint. Sownds man, hee's turnd swaggerer.

Leo. Ist possible?

Quint. Swaggerer by this light he; and is in the next roome writing   215
a challenge to this tall Gentleman my Antient here.

Leo. What, mutinous in your owne company?

Quint. S'fut man, who can bridle the asses valour?

Giou. S'blood and any man thinke to bridle me.

Leo. But what was the quarrell?   220

Quint. Why sir, because I entertaind this Gentleman for my Antient
(being my deare friend and an excellent scholler), he takes pepper ith'
nose and sneeses it out vpon my Antient; now sir he (being of an vn-
cole-carrying spirit) fals foule on him, cals him gull openly; and euer
since I am faine to drinke with 'em in two roomes, dare not let 'em   225
come together for my life, but with pen and inke-hornes, and so my
Lieftenant is in the next chamber casting cold Inke vpon the (*Enter
Innocentio.*) flame of his courage, to keepe him from the blot of cowardise; see where he comes with his challenge: good *Clarissimo* hold
my Antient.   230

Leo. Good Antient, forbeare in a Tauerne.

Quint. Reuenge noble Lieftenant, hast thou done it?

---

194 *Giou.*] *Geo.* | sir;] ~, || **203-4** *And . . . bed*] and . . . bed || **205** practis'd,] ~∧ || **210** Sirha]
~, || **212** Lieftenant,] ~∧ || **221** Antient] ~, || **222** scholler),] ~)∧ || **223** he (being] (~ ~ ||
223-24 vn-cole] vncole || **228-29** cowardise;] ~, ||

Innoc. S'light I thinke I haue pepperd him, but twas his owne seeking you know.

 Quint. Thats certaine.   235

 Giou. Sownds, my seeking sir?

 Quint. Hold him *Leonoro*; and if it be possible, perswade him to
heare the challenge from the enemies owne mouth.

 Leo. Ile vndertake he shall Captaine: Good Antient let me entreate you. /   240

 Giou. Well sir, because y'are a stranger to me, you shall doe more   [G3ᵛ]
with me.

 Leo. Thanke you good ancient.

 Quint. Reade fiery Lieftenant, reade boy, legibly.

 Innoc. Here it is sir: Signior *Giouenelli,* it is not ignorant vnto you,   245
that euen now you crost me ouer the cocks-comb.

 Giou. I did so sir: I will not denie it I warrant you.

 Leo. Good Ancient peace.

 Innoc. And that openly, or else it would neuer haue greeu'd me.

 Quint. That openly was all indeede.   250

 Innoc. And moreouer, very vnreuerendly to call me gull, and asse to
my face: And therefore, though I held it good discretion in me to
winke at the blow, not seeing to take notice of it —

 Leo. Good discretion in deede.

 Innoc. Yet know that I will haue satisfaction from you.   255

 Giou. Well sir, and you shall.

 Quint. Nay good Ancient heare him.

 Innoc. And desire you to send me word, whether you will maintaine
it or no, hoping that you will not offer that discourtesie to doe me
wrong, and stand to it when you haue done.   260

 Leo. That were foule indeede.

 Innoc. And as for the words, in that you call'd me gull, and Asse to
my face, resolue me by letter (for I do not thinke fit we should meete)
first whether you spake any such words or no: and secondly by whom
you meant 'em. And if by me (as I thinke you durst not) confesse you   265
are sorry for 'hem: and if I haue offended you, I heartily aske you forgiuenesse. And so farewell.

 Quint. Afore heauen Ancient, this would haue tickled you, but
good *Leonoro,* and thou bee'st a right *Clarissimo,* lets make 'em friends,
and drinke to one another: S'fut, we haue no wine here me thinks,   270
where's this Aperner?

 Draw. Here Sir. /

 Quint. Haue you mended your hand sir?   [G4]

---

236 Sownds,] ∼∧ ‖ **253** it—] ∼. ‖ **273** sir?] ∼. ‖

Draw. I Captaine, and if this please not your taste, either you or I
cannot tast a cup of wine.   275

Quint. Sounds y'are very saucy sir, here Lieftenant, drink to thy
Ancient, and voide mutinies with your officer, marshall law is dangerous.

Innoc. Is he content I shoud drinke to him?

Leo. He is I warrant thee.   280

Innoc. Why then Ancient good lucke t'ee.

Giou. Let come Lieftenant, I pledge you.

Quint. Why so, now my company is cur'de againe, afore 'twas
wounded. Come honorable *Clarissimo,* lets retire to our strength, taste
a fresh carouse or two, and then march home with Musicke. Tapster,   285
call vs in some Musicke.

Draw. I will sir.   [*Exeunt.*]

Finis Actus Tertii.

Actus Quartus.

Enter Quintiliano, Leonoro, Innocentio, Lionell,
Fannio, with Musicians.

Quint. Strike vp Scrapers; honorable *Clarissimo,* and thy sweet
Adonis, adieu, remember our deuice at the show soone.

Leo. I will not faile Captaine, farewell t'ee both: come *Lionel,* now
let vs trie the truth of Madam *Temperance,* and see if shee attend vs.

Innoc. I hope by this time shee remembers her promise sir.   5
                                                        Exeunt Leo and Lio.

Quint. How now Lieftenant, where's my Ancient?

Innoc. Marry Captaine y'aue left him casting the reckoning ith'
chimney.

Quint. Why then his purse and his stomacke wil be emp- / ty to-   [G4ᵛ]
gether, and so I cashier him; let the scholler report at Padua, that   10
Venice has other manner of learning belongs to it: what does his
Continuum & Contiguum here? let 'em goe to the Inke pot and beware of the wine pot.

Fill red cheek't *Bacchus,* let the *Burdeux* grape
Skip like *la voltos* in their swelling vaines.   15

Te dan, dan tidle, te dan de dan tidle didle, &c.   [*Dances.*]

Innoc. O God Captaine that I could dance so.

Quint. He tooke her by (strike vp fidlers) *the lilly white hand and*
he laid her vpon the bedde. Oh what a spirit haue I now? I long to

287 SD *Exeunt.*] *Dilke* ‖ SD *Lionell*] *Lionello* | *Musicians*] *Musicke* ‖ **1** Scrapers;] ∼, ‖ **5** *Innoc.*] *stet*
(*See Textual Note*) ‖ **16** SD *Dances.*] *Dilke* ‖ **18-19** *He . . . bedde*] He . . . bedde ‖

357

meete a Sergeant in this humor, I would but haue one whiffe at one   20
of these same peuter button'd shoulder-clappers, to trie whether this
chopping knife or their pestels were the better weapons. Here's a
blade Boy, it was the old Dukes first predecessors; Ile tell thee what
Lieftenant, this sword has dubd more Knights then thy knife has
opened Oysters.   25

    Innoc. Ist possible Captaine? and me thinks it stands a little.

    Quint. No matter for that, your best mettald blades will stand
soonest:
So, now we haue attaind our Mansion house.
At which Ile sing a verse shall breake the dores.   30
O noble *Hercules,* let no Stygian lake —
Te dan dan tidle, te dan de dan tidle didle, &c.
Farewell scrapers, your reward now shall be that I will not cut your
strings nor breake your fidles, *via,* away.   *[Exeunt Musicians.]*

    Innoc. Come Captaine, lets enter, I long to see my Mistris, I war-   35
rant shee's a heauy Gentlewoman for your absence.

    Quint. S'fut she's an Asse, honour wooes me, preferment cals me,
and I must lye pampred in a wenches lap, because shee dotes on me.
Honour saies no, Lieftenant. *Pugna pro patria,* we must too't yfaith
and seeke our portion amongst the scratcht faces.   40

    Lorenzo within. Mistris, Mistris, is he gone?

    Quint. Whoe's that cals there? /

    Innoc. I heard no body.   [H1]

    Quint. No? there was one cald Mistris: I say who cald Mistris?
s'blood I hope I am not drunke.   45

    Fann. In truth sir I heard no body.

    Quint. I tell thee I smelt a voice here in my entry, s'fut Ile make it
smell worse and 'cheare it againe.   *[Exit.]*

    Innoc. O me, hee'll draw vpon his owne shaddow in this humour, if
it take the wall of him. Follow him *Fannio,* looke he doe no harme for   50
God sake.

    Lor. *[Within.]* Helpe, helpe, helpe.

    Innoc. Name of God, what's there to doe?

              (Enter Quintil. and Lorenzo.)

    Lor. Good Captaine doe not hurt me.

    Quint. Sounds is hell broke loose? why *Snaile,* though you can sing   55
songs and doe things *Snaile,* I must not allow yee to creepe into my
wiues cole-house; what, *Snaile,* into my withdrawing chamber?

---

26 Captaine?] ~, ‖ **29-31** So . . . lake—] *Parrott; as prose* (so) ‖ **31** O noble] *O noble* | lake—]
~. ‖ **34** SD *Exeunt Musicians.*] ‖ **44** Mistris?] ~, ‖ **48** and 'cheare] *stet* (*See Textual Note*) | SD
Exit.] *Dilke* ‖ **52** SD *Within.*] *Parrott* ‖ **57** house;] ~, | what,] ~∧ | *Snaile,*] ~∧ ‖

Lor. I beseech your Worship heare me speake.

Quint. O *Snaile,* this is a hard case; no roome serue your turne, but my wiues cole-house, and her other house of office annext to it? a   60
priuy place for her selfe, and me sometimes, and will you vse it being a stranger? s'light how comes this about? vp sirha and call your Mistris.

Lor. [*Aside.*] A plague of all disguises.   *Exit Fannio.*

Innoc. Alas poore *Snaile,* what didst thou make here?

Lor. I protest sir for no harme, my Mistris cald me in to sweepe her   65
chimney, and because I did it not to her minde, shee made me doe pennance in her cole-house.

Innoc. Search him Captaine and see, if he haue stolen nothing.

Lor. Kill me, hang me, if I haue.

Quint. Yes *Snaile,* and besides I heare complaints of you, y'are an   70
old luxurious hummerer about wenches *Snaile,* does this become your grauity sir? Lieftenant, fetch me a cole-sacke, Ile put him in it and hang him vp for a signe.

Lor. I beseech your Worship be good to me. /

Innoc. Good Captaine pardon him, since he has done nothing but [H1ᵛ] 75
swept your chimney worse then my Mistris would haue it swept, he will doe it better another time.

Quint. Well *Snaile,* at this Gentlemans request, (to whom I can denie nothing) I release you for this once, but let me take you no more thus I aduise you.   80

Lor. Not while I liue good Captaine.

Quint. Hence, trudge you drudge, goe away.

Lor. [*Aside.*] A plague of all disguises.   *Exit Lorenzo.*

(Enter Fannio.)

Fann. I haue look't about all the house for my Mistris sir, but I cannot finde her.   85

Quint. Goe then, looke all about the towne for her too; come in Lieftenant, lets repose a little after our liquor.   *Exeunt.*

[IV.ii]

Enter Aurelio and AEmilia, aboue.

Aur. Deare life, be resolute, that no respect
Heighted aboue the compasse of your loue,
Depresse the equall comforts it retaines;
For since it finds a firme consent in both,

63, 83 SD *Aside.*] *Dilke* ‖ IV.ii] *Shepherd* ‖

And both our births and yeares agree so well,   5
If both our aged parents should refuse,
For any common obiect of the world,
To giue their hands to ours, let vs resolue
To liue together like our liues and soules.
    AEm. I am resolu'd my loue; and yet alas,   10
So much affection to my fathers will
Consorts the true desires I beare to you,
That I would haue no sparke of our loue seene,
Till his consent be ask'd, and so your fathers.
    Aur. So runnes the mutuall current of my wish,   15
And with such staid and circumspect respects,
We may so serue and gouerne our desires,
That till fit obseruation of our fathers /
Preferre the motion to them, we may loue   [H2]
Without their knowledge and the skill of any,   20
Saue only of my true friend *Lodowicke.*
    AEm. I wonder where he is.
    Aur.   Not farre I know,
For in some place, he watcheth to preuent
The feared danger of your fathers presence.

        Enter Lorenzo and Angelo below, running.

    Ang. Sounds stay for the loue of your honour sir.   25
    Lor. A plague of all disguises *Angelo.*
    Ang. What reason haue you to curse them? has not one of them
kept you safe from the shame of the world, as much as a poore disguise might doe? but when your ridiculous feares will cast it off, euen
while it is on, so running through the streets, that they rise all in an   30
vprore after you, alas what is the poore disguise to blame sir?
    Lor. Well then fortune is to blame, or some thing; come, as thou
didst helpe to dawbe me, helpe to cleanse me, I pre thee.
    Ang. Let alone a while sir for Gods sake, Ile goe see whether the
Captaine be gone from home or no.   35
    Lor. Out vpon that course *Angelo;* I am frighted out of it, come
enter my house, enter.
    Ang. What, will you enter your house sir afore you know who is in
it? keepe your selfe close, and let me first enter and discouer.
    Lor. I know there is no body.   40
    Ang. You cannot know it sir, I heard euen now that diuers of the
Senate were determin'd to come and sit in Counsell there.
    Lor. A tale, a very tale *Angelo,* enter for the loue of heauen, enter
and vnsmother me.   *Exit. /*

---

18 fathers] ∼, ‖ **19** them,] ∼; ‖ **24** SD *Angelo below*] *Angelo* ‖ **29** doe?] ∼; ‖ **31** you,] ∼; ‖ **32**
come,] ∼∧ ‖ **39** it?] ∼: ‖

Ang. What shall I doe? my poore Master is berai'd, O that same [H2ᵛ] 45
faithlesse *Lodowicke,* that could drowne the swaggering Captaine no
better in his drunkennesse; alas how should I salue this?   *Exit.*

(*Enter Lorenzo and after him Angelo.*)

Lor. How now? whom doe I see? my daughter and a yonker together? passion of death, hell and damnation, what lecherous capri-
corne raignes this vnhappy day? old and yong in a predicament? O   50
fie of filthy sinne and concupiscence, I will conceale my rage a while
that it may breake forth in fury; Ile shift me presently *Angelo,* and goe
fetch the Prouost.

Ang. O vnspeakable madnesse, will you for euer dishonour your
daughter, and in her your selfe sir?   55

Lor. Talke not to me, out vpon this abhominable concupiscence, the
pride of the flesh, this witchcraft of the Diuell: talke not to me, iustice
cries out an't in the streets, and I will see it punish't, come good *Angelo*
to helpe to shift me.   [*Exit.*]

Ang. Ile follow you Sir instantly. — Master, Master.   60

Aur. Angelo? what newes?

Ang. Miserable Master, cast downe your ladder, and come downe
instantly.

AEm. Alas, why, *Angelo,* is my father comming?

Ang. Let vs not talke but come downe I say.   65

Aur. Deere life, farewell, wee'll shortly meete againe;
So parts the dying body from the soule,
As I depart from my *AEmilia.*

AEm. So enter frighted soules to the low world,
As my poore spirit vpon this soddaine doubt,   70
What may succeede this danger.

Ang. Come away, you'll be whipt anone for your amourosity, hast
for shame hast, &c.

AEm. Once more and euer, fare my deere life well.   *Exit AEmil.*

Ang. Leaue your amorous congeis and get you in Dame; / sir you [H3] 75
and I will talke as 'twere betwixt the pales, now, get you and shift you
of this sute presently.

Aur. Shift me *Angelo?* why man?

Ang. Aske me no questions, but goe home and shift you presently,
and when I haue done a little businesse here within, Ile come and tell   80
you my deuice: there hath more chanc't then you are aware of, and
then I can stand to tell you; away therefore presently goe home and
shift you.

Aur. Very good sir, I will be ruld by you, and after learne the
misteries.   *Exit Aurel.*

59 SD *Exit.*] *Dilke* ‖ **60** instantly.—] ∼; ‖ **64** *Angelo,*] ∼∧ | comming?] ∼. ‖ **66** againe;] ∼,
‖ **67** soule,] ∼; ‖

Ang. Now will I let the little squire shift and cleanse himselfe without me, that he may be longer about fetching the Prouost, and in the
meane time will I take my Masters sute (of which the little squire
tooke note) and put it on my sweet heart *Francischina,* who shall
presently come and supply my Masters place, with his Mistris; for the   90
little squire, amaz'd with his late affrights and this suddaine offence-
full spectacle of his daughter, tooke no certaine note who it was that
accosted her; for if he had, he would haue blam'd me for my Master;
only the colour of his garment sticks in his fancie, which when he shall
still see where he left it, he will still imagine the same person weares it,   95
and thus shall his daughters honour and my Masters be preseru'd with
the finest sugar of inuention. And when the little squire discouers my
sweet heart, shee shall sweare, shee so disguised her selfe, to follow
him, for her loue to him; ha, ha ha, O the wit of man when it has the
winde of a woman.   *Exit.*

[IV.iii]

Enter Lodouico and Lucretia, with Rapiers fighting.

Lod. Hold, hold, I pre thee hold; I yeeld my rapier,
Let my submission, my presumption salue.
   Lucr. Ignoble *Lodwicke,* should I take thy life,
It were amends too little for the wrong. /
   Lod. O the precious heauens: [H3ᵛ] 5
How was I gul'd? hand, hide thy selfe for shame.
And henceforth haue an eye before thy fingers.
   Lucr. Well do not ieast it out, for I protest
If this disguise, which my inhumane fate
Puts on my proper sexe, be by thy meanes   10
Seene through, by any other then thy selfe,
The quarrell twixt vs shall be more then mortall.
And thy dishonour to a friendlesse stranger
(Exild his natiue countrey, to remaine
Thrall to the mercy of such vnknowne minds   15
As fortune makes the rulers of my life)
Shall spread it selfe beyond my misery.
   Lod. Nay, mixe not cause of mirth with passion,
Do me the grace t'vnfold thy name and state,
And tell me what my whole estate may doe,   20
To salue this wrong vnwittingly I did thee,
And set the plantife thoughts of thy hard fate
In such peace, as my friendship may procure:

---

91 squire,] ∼∧ ‖ **93** Master;] ∼, ‖ IV.iii] *Shepherd* ‖ **6** hand] haud ‖ **14** remaine] remnine ‖
15 minds] miads ‖ **17** misery.] ∼, ‖ **21** thee,] *Dilke;* ∼? ‖

And if I faile thee, let *Ioue* fayle my soule,
When most this earth makes it need help of heauen.   25
   Lucr. In this you more then temper my late rage
And show your vertues perfectly deriu'd
From the Venetian noblesse; for my name,
It is *Lucretio,* which to fit this habit
I turn'd *Lucretia*: the rest that rests   30
To be related of my true estate,
Ile tell some other time: least now your presence
Might dumbly tell it (if it should be seene)
To all the world, or else make it suspect
My femall life of lightnesse: then with thanks   35
And vow of all true friendship, for th'amends
Your kindnesse makes me, take your sword againe,
And with it while I liue the power of mine
In any honor'd vse [you] shall commaund.
Then till we meete, and may laugh at this error, /   40
Ile once more trie the free peace of my chamber.   *Exit.* [H4]
   Lod. Do so sweet friend. — A plague of *Gingerly?*
Where is that stale and fulsome *Gingerly?*
She brought me to a fury, Ile be sworne
Rather then man or woman: a flat beating: 45
I found her suppos'd mistresse fast asleepe,
Put her to the touchstone, and she prou'd a man.
He wak't, and with a more then manly spirit
Flew in my face, and gaue me such a dash
In steed of kissing, of these licorish lips   50
That still my teeth within them bled I sweare.   *(He spits.*
Gingerly, Gingerly, a plague a you.   *(He spits againe.*
But now how does my louers on the Tarrasse?

     Enter Aurelio with Angelo, shifting his Apparell.

   Aur. Hold, take my dublet too, my hat and all,
And quickly hie thee to thy sweete.   55
   Ang. S'ounds, see sir see, your proper Sentinell,
That when you needed him, gaue you a slip.
   Aur. Friend *Lodouico,* by my life, well welcome
To this my fathers backeside.
   Lod.   Well sir, well,
I would I had kist almost your fathers backeside   60
So I had neuer knowne it.
   Ang.   A my life
He faints extremely, he left you euen now

---

26 this you] *Dilke*; the (*See Textual Note*) ‖ **28** name,] ∼∧ ‖ **39** you] *Dilke* ‖ **42** friend.—A] ∼:∧
a | *Gingerly*] roman ‖ **43** *Gingerly?*] Gingerly, ‖ **47** prou'd] *Dilke*; prou' ‖ **51** sweare.] ∼∧ ‖ **52**
Gingerly, Gingerly] Gengerly, ∼ ‖ **54-71** Hold . . . friend?] *as prose* (and . . . that . . . to . . . so
. . . he . . . to . . . of . . . to . . . who) ‖

To purchase him the amorous enteruiew
Of your fayre cuze *Lucretia* that lies heere.
    Aur. Gods me, sweete friend, would'st thou vse such a slight   65
To any one that lay within my walke?
Who was thy meane to her?
    Ang.   I lay my life,
Tame madam *Temperance,* the notorious Pandar.
    Aur. S'fut friend,
Wat a notorious ouersight was that?   70
And what a violent iniury vnto thy friend?
    Lod. A plague vpon you both; you scuruy hinde,
Haue / you no gull but me to whet your wit vpon?   [H4ᵛ]
    Aur. My friend a priuie louer? I'de haue sworne
Loue might spend all his shafts at butterflies   75
As well as at his bosome.
    Ang.   'Twas your fault then,
For I haue noted a most faithfull league
Betwixt him and his barber now of late,
And all the world may see, he does not leaue
One haire on his smooth chinn, as who should say,   80
His haplesse loue was gone against the hayre.
    Lod. [*Aside.*] S'bloud and these rogues knew how I was deceiu'd,
They'd flout me into motley, by this light.
    Ang. Well sir, I euer thought y'ad the best wit
Of any man in Venice next mine owne,   85
But now Ile lay the bucklers at your feete.
    Lod. A poxe vpon thee, tame your bold hewed tongue,
Or by the Lord of heauen Ile pull it out.
    Aur. O my sweet friend, come Ile know more of this,
And tell thee all our fortune, hence good *Angelo.*   90
    Ang. O, if this man had patience to his braine,
A man might load him till he smart againe.   *Exit Ang.*
    Lod. Patience worthy friend,
Hee knowes you loue him for his knauish wit.   *Exeunt.*

[IV.iv]

Enter Leonoro, Temperance and Lyonell.

    Leo. Thou shalt not stay sweet *Temperance,* tell vs the manner of
our warre and wee'll leaue thee presently.
    Temp. Why that perlous man *Lodowicke,* according to your ap-

---

72-73 A . . . vpon?] *Parrott; as prose* (haue) ‖ **72** both;] ∼, ‖ **82** SD *Aside.*] *Parrott* ‖ **86** feete.]
∼, ‖ **87** bold] *Parrott;* bald (*See Textual Note*) ‖ **93-94** Patience . . . wit.] *Parrott; as prose* (hee) ‖
3 perlous] *Parrott;* perl's ‖

pointment was iumpe at three with mee, iust, eene full at your hower; Muffled as I wild you, ee'ne your fashion and your very leg for all the   5
earth, and followed me in so gingerly, that by my troth I must needs say, he was worthy the pleasuring; but in what a taking was I when I perceiued / his voyce? and when I saw my mistresse and he together   [I1]
by the eares?

Leo. What, did thy mistresse fight with him?   10

Temp. O king a heauen, she ranne vpon his naked weapon the most finely that euer liu'd, and I ran away in a swoone for feare.

Leo. Has she a good courage?

Lio. It seemes she is too honest for our companies, a little more good *Temperance.*   15

Temp. And when he saw me, he call'd me punke, and pandor, and doxie, and the vilest nicknames as if I had bene an arrand naughty-packe.

Leo. 'Tis no matter *Temperance,* hee's knowne and thou art knowne.   20

Temp. I thanke heauen for it, and ther's all indeed, I can stay no longer.   *Exit.*

Leo. Farewell honest *Temperance*: how was it possible, *Lodouico* should fit all these circumstances without the confederacy and trechery of this beldam? well, *Lodouico* must satisfie this doubt when   25
I see him.

Lio. That will be at the May night shew at Signior *Honorios.*

Leo. I would not meet him there, I shall offend him; but there I must needs be, and haue thee disguis'd like a woman.

Lio. Me sir?   30

Leo. No remedy, the Captain *Quintilliano* and I haue deuis'd it to gull his Lieutenant: for thou shalt dance with him, we will thrust him vpon thee, and then for his courting and gifts, which we will tell him he must win thee withall, I hope thou wilt haue wit enough to receiue the tone, and pay him againe with the tother, come   35
Lionell let me see how naturally thou canst play the woman.   *Exit.*

Lio. Better then you thinke for.   [*Exit.*]

[IV.v]

Enter Quintiliano and Innocentio.

Quint. Come Lieutenant, this nap has set a nap of sobriety vpon our braines, now lets sit heere and consult, what course were best for vs to take in this dangerous mansion of mans life. /

---

10 What,] ~∧ | mistresse] mistesse ‖ 17 nicknames] *Q(c);* nickname *Q(u)* (*See Textual Note*) | bene an] benena *Q(u);* ben an *Q(c)* (*See Textual Note*) ‖ 23 *Temperance*:] *Q(c);* ~, *Q(u)* ‖ 25 well,] ~∧ ‖ 37 SD *Exit.] Parrott* ‖ 2 were best] *Q(c);* wbest *Q(u)* ‖

Innoc. I am for you yfaith Captaine and you go to consult once.   [I1ᵛ]

Quint. I know it Lieutenant, say then what think'st thou? we   5
talk't of employment, of action, of honor, of a company and so forth.

Innoc. Did we so Captaine?

Quint. Did we so Asse? S'fut, wert thou drunke afore thou went'st
to the tauerne, that thou hast now forgotten it?

Innoc. Crie you mercy good Captaine, I remember I am your   10
Lieutenant.

Quint. Well sir, and so thou shalt be called stil, and I Captaine,
though we neuer leade other company then a sort of quart pots.

Innoc. Shall we Captaine? bith masse then lets neuer haue other
company in deed.   15

Quint. Why now th'art wise, and hast a minde transform'd with
maine right, and to confirme thee, I will compare the noble seruice
of a feast with the honourable seruice of the field, and then put on thy
hand to which thou wilt.

Innoc. Thanke you good Captaine, but do you thinke that warre   20
is naught sir?

Quint. Exceeding naught.

Innoc. Why then sir take heede what you say, for 'tis dangerous
speaking against any thing that is naught, I can tell you.

Quint. Thou saist wisely Lieutenant, I will not then vse the word   25
naught, nor speake ill of eyther, but compare them both, and choose
the better.

Innoc. Take heede then good Captaine, there be some pricke-ear'd
intelligencers conuaid into some wall or other about vs.

Quint. If there were I care not, for to say true, the first modell   30
of a battell was taken from a banquet. And first touching the offices
of both: for the generall of the field, there is the master of the feast,
for the Lieutenant Generall, the mistresse, for the Sergeant Maior,
the Steward, for the Gentleman vsher, the Marshall, for master oth'
Ordinance the Sewer, and all other officers.   35

Innoc. Yet y'are reasonable well Captaine.

Quint. Then for the preparation, as in a field is all kinde of artillery, your Cannon, your Demicannon, Culuerings, falkons, Sacres,
minions, and such goodly ornaments of a field, I speake no hurt of
em thou seest, Ile haue nothing to do with 'am.   40

Innoc. Hold you still there Captaine.

Quint. Besides other munition of powder and shot, and so for /
the feast, you haue your Court cubbords planted with flagons, cannes,   [I2]

14 Captaine?] ∼, ‖ **40** do] do do ‖ **43** Court] ∼, ‖

cups, beakers, bowles, goblets, basens and ewers: And more glorious
shew I wisse then the tother, and yet I speake no hurt of the other.   45

Innoc. No Ile be sworne Captaine.

Quint. Besides your munition of manchet, napery, plats, spoons,
glasses and so forth; Then for your kitchen artillerie, there shall you
see all your brasse peeces mounted in order, as your beefe-pots, your
chaldrons, your kettles, chafingdishes, ladles, spits, a more edifying   50
spectacle then your Cannon and Culuering, and yet I speake no hurt
of them neither.

Innoc. No Captaine, thus farre, I goe w'ee.

Quint. Then sir, as in the field the drumme, so to the feast the
dresser giues the Alarme, Ran tan tara, tan tan tantara tan.   55

Innoc. O how it stirres my stomacke?

Quint. First then sets forward a wing of light horse, as sallads,
brothes, sauces, stew'd meats, and other kickshores, and they giue a
charge, then do the battell ioyne Captaine Capon in white-brith,
Lieutenant calues head —   60

Innoc. Thats my place.

Quint. Ancient Surloigne, a man of a goodly presence, and full
of expectation, as your ancient ought to bee, then haue you *Sergeant
Piemeat, Corporall Conny, Lanceprizado Larke,* Gentlemen Pancakes,
and all the species of a company.   65

Innoc. Would we might fall to the fight once.

Quint. Why now growes the fight hot man, now shall you see many
a tall piece of beefe, many a tough capon go downe, and hee'rs the
triall of a mans stomacke; all the while the Artillery playes on both
hands, the Canons lay about them, the flagons go off, thicke and three-   70
fold, and many a tall man goes halting off, some quite ouerthrowne
both horse and foote.

Innoc. O my heart bleeds.

Quint. That is, thy teeth water. In conclusion, as the remnant
of the feast, (I meane such dishes as scap't the fury of the fight)   75
if they be seruiceable, are reseru'd to furnish out another day; if
they be maim'd or spoyld, they are sent abroad to relieue prisons and
hospitals. So the remainder of the fight, if they be seruiceable, they
are reseru'd to supply a second field; for the / fragments of the fight,   [12ᵛ]
viz. the maimd soldiers, they are sent likewise to furnish prisons and   80
hospitals; how sayest thou now Lieutenant, shall we to the feast, or
to the fight?

Innoc. No fighting good Captain, to the feast for Gods sake.

---

47 napery,] ∼∧ ‖ 53 w'ee] wee ‖ 60 head—] ∼. ‖ 63 your] *Dilke*; you ‖ 64 Gentlemen] ∼,
| Pancakes] *Dilke*; Panbakex ‖ 69 stomacke;] ∼, ‖ 76 day;] ∼, ‖ 79 field;] ∼, ‖ 81 hospitals;]
∼, ‖

Quint. Tha'rt a my mind right, and so will we presently march on to the sacke of the Emperours head, then to the May-night feast, and 85 shew at Signior *Honorios,* and there will be a wench there boy, a delicate yong morsell, a kinswoman of Signior *Honorios,* and her fathers only child, he a mighty rich *Clarissimo,* and her shalt thou court, winne her and weare her, thou hast wit at will.

Innoc. But shall that wench be her fathers sonne and heire 90 Captaine?

Quint. Shee shall be his heire, a mine honesty.

Innoc. But shall not my Mistris your wife bee at that show?

Quint. Shee shall, and we could finde her; *Fannio* has beene abroad this houre to seeke her: the Asse is stept into some corner or 95 other mourning for my absence. (*Enter Angelo and Francischina in disguise.*) See who comes here?

Ang. Come Cuze, march faire, me thinks thou becom'st a Page excellent naturally, cheere vp thy heart wench.   *Kisse her.*

Fran. Fie for shame, kisse in the streets? 100

Ang. Why not? truth seekes no corners, and 'twas a true loues kisse, and so is this.   [*Kiss again.*]

Quint. Ware riot, do'st thou marke Lieftenant?

Fran. Gods pitty, my husband.   *Exeunt Franc. Ang.*

Innoc. What were these Captaine? 105

Quint. Vpon my life the hindermost of them, is a wench in mans attire, didst thou not marke besides his slabbering about her, her bigge thighs and her splay feete?

Innoc. By the meskin me thought they were so indeede.

Quint. S'life, the hungry knaue her squire, could not hold in the 110 open streets.

Innoc. What should shee be?

Quint. The Doxie was muffeld in her cloake, I had but a glimpse of her; but s'light I will know her, shee passes not so, come wee'll follow. Ile beate the Rogue and take away's whore from him.   *Exeunt. /*

[IV.vi]

Enter Angelo and Francischina (AEmilia aboue).   [I3]

Ang. Come, courage Cuze, wee haue sailed the man of Warre out of sight, and here wee must put into harbour. Hist, ha'we *AEmilia?*

AEm. O welcome good *Angelo.*

---

85 the Emperours] *Q(c);* the the ~ *Q(u)* ‖ 88 *Clarissimo*] *Q(c); Charissimo Q(u)* ‖ 100 shame,] ~∧ ‖ 102 SD *Kiss again.*] ‖ 108 feete?] ~. ‖ SD *(Æmilia aboue).*] *Parrott subs.* ‖ 1 Come,] ~∧ ‖ 2 ha'we] hawe *(See Textual Note)* │ Æmilia] *Amila* ‖

Ang. Here take in, goe, get vp lightly, away, take heed you slip not
Cuze, remember y'are short heel'd.   5
Fran. Hold fast for Gods sake.
Ang. Nay hold you fast, you'll shame vs all else; so *Ioue* receiue thy
soule; I take away the ladder: Now till you haue deceiued the
Prouost, farewell, remember your lesson Cuze.   *Exit.*
Fran. I warrant you.   [*Exit with AEmilia.*]

(*Enter Quintil. and Innocentio.*)

Quint. How vnhappily did we misse 'em? they slipt into some
vaulting house, I hold my life.
Innoc. Faith it's good we mist 'em, she was some stale punke
I warrant her.
Quint. Twenty to one shee is some honest mans wife of the Parish   15
that steales abroade for a trimming, while he sits secure at home,
little knowing, God knowes, what hangs ouer his head; the poore
Cuckold esteeming her the most vertuous wife in the world. And
shoude one tell him, he had seene her drest like a Page following a
knaue thus, Ile lay my life he would not beleeue it.   20
Innoc. Why no Captaine, wiues take all the faith from their
husbands. And that makes 'em doe so many good workes as they doe.
Quint. Mercy for that yfaith Lieftenant, stand close.

(*Enter Fannio and Giacono.*)

Fann. My Mistris in mans apparell saist thou?
Giac. Thy Mistris in mans apparell I assure thee, and attended   25
by *Angelo.*
Fann. Would to heauen I had seene her, canst tell whither shee
went?
Giac. Full butt into *Lorenzoes* house, and if thou knewst him, thou
know'st wherefore, an ill-fauourd trimming is her errand.   30
Fann. 'Tis very well, shee trims my Captaine prettily, in the /
meane time his head paies for all, and yet alas poore hornestocke, he   [13ᵛ]
thinks her to haue no fault, but her too much dotage vpon him, well,
my conscience will not let me keepe her counsaile, he shall know on't.
Giac. Why man if both of vs should tell him her fault he will not   35
beleeue vs.
Fann. No, nor if he had seene it with his owne eyes I thinke,
I shal neuer forget how the profound Cockatrice hung on his sleeue
to day, and he shoude not from her sight, shee'd follow him into the

warres, one day should make an end of both their loues and liues; 40
and then to see him the wittall, my Captaine began to stroote, and
batle the pride of his merits that so heightned her affection.

Giac. True, and how the foppasty his Lieftenant, stept in to perswade with her, to take it patiently, for friends must part, we came not
all together, and we must not goe all together. 45

Fann. Well, 'twill not be for any man to follow him, if this were
knowne once.

Giac. Lord how all the boyes in the towne would flocke about him
as he walks the streets, as 'twere about a bagge-pipe, and hoote the
poore Cuckold out of his hornecase. 50

Fann. Well, and I were worthy to giue him counsaile, he should
e'ne faire and well hang himselfe.

Giac. No, no, keepe it from him, and say thou found'st her at a
womans labour.

Fann. A plague of her labour, the Captaines browes sweate while 55
shee labours.

Giac. If I were in thy case, I should laugh out right when I saw
him.

Fann. That dare not I doe, but as often as he turnes his backe to
me, I shall be here [*makes* V] with him thats certaine: or when I 60
follow him and his cheating stocke *Innocentio,* in the streets, I shall
imagine still I am driuing an Oxe and an Asse before me, and cry
phtroh, ho, ptrough.

Innoc. S'light Captaine take this and take all.

Quint. Not a word for the world, for if we should take notice of 65
his words the slaue would denie all, leaue it to me to sift it in priuate.
—Now sir, what newes with you? where's your Mistris, / that you [14]
range thus at your pleasure?

Fann. In health sir I trust.

Quint. Come forward you rogue you: come forward, whither 70
creepe you behinde so? where's your Mistris sir?

Fann. At a poore womans labour sir.

Quint. Very well sir, come Lieftenant, goe you afore, and doe you
follow him sir.

Fann. What, afore my Captaine sir? you shall pardon me. 75
Quint. Afore you rogue, afore. *Exeunt*

Finis Actus Quarti.

40 liues;] ∼, ‖ 60 SD *makes* V] *Dilke subs.*; V ‖ 66 priuate.—] ∼. ‖ 75 What,] ∼∧ | sir?] ∼: ‖

Actus Quintus.

Enter Honorio, Lorenzo, Gasparo and Angelo.

Hon. Signior *Lorenzo,* and *Gasparo,* y'are very welcome, we shall haue good company and sport to entertaine you ere long I hope, shall we not *Angelo?*

Ang. Yes sir, I haue enuited all you commanded me.

Lor. This is the honest man indeede, that tooke the paines to 5 come for me.

Gasp. And for me also.

Ang. No paines but pleasure sir, I was glad I had such good meanes to be knowne to your Worship.

Lor. Nay, I haue knowne you before, to be the seruant of Signior 10 *Honorio* here, I take it.

Hon. Not my seruant Signior *Lorenzo,* but my sonnes.

Lor. O, your sonne *Aurelios* seruant? beleeue me you or your sonne (in mine opinion, though I say it before him) made good choice of him: for he hath a good honest face, and to a man of iudgement 15 (I tell you) that's as good as a good surety for him. I will be better acquainted with you sir, pray you giue me your hand.

Ang. Both my hand and heart sir, shall be euer at your seruice. /

Lor. Thanks my good friend, Ile make thee laugh anone *Angelo.* [14ᵛ]

Ang. I thanke your Worship, you haue done so often. 20

Hon. [*Aside to Gasp.*] A notable wagge Signior *Gasparo.*

Gasp. [*Aside to Hon.*] How curiously *Lorenzo* thinks he carries the matter?

Lor. How now Gentlemen, ist a merry secret, that you smile so?

Hon. No secret Signior *Lorenzo,* but a merry conceipt we were 25 thinking on, to furnish our show anone, if it had beene thought on in time.

Lor. What was that I pray?

Hon. Marry sir, we had good sport to day with *Snayle* the chimney-sweeper. 30

Lor. Had you so sir?

Gasp. That euer was.

Lor. Lord that I had beene amongst you, but what more of him sir?

Hon. Marry sir, we were thinking how we might merrily deceaue 35 our company that is to come, if we could haue gotten him some

Magnificoes sute of the Citty, whom for his little stature and leane face he might resemble, that in that habit he might haue stolen some kinde fauours from the Ladies, to make him amends and please him for the anger we put him in.   40

Lor. It would haue made excellent merriment.

Ang. You are his best Master sir, and if it please you to send me for him by some token, Ile goe for him; otherwise he will not come to these Gentlemen.

Lor. Shall he come Gentlemen?   45

Amb. If you please sir.

Lor. Why then hearke thee *Angelo*; [*Aside to Ang.*] not for the world.

Ang. [*Aside to Lor.*] Thinke you me such an Asse sir?

Lor. Shall he haue one of my little brothers suites, and come in   50
amongst the Dames for him?

Hon. If you could, it would fit him exceedingly.

Lor. Much; now laugh *Angelo*: [*Aside to Ang.*] what Gentleman was that I spi'd aloft with my daughter think'st thou?

Ang. [*Aside to Lor.*] I know not sir; I beseech your Worship who   55
was it?

Lor. [*Aside to Ang.*] *Franke,* in mans apparell *Angelo.* /

Ang. O wonderfull.   [K1]

Lor. We cannot inuent a token, [*Aside to Ang.*] for my loue
Angelo.   60

Ang. O excellent.

Lor. We will hit it anone Gentlemen.

Amb. At your leasure sir.

Lor. [*Aside to Ang.*] The swaggerer her husband, had note of it
by his Page, and yet the same Page hath perswaded him since, that   65
'twas but a gullery.

Ang. 'Tis a notable cracke; [*Aside to Lor.*] and his Master hath such a pure beleefe in his wife, that hee's apt to beleeue any good of her.

Lor. True *Angelo,* enough for this time; [*Aside to Ang.*] thou shalt   70
make as if thou went'st for *Snaile,* and returne without him, saying thou canst not finde him.

Ang. Agreed sir.

Lor. Now Gentlemen, we haue deuis'd a wile to bring *Snaile* amongst vs, and I haue giuen *Angelo* order for a sute for him, that   75
is my little brothers, and him he shall counterfeit; goe *Angelo* seeke him out.

Ang. I will sir.   *Exit Ang.*

---

47 SD *Aside to Ang.*] *Dilke subs.* ‖ **49** SD *Aside to Lor.*] *Dilke subs.* ‖ **53** SD *Aside to Ang.*] *Parrott subs.* ‖ **55** SD *Aside to Lor.*] *Dilke subs.* ‖ **57** SD *Aside to Ang.*] *Dilke subs.* ‖ **59** SD *Aside to Ang.*] *Parrott subs.* ‖ **64** SD *Aside to Ang.*] *Dilke subs.* ‖ **65** him since,] ∼, ∼∧ ‖ **67** SD *Aside to Lor.*] *Dilke subs.* ‖ **70** SD *Aside to Ang.*] *Dilke subs.* ‖

Hon. Thanke you for this good Signior *Lorenzo.*

Gasp. It will quicken the company well. 80

(*Enter AEmilia, Lionell in womans dress, Francischina and another woman.*)

Lor. For their sakes and yours, I haue done it Gentlemen; and see the faire flocke come vpon vs.

Hon. Welcome faire Ladies, but especially you Lady, that are so meere a stranger; Signior *Lorenzo* you know yong *Leonoro?*

Lor. Very well sir, a gallant sparke. 85

Gasp. And I thinke you know his father.

Lor. Know him? Ifaith sir there was a reueller, I shall neuer see man doe his lofty tricks like him while I liue.

Hon. This Gentlewoman is his Neice sir.

Lor. His Neice? shee shall doe her selfe wrong not to be acquainted 90
with her deere vnkles companion. *Kisse her.*

Gasp. You know not this Gentlewoman sir?

Lor. Not very well sir indeede, but entertainement must be giuen, [*Aside to Fran.*] mercy *Franke* for thy mans apparell, a plague of all / swaggering husbands. Nay I must forth yfaith. — Signior *Honorio,* [K1ᵛ] 95 this is for your sake, am I not a kinde helpe to your entertainement?

Hon. An exceeding kinde one sir, and I exceedingly thanke you.

(*Enter Messenger.*)

Mess. The maskers are come sir.

Hon. Doe you and your fellowes attend them in.

Mess. We will sir. *Exit Mess.*

Hon. Sit gentle Ladies till the maskers raise you to dance.

Enter Aurelio, Leonoro, Quintiliano, and Innocentio,
in a maske dancing.

Hon. Welcome Gallants, O the roome's too scant, a hall Gentlemen.

Leo. [*Aside to Quint.*] See how womanly my Boy lookes *Quintiliano.*

Quint. [*Aside to Leo.*] 'Twill be rare sport. — Lieftenant, that sweet wench in the brancht gowne is the heire I told thee of. 105

Innoc. Gods me, Ile to her and kisse her.

Quint. O no, you must not vnmaske.

Innoc. No, no, Ile kisse her with my maske and all.

Leo. No Lieftenant, take her and court her first, and then kisse her.

Amb. To her, slaue. 110

Aur. There's thy wife too, *Quintiliano.*

Quint. True, little knowes shee I am so neere her; Ile single her out, and trie what entertainement a stranger may finde with her.

Aur. Doe so, and wee'll take vp the tother.

---

80 SD *Lionell . . . Francischina*] *Dilke subs.*; *Lionell, Francischina* ‖ **84** stranger;] ∼, ‖ **88** liue.] ∼: ‖ **91** companion.] ∼: ‖ **94** SD *Aside to Fran.*] *Dilke subs.* ‖ **95** yfaith.—] ∼, ‖ **103** SD *Aside to Quint.*] *Dilke subs.* ‖ **104** SD *Aside to Leo.*] *Dilke subs.* | sport.—] ∼; ‖ **110** *Amb.*] *Omnes.* ‖ **113** her.] ∼∧ ‖

     (Enter Angelo.)   *They dance.*

Ang. I can by no meanes finde *Snaile* sir.   115
Hon. The worse lucke, but what remedy?
Lor. [*Aside to Ang.*] Gramercy *Angelo.* — But Signior *Honorio,*
mee thinks I misse one flower in this femall garland.
 Hon. Whose that?
 Lor. Your Neice *Lucretia.*   120
 Hon. By my soule 'tis true; whats the reason *Angelo, Lucretia* is not
here? /
 Ang. I know no reason but her owne will sir.   [K2]
 Gasp. Ther's somewhat in it certaine.   *They dance againe.*
 Innoc. Did you see the play to day I pray?   125
 Lio. No, but I see the foole in it here.
 Innoc. Doe you so forsooth? where is he pray?
 Lio. Not farre from you sir, but we must not point at any body here.
 Innoc. Thats true indeede, cry mercy forsooth, doe you know me
through my maske?   130
 Lio. Not I sir, shee must haue better skill in bak't meats then I, that
can discerne a woodcocke through the crust.
 Innoc. Thats true indeede, but yet I thought I'de try you.

     (Enter Lodouico.)   *They dance.*

 Lor. What Nephew *Lodowicke,* I thought you had beene one of the
maskers.   135
 Lod. I vse no masking sir with my friends.
 Hon. No signior *Lodowick,* but y'are a very truant in your schoole
of friendship, that come so late to your friends.
 Gasp. Somewhat has crost him sure.
 Leo. Somewhat shall crosse him; *Lodouico* let me speake with 140
you.
 Lod. With me sir?
 Leo. You are the man sir, I can scarse say the Gentleman, for you
haue done a wrong the credit of a Gentleman cannot answere.
 Lod. Would I might see his face, that durst say so much.   145
 Leo. Obserue him well, [*unmasks*] he shoes his face that will proue
it when thou dar'st.
 Aur. How now *Leonoro,* you forget your selfe too much, to grow
outragious in this company.
 Leo. *Aurelio,* doe not wrong me, and your selfe, I vndertake your 150
quarrell; this man hath dishonord your Kinswoman *Lucretia,* whom
(if I might) I intended to marry.

---

117 SD *Aside to Ang.*] | *Angelo.*—But] ~; but | *Honorio*] *Parrott; Lorenzo* ‖ 121 *Angelo,*] ~∧ ‖
134 *Lodowicke*] *Lodwicke* ‖ 146 *Leo.*] *Dilke; Lod.* | SD *unmasks*] *Dilke subs.* ‖ 151 quarrell;] ~, ‖

Aur. Some error makes you mistake, *Leonoro,* I assure my selfe.

Hon. What interruption of our sport is this, gentlemen?

Lor. Are not my Nephew and *Leonoro* friends? 155

Lod. He charges me with dishonoring his mistris *Lucretia.* /

Hon. Birlady *Lodouico,* the charge touches you deeply, you must [K2ᵛ]
answere it.

Lod. I only desire I may sir, and then will referre me to your
censures. 160

Lor. Well Nephew, well; will you neuer leaue this your haunt of
fornication? I schoole him, and doe all I can, but all is lost.

Lod. Good Vnkle giue me leaue to answere my other accuser, and
then Ile descend, and speake of your fornication, as the last branch of
my diuision. 165

Lor. Very well, be briefe.

Lod. I will sir; The ground vpon which this man builds his false
imagination, is his sight of me at *Honorios* backe gate, since dinner,
where muffled in my cloke, kinde Madam *Temperance,* the attendant
of *Lucretia,* from the Tarrasse, wafted me to her with her hand; taking 170
me (as now I vnderstand) for this honest Gentleman; I, not knowing
what vse shee had to put me to, obaid the attraction of her signall, as
gingerly as shee bad me, (A plague vpon her gingerly) till shee lockt
me into *Lucretias* chamber, where *Lucretia* lying asleepe on her bed,
I thought it rudenesse to wake her; and (imagining when shee wak't 175
shee had something to say to me) attended her leasure at my ease, and
lay downe softly by her; when (hauing chaster and simpler thoughts
then *Leonoro* imagines because he measures my wast by his owne) in
the very coldnesse and dulnesse of my spirit, I fell sodainly a-sleepe. In
which my fancy presented me with the strangest dreame, that euer yet 180
possest me.

Lor. Pray God you did but dreame Nephew.

Lod. You shall know that by knowing the euent of it.

Hon. Goe to, pray let vs heare it.

Lod. Me thought *Lucretia* and I were at mawe, a game Vnkle that 185
you can well skill of.

Lor. Well sir I can so.

Lod. You will the more muse at my fortune; or my ouersights. For
my game stood, me thought, vpon my last two tricks, when I made
sure of the set, and yet lost it, hauing the varlet and the fiue finger to 190
make two tricks.

Lor. How had that beene possible? /

Hon. That had beene no misfortune sure but plaine ouersight. [K3]

---

153 mistake,] ∼∧ ‖ **154** this,] ∼∧ ‖ **171** Gentleman;] ∼, | I,] ∼∧ ‖ **173** me,] *Q(c)*; ∼. *Q(u)*
‖ **178** imagines] ∼) ‖

Gasp. But what was the reason you thought you lost it sir?

Lod. You shall heare; shee had in her hand the Ace of Hearts, me 195
thought, and a Coate-carde, shee led the bord with her coate, I plaid
the varlet, and tooke vp her coate, and meaning to lay my fiue finger
vpon her Ace of hearts, vp start a quite contrary card; vp shee rises
withall, takes me a dash a the mouth, drew a rapier he had lay by him,
and out of dores we went together by the eares. 200

Hon. A rapier he had lay by him?

Lor. What, a shee turned to a he? do'st thou not dreame all this
while Nephew?

Lod. No nor that time neither, though I pretended it; let him
be fetcht, I warrant you he will show as good cards as the best on you, 205
to proue him an heir Male, if he be the eldest child of his father.

Hon. This is exceeding strange: goe *Angelo,* fetch her and her
hand-maide.

Ang. I will sir, if her valure be not too hot for my fingers. *Exit.*

Hon. Could such a disguise be made good all this while without my 210
knowledge? to say truth, shee was a stranger to me, her father being
a Sicilian: fled thence for a disausterous act, and comming hither
grew kindly acquainted with me, and called me brother, at his death
committing his supposed daughter to my care and protection, till she
were restor'd to her estate in her natiue Country. 215

Lor. Was he in hope of it?

Hon. He was, and in neere possibility of it himselfe, had he liu'd
but little longer.

(*Enter Angelo, Lucretia in mans dress, and Temperance.*)

Ang. Here's the Gentlewoman you talkt of sir; nay you must come
forward too, graue Mistris *Temperance.* 220

Lod. How now sir? who wants gentility now I beseech you?

Leo. Who haue we here?

Lucr. Stand not amaz'd, nor disparage him: you see sir, this habit
truly doth sute my sexe, howsoeuer my hard fortunes haue made me a
while reiect it. 225

Hon. What hard fortunes? /

Lucr. Those you know of my father sir: who feard my following of [K3ᵛ]
him in my natiue likenesse, to the hauen, where he by stealth em-
barqu't vs, would haue discouer'd him, his offence being the slaughter
of a Gentleman, that would haue slaine him. 230

Hon. But did you not tell me you were betroth'd before this misfortune hapned, to a yong Gentleman of Sicily, call'd *Theagines*?

202 What,] ∼∧ ‖ **203** Nephew?] ∼. ‖ **206** heir] *Q(u)*; heire *Q(c)* ‖ **213** brother, at] ∼. At ‖
218 *Enter . . . Temperance.*] Parrott subs.; *Enter Angelo and Lucretia.* ‖ **219** sir;] ∼, ‖ **220** too,] ∼∧
‖ **229** vs, would] *Dilke*; vs, and would (*See Textual Note*) ‖

Lucr. I told you I was betroth'd to one *Theagine,* not *Theagines,* who indeed was a woman.

Lio. And yet whosoeuer had seene that *Theagine* since might haue   235
taken him for a man.

Lucr. Do you know her, Gentlewoman?

Lio. It seemes you will not know her.

Leo. [*Aside to Quint.*] Hearke how my boy plaies the knaue with
him.   240

Quint. A noble rogue. S'fut Lieutenant, wilt thou suffer thy nose to
be wipt of this great heire?

Innoc. S'light sir you are no handkercher are you?

Lucr. Pre thee forbeare; more happy then vnlookt for is this deere
accident: adopted and noble father, this is the Gentlewoman to whom   245
I told you I was betroth'd; the happy newes she had to relate to me,
made her a traueller, the more search of her passage made her a Page,
and her good fortune obtaind her —— this honest Gentleman to her
Master, who, I thanke him, (I being as he supposed me) lou'd me;
accept vs both for your children.   250

Hon. Most gladly, and with no lesse care then mine owne protect
you.

Quint. S'fut, how now *Leonoro*? new fireworkes?

Lod. Now sir, who wants gentility? this is a gentlemanly part of
you to keepe a wench in a Pages furniture?   255

Leo. It was more then I knew Sir, but this shall be a warning to me
while I liue, how I iudge of the instrument by the case againe.

Lucr. Nay it is you friend *Lodouico* that are most to blame, that
holding the whole feminine sexe in such contempt, would yet play the
pickpurse, and steale a poore maids maidenhead out of her pocket   260
sleeping. /

Leo. 'Twas but to cousen mee.   [K4]

Aur. And to be before me in loue.

Lor. And to laugh at me.

Lod. Nay, ieast not at me sweete Gentles, I v'sd plaine and man-   265
nerly dealing, I neither v'sd the brokage of any, as you know who did,
Leonoro, nor the help of a ladder to creep in at a wenches chamber
window (as you know who did, *Aurelio.*) Nor did I case my selfe in
buckrame, and crie Chimney sweepe (where are you vncle?) but I
was train'd to it by this honest matron here.   270

Temp. Meddle not with me sir.

234 woman.] ∼, ‖ **237** her,] ∼∧ ‖ **239** SD *Aside to Quint.*] ‖ **240** him] her (*See Textual Note*)
‖ **241** rogue.] ∼, ‖ **244** forbeare;] ∼, ‖ **246** betroth'd;] ∼, ‖ **249** who,] ∼∧ | (I being as]
Parrott; being (as | me;] ∼, ‖ **251** gladly,] ∼∧ | care] ∼, ‖ **253** *Leonoro*] *Leonora* ‖ **254** Now] *Dilke*;
New ‖ **266, 268** did,] ∼∧ ‖ **269** Chimney] chimney ‖

Lucr. I am beholding to her, she was loth to haue me leade apes in hell.

Quint. Looke that you keepe promise with me Ladie, when will thy husband be from home? 275

Fran. Not so soone as I would wish him, but whensoeuer you shall be welcome.

Quint. I very kindly thanke you Lady. [*unmasks*]

Fran. Gods me, I tooke you for Signior *Placentio.*

Quint. S'fut, thou liest in thy throte, thou knewst me as well as my 280 selfe.

Hon. What, Signior *Quintilian,* and friend *Innocentio?* I look't not for you here, and y'are much the better welcome.

Quint. Thanks dad *Honorio.* — And liues my little squire? when shall I see thee at my house lad? 285

Lor. A plague a your house, I was there too lately.

Lod. See Lordings, her's two will not let go till they haue your consents to be made surer.

Lor. By my soule, and because old *Gasparo* heere has bene so cold in his loue sute, if she be better pleas'd with *Aurelio,* and his father 290 with her, heauen giue abundance of good with him.

Hon. So you stand not too much vpon goods, I say, Amen.

Lor. Faith, vse him as your sonne and heire, and I desire no more.

Hon. So will I of mine honour, are you agreed youths?

Amb. And most humbly gratulate your high fauours. 295

Gasp. Faith, and *Ioue* giue 'em ioy together for my part. /

Lod. Yet is heere another nayle to be driuen, heer's a vertuous [K4ᵛ] Matron, Madam *Temperance,* that is able to doe much good in a commonwealth, a woman of good parts, sels complexion, helpes maids to seruices, restores maidenheads, brings women to bed, and men to 300 their bedsides.

Temp. By my faith, but saue votre grace sir.

Lod. Hath drinks for loue, and giues the diet.

Temp. Birladie, and thats not amisse for you sir.

Lod. For me, with a plague t'ee? 305

Temp. No nor for any man thats not sound I meane sir.

Quint. S'fut masters these be good parts in the old wench, wilt thou haue her Lieutenant? sheele be a good stay to the rest of thy liuing, the gallants will all honour thee at thy house I warrant thee.

Innoc. Fore God Captaine I care not if I haue. 310

Temp. Well yong Gentleman, perhaps it should not be the worst for you.

278 SD *unmasks*] *Dilke subs.* ‖ **284** *Honorio.*—And] ∼, and ‖ **293** Faith,] ∼∧ ‖ **299** complexion,] *Q(c);* complexionn *Q(u)* ‖ **305** t'ee] tee ‖ **307** *Quint.*] *Dilke; Lod.* ‖

Quint. Why law, thy vertues haue won her at first sight, shee shall
not come to thee emptie, for Ile promise thee that Ile make her able to
bid any Gentleman welcome to a peece of mutton and rabbet at all   315
times.

   Lor. Birladie, a good Ordinarie.

   Quint. Thow't visit sometimes *Dad.*

   Lor. That I will yfaith boy, in authority wise.

   Quint. Why then strike hands, and if the rest be pleas'd,   320
Let all hands strike as these haue strucke afore,
And with round Ecchoes make the welken rore.   *Exeunt.*

Finis Actus Quinti et vltimi.

319 boy,] ∼∧ ‖

HISTORICAL COLLATION

[Editions collated: Dilke (=*D* in *Old English Plays*, IV, 1814, pp. 3-114; Shepherd (=*S* in *The Works of George Chapman: Plays*, 1875, pp. 275-306); and Parrott (=*P* in *The Plays and Poems of George Chapman: The Comedies* [1914], pp. 164-232). Only substantive and semi-substantive variants are recorded; obvious errors are not recorded. Lemmata are taken from the present text. Where lemma represents the reading of Q copy-text, omission of siglum indicates agreement with lemma.]

I.i

SD] *A street in Venice P*

SD *Chorus . . . hand.] A number of young Persons are discovered singing and dancing; Lorenzo enters with Papers in his Hand: after some time they go out dancing. D*

22-24 How . . . we?] *as aside P*

22 wonder] wonder'd *D, S*

24 trow we] trow *P (Brereton conj.)*

28-29 Out . . . cranion.] *as aside P*

31 And . . . one.] *as aside P*

33 True . . . matches.] *as aside P*

35 Painted . . . you.] *as aside P*

37 It . . . deede.] *as aside P*

39 A . . . sincerity.] *as aside P*

45 O . . . whyniard.] *as aside P*

47 well] ~, *D, S, P*

50 man] man's *D*

53-55 A . . . businesse.] *as aside P*

56 you.] ~. *Running after* Angelo *and catching him P*

86 these] this *D*

110 thy] the *D, S, P*

112-13 hell; I] *S*; hell, hell I *Q, D, P*

113 thee—] *S*; ~. *Q, D, P*

115 parlous] *P*; parlesse *Q*; peerless *D, S*

116 t'ee] t'thee *D*

119 SD *Aside.] D, P; om. Q, S*

120 to] though I *D*

123 vnwieldy] unwieldly *D*

144 God . . . God] god . . . god *P*; good . . . good *D*

145 God] Good *D*

147 I thinke . . . rotten,] *as aside D; set off with hyphens P*

155 portion] *D, S, P*; potion *Q*

158 a] on *D*; o' *P (not hereafter recorded)*

160 profest;] ~_∧ S
170 SD *Falls prostrate.*] *Throws himself on the ground. D; He falls prostrate P; om. Q, S*
203 heeles] ears *D, P*
213 stormes] scorns
238 at the least] at least *S*
241 SD *Exeunt.*] *Exit* Lodovico *with the others P; Exit. Q, D, S*

I.ii

1-2 Thou . . . me] A purse of twenty pound in gold (*as marginal note*) *Q, P;* (*as SD after "gold" l. 148*) *S*
21 SD *Aside to Fran.*] *Aside. D, P; om. Q, S*
23 SD *Exit with Fran.*] *Exeunt Ang. and Fran. D; Exit* Angelo *with* Franceschina *P; Exit. Q, S*
37 SD *Aside.*] *D, P; om. Q, S*
54 throughly] thoroughly *D*
82 anger] hunger *S*
88 not you] you not *S, P*
91 th'art] thou'rt *D* (*not hereafter recorded*)
124 with] without *D, P*
146 Is] Is't *D*

II.i

SD] *A street in Venice P*
7 a] in *D;* o' *P*
8 say] say you *D*
32 you] *D, P; om. Q, S*
33 SD *Aside.*] *D; om. Q, S, P*

II.ii

23 tottred] tattered *D, S, P*
33 chickeene] zequine *S;* chequeen *P*
43 SD *Gasparo crosses*] *Gasparo crosses the stage D;* Gasparo *crosses over P; Enter Gasparo Q, S*
57 SD *Aside.*] *D, P; om. Q, S*
61 *Aurelio*] *D, P; Aurelia Q, S*
65 look'st] lookedst *S*
ador'd] adore *D*
74 SD *Exiturus.*] *Is going D*
83 harme an you,] ~, ~ ~_∧ *D*
an] on *S*
93 continue] contain *S*
96 disgracings] *Q(c);* disgracing *Q(u)*
132 If doe] If I doe *D, S, P*
147 knot] not *Q, D, S, P*
148 wenches.] ~? *D*
151 any] *P;* my *Q, D, S*
153 SD *Exit . . . AEmilia.*] *Exeunt D*

II.iii

1 God morrow] god morrow *P;* good morrow *D*
7 say Sir] say you Sir *D*

19 withall] *D, S, P*; with all *Q*
24 And . . . hundred.] *as aside D*
65 clocke, now; now] *P*; ∼, ∼, ∼ *Q*; ∼; ∼, ∼ *D*; ∼, ∼, *S*
68 *Lio.*] *Leo. Q, D, S, P*
   SD *Aside.*] *om. Q, D, S, P*

II.iv

14 *Ang.*] ∼. *Not observing them. D*; ∼. *Aside P*
22 make] to make *D*
41 waies] *Q(u)*; waie *Q(c), D, S, P*
43 enforce] inform *P*
44 away] a way *D*
51 SD *holds vp bracelets*] *Holds up the bracelets* (*after l. 53*) *D, S; Hold vp the bracelets Q* (*as marginal note*), *P* (*after l. 53*)
59 *Lorenzo, Lorenzo*] Lorenzo's, Lorenzo's *D*
84-85 Now . . . eare-shot.] *as aside D, P*
85 SD *Exit Fran.*] *after* "prayers" *l. 83 P*
   Well, beauty may] *P*; ∼∧ ∼ ∼ *D*; well may beauty *Q, S*
88 an] on *D, S, P*
106 cock] *D*; colt *Q, S, P*
130 *Lor.*] *D, S, P; Ang. Q*
147 villany] villany's *D*
153 in earnest to carry] it earnest to carry *Q, S*; in earnest carry *D, P*
166 *Snaile*] *D, S, P*; snaile *Q*
168 flues] fluds *Q(u), D*; fludgs *Q(c)*; *sings P* (*Brereton conj.*); *om. S*
169 weeds] *D conj., P*; words *Q, D, S*
176 Oyster] *D, S, P*; Oysters *Q*
   Eringos] *Q(c)*; Eringes *Q(u), D*
188 SD *Exit Lor.*] *D*; *Exit. Q*; *Exit* (*after l. 187*) *S, P*
   Signior *Lodouico.*] *om. D*
192 so] to *P*
199 mile] miles *D*
206 SD *Enter . . . sonne.*] *Enter Quintiliano, Innocentio, Fannio, Tailor, Tailor's Son: Quintiliano is reading a Bill. D; Enter Quintiliano, Innocentio, Fannio, Taylor, Taylors sonne, he Reades a bill. Q, S, P*
220 quartridge] quarterage *D, P*
237-38 him at night,] *S, P*; ∼, ∼ ∼∧ *Q, D*
243 SD *Exit cum filio.*] *Exeunt Tailor and Son. D*
252 And . . . halter.—] *as aside D, P*
255 health] healths *D, P*
271 th'ast] thou'st *D* (*not hereafter recorded*)
276 new] now *S, P*
281 not. My] *Q(u)*; not, my *Q(c), D, S, P*
283 childes] children *D*
   SD *Cuthbert Barber.*] *Cuthbert, a Barber. D; Cutbeard Barber P*
301 they] ye *D*
   themselues] yourselves *D*
302 you not] not you *D*

318 as good] of ~ ~ *D*
335 now? ... scrowle.] ~_∧ ... ~? *P*
342 wilt] thou wilt *D, S, P*
344 a] ha' *D*
347 Gentlemen] *S, P*; Gentleman *Q, D*
349 SD *Exit.*] *P*; *om. Q, D, S*
350 *Giouenelle;*] ~; (*aside to him*) *D, P*

III.i

SD] *Before the House of* Lorenzo *P*
22 at] then at *P conj.*
    SD *Exit.*] *D*; *Exit* Angelo *P*; *om. Q, S*
25 and tell] but will tell *D*
48 Aye] ah *D*
51 any] *D, P*; my *Q, S*
55 towne] towns *D*
57 SD *Exit.*] *D, P*; *om. Q, S*
72 *pace*] *paix D, P*
74 SD *stands aside*] *Exit P* (*after* place); *om. Q, D, S*
76 earnest] right earnest *S, P*
77 SD *stands aside*] *Exit P*; *om. Q, D, S*
    SD *Enter*] ~ *at the door of his house P*
96 a doore] the ~ *D*
123 life] long life *D*
128 venery] Venice *D*
162 *Lor.*] *D, S, P*; *Lod. Q*
    sweeper] sweep *D*
    SD *Aside.*] *D, P*; *om. Q, S*
172 hast] hadst *S, P*
186 ye] you *S, P*
    tro'e] troe *Q*; trow *D, S, P*
192 neuer] ever *D*

III.ii

SD] *Before the house of* Quintiliano *P*
4 whiles] while *D*
5 of] off *D, S*
6 bewrayed] betrayed *D*
10 SD *Aside.*] *om. Q, D, S, P*
16 y'aue] you've *D*
    Iayes] Iayles *Q, D, S*; Ioyes *P* (*D conj.*); toyles *Brereton conj.*
20 you;] *D, P*; ~, *Q, S*
23 torch] the torch *D*
30 SD *Lorenzo.*] ~_∧ *into the house P*

III.iii

SD] *Behind the house of* Lorenzo *P*
8 houses] horses *D, S, P*
11 you slaue] slave *D*

12 not,] ~∧ S
13 here.] ~. Aurelio *retires* P
25-26 Ile . . . better;] *as aside* D, P
33 cut] cut it S, P
45 loose] lose D
55 last] lasts S, P
57 does so distract] so distracts S
60 safe?] ~? *Aurelio comes forward.* D
61 *Aurelio?*] ~? Aurelio *advances* P
87 spurblinde] purblind D, S, P
91 agree.] ~. Aurelio *mounts* P
93 mouse.] ~. *Aurelio goes up.* D
104 SD *Exeunt Aur. and AEm.*] *Exeunt* Aurelio *and* AEmilia *into the house* P; *Exeunt.*
  Q, D, S
112 sunne] D, S, P; summe Q
123 a wench dreams] D, P; wench dreams Q; wench dreams not S
134 yet.] ~. *Makes signs.* D
139 SD *Exit Temp.*] P; D (*after* "in" *l. 138*); *om.* Q, S
149 tro'e] troe Q; trow D, S, P
150 SD *Exit with Lio.*] P; *Exeunt.* D; *Exit.* Q, S
161 what] who D
180 Arbor] harbour D
181 desire you] I desire your D
194 sir;] ~: *tastes it* D
199 SD (*He stands close.*)] *Retires behind the scene.* D
203 *And*] and (*sings*) D
205 she] he D
215 is] he is D
251 to call] did ~ D
253 seeing] seeming S, P
283 againe,] ~∧ S, P

IV.i

SD] *Before the House of* Quintiliano P
SD *Musicians*] Musicke Q, D, S, P
5 *Innoc.*] *Lio.* D, P
16 SD *Dances.*] D, P; *om.* Q, S
18 *Quint.*] ~. (*Sings.*) D
26 stands] bends D (*conj.*)
30 dores.] ~. *Sings.* D
34 SD *Exeunt Musicians.*] *om.* Q, D, S, P
48 and 'cheare] and I hear S, P; an I hear D
  SD *Exit.*] D, P; *om.* Q, S
51 God] God's D, S, P
52 SD *Within.*] P; *om.* Q, D, S
53 SD (*Enter . . . Lorenzo.*)] Quintiliano *enters dragging in Lorenzo.* D; *Enter* Quin-
  tilano *dragging in* Lorenzo P
63 SD *Aside.*] D, P; *om.* Q, S

71 hummerer] humourer *D*
83 SD *Aside.*] *D, P; om. Q, S*

IV.ii

SD] *Behind the House of* Lorenzo *P*
2 Heighted] Heighten'd *D*
12 desires] desire *D*
24 presence.] ∼. *They retire P*
   SD *Enter . . . running.*] *Enter* Lorenzo *hastily, and* Angelo *running after him. D*
44, 47 SD *Exit.*] *Exit into the house P*
45 berai'd] betrayed *D*
56-57 the pride] this ∼ *S, P*
59 SD *Exit.*] *D; Exit into the house P; om. Q, S*
60 Master.] ∼. *Enter* Aurelio *and* AEmilia *above P*
73 hast, &c.] *haste! D*
74 SD *Exit AEmil.*] ∼ ∼. Aurelio *descends P (after* "Dame;" *l. 75)*
76-77 shift you of this] shift this *D*
99 man] a man *D*

IV.iii

16 fortune makes] fortunes make *S*
21 thee,] *D, S, P;* ∼? *Q*
26 this you] *D, S, P;* the *Q*
39 you] *D, S, P; om. Q*
47 prou'd] *D, S, P;* prou' *Q*
53 does] do *D*
61 A] Oh *D*
82 SD *Aside.*] *P; om. Q, D, S*
84 y'ad] you'd *D*
86 Ile] I *D*
   your] thy *D*
87 bold hewed] *P;* bald ∼ *Q, D, S;* bald haired *Deighton conj.*; gall-dewed,
   Brereton conj.
89 know] no *S*
92 load] lead *D*
93 *Lod.*] *Aur. P*

IV.iv

SD *Lyonell.*] Lionello *P*
3 perlous man] per'lous ∼ *P;* perl'sman *D;* pearl's man *S;* perl's man *Q*
4 eene full] e'en *D*
5 ee'ne] e'er *D*
10 with] *om. S*
17 nicknames] *Q(c);* nickname *Q(u)*
35 tone] the one *D, S*
37 SD *Exit.*] *P; om. Q, D, S*

IV.v

SD] *Before the house of* Quintiliano *P*
42 and so] so *D*
44 And] *om. D*
   more] a more *D, P*

57 sets] set's *S*
58 kickshores] kickshaws *D, S, P*
59 white-brith] white-broth *D, S, P*
63 your] *D, P*; you *Q, S*
64 Gentlemen] Gentleman *S, P*
    Pancakes] *D*; Panbakex *Q*; Pancake *S, P*
74 teeth water] ~-~ *D*
84 my] *om. D*
96 SD *in disguise.*] *in Boy's Clothes D*
99 SD *Kisse*] *Kisses D, S*
102 SD *Kiss again.*] *om. Q, D, S, P*
104 Gods . . . husband.] *as aside D*
109 meskin] maskin *D*
111 streets] street *D*

IV.vi

SD] *Behind the house of* Lorenzo *P*
SD (*AEmilia aboue*).] *om. Q, D, S, P*
2 ha'we] hawe *Q*; ha *D, S, P*
    AEmilia?] ~! *Enter* AEmilia *above P*
6 sake.] ~! *Goes up the ladder. D*; ~! *She mounts P*
10 SD *Exit with AEmilia.*] *P*; *om. Q, D, S*
23 close.] ~. *They retire P*
29 knewst] knowst *D*
41 stroote] strut *D, S, P*
45 all together] altogether *D*
60 SD *makes* V] makes horns *D*; making horns *P*; V *Q, S*
64 S'light . . . all.] *as aside D*
65-66 Not . . . priuate.—] *as aside D*
66 priuate.—] ~.ₐ *advancing P*
67-68 you range] you can range *S, P*

V.i

SD] *A Hall in the House of* Honorio *P*
21 SD *Aside to Gasp.*] aside *P*; *om. Q, D, S*
22 SD *Aside to Hon.*] aside *P*; *om. Q, D, S*
46 *Amb.*] *An. S*
47 SD *Aside to Ang.*] aside *P*; (*whispers*) *D*; *om. Q, S*
49 SD *Aside to Lor.*] aside *D, P*; *om. Q, S*
53 SD *Aside to Ang.*] aside *D*; Aside (*after* Much;) *P*; *om. Q, S*
55 SD *Aside to Lor.*] *Aside. D, P*; *om. Q, S*
57 SD *Aside to Ang.*] *Aside. D, P*; *om. Q, S*
59 SD *Aside to Ang.*] aside *P*; We . . . Angelo. *as aside D*; *om. Q, S*
63 *Amb.*] *An. S*
64 SD *Aside to Ang.*] *Aside. D, P*; *om. Q, S*
67 SD *Aside to Lor.*] *Aside.* (*after* "Ang.") *D, P*; *om. Q, S*
70 SD *Aside to Ang.*] *Aside.* (*after* "Lor.") *D, P*; *om. Q, S*
73 Agreed sir.] *as aside D, P*

80 SD *in . . . dress,*] *dressed in Woman's Clothes D; in a woman's dress P; om. Q, S*
83 Lady,] ~, *to* Lionello *P*
91 SD *Kisse*] *Kisses D, S*
94 SD *Aside to Fran.*] *Aside. D, P; om. Q, S*
101 SD *a maske*] *masks D*
103 SD *Aside to Quint.*] *Aside. D, P; om. Q, S*
104 SD *Aside to Leo.*] *Aside. D, P; om. Q, S*
110 *Amb.*] *Omnes. Q, D, S, P*
117 SD *Aside to Ang.*] *om. Q, D, S, P*
    Honorio,] *P; Lorenzo, Q, D, S*
146 SD *unmasks*] *Unmasking D, P (D places SD before "Obserue"); om. Q, S*
162 fornication?] ~? (*To the others.*) *D*
189 my game] the ~ *D*
198 start] starts *P*
    a quite] quite a *S*
205 on] of *D*
209 valure] valour *D, S, P*
218 SD *Enter . . . Temperance.*] *P (Lucretio); Enter Angelo and Lucretio in his Male Dress. D; Enter Angelo and Lucretia. Q, S*
221 *Lod.*] ~. (*To Leo.*) *D*
223 him:] ~. (*To Leo.*) *D*
229 vs, would] *D, P; vs, and would Q, S*
235 *Lio.*] *Leo. S*
238 her.] ~. *unmasking and embracing Lucretio. P*
239 SD *Aside to Quint.*] *om. Q, D, S, P*
240 him] her *Q, D, S, P*
243 *Innoc.*] ~. (*To Lucretio*) *D*
244 more] not more *D conj., P*
248 her——] ~∧ (*to* Leonoro) *P*
249 (I being as] *P; being (as Q, D, S*
254 Now] *D, P; New Q, S*
274 Looke . . . Ladie,] *as aside D; as aside to Franceschina P*
276-77 Not . . . welcome.] *as aside D*
278 SD *unmasks*] *D (before "I"); unmasking P (before "I"); om. Q, S*
284 *Honorio.*—] ~.∧ *to* Lorenzo *P*
286 A . . . lately.] *as aside D, P*
295 *Amb.*] *Both D*
299 complexion] *Q(c); complexionn Q(u); complexions D*
302 saue] *sauve P*
307 *Quint.*] *D, P; Lod. Q, S*
315 rabbet] a rabbit *D*
318 Thow't] Thou'lt *D*

PRESS-VARIANTS

[Copies collated:[1] BM¹ (British Museum 644 d. 47); BM² (British Museum C. 12. g. 5 (4)); Bodl¹ (Bodleian Douce c. 249); Bodl² (Bodleian Mal. 241 (4)); CSmH (Huntington Library); DFo (Folger Shakespeare Library); Dyce (Victoria and Albert Museum); ICU (University of Chicago); IU (University of Illinois); MH (Harvard University); NN (New York Public Library); PU (University of Pennsylvania); TxU (University of Texas); Worc (Worcester College, Oxford)]

Sheet C (outer forme)

Corrected: BM¹, Bodl¹, Bodl², Dyce, Worc, CSmH, DFo, NN, PU, MH, TxU, ICU, IU

Uncorrected: BM²

Sig. C3

   II.ii.96 disgracings?] disgracing?

Sheet D (outer forme)

Corrected: BM¹, BM², Bodl¹, Bodl², Dyce, Worc, CSmH, DFo, NN, PU, MH, TxU, IU

Uncorrected: ICU

Sig. D2ᵛ

   II.iv.84 loue-squire.] loue-squire,

Sig. D3

        109 ouer-come] oner-come
        115 slander;] slander,
        119 tickil'st] ticki'st
        120 auoid] auod
        122 Citie,] Citie

Sheet D (inner forme)

Corrected: BM¹, BM², Bodl¹, Bodl², Dyce, DFo, NN, PU, MH, TxU, IU

Uncorrected: Worc, CSmH, ICU

[1] All variant states of Q preserved in extant copies are represented in the copies collated for the present edition. In addition to those listed above, copies from the British Museum (Ashley 379), University of Glasgow, National Library of Scotland, Yale University, Chapin Library, and the Pforzheimer Library have been collated by Professor Akihiro Yamada; but none of these contains additional variants. See the table of press-variants in Professor Yamada's "Bibliographical Studies of George Chapman's *May-Day* (1611) Printed by William Stansby," *Journal of the Faculty of Liberal Arts and Science,* Shinshu University, No. 15 (December, 1965), 13-34. (Professor Yamada's report that a variant state of A inner exists in the University of Illinois copy is erroneous; several words on sig. A2 of that copy have been altered by hand.)

Sig. D1ᵛ

    II.iv.13 SD *Angelo.*)] *Angelo.*

        41 waie] waies

Sig. D4

        168 fludgs] fluds

        176 Eringos] Eringes

Sheet E (inner forme)

Corrected: Bodl¹, CSmH, Dyce, ICU, IU, MH, NN, TxU

Uncorrected: BM¹, BM², Bodl², DFo, PU, Worc

Sig. E1ᵛ

    II.iv.281 not, my] not. My

Sig. E3ᵛ

    III.i.8 him-selfe] him‾selfe

        10 Snaile] snaile

          he triumphes] hetriumphes

        11 as curiously] ascuriously

        12 sweepers)] sweepers,

        13 beautifull] beautifull)

          lips] lipst

        18 world] worl

        20 one by one to] one to by one

        25 *Lorenzo*] *Loreuzo*

Sig. E4

    III.i.38 imagine] Imagine

        44 neither] nerther

        63 case:] case

        64 case] case:

Sheet F (outer forme)

Corrected: BM¹, BM², Bodl¹, Bodl², CSmH, DFo, Dyce, ICU, IU, MH, PU, TxU, Worc

Uncorrected: NN

Sig. F1

    III.i.100 me?] me.

Sheet G (outer forme)

Corrected: BM¹, BM², Bodl¹, CSmH, DFo, Dyce, ICU, IU, MH, NN, PU, TxU

Uncorrected: Bodl², Worc

Sig. G1

    III.iii.114 it,] it

Sheet I (outer forme)

Corrected: BM¹, BM², Bodl¹, Bodl², CSmH, DFo, Dyce, ICU, IU, NN, PU, TxU, Worc

Uncorrected: MH

Sig. I1
    IV.iv.17 nicknames] nickname
          ben an] benena
       23 *Temperance*:] *Temperance*,
    IV.v.2 were best] wbest
Sig. I2ᵛ
    IV.v.85 the] the the
       88 *Cla-rissimo*] *Cha-rissimo*

Sheet K (outer forme)

Corrected: BM¹, BM², Bodl¹, Bodl², DFo, Dyce, ICU, IU, MH, NN, TxU,
    Worc
Uncorrected: CSmH, PU
Sig. K2ᵛ
    V.i.173 me,] me.
Sig. K3
    V.i.206 heire] heir
Sig. K4ᵛ
    V.i.299 complexion,] complexionn

TEXTUAL NOTES

I.i

112-13 hell; I beseech thee —] I accept Shepherd's emendation on the assumption that Lorenzo, having mentioned "the good Deuill" earlier in the line, would not then address "hell" with the personal pronoun "thee"; Lorenzo has been beseeching Angelo (to be his emissary to Francischina) throughout this scene, and I conjecture, *contra* Parrott, that he is doing so here also. Compositor X, who set this passage, erroneously repeated a word at IV.vi.37, and I conjecture that he made a similar mistake here.

144 Godge you God morrow . . . godge you God morrow] Since the phrase "God morrow" appears twice in this line, again in l. 145, and again at II.iii.1, it almost certainly has MS authority. The real problem here concerns the pronunciation of Q's "Godge": should it be divided clearly into subject and verb, as Parrott believes, or might Gasparo have pronounced it as a one-syllable word with a soft *g*? I raise the latter possibility because Gasparo is introduced in the stage direction of l. 138 as "an olde Clowne," and I think we might expect an unusual form of address from him. Further, Madam Temperance at II.iii.1 uses the greeting "God yee God Morrow," which omits the verb entirely. I therefore see no justification for either Dilke's or Parrott's emendation, and I allow the Q reading to stand.

I.ii

124 with] If we assume that Quintiliano is giving Innocentio straightforward advice on how to behave, the "without" must be the accepted reading; but I would argue that Quintiliano is here making contradictory suggestions, talking near-nonsense, to his foolish lieutenant. Each of the three statements of advice in this speech (ll. 123-28) is in a sense a balance of two contradictions:
(1) "for your place, take it as it fals, // but so as you thinke no place to good for you;"
(2) "fall too with ceremony whatsoeuer the company be: // and as neere as you can, when they are in their Mutton, be thou in thy Wood-Cocke, it showes resolution."
(3) "Talke any thing, thou car'st not what, // so it be without offence, and as neere as thou canst without sence."
The riddling non-sequiturs of Quintiliano's speech at ll. 137-43 confirm that Quintiliano's purpose in this conversation is to befuddle Innocentio rather than to instruct him.

II.ii

147 knot] The MS form may well have been Q's "not," but I conjecture that the intended word is "knot," glossed by the *NED* as an adjective meaning "knitted" and/or "fastened."

151 any] I adopt Parrott's emendation in this doubtful case chiefly because this same emendation is clearly required in a later passage, III.i.51 (see note); the fact that Compositor Y misread MS "any" as "my" at III.i.51 increases the likelihood that Compositor X did so here. (Cf. also III.iii.112, where Compositor Y set "summe" for MS "sunne.")

II.iii

68 *Lio.*] The word "Boy" in this line, as in l. 67, clearly refers to Lionell, a woman disguised as Leonoro's boy page, and the words "him" and "he" to Leonoro, who is of course unaware of Lionell's true identity. Thus the speaker must be Lionell and not Leonoro.

II.iv

41 waies] Although "out of the waies" did not suit the proofreader, we may be fairly certain that it was the MS reading. In another speech in this scene, Angelo says, "go thy waies in" (l. 69), and the phrase "go thy waies" appears also in *The Widow's Tears* (sigs. C4, D4), *The Gentleman Usher* (sig. H1), *Monsieur D'Olive* (sig. D4^v), and *Humorous Day's Mirth* (sig. E1). In light of this evidence of Chapman's fondness for "waies," one who conjectures that Q(c)'s "waie" restores the MS reading must assume an amazing coincidence between Chapman's demonstrated habit and Compositor Y's "mistake" here.

43 enforce] Although for Parrott the Q reading "makes nonsense," the preceding exchange between Angelo and his masters makes "enforce" perfectly appropriate here. Angelo is being asked to do his master Aurelio a favor, in anticipation of which Aurelio says to him (1.22), "make me no more thy master, but thy friend," and (l. 35) "Which if thou do'st *Angelo,* be sure of reward to thy wishes." Thus Lodowick might well say that once the favor is done, Angelo should "enforce" them (i.e., demand of them, press them, urge them) in claiming his promised reward. This reading also gives added point to Angelo's response (l. 44), "I will not faile sir."

85 Well, beauty may] The emendation restores the passage in two ways: first, the parallelism of the clause with the following clause, "riches may tempt others," is restored; second, and perhaps more important, the introductory "Well," in being changed from adverb to interjection, is restored to conformity with many other, similar uses of this word in the play. Apparently the compositor erroneously anticipated the "mays" that occur later in the line.

Further justification for reversing the word order here is provided by the fact that Compositor Y elsewhere in Q reverses the proper order both of letters (IV.iv.17) and of words (III.i.20). Perhaps significant also, is the fact that Compositor Y was obviously having difficulty in justifying this line: an unusually large quad separates "may" and "beauty," the last two complete words in the line.

106 cock] Dilke gives two reasons for the emendation: that the phrase "old colt" is a contradiction in terms; and that Angelo's reference to "fethers" in the next line more logically follows "cock" than "colt." I would also argue that the verb "strike" in l. 106 accords with "cock" and not with "colt."

There are two possibilities as to how MS "cock" became "colt" in Q. One is misreading, the other results from the fact that the word preceding "Colt" in Q is "old": Compositor Y, frequently prone to the corrupting influence of proximate forms (see note to II.iv.153), may have set "colt" because the "ol" combination (letter sequence and/or sound) carried over from the preceding word.

153 doe in earnest] I emend here because the unusual use of the word "earnest" (apparently adverbial) in the Q reading makes it suspect, and because Y is the compositor. "Earnest" can be restored to its frequent use following "in" by conjecturing that Compositor Y set the word "it," which appears correctly four words later, rather than MS "in" before "earnest." This conjecture is the more likely because of the fact that at least nine of Compositor Y's errors elsewhere in Q are obviously due to the corrupting influence of a proximate form.

168 flues?] The question here is whether the Q(u) or Q(c) reading, both of which are obviously erroneous, is closer to MS; that is, whether the "g" added by the proofreader has MS authority. I conjecture that the Q(c) reading "fludgs" does not derive from a fresh MS consultation for two reasons: first, we know that at least one other of the four proof corrections in this forme (D inner) derives from the proofreader's judgment rather than from MS (see note to II.iv.41); second, I know of no reasonable emendation here which includes Q(c)'s "g." (Parrott's conjecture that the direction "sings" was the MS form is highly unlikely. The word appears in correct form in the preceding line; and one would have to conjecture that Compositor Y misread four consecutive letters in setting "fluds." Another difficulty involves the principle of the *difficilior lectio;* it is most unlikely that a common form like "sings" would be set as "fluds.")

If we use Q(u)'s "fluds" as a basis for conjecture, we very easily reach the form "flues" (chimneys) as a likely MS reading; the word would be spoken as an exclamation or indignant question by Lorenzo in a tone of shock and disgust at the demeaning prospect of a chimney-sweeper's disguise. This emendation would require only the modest conjecture of an "e-d" misreading, a likely graphic confusion which might have been strengthened by Compositor Y's ignorance of the rather obscure word "flues."

There remains the question of why the proofreader altered "fluds" to the totally unintelligible "fludgs" (*NED* records no other appearances of the word). To this there is no clear answer other than to note that he did the same kind of thing at III.i.12,13 (E inner), where he incorrectly moved a parenthesis.

169 weeds] The context of the reading requires the emendation of borrowed speech ("words") to borrowed apparel ("weeds"): it is clothing, not words, which will cause Lorenzo to *resemble* (1. 171) Snail's person; Lorenzo immediately (1. 171) questions Angelo's suggestion in terms which suggest clothing ("But is that a fit resemblance to please a louer *Angelo?*") and Angelo's answer (ll. 172-74) refers specifically to clothing ("you shall no sooner enter but off

goes your rustie skabberd . . . a bath of fernebraks for your fustie bodie . . .").
This misreading is a plausible one, both graphically (cf. the same "e-o" confusion in the Q form "Eringes" at l. 176 of this scene) and because of the fact
that Q's "words" is so much more common a word than the conjectured MS
"weeds."

281 not. My] At first glance the uncorrected form seems abrupt and incomplete.
But more careful scrutiny shows the uncorrected form to be the preferred form.
The construction here is identical to that at I.ii.78,79 (except that here the
word "not," rather than the word "if," receives the emphasis), in which the
"if"-clause, left incomplete, is said indignantly and scornfully, almost mockingly,
by Quintiliano in reply to his doubting lieutenant. That is, the uncorrected
state here shows the Captain to be confident and scornful of all doubts as to
his prowess. In contrast, the corrected form, in which the "if"-clause is a true
conditional, shows him uncertain of initial success. In the corrected reading,
his plan to secure his "Valentine" is a provisional plan which would follow a
possible failure; in the uncorrected reading the Captain scoffs at the possibility
of failure and then outlines his plan. The latter alternative seems to me much
more characteristic of the blustering Captain, who in this scene is quite eager
to impress his companions with his prowess.

III.i

51 any] The emendation is required because (as far as we know) Lodowick has
no "man," or servant. Further, the phrase "any man" anticipates Lodowick's
next speech in which he speaks of making a public display of Lorenzo. Cf.
II.ii.151, where the same misreading of MS "any" as "my" appears in the work
of the other compositor, X.

72 *de la pace*] The pronunciation of Q's "pace," an Englished version of French
"pas," makes a pun with *"Pax"* in the following phrase. I retain Q's *"de la
pace"* because it includes the concept of time which accords with the word
"patient" in the next line: in a sense all three of the clauses here are a repetition of the idea of being humble or patient: "take fortune *de la pace,* kisse the
Paxe, and be patient like your other neighbours." Though Dilke's emendation
has the advantage of creating an exact correspondence of *"paix"* and *"Pax,"* it
has as well the liability of removing the time element from the French phrase.
(The fact that it also makes good French of the Q reading does not particularly
increase its plausibility: at V.i.302 Temperance mixes the two languages with
her "saue votre grace."

186 tro'e] The verb "trow" appears three times in Q, once in the form "trow
we" (I.i.24) and twice in the form "troe" (here and at III.iii.149), the word(s)
concluding a question in all three instances. Because the pronoun is present at
I.i.24, and since the elided form of "ye" appended to another word appears
without apostrophe elsewhere in Q ("wee" for "wi'ye," "tee," "dee"), I punctuate Q's "troe" both here and at III.iii.149 to indicate clearly that the final "e"
should be sounded.

III.ii

16 Iayes] The verb "swarme" renders the Q reading absurd; and Parrott's

"joys" is only slightly better. That jays should swarm to salute Lorenzo's arrival at Francischina's house is particularly fitting, since "jay" in current usage designated not only a bird but (*NED*) "a person absurdly dressed; a stupid or silly person; a simpleton." Lorenzo is of course all of these as he approaches Francischina's house in the disguise of a chimney-sweep.

III.iii

8 houses] Previous editors have apparently missed the point of this exchange between Lodowick and Aurelio which culminates in Lodowick's statement that "we haue watred our houses in Helicon." Lodowick had introduced the subject of the lovers' meeting place with his question (ll. 2,3), "This is the Tarrasse where thy sweet heart tarries; what wouldst thou call it in Rime?" Aurelio then calls it (l. 4) a "celestiall spheare" containing more beauty than "Dardanian Ida" (l. 6). This exchange leads directly to Lodowick's reference to houses watered in Helicon; Aurelio has indeed been showering the house, the place of his meeting with AEmilia, with the water of Helicon.

IV.i

5 *Innoc.*] I see no need to emend Q here; possibly Innocentio learned of Leonoro's planned meeting with Lucretia in the off-stage conversation just completed by the group.

48 and 'cheare] Parrott thought it "unlikely that Chapman meant Quintiliano to use, in this place only, the rustic form of the pronoun, *Ich*." However, the dramatic context corroborates the Q reading. Quintiliano is obviously drunk; he speaks of smelling a voice (l. 47), and, as he leaves the stage, Innocentio says "O me, hee'll draw vpon his owne shaddow in this humour, if it take the wall of him." This special emphasis upon Quintiliano's drunkenness and anger support my conjecture that the rustic form of the pronoun is correct.

IV.iii

26 this you] The line in Q is obviously corrupt, and Dilke's emendation seems the simplest way of restoring both sense and meter.

87 bold] The only meaning of "bald" which could apply here is that of "palpable" or "evident," which is hardly satisfactory when coupled with "hewed." "Bold ("presumptive," "forward") fits the context perfectly. Misreading of MS. "o," by the way, occurs elsewhere in Compositor Y's work (II.iv.169, V.i.253).

IV.iv

17 nicknames . . . bene] Here again Compositor Y's errors relate to problems of spacing and justification. Probably his preoccupation with justifying the line caused him to reverse (and crowd) the two letters in "an," which is the third word from the end of this very crowded line. (Cf. his similar errors involving reversal of proper order at II.iv.85 and III.i.20.) The omission of "s" from the obviously correct "nicknames" could have resulted either from lack of space (cf. his omissions at III.iii.123 and IV.iii.26) or from the fact that "as," which follows "nickname" in Q, contains the "s" sound (cf. his error at IV.iii.39).

In order to add an "s" to "nickname," the proofreader had to eliminate a letter from the severely crowded line; thus "ben," rather than Y's customary "bene," appears in Q(c).

IV.vi

2 ha'we] Previous editors considered "hawe" an interjection (i.e., a form of "ha"); but in all other occurrences in Q where this word is unmistakably an interjection, it is spelled "ha." Furthermore, the occurrence of "ha" as a verb ("haue") at I.ii.40 provides additional support for my conjecture that Q's "hawe" is two words.

V.i

229 vs, would] The Q reading cannot be right; I accept Dilke's emendation as the likeliest retoration.

240 him] Lucretio, though formerly disguised as a woman, appears in male dress in this scene (ll. 223-24, "this habit truly doth sute my sexe") and there seems to be no reason for Leonoro to refer to him as "her" here. I conjecture that this error, like others in the work of Compositor Y, resulted from the influence of a proximate form: the last word of the preceding line is "her." (Cf. l. 254 of this scene, also set by Y, in which occurs a similar error.)

Monsieur D'Olive

edited by Allan Holaday

❖

TEXTUAL INTRODUCTION

To convincing arguments by Fleay and Stoll that link *Monsieur D'Olive* with the early reign of James I, Parrott added a further observation that since plague had closed the theaters from May, 1603, until April, 1604, and since throughout the following autumn London had hummed with talk of three elaborate embassies — the probable originals of D'Olive's abortive expedition — composition must have occurred during the fall or early winter of 1604-05.[1] Publication in 1606, according to the quarto title page, followed "sundrie" performances at Blackfriars, only one edition appearing in the seventeenth century.[2] But William Holmes, for whom T. C. (presumably Thomas Creede) printed the quarto, did not record his title at Stationers' Hall. Indeed, a lack of unequivocal reference to *Monsieur D'Olive* in either the stationers' registers or Henslowe's *Diary* has fostered its conjectural identification with various "lost" plays. Fleay, for example, supposed it to be the work to which two of Henslowe's puzzling titles, the "ylle [i.e., isle?] of A woman" and the "ffounte of new facianes," refer. But though, as the *Diary* makes clear, both the "ylle" and the "ffounte" were Chapman's, and though both titles may refer to one play, that play almost certainly is not *Monsieur D'Olive*. Fleay's hypothesis, which rests upon an inconsequential correspondence (i.e., "D'Olive's speech about teaching fashions to younger sons"), proves completely unconvincing.[3]

[1] F. G. Fleay, *A Biographical Chronicle of the English Drama, 1559-1642* (London, 1891), I, 59; E. E. Stoll, "On the Dates of Some of Chapman's Plays," XX, *MLN* (Nov., 1905), 206-09; T. M. Parrott, *The Comedies,* II, 773 ff. Fleay, noting that the play "alludes to King James' Knights," remarked that it "appears to belong to 1604." A reference to the calling in of monopolies (an event of May 7, 1603) and the fact of Chapman's imprisonment in 1605 provide Stoll's *terminus a quo* and *terminus ad quem*.
[2] For bibliographical description, see W. W. Greg, *A Bibliography of the English Printed Drama to the Restoration,* I, 236. Sheets from this edition, together with those for several other Chapman plays, figured in a nonce edition of 1652.
[3] Foakes and Rickert, *Henslowe's Diary,* pp. 91, 99, 101. G. A. Wilkes, in "Chapman's 'Lost' Play, *The Fount of New Fashions,*" *JEGP,* LXII (Jan., 1963), 77-81, suggests that *The Fount* was an early version of *Sir Gyles Goosecap.* His hypothesis rests on references to new fashions in *Sir Gyles* and on the appropriateness of the earlier title to the later play.

Preservation in the quarto of a special Chapman spelling,[4] some irregularities in the speech heads (e.g., "Duke" is substituted for "Phil." and "Pag." for "Dig."), numerous stage directions in Latin, and others which, though in English, are not sufficiently explicit, one assumes, to suit a bookkeeper,[5] plus an occurrence in the stage directions of a particular Chapman word, *exiturus*,[6] all imply that the printer worked from some sort of author's papers. And one finds corroboration for this assumption in the conclusions of Professor Akihiro Yamada, who has sought in detail to describe the manuscript that served as printer's copy.[7] Yamada calls particular attention to an allegedly irrelevant comment by Eurione, to mention of several mute characters, particularly Ieronime, and to the unusual location on the printed page of several stage directions. These and other characteristics of the quarto support his conclusion that Chapman, in transcribing his original draft, effected minor textual alterations through cancellations, interlineations, and marginal additions. To this text transcribed and modified by Chapman, he suggests, a bookkeeper made further additions, chiefly marginal, before a scribe prepared a third copy for the theater. Later, this intermediate manuscript, containing Chapman's authentic revisions as well as the bookkeeper's notations, served for printer's copy.

Although the supposedly irrelevant remark by Eurione strikes me as quite appropriate within its context,[8] I find Professor Yamada's hypothesis in general highly plausible. For example, a superfluous duplication of the direction *Within* on C1^v probably does reflect, as he suggests, someone's concern about the possibility of a mistake here during performance. The compositor of sheet C uncritically printed both the bookkeeper's warning notation and, in the following line, Chapman's original direction. And several marginal entries (e.g., those on G3: "He looks out with a light" and *"Redit cum lumine"*), plus the centered direction "An other within," on C1, which surely began as someone's interlinear addition, also tend to support Yamada, since the compositor has apparently continued to pattern his pages after those of the manuscript. But whether or not one accepts all these hypotheses, their overall effect is to confirm our assumption that the quarto text does derive from holographic copy.

Despite several contradictory details, we can detect within the quarto, work stints of five compositors, a notably large number; and, through an error in imposition that necessitated the reprinting of sheet B, we can define not only the original stints, discoverable in the unique Clark Library copy, but also those of the reprint. In the Clark copy, which by accident preserves a sheet printed before the error in imposition had been corrected, I identify the following work units: Compositor I — sheet A; II — sheet B; III — sheets C-D; IV — sheets

---

[4] Chapman's unusual spelling, "ahlas," which rarely occurs outside the quartos of his plays, appears here on sigs. C2, C3, D1, D2, and E1^v.

[5] E.g., "An other within" on C1 and "Enter Muge, and two others" on E3^v.

[6] It occurs on H3. For other instances, see *The Widdowes Teares*, sigs. D1, H4, I4, and K4.

[7] "Bibliographical Studies of George Chapman's *Monsieur D'Olive* (1606), Printed by Thomas Creede," *Studies in English Literature* (The English Literary Society of Japan, 1963).

[8] In the remark which Yamada cites ("A trauaile quoth you?" sig. C3), Eurione, as she has done twice before in this scene, again alludes to Vandome's recent travels and their effect upon him.

E-F; and V — sheets G-H. This hypothetical division, as we shall note later, is strongly supported by evidence from the running titles; and despite the improbable number of compositors that it assumes, it is further corroborated by such accidentals as spelling, punctuation, contrasting type fonts, and the abbreviations in speech-prefixes and stage directions.[9]

The faulty imposition of inner B, which probably occurred during press work on the outer forme of the sheet, resulted from transposition within the forme of type pages for sigs. B1^v and B3^v. Since, to correct the error, the printer reset type for all of outer B and for one page, B1^v, of inner B, one concludes that no one discovered the mistake until both formes had been wrought off and type for the outer forme and for one page, B1^v, of the inner forme had been distributed. While outer B was in press, the compositor apparently set type for inner B, then incorrectly imposed the forme. During the perfecting of sheet B (with the faulty inner forme), he distributed type from the stripped outer forme. Later, when he had also distributed one type page, B1^v, of the inner forme, someone discovered the error in imposition that had ruined the entire sheet B impression. Thus, a complete, new impression of both formes of the sheet was required, though of the inner forme, only B1^v had to be reset. Compositor II thereupon composed a new B1^v (the other three pages of the inner forme were, of course, still standing), and another workman, Compositor V, reset the entire outer forme.

One assumes, from all this, that no one pulled a proof during the original printing of inner B. Had discovery of the error occurred before completion of the press work, presumably the compositor would have destroyed the faulty sheets and immediately corrected the inner forme so that the pressman could have properly perfected the remaining sheets and printed the inner forme of additional new sheets to replace those that had been destroyed. After type for the outer forme had been reset, these additional, unperfected sheets would then have been perfected with the reset outer forme. By this procedure, all copies of the quarto would have contained the correctly imposed inner forme of B printed from the original setting of type; but the outer forme would have represented in some copies the original; in others, the resetting, a distinction

---

[9] Particularly because of the two-sheets-to-a-compositor pattern, one is strongly tempted to see both sheets A and B as the work of one man. And, unlike any of the other three, these compositors did share a set of running titles, two of the five made for sheet A reappearing in the inner and also in the outer forme of B. They shared also a variety of characteristic spellings (e.g., "mistresse," "syr," "honour," and "onely," and the fondness for a final "e" on such words as "sweete," "farre," etc.). But distinctions between them, though not immediately apparent, prove convincing. Compositor I used a wider measure than did his fellow and in contrast with Compositor II, roman type for names in his stage directions. And in the spelling of "he," "she," "we," "me," and "be," the contrasts are marked. By my count, Compositor I used these words thirty-two times, the "double e" spelling occurring only twice. But in the work of Compositor II, the words occur seventy-seven times, and, with four exceptions, always as "hee," "shee," "wee," "mee," and "bee."

My identification of compositors' work stints accords with that of Professor Yamada, except that he assigns C and D to separate workmen. Our conclusions about the faulty imposition of inner B also, in general, agree. He, however, was first to notice this rare error. See his "The Printing of Sheet B in the W. A. Clark Library Copy of *Monsieur D'Olive* (1606)," *Journal of the Faculty of Liberal Arts and Science,* Shinshu University (Dec., 1963).

which would probably have survived among the two dozen or so extant copies. Also, of course, B1^v would not have been reset. Existence of the reset outer forme plus B1^v of the inner forme implies a late discovery of the error.

In many details, the reset B1^v agrees with its original; presumably one man, Compositor II, set type for both. By contrast, the reset version of the outer forme differs sharply from its earlier counterpart. It lacks, for example, many of the wrong-font letters found in the original; and it fails to exhibit such other of Compositor II's traits as a preference for "hee," "shee," "wee" over "he," "she," "we" and for the "y" over "i" in such words as "admyrer," "syr," "bytter," "syres," "myrth," and "receyue." I consider it, therefore, to be the work of another typesetter.

From several bits of evidence, I suppose the new workman to be Compositor V, whose stint also includes sheets G and H. These sheets share a new set of running titles with the reset version of outer B and, like it, they demonstrate their compositor's preference for the "he," "she," "we" spellings; they also tend, as it does, to use the "VV" and the exclamation point, though these are generally scarce throughout other parts of the quarto. And both, again like the reset passage, occasionally use "am" (for "them") but, in contrast to the practice of the original sheet B compositor, never with the apostrophe (i.e., "'am"). On the basis of such similarities, I suggest that the reset outer B plus sheets G and H comprise the stint of Compositor V.

Since lineation in the reset version generally accords with that of the original — the compositor, on occasion, even hyphenating the same final words — I conclude that the printer did not return to the manuscript for copy. The original printing of B1^v and of outer B, therefore, provides my copy-text for this part of the play.

Compositor III's work (sheets C and D) contrasts in several ways with the rest of the volume, standing out as the most distinct typographic unit within the quarto. And since C and D share a profusion of characteristics peculiar to themselves, I judge them to be the work of one man. Employment throughout both sheets of the same running titles and type font, neither of which was used anywhere else in the quarto, and of upper case roman instead of the customary italics, the frequent occurrence of unusual spellings[10] and of the colon after speech-prefixes, use of similar abbreviations in the prefixes, and the uniquely ragged indentations, all corroborate this supposition.

Nonetheless, an abrupt change in punctuation needs examination. Throughout both formes of sheet C, the compositor tended to terminate single-line speeches and all verse lines with a colon; but in D he often employed no end punctuation whatever.[11] So sharp a contrast between these sheets, one supposes, might well signal a change in workmen.

Perhaps what happened is that, having depleted his case through excessive use of the colon in sheet C, the compositor, though continuing to use a few

---

[10] E.g., y-faith, theise, and *Mvg.*, the first two of which are peculiar to sheets C and D.

[11] For example, on C1, he ends five lines with a colon, six on C1^v, eight on C2, eleven on C2^v and C3, nine on C3^v, and six on C4 and C4^v, in contrast with one each on D1 and D1^v, two each on D2^v and D3^v, one on D4^v, and none on D2, D3, and D4. Most verse in this sheet, as we noticed, has no final punctuation whatever.

colons, particularly following speech heads, omitted from sheet D nearly all terminal punctuation. The failure of several defective types used in sheet C to reappear in D implies that composition of D preceded complete distribution of the C formes. Thus, on D1 twenty-seven lines end with no mark whatever, as do twenty-nine on D1^v. The greatest number, thirty-two, occurs on D3; and if we except D3^v and D4, which contain chiefly long prose speeches, every relevant page in sheet D includes well over twenty such lines. A few similar instances occur, of course, in sheet C and in every other sheet, but nowhere with anything like the frequency characteristic of D.

Evidence for Compositor IV's presence, though less conspicuous than that for Compositor III, still proves convincing. First of all, the sheets that we assign him, E and F, bear running titles that appear nowhere else. And his difficulties with Latin, his consistent use of the apostrophe, his unusual spellings, particularly *Monseuer* and *saena,* and his unique method for closing one act and starting another seem to be characteristics numerous and significant enough to distinguish his work from that of his fellows. The final sheets, G and H, belong, as we noted, to Compositor V, originally employed to reset outer B.

Printing of the quarto may have begun with copy cast off by sheets, though evidence for this assumption appears only in the final pages of B. Demarkation of copy for sheet A — since the opening scene of the play occurs in verse — would have posed few problems. But achieving similar accuracy in casting off sheet B was clearly more difficult, since this portion of the text is all prose. And, indeed, the conspicuously expanded blank spaces and the reduced amount of dialogue in the final pages of the sheet all suggest the printer's need to stretch his copy. Unlike the full thirty-six-line pages common in sheet A, B3^v contains thirty-two, B4 thirty-one, and B4^v thirty.

Evidence from the running titles, as I have several times insisted, tends to corroborate our definition of the work stints; apparently each of three compositors had his private complement of titles. Because the head title and the title page (with blank verso) occur in sheet A, the outer forme of this sheet required but three running titles, the inner only two. Of these five, two reappear in the B formes. A new set — that is, eight new titles incorporated in two skeletons — appears in the next two sheets. Peculiar to sheets C-D and particularly conspicuous because of their small capitals, these prove immediately recognizable even though surviving copies preserve them in several states. Like C-D, sheets E-F also introduce a set of eight new titles that never recur in the volume. And finally, as we have already noticed, the four titles originally assembled for the reset outer B reappear in the skeleton that printed all formes of G-H.

By happy accident, a British Museum copy of the quarto (C. 34. c. 15) preserves sheet D in proof state, the inked corrections clearly legible on the inner forme. Authenticity of the markings was established by W. W. Greg,[12] who pointed out that, although errors abound, one state of the forme preserved in a Dyce copy contains eleven of the twelve indicated corrections and no others. Greg, having examined only the British Museum and Dyce copies, thought the existence of other states improbable. But, as my collation indicates, several

[12] "A Proof-Sheet of 1606," *The Library,* XVII (March, 1937), 454-57.

others do exist. Greg further remarked that, "though we may still fairly call the sheet a proof, it was a very belated one; the corrections were not made till most of the impression had been taken, and are found in only a quarter of the extant copies." My notes indicate that in only four of twenty-three copies examined do the corrections appear. The first corrected state of the forme occurs in nineteen copies, the second that involves the text of the play in sixteen. Not improbably, therefore, the first two corrections occurred close together and reasonably early in the run, and the most thorough, as Greg suggests, came late.

Greg further mentions[13] the occurrence of an incomplete persona list on H4 representing a second state of this forme, the page originally occurring as a blank. Early in the printing of inner H the list was inserted and thus appears in most copies. But determining which state is represented by a particular copy is sometimes difficult, as both Greg and Yamada recognize; substitution of a leaf that bears the list for one that may have lacked it, we know, did occur. And rebinding can make such a change difficult to detect.[14] Existence of the original state is established, however, by a Bodleian copy (4T. 39 (2) ART.) in which H4 occurs as a blank.

My determination of press-variants derives from a collation of thirteen copies from the Bodleian Library, Boston Public Library, the British Museum, the W. A. Clark Library, the Folger Shakespeare Library, the Huntington Library, the University of Illinois Library, the University of Texas Library, and the library of Worcester College, Oxford, and from an examination of uncorrected formes in additional copies from the Library of Congress, the Houghton Library, Harvard, and the New York Public Library.

[13] *Bibliography,* p. 366.
[14] Yamada points out that in Huntington copy 98556, H4 may not be the conjugate of H1. And Greg notes that in Huntington copy 98557, H4 is clearly from some other copy.

MONSIEVR

D'OLIVE.

A

Comedie, as it was fundrie times aʃted by her
Maieʃties children at the Blacke-
Friers.

By George Chapman.

LONDON
Printed by **T. C.** for *William Holmes*, and are to be ʃold at
his Shop in Saint *Dun-ʃtons* Church-yard in
Fleete-ʃtreete, **1606.**

ACTORS.

Monsieur D'Oliue.

Philip the Duke.

S. Anne Count.

Vaumont Count.

Vandome.

Rhodoricke.

Mugeron.

Pacque,
Dicque, two pages.

[Digue, Page to Marcellina.

Cornelius, a Surgeon.

Fripper.

Servants and Sailors.]

Gueaquin the Dutchesse.

Hieronime Ladie.

Marcellina Countess

Eurione her sister.

[Licette, Marcellina's Maid.]

MONSIEVR D'OLIVE. [A2]

Actvs Primi. Scæna Prima.

Vandome with seruants and saylors laden,
Vavmont, another way walking.

Vand.

Conuey your carriage to my brother in Lawes,
Th'Earle of *Saint Anne,* to whome and to my Sister,
Commend my humble seruice, tell them both
Of my arriuall, and intent t'attend them
When in my way, I haue performd fit duties,   5
To Count Vaumont, and his most honoured Countesse.
   Ser. We will Syr; this way, follow honest Saylors.   *Exeunt Seruants.*
   Vand. Our first obseruance, after any absence
Must be presented euer to our Mistresse:
As at our parting she should still be last,   10
Hinc Amor vt circulus, from hence tis said
That loue is like a circle, being th'efficient
And end of all our actions; which, excited
By no worse obiect then my matchlesse mistresse
Were worthy to employ vs to that likenesse,   15
And be the onely Ring our powers should beate;
Noble she is by birth, made good by vertue,
Exceeding faire, and her behauiour to it,
Is like a singular Musitian
To a sweete Instrument, or else as doctrine   20
Is to the soule, that puts it into Act, /
And prints it full of admirable formes   [A2ᵛ]
Without which twere an emptie, idle flame.
Her eminent iudgement to dispose these parts,
Sits on her browe and holds a siluer Scepter,   25
With which she keepes time to the seuerall musiques,
Plac't in the sacred consort of her beauties:
Loues compleat armorie is managde in her
To stirre affection, and the discipline

---

2 *Saint*] roman ‖ 4 them] ~: ‖ 7 Syr;] ~, ‖ 13 which,] ~∧ ‖ 14 obiect] *Dilke*; abiect ‖ 15
likenesse,] ~; ‖ 16 beate;] ~, ‖ 23 flame.] ~∧ ‖ 26 With] with ‖ 28 managde] *Q(c)*; manadgd
Q(u) | her] ~. ‖

405

To checke and to affright it from attempting   30
Any attaint might disproportion her,
Or make her graces lesse then circular;
Yet her euen carriage, is as farre from coynesse
As from Immodestie, in play, in dancing,
In suffering court-ship: in requiting kindnesse.   35
In vse of places, houres, and companies
Free as the Sunne, and nothing more corrupted,
As circumspect as *Cynthia,* in her vowes,
And constant as the Center to obserue them,
Ruthfull and bountious, neuer fierce nor dull,   40
In all her courses euer at the full.
These three yeares, I haue trauaild, and so long
Haue beene in trauaile with her dearest sight,
Which now shall beautifie the enamour'd light.
This is her house, what? the gates shut and cleere   45
Of all attendants? Why, the house was wont
To hold the vsuall concourse of a Court,
And see, me thinks through the encourtaind windowes
(In this high time of day) I see light Tapers,
This is exceeding strange. Behold the Earle   50
Walking in as strange sort before the dore,
Ile know this wonder sure: My honoured Lord?

                                     [He starts to embrace Vaumont.]
    Vau. Keepe of Sir and beware whom you embrace.
    Vand. Why flyes your Lordship back?
    Vau.   You should be sure
To knowe a man your friend ere you embrac't him.   55
    Vand. I hope my knowledge cannot be more sure
Then of your Lordships friendship. /
    Vau.   No mans knowledge   [A3]
Can make him sure of any thing without him,
Or not within his power to keepe, or order.
    Vand. I comprehend not this; and wonder much   60
To see my most lou'd Lord so much estrang'd.
    Vau. The truth is, I haue done your knowne deserts
More wrong, then with your right should let you greet me
And in your absence, which makes worse the wrong,
And in your honour, which still makes it worse.   65
    Vand. If this be all my Lord, the discontent
You seeme to entertaine, is meerely causelesse:

---

31 her,] *Q(c);* ∼∧ *Q(u)* ‖ **34** dancing,] *Q(c);* ∼∧ *Q(u)* ‖ **40** Ruthfull and bountious,] ∼,
∼ ∼∧ ‖ **41** full.] *Q(c);* ∼∧ *Q(u)* ‖ **49** this] *Q(c);* thls *Q(u)* ‖ **52** SD *He . . . Vaumont.*] ‖ **53**
embrace.] ∼, ‖ **57** knowledge] *Q(c);* ∼, *Q(u)* ‖ **58** him,] *Q(c);* ∼∧ *Q(u)* ‖

Your free confession, and the manner of it,
Doth liberally excuse what wrong soeuer
Your mis-conceit could make you lay on me.   70
And therefore, good my Lord discouer it,
That we may take the spleene and corsey from it.
   Vau. Then heare a strange report and reason, why
I did you this repented iniurie.
You know my wife is by the rights of courtship,   75
Your chosen Mistresse, and she not disposde
(As other Ladies are) to entertaine
Peculiar termes, with common acts of kindnesse:
But (knowing in her, more then womens iudgement,
That she should nothing wrong her husbands right,   80
To vse a friend, onely for vertue chosen,
With all the rights of friendship) tooke such care
After the solemne parting to your trauaile,
And spake of you with such exceeding passion,
That I grew iealous, and with rage excepted   85
Against her kindnesse, vtterly forgetting
I should haue waied so rare a womans words,
As duties of a free and friendly iustice:
Not as the head-strong and incontinent vapors
Of other Ladies bloods, enflamed with lust,   90
Wherein I iniured both your innocencies,
Which I approue, not out of flexible dotage, /
By any cunning flatteries of my wife,   [A3ᵛ]
But in impartiall equitie, made apparant
Both by mine owne well-waid comparison   95
Of all her other manifest perfections,
With this one onely doubtfull leuitie,
And likewise by her violent apprehension
Of her deepe wrong and yours, for she hath vowde,
Neuer to let the common Pandresse light,   100
(Or any doome as vulgar) censure her
In any action she leaues subiect to them,
Neuer to fit the day with her attire,
Nor grace it with her presence; Nourish in it,
(Vnlesse with sleepe) nor stir out of her chamber: 105
And so hath muffled and mewd vp her beauties
In neuer-ceasing darkenesse, Neuer sleeping,
But in the day transform'd by her to night:

---

69 soeuer] ∼, ‖ **72** spleene] *Q(c)*; ∼, *Q(u)* ‖ **81** friend,] ∼∧ | vertue chosen,] *Dilke*; ∼, ∼∧ ‖

With all Sunne banisht from her smootherd graces:
And thus my deare and most vnmatched wife,   110
That was a comfort and a grace to me,
In euery iudgement, euery companie,
I, by false Iealousie, haue no lesse then lost,
Murtherd her liuing, and emtoomd her quicke.
   Vand. Conceit it not so deepely, good my Lord,   115
Your wrong to me or her, was no fit ground
To beare so waightie and resolu'd a vowe,
From her incensed and abused vertues.
   Vau. There could not be a more important cause,
To fill her with a ceaslesse hate of light,   120
To see it grace grose lightnesse with full beames,
And frowne on continence with her oblique glances.
As nothing equalls right to vertue done,
So is her wrong past all comparison.
   Vand. Vertue is not malitious, wrong done her   125
Is righted euer when men grant they Erre,
But doth my princely mistresse so contemne
The glorie of her beauties, and the applause /
Giuen to the worth of her societie,   [A4]
To let a voluntarie vowe obscure them?   130
   Vau. See all her windowes, and her doores made fast,
And in her Chamber lights for night enflam'd,
Now others rise, she takes her to her bed.
   Vand. This newes is strange, heauen grant I be encounterd
With better tydings of my other friendes,   135
Let me be bold my Lord t'enquire the state
Of my deare sister, in whose selfe and me,
Surviues the whole hope of our familie,
Together with her deare and princely husband
Th'Earle of Saint *Anne*.
   Vau.   Vnhappie that I am,   140
I would to heauen your most welcome steppes
Had brought you first vpon some other friend,
To be the sad Relator of the changes
Chanc't your three yeares most lamented absence;
Your worthy sister, worthier farre of heauen   145
Then this vnworthy hell of passionate Earth,
Is taken vp amongst her fellow Starres.

123 equalls] ∼, ‖ 130 them?] ∼; ‖ 144 absence;] ∼, ‖

Vand. Vnhappie man that euer I returnd
And perisht not ere these newes pierst mine eares.
    Vau. Nay be not you that teach men comfort, grieued;   150
I know your iudgement will set willing shoulders
To the knowne burthens of necessitie:
And teach your wilfull brother patience,
Who striues with death, and from his caues of rest
Retaines his wiues dead Corse amongst the liuing,   155
For with the rich sweetes of restoring Balmes,
He keepes her lookes as fresh as if she liu'd,
And in his chamber (as in life attirde)
She in a Chaire sits leaning on her arme,
As if she onely slept: and at her feete   160
He like a mortified hermit clad,
Sits weeping out his life, as hauing lost
All his lifes comfort: And that, she being dead /
(Who was his greatest part) he must consume,   [A4ᵛ]
As in an Apoplexy strooke with death.   165
Nor can the Duke nor Dutchesse comfort him,
Nor messengers with consolatory letters
From the kinde King of *France,* who is allyed
To her and you. But to lift all his thoughts
Vp to another world, where she expects him,   170
He feedes his eares with soule-exciting musicke,
Solemne and Tragicall, and so Resolues
In those sadde accents to exhale his soule.
    Vand. O what a second Ruthles Sea of woes
Wracks mee within my Hauen, and on the Shore?   175
What shall I doe? mourne, mourne, with them that mourne,
And make my greater woes their lesse expell;
This day Ile consecrate to sighes and teares,
And this next Euen, which is my mistresse morning
Ile greete her, wondring at her wilfull humours,   180
And with rebukes, breaking out of my Loue,
And duetie to her honour, make her see
How much her too much curious vertue wrongs her.
    Vau. Sayd like the man the world hath euer held you,
Welcome, as new liues to vs; our good now   185
Shall wholly be ascrib'de and trust to you.   *Exeunt.*

---

163 that,] *Lowell;* ∼∧ ‖ **167** messengers] *Q(c);* messagers *Q(u)* | letters] ∼, ‖ **168** *France*]
roman ‖ **173** soule.] *Q(c);* ∼, *Q(u)* ‖ **174** second] *Q(c);* ∼, *Q(u)* ‖ **177** expell;] ∼, ‖ **178** teares,]
Q(c); ∼∧ *Q(u)* ‖ **179** next] *Q(c);* Next *Q(u)* ‖ **183** her.] *Q(c);* ∼∧ *Q(u)* ‖ **185** liues] *Q(c);*
lines *Q(u)* | vs; our good now] *Lowell;* vs, our good Now *Q(u);* vs, our good. Now *Q(c)* ‖

[I.ii]

Enter Rhoderique *and* Mugeron.

Mug. See, see, the vertuous Countesse hath bidden our day Good night, her starres are now visible: when was any Ladie seene to be so constant in her vowe, and able to forbeare the society of men so sincerely?

Rho. Neuer in this world, at least exceeding seldome. What shame   5
it is for men to see women so farre surpasse them: for when was any man knowne (out of iudgement) to performe so staied an abstinence, from the society of women?

Mug. Neuer in this world. /

Rho. What an excellent Creature an honest woman is? I warrant   [B1] 10
you the Countesse, and her Virgine sister, spende all their times in Contemplation, watching to see the Sacred Spectacles of the night, when other Ladies lye drownd in sleepe or Sensualitie. Ist not so, thinck'st?

Mug. No Question.   15

Rho. Come, come, letts forgette wee are Courtiers, and talke like honest men, tell truth, and shame all trauaylers and tradesmen: Thou beleeu'st all's naturall beautie that shewes faire, though the paynter enforce it, and sufferst in soule I know for the honourable Ladie.

Mug. Can any heart of Adamant not yeelde in compassion to see   20
spottelesse innocencie suffer such bitter pennance?

Rho. A very fitte stocke to grafte on: Tushe man thinke what shee is, thinke where shee liues, thinke on the villanous cunning of these times. Indeede did wee liue nowe in olde *Saturns* time: when women hadde no other Arte, then what Nature taught am (and yet there   25
needes little Arte I wisse to teache a woman to dissemble) when lux-urie was vnborne, at least vntaught, the arte to steale from a forbidden tree; when Coaches, when Perwigges, and paynting, when Maskes, and Masking, in a worde when Court and Courting was vnknowne, an easie mist might then perhappes haue wrought vpon my sence as it   30
does now on the poore Countesse and thine.

Mug. O world!

Rho. O fleshe!

Mug. O Deuill!

Rho. I tell thee *Mugeron,* the Fleshe is growne so great with the   35
Deuill, as there's but little Honestie lefte ith worlde. That, that is, is in Lawyers, they engrosse all: S'foote what gaue the first fier to the Counts Iealousie? /

I.ii] ‖ **2** Ladie] *Q(c)*; Lady *Q(u)* ‖ **3** vowe] *Q(c)*; vow *Q(u)* ‖ **4** sincerely] *Q(c)*; sinceerely *Q(u)* ‖ **8** of women] *Q(c)*; ef women *Q(u)* | women?] ~. ‖ **13** Sensualitie.] ~, Q, *Q(r)* | so,] ~∧ Q, *Q(r)* ‖ **18** all's] alls Q, *Q(r)* ‖ **21** pennance?] ~. Q, *Q(r)* ‖ **22** grafte] Q; graffe *Q(r)* ‖ **24** times.] ~, Q, *Q(r)* ‖ **32** world!] *Q(r)*; ~. Q ‖ **33** fleshe!] *Q(r)*; ~. Q ‖ **34** Deuill!] *Q(r)*; ~. Q ‖ **36** there's] theres Q, *Q(r)* | but little] Q; but a little *Q(r)* ‖

Mug. What but his misconstruction of her honourable affection to [B1ᵛ]
Vandome? 40

Rho. Honourable affection? first shee's an ill huswife of her honour, that puts it vpon construction; but the presumption was violent
against her, no speeche but of *Vandome,* no thought but of his memorie, no myrth but in his company, besides the free entercourse of
Letters, Fauours, and other entertainments, too too manifest signes 45
that her heart went hand in hand with her tongue.

Mug. Why, was shee not his mistresse?

Rho. I, I, a Court terme, for I wote what! Slight, *Vandome* the
stallion of the Court, her deuoted seruant, and forsoothe loues her
honourablie: Tush, hee's a foole that beleeues it; for my part I loue 50
to offend in the better part still, and that is, to iudge charitablie:
But now forsoothe to redeeme her Honour, shee must by a laborious
and violent kinde of Purgation, Rubbe off the Skinne, to washe out
the spotte, Turne her Chamber to a Cell, the Sunne into a Taper, And
(as if shee liu'd in another World amongst the *Antipodes,*) make our 55
night her day, our day her night, that vnder this curtaine, shee may
laye his iealousie a sleepe, whiles shee turnes poore *Argus* to *Acteon,*
and makes his Sheets common to her Seruant *Vandome.*

Mug. Vandome? Why hee was mette ith streete but euen now,
newly arriv'd after three yeares trauaile. 60

Rho. Newely arriv'd? hee has beene arriv'd this twelue-month, and
has euer since lyne close in his mistresse cunning darkenesse, at her
seruice.

Mug. Fye a the Deuill, who will not enuie slaunder? O the
miserable condition of her Sexe; borne to liue vnder all construction. 65
If shee be courteous, shee's thought to bee wanton, if shee be kinde,
shee's too willing, if coye, too wilfull, if shee be modest, shee's a
clowne, if shee be honest, shee's a foole: *Enter D'oliue.* And so
is hee. *[Pointing to D'Olive.]* /

Rho. What *Monsieur D'oliue,* the onely admyrer of wit and good [B2] 70
words.

D'Ol. Morrowe wits, morrowe good wits: my little parcell of wit,
I haue Roddes in pisse for you; how doest *Iacke,* may I call thee
Syr Iack yet?

Mug. You may Syr: Syr's as commendable an addition as *Iacke,* 75
for ought I knowe.

D'Ol. I know it *Iacke,* and as common too.

Rho. Go too, you may couer; wee haue taken notice of your
embroydered Beuer.

---

40 *Vandome*?] ∼. *Q, Q(r)* ‖ **41** shee's] shees *Q, Q(r)* ‖ **47** Why] *Q(r)*; why *Q* ‖ **48** what! Slight,] *Parrott*; what, slight∧ *Q, Q(r)* ‖ **50** hee's] hees *Q, Q(r)* ‖ **56** day, our] *Q*; day, and our *Q(r)* ‖ **58** makes] *Q(r)*; make *Q* ‖ **59** streete] *Q(r)*; streetes *Q* ‖ **66, 67** *(twice),* **68** shee's] shees *Q, Q(r)* ‖ **68** SD *Enter D'oliue.*] *Parrott; follows Mugeron's speech* | SD *Pointing to D'Olive.*] ‖ **73** *Iacke*] *roman throughout* ‖ **75** Syr's] Syrs ‖ **79** Beuer.] ∼: ‖

D'Ol. Looke you: by Heauen tha'art one of the maddest bitter   80
slaues in *Europe,* I doe but wonder how I made shifte to loue thee
all this while.

Rho. Go too what might such a parcell guild couer be worth?

Mug. Perhappes more then the whole peece besides.

D'Ol. Good yfaith, but bytter; O you madde slaues, I thinke you   85
had *Satyres,* to your syres, yet I must loue you, I must take pleasure
in you, and yfaith tell mee, how ist? Liue I see you doe, but how?
but how? witts?

Rho. Faith as you see, like poore younger Brothers.

D'Ol. By your wittes?   90

Mug. Nay not turnd Poets neither.

D'Ol. Good, soothe: but indeede to say truth, Time was when the
sonnes of the *Muses* had the priuiledge to liue onlie by their wits,
but times are altered, *Monopolies* are nowe calld in, and wit's become
a free trade for all sorts to liue by, Lawyers liue by wit and they liue   95
worshipfully: Souldiers liue by wit, and they liue honourably:
Panders liue by wit, and they liue honestlie. In a word there are
fewe trades but liue by wit, onely bawdes and Midwifes liue by
Womens labours, as Fooles and Fidlers do by making myrth, Pages
and Parasits by making legges: Paynters and Players by / making [B2ᵛ] 100
mouthes and faces; ha, doest well witts?

Rho. Faith thou followest a figure in thy iests, as countray Gentlemen followe fashions when they bee worne threed-bare.

D'Ol. Well, well, letts leaue these wit skirmishes, and say when
shall wee meete?   105

Mug. How thinke you, are wee not met now?

D'Ol. Tush man, I meane at my chamber, where wee may take
free vse of ourselues, that is, drinke sacke, and talke *Satyre,* and let
our witts runne the wilde-goose chase ouer Court and Countrey.
I will haue my chamber the Rende-vous of all good wittes, the   110
shoppe of good wordes, the Minte of good iestes, and Ordinary of
fine discours; Critickes, Essayists, Linguists, Poets, and other professors
of that facultie of witte, shall at certaine houres ith day resorte thither,
it shall bee a second *Sorbonne,* where all doubts or differences of
Learning, Honour, Duellisme, Criticisme, and Poetrie, shall bee dis-   115
puted. And how witts, doe ye follow the Court still?

Rho. Close at heeles Syr, and I can tell you, you haue much to
aunswere for to your Starres, that you doe not so too.

D'Ol. As why wittes, as why?

85 bytter;] *Dilke subs.*; ~, ‖ 87 Liue] liue ‖ 92 Good,] ~∧ ‖ 94 wit's] wits ‖ 101 ha,] ~∧ Q,
Q(r) ‖ 102 countray] Q; counttey Q(r) ‖ 107-8 take free] Q(r); take the free Q ‖ 109 Coun-
trey.] ~, Q, Q(r) ‖ 112 discours;] ~, Q, Q(r) ‖ 115-16 disputed. And] ~, and Q; ~: and
Q(r) ‖ 116 ye] Q(r); om. Q ‖ 118 to] Q; om. Q(r) ‖

Rho. Why Syr, the Court's as t'were the stage; and they that haue a 120
good suite of partes, and qualities, ought to preasse thither to grace
them, and receyue theyr due merit.

D'Ol. Tush, let the Court follow mee; hee that soares too neere
the Sunne, melts his wings many times; As I am, I possesse my selfe,
I enioy my libertie, my learning, my wit. As for wealth and honour 125
let am goe, Ile not loose my learning to bee a Lord, nor my wit to
be an Alderman.

Mug. Admirable *D'oliue.*

D'Ol. [*Indicating Marcellina's house.*] And what! you stand
gazing at this Comet here, and admyre it, I dare say. 130

Rho. And do not you?

D'Ol. Not I, I admyre nothing but wit. /

Rho. But I wonder how she entertaines time in that solitarie Cell: [B3]
does shee not take *Tabacco* thinke you?

D'Ol. Shee does, shee does: others make it their physicke, shee 135
makes it her foode. Her sister and shee take it by turne, first one,
then th'other: and *Vandome* ministers to them both.

Mug. How sayst thou by that *Helene* of *Greece,* the Countesses
Sister? There were a Paragon *Monsieur D'oliue,* to admyre and
marrie too. 140

D'Ol. Not for mee.

Rho. No: what acceptions lyes against the choice?

D'Ol. Tush, tell not mee of choice, if I stood affected that way, I
would chuse my wife as men doe *Valentines,* blindefolde, or drawe
cuttes for them, for so I shall bee sure not to bee deceiued in choosing: 145
for take this of mee, there's tenne times more deceipt in women, then
in Horse-fleshe, and I say still, that a prettie well pac't Chamber-maide
is the onely fashion: if shee growe full or fulsome, giue her but sixe
pence to buye her a handbasket, and sende her the way of all fleshe:
there's no more but so. 150

Mug. Indeede that's the sauingst way.

D'Ol. O mee, what a Hell t'is for a man to bee tyed to the continuall charge of a Coache, with the appurtenances, horse, men, and
so forth; and then to haue a Mans house pestered with a whole country of Guests, Groomes, Panders, Wayting Maydes, *&c.* I carefull 155
to please my wife, shee carelesse to displease mee, shrewish if shee be
honest, intollerable if shee be wise: Imperious as an Empresse, all shee
does must be lawe, all shee sayes Gospell: O what a pennance tis

---

120 Court's] *Q(r)*; Courts *Q* ‖ **125** wit. As] wit, as *Q, Q(r)* ‖ **129** SD *Indicating . . . house.*] *om.*
Q, Q(r) ‖ **136** foode.] ~, *Q*; ~: *Q(r)* | by] *Q*; my *Q(r)* ‖ **137** th'other] *Q*; the other *Q(r)* ‖
139 Sister? There] ~, there *Q*; sister, there *Q(r)* | Paragon *Monsieur*] *Q(r)*; Paragon for
Monsieur Q ‖ **143** not mee] *Q*; me not *Q(r)* ‖ **146** there's] *Q(r)*; theres *Q* ‖ **148** fashion:] ~,
Q, Q(r) ‖ **150** there's] theres *Q, Q(r)* ‖ **151** that's] thats *Q, Q(r)* ‖ **155** Maydes,] *Q*; ~? *Q(r)*
‖ **158** Gospell:] *Q(r)*; ~, *Q* ‖

to endure her. I glad to forbeare still, all to keepe her loyall, and yet
perhappes when all's done, my heyre shall bee like my Horse-keeper: 160
Fye ont, the verie thought of Marriage, were able to coole the hottest
Liuer in *France*.

    Rho. Well, I durst venture twice the price of your guilt Connies
wooll, wee shall haue you change your coppie ere a twelue months
day. / 165

    Mug. We must haue you dubd ath order, ther's no remedie; you [B3ᵛ]
that haue vnmarryed, done such honourable seruice in the commonwealth, must needes receyue the honour due too't in marriage.

    Rho. That hee may doe, and neuer marrie.

    D'Ol. As how wits, yfaith as how? 170

    Rho. For if hee can prooue his father was free ath order, and that
hee was his fathers sonne, then by the laudable custome of the Cittie,
hee may bee a cuckold by his fathers coppie, and neuer serue fort.

    D'Ol. Euer good yfaith.

    Mug. Nay howe can hee pleade that, when t'is as well knowne his 175
father dyed a batcheler?

    D'Ol. Bitter, in verity, bitter. But good still in its kinde.

    Rho. Goe too, we must haue you follow the lanthorne of your fore-
fathers.

    Mug. His forefathers? S'body had hee more fathers then one? 180

    D'Ol. Why this is right: heer's wit canuast out ans coate, into's
Iacket: the string sounds euer well, that rubs not too much ath frets:
I must loue your Wits, I must take pleasure in you. Farewell good
wits; you know my lodging, make an Errand thether now and than,
and saue your ordinarie, doe wits, doe. 185

    Mug. Wee shall be troublesome tee.

    D'Ol. O God Syr, you wrong mee, to thinke I can bee troubled
with wit, I loue a good wit, as I loue my selfe. If you neede a brace
or two of Crownes at any time Addresse but your Sonnet, it shall bee
as sufficient as your bonde at all times. I carrie halfe a score byrdes 190
in a Cage, shall euer remaine at your call: Farewell wits, farewell
good wits. *Exit.* /

    Rho. Farewell the true mappe of a gull: by Heauen hee shall [B4]
too'th Court: t'is the perfect model of an impudent vpstart: the
compound of a Poet, and a Lawyer, hee shall sure too'th Court. 195

    Mug. Naye for Gods sake, letts haue no fooles at Court.

    Rho. Hee shall too't that's certaine, the Duke had a purpose to
dispatch some one or other to the French King, to entreat him to
send for the bodie of his Neece, which the melancoly Earle of

---

159 her.] ∼, Q, Q(r) ‖ **166** order,] ∼∧ | remedie;] ∼, ‖ **168** too't] t'oot ‖ **174** yfaith.] ∼: ‖
176 batcheler?] ∼. ‖ **177** its] *Dilke*; it ‖ **180** one?] ∼. ‖ **181** heer's] heers ‖ **187** God] Q(c);
good Q(u) | can] ∼, ‖ **188** selfe. If] ∼, if ‖ **189** time] Q(c); ∼, Q(u) ‖ **190** times.] ∼, ‖ **192**
SD *Exit*] *Exjt* ‖ **197** that's] thats ‖

Saint Anne, her husband hath kept so long vnburied, as meaning one 200
graue should entombe himselfe and her together.

Mug. A very worthy subiect for an Ambassage, as *D'oliue* is for
an Ambassador Agent, and t'is as sutable to his braine, as his parcell
guilt Beuer to his fooles head.

Rho. Well it shall goe hard but hee shall bee employd, O tis a most 205
accomplisht asse, the mungrill of a Gull, and a villaine, the very
essence of his soule is pure villany: The substance of his braine, fool-
ery: one that beleeues nothing from the starres vpward. A Pagan in
beleefe, an Epicure beyond beleefe, Prodigious in lust, Prodigall in
wastfull expence, in necessary most penurious, his wit is to admire 210
and imitate, his grace is to censure, and detract; he shall to'th Court,
yfaith hee shall thither. I will shape such employement for him, as that
hee himselfe shall haue no lesse contentment, in making myrth to the
whole Court, then the Duke and the whole Court shall haue pleasure
in enioying his presence. A knaue if hee be riche, is fit to make an 215
Officer, As a Foole if hee bee a knaue is fit to make an Intelligencer.

Exeunt. /

Actus secundi. Scæna prima. [B4ᵛ]

Enter Digue, Licette, with Tapers.

Dig. What an order is this? Eleuen a clocke at night is our Ladies
morning, and her houre to rise at; as in the morning, it is other Ladies
houre: these Tapers are our Sunnes, with which wee call her from her
bed. But I pray thee *Licette* what makes the virgin Lady, my Ladies
sister, breake winde so continually, and sigh so tempestuouslie? I 5
beleeue shee's in loue.

Lic. With whome, can you tell?

Dig. Not very well, but certes that's her disease, a man may cast her
water in her face: The truth is, t'is no matter what she is, for there
is little goodnes in her, I could neuer yet finger one *Cardecue* of her 10
bountie; And indeede all bountie now a dayes is dead amongst Ladies.
This same *Bonitas* is quite put downe amongst am. But see, Now we
shall discouer the heauines of this virgine Ladie. Ile eauesdroppe, and
if it bee possible, heare who is her Louer: For when this same amorous
spirite possesses these young people, they haue no other subiect to talke 15
of. [*They retire.*]

Enter Marcelina and Euriony.

Eur. O sister, would that matchlesse Earle euer haue wrongd his
wife with iealousie?

---

206 mungrill] *Dilke (i.e., mongrel);* mugrill ‖ **207** braine,] ∼- ‖ **212** thither.] ∼, ‖ secundi.
Scæna] ∼∧ Scena ‖ SD *Digue, Licette,*] *Q(r); Diqve*∧ *Licette*∧ *Q (See Textual Note)* ‖ **1** *Dig.*]
Q(r); Diq. Q | this?] *Q(r);* ∼, *Q* ‖ **5** tempestuouslie?] ∼, *Q, Q(r)* ‖ **6** shee's] shees *Q, Q(r)* |
loue.] *Q;* ∼? *Q(r)* ‖ **8** *Dig.*] *Q(r); Diq. Q* | that's] thats *Q, Q(r)* ‖ **13** Ladie.] ∼, *Q, Q(r)* ‖
16 SD *They retire.*] *Parrott (after Dilke);* om. *Q, Q(r)* ‖

Mar. Neuer.

Eur. Good Lord what difference is in men? but was such a man as 20
this euer seene, to loue his wife euen after death so deerely, to liue
with her in death? To leaue the world and all his pleasures: all his
friends and honours, as all were nothing, now his wife is gone: is it
not strange? /

Mar. Exceeding strange. [C1] 25

Eur. But sister should not the noble man be Chronicled if he had
right, I pray you sister, should he not?

Mar. Yes, yes he should.

Eur. But did you euer heare of such a Noble gentleman: did you
sister? 30

Mar. I tell you no.

Eur. And doe not you delight to heare him spoken of? and prais'd,
and honord? Doe you not Madame?

Mar. What should I say? I doe.

Eur. Why very well: and should not euery woman that loues the 35
Soueraigne honour of her Sexe, delight to heare him praisd as well
as wee? Good Maddam answere hartely?

Mar. Yet againe? who euer heard one talke so?

Eur. Talk so? Why should not euery Lady talke so?
You thinke belike I loue the Noble man: 40
Heauen is my iudge if I: indeede his loue
And honour to his Wife so after death
Would make a Fayry loue him, yet not loue,
But thinke the better of him, and sometimes,
Talke of his loue or so; But you know Maddam: 45
I cald her sister, and if I loue him,
It is but as my Brother I protest.

Vand. [*Within.*] Let me come in!

An other within. Sir you mvst not enter!

Mar. What rude disordred noise is that within? 50

Lic. I know not Maddam.

[*Enter a seruant.*]

Dig. How now?

Ser. Wher's my Lady?

Mar. What hast with you?

Ser. Maddame ther's one at doore that askes to speake with you, 55
admittes no answere but will enforce his passage to your honor. /

20 was] *Dilke; om.* Q, *Q(r)* ‖ 21 this euer seene,] this was euer seene Q, *Q(r)* (*See Textual Note*) ‖
23 nothing, now] *Q(r)*; ∼: Now Q | gone:] ∼, Q, *Q(r)* ‖ 25 Exceeding] *Q(c)*; Eaceeding
Q(u) ‖ 31 no.] ∼: ‖ 32 doe not you] *Q(c)*; doe you not *Q(u)* ‖ 34 doe.] ∼; ‖ 36 Sexe,] *Q(c)*;
∼∧ *Q(u)* ‖ 37 wee?] *Q(c)*; ∼. *Q(u)* ‖ 38 *Mar.*] *Q(c)*; *Mvg*: *Q(u)* | againe?] *Parrott*; ∼, ‖ 40
loue the Noble] *Q(c)*; loue you loue the Noble *Q(u)* ‖ 42 death] ∼: ‖ 43 loue,] ∼. ‖ 48 SD
Within.] *Lowell* | in!] ∼; ‖ 49 *An other within*] *Shepherd; roman, centered as SD following* protest |
Sir . . . enter!] *Dilke; part of the preceding line* | enter!] enrer: *Q(u)*; enter: *Q(c)* ‖ 51 Maddam.]
∼, | SD *Enter a seruant.*] *Dilke* ‖ 52 *Dig.*] *Dilke; Diq.* | now?] ∼; ‖ 53 *Ser.*] *Dilke; Sic:* | Wher's]
Whers ‖ 55 *Ser.*] *Dilke; Sdc:* *Q(u); Sic:* *Q(c)* | ther's] thers ‖ 56 your] *Q(c)*; yodr *Q(u)* ‖

Mar. What insolent guest is that?   [C1ᵛ]

Eur.   Who should he be

That is so ignorant of your worth and custome?

Enter an other Seruant.

2nd Ser. Maddam her's one hath drawne his rapier on vs and will
come in he sayes.   60

Mar. This is strange Rudenes,

What is his name, doe you not know the man?

2nd Ser. No Maddam, tis too darke.

Mar. [*To Licette.*]   Then take a light,

See if you know him, if not raise the streetes.

                         Exeunt seruants. *Lycitte* walkes with a candle.

Eur. And keepe the doore safe: what night-walker's this,   65

That hath not light enough to see his rudenes?

Enter *Lycitte* in hast.

Lic. O Maddame tis the Noble gentleman,

Monsieur *Vandome* your Seruant.

Eur. Is it he? is he returnd?

Mar.   Hast, commend me to him.

Tel him I may not nor will not see him: 70

For I haue vowd the contrary to all.

Lic. Maddam, we told him so a hundred times yet he will enter.

Within. Hold, hold, keepe him back there.

Mar. What rudenes, what strange insolence is this?

Enter *Vandome.*

Vand. What hower is this? what fashion? what sad life?   75

What superstition of vnholy vow?

What place is this? O shall it ere be said

Such perfect Iudgement should be drownd in Humor?

Such beauty consecrate to Batts and Owles?   [*Throwing down his sword.*]

Here lyes the weapon that enforst my passage,   80

Sought in my loue, sought in regard of you:

For whom I will indure a thousand deaths,

Rather then suffer you to perish thus

And be the fable of the scornefull world;

Yf I offend you Lady kill me now. /   85

Mar. What shall I say? Ahlas my worthy Seruant,   [C2]

I would to God I had not liu'd to be

A fable to the worlde, a shame to thee.

---

57 What] what | be] ~; ‖ **58** custome?] ~: ‖ **59** *2nd Ser.*] *Dilke*; *2 Lec.* | her's] hers ‖ **61** This]
Dilke; Tis ‖ **63** *2nd Ser.*] *Parrott*; *Sig.* | SD *To Licette.*] ‖ **64** streetes.] ~∧ | SD Exeunt seruants.]
Dilke subs.; *Exit*∧ ‖ **65-66** And . . . rudenes?] *Parrott*; *as prose* (that) | rudenes?] ~. ‖ **65** night-
walker'] *Dilke*; night-walker' ‖ **69-71** Hast . . . all.] *Parrott*; *as prose* (tel . . . for) ‖ **69** Hast,]
~∧ | him.] ~∧ ‖ **72** *Lic.* . . . enter.] ~. . . . ~: within ‖ **73** *Within.*] Within: | there.] ~: ‖
74 rudenes,] ~∧ | this?] ~: ‖ **79** Owles?] ~: | SD *Throwing . . . sword.*] *Dilke subs.* ‖ **85** now.]
~, ‖

Vand. Deare mistris heare me and forbeare these humors.

Mar. Forbeare your vaine disswasions.

Vand.   Shall your iudgement —   90

Mar. I will not heare a word.   *Exit Marc. and Licette.*

Vand.   Strange will in women;

What sayes my honorable virgin sister?

How is it you can brooke, this Batt-like life?

And sit as one withovt life?

Eur.   Would I were.

If any man would kill me, I'de forgiue him.   95

Vand. O true fit of a maiden Melancholy?

Whence comes it, louely sister?

Eur.   In my minde

Your selfe hath small occasion to be merry:

That are arriu'd on such a haples Shore:

As beares the dead waight of so deare a Sister: 100

For whose decease, being my deare Sister vow'd,

I shall for euer leade this desolate life.

Vand. Now heauen forbid; women in Loue with women;

Loues fire shines with too mutuall a refraction,

And both wayes weakens his colde beames too much   105

To pierce so deeply; tis not for her I know

That you are thus impassiond.

Eur. For her I would be sworne and for her husband.

Vand. I mary Sir, a quick man may doe much,

In theise kinde of impressions.

Eur.   See how Idely   110

You vnderstand me? theise same travailers,

That can liue any where, make iests of any thing:

And cast so farre from home, for nothing else:

But to learne how they may cast of their friends;

She had a husband does not cast her of so: 115

O tis a rare, a Noble gentleman. /

Vand. Well well, there is some other Humor stirring,   [C2ᵛ]

In your young bloud then a dead womans Loue.

Eur. No, ile be sworne.

Vand.   Why, is it possible?

That you, whose frolicke brest was euer filde,   120

With all the spirits of a mirthfull Lady:

Shovld be with such a sorrow so transform'd?

Your most sweet hand in touch of Instruments:

Turnd to pick strawes, and fumble vpon Rushes;

---

90 Shall] shall | iudgement—] ∼? ‖ 91 SD *Exit . . . Licette.*] *Dilke; Exit Mard:* | *Strange . . .*
women;] *Dilke;* ∼ . . . ∼; *Exit Marc.* ‖ 94 were.] ∼, ‖ 95 him.] ∼, ‖ 97 minde] ∼: ‖ 101
decease, . . . vow'd,] ∼∧ . . . ∼. ‖ 105 much] ∼: ‖ 106 deeply;] ∼∧ ‖ 107 That] that ‖ 108
husband.] ∼, ‖ 110 Idely] *Dilke;* ∼. ‖ 114 friends;] ∼, ‖ 117 *Vand.*] *Dilke* ‖ 118 Loue.] ∼: ‖
119 sworne.] ∼: | Why,] ∼∧ | possible?] *Q(c);* ∼. *Q(u)* ‖ 120 was] *Q(c);* wa: *Q(u)* ‖ 121
spirits] *Q(c);* spitits *Q(u)* ‖

Your heauenly voice, turnd into heauy sighes,   125
And your rare wit to in a manner tainted?
This cannot be, I know some other cause,
Fashions this strange effect, and that my selfe
Am borne to find it out and be your cure
In any wound it forceth whatsoeuer.   130
But if you wil not tell me, at your perill.   [*He offers to go.*]
   Eur. Brother.
   Vand.   Did you call?
   Eur. No, tis no matter.
   Vand.   So then: [*Going.*]
   Eur.   Doe you heare?
Assur'd you are my kind and honor'd Brother,
Ile tell you all.
   Vand.   O will you? doe so then.   135
   Eur. You will be secret?
   Vand.   Secret? ist a secret?
   Eur. No tis a triffle that torments one thus:
Did euer man aske such a question,
When he had brought a woman to this passe?
   Vand. What, tis no Treason is it?
   Eur.   Treason quoth he?   140
   Vand. Well if it be, I will engage my quarters
With a faire Ladies euer, tell the secret.
   Eur. Attending oftentimes the Duke and Dutchesse
To visit the most passionate Earle your Brother: /
That Noble Gentleman.   [C3]
   Vand.   Well said put in that.   145
   Eur. Put it in? why? y'faith y'are such a man,
Ile tell no further, you are changed indeede.
A trauaile quoth you?
   Vand.   Why what meanes this?
Come Lady fourth, I would not loose the thankes
The credit and the honor I shall haue   150
For that most happy Good I know in Fate,
I am to furnish thy desires withall:
For all this house in Gold.
   Eur.   Thanke you good Brother:
Attending (as I say) the Duke and Dutchesse
To the sad Earle —
   Vand.   That noble gentleman?   155

---

126 tainted?] ~. ‖ **128** selfe] *Dilke*; ~: ‖ **129** cure] *Lowell*; ~: ‖ **130** whatsoeuer.] ~, ‖ **131** not tell me,] *Dilke*; ~, ~ ~∧ | SD *He . . . go.*] *Parrott* ‖ **133** No,] ~∧ | SD *Going.*] *Parrott* | you] *Q(c)*; yon *Q(u)* ‖ **135** you] *Q(c)*; ynu *Q(u)* | all.] ~: | you?] *Dilke*; ~∧ | then.] *Dilke*; ~? ‖ **136** You] you ‖ **140** What,] ~∧ ‖ **141** quarters] ~: ‖ **143** Dutchesse] ~. ‖ **145** that.] ~, ‖ **150** haue] ~: ‖ **155** Earle—] ~. ‖

Eur. Why I, is he not?
Vand.   Beshrew my hart else,
The Earle quoth you, he cast not of his Wife.
   Eur. Nay looke you now —
Vand.   Why, does he pray?
Eur.   Why no.
   Vand. Foorth then I pray, you louers are so captious.
   Eur. When I obseru'd his constancie in Loue: 160
His honor of his deere wiues memory,
His woe for her, his life with her in death:
I grew in loue, euen with his very mind.
   Vand. O, with his mind?
Eur.   I by my soule no more.
   Vand. A good mind certainly is a good thing: 165
And a good thing you know —
   Eur.   That is the chiefe:
The body without that, Ahlas is nothing:
And this his mind cast such a fier into me
That it hath halfe consum'd me, since it lou'd
His Wife so dearely, that was deere to me.   170
And euer I am saying to my selfe: /
How more then happy should that woman be   [C3ᵛ]
That had her honord place in his true loue:
But as for me I know I haue no reason
To hope for such an honor at his hands.   175
   Vand. What, at the Earles hands? I thinke so indeede,
Heauen I beseech thee, was your loue so simple
T'n flame it selfe with him? why hee's a husband:
For any Princesse any Queene or Empresse:
The Ladies of this land would teare him peece-meale: 180
(As did the drunken Froes, the *Thratian Harper*)
To mary but a lymbe, a looke of him,
Heauen's my sweet comfort: Set your thoughts on him?
   Eur. O cruell man, dissembling trauailer,
Euen now you took vpon you to be sure   185
It was in you to satisfie my longings,
And whatsoeuer t'were, you would procure it,
O you were borne to doe me good, you know.
You would not loose the credit and the honor
You should haue by my satisfaction   190

---

158 now—] ~, | Why,] *Dilke*; ~∧ | no.] ~: ‖ 159 louers] *Q(c)*; loners louers *Q(u)* | captious.]
~∧ ‖ 160 obseru'd] *Q(c)*; obseru'n *Q(u)* ‖ 164 O,] ~∧ | more.] ~, ‖ 166 know—] ~. ‖ 168
me] ~: ‖ 172 be] ~: ‖ 174 reason] ~. ‖ 175 an] *Dilke*; a ‖ 176 What,] ~∧ | hands?] ~: ‖
177 thee,] ~∧ | simple] ~: ‖ 183 Heauen's] Heauens ‖ 189 honor] ~. ‖ 190 satisfaction] ~? ‖

For all this house in Gold. The very Fates
And you were all one in your power to help me.
And now to come and wonder at my folly,
Mocke me, and make my Loue impossible?
Wretch that I was, I did not keepe it in.   195
    Vand. Alas poore sister; when a greefe is growne
Full home, and to the deepest then it breakes
And ioy (Sunn like) out of a black cloude shineth.
But couldst thou thinke yfaith I was in earnest:
To esteeme any man without the reach   200
Of thy far-shooting beauties? any name
Too Good to subscribe to *Evrione?*
Here is my hand; if euer I were thought
A gentleman or would be still esteemd so
I will so vertuously solicite for thee: 205
And with such cunning wind into his heart,
That I sustaine no doubt I shall dissolue /
His setled Melancholy be it nere so grounded,   [C4]
On rationall loue, and graue Philosophy.
I know my sight will cheere him at the heart: 210
In whom a quick forme of my deare deade Sister
Will fire his heauy spirrits. And all this
May worke that change in him, that nothing else
Hath hope to ioy in, and so farewel Sister
Some few dayes hence, Ile tell thee how I speed.   215
    Eur. Thankes honord Brother: but you shall not goe
Before you dine with your best loued Mistris.
Come in sweet Brother:
    Vand.   In to dinner now?
Midnight would blush at that, farewell, farewell.
    Eur. Deere Brother doe but drinke or tast a Banquet;   220
Y-faith I haue most excellent conserues.
You shall come in; in earnest, stay a little
Or will you drinke some Cordial stilld waters,
After your trauel? pray thee worthy brother
Vpon my loue you shall stay? sweet now enter.   225
    Vand. Not for the world, commend my humble seruice,
And vse all meanes to bring abroad my Mistris.
    Eur. I will in sadnes; farewell happy brother.   *Exeunt.*

---

191 Gold. The] ∼∧ the | Fates] ∼, ‖ **193** folly,] ∼. ‖ **194** me,] ∼? | impossible?] ∼∧ ‖ **195** in.] ∼, ‖ **196** growne] ∼. ‖ **198** like] *followed by a square bracket* ‖ **201** beauties? any name] *Dilke;* ∼∧ ∼ ∼? ‖ **202** *Evrione?*] ∼: ‖ **203** hand;] ∼, ‖ **208** grounded,] ∼. ‖ **209** Philosophy.] ∼, ‖ **215** Ile] ile ‖ **217** Before] before ‖ **219** blush at that,] *Dilke;* ∼, ∼ ∼∧ | farewell.] ∼: ‖ **220** Banquet;] ∼∧ ‖ **221** Y-faith] y-faith | conserues.] ∼∧ ‖ **222** in;] ∼, ‖ **224** trauel?] ∼, ‖

[II.ii]

Enter Phillip. Gveaq. Ieronnime. and Mvgeron. Gveaq. and Iero.
sit down to worke.

Phil. Come *Mvgeron*, where is this worthy statesman,
That you and *Rhoderique* would perswade
To be our worthy Agent into *France*?
The couller we shal lay on it, t'inter
The body of the long deceased Countesse,   5
The French Kings neece, whom her kind husband keepes
With such great cost, and care from buriall,
Will shew as probable as can be thought.
Thinke you he can be gotten to performe it?
   Mug. Feare not my Lord. The wizzard is as forward,   10
To vsurpe greatnes, as all greatnes is
To abuse vertue, or as riches honor.
You cannot loade the Asse with too much honor. /
He shall be yours my Lord; *Rhoderique* and I,   [C4ᵛ]
Will giue him to your highnes for your foote-cloth.   15
   Phil. How happens it, he liud conceald so long?
   Mug. It is his humor sir; for he sayes still,
His iocund mind loues pleasure aboue honor,
His swindge of liberty, aboue his life,
It is not safe (sayes he) to build his nest   20
So neere the Eagle; his mind is his Kingdome
His chamber is a Court, of all good witts;
And many such rare sparkes of Resolution,
He blesseth his most loued selfe withall,
As presently, your excellence shall heare.   25
But there is one thing I had halfe forgotten,
With which your highnes needs must be prepar'd,
I haue discourst with him about the office
Of an Ambassador, and he stands on this.
That when he once hath kist your Highnes hand,   30
And taken his dispatch he then presents
Your Highnes parson, hath your place and power,
Must put his hat on, vse you, as you him:
That you may see before he goes how well,
He can assume your presence and your greatnes.   35
   Phil. And will he practise his new state before vs?

II.ii] *Parrott subs.* ‖ **2** *Rhoderique*] *roman throughout act* | perswade] ∼: ‖ **3** *France?*] *Dilke*; ∼,
roman throughout act ‖ **4** it, t'inter] ∼∧ ∼, ‖ **7** buriall,] ∼: ‖ **9** it?] ∼∧ ‖ **10** Lord.] Lo: ‖ **11**
is].∼: ‖ **14** Lord;] *Dilke*; ∼∧ ‖ **15** foote-cloth.] ∼: ‖ **16** long?] ∼, ‖ **20** he] *followed by a square
bracket* ‖ **21** Eagle;] ∼, ‖ **22** witts;] *Dilke*; ∼, ‖ **26** there] *Dilke*; this | forgotten,] ∼. ‖ **28** office]
∼: ‖ **31** presents] ∼: ‖ **35** greatnes.] ∼∧ ‖

Mug. I and vpon you too, and kisse your Dutchesse,
As you vse at your parting.
    Phil.   Out vpon him,
She will not let him kisse her.
    Mug.   He will kisse her,
To doe your parson right.
    Phil.   It will be excellent: 40
She shall not know this till he offer it.
    Mug. See see, he comes.

        Enter Rhod: Mons: Doliue *and* Pacque.

    Rho.   Heere is the gentleman
Your highnes doth desire to doe you honor
In the presenting of your princely parson
And going Lord Ambassador to th' French King. /   45
    Phil. Is this the gentleman whose worth so highly   [D1]
You recommend to our election?
    Ambo. This is the man my Lord.
    Phil.   Wee vnderstand Sir
We haue beene wrongd, by being kept so long
From notice of your honorable parts   50
Wherein your country claimes a deeper intrest
Then your meere priuate selfe; what makes wise Nature
Fashion in men thiese excellent perfections
Of haughty courage, great wit, wisedome incredible —
    D'Ol. It pleaseth your good excellence to say so.   55
    Phil. But that she aymes therein at publique good
And you in duty thereto of your selfe
Ought to haue made vs tender of your parts
And not entombd them tirant-like aliue.
    Rho. We for our parts, my Lord are not in fault,   60
For we haue spurnd him forward euermore
Letting him know how fit an instrument
He was to play vpon in stately Musique.
    Mug. And if he had bin ought else but an Asse
Your Grace ere this time long had made him great   65
Did not we tell you this?
    D'Ol.   Oftentimes,
But sure my honord Lord the times before
Were not as now they be, thankes to our fortune

38-39 Out . . . her.] *Parrott; one line* (she) ‖ **39** her.] ∼∧ ‖ **39-40** He . . . right.] *Parrott; one line*
(to) ‖ **40** right.] ∼, ‖ **41** it.] ∼: ‖ **42** comes.] ∼, ‖ **45** to th'] to'th | King.] ∼, ‖ **48** Lord.] ∼∧
| Sir] ∼: ‖ **54** incredible—] ∼∧ ‖ **55** so.] ∼∧ ‖ **59** entombd] entombe | aliue.] ∼∧ ‖ **61**
spurnd] *Parrott;* spnrnd ‖

That we inioy so sweet and wise a prince
As is your gratious selfe; for then t'was pollicie   70
To keepe all witts of hope still vnder hatches
Farre from the Court, least their exceeding parts
Should ouer shine those that were then in place
And t'was our happines, that we might liue so
For in that freely choos'd obscuritie   75
Wee found our safetie, which men most of Note
Many times lost, and I ahlas for my part,
Shrunk my despised head in my poore shell,
For your learnd excellence, I know knows well /

              Qui bene latuit, bene vixit, still.   [D1ᵛ] 80

    Phil. Twas much you could containe your selfe, that had
So great meanes to haue liu'd in greater place.
    D'Ol. Faith Sir I had a poore roofe, or a paint-house
To shade me from the Sunne, and three or foure tyles
To shrow'd me from the Rayne, and thought my selfe   85
As private as I had King *Gyges* Ring
And could haue gone invisible, yet saw all
That past our states rough Sea both neere and farre,
There saw I our great Galliasses tost
Vpon the wallowing waues, vp with one billow   90
And then downe with another: Our great men
Like to a Masse of clowds that now seeme like
An Elephant, and straight wayes like an Oxe
And then a Mouse, or like those changeable creatures
That liue in the Burdello, now in Satten   95
Tomorrow next in Stammell.
When I sate all this while in my poore cell
Secure of lightning, or the sodaine Thunder,
Conuerst with the poore Muses, gaue a scholler
Forty or fiftie crownes a yeare to teach me   100
And prate to me about the predicables
When indeede my thoughts flew a higher pitch
Then Genus and Species as by this tast
I hope your highnes happyly preceiues
And shall hereafter more at large approue   105
If any worthy opportunitie

---

78 shell,] ∼∧ ‖ **79** know] konow | well] ∼. ‖ **80** *Qui . . . vixit*] roman ‖ **82** place.] ∼∧ ‖ **86** *Gyges*] Dilke; *Giris* ‖ **98** Thunder,] *Lowell;* ∼∧ ‖ **100** or] *Q(c);* of *Q(u)* ‖

Make but her fore topp subiect to my hold
And so I leaue your Grace to the tuition
Of him that made you.
    Rho.   Soft good Sir I pray:
What sayes your Excellence to this gentleman?   110
Haue I not made my word good to your highnes?
    Phil. Well Sir, how euer Enuious policie
Hath rob'd my predicessors of your seruice
You must not scape my hands, that haue design'd /
Present employment for you; and tis this: [D2] 115
T'is not vnknowne vnto you with what griefe
Wee take the sorrow of the Earle *Saint Anne*
For his deceased wife; with whose dead sight
Hee feeds his passion, keeping her from right
Of christian buriall, to make his eyes   120
Doe pennance by their euerlasting teares
For loosing the deare sight of her quick bewties.
    D'Ol. Well spoke y-faith, your grace must giue me leaue
To praise your witt, for faith tis rarely spoken.
    Phil. The better for your good commendation   125
But Sir your Ambassy to the French King
Shall be to this effect; thus you shall say —
    D'Ol. Not so, your Excellence shall pardon me
I will not haue my tale put in my mouth.
If you'le deliuer me your mind in grose   130
Why so; I shall expresse it as I can
I warrant you t'wilbe sufficient.
    Phil. T'is very good, then Sir my will in grose
Is that in pitty of the sad Countes case
The King would aske the body of his Neece   135
To giue it Funerall fitting her high blood,
Which (as your selfe requires and reason wills)
I leaue to be enforst and amplyfied
With all the Ornaments of Arte and Nature
Which flowes I see in your sharp intellect.   140
    D'Ol. Ahlas you cannot see't in this short time
But there be some not far hence that haue seene
And heard me too ere now: I could haue wisht

---

113 rob'd] ∼? ‖ **115** Present] present | this:] ∼∧ ‖ **116** you] ∼; ‖ **117** *Saint Anne*] *roman* ‖ **122**
bewties.] ∼∧ ‖ **124** spoken.] ∼∧ ‖ **127** say—] ∼∧ ‖ **129** mouth.] ∼∧ ‖ **131** so;] *Dilke*; ∼∧
‖ **134** Countes] *stet* (*See Textual Note*) ‖ **140** intellect.] ∼∧ ‖ **142** But] Bur | be] ∼, ‖

Your highnes presence in a priuat Conuenticle
At what time the high point of state was handled.   145
   Phil. What was the point?
   D'Ol. It was my happ to make a number there
My selfe (as euery other Gentleman)
Beeing interested in that graue affayre
Where I deliuer'd my opinion: how well — /   150
   Phil. What was the matter pray?   [D2ᵛ]
   D'Ol.   The matter, Sir,
Was of an antient subiect, and yet newly
Cald into question; And t'was this in breefe
We sate as I remember all in rowt,
All sorts of men together,   155
A Squier and a Carpenter, a Lawier and a Sawier.
A Marchant and a Broker, a Iustice and a peasant
And so forth without all difference.
   Phil. But what was the matter?
   D'Ol. Faith a stale argument though newly handled   160
And I am fearefull I shall shame my selfe:
The subiect is so thred bare.
   Phil.   Tis no matter
Be as it wil; go to the point I pray.
   D'Ol. Then thus it is: the question of estate
(Or the state of the question) was in briefe   165
Whether in an Aristocratie
Or in a Democriticall estate
Tobacco might be brought to lawfull vse.
But had you heard the excellent speeches there
Touching this part: 170
   Mug. Rho. Pray thee to the point.
   D'Ol. First to the point then,
Vpstart a weauer, blowne vp b'inspiration,
That had borne office in the congregation
A little fellow and yet great in spirit   175
I neuer shall forget him; for he was
A most hot liuer'd enemie to Tobacco.
His face was like the ten of Diamonds
Pointed each where with pushes, and his Nose
Was like the Ase of clubs (which I must tell you   180
Was it that set him, and Tobacco first
At such hot Enmitie) for that nose of his

---

145 handled.] ∼? ‖ **150** well—] ∼? ‖ **151** *Phil.*] *Dilke*; *Dol*: | pray?] ∼∧ | *D'Ol.*] *Dilke* |
Sir,] ∼. ‖ **158** And] and | difference.] ∼∧ ‖ **162** bare.] ∼∧ ‖ **162-63** Tis . . . pray.] *Shepherd*;
one line (be) ‖ **163** wil;] *Lowell*; ∼∧ | the point] y'point | pray.] ∼, ‖ **166** Whether] whether ‖
168 vse.] ∼∧ ‖ **17 1** point.] ∼∧ ‖ **173** *Vpstart*] *roman* | b'inspiration,] ∼∧ ‖ **177** Tobacco.] ∼∧
‖ **18 1-87** Was . . . Pett.] *Dilke*; *as prose* (at . . . according . . . hauing . . . being . . . his . . . and)
‖ **182** Enmitie] Enmitle ‖

(According to the Puritannick cut)
Hauing a narrow bridge, and this Tobacco,
Being in drink durst not passe by and finding stopt   185
His narrow passage fled backe as it came
And went away in Pett. /

    Mug.   Iust cause of quarrell.   [D3]

    Phil. But pray thee, briefely say what said the weauer?

    D'Ol. The weauer Sir much like a virginall iack
Start nimbly vp; the culler of his beard   190
I scarse remember; but purblind he was
With the *Geneva* print, and wore one eare
Shorter then tother for a difference.

    Phil. A man of very open note it seemes.

    D'Ol. He was so Sir, and hotly he envaid   195
Against Tobacco (with a most strong breath
For he had eaten garlicke the same morning
As t'was his vse partly against ill ayres
Partly to make his speeches sauorie)
Said t'was a pagan plant, a prophane weede   200
And a most sinful smoke, that had no warrant
Out of the word; inuented sure by *Sathan*
In theise our latter dayes, to cast a mist
Before mens eyes, that they might not behold
The grosenes of olde superstition   205
Which is as t'were deriu'd into the church
From the fowle sinke of Romish popery
And that it was a iudgement on our land
That the svbstantiall commodities
And mighty blessings of this Realme of *France*   210
Bells, Rattles, hobby horses and such like
Which had brought so much wealth into the Land
Should now be changd into the smoke of vanitie
The smoke of superstition; for his owne part
He held a Garlick cloue being sanctifyed   215
Did edifie more the body of a man
Then a whole tun of this prophane Tobacco
Being tane without thankes-giuing; in a word
He said it was a ragge of Popery,
And none that were truely regenerate would   220
Prophane his Nosthrils with the smoke thereof.
And speaking of your grace behind your back, /

---

183 cut] *followed by a square bracket* ‖ **184** Tobacco,] *Lowell*; ∼: ‖ **187** quarrell.] ∼∧ ‖ **188** thee,] ∼∧ | weauer?] ∼∧ ‖ **193** difference.] ∼∧ ‖ **194** seemes.] ∼∧ ‖ **199** sauorie)] ∼∧ ‖ **202** *Sathan*] *roman* ‖ **209** commodities] ∼. ‖ **219** Popery,] ∼? ‖ **221** thereof.] ∼∧ ‖

He chargd and coniur'd you to see the vse,   [D3ᵛ]
Of vaine Tobacco banisht from the land
For feare least for the great abuse thereof   225
Our candle were put out; and therewithall
Taking his handker-chiefe to wipe his mouth
As he had told a lie, he tun'd his nose
To the olde straine as if he were preparing
For a new exercise. But I my selfe   230
(Angry to heare this generous Tabacco
The Gentlemans Saint and the souldiers idoll
So ignorantly poluted) stood me vp
Tooke some Tabacco for a complement
Brake fleame some twice or thrice, then shooke mine eares   235
And lickt my lipps, as if I begg'd attention
And so directing me to your sweet Grace
Thus I replyed,
    Rho. Mug. Rome for a speach there. Silence.
    D'Ol. I am amused, or I am in a quandarie gentlemen (for in good   240
faith I remember not well whether of them was my words)
    Phil. Tis no matter either of them will serue the turne.
    D'Ol. Whether I should (as the Poet sayes) *eloquar, an siliam*;
whether by answering a foole I should my selfe seeme no lesse; or by
giuing way to his winde (for words are but winde) I might betray the   245
cause; to the maintaynance whereof, all true Troyans (from whose
race we claime our decent) owe all their patrimonies; and if neede be
their dearest blood, and their sweetest breath; I would not be tedious
to your highnes:
    Phil. You are not Sir: Proceede: 250
    D'Ol. Tabacco that excellent plant, the vse whereof (as of fift
Element) the world cannot want, is that little shop of Nature, wherein
her whole workeman-ship is abridg'd; where you may see Earth kindled into fier, the fire breath out an exhalation, which entring in at the
mouth walkes through the Regions of a mans brayne, driues / out all [D4] 255
ill Vapours but itselfe, drawes downe all bad Humors by the mouth,
which in time might breed a Scabbe ouer the whole body if already
they haue not; a plant of singular vse, for on the one side, Nature being
an Enemie to Vacuitie and emptines, and on the other, there beeing
so many empty braines in the World as there are, how shall Natures   260
course be continued? How shall thiese empty braines be filled, but
with ayre Natures immediate instrument to that purpose? If with

225 For feare] Forfeare ‖ **226** Our] *Dilke;* Or ‖ **228** nose] *Dilke;* noise ‖ **230** exercise.] ∼, ‖
231-33 Angry . . . poluted] *in square brackets* ‖ **237** And] and ‖ **239** Silence.] ∼∧ ‖ **240-41** for
. . . words] *in square brackets* ‖ **242** turne.] ∼∧ ‖ **243** *eloquar, an siliam*;] eloquar, an siliam? ‖ **247**
decent] *followed by a square bracket* ‖ **248** breath;] ∼, ‖ **251-52** as . . . Element] *in square brackets* ‖
255 brayne,] *Q(c);* ∼∧ *Q(u)* ‖ **256** the] *Dilke;* the the ‖ **260** there] *Q(c);* thete *Q(u)* ‖

ayre, what so proper as your fume: what fume so healthfull as your
perfume? what perfume so soueraigne as Tabacco? Besides the excellent edge it giues a mans wit, (as they can best iudge that haue beene   265
present at a feast of Tobacco where commonly all good witts are con-
sorted) what varietie of discourse it begetts? What sparkes of wit it
yeelds, it is a world to heare: as likewise to the courage of a man, for
if it be true, that *Iohannes de Sauoret* writes, that hee that drinkes
Veriuice pisseth vinegere, Then it must needs follow to be as true,   270
that hee that eates smoke, farts fire; for Garlicke I will not say because
it is a plant of our owne country; but it may cure the diseases of the
country, but for the diseases of the Court, they are out of the Element
of Garlick to medicine; to conclude, as there is no enemy to Tabacco
but Garlick, so there is no friend to Garlick, but a sheeps head, and so   275
I conclude.

   Phil. Well Sir, Yf this be but your Naturall vaine
I must confesse I knew you not indeede
When I made offer to instruct your brayne
For the Ambassage, and will trust you now   280
If t'were to send you foorth to the great Turke
With an Ambassage.

   D'Ol.   But Sir in conclusion
T'was orderd for my speach, that since Tobacco
Had so long bin in vse, it should thence foorth /
Be brought to lawfull vse; but limitted thus   [D4ᵛ] 285
That none should dare to take it but a gentleman
Or he that had some gentlemanly humor
The Murr, the Head-ach, the Cattar, the bone-ach
Or other branches of the sharpe salt Rhewme
Fitting a gentleman.   290

   Rho. Your grace has made choise
Of a most simple Lord Ambassador.

   Phil. Well Sir you neede not looke for a commission
My hand shall well dispatch you for this busines
Take now the place and state of an Ambassador   295
Present our parson and performe our charge
And so farewell good Lord Ambassador.

   D'Ol. Farewell good Duke and *Gveaqvin* to thee.   [*Kisses her.*]
   Gue. How now you foole? out you presumptious gull.

265-67 as . . . consorted] *in square brackets* ‖ 269 *Iohannes*] Iehannes *Q(u)*; Iohannes *Q(c)* |
de Sauoret] de sauo et sauo et (*See Textual Note*) ‖ 272 country;] ∼? ‖ 274 conclude,] ∼∧ ‖
275 to Garlick] *Q(c)*; to GarIck *Q(u)* | head,] ∼∧ ‖ 282 Ambassage.] ∼∧ ‖ 288 bone-ach]
∼.∼ ‖ 292 Lord Ambassador.] Lo: ∼∧ ‖ 295 Ambassador] Anbassador ‖ 297 Ambassador.]
∼∧ ‖ 298 thee.] ∼∧ | SD *Kisses her.*] *Dilke subs.* ‖ 299 gull.] ∼∧ ‖

D'Ol. How now you baggage? sfoote, are you so coy   300
To the Dukes parson, to his second selfe?
Are you to good dame to enlarge your selfe
Vnto your proper obiect? slight twere a good deede —
    Gue. What meanes your grace to suffer me abus'd thus?
    Phil. Sweet Loue be pleas'd; you do not know this Lord.   305
Giue me thy hand my Lord:
    D'Ol.   And giue me thine:
    Phil. Farewell againe.
    D'Ol.   Farewell againe to thee.
    Phil. Now go thy wayes for an ambassador.   *Exiunt* Phil. Gueaq; Iero:
    D'Ol. Now goe thy wayes for a Duke.
    Mug. Rho. Most excellent Lord.   310
    Rho. Why this was well performd and like a Duke
Whose parson you most naturally present.
    D'Ol. I told you I would doo't, now Ile begin
To make the world take notice I am noble;
The first thing I will doe ile sweare to pay   315
No debts, vpon my honor.
    Mug. A good cheape proofe of your Nobilitie. /
    D'Ol. But if I knew where I might pawne mine honor,   [E1]
For some odd thousand Crownes, it shalbe layd:
Ile pay't againe when I haue done withall: 320
Then twill be expected I shalbe of some Religion,
I must thinke of one for fashion, or for faction sake,
As it becomes great personages to doe:
Ile thinke vpon't betwixt this and the day.
    Rho. Well sayd my Lord; this Lordship of yours wil worke a mighty   325
alteration in you: do you not feele it begins to worke alreadie?
    D'Ol. Fayth onely in this; it makes mee thinke, how they that were
my Companions before, shall now be my fauorites: They that were
my Friends before, shall now be my followers: They that were my
Seruants before, shall now be my knaues: But they that were my   330
Creditors before, shall remaine my Creditors still.
    Mug. Excellent Lord: Come, will you shew your Lordship in the
Presence now?
    D'Ol. Faith, I do not care if I go and make a face or two there, or
a few gracefull legges; speake a little Italian, and away; there's all a   335
Presence doth require.   *[Exeunt.]*

Finis Actvs Secvndi.

---

302 Are] are ‖ **303** deede—] ~∧ ‖ **304** thus?] ~∧ ‖ **305** Lord.] ~∧ ‖ **306** thine:] ~∧ ‖ **307**
againe.] ~∧ | thee.] ~∧ ‖ **308** ambassador.] ~∧ | SD Phil.] ~∧ ‖ **309** Duke.] ~∧ ‖ **310**
Lord.] ~, ‖ **312** present.] ~∧ ‖ **313** Ile] ile ‖ **314** noble;] ~∧ ‖ **316** debts,] *Shepherd;* ~∧ ‖
317 Nobilitie.] ~∧ ‖ **322** one] some ‖ **334** Faith,] ~∧ | care] ~, ‖ **336** SD *Exeunt.*] *Parrott* ‖

Actvs Tertii. Scæna prima.

Enter Vandome, and St. Anne.

St. Anne.

You haue enclinde me more to leaue this life,
Then I supposde it possible for an Angell;
Nor is your iudgement to suppresse your passion
For so deare lou'd a Sister (being as well
Your blood and flesh, as mine) the least enforcement   5
Of your disswasiue arguments. And besides,
Your true resemblance of her, much supplies
Her want in my affections; with all which,
I feele in these deepe griefes, to which I yeeld
A kind of falce sluggish (and rotting sweetnes,) /   10
Mixt with an humour where all things in life,   [E1ᵛ]
Lie drownd in sower, wretched, and horred thoughts:
The way to cowardly desperation opened.
And whatsoeuer vrgeth soules accurst,
To their destruction, and sometimes their plague,   15
So violently gripes me, that I lie
Whole dayes and nightes bound at his tirranous feete:
So that my dayes are not like life or light,
But bitterest death, and a continuall night.
    Vand. The ground of all is vnsuffised Loue,   20
Which would be best easd with some other obiect:
The generall rule of *Naso* being autentique

Quod successore nouo vincitur omnis Amor:

For the affections of the minde drawne foorth
In many currents, are not so impulsiue   25
In anie one; And so the *Persian* King
Made the great Riuer *Ganges* runn distinctly
In an innumerable sort of Channels;
By which meanes, of a fierce and dangerous Flood,
He turnd it into many pleasing Riuers: 30
So likewise is an Armie disarayd,
Made penetrable for the assaulting foe:
So huge fiers being deffused, grow asswadgd:
Lastly, as all force being vnite, increaseth;
So, being dispearst, it growes lesse sharpe, and ceaseth.   35

Scæna] *Sæna* ‖ **3** passion] ∼: ‖ **13** opened.] ∼, ‖ **14** accurst,] ∼: ‖ **17** tirranous] *Q(c)*; terrinous
Q(u) ‖ **23** vincitur] *Q(c)*; viuatur *Q(u)* ‖

St. Anne. Ahlas, I know I cannot loue another,
My hart accustomd to loue onely her,
My eyes accustomd to view onely her,
Will tell me whatsoeuer is not her,
Is foule and hatefull.

Vand.   Yet forbeare to keepe her   40
Still in your sight: force not her breathles body
Thus against Nature to suruiue; being dead,
Let it consume, that it may reassume
A forme incorruptible; and refraine
The places where you vsde to ioy in her: 45

        Heu fuge dilectas terras, fuge littus Amatum:

For how can you be euer sound or safe,
Wherein so many red lips of your wounds, /
Gaspe in your eyes? with change of place be sure,   [E2]
Like sicke men mending, you shall find recure.   50

    Enter the Duke, D'oliue, Gueaquin, Ieronime, Muge, Rhod. to see the
        dead Countesse that is kept in her attire vnburied.

D'Ol. Fayth Madam, my companie may well be spard at so mournefull a visitation: For, by my soule, to see *Pigmalion* dote vpon a Marble Picture, a senceles Statue, I should laugh and spoyle the Tragedie.

Gue. Oh, tis an obiect full of pittie my Lord.

D'Ol. Tis pittie in deed, that any man should loue a woman so   55
constantly.

Phil. Bitterly turnd my Lord: we must still admire you.

D'Ol. Tush my Lord, true Manhood can neither mourne nor
admire: It's fitt for Women, they can weepe at pleasure, euen to
admiration.   60

Gue. But men vse to admire rare things, my Lord.

D'Ol. But this is nothing rare; Tis a vertue common for men to
loue their Wiues after death: The value of a good Wife (as all good
things else) are better knowne by their want, then by their fruition:
for no man loues his Wife so well while she liues, but he loues her ten   65
times better when shee's dead.

Rho. This is sound Philosophie, my Lord.

D'Ol. Faith, my Lord, I speake my thoughts; and for mine owne
part, I should so ill indure the losse of a Wife (always prouided, I
lou'd her) that if I lost her this weeke, I'de haue another by the begin-   70
ning a'th next: And thus resolu'd, I leaue your Highnes to deale with
Atropos, for cutting my Ladyes threed: I am for *France*; all my care

---

39-40 Will . . . hatefull.] *Shepherd; one line* (is) ‖ **42** suruiue; being dead,] ∼, ∼ ∼: ‖ **46** *dilectas*]
Q(c); delectas Q(u) | *littus*] *Q(c); actus Q(u)* ‖ **48** Wherein] Where in | lips] *Deighton conj.*; steps
‖ **50** SD *Gueaquin*] *Q(c); Guraquin Q(u)* | *Ieronime*] *Q(c); Ierommie Q(u)* ‖ **57** Phil.] Duke. ‖ **61**
Lord.] ∼, ‖ **72** threed] *Q(c);* throat *Q(u)* ‖

is for Followers to Imp out my Traine: I feare I must come to your
Grace for a Presse; for I will be followd as becomes an honorable
Lord: and that is, like an honest Squire: for with our great Lords,   75
followers abrod, and Hospitalitie at home, are out of date: The
world's now growne thriftie: He that fils a whole Page in folio, with
his Stile; thinkes it veriest Noble, to be mand with one bare Page and
a *Pandare*; and yet *Pandare* in auntient time, was the name of an honest Courtier; what tis now, *Viderit vtilitas*: Come Witts, let's to my   80
Chamber.   *Exeunt. Manent Vando. S. An. /*

  Vand. Well now my Lord, remember all the reasons   [E2ᵛ]
And arguments I vsde at first to you,
To draw you from your hurtfull passions:
And therewithall, admit one further cause,   85
Drawne from my loue, and all the powers I haue;
Euryone, vow'd sister to my sister,
Whose vertues, beauties, and perfections,
Adorne our Countrie, and do neerest match
With her rich graces, that your loue adores,   90
Hath wounded my affections; and to her
I would intreat your Lordships gracefull word.
  St. Anne. But is it true? Loues my deare brother now?
It much delights me, for your choyce is Noble:
Yet need you not vrge me to come abrode,   95
Your owne worth will suffize for your wisht speed.
  Vand. I know my Lord, no man aliue can winn
Her resolu'd iudgment from virginitie,
Vnlesse you speake for him, whose word of all Dames
Is held most sweet, and worthie to perswade them.   100
  St. Anne. The world will thinke mee too phantasticall,
To ope so sodenly my vow'd obscurenes.
  Vand. My Lord, my loue is suddaine, and requires
A suddaine remedie: If I be delayed,
Consider Loues delay breedes desperation,   105
By waighing how strongly Loue workes in your selfe.
  St. Anne. Deare Brother, nothing vnderneath the Starres,
Makes mee so willing to pertake the ayre,
And vndergo the burden of the world,
As your most worthy selfe, and your wisht good: 110
And glad I am that by this meanes I may
See your descent continued, and therein
Behold some new borne Image of my wife: *[Addressing his dead wife.]*

92 word.] ∼: ‖ **113** SD *Addressing . . . wife.*] ‖

433

Deare life, take knowledge that thy Brothers loue,
Makes me dispaire with my true zeale to thee: 115
And if for his sake I admit the Earth
To hide this treasure of thy pretious beauties;
And that thy part suruiuing, be not pleasd,
Let it appeare to mee ye iust assisters /
Of all intentions bent to soueraigne iustice; [E3] 120
And I will follow it into the Graue,
Or dying with it; or preserue it thus,
As long as any life is left betwixt vs. *Exeunt.*

[III.ii]

Enter Monseuer D'oliue, Rhoderique.

D'Ol. But didst note what a presence I came of with-all?

Rho. Sfoot, you drew the eyes of the whole presence vpon you:
There was one Ladie a man might see her hart Readie to start out of
her eyes to follow you.

D'Ol. But *Monseuer Mustapha* there kept state, when I accosted 5
him; s'light the Brasen head lookt to be Worshipt I thinke: No Ile
commit no Idolatrie for the proudest Image of 'am all, I.

Rho. Your Lordship has the right garbe of an excellent Courtier;
respect's a Clowne, supple ioynted courtesie's a verie peagoose; tis stiffe
ham'd audacity that carries it; get once within their distance, and you 10
are in their bosoms instantly.

D'Ol. S'hart doe they looke I should stande aloofe, like a Scholar,
and make leggs at their greatnes? No Ile none of that; come vp close
to him, giue him a clap a'th shoulder shall make him crie oh againe:
it's a tender place to deale withal, and say, Well encounterd noble 15
Brutus.

Rho. That's the onely way indeed to be familiar.

D'Ol. S'foot Ile make leggs to none, vnlesse it be to a Iustice of
peace when he speakes in's Chaire, or to a Cunstable when he leanes
on's Staffe, that's flat: softnes and modestie sauors of the Cart, tis 20
boldnes boldnes does the deed in the Court: and as your Camelion
varries all cullours a'th Rainebow but white and red, so must your true
Courtier be able to varrie his countenance through all humors; State,
Strangnes, Scorne, Mirth, Melanchollie, Flatterie, and so foorth: some
cullours likewise his face may change vpon occasion, Blacke or Blew it 25
may, Tawnie it may; but Redd and White at no hand, auoyde that like
a Sergeant: keepe your cullour still unguiltie of passion or disgrace,

---

III.ii] *Parrott* ‖ SD *Monseuer*] ∼, ‖ 2-4 Sfoot . . . you.] *Dilke*; Sfoot . . . you: / There . . . hart /
Readie . . . you. / ‖ 5 when] When ‖ 8-9 Courtier; respect's] *Dilke*; ∼, respects ‖ 9 ioynted
courtesie's] *Shepherd*; ∼, courtesies ‖ 12 looke] *Dilke*; ∼? | Scholar] Scholares ‖ 13 greatnes?]
∼: ‖ 17 That's] Thats ‖ 20 that's] thats ‖ 22 but] both ‖ 27 still] stiffe, ‖

not changing White at sight of your Mercer, nor Red at sight of your Surgeon: aboue all sinnes, heauen sheild mee from the sinne of blushing; it does ill in a young Waighting / woman, but monstrous mon- [E3ᵛ] 30 strous, in an old Courtier.

Rho. Well, all this while your Lordship forgets your Ambassage; you haue giuen out, you will be gone within this moneth, and yet nothing is readie.

D'Ol. It's no matter, let the Moone keepe her course: and yet to   35 say trueth, t'were more then time I were gone, for by heauen I am so haunted with Followers, euerie day new offers of Followers: But heauen shield me from any more Followers. How now, what's the newes?

Enter Muge, and two others.

Mug. My Lord, heere's two of my speciall Friends, whom I would   40 gladly commend to follow you in the honorable action.

D'Ol. S'foote, my eares are double lockt against Followers, you know my number's full, all places vnder mee are bestowde: Ile out of towne this night, that's infallible; Ile no more Followers, a mine honour.   45

Mug. S'light my Lord, you must entertaine them, they haue paid me their income, and I haue vndertaken your Lordshippe shall grace them.

D'Ol. Well my Maisters, you might haue come at a time when your entertainement would haue proou'd better then now it is like: but   50 such as it is, vpon the commendation of my Steward here —

Mug. A pox a your Lordship! Steward?

D'Ol. Y'are welcome in a word: deserne and spie out.

Ambo. Wee humbly thanke your Lordship.

D'Ol. Mugeron, let 'am be enterd.   55

Mug. In what rancke my Lord, Gentlemen or Yomen?

D'Ol. Gentlemen, Their bearing berayes no lesse, it goes not alwayes by apparrell: I do alow you to suite your selues anew in my Cullours at your owne charges.

Ambo. Thanke your good Lordship.   60

D'Ol. Thy name first, I pray thee?

Cor. Cornelius, My Lord.

D'Ol. What profession? /

Cor. A Surgeon an't please your Lordship. [E4]

D'Ol. I had rather th'hadst been a Barber, for I thinke there wilbe   65 little blood-shed amongst my Followers, vnlesse it be of thy letting: Ile see their nailes parde before they goe. And yet now I bethinke my

35 It's] Its ‖ **38** what's] whats ‖ **44** night,] *Lowell*; ∼∧ | that's] tha'ts ‖ **46** my] *See Textual Note* ‖ **47** their] *Q(c)*; my *Q(u)* ‖ **51** here—] ∼∧ ‖ **52** Lordship!] *Shepherd*; Lor. ‖

selfe, our Ambassage is into *Fraunce,* there may be employment for
thee: hast thou a Tubbe?

Cor. I would be loth, my Lord, to be dislocated or vnfurnisht of any 70
of my properties.

D'Ol. Thou speak'st like thy selfe *Cornelius:* booke him downe
Gentleman.

Mug. Verie well Sir.

D'Ol. Now your profession, I pray? 75

Frip. Fripperie, my Lord, or as some tearme it, *Petty Brokery.*

D'Ol. An honest man Ile warrant thee, I neuer knew other of thy
trade.

Frip. Trulie a richer your Lordship might haue, An honester I hope
not. 80

D'Ol. I beleeue thee *Pettie Broker:* canst burne Gold-lace?

Frip. I can do anie thing, my Lord, belonging to my trade.

D'Ol. Booke him downe Gentleman, heele do good vpon the voyage I warrant him: prouide thee a Nagge *Pettie Broker,* thou'l finde
employment for him doubt not: keepe thy selfe an honest man, and 85
by our returne I doe not doubt but to see thee a rich Knaue: Farewel
Pettie Broker, prepare your selues against the day; this Gentleman
shall acquaint you with my Cullours: Farewell *Fripper,* Farewell
Pettie Broker: Deserne and spie out is my *Motto.*

Ambo. God continue your Lordship. *Exeunt.*

Rho. [*Aside.*] A verie seasonable praier, for vnknowne to him, it
lies now vpon his death-bedd.

D'Ol. And how like you my Chamber good Witts?

Rho. Excellent well Sir.

D'Ol. Nay beleeue it, it shall do well (as you will say) when you 95
see't set foorth sutable to my proiect: Here shall stand my Court Cup-
bord, with its furniture of Plate: Heere shall runne a Wind Instrument: Heere shall hang my base Viall: Heere my Theorbo: and
heere will I hang my selfe. /

Ambo. Twill do admirable well. [E4ᵛ] 100

D'Ol. But how will I hange my selfe good witts? Not in person,
but in Picture; I will be drawne.

Rho. What hangd and drawne too?

D'Ol. Good againe: I say I wilbe drawne, all in compleat Satten of
some Courtly cullour, like a Knight of *Cupids* band: On this side 105
shalbe ranckt Chaires and Stooles, and other such complements of a
Chamber: This corner will be a conuenient roome for my Close
stoole: I acquaint you with all my priuities, you see.

---

76 *Brokery*] *Prokery* ‖ **89** spie out is] *Q(c);* spieout an't is *Q(u)* ‖ **90** SD *Exeunt.*] *Dilke; follows
preceding line* ‖ **91** SD *Aside.*] *Parrott* ‖ **91-92** A . . . death-bedd.] *Parrott;* A . . . praier, / For
. . . death-bedd. / ‖ **91** seasonable] *stet (See Textual Note)* | for] For ‖ **96** Here] *Q(c);* Heere
Q(u) ‖ **97** its] *Lowell; om. Q(u);* it *Q(c)* ‖ **105** Courtly] *Q(c);* Gourtly *Q(u)* ‖

Mug. I Sir, we smell your meaning.

D'Ol. Heere shalbe a Peartch for my Parrat; while I remaine vn-   110
married, I shall haue the lesse misse of my Wife: Heere a Hoope for
my Munckie; when I am married, my wife will haue the lesse misse of
mee: Heere will I haue the statue of some excellent Poet, and I will
haue his Nose goe with a Vice (as I haue seene the experience) And
that (as if t'had taken cold i'th head,)   115

Rho. For want of a guilt Nightcap.

D'Ol. Bitter still, shall like a Spout runne pure Witt all day long;
and it shalbe fedd with a Pipe brought at my charge, from *Helicon,*
ouer the Alpes, and vnder the Sea by the braine of some great Enginer;
and I thinke twill do excellent.   120

Mug. No question of that, my Lord.

D'Ol. Well, now Witts about your seuerall charges touching my
Ambassage: *Rhoderique,* is my Speach put out to making?

Rho. It's almost done.

D'Ol. Tis well, tell him he shall haue fourtie Crownes; promisse,   125
promisse; want for no promising: And well remembred, haue I ere a
Gentleman Vsher yet? a strange thing, amongst all my followers, not
one has witt enough to be a Gentleman Vsher; I must haue one ther's
no remedie; Fare-well: haue a care of my Followers, all but my pettie
Broker, heele shift for him selfe.   130

Rho. Well, let vs alone for your followers.

D'Ol. Well said, deserue and spie out.

Ambo. We thanke your Lordship.   *Exeunt. Manet D'oliue.*

D'Ol. Heauen I beseech thee, what an abhominable sort of / Fol-   [F1]
lowers haue I put vpon mee? These Courtiers feed on 'am with my   135
countenaunce: I can not looke into the Cittie, but one or other makes
tender of his good partes to me, either his Language, his Trauaile, his
Intelligence, or something: Gentlemen send me their younger Sonnes
furnisht in compleat, to learne fashions for-sooth; as if the riding of
fiue hundred miles, and spending 1000. Crownes would make 'am   140
wiser then God meant to make 'am. Others with-child with the trauailing humor, as if an Asse for going to *Paris,* could come home a
Courser of *Naples*: Others are possest with the humor of Gallantrie,
fancie it to be the onelie happinesse in this world, to be enabled by
such a coolor to carrie a Feather in his Crest, weare Gold-lace, guilt   145
Spurs, and so sets his fortunes ont: Turnes two or three Tenements
into Trunckes, and creepes home againe with lesse then a Snayle, not a
House to hide his head in: Three hundred of these Gold-finches I
haue entertaind for my Followers; I can go in no corner, but I meete

---

110 Parrat;] ∼, ‖ 112 Munckie;] ∼∧ ‖ 124 It's] Its ‖ 127 yet?] ∼; ‖ 128 Vsher;] ∼, ‖ 132
out.] ∼∧ ‖ 133 We] *Dilke*; Me | SD *Exeunt . . . D'oliue.*] *Dilke; follows preceding line* ‖ 135 mee?]
∼: ‖

with some of my Wifflers in their accoutraments; you may heare 'am   150
halfe a mile ere they come at you, and smell 'am halfe an hower after
they are past you; sixe or seauen make a perfect Morrice-daunce;
they need no Bells, their Spurs serue their turne: I am ashamd to
traine 'am abroade, theyle say I carrie a whole Forrest of Feathers
with mee, and I should plod afore 'am in plaine stuffe, like a writing   155
Schole-maister before his Boyes when they goe a feasting: I am afraid
of nothing but I shall be Ballated, I and all my Wifflers: But it's no
matter, Ile fashion 'am, Ile shew 'am fashions: By heauen Ile giue
three parts of 'am the slipp, let 'am looke fort: and yet to say trueth,
I shall not need, for if I can but linger my Iorney another moneth, I   160
am sure I shall mute halfe my Feathers; I feele 'am begin to weare
thinne alreadie: There's not tenne Crownes in twentie a their purses:
And by this light, I was told at Court, that my greasie Host of the
Porcupine last Holiday, was got vp to the eares in one of my Followers
Satten suites; And *Vandome* went so farre, that he swore he saw two   165
of them hangd: My selfe indeed passing yesterday by the *Fripperie*,
spide two of them hang out at a stall with a gambrell thrust from
shoulder to shoulder, like a / Sheepe that were new flead: Tis not   [F1ᵛ]
for nothing that this Pettie Broker followes me; The Vulture smels a
pray; not the Carcases, but the Cases of some of my deceassed Follow-   170
ers; S'light, I thinke it were my wisest course, to put tenne poundes in
stocke with him, and turne pettie Broker; certainelie there's good to be
done vpon't; if we be but a day or two out of towne heele be able to
load euerie day a fresh Horse with Satten suites, and send them backe
hither: indeed tis like to be hot trauaile, and therefore t'wilbe an ease 175
to my Followers to haue their cloathes at home afore 'am; Theyle on,
get off how they can: Little know they what Pikes their Feathers must
passe: Before they goe, the Sergeants; when they come home, the
Surgeons: but chuse them, Ile wash my hands on 'am.   *Exit.*

Finis Actvs Tertii.

Actvs Qvarti. Scœna prima.

Vandome solus.

My Sisters Exequies are now performed
With such pompe as exprest the excellence
Of her Lords loue to her: And firde the enuie
Of our great Duke, who would haue no man equall

---

157 it's] its ‖ **178** goe, the Sergeants;] *Lowell;* ∼∧ ∼ ∼, | home,] *Dilke;* ∼∧ ‖ *Scœna*] *Sæna* ‖

The honour he does t'his adored wife: 5
And now the Earle (as he hath promist mee)
Is in this sad Cell of my honord Mistresse,
Vrging my loue to faire *Euryone,*
Which I framde, onely to bring him abrode,
And (if it might succeed) make his affectes   10
With change of obiectes, change his helples sorrow
To helpfull loue. I stood where I obseru'd
Their wordes and lookes, and all that past betwixt them:
And shee hath with such cunning borne her selfe,
In fitting his affection, with pretending   15
Her mortified desires: her onely loue
To Vertue and her louers: and, in briefe, /
Hath figurd with such life my deare dead Sister,   [F2]
Enchasing all this, with her heightned Beautie,
That I beleeue she hath entangld him,   20
And wonn successe to our industrious plot.
If he be toucht, I know it greiues his soule,
That hauing vndertane to speake for mee,
(Imagining my loue was as I fainde)
His owne loue to her should enforce his tongue   25
To court her for himselfe, and deceaue mee:
By this time, we haue tried his passionate blood:
If he be caught (as heauen vouchsafe he be)
Ile play alittle with his Phantasie.   [*Retires.*]

Enter St. Anne.

St. Anne. Am I alone? Is there no Eye nor Eare   30
That doth obserue mee? Heauen how haue I graspt,
My Spirrits in my hart, that would haue burst
To giue wisht issue to my violent loue?
Dead Wife excuse me, since I loue thee still,
That liu'st in her, whom I must loue for thee: 35
For he that is not mou'd with strongest passion
In viewing her; that man did ne're know thee:
Shee's thy suruiuing Image: But woo's mee;
Why am I thus transported past my selfe?
Vand. [*Aside.*] Oh, are your dull vxorious spirrits raisd?   40
One madnesse doth beget another still.
St. Anne. But stay, Aduise mee Soule; why didst thou light me
Ouer this threshold? was't to wrong my Brother?
To wrong my Wife, in wronging of my Brother?

---

12 obseru'd] obserud ‖ **25** her] ∼, ‖ **29** SD *Retires.*] *Parrott* ‖ **33** my] *Dilke*; any ‖ **40** SD *Aside.*] *Dilke* ‖ **43** Ouer] ouer ‖

Ile die a miserable man, no villane: 45
Yet in this case of loue, who is my Brother?
Who is my Father? Who is any kinn?
I care not, I am nearest to my selfe:
I will pursue my Passion; I will haue her.
    Vand. [*Advancing.*] Traytor, I heere arrest thee in the names   50
Of Heauen, and Earth, and deepest *Acheron*:
Loues traytor, Brother's; traytor to thy Wife. /
    St. Anne. O Brother, stood you so neare my dishonour?   [F2ᵛ]
Had you forborne awhile, all had been changd:
You know the variable thoughts of Loue,   55
You know the vse of Honour, that will euer
Retire into it selfe; and my iust blood
Shall rather flow with Honour then with Loue:
Be you a happie Louer, I a friend,
For I will die for loue of her and thee.   60
    Vand. My Lord and brother, Ile not challenge more,
In loue and kindnes then my loue desernes:
That you haue found one whom your hart can like,
And that, One whom we all sought to preferre
To make you happie in a life renewde: 65
It is a heauen to mee, by how much more
My hart imbrac't you for my Sisters loue:
Tis true, I did dissemble loue t'*Euryone,*
To make you happie in her deare affection,
Who more dotes on you, then you can on her: 70
Enioy *Euryone,* shee is your owne,
The same that euer my deare Sister was:
And heauen blesse both your loues as I release
All my faind loue, and interest to you.
    St. Anne. How Noblie hath your loue deluded mee?   75
How iustlie haue you beene vniust to mee?
Let mee embrace the Oracle of my good,
The Aucthor and the Patron of my life.
    Vand. Tush, betwixt vs my Lord, what need these tearmes?
As if we knew not one another yet?   80
Make speed my Lord, and make your Nuptials short,
As they are sodaine blest in your desires.
    St. Anne. Oh I wish nothing more then lightning hast.

---

45 man, no] *Dilke;* ∼: No ‖ **50** SD *Advancing.*] *Parrott* ‖ **52** Brother's] Brothers ‖ **62** desernes:]
∼∧ (*See Textual Note*) ‖ **63** like,] ∼: ‖ **64** that, One] *Shepherd subs.;* ∼∧ ∼, ‖ **68** *Euryone,*] ∼.
‖ **82** desires.] ∼' ‖

Vand. Stay, one word first my Lord; You are a sweet brother
To put in trust, and woo loue for another?   85
   St. Anne. Pray thee no more of that.
   Vand.   Well then be gone,
My Lord; her brother comes.   *Exit S. Anne.*

                Enter Vaum.

   Vau.   Most happie Friend, /
How hath our plot succeeded?   [F3]
   Vand.   Hee's our owne.
His blood was framde for euerie shade of vertue,
To rauish into true inamourate fire: 90
The Funerall of my Sister must be held
With all solemnitie, and then his Nuptialls,
With no lesse speed and pompe be celebrate.
   Vau. What wonders hath your fortunate spirrite and vertues
Wrought to our comforts? Could you crowne th'enchantments   95
Of your diuine Witte with another Spell,
Of powre to bring my Wife out of her Cell,
You should be our quicke *Hermes,* our *Alcides.*
   Vand. That's my next labour: come my Lord, your selfe
Shall stand vnseene, and see by next morns light   100
(Which is her Beddtime) how my Braine's bould valoure
Will rouse her from her vowes seueritie:
No Will, nor Powre, can withstand Pollicie.   *Exeunt.*

                 [IV.ii]

        Enter D'oliue, Pacque, Dique.

   D'Ol. Welcome little Witts, are you hee my Page *Pacque* here
makes choice of, to be his fellow Coch-horse?
   Diq. I am my Lord.
   D'Ol. What Countrie man?
   Diq. Borne i'th Cittie.   5
   Pac. But begot i'th Court: I can tell your Lordship, he hath had as
good Court breeding, as anie Impe in a Countrie: If your Lordship
please to examine him in anie part of the Court Accidence, from a
Noune to an Interiection, Ile vndertake you shall finde him sufficient.

87 Lord;] *Shepherd;* ∼, | SD *Exit S. Anne.*] *Shepherd; follows preceding line* ‖ **99** That's] Thats |
labour] lobour ‖ **101** Braine's bould] Braines-bould ‖ **103** SD *Exeunt*] *Exit* ‖ IV.ii] *Parrott* ‖
2 makes] Makes ‖

D'Ol. Saist thou so little Witt? Why then Sir, How manie Pro-   10
nounes be there?

Diq. Faith my Lord there are more, but I haue learned but three
sorts; the Goarde, the Fulham, and the Stop-kater-tre; which are all
demonstratiues, for heere they be: [*Showing a set of dice.*] There are
Relatiues too, but they are nothing without their Antecedents.   15

D'Ol. Well said, little Witt I'faith. How manie Antecedents are
there? /

Diq. Faith my Lord, their number is vncertaine; but they that are,   [F3ᵛ]
are either Squires, or Gentlemen vshers.

D'Ol. Verie well said: when all is done, the Court is the onely   20
Schoole of good education; especially for pages and Waighting women;
Paris, or *Padua,* or the famous Schoole of England called *Winchester,*
famous (I meane) for the Goose, Where Schollers weare Petticoates so
long, till their Penn and Inckhorns knocke against their knees: All
these I say, are but Belfries to the Bodie or Schoole of the Court: Hee   25
that would haue his Sonne proceed Doctor in three dayes, let him
sende him thither; there's the Forge to fashion all the parts of them:
There they shall learne the true vse of their good Partes indeed.

Pac. Well my Lord, you haue said well for the Court, What sayes
your Lordshippe now to vs Courtiers, Shall we goe the voyage?   30

D'Ol. My little *Hermophrodites,* I entertaine you heere into my
Chamber; and if need be, nearer: your seruice you know. I will not
promise Mountaines, nor assure you Annuities of fourtie or fiftie
Crownes; in a word, I will promise nothing: but I will be your good
Lord, do you not doubt.   35

Diq. We do not my Lord, but are sure you will shew your selfe
Noble: and as you promise vs nothing, so you will Honorably keepe
promise with vs, and giue vs nothing.

D'Ol. Prettie little Witt, y'faith; Can he verse?

Pac. I and sett too, my Lord; Hee's both a Setter and a Verser.   40

D'Ol. Prettie in faith; but I meane, has he a vaine Naturall?

Pac. O my Lord, it comes from him as easelie,

Diq. As Suites from a Courtier, without money: or money from a
Cittizen without securitie, my Lord.

D'Ol. Wel, I perceiue nature has suited your Witts; and Ile suite   45
you in Guarded coates, answerable to your Witts: for Witt's as sutable
to guarded Coates, as Wisedome is to welted Gownes. My other Followers Horse themselues; my selfe will horse you. And now tell me

---

10 Witt?] ∼: ‖ **13** Goarde] *Parrott* (gourd); Goade (*See Textual Note*) ‖ **14** SD *Showing ...
dice.*] *Parrott* ‖

(for I will take you into my bosome) What's the opinion of the many headed Best touching my new adition / of Honour?   [F4] 50

Diq. Some thinke, my Lord, it hath giuen you adition of pride, and outercuidance.

D'Ol. They are deceaud that thinke so: I must confesse, it would make a Foole proude; but for me, I am *semper idem.*

Pac. We beleeue your Lordship.   55

D'Ol. I finde no alteration in my selfe in the world, for I am sure I am no wiser then I was, when I was no Lord, nor no more bountifull, nor no more honest; onely in respect of my state, I assume a kinde of State; to receiue Suters now, with the Nodd of Nobilitie; not (as before) with the Cappe of courtesie; the knee of Knighthood: And why   60 knee of Knighthood, little Witte? there's another Question for your Court Accidence.

Diq. Because Gentlemen, or Yoemen, or Pessantes, or so, receiue Knighthood on their knees.

Pac. The signification of the Knee of Knighthood in Heraldie an't   65 please your Lordship, is, that Knights are tyed in honour to fight vp to the knees in blood, for the defence of faire Ladyes.

D'Ol. Verie good: but if it be so, what honour doe they deserue, that purchase their Knighthood?

Diq. Purchase their Knighthood my Lord? Mary I thinke they   70 come truely by't, for they pay well for't.

D'Ol. You cut mee off by the knees, little Witte: but I say, (if you will heare mee) that if they deserue to be Knighted, that purchase their Knighthood with fighting vp to the knee, What doe they deserue, that purchase their Knighthood with fighting aboue the knee?   75

Pac. Mary my Lord, I say the purchase is good, if the conueyance will hold water.

D'Ol. Why this is excellent: by heauen twentie poundes annuitie shal not purchase you from my heeles. But foorth now: What is the opinion of the world touching this new Honour of mine? Doe not   80 Fooles enuie it?

Diq. No my Lord, but wise men wonder at it: you hauing so buried your wisedome heretofore in Tauerns, and Vaulting- / houses, that   [F4ᵛ] the world could neuer discouer you to be capable of Honour.

D'Ol. As though *Achilles* could hide himselfe vnder a Womans   85 clothes: was he not discouered at first? This Honor is like a Woman, or a Crocadile (chuse you whether) it flies them that follow it; and

followes them that flie it: For my selfe, how euer my worth for the
time kept his bedd; yet did I euer prophecie to my selfe that it would
rise, before the Sun-set of my dayes: I did euer dreame, that this head   90
was borne to beare a breadth, this shoulder to support a State, this
face to looke bigg, this bodie to beare a presence, these feete were
borne to be reuellers, and these Calues were borne to be Courtiers:
In a word, I was borne Noble, and I will die Noblie: neither shall my
Nobilitie perish with death; after ages shall resounde the memorie   95
thereof, while the Sunne sets in the East, or the Moone in the West.

    Pac. Or the Seuen Starres in the North.

    D'Ol. The Siege of *Bullaine* shall be no more a landmarke for
Times: *Agencourt* Battaile, *St. Iames* his Fielde, the losse of *Calice,*
and the winning of *Cales,* shal grow out of vse: Men shal reckon their   100
yeares, Women their mariages, from the day of our Ambassage: As, I
was borne, or married two, three, or foure yeares before the great
Ambassage. Farmers shall count their Leases from this day, Gentlemen their Morgages from this day: Saint *Dennis* shall be rac't out of
the Kallender, and the day of our Enstalment enterd in redd letters: 105
And as St. *Valentines* day is fortunate to choose Louers, St. *Lukes* to
choose Husbandes; So shall this day be to the choosing of Lordes: It
shall be a Critticall day, a day of Note: In that day it shall be good to
quarrell, but not to fight: They that Marrie on that day, shall not
repent; marie, the morrow after perhappes they may: it shal be hol-   110
some to beat a Sergeant on that day: Hee that eates Garlicke on that
morning, shall be a rancke Knaue till night.

    Diq. What a day will this be, if it hold?

    D'Ol. Hold? S'foote it shall hold, and shall be helde sacred to im-
mortalitie: let all the Chroniclers, Ballet makers, and / Almanack-[G1]   115
mungers, do what they dare.

Enter Rhoderique.

    Rho. S'foote (my Lord) al's dasht, your voyage is ouerthrowne.

    D'Ol. What ayles the franticke Tro?

    Rho. The Lady is entoombde, that was the Subiect of your Ambas-
sage: and your Ambassage is beraid.   120

    Pac. Dido is dead, and wrapt in lead.

    Diq. O heauy herse!

    Pac. Your Lordships honor must waite vpon her.

    Diq. O scuruy verse! Your Lordship's welcome home: pray let's
walke your horse my Lord.   125

    D'Ol. A prettie gullery. Why my little wits, doe you beleeue this to
be true?

    Pac. For my part my Lord, I am of opinion you are guld.

---

88 worth] ∼, ‖ **99** *Agencourt*] roman │ *St. Iames*] S. Iames │ *Calice*] roman ‖ **100** *Cales*] roman ‖ **110**
marie,] *Dilke* (marry); ∼∧ ‖ **124** *Diq.*] Dig. ‖

Diq. And I am of opinion that I am partly guiltie of the same.

Enter Muge.

Mug. Where's this Lord foole here? S'light you haue made a pret-   130
tie peece of seruice an't: raisd vp all the countrey in gold lace and
feathers; and now with your long stay, there's no employment for
them.

D'Ol. Good still.

Mug. S'light I euer tooke thee to be a hammer of the right feather: 135
but I durst hane layed my life, no man could euer haue cramd such a
Gudgeon as this downe the throate of thee: To create thee a Christmas Lord, and make thee laughter for the whole Court: I am
ashamde of my selfe that euer I chusde such a Grosseblocke to whet
my wits on.   140

D'Ol. Good wit yfaith. I know all this is but a gullery now: But
since you haue presumde to go thus farre with me, come what can
come to the State, sincke or swimme, Ile be no more a father to it, nor
the Duke; nor for the world wade one halfe steppe further in the
action. /   145

Pac. But now your Lordship is gone, what shall become of your   [G1ᵛ]
followers?

D'Ol. Followers? let them follow the Court as I haue done: there
let them raise their fortunes: if not, they know the way to the pettie
Brokers, there let them shift and hang.   *Exit cum suis.*

Rho. Here we may strike the *Plaudite* to our Play, my Lord foole's
gone: all our audience will forsake vs.

Mug. Page, after, and call him againe.   [*The page starts to leave.*]

Rho. Let him go: Ile take vp some other foole for the Duke to employ: euery Ordinary affoords fooles enow: and didst not see a paire   155
of Gallants sit not far hence like a couple of Bough-pots to make the
roome smell?

Mug. Yes, they are gone: But what of them?

Rho. Ile presse them to the Court: or if neede be, our Muse is not
so barren, but she is able to deuise one tricke or other to retire *D'oliue*   160
to Court againe.

Mug. Indeed thou toldst me how gloriously he apprehended the
fauour of a great Lady ith Presence, whose hart (he said) stood a tipto
in her eye to looke at him.

Rho. Tis well remembred.   165

Mug. O, a Loue-letter from that Ladie would retriue him as sure as
death.

Rho. It would of mine honor: Weele faine one from her instantly:
Page, fetch pen and inke here.   *Exit Pag.*

---

129 *Diq.*] *Dig.* ‖ **136** hane] *stet* (*See Textual Note*) ‖ **153** SD *The . . . leave.*] ‖

Mug. Now do you and your Muse engender: my barren skonce   170
shall prompt something.

Rho. Soft then: The Lady *Ieronime,* who I said viewed him so in
the Presence, is the Venus that must enamour him: Weele go no
further for that. But in what likenesse must he come to the Court to
her now? As a Lord he may not: in any other shape he will not.   175

Mug. Then let him come in his owne shape like a gull.

[*Enter page with ink and quills.*]

Rho. Well, disguisde he shall be: That shall be his mistrisses
direction: [*Taking the ink.*] this shall be my Helicon: [*Selecting a
quill.*] and from this quiuer will I draw the shaft that shall wound
him.   180

Mug. Come on: how wilt thou begin?

Rho. Faith thus: Dearely Beloued.

Mug. Ware ho, that's prophane. /

Rho. Go to then: Diuine *D'oliue:* I am sure that's not prophane.   [G2]

Mug. Well, forward.   185

Rho. I see in the powre of thy beauties.

Mug. Breake of your period, and say, Twas with a sigh.

Rho. Content: here's a full pricke stands for a teare too.

Mug. So, now take my braine.

Rho. Poure it on.   190

Mug. I talke like a foole, but alas thou art wise and silent.

Rho. Excellent: And the more wise, the more silent.

Mug. That's something common.

Rho. So should his mistris be.

Mug. That's true indeed: Who breakes way next?   195

Rho. That will I sir: But alas, why art not thou noble, that thou
mightst match me in Blood?

Mug. Ile answer that for her.

Rho. Come on.

Mug. But thou art noble, though not by birth, yet by creation.   200

Rho. That's not amisse: forth now: Thy wit proues thee to be a
Lord, thy presence showes it: O that word Presence, has cost me deare.

Mug. Well said, because she saw him ith Presence.

Rho. O do but say thou lou'st me.

Mug. Soft, there's too many OOs.   205

Rho. Not a whit: O's but the next doore to P. And his mistris may
vse her O with modestie: or if thou wilt, Ile stop it with another
brachish teare.

Mug. No, no, let it runne on.

176 SD *Enter . . . quills.*] *Parrott subs.* ‖ **178** SD *Taking the ink.*] ‖ **178-79** SD *Selecting a quill.*] ‖
196 not thou] *stet* (*See Textual Note*) ‖ **201** That's] Thats ‖ **207** with modestie] *Lowell*; with
with ∼ (*See Textual Note*) ‖

Rho. O do but say thou lou'st me, and yet do not neither, and   210
yet do.

Mug. Well said, let that last stand, let him doe in any case: now
say thus, do not appeare at Court.

Rho. So.

Mug. At least in my companie.   215

Rho. Well.

Mug. At lest before folkes.

Rho. Why so? /

Mug. For the flame will breake forth.   [G2ᵛ]

Rho. Go on: thou doest well.   220

Mug. Where there is fire ith harth:

Rho. What then?

Mug. There will be smoke ith chimney.

Rho. Forth.

Mug. Warme, but burne me not: there's reason in all things.   225

Rho. Well said, now doe I vie it: Come to my chamber betwixt
two and three.

Mug. A very good number.

Rho. But walk not vnder my window: if thou doest, come disguisde: in any case weare not thy tuft taffeta cloke: if thou doest,   230
thou killest me.

Mug. Well said, now to the *L'envoye*.

Rho. Thine, if I were worth ought; and yet such, as it skils not
whose I am if I be thine; *Ieronime*: Now for a fit Pandar to trans-
port it, and haue at him.   *Exeunt.*

Finis Actus quarti.

Actvs Qvinti Scæna prima.

Enter Vaumont, and Vandome.

Vand.

Come my good Lord, now will I trie my Braine,
If it can forge another golden chaine,
To draw the poore Recluse, my honord mistris
From her darke Cell, and superstitious vow.
I oft haue heard there is a kind of cure   5
To fright a lingring Feuer from a man
By an imaginous feare, which may be true,
For one heate (all know) doth driue out another,

225 there's] theres ‖

One passion doth expell another still,
And therefore I will vse a fainde deuice   10
To kindle furie in her frozen Breast,
That rage may fire out griefe, and so restore her
To her most sociable selfe againe. /
    Vau. Iuno Lucina fer opem,   [G3]
And ease my labouring house of such a care.   15
    Vand. Marke but my Midwifery: the day is now
Some three houres old, and now her night begins:
Stand close my Lord, if she and her sad meany
Be toward sleepe, or sleeping, I will wake them
With orderly alarmes; Page? Boy? sister?   20
All toong-tied? all asleepe? page? sister?
    Vau. Alas *Vandome,* do not disturbe their rest
For pittie sake, tis yong night yet with them.
    Vand. My Lord, your onely way to deale with women
And Parrets, is to keepe them waking still.   25
Page? who's aboue? are you all dead here?
    Dig. S'light is hell broke loose? who's there?   *He looks out with a light.*
    Vand. A friend.
    Dig. Then know this Castle is the house of wo,
Here harbor none but two distressed Ladies   30
Condemn'd to darknesse, and this is their iayle,
And I the Giant set to guard the same:
My name is *Dildo.*   *Retrahit se.*
    Vand. Sirra leaue your rogerie, and hearken to me: what Page,
I say.   35

Redit cum lumine.

    Dig. Tempt not disasters: take thy life: Be gone.
    Vau. An excellent villanie.
    Vand. Sirra? I haue businesse of waight to impart to your Ladie.
    Dig. If your businesse be of waight, let it waite till the afternoone,
for by that time my Ladie will be deliuered of her first sleepe: Be   40
gone, for feare of watery meteors.
    Vand. Go to sir, leaue your villany, and dispatch this newes to your
Ladie.
    Dig. Is your businesse from your selfe, or from some body besides?
    Vand. From no body besides my selfe.   45
    Dig. Very good: then Ile tel her, here's one besides himselfe has
businesse to her from no body.   *Retrahit se.*

27 SD *He . . . light.*] *roman, and in margin* ‖ **35** SD *Redit . . . lumine.*] *Dilke; in margin after next line* ‖

Vau. A perfect yong hempstring.

Vand. Peace least he ouerheare you.

Redit Dig. /

Dig. You are not the Constable sir, are you?   [G3ʳ] 50

Vand. Will you dispatch sir? you know me well enough, I am
Vandome.

[Enter Eurione aboue.]

Eur. What's the matter? who's there? Brother *Vandome*!

Vand. Sister?

Eur. What tempest driues you hither at such an hower?   55

Vand. Why I hope you are not going to bed, I see you are not yet
vnready: if euer you will deserue my loue, let it be now, by calling
forth my mistris; I haue newes for her, that touch her nearely.

Eur. What ist good brother?

Vand. The worst of ils: would any tongue but mine had bene   60
the messenger.

[Enter Marcellina aboue.]

Mar. What's that, seruant?

Vand. O Mistris come downe with all speed possible, and leaue that
mournfull cell of yours; Ile shew you another place worthy of your
mourning.   65

Mar. Speake man, my heart is armed with a mourning habit of
such proofe, that there is none greater without it, to pierce it.

Vand. If you please to come downe, Ile impart what I know: if
not, Ile leaue you.

Eur. Why stand you so at gaze sister? go downe to him. Stay   70
brother, she comes to you.   *[Exeunt Marcellina and Eurione.]*

Vand. Twill take I doubt not; though her selfe be ice,
There's one with her all fire, and to her spirit
I must apply my counterfeit deuice:
Stand close my Lord.

Vau.   I warrant you, proceed.   *[He retires.]*

[Enter Marcellina and Eurione below.]

Vand. Come silly mistris, where's your worthy Lord?
I know you know not, but too well I know.

Mar. Now heauen grant all be well.

Vand.   How can it be?
While you poore Turtle sit and mourne at home,

---

52 SD *Enter . . . aboue.*] *Parrott* ‖ **53** What's] Whats | *Vandome*!] ∼. ‖ **58** mistris;] ∼, ‖ **61** SD
Enter . . . aboue.] *Parrott* ‖ **62** What's that,] *Dilke*; Whats ∼∧ ‖ **64** yours;] ∼∧ ‖ **71** brother]
Dilke; bother | SD *Exeunt . . . Eurione.*] *Parrott* ‖ **72** not;] *Lowell*; ∼, ‖ **73** There's] Theres ‖
75 SD *He . . . below.*] *Dilke subs.* ‖

Mewd in your cage, your mate he flies abroade,   80
O heauens who would haue thought him such a man?

   Eur. Why what man brother? I beleeue my speeches will proue
true of him.

   Vand. To wrong such a beautie, to prophane such vertue, / and to [G4]
proue disloyall.   85

   Eur. Disloyall? nay nere gilde him ore with fine termes, Brother,
he is a filthy Lord, and euer was, I did euer say so, I neuer knew any
good ath haire, I do but wonder how you made shift to loue him,
or what you saw in him to entertaine but so much as a peece of a
good thought on him.   90

   Mar. Good sister forbeare.

   Eur. Tush sister, bid me not forbeare: a woman may beare, and
beare, and be neuer the better thought on neither: I would you had
neuer seene the eyes of him, for I know he neuer lou'd you in's life.

   Mar. You wrong him sister, I am sure he lou'd me   95
As I lou'd him, and happie I had bene
Had I then dide, and shund this haplesse life.

   Eur. Nay let him die, and all such as he is; he lay a catterwalling
not long since: O if it had bene the will of heauen, what a deare
blessing had the world had in his riddance?   100

   Vand. But had the lecher none to single out
For obiect of his light lasciuious blood,
But my poore cosin that attends the Dutchesse,
Lady *Ieronime*?

   Eur.   What, that blaberlipt blouse?

   Vand. Nay no blouse, sister, though I must confesse   105
She comes farre short of your perfection.

   Eur. Yes by my troth, if she were your cosin a thousand times,
shee's but a sallow freckld-face peece when she is at the best.

   Vand. Yet spare my cosin, sister, for my sake,
She merits milder censure at your hands,   110
And euer held your worth in noblest termes.

   Eur. Faith the Gentlewoman is a sweete Gentlewoman of her selfe,
I must needs giue her her due.

   Vand. But for my Lord your husband, honor'd mistris,
He made your beauties and your vertues too,   115
But foyles to grace my cosins, had you seene
His amorous letters — But my cosin presently
Will tell you all, for she reiects his sute;
Yet I aduisde her to make a shew she did not,

98 as] *Dilke*; as as | is;] ∼, ‖ **103-4** But . . . *Ieronime*?] *Dilke*; one line ‖ **108** shee's] shees |
freckld-face peece] *Lowell*; freckld face peece ‖ **117** letters—] ∼, ‖ **117-21** But . . . houre.]
Dilke; *as prose* (will . . . yet . . . and) ‖ **118** sute;] ∼, ‖ **119** not,] ∼. ‖

But point to meet him when you might surprise him, 120
And this is just the houre. /

   Eur. Gods my life sister, loose not this aduantage, it wil be a good   [G4ᵛ]
Trumpe to lay in his way vpon any quarrell: Come, you shall go:
S'bodie will you suffer him to disgrace you in this sort? dispraise your
beautie? And I do not think too, but he has bin as bold with your 125
Honor, which aboue all earthly things should be dearest to a woman.

   Vand. Next to her Beautie.

   Eur. True, next to her beautie: and I doe not thinke sister, but hee
deuiseth slaunders against you, euen in that high kinde.

   Vand. Infinite, infinite. 130

   Eur. And I beleeue I take part with her too: would I knew that
yfaith.

   Vand. Make your account, your share's as deepe as hers: when
you see my cosin, sheele tell you all: weele to her presently.

   Eur. Has she told you, she would tell vs? 135

   Vand. Assurde me, on her oath.

   Eur. S'light I would but know what he can say: I pray you brother
tell me.

   Vand. To what end? twill but stirre your patience.

   Eur. No I protest: when I know my carriage to be such, as no 140
staine can obscure, his slaunders shall neuer moue me, yet would I
faine know what he faines.

   Vand. It fits not me to play the gossips part: weel to my cosin,
sheele relate all.

   Eur. S'light what can he say? pray let's haue a taste an't onward. 145

   Vand. What can he not say, who being drunke with lust, and sur-
fetting with desire of change, regards not what he sayes: and briefly I
will tell you thus much now; Let my melancholy Lady (says he) hold
on this course till she waste her selfe, and consume my reuenew in
Tapers, yet this is certaine, that as long as she has that sister of hers at 150
her elbow —

   Eur. Me? why me? I bid defiance to his foule throate.

   Vau. [*Aside.*] Hold there *Vandome*, now it begins to take.

   Eur. What can his yellow iealousie surmise against me? if you loue
me, let me heare it: I protest it shall not moue me. / 155

   Vand. Marry forsooth, you are the shooing horne, he sayes, to draw   [H1]
on, to draw on sister.

   Eur. The shooing horne with a vengeance? what's his meaning in
that?

---

145 he] *Lowell*; she ‖ **151** elbow—] ∼. ‖ **153** SD *Aside.*] *Dilke* ‖

Vand. Nay I haue done, my cosin shall tell the rest: come shal   160
we go?

Eur. Go? by heauen you bid me to a banquet: sister, resolue your
selfe, for you shall go; loose no more time, for you shall abroade on my
life: his licorice chaps are walking by this time: but for heauens
sweete hope what meanes he by that shooing horne? As I liue it shall   165
not moue me.

Vand. Tell me but this, did you euer breake betwixt my mistris and
your sister here, and a certaine Lord ith Court?

Eur. How? breake?

Vand. Go to, you vnderstand me: haue not you a Petrarch in   170
Italian?

Eur. Petrarch? yes, what of that?

Vand. Well, he sayes you can your good, you may be waiting
woman to any dame in Europe: that Petrarch does good offices.

Eur. Marry hang him, good offices? S'foot how vnderstands he that?   175

Vand. As when any Lady is in priuate courtship with this or that
gallant, your Petrarch helpes to entertaine time: you vnderstand his
meaning?

Eur. Sister if you resolue to go, so it is: for by heauen your stay
shall be no barre to me, Ile go, that's infallible; it had bene as good he   180
had slandered the diuell: shooing horne? O that I were a man for's
sake.

Vand. But to abuse your person and your beautie too: a grace
wherein this part of the world is happie: but I shall offend too much.

Eur. Not me, it shall neuer moue me.   185

Vand. But to say, ye had a dull eye, a sharpe nose (the visible
markes of a shrow) a drie hand, which is a signe of a bad liuer; as he
said you were being toward a husband too, this was intolerable.

Vau. [*Aside.*] This strikes it vp to the head.

Vand. Indeed he said you drest your head in a pretie strange /   190
fashion: but you would dresse your husbands head in a far stranger;   [H1ᵛ]
meaning the Count of *saint Anne* I thinke.

Eur. Gods precious, did he touch mine honor with him?

Vand. Faith nothing but that he weares blacke, and sayes tis his
mistris colours: and yet he protests that in his eye your face shewes   195
well enough by candle light, for the Count neuer saw it otherwise,
vnlesse twere vnder a maske, which indeed he sayes becomes you aboue
all things.

Eur. Come Page, go along with me, Ile stay for no body: Tis at
your cosins chamber, is it not?   200

---

187 liuer;] ∼, (*See Textual Note*) ‖ 188 were] ∼, | too,] ∼: ‖ 189 SD *Aside.*] *Dilke* ‖ 192 *saint
Anne*] *roman* ‖

Vand. Marry is it, there you shall find him at it.

Eur. That's enough: let my sister go waste his reuenew in tapers, twill be her owne another day.

Mar. Good sister, seruant, if euer there were any loue or respect to me in you both —   205

Eur. Sister? there is no loue, nor respect, nor any coniuration, shall stay me: and yet by my part in heauen, Ile not be moued a whit with him: you may retire your selfe to your old cell, and there waste your eyes in teares, your heart in sighes, Ile away certaine.

Vand. But soft, let's agree first what course we shal take when we   210
take him.

Eur. Marry euen raise the streetes on him, and bring him forth with a flocke of boyes about him, to whoote at him.

Vand. No, that were too great a dishonor: Ile put him out on's
paine presently.   *Stringit ensem.*

Dig. Nay good sir spare his life, cut of the offending part, and saue the Count.

Mar. Is there no remedie? Must I breake my vow?
Stay Ile abroad, though with another aime
Not to procure, but to preuent his shame.   220

Vand. Go Page, march on, you know my cosins chamber,
[*To Martia and Eurione.*] My company may wrong you, I will crosse
The nearer way, and set the house afore you:
But sister see you be not mou'd for Gods sake.

Eur. Not I by heauen: Come sister, be not moued,   225
But if you spare him, may heauen nere spare you.   *Exeunt. man. Van. et Vau.*

Vand. So now the solemne votary is reuiu'd. /
Vau. Pray heauen you haue not gone a step too farre,   [H2]
And raisde more sprites, then you can coniure downe.

Vand. No my Lord, no, th' Herculean labor's past,   230
The vow is broke, which was the end we sweat for,
The reconcilement will meet of it selfe:
Come lets to Court, and watch the Ladies chamber,
Where they are gone with hopefull spleene to see you.   [*Exeunt.*]

[V.ii]

*Enter Roderique, Mugeron, D'oliue in disguise towards
the Ladies chamber.*

Rho. See *Mugeron*, our counterfait letter hath taken: who's yonder
think'st?

---

205 both—] ∼. ‖ **216** *Dig.*] *Parrott; Pag.* ‖ **222** SD *To . . . Eurione.*] ‖ **230** th'Herculean] *Dilke;*
t'Herculean ‖ **234** SD *Exeunt.*] ‖ V.ii] *Lowell* ‖

Mug. Tis not *Doliue?*

Rho. Ift be not he, I am sure hee's not farre off:
Those be his tressels that support the motion. 5

Mug. Tis he by heauen, wrapt in his carelesse cloke: See the Duke
enters: Let him enioy the benefite of the inchanted Ring, and stand a
while inuisible: at our best oportunitie weele discouer him to the
Duke.

> *Enter Duke, Dutchesse, Saint Anne, Vaumont, Vandome,*
> *to them Digue, whispering Vandome in the eare,*
> *and speakes as on the other side.*

Dig. [*Aside.*] *Monsieur Vandome,* yonders no Lord to be found: 10
my Ladie stayes at hand and craues your speech.

Vand. [*Aside.*] Tell her she mistook the place, and conduct her
hither: *Exit Dig.* How will she looke when she findes her expectation
mockt now?

Vau. What's that, *Vandome?* 15

Vand. Your wife and sister are coming hither, hoping to take you
and my cosin together.

Vau. Alas, how shall we appease them, when they see themselues so
deluded?

Vand. Let me alone, and stand you off my Lord: 20

> *Enter Mar: and Eurione.*

[*To Marcellina.*] Madame, y'are welcome to the Court: doe you see
your Lord / yonder? I haue made him happie by training you forth: [H2ᵛ]
In a word, all I said was but a traine to draw you from your vow:
[*She starts to leave.*] Nay, there's no going backe: Come forward and
keepe your temper. [*To Eurione.*] Sister, cloud not you your forhead: 25
yonder's a Sunne will cleare your beauties I am sure. Now you see the
shooing-horne is expounded: all was but a shooing-horne to draw you
hither: now shew your selues women, and say nothing.

Phil. [*To Roderique and Mugeron.*] Let him alone awhile. *Van-*
dome, who's there? 30
What whisper you?

Vand.   Y'aue done? come forward:
See here my Lord, my honorable mistris,
And her faire sister, whom your Highnesse knowes
Could neuer be importunde from their vowes
By prayer, or th'earnest sutes of any friends, 35
Now hearing false report that your faire Dutchesse
Was dangerously sicke, to visit her

---

3 *Doliue?*] ~: ‖ **10** SD *Aside.*] *Parrott* ‖ **12** SD *Aside.*] *Parrott* ‖ **13** SD *Exit Dig.*] *Parrott;* ~. ~.
follows now? ‖ **21** SD *To Marcellina.*] ‖ **24** SD *She . . . leave.*] ‖ **25** SD *To Eurione.*] ∣ you] *stet*
(*See Textual Note*) ‖ **29** SD *To . . . Mugeron.*] *Dilke* ‖ **29-31** Let . . . you?] *Dilke;* one line (what)
‖ **29-30** awhile. *Vandome,*] *Dilke;* ~∧ ~: ‖ **31** What] what ‖

Did that which no friend else could winne her to,
And brake her long kept vow with her repaire.

    Phil. Madam you do me an exceeding honor,   40
In shewing this true kindnesse to my Dutchesse,
Which she with all her kindnesse will requite.

    Vand. To S. An. Now my good Lord, the motion you haue made,
With such kind importunitie by your selfe,
And seconded with all perswasions   45
On my poore part, for mariage of this Ladie,
Her selfe now comes to tell you she embraces,
And (with that promise made me) I present her.

    Eur. Sister, we must forgiue him.

    St. Anne.   Matchlesse Ladie,
Your beauties and your vertues haue atchieu'd   50
An action that I thought impossible,
For all the sweete attractions of your sex,
In your conditions, so to life resembling
The grace and fashion of my other wife:
You haue reuiu'd her to my louing thoughts,   55
And all the honors I haue done to her,
Shall be continude (with increase) to you. /

    Mug. Now let's discouer our Ambassador, my Lord.   [H3]

    Phil. Do so.   *Exiturus D'oliue.*

    Mug. My Lord? my Lord Ambassador?   60

    D'Ol. My Lord foole, am I not?

    Mug. Go to, you are he: you cannot cloke your Lordshippe from
our knowledge.

    Rho. Come, come: could *Achilles* hide himselfe vnder a womans
clothes? Greatnesse will shine through clouds of any disguise.   65

    Phil. Who's that *Rhoderique?*

    Rho. Monsieur D'oliue, my Lord, stolne hither disguisde, with what
minde we know not.   *[D'Olive tries to leave.]*

    Mug. Neuer striue to be gone sir: my Lord, his habite expounds his
heart: twere good he were searcht.   70

    D'Ol. Well rookes wel, Ile be no longer a blocke to whet your dull
wits on: My Lord, my Lord, you wrong not your selfe onely, but your
whole state, to suffer such vlcers as these to gather head in your Court;
neuer looke to haue any action sort to your honor, when you suffer
such earewigs to creepe into your eares thus.   75

    Phil. What's the matter *Rhoderique?*

---

40 *Phil.*] *Shepherd; Duke.* ‖ **43** SD *To S. An.*] *in margin* ‖ **59** *Phil.*] *Shepherd; Duke.* ‖ **68** SD *D'Olive
. . . leave.*] ‖

Rho. Alas my Lord, only the lightnesse of his braine, because his hopes are lost.

Mug. For our parts, we haue bene trustie and secret to him in the whole manage of his ambassage.   80

D'Ol. Trustie? a plague on you both, there's as much trust in a common whore as in one of you: and as for secrecy, there's no more in you then in a profest Scriuener.

Vand. Why a Scriuener, *Monsieur D'oliue?*

D'Ol. Marry sir a man cannot trust him with borrowing so much as   85 poore fortie shillings, but he will haue it Knowne to all men by these presents.

Vand. That's true indeed, but you employed these gentlemen very safely.

D'Ol. Employed? I mary sir, they were the men that first kindled   90 this humor of employment in me: a pox of employment I say: it has cost me — but what it has cost me, it skils not: they haue thrust vpon me a crew of thredbare, vnbutton'd fellowes, / to be my followers: [H3ᵛ] Taylers, Frippers, Brokers, casheerd Clarks, Pettifoggers, and I know not who I: S'light I thinke they haue swept all the bowling allies ith   95 citie for them: and a crew of these, rakt like old ragges out of dunghils by candle light, haue they presented to me in very good fashion, to be gentlemen of my traine, and solde them hope of raising their fortunes by me: A plague on that phrase, Raising of fortunes, it has vndone more men then ten dicing houses: Raise their fortunes with a ven-   100 geance? And a man will play the foole and be a Lord, or be a foole and play the Lord, he shall be sure to want no followers, so there be hope to raise their fortunes. A burning feuer light on you, and all such followers. S'foote they say followers are but shadowes, that follow their Lords no longer then the sun shines on them: but I finde it not so: 105 the sunne is set vpon my employment, and yet I cannot shake off my shadowes; my followers grow to my heeles like kibes, I cannot stir out of doores for am. And your grace haue any employment for followers, pray entertaine my companie: theyle spend their bloud in your seruice, for they haue little else to spend; you may soone raise their   110 fortunes.

Phil. Well *Monsieur D'oliue,* your forwardnesse
In this intended seruice, shall well know
What acceptation it hath wonne it selfe
In our kind thoughts: nor let this sodaine change   115
Discourage the designements you haue laid

---

88 That's] Thats ‖ 92 me—] ∼, ‖ 110 spend;] ∼, ‖

For our States good: reserue your selfe I pray,
Till fitter times: meane time will I secure you
From all your followers: follow vs to Court.
And good my Lords, and you my honor'd Ladies,   120
Be all made happie in the worthy knowledge
Of this our worthy friend *Monsieur D'oliue.*
   Omnes. Good *Monsieur D'oliue.*   *Exeunt.*

       Finis Actus quinti et vltimi. /

123 SD *et*] *&* ‖

457

HISTORICAL COLLATION

[Editions collated: Dilke (=D, in *Old English Plays*, III, 1814, pp. 343-432); Lowell (=L, proof sheets preserved in the Widener Library, Harvard, for an edition, never published, edited by James Russell Lowell); Shepherd (=S, in *The Works of George Chapman: Plays*, 1875, pp. 113-39); and Parrott (=P, in *The Plays and Poems of George Chapman: The Comedies* [1914], pp. 307-61). The siglum Q identifies the quarto of 1606, with Q(c) and Q(u) designating corrected and uncorrected states of that text and Q(r) the reset outer forme of B as well as B1ᵛ of the inner forme. In addition, emendations suggested by K. Deighton in *The Old Dramatists: Conjectural Readings* (Westminster, 1896), pp. 128-30, and by J. Brereton in "Notes on the Text of Chapman's Plays," *MLR*, III (1907), 56-68, are also included. Only substantive and semi-substantive variants are recorded; obvious errors are not recorded. Lemmata are taken from the present text. Where lemma represents the reading of Q copy-text, omission of a siglum indicates agreement with lemma.]

I.i

Scæna Prima.] ~ ~. Paris *L*; ~ ~. *Before the House of Vaumont P*
2 Th'] The *L*
4 t'attend] to attend *L*
7 SD *Exeunt Seruants.*] *Exeunt* Servants *with* sailors *P*
12 th'] the *L*
13 actions;] ~, *L*
14 obiect] *D, L, S, P*; abiect *Q*
15 to that] that *D*
35 kindnesse.] ~, *D, L, S*; ~; *P*
52 SD *He . . . Vaumont.*] *om. Q, D, L, S, P*
55 embrac't] embraced *L*; embrace *S*
79 womens] woman's *L*
81 vertue chosen,] *D, L, P*; ~, ~ₐ *Q, S*
138 Surviues] Together *P*
139 Together] Survives *P*
144 Chanc't your] Chanced in your *D, L, S, P*
163 that,] *L, P*; ~ₐ *Q, D, S*
185 vs; our good now] *D, L, S, P*; ~, ~ ~ Now *Q(u)*; ~, ~ ~. Now *Q(c)*

I.ii

I.ii] *om. Q, D, L, S, P*
11 times] time *L, S*

21 innocencie] innocence *S*
22 grafte] *Q*, *L*; graffe *Q(r)*, *D*, *S*, *P*
25 am] them *L*
31 Countesse] Countess's *D*, *L*
36 but little] *Q*; but a little *Q(r)*, *D*, *L*, *S*, *P*
    is, is] is *L*
48 what! Slight,] *P*; ∼, ∼∧ *Q*; ∼. '∼! *D*; ∼. '∼; *L*; ∼; '∼! *S*
55 amongst] among *S*, *P*
56 day, our] *Q*; day, and our *Q(r)*, *D*, *L*, *S*, *P*
57 whiles] while *L*, *S*, *P*
58 makes] *Q(r)*; make *Q*
59 streete] *Q(r)*; streetes *Q*
62 lyne] laid *D*; lain *L*
64 a] at *L*
68 SD *Enter D'oliue.*] *P*; *follows Mugeron's speech Q*, *Q(r)*, *D*, *L*, *S*
68-69 so is hee] so he is *P*
69 SD *Pointing to D'olive.*] *om.* *Q*, *Q(r)*, *D*, *L*, *S*, *P*
72 parcell] parcels *D*
73 pisse] pickle *L*
85 bytter;] ∼, *Q*; ∼. *D*, *L*, *S*; ∼! *P*
92 Good, soothe] Good in sooth *D*
102 countray] *Q*; counttey *Q(r)*
107-8 take free] *Q(r)*; take the free *Q*
111 and] an *L*
116 ye] *Q(r)*; *om.* *Q*
118 for to your] *Q*, *L*; for your *Q(r)*, *S*, *P*; to your *D*
129 SD *Indicating . . . house.*] *om.* *Q*, *Q(r)*, *D*, *L*, *S*, *P*
136 by] *Q*; my *Q(r)*
139 Paragon *Monsieur*] *Q(r)*; Paragon for *Monsieur Q*
142 lyes] lie *D*, *L*
143 not mee] *Q*; me not *Q(r)*, *D*, *L*, *S*, *P*
177 its] *D*, *L*, *P*; it *Q*, *S*
181 into's] into his *L*
183 your] you, *S*
187 God] *Q(c)*; good *Q(u)*, *L*
206 mungrill] *D*, *L*, *P* (i.e., mongrel); mugrill *Q*, *S*

II.i

SD *Scæna prima.*] ∼ ∼. *A Room in the House of Vaumont P*
SD *Digue*] Dique (Dicque) *throughout scene Q*, *S*, *P*
14 it bee] *om.* *D*
16 SD *They retire.*] *D*, *L*, *P*; *om.* *Q*, *Q(r)*, *S*
20 but was such] *D*, *S*; but such *Q*, *Q(r)*, *P*; That *L*
21 this euer seene,] this was euer seene∧ *Q*, *Q(r)*; ever such a man as this seen?
    D; this was ever seen! *L*, *S*; this was never seen, *P*
23 nothing, now] *Q(r)*; ∼: Now *Q*
    is it] is't *S*, *P*

32 doe not you] *Q(c)*; doe you not *Q(u), D*
38 *Mar.] Q(c); Mvg: Q(u)*
    againe?] *P*; ~, *Q, L*; ~! *D*; ~; *S*
40 loue the Noble] *Q(c)*; loue you loue the Noble *Q(u)*
48 SD *Within.] L, P; om. Q, S; Vandome heard within. D*
49 *An other within] S, P; as a separate line following* protest *Q; Vandome heard within follows* protest *D, L*
51 SD *Enter a seruant.] D, L; om. Q, S; follows next line P*
52 *Dig.] D, L; Diq. Q; Di. S; Dic. P*
53 *Ser.] D, S, P; Sic: Q, L*
55 *Ser.] D, S, P; Sic: Q(c), L; Sdc: Q(u)*
    at doore] at the door *D*
59 *2nd Ser.] D, L, S, P; 2 Lec. Q*
61 This] *D, L, S, P*; Tis *Q*
63 *2nd Ser.] P; Sig. Q; 1 Serv. D; Sic. L; Ser. S*
    SD *To Licette.] om. Q, D, L, S, P*
64 SD *Exeunt seruants.] D; Exit. Q, L, S, P*
65 night-walker's] *D, L, S, P*; night-walker' *Q*
72 *Lic. . . . enter.] D, L, S, P*; ~ . . . ~. within *Q*
79 SD *Throwing . . . sword.] P; om. Q, L, S; Lays his sword at her feet. D*
91 SD *Exit . . . Licette.] D, L, S, P; Exit Mard: Q*
    Strange . . . women;] *D, L*; ~ . . . ~; *Exit Marc. Q, S*; ~ . . . ~; *Exit Marcellina with Licette, Dicque, and Servants P*
106 tis] it is *L*
110 Idely] *D, L, S, P*; ~. *Q*
117 *Vand.] D, L, S, P; om. Q*
128 selfe] *D, L, S, P*; ~: *Q*
129 cure] *L, S, P*; ~: *Q*; ~, *D*
131 not tell me,] *D, L, S, P*; ~, ~ ~∧ *Q*
    SD *He . . . go.] P; om. Q, D, L, S*
133 SD *Going.] P; om. Q, D, L, S*
135 you?] *D*; ~∧ *Q, L, S, P*
    then.] *D*; ~? *Q, L, S, P*
137 one] me *S*
146 y'are] you're *D*; you are *L*
148 trauaile] traveller *D, L, P*
154 sad] said *L*
158 Why, does he] *D, S*; ~∧ ~ ~ *Q*; ~ ~ ~, *L*; ~, ~ ~, *P*
159 you louers] *Q(c)*; you loners louers *Q(u)*
175 an] *D, L, S, P*; a *Q*
201 beauties? any name] *D, L, S, P*; ~∧ ~ ~? *Q*
209 On] To *D*
219 blush at that,] *D, L, S, P*; ~, ~ ~∧ *Q*

II.ii

II.ii] *P; om. Q, D, L, S*
SD *Enter . . . worke.]* ~ . . . ~. *A Room at the Court P*

SD *Gveaq.*] Jacqueline *throughout P*; Duchess *throughout D, L*
1 *Phil.*] Duke *throughout D, L, P*
3 *France?*] *D, L*; France, *Q*; France. *S, P*
4 t'inter] to inter *L*
10 wizzard] buzzard *Brereton conj.*
14 Lord;] *D, S, P*; ∼∧ *Q, L*
20 sayes he] he says *D*
22 witts;] *D, S, P*; ∼, *Q, L*
26 there] *D*; this *Q, L, S, P*
48 Sir] ∼: *Q*; ∼, *D, L, S, P*
59 entombd] entombe *Q, D, L, S, P*
61 spurnd] *P*; spnrnd *Q*; spurred *D, L*; spurr'd *S*
66 not we] we not *D*
75 choos'd] chosen *L*
86 *Gyges*] *D, L, P, Deighton conj.*; *Giris Q, S*
98 Thunder,] *L, S, P*; ∼∧ *Q*; ∼; *D*
100 or] *Q(c)*; of *Q(u)*
109 Of . . . you.] ∼ . . . ∼. Going *L, P*
131 Why so;] *D, P*; ∼, ∼∧ *L*; ∼ ∼∧ *Q, S*
134 Countes] Countess's *D, L, P*
150 well —] *om. L*
151 *Phil.*] *D, L, S, P*; *Dol: Q*
    D'Ol.] *D, L, S, P*; *om. Q*
163 wil;] *L, S, P*; ∼∧ *Q*; ∼, *D*
166 Aristocratie] aristocratical *D*
173 vp] *om. L*
    b'inspiration] by inspiration *L, S*
179 where] way *D*
184 Tobacco,] *L, P*; ∼: *Q*; ∼∧ *D, S*
185-86 finding stopt/ His narrow passage] finding/ His narrow passage stopp'd
    D
217 tun] ton *L, S, P*
220 were truely] truly were *L*
226 Our] *D, L, S, P*; Or *Q*
228 tun'd his nose] *D, L*; tun'd his noise *Q, P*; turned his nose *S*
243 *siliam*] *sileam L*
245 I] *om. S, P*
251 of fift] of a fifth *D*; of first *L*
256 the] *D, L, S, P*; the the *Q*
269 true, that *Iohannes*] ∼, what ∼ *D*; ∼∧ ∼ ∼ *L*
    de Sauoret] de sauo et sauo et *Q, D, L*; Savonarola *S, P*
270 pisseth] passeth *L*
271 farts] voids *L*
298 *Gveaquin*] Jacqueline *L*
    SD *Kisses her.*] *P*; *om. Q, S*; *Offers to salute her. D, L*
310 *Rho.*] *om. L*
316 debts,] *S, P*; ∼∧ *Q, D, L*

322 one] some *Q, D, L, S, P*
336 SD *Exeunt.*] *P; om. Q, D, L, S*

III.i

Actvs . . . prima.] ∼ . . . ∼. *A Room in the House of* St. Anne *P*
11 an] a *D*
17 tirranous] *Q(c);* terrinous *Q(u)*
23 *vincitur*] *Q(c); viuatur Q(u)*
42 suruiue; being dead,] ∼, ∼ ∼: *Q, D, L, S, P*
45 where] were *S*
46 *littus*] *Q(c); actus Q(u)*
48 lips] *Deighton conj.;* steps *Q, D, L, S, P*
49 Gaspe] Gape *Deighton conj.*
50 Like . . . recure.] ∼ . . . ∼. They retire *D*
57 *Phil.*] Duke. *Q, D, L, S, P*
63 all] of ∼ *L*
64 are] is *L*
72 threed] *Q(c);* throat *Q(u), D*
75 is,] ∼∧ *S, P*
113 SD *Addressing . . . wife.*] *om. Q, D, L, S, P*
114 life] wife *D*
115 dispaire] dispense *D*

III.ii

III.ii] *L; om. Q, D, S;* ∼. ∼ D'Olive's *Chamber P*
8-9 Courtier; respect's] *D, L, S, P;* Courtier, respects *Q*
9 ioynted courtesie's] *S, P;* ∼, courtesies *Q;* jointed; courtesy's *D;* ∼, Courtesy *L*
12 looke] *D, L, S, P;* ∼? *Q*
22 but] both *Q, D, L, S, P*
27 still] stiffe, *Q, D, L, S, P*
37 with] by *D*
44 night,] *L, S, P;* ∼∧ *Q, D*
46 my] *om. Q, D, L, S, P*
47 their] *Q(c);* my *Q(u), D*
52 A . . . Steward?] *as aside L*
    Lordship! Steward?] *S, P;* Lor. ∼? *Q;* lordship's steward! *D;* Lord ∼! *L*
53 welcome in a word:] ∼: ∼ ∼ ∼, *D*
57 berayes] betrays *D, L*
65 th'] thou *L*
89 spie out is] *Q(c);* spieout an't is *Q(u), D*
90 SD *Exeunt.*] *D, L, P; follows preceding line Q, S*
91 SD *Aside.*] *P; om. Q, D, L, S*
    seasonable] reasonable *P*
92 his] its *D*
97 its] *L, P; om. Q(u), D;* it *Q(c), S*
100 admirable] admirably *L*
133 We] *D, S, P;* Me *Q, L*
    SD *Exeunt . . . D'oliue.*] *D, L, S, P; follows preceding line Q*
    SD *Manet D'oliue.*] *om. D, L*

141 Others with] Others are with *D*
146 ont] out *L*
154 theyle] they *S*
161 mute] moult *S*
168 were] was *D*
178 goe, the Sergeants;] *L, P;* ~∧ ~ ~, *Q, S;* ~, ~ ~, *D*
    home,] *D, P;* ~∧ *Q, L, S*

IV.i

Actvs . . . prima.] ~ . . . ~. *A Room in the House of* Vaumont *P*
5 t'his] to his *L, S*
29 SD *Retires.*] *P; om. Q, D, L, S*
33 my] *D, L, S, P;* any *Q*
40 SD *Aside.*] *D; om. Q, L, S, P*
45 man, no] *D, L, S, P;* ~: No *Q*
50 SD *Advancing.*] *P; om. Q, D, L, S*
61 more,] ~; *S;* ~∧ *L, P*
62 desernes:] ~, *Q, L;* ~∧ *S;* deserves: *D, P*
64 that, One] ~∧ ~, *Q, D;* ~∧ ~∧ *L, S, P*
87 Lord;] *S, P;* ~, *Q, D, L*
    SD *Exit S. Anne.*] *follows* Well . . . gone *D, L*
91 must be] has been *D*
92 and then] now must *D*
103 SD *Exeunt.*] *D; Exit Q, L, S; Exit with* Vaumont *P*

IV.ii

IV.ii] *om. Q, D, L, S;* ~. ~ D'Olive's *Chamber P*
3 *Diq.*] *Dig. throughout L*
6 had] *om. L*
13 Goarde] *P;* Goade *Q, D, L, S*
14 SD *Showing . . . dice.*] *P; om. Q, D, L, S*
27 thither] hither *L*
41 in faith] i'faith *S, P*
79 now] how *S*
91 breadth] brain *Deighton conj.*
98 *Bullaine*] Boulogne *L*
99 *St. Iames* his] St. James's *D, L*
    Calice] Calais *D, L, S, P*
104 rac't] rased *L;* razed *S*
110 marie,] marie∧ *Q;* marry∧ *S;* marry, *D, L, P*
120 beraid] buried *D*
124 *Diq.*] *Dig. here and throughout remainder of scene Q*
129 SD *Enter Muge.*] ~ ~ *and a Page D, P*
136 hane] have *D, L, S, P*
153 SD *The . . . leave.*] *om. Q, D, L, S, P*
160 retire] retrieve *D*
169 SD *Exit Pag.*] *The Page goes out, and returns with pens and ink D*
176 SD *Enter . . . quills.*] *P; om. Q, D, L, S*

178 SD *Taking the ink.*] *om.* Q, D, L, S, P
178-79 SD *Selecting a quill.*] *om.* Q, D, L, S, P
196 not thou] thou not S, P
207 with modestie] L, S; with with modestie Q; with—with modesty D, P
221 there is] there's D

V.i

Actvs . . . prima.] ~ . . . ~. *Before the House of* Vaumont P
26 here?] ~? *Enter Digue above.* L
27 SD *He . . . light.*] *om.* L
35 SD *Redit cum lumine.*] D; *follows next two lines* Q, S; *om.* L
37 villanie.] ~! *Coming forward again* L
46 besides] beside D
52 SD *Enter Eurione aboue.*] P; *om.* Q, L, S; *Within* D
58 touch] touches L
61 SD *Enter Marcellina aboue.*] P; *om.* Q, L, S; *Within* D
62 that,] D, L, S, P; ~∧ Q
71 brother] D, L, S, P; bother Q
   SD *Exeunt . . . Eurione.*] P; *om.* Q, D, L, S
72 *Vand.*] ~. *To Vaum.* D
   not;] L, P; ~, Q, S; ~: D
75 SD *He . . . below.*] D, P; *om.* Q, L, S
98 as] D, L, S, P; as as Q
108 freckld-face peece] L, S, P; freckld face peece Q; freckled face-piece D
123 Trumpe] triumph S
145 he] L, S, P; she Q, D
153 SD *Aside.*] D, L, P; *om.* Q, S
187 liuer;] ~, Q, D, L, S, P
188 were] ~, Q, L, S; ~), D; ~)∧ P
189 SD *Aside.*] D, L, P; *om.* Q, S
215 SD *Stringit ensem.*] *Drawing.* L
216 *Dig.*] P; *Pag.* Q, D, L, S
222 SD *To . . . Eurione.*] *om.* Q, D, L, S, P
223 afore] before L
226 SD *Exeunt . . . Vau.*] *Exeunt Mar. Eury. and Page. Vaum. comes forward.* D; *Exeunt* Marcellina, Eurione, *and* Dicque. *Manent* Vandome *and* Vaumont P
230 th' Herculean] D, P; t'Herculean Q; the Herculean L, S
234 SD *Exeunt.*] *om.* Q, D, L, S, P

V.ii

V.ii] L; *om.* Q, D, S; ~. ~ *A Street Before the Court* P
4 I am] I'm P
10 SD *Aside.*] P; *om.* Q, D, L, S
11 stayes] stands S
12 SD *Aside.*] P; *om.* Q, D, L, S
13 SD *Exit Dig.*] *at conclusion of speech* D, L, S
21 SD *To Marcellina.*] *om.* Q, D, L, S, P
   y'are] you're D; you are L

24 SD *She . . . leave.*] *om. Q, D, L, S, P*
25 SD *To Eurione.*] *om. Q, D, L, S, P*
    you] *om. S, P*
26 Sunne] ~ *pointing to St. Anne D*
29 SD *To . . . Mugeron.*] *D, L, P; om. Q, S*
    awhile. *Vandome,*] *D, L, P;* ~∧ ~: *Q;* ~, ~. *S*
31 Y'aue . . . forward:] You have . . . ~. *as part of preceding speech by Phil. L*
33 whom] who *L*
40 *Phil.*] *S; Duke. Q, D, L, P; Duke throughout scene D*
59 *Phil.*] *S; Duke. Q, D, L, P*
68 SD *D'Olive . . . leave.*] *om. Q, D, L, S, P*

PRESS-VARIANTS

[Copies collated: BM[1] (British Museum C. 34. c. 15); BM[2] (British Museum Ashley 372); Bodl (Bodleian Library 4 T. 39 [2] ART., wants D3); CLUC (W. A. Clark Library, the University of California at Los Angeles); CSmH[1] (Huntington Library C 4983 98556); CSmH[2] (Huntington Library C 4983 98557); DFo[1] (Folger Shakespeare Library 7867); DFo[2] (Folger Shakespeare Library 4983); IU (University of Illinois Library); MB[1] (Boston Public Library 149.577); MB[2] (Boston Public Library 151.506); TxU (University of Texas Library); Worc (Worcester College Library, Oxford)]

Sheet A (outer forme)

First State Corrected: BM[1], CSmH[2], DFo[2], IU, MB[1], TxU
Uncorrected: CSmH[1], Worc

Sig. A1

Title page D'OLIVE.] D'OLIVE

George Chapman] Geo. Chapmon
Shop] $_S$hop

Dun-stons] Dun-Stons
Fleete-streete] Fleete streete

Sig. A2[v]

I.i.28 managde] manadgd
31 her,] her
34 dancing,] dancing
41 full.] full
43 Haue] Have
49 this] thls

Sig. A3

I.i.57 knowledge] knowledge,
58 without him,] without him
72 spleene] spleene,

Sig. A4[v]

I.i.167 messengers] messagers
173 soule.] soule,
174 second] second,
178 teares,] teares$_\wedge$
179 next] Next
183 wrongs her.] wrongs her
185 liues] lines
good. Now] good Now

466

I.ii.1 SD Rhoderique] Rhoderiqne
   2 La-/ die] Lady
   3 vowe] vow
     to forbeare] to for-/ beare
   4 sincerely] sinceerely
   8 of] ef
Second State Corrected: BM², Bodl, CLUC, DFo¹, MB²

Sig. A1

Title page *Comedie, as it was sundrie times acted by her/* Maiesties children at the Blacke-/ *Friers.*] Comedie, as it vvas/ sundrie times acted by her/ *Maiesties children at the Blacke-/* Friers.

Sheet B (inner forme)

Corrected: BM¹, BM², Bodl, CSmH¹, CSmH², DFo¹, DFo², IU, MB¹, MB², TxU, Worc
Uncorrected: CLUC

Sig. B3ᵛ

I.ii.187 God] good
       can,] can
   189 time] time,
catchword *Rho.] Enter*

Sheet C (outer forme)

Corrected: BM¹, BM², Bodl, CLUC, CSmH¹, CSmH², DFo¹, DFo², MB¹, MB², TxU, Worc
Uncorrected: IU

Sig. C1

running title D'OLIVE] DELIVE
II.i.25 Exceeding] Eaceeding
   32 doe not you] doe you not
   36 Sexe,] Sexe∧
   37 wee?] wee.
   38 *Mar:] Mvg:*
   40 loue the Noble] loue you loue the Noble
   48 *Vand.] Vavd.*
   49 enter] enrer
   55 *Sic:] sdc:*
   56 your] yodr

Sig. C2ᵛ

running title D'OLIVE] DOLIVE
II.i.119 possible?] possible.
   120 was] wa:
   121 spirits] spitits
   133 you] yon
   135 you] ynu
   137 Evry] Evey

Sig. C3

    running title D'OLIVE] DOLIVE

    II.i.159 you louers] you loners louers

                captious] captious.

        160 obseru'd] obseru'n

        167 without] wlthout

Sig. C4^v

    running title D'OLIVE] DOLIVE

    II.ii.32 Highnes] Highues

        33 his] h!s

Sheet D (inner forme)

First State Corrected: CLUC, DFo^2

Uncorrected: MB^1, MB^2

Sig. D2

    II.ii.127 Shall be] Sha ll be

    Second State Corrected: BM^1, BM^2, Bodl, CSmH^2, TxU

Sig. D4

    II.ii.269 Iohannes] Iehannes

    Third State Corrected: CSmH^1, DFo^1, IU, Worc

Sig. D1^v

    II.ii.81 vour] your (*imperfect y*)

        91 m n] men

      100 or] os

Sig. D2

    II.ii.130 you'le] you'le

      136 high] h!gh

Sig. D3^v

    II.ii.248 breat] breath

      255 brayne,] brayne$_\wedge$

Sig. D4

    II.ii.260 as there] as thete

      267 begetts] bege ts

      272 country?] country¿

      275 to Garlick] to GarIck

Sheet D (outer forme)

First State Corrected: BM^1, Bodl, CSmH^2, DFo^1, IU, MB^2, TxU, Worc

Uncorrected: CLUC, DFo^2, MB^1

Sig. D2^v

    running title MONSIEVR] MO$_N$SIEVR

Second State Corrected: BM^2

Sig. D4^v

    running title D'OLIVE.] D'OLIVE:

    Third State Corrected: CSmH^1

Sig. D2^v
  running title D'OLIVE.] D'OLIVE$_\wedge$
Sig. D3
  running title D'OLIVE.] D'OLIVE$_\wedge$

Sheet E (inner forme)

First State Corrected: IU
Uncorrected: Bodl, CSmH^2, MB^2
Sig. E1^v
  III.i.17 tirranous] terrinous
      23 *vincitur*] *viuatur*
      46 *dilectas*] *delectas*
        littus] *actus*
Sig. E2
  III.i.50 SD *Gueaquin*] *Guraquin*
        Ieronime] *Ierommie*
      72 threed] throat
Second State Corrected: BM^1, BM^2, CLUC, CSmH^1, DFo^1, DFo^2, MB^1, TxU,
                Worc
Sig. E3^v
  III.ii.47 their] my
Sig. E4
  III.ii.89 spie out is] spieout an't is
      96 Here] Heere
      97 with it furniture] with furniture

Sheet E (outer forme)

Corrected: BM^2, CLUC, MB^1, TxU
Uncorrected: BM^1, Bodl, CSmH^1, CSmH^2, DFo^1, DFo^2, IU, MB^2, Worc
Sig. E4^v
  III.ii.105 Courtly] Gourtly
Stop-press repositioning of the running titles occurred on the following
pages: sigs. A4^v, B1^v, C1^v, C2^v, C3^v, C4, C4^v, D1, D3^v, D4, D4^v, E3.

TEXTUAL NOTES

II.i

1 SD *Digue*] Dilke, Shepherd, and Parrott fail to distinguish Digue and Dique. Dilke identifies both as one servant named Digue; Parrott does the same but calls him Dicque throughout. But Digue, as we see in IV.ii and again in V.i and V.ii, is page to Marcellina; Dique, companion of Pacque and one of D'Olive's followers, appears only in IV.ii.

20-21 but was such a man as this euer seen,] Parrott emends to "But such a man as this was never seen," a plausible reading that requires minimal interference with the copy-text. The interrogation point at the end of the sentence, however, and the function of this clause in a long series of closely parallel questions insistently asked by Eurione imply, I think, that it also is a question. By slightly modifying the syntax, I convert the statement into a question that perfectly continues Eurione's series.

II.ii

134 Countes] Clearly the duke here refers to St. Anne, and not, as Dilke and Parrott assume, to the dead countess.

269 de Sauoret] Probably D'Olive here alludes (as Shepherd suggests) to Giovanni Michele Savonarola and his *Practica Canonica de Febribus,* several editions of which appeared in the sixteenth century. But in emending to *Savonarola,* Shepherd and Parrott have obscured D'Olive's unintentional witticism in calling the Paduan doctor "sauoret" (i.e., *savouret* or marrow-bone). This supposition has also the virtue of accounting for the otherwise superfluous *et* in the copy-text, which reads "de sauo et."

III.ii

46 my] Since the compositor erroneously substituted "my" for "their" later in the line (an error which the proofreader caught), I think it highly probable that the "my" belongs with "Lord."

91 seasonable] Parrott emends to "reasonable"; but the context establishes "seasonable," in the sense of "timely," as the correct reading.

IV.i

62 desernes:] Dilke and Parrott emend to "deserves" (i.e., deserues). But here the copy-text appears to be correct. The clause which follows l. 62 is the object of "desernes."

IV.ii

13 Goarde] Although "goade" as it appears in Q may represent a variant form of "goarde," I think it more likely that "goarde" is correct, particularly since the compositor tended to such errors.

136 hane] Parrott emends to "have" (i.e., "haue"). But the colloquial tone of the speech strongly supports the copy-text reading. Mugeron uses a common expression that often occurs as "I durst han swore" or "I durst han vowed" or, as here, "I durst han layed my life."

196 not thou] Shepherd and Parrott improve the syntax by emending to "thou not"; but the intentionally affected style of Rhoderique and Mugeron's letter is heightened by the awkward copy-text version.

207 with modestie] Dilke and Parrott, by employing a dash to separate the two "with's" of the quarto, indicate that Rhoderique, in groping for a conclusion to his witticism, repeated himself. But both Rhoderique and Mugeron's sophisticated articulateness and the lack of similar passages in the play strongly imply that the compositor simply once again erroneously duplicated a word as he does, for example, with "as" a few pages later.

V.i

187 liuer;] Dilke's suggestion that the phrase "as he said you were" has been transposed from its proper position following "shrow" implies a misunderstanding of "liuer" and hence of the whole passage. Although they do not transpose the phrase, Shepherd and Parrott, by their punctuation, indicate that they follow Dilke in his misreading.

V.ii

25 you] Omitted by Shepherd and Parrott. But since Vandome, who has been addressing Marcellina, here abruptly turns to Eurione, he intentionally employs the "you your" phrase to emphasize the shift.

The Widow's Tears

edited by Robert Ornstein

❖

TEXTUAL INTRODUCTION

The only contemporary edition of *The Widow's Tears* was printed in quarto (Q) by William Stansby for John Browne in 1612, perhaps to capitalize on a successful revival of the work some years after its composition. Chapman speaks of the play in his Dedication as one "of manie desired to see printed," and not long after its publication, on February 27, 1613, it was performed at Court. The legend on the title page (see Greg, *Bibliography,* pp. 439-40), "As it was often presented in the blacke and white Friers," suggests that it was first staged at the Blackfriars by the Chapel or Revel players, and was printed after performance at the Whitefrairs. No entry in the *Stationers' Register* provides any clue to a specific date of composition. Wallace's strained attempt to identify *The Widow's Tears* with a Chapel play seen by the Duke of Stettin in 1602 was thoroughly demolished by Parrott, and by Chambers, who particularly points out the Jacobean character of topical references to strange knights abroad. Unless we assume that such references were added in revivals of the play, they seem to imply that composition occurred early in the reign of James. Chambers argues for a date before 1608. Parrott voices the scholarly consensus that the play was written about 1605.

Although Q contains Chapman's dedicatory preface and a haphazard list of "Actors" — very probably part of the manuscript from which the play was printed — the text is extremely inaccurate. As the press corrections indicate, the printers did what they could with difficult copy. Their problems seemed to increase as they progressed through the manuscript until, in the final sheets, the attempt to print the lines as verse almost breaks down, and the pages are marred by omission of words or lines and by other corruptions of the text. Since, on the other hand, the printing seems fairly careful, with few obvious errors escaping proof correction, we can ascribe the frequent mislining and the confusion of verse and prose to foul copy rather than to compositorial ineptitude. There are various signs, in fact, that the manuscript copy included many revised and interlined passages. For example, the existence of such interlinear insertions may well explain the printing in Q (on sig. D2^v) of two successive lines assigned to the same character (II.ii.5). Similarly, revisions in the manuscript rather than careless typesetting seem to be responsible for the several metatheses corrected during the proofing: e.g. "ith place speeding" (I.iii.119), and "how know you" (II.iii.44).

But not all difficulties in the quarto text can be explained by a hypothesis of foul copy. In many instances verse arbitrarily turns to prose, and prose to verse. Worse still are the passages that are not quite prose or finished verse but either rough-hewn poetry or prose unconsciously cast in clauses that approximate iambic pentameter. As Parrott points out, the last act in particular shows signs of hasty or careless composition. In view of this evidence, one may reasonably assume that the copy for Q was not only Chapman's foul papers but also that these papers represented something less than a finished draft of the play. The list of actors suggests that at one time Chapman had no names for the Spartan lords; and at I.ii.151 (sig. C2) we find the speech head "Lurd," apparently a misprint for "Lord," though the speaker seems to be Psorabeus. Similarly the Usher Clinias does not enter the play until Act II, though he is evidently supposed to be present in Act I, and may be the "other Usher" mentioned in the stage direction at I.ii.32.

The stage directions seem to be authorial: they are permissive about the number of minor characters in a scene, occur frequently in Latin, and, on occasion, elaborately prescribe the actors' gestures. Moreover, because two of the directions in the manuscript were apparently insufficiently distinct from the rest of the text, the compositor set them in roman type as part of the dialogue. On the other hand, the stage directions are virtually complete; only one entrance — that of a minor character — is missing. And we also find such abrupt directions as *"shee strikes"* and *"Shut the tomb"* which, presumably, characterize prompt copies. The characteristics of the stage directions, then, raise the possibility that Q was printed from Chapman's foul papers which had been marked by the prompter before the author made a clean and possibly somewhat revised copy for the company. One should further note in support of this hypothesis that the play was being performed successfully at the time of its printing; thus the company might well have preferred to surrender foul papers, rather than its fair copy, to the printer.

Two sets of running titles appear regularly throughout Q: one set used consistently for the inner formes, another for the outer. In addition, convincing evidence, particularly in the early sheets, points to composition by formes from cast-off copy. For example, B3 is one line short; D2 is three lines short. The prose is obviously spaced out on B3, C4, D3ᵛ, D4, and F4; but on other pages the type is crowded. Furthermore, in each sheet the evident signs of casting-off are limited to one forme, presumably the second forme set, since the compositor could, to some extent, ignore the demarcations of the cast-off copy in setting the first forme of a sheet so long as he compensated in the second forme. From such evidence we can hypothesize, then, that for sheets B, G, H, the printer set the inner formes first; for sheets C, D, E, and F, he reversed the order. Clear-cut evidences of casting-off are not present on sheets I, K, and L for the interesting reason that beginning with I3, the number of lines per page increases from 37 to 38, and the typography becomes consistently dense and crowded. If we assume that these sheets, like the earlier ones, were set from cast-off copy, then the increased density of the typography that begins on I3 indicates a changed method of casting off the copy — an attempt to crowd more copy on each page — rather than the presence of a new workman with different habits of composition.

Since the signs of casting-off suggest two orders of composition in the formes, it is possible that two compositors worked on Q, one who started his sheets with the inner formes, the other who set outer formes first. But I find no variant patterns of spelling and punctuation that point to more than one compositor. On the contrary, two typographical peculiarities suggest that one compositor set all the formes. First, throughout Q the speech heads, in contrast to the usual practice of Jacobean printers, are not indented. And second, the compositor has troubled to align the speeches on almost every page,[1] and to that end he has varied the spellings of the speech heads so that those on any page approximate each other in length.

Some of the press corrections in Q remind one of those in the Pied Bull quarto of *King Lear*. Most of the variants in the outer forme of C, for example, are not corrections of obvious misprints or nonsense phrases; on the contrary, they result from changes made in words and phrases that appear correct in their context. Thus the proofreader either was checking the proofsheets so carefully against the manuscript that he was able to spot and refine upon the guesses made by the compositors; or, as I think more likely, he knew that these particular words and phrases were guesses, made in the relative haste of composition, that required further scrutiny. If the latter is true, then it is quite possible that such corrections derive from the compositors themselves.

Since publication of the original quarto, five editions of *The Widow's Tears* have appeared. The play was edited successively by Dodsley, Reed, and Collier in the 1744, 1780, and 1825 editions of *A Select Collection of Old Plays*. And it appears also in Shepherd's and Parrott's editions of Chapman. Although the editors of Dodsley's *Collection* introduced additional corruptions and made unnecessary changes in the text of Q, they began the necessary process of emendation, which Shepherd and Parrott continued. As the footnotes indicate, I have drawn heavily on the work of earlier editors, and I have made other emendations and corrections which seemed to me essential.

[1] In printing *May-Day*, also a product of Stansby's shop, one of two compositors involved in the project also aligned his speeches. See the textual introduction to that play.

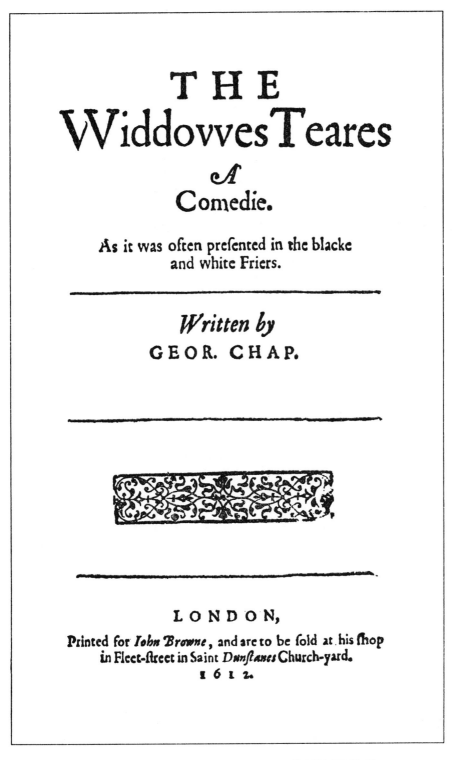

THE
VViddovvesTeares

A
Comedie.

As it was often prefented in the blacke
and white Friers.

Written by
GEOR. CHAP.

LONDON,

Printed for *Iohn Browne*, and are to be fold at his fhop
in Fleet-ftreet in Saint *Dunftanes* Church-yard.
1 6 1 2.

The Actors.

Tharsalio the wooer.

Lysander his brother.

Gouernour of Cyprus.

Lycus, ser. to the widdow Countesse.

Argus, Gent. Vsher.

[Clinias, a servant of Eudora.

Rebus, a suitor of Eudora.

Hiarbas ⎫
       ⎬ his friends.]
Psorabeus ⎭

Eudora the widdow Countesse.

Cynthia, wife to Lysander.

Sthenio ⎫ gentlewomen atending
Ianthe ⎭ on Eudora.

Ero, waiting woman to Cynthia.

[Laodice, daughter to Eudora.

Arsace, a pandress.

Tomasin, a courtesan.]

Hylus, Nephew to Tharsalio, and Sonne to Lysander.

Captaine of the watch.

2. Souldiers.

To the right Vertuous and truly *noble Gentleman,*
Mʳ Io. REED of Mitton, in the countie of Glocester Esquire.

Sir, if any worke of this nature be worth the presenting to Friends
Worthie, and Noble; I presume this, will not want much of that value.
Other Countrie men haue thought the like worthie of Dukes and
Princes acceptations; Iniusti sdegnij; Il Pentamento Amorose: Calis-
the, Pastor fido, &c. *(all being but plaies) were all dedicate to Princes*   5
of Italie. And therefore [I] only discourse to shew my loue to your
right vertuous and noble disposition. This poor Comedie (of many
desired to see printed) I thought not vtterly vnworthie that affection-
ate designe in me: Well knowing that your free iudgement weighs
nothing by the Name, or Forme; or any vaine estimation of the vulgar;   10
but will accept acceptable matter, as well in Plaies; as in many lesse
materialls, masking in more serious Titles. And so, till some worke
more worthie I can select, and perfect, out of my other Studies, that
may better expresse me; and more fit the grauitie of your ripe inclina-
tions, I rest,   15

Yours at all parts most truly affected,
Geo. Chapman.

---

6 *therefore I only*] Parrott; *therefore only* ‖ 7 *disposition.*] Parrott; ∼; ‖ **15** *rest,*] ∼. ‖ **16** affected,] ∼. ‖

The Widdowes Teares.

A COMEDIE

Actus Primi: Scœna Prima.

Tharsalio Solus, with a Glasse in his hand making readie.

Thow blinde imperfect Goddesse, that delights
(Like a deepe-reaching Statesman) to conuerse
Only with Fooles: Iealous of knowing spirits;
For feare their piersing Iudgements might discouer
Thy inward weaknesse, and despise thy power;   5
Contemne thee for a Goddesse; Thou that lad'st
Th'vnworthy Asse with gold; while worth and merit
Serue thee for nought; (weake Fortune) I renounce
Thy vaine dependance, and conuert my dutie
And sacrifices of my sweetest thoughts,   10
To a more Noble Deitie. Sole friend to worth,
And Patronesse of all good Spirits, *Confidence.*
Shee be my Guide, and hers the praise of these
My worthie vndertakings.

Enter Lysander with a Glasse in his hand, Cynthia,
Hylus, Ero.

Lys. Morrow Brother; Not readie yet?   15
Thar. No; I haue somewhat of the Brother in me; / I dare say, [B1ᵛ]
your Wife is many times readie, and you not vp. Saue you sister; how,
are you enamoured of my presence? how like you my aspect?
Cynth. Faith no worse then I did last weeke, the weather has noth-
ing chang'd the graine of your complexion.   20
Thar. A firme proofe, 'tis in graine, and so are not all complexions.
A good Souldiers face Sister.
Cynth. Made to be worne vnder a Beuer.
Thar. I, and 'twould shew well enough vnder a maske too.

---

22 A . . . Sister.] *Parrott; on separate line* ‖

Lys. So much for the face.   25

Thar. But is there no obiect in this suite to whet your tongue vpon?

Lys. None, but Fortune send you well to weare it: for shee best knowes how you got it.

Thar. Faith, 'tis the portion shee bestowes vpon yonger Brothers, valour, and good clothes: Marry, if you aske how we come by this new   30 suite, I must take time to answere it: for as the Ballad saies, in written Bookes I find it. Brother these are the blossomes of spirit: and I will haue it said for my Fathers honour, that some of his children were truly begotten.

Lys. Not all?   35

Thar. Shall I tell you brother that I know will reioyce you? my former suites haue been all spenders, this shall be a speeder.

Lys. A thing to bee heartily wisht; but brother, take heede you be not gull'd, be not too forward.

Thar. 'T had beene well for me, if you had follow'd that counsaile: 40 You were too forward when you stept into the world before me, and gull'd me of the Land, that my spirits and parts were indeed borne too.

Cynth. May we not haue the blessing to know the aime of your fortunes, what coast, for heauens loue?

Thar. Nay, tis a proiect of State: you may see the preparation; but   45 the designe lies hidden in the brests of the wise. /

Lys. May we not know't?   [B2]

Thar. Not vnlesse you'le promise mee to laugh at it, for without your applause, Ile none.

Lys. The qualitie of it may bee such as a laugh will not be ill be-   50 stow'd vpon't; pray heaven I call not *Arsace* sister.

Cyn. What? the Pandresse?

Thar. Know you (as who knowes not) the exquisite Ladie of the Palace? The late Gouernours admired Widdow? The rich and haugh-tie Countesse *Eudora*? Were not shee a Iewell worth the wearing, if a   55 man knew how to win her?

Lys. How's that? how's that?

Thar. Brother, there is a certaine Goddesse called *Confidence,* that carries a maine stroke in honourable preferments. Fortune waits vpon her; *Cupid* is at her becke; shee sends them both of errands. This   60 Deitie doth promise me much assistance in this businesse.

Lys. But if this Deitie should draw you vp in a basket to your Countesses window, and there let you hang for all the wits in the Towne to shoot at: how then?

Thar. If shee doe, let them shoote their bolts and spare not: I haue   65
a little Bird in a Cage here that sings me better comfort. What should
be the barre? you'le say, I was Page to the Count her husband. What
of that? I haue thereby one foote in her fauour alreadie; Shee has
taken note of my spirit, and suruaid my good parts, and the picture of
them liues in her eie: which sleepe, I know, can not close, till shee   70
haue embrac't the substance.

Lys. All this sauors of the blind Goddesse you speake of.

Thar. Why should I despaire, but that *Cupid* hath one dart in store
for her great Ladiship, as well as for any other huge Ladie, whom she
hath made stoope Gallant, to kisse their worthie followers. In a word,   75
I am assured of my speede. Such faire attempts led by a braue resolue,
are euermore seconded by Fortune.

Cynth. But brother? haue I not heard you say, your own eares haue
been witnesse to her vowes, made solemnely to your late Lord; in memorie of him, to preserue till death, / the vnstain'd honour of a Wid- [B2ᵛ] 80
dowes bed. If nothing else, yet that might coole your confidence.

Thar. Tush sister, suppose you should protest with solemne oath (as
perhaps you haue done) if euer Heauen heares your praiers, that you
may liue to see my Brother nobly interred, to feede only vpon fish, and
not endure the touch of flesh, during the wretched Lent of your miser-   85
able life; would you beleeue it Brother?

Lys. I am therein most confident.

Thar. Indeed, you had better beleeue it then trie it: but pray Sister
tell me, you are a woman: doe not you wiues nod your heads, and
smile one vpon an other when yee meete abroade?   90

Cynth. Smile? why so?

Thar. As who should say, are not we mad Wenches, that can lead
our blind husbands thus by the noses? do you not brag amongst your
selues how grosly you abuse their honest credulities? how they adore
you for Saints: and you beleeue it? while you adhorne their temples,   95
and they beleeue it not? how you vow Widdow-hood in their life time,
and they beleeue you, when euen in the sight of their breathlesse corse,
ere they be fully cold, you ioine embraces with his Groome, or his Phisition, and perhaps his poisoner; or at least by the next Moone (if you
can expect so long) solemnely plight new Hymineall bonds, with a   100
wild, confident, vntamed Ruffine?

Lys. As for example?

Thar. And make him the top of his house, and soueraign Lord of
the Palace, as for example. Looke you Brother, this glasse is mine.

83 done)] ∼, ‖ 84 interred,] ∼) ‖ 102 example?] ∼. ‖

Lys. What of that?   105

Thar. While I am with it, it takes impression from my face; but can
I make it so mine, that it shall be of no vse to any other? will it not
doe his office to you or you: and as well to my Groome as to my selfe?
Brother, Monopolies are cryed downe. Is it not madnes for me to beleeue, when I haue conquer'd that Fort of chastitie the great / Coun- [B3] 110
tesse; that if another man of my making, and mettall, shall assault her:
her eies and eares should lose their function, her other parts their vse,
as if Nature had made her all in vaine, vnlesse I only had stumbl'd into
her quarters?

Cynth. Brother: I feare me in your trauaile, you haue drunck too   115
much of that Italian aire, that hath infected the whole masse of your
ingenuous Nature; dried vp in you all sap of generous disposition,
poisond the very Essence of your soule, and so polluted your senses,
that whatsoeuer enters there, takes from them contagion, and is to your
fancie represented as foule and tainted, which in it selfe perhaps is   120
spotlesse.

Thar. No sister, it hath refin'd my senses, and made mee see with
cleare eies, and to iudge of obiects, as they truly are, not as they seeme,
and through their maske to discerne the true face of thinges. It tells
me how short liu'd Widdowes teares are, that their weeping is in truth   125
but laughing vnder a Maske, that they mourne in their Gownes, and
laugh in their Sleeues, all which I beleeue as a Delphian Oracle: and
am resolu'd to burne in that faith. And in that resolution doe I march
to the great Ladie.

Lys. You lose time Brother in discourse, by this had you bore vp   130
with the Ladie y'ad clapt her aboord, for I knowe your confidence will
not dwell long in the seruice.

Thar. No, I will performe it in the Conquerours stile. Your way is,
not to winne *Penelope* by suite, but by surprise. The Castle's carried
by a sodaine assault, that would perhaps sit out a twelue-moneths siege.   135
It would bee a good breeding to my yong Nephew here, if hee could
procure a stand at the Palace, to see with what alacritie Ile a-coast her
Countesship, in what garbe I will woo her, with what facilitie I will
winne her. /

Lys. It shall goe hard but weele heare your entertainement for your [B3ᵛ] 140
confidence sake.

Thar. And hauing wonne her, Nephew, this sweet face
Which all the Citie saies, is so like me,
Like me shall be preferr'd, for I will wed thee

114 quarters?] ∼. ‖ 128 faith.] ∼, ‖ 131 y'ad] and ‖ 142 her, Nephew, this] ∼∧ ∼; This ‖

To my great widdowes Daughter and sole Heire,   145
The louely sparke, the bright *Laodice.*
   Lys. A good pleasant dreame.
   Thar.   In this eie I see
That fire that shall in me inflame the Mother,
And that in this shall set on fire the Daughter.
It goes Sir in a bloud; beleeue me brother,   150
These destinies goe euer in a bloud.
   Lys. These diseases doe, brother, take heede of them:
Fare you well; take heede you be not baffeld.
                              Exeunt. Lys. Cynth. Hyl. Ero. manet Thars.
   Thar. Now thou that art the third blind Deitie
That gouernes earth in all her happinesse,   155
The life of all endowments, *Confidence;*
Direct and prosper my intention.
Command thy seruant Deities, Loue and Fortune
To second my attempts for this great Ladie,
Whose Page I lately was; That shee, whose bord   160
I might not sit at, I may boord a bed
And under bring, who bore so high her head.   *Exit.*

[I.ii]

Lysander, Lycus.

   Lyc. 'Tis miraculous that you tell me Sir: he come to woo our
Ladie Mistris for his wife?
   Lys. 'Tis a phrensie he is possest with, and wil not be cur'd but by
some violent remedie. And you shall fauour me so much to make me
a spectator of the Scene. But is shee (say you) alreadie accessible for   5
Suiters? I thought shee would have stood so stifly on her Widdow vow,
that shee would not endure the sight of a Suiter.
   Lyc. Faith Sir, *Penelope* could not barre her gates against / her   [B4]
woers, but shee will still be Mistris of her selfe. It is as you know, a
certaine Itch in femall bloud, they loue to be su'd to: but sheele   10
hearken to no Suiters.
   Lys. But by your leaue *Lycus, Penelope* is not so wise as her husband
Ulysses, for he fearing the iawes of the *Syren,* stopt his eares with waxe
against her voice. They that fear the Adders sting, will not come neare
her hissing. Is any Suiter with her now?   15
   Lyc. A Spartan Lord, dating himselfe our great Viceroies Kinsman,
and two or three other of his Countrie Lords, as spots in his train. He

I.ii] *Parrott* ‖

484

comes armed with his Altitudes letters in grace of his person, with
promise to make her a Duchesse if shee embrace the match. This is no
meane attraction to her high thoughts; but yet shee disdaines him.   20

Lys. And how then shall my brother presume of acceptance? Yet
I hold it much more vnder her contentment, to marrie such a Nastie
braggart, then vnder her honour to wed my brother: A Gentleman
(though I sai't) more honourably descended than that Lord: who
perhaps, for all his Ancestrie would bee much troubled to name you   25
the place where his Father was borne.

Lyc. Nay I hold no comparison betwixt your brother and him. And
the Venerean disease, to which they say, he has beene long wedded,
shall I hope first rot him, ere shee endure the sauour of his Sulphurous
breath. Well, her Ladiship is at hand; y'are best take you to your   30
stand.

Lys. Thankes good friend *Lycus*.   *Exit.*

Enter Argus barehead, with whome another Vsher Lycus ioynes, going
ouer the Stage. Hiarbas, and Psorabeus next, Rebus single before
Eudora, Laodice, Sthenio bearing her traine, Ianthe following.

Reb. I admire Madame, you can not loue whome the Viceroy loues.

Hiar. And one whose veines swell so with his bloud, Madam, as they
doe in his Lordship. /   35

Pso. A neare and deare Kinsman his Lordship is to his Altitude, the   [B4ᵛ]
Viceroy; In care of whose good speede here, I know his Altitude hath
not slept a sound sleepe since his departure.

Eud. I thanke *Venus* I haue, euer since he came.

Reb. You sleepe away your Honour, Madam, if you neglect me.   40

Hiar. Neglect your Lordship? that were a negligence no lesse than
disloialtie.

Eud. I much doubt that Sir; It were rather a presumption to take
him, being of the bloud Viceroiall.

Reb. Not at all, being offered Madame.   45

Eud. But offered ware is not so sweet you know. They are the
graces of the Viceroy that woo me, not your Lordships, and I conceiue
it should be neither Honor nor Pleasure to you, to be taken in for an
other mans fauours.

Reb. Taken in Madam? you speake as I had no house to hide my   50
head in.

Eud. I haue heard so indeed, my Lord, unlesse it be another mans.

Reb. You haue heard vntruth then; These Lords can well witnesse
I can want no houses.

Hiar. Nor Palaces neither my Lord.   55

21 Yet] yet ‖ **32** SD *another Vsher*] stet | SD *Sthenio*] *Sthenia* ‖ **43** Sir;] ∼, ‖

Pso. Nor Courts neither.

Eud. Nor Temples I thinke neither; I beleeue wee shall haue a God of him.

Enter Tharsalio.

Arg. See the bold fellow; whether will you Sir?

Thar. Away, all honour to you Madam?　　　　　　　　　　　　　60

Eud. How now base companion?

Thar. Base Madame? hees not base that sights as high as your lips.

Eud. And does that beseeme my seruant?

Thar. Your Court-seruant Madam.

Eud. One that waited on my boord? /　　　　　　　　　　　　　65

Thar. That was only a preparation to my weight on your bed　　[C1]
Madam.

Eud. How dar'st thou come to me with such a thought?

Thar. Come to you Madam? I dare come to you at midnight, and
bid defiance to the proudest spirit that haunts these your loued shad-　70
owes; and would any way make terrible the accesse of my loue to you.

Eud. Loue me? loue my dogge.

Thar. I am bound to that by the prouerb Madam.

Eud. Kennell without with him, intrude not here. What is it thou
presum'st on?　　　　　　　　　　　　　　　　　　　　　　　　75

Thar. On your iudgement Madam, to choose a Man, and not a
Giant, as these are that come with Titles, and Authoritie, as they
would conquer, or rauish you. But I come to you with the liberall and
ingenuous Graces, Loue, Youth, and Gentrie; which (in no more deform'd a person then my selfe) deserue any Princesse.　　　　　　80

Eud. In your sawcie opinion Sir, and sirha too; get gone; and let
this malipert humour returne thee no more, for afore heauen Ile haue
thee tost in blanquets.

Thar. In blanquets Madam? you must adde your sheetes, and you
must be the Tosser.　　　　　　　　　　　　　　　　　　　　85

Reb. Nay then Sir y'are as grosse as you are sawcie.

Thar. And all one Sir, for I am neither.

Reb. Thou art both.

Thar. Thou liest; keepe vp your smiter Lord *Rebus*.

Hiar. Vsest thou thus his Altitudes Cosen?　　　　　　　　　　90

Reb. The place thou know'st protects thee.

Thar. Tie vp your valour then till an other place turne me loose to
you, you are the Lord (I take it) that wooed my great Mistris here
with letters from his Altitude; which while she was reading, your

Lordship (to entertaine time) strodl'd and skal'd your fingers; as you   95
would shew what an itching desire you had to get betwixt her sheetes.

Hiar. Slight, why does your Lordship endure him?

Reb. The place, the place my Lord.

Thar. [*to Hiar.*] Be you his Attorney Sir. /

Hiar. What would you doe Sir?   [C1ᵛ] 100

Thar. Make thee leape out at window, at which thou cam'st in:
Whores-sonne bag-pipe Lords.

Eud. What rudenesse is this?

Thar. What tamenesse is it in you Madam, to sticke at the discard-
ing of such a suiter? A leane Lord, dub'd with the lard of others? A   105
diseased Lord too, that opening certaine Magick Characters in an vnlawfull booke, vp-start as many aches in's bones, as there are ouches
in's skinne. Send him (Mistris) to the Widdow your Tennant; the
vertuous Pandresse *Arsace.* I perceiue he has crownes in's Purse, that
make him proud of a string; let her pluck the Goose therefore, and   110
her maides dresse him.

Pso. Still my Lord suffer him?

Reb. The place Sir, beleeue it the place.

Thar. O good Lord *Rebus*; The place is neuer like to be yours that
you neede respect it so much.   115

Eud. Thou wrong'st the noble Gentleman.

Thar. Noble Gentleman? A tumor, an impostume hee is Madam;
a very hault-boy, a bag-pipe; in whom there is nothing but winde, and
that none of the sweetest neither.

Eud. Quitt the House of him by 'thead and Shoulders.   120

Thar. Thankes to your Honour Madame, and my Lord Cosen the
Viceroy shall thanke you.

Reb. So shall he indeede sir.

Lyc. Arg. Will you be gone sir?

Thar. Away poore Fellowes.   125

Eud. What is he made of? or what Deuill sees
Your childish, and effeminate spirits in him,
That thus yee shun him? Free vs of thy sight;
Be gone, or I protest thy life shall goe.

Thar. Yet shall my Ghost stay still; and haunt those beauties,   130
And glories, that haue rendered it immortall.
But since I see your bloud runnes (for the time) /
High, in that contradiction that fore-runs   [C2]
Truest agreements (like the Elements

99 SD *to Hiar.*] ‖ **120** Shoulders] *Dodsley*; Soulders ‖ **126-28** What . . . sight;] *Collier; as prose*
(your . . . that) ‖ **130-31** Yet . . . immortall.] *Reed; as prose* (and) ‖

Fighting before they generate;) and that Time   135
Must be attended most, in thinges most worth;
I leaue your Honour freely; and commend
That life you threaten, when you please, to be
Aduentur'd in your service; so your Honour
Require it likewise.
    Eud.   Doe not come againe.   140
    Thar. Ile come againe, beleeue it, and againe.   *Exit.*
    Eud. If he shall dare to come againe, I charge you
Shut dores vpon him.
    Arg.   You must shut them (Madam)
To all men else then, if it please your Honour,
For if that any enter, hele be one.   145
    Eud. I hope, wise Sir, a Guard will keepe him out.
    Arg. Afore Heaven, not a Guard (ant please your Honour.)
    Eud. Thou liest base Asse; One man enforce a Guard?
Ile turne yee all away (by our Iles Goddesse)
If he but set a foote within my Gates.   150
    Pso. [*to Rebus*] Your Honour shall doe well to haue him poison'd.
    Hiar. Or begg'd of your Cosen the Viceroy.   *Exeunt.*

[I.iii]

Lysander from his stand.

    Lys. This brauing wooer, hath the successe expected; The fauour I
obtain'd, made me witnesse to the sport; And let his Confidence bee
sure, Ile giue it him home. The newes by this, is blowne through the
foure quarters of the Cittie. Alas good Confidence: but the happinesse is he has a forehead of proofe; the staine shall never stick there   5
whatsoeuer his reproch be.

Enter Tharsalio.

    Lys. [*Aside.*] What? in discourse?
    Thar. Hell and the Furies take this vile encounter. /
Who would imagine this Saturnian Peacock   [C2ᵛ]
Could be so barbarous to vse a spirit   10
Of my erection, with such lowe respect?
Fore heauen it cuts my gall; but Ile dissemble it.
    Lys. What? my noble Lord?
    Thar. Well Sir, that may be yet, and meanes to be.

142-43 If . . . him.] *Parrott; as prose* (shut) ‖ 151 *Pso*] *Parrott; Lurd* | SD *to Rebus*] ‖ 152 SD
Exeunt] *Reed; Exit* ‖ I.iii] *Parrott* ‖ 7 SD *Aside.*] *Parrott* ‖ 11 erection,] *Q(c)*; direction, *Q(u)* |
lowe] *Q(c)*; loued *Q(u)* ‖

Lys. What meanes your Lordship then to hang that head that hath 15
beene so erected; it knocks Sir at your bosome to come in and hide it
selfe.

Thar. Not a iot.

Lys. I hope by this time it needes feare no hornes.

Thar. Well Sir, but yet that blessing runs not alwaies in a bloud. 20

Lys. What blanqueted? O the Gods! spurn'd out by Groomes like
a base Bisogno? thrust out by'th head and shoulders?

Thar. You doe well Sir to take your pleasure of me, (I may turne
tables with you ere long.)

Lys. What has thy wits fine engine taken cold? art stuff't inth head? 25
canst answere nothing?

Thar. Truth is, I like my entertainment the better that 'twas no
better.

Lys. Now the Gods forbid that this opinion should run in a bloud.

Thar. Haue not you heard this principle, All thinges by strife 30
engender?

Lys. Dogges and Cats doe.

Thar. And men and women too.

Lys. Well Brother, in earnest, you haue now set your confidence to
schoole, from whence I hope't has brought home such a lesson as will 35
instruct his master neuer after to begin such attempts as end in
laughter.

Thar. Well Sir, you lesson my Confidence still; I pray heauens
your confidence haue not more shallow ground (for that I know) then
mine you reprehend so. 40

Lys. My confidence? in what?

Thar. May be you trust too much. /

Lys. Wherein? [C3]

Thar. In human frailtie.

Lys. Why brother know you ought that may impeach my confidence, 45
as this successe may yours? hath your obseruation discovered any such
frailtie in my wife (for that is your aime I know) then let me know it.

Thar. Good, good. Nay, Brother, I write no bookes of Obseruations,
let your confidence beare out it selfe, as mine shall me.

Lys. That's scarce a Brothers speech. If there be ought wherein 50
your Brothers good might any way be question'd, can you conceale it
from his bosome?

Thar. So, so. Nay my saying was but generall. I glanc't at no
particular.

27 like] *Q(c);* tooke *Q(u)* ‖ **31** engender?] *Q(c);* ∼. *Q(u)* ‖ **38** Well] *Q(c);* What *Q(u)* ‖ **51**
question'd,] ∼∧ ‖

Lys. Then must I presse you further. You spake (as to your selfe,   55
but yet I ouer-heard) as if you knew some disposition of weaknesse
where I most had fixt my trust. I challenge you to let me know what
'twas.

Thar. Brother? are you wise?

Lys. Why?   60

Thar. Be ignorant. Did you neuer heare of *Actæon*?

Lys. What then?

Thar. Curiositie was his death. He could not be content to adore
Diana in her Temple, but he must needes dogge her to her retir'd
pleasures, and see her in her nakednesse. Doe you enioy the sole   65
priuiledge of your wiues bed? haue you no pretie *Paris* for your Page?
No mysticall *Adonis* to front you there?

Lys. I thinke none: I know not.

Thar. Know not still Brother. Ignorance and credulitie are your
sole meanes to obtaine that blessing. You see your greatest Clerkes,   70
your wisest Politicians, are not that way fortunate, your learned Lawyers would lose a dozen poore mens causes to gaine a lease ant, but
for a Terme. Your Phisition is ielous of his. Your Sages in generall,
by seeing too much ouersee that happinesse. Only your block-heally
Tradesman; your honest meaning Cittizen; your not- / headed Coun- [C3ᵛ] 75
trie Gentleman; your vnapprehending Stinckerd is blest with the sole
prerogatiue of his Wiues chamber. For which he is yet beholding, not
to his starres, but to his ignorance. For if he be wise, Brother, I must
tell you the case alters. How doe you relish these thinges Brother?

Lys. Passing ill.   80

Thar. So do sick men solid meates: hearke you brother, are you not
ielous?

Lys. No: doe you know cause to make me?

Thar. Hold you there; did your wife neuer spice your broth with a
dramme of sublimate? hath shee not yeelded up the Fort of her Hon-   85
our to a staring Soldado? and (taking courage from her guilt) plaid
open banckrout of all shame, and runne the Countrie with him?
Then blesse your Starres, bow your knees to *Iuno*. Looke where shee
appeares.

Enter Cynthia, Hylus, and Ero.

Cynth. We haue sought you long Sir, there's a Messenger within,   90
hath brought you letters from the Court, and desires your speech.

Lys. [*Aside.*] I can discouer nothing in her lookes. — Goe, Ile not
be long.

Cynth. Sir, it is of weight the bearer saies: and besides, much

67 mysticall] *Q(u)*; yong *Q(c)* (*See Textual Note*) ‖ 79 How . . . Brother?] *Parrott*; *on separate line*
‖ 89 SD *Hylus, and Ero.*] *Parrott*; *Hylus.* ‖ 92 SD *Aside.*] *Parrott* | lookes.—] ~.∧ ‖

hastens his departure. Honourable Brother! crie mercie! what, in a   95
Conquerours stile? but come and ouercome?

Thar. A fresh course.

Cynth. Alas you see of how sleight mettall Widdowes vowes are
made.

Thar. [*Aside.*] And that shall you proue too ere long.   100

Cynth. Yet for the honour of our sexe, boast not abroade this your
easie conquest; another might perhaps have staid longer below staires,
it but was your confidence, that surpris'd her loue. /

Hyl. My vncle hath instructed me how to accoast an honorable   [C4]
Ladie; to win her, not by suite, but by surprise.   105

Thar. The Whelp and all.

Hyl. Good Vncle let not your neare Honours change your manners,
bee not forgetfull of your promise to mee, touching your Ladies daughter *Laodice*. My fancie runns so vpon't, that I dreame euery night
of her.   110

Thar. A good chicken, goe thy waies, thou hast done well; eate
breade with thy meate.

Cynth. Come Sir, will you in?

Lys. Ile follow you.

Cynth. Ile not stirre a foot without you. I can not satisfie the mes-   115
sengers impatience.

Lys. *He takes Thar. aside.* Wil you not resolue me brother?

Thar. Of what?

Lysander stamps and goes out vext with Cynth. Hyl. Ero.

So, there's venie for venie, I haue giuen't him 'ith speeding place for
all his confidence. Well out of this perhaps there may bee moulded   120
matter of more mirth, then my baffling. It shall goe hard but Ile make
my constant sister act as famous a Scene as *Virgil* did his Mistris; who
caus'd all the Fire in Rome to faile so that none could light a torch
but at her nose. Now forth: At this house dwells a vertuous Dame,
sometimes of worthy Fame, now like a decai'd Merchant turn'd Broker,   125
and retailes refuse commodities for vnthriftie Gallants. Her wit I
must imploy upon this businesse to prepare my next encounter, but in
such a fashion as shall make all split. Ho? Madam *Arsace*? pray
heauen the Oister-wiues haue not brought the newes of my woing
hether amongst their stale Pilcherds.   130

Enter Arsace, Tomasin.

Ars. What? my Lord of the Palace?

Thar. Looke you.

---

96 ouercome] ouer-/ come ‖ **100** SD *Aside.*] *Parrott* ‖ **103** it but was] *Q* (*c second state*); but
vpon *Q* (*u second state*) ‖ **119** speeding place] *Q* (*c first state*); place speeding *Q* (*u first state*) ‖
123 so] *Q* (*c second state*); ~; *Q* (*u second state*) ‖ **124** Now forth] Nowforth ‖ **126** commodities]
commodoties ‖

Ars. Why, this was done like a beaten Souldier.

Thar. Hearke, I must speake with you. I haue a share for you in this rich aduenture. You must / bee the Asse chardg'd with Crownes[C4ᵛ] 135 to make way to the Fort, and I the Conquerour to follow, and seise it. Seest thou this iewell?

Ars. Is't come to that? why *Tomasin!*

Tom. Madam.

Ars. Did not one of the Countesses Seruing-men tell vs that this   140 Gentleman was sped?

Tom. That he did, and how her honour grac't and entertained him in very familiar manner.

Ars. And brought him downe staires her selfe.

Tom. I forsooth, and commanded her men to beare him out of   145 dores.

Thar. Slight, pelted with rotten egges?

Ars. Nay more, that he had alreadie possest her sheetes.

Tom. No indeede Mistris, twas her blanquets.

Thar. Out you yong hedge-sparrow, learne to tread afore you be   150 fledge.   *He kicks her out.* Well haue you done now Ladie?

Ars. O my sweet kilbuck.

Thar. You now, in your shallow pate, thinke this a disgrace to mee, such a disgrace as is a battered helmet on a souldiers head, it doubles   155 his resolution. Say, shall I vse thee?

Ars. Vse me?

Thar. O holy reformation! how art thou fallen downe from the vpper-bodies of the Church to the skirts of the Citie! honestie is stript out of his true substance into verball nicetie. Common sinners   160 startle at common termes, and they that by whole mountaines swallow downe the deedes of darknesse; A poore mote of a familiar word, makes them turne up the white o'th eie. Thou art the Ladies Tennant.

Ars. For terme Sir.

Thar. A good induction, be successefull for me, make me Lord of   165 the Palace, and thou shalt hold thy Tenement to thee and thine heirs for euer, in free smockage, as of the manner of Panderage, prouided alwaies — /

Ars. Nay if you take me vnprouided —   [D1]

Thar. Prouided I say, that thou mak'st thy repaire to her presently   170 with a plot I will instruct thee in; and for thy surer accesse to her greatnesse, thou shalt present her, as from thy selfe with this iewell.

138 *Tomasin!*] ∼. ‖ **151** SD *out.*] ∼: ‖ **152** Ladie?] ∼. ‖ **166** heirs] *Dodsley;* ears ‖ **168** alwaies—] ∼. ‖ **169** vnprouided—] ∼. ‖

Ars. So her old grudge, stand not betwixt her and me.

Thar. Feare not that.

Presents are present cures for femall grudges,   175

Make bad, seeme good; alter the case with Iudges.   *Exeunt.*

Finis Actus Primi

Actus Secundi Scœna Prima.

Lysander, Tharsalio.

Lys. So now we are our selues. Brother, that ill relisht speech you
let slip from your tongue, hath taken so deepe hold of my thoughts,
that they will neuer giue me rest, till I be resolu'd what 'twas you said,
you know, touching my wife.

Thar. Tush: I am wearie of this subiect, I said not so.   5

Lys. By truth it selfe you did: I ouer-heard you. Come, it shall
nothing moue me, whatsoeuer it be; pray thee vnfold briefly what you
know.

Thar. Why briefly Brother, I know my sister to be the wonder of
the Earth; and the Enuie of the Heauens; Vertuous, Loiall, and what   10
not. Briefly, I know shee hath vow'd, that till death and after death,
sheele hold inuiolate her bonds to you, and that her black shall take
no other hew; all which I firmely beleeue. In briefe Brother, I know
her to be a woman. But you know brother, I haue other yrons on th'
anuile.   *Exiturus.*

Lys. You shall not leave mee so vnsatisfied; tell mee / what tis   [D1ᵛ]
you know.

Thar. Why Brother; if you be sure of your wiues loialtie for terme
of life: why should you be curious to search the Almanacks for after-
times: whether some wandring *Aeneas* should enioy your reuersion;   20
or whether your true Turtle would sit mourning on a wither'd branch,
till *Atropos* cut her throat: Beware of curiositie, for who can resolue
you? youle say perhaps her vow.

Lys. Perhaps I shall.

Thar. Tush, her selfe knowes not what shee shall doe, when shee is   25
transform'd into a Widdow. You are now a sober and staid Gentleman. But if *Diana* for your curiositie should translate you into a mon-
ckey; doe you know what gambolds you should play? your only way to
bee resolu'd is to die and make triall of her.

---

176 seeme] *Q(c)*; few *Q(u)* | SD *Exeunt.*] *Parrott subs.*; *Exit.* ‖ **10** Heauens;] ∼. ‖ **12** to you,
and] *Q(c)*; too, and *Q(u)* | shall] *Q(u)*; shal *Q(c)* ‖ **13** firmely] *Q(c)*; firme *Q(u)* ‖

Lys. A deare experiment! then I must rise againe to bee resolu'd.   30
   Thar. You shall not neede. I can send you speedier aduertisement
of her constancie, by the next Ripier that rides that way with Mack-
erell. And so I leaue you.   *Exit. Thar.*
   Lys. All the Furies in hell attend thee; h'as giuen me
A bone to tire on with a pestilence; slight know?   35
What can he know? what can his eie obserue
More then mine owne, or the most piersing sight
That euer viewed her? by this light I thinke
Her priuat'st thought may dare the eie of heauen,
And challenge th'enuious world to witnesse it.   40
I know him for a wild corrupted youth,
Whom prophane Ruffins, Squires to Bawds, and Strumpets,
Drunckards, speud out of Tauerns, into'th sinkes
Of Tap-houses, and Stewes, Reuolts from manhood,
Debaucht perdu's, have by their companies   45
Turn'd Deuill like themselues; and stuft his soule
With damn'd opinions, and vnhallowed thoughts
Of womanhood, of all humanitie,
Nay Deitie it selfe. /
              Enter Lycus.   [D2]
Lys.   Welcome friend *Lycus.*
   Lyc. Haue you met with your capricious brother?   50
   Lys. He parted hence but now.
   Lyc.   And has he yet resolu'd
You of that point you brake with me about?
   Lys. Yes, he bids me die for further triall of her constancie.
   Lyc. That were a strange Phisicke for a iealous patient; to cure his
thirst with a draught of poison. Faith Sir, discharge your thoughts   55
an't; thinke 'twas but a Buzz deuis'd by him to set your braines a work,
and diuert your eie from his disgrace. The world hath written your
wife in highest lines of honour'd Fame: her vertues so admir'd in this
Ile, as the report thereof sounds in forraigne eares; and strangers oft
arriuing here, (as some rare sight) desire to view her presence, thereby   60
to compare the Picture with the originall.
Nor thinke he can turne so farre rebell to his bloud,
Or to the Truth it selfe to misconceiue
Her spotlesse love and loialtie; perhaps
Oft hauing heard you hold her faith so sacred   65
As you being dead, no man might stirre a sparke
Of vertuous love, in way of second bonds;

30 experiment!] ∼, ‖ 34 h'as] has ‖ 34-35 All ... know?] *Reed*; All ... a / Bone ... know?
‖ 44 manhood,] ∼; ‖ 46 themselues;] ∼, ‖ 51-52 And ... about?] *as prose* (you) ‖ 62 Nor
... bloud,] *Shepherd*; *as prose* ‖

As if you at your death should carrie with you
Both branch and roote of all affection.
T'may be, in that point hee's an Infidell,   70
And thinkes your confidence may ouer-weene.
   Lys. So thinke not I.
   Lyc. Nor I : if euer any made it good.
I am resolu'd of all, sheele prove no changling.
   Lys. Well, I must yet be further satisfied;   75
And vent this humour by some straine of wit,
Somewhat Ile doe; but what, I know not yet.   *Exeunt.* /

[II.ii]

                                                       [D2ᵛ]

Enter Sthenio, Ianthe.

   Sthe. Passion of Virginitie, *Ianthe,* how shall we quit our selues of
this Pandresse, that is so importunate to speake with vs? Is shee
knowne to be a Pandresse?
   Ian. I, as well as we are knowne to be waiting women.
   Sthe. A shrew take your comparison. Lets cal out *Argus* that bold   5
Asse that neuer weighs what he does or saies; but walkes and talkes
like one in a sleepe; to relate her attendance to my Ladie, and present her.
   Ian. Who? ant please your Honour? None so fit to set on any dangerous exploit. Ho? *Argus?*   10

Enter Argus bare.

   Arg. Whats the matter Wenches?
   Sthe. You must tell my Ladie here's a Gentle-woman call'd *Arsace,*
her Honours Tennant, attends her, to impart important businesse to
her.
   Arg. I will presently.   *Exit Arg.*
   Ian. Well, shee has a welcome present, to beare out her vnwelcome
presence: and I neuer knew but a good gift would welcome a bad
person to the purest. *Arsace?*

Enter Arsace.

   Ars. I, Mistris.
   Sthe. Giue me your Present, Ile doe all I can, to make way both for   20
it and your selfe.
   Ars. You shall binde me to your seruice Ladie.
   Sthe. Stand vnseene.

II.ii] *Parrott* ‖ SD *Sthenio,*] *Q(c)*; *Sthenia, Q(u)* ‖ **5-8** *Sthe.* A . . . her.] *Sthe.* A . . . comparison.
/ *Sthe.* Lets . . . her. (*See Textual Note*) ‖ **9** Who?] *Q(c)*; ∼∧ *Q(u)* ‖ **10** Ho? *Argus?*] *on separate
line* ‖

Enter Lyc., Eudora, Laodice, Argus comming to Eudora.

Arg. Here's a Gentle-woman (ant please your Honour) one of your
Tennants, desires accesse to you.   25

Eud. What Tennant? what's her name? /

Arg. Arsace, she saies Madam.   [D3]

Eud. Arsace? what the Bawde?

Arg. The Bawd Madam? *shee strikes.* that's without my privitie.

Eud. Out Asse, know'st not thou the Pandresse *Arsace?*   30

Sthe. Shee presents your Honour with this Iewell.

Eud. This iewell? how came shee by such a iewell? Shee has had
great Customers.

Arg. Shee had neede Madam, shee sits at a great Rent.

Eud. Alas for your great Rent: Ile keepe her iewell, and keepe you   35
her out, yee were best: speake to me for a Pandresse? [*walks aside.*]

Arg. What shall we doe?

Sthe. Goe to; Let vs alone. *Arsace?*

Ars. I Ladie.

Sthe. You must pardon us, we can not obtaine your accesse.   40

Ars. Mistris *Sthenio,* tell her Honour, if I get not accesse to her, and
that instantly, shee's vndone.

Sthe. This is some thing of importance. Madam, shee sweares your
Honour is vndone if she speake not with you instantly.

Eud. Vndone?   45

Ars. Pray her for her Honours sake to give mee instant accesse
to her.

Sthe. Shee makes her businesse your Honour Madame, and en-
treates for the good of that, her instant speech with you.

Eud. How comes my Honour in question? Bring her to mee.   50

Arsace approaches to Eudora.

Ars. Ovr *Cypriane* Goddesse saue your good Honor.

Eud. Stand you off I pray: How dare you Mistris importune accesse to me thus, considering the last warning I gaue for your absence?

Ars. Because, Madam, I have been mou'd by your Honours last
most chast admonition, to leaue the offensiue life / I led before.   [D3ᵛ] 55

Eud. I? haue you left it then?

Ars. I, I assure your Honour, vnlesse it be for the pleasure of two or
three poore Ladies, that haue prodigall Knights to their husbands.

Eud. Out on thee Impudent.

Ars. Alas Madam, wee would all bee glad to liue in our callings.   60

Eud. Is this the reform'd life thou talk'st on?

---

23 SD *Laodice, Argus*] *Laodice, Reb, Hiar Psor. comming after, Argus (See Textual Note)* ‖ **24-25**
Here's . . . you.] *Collier;* Here's . . . ant / Please . . . Tennants / Desires . . . you. ‖ **29** SD
shee strikes.] ∼ ∼, *(See Textual Note)* ‖ **31** Iewell.] ∼? ‖ **36** SD *walks aside.*] ‖ **41** *Sthenio*] *Q(c);*
Sthenia Q(u) ‖ **42** instantly,] *Dodsley;* ∼∧ ‖ **49** that,] *Q(c);* ∼∧ *Q(u)* ‖ **50** SD *Arsace . . . Eudora.*]
Parrott subs.; Enter Arsace. ‖

Ars. I beseech your good Honour mistake me not, I boast of nothing but my charitie, that's the worst.

Eud. You get these iewels with charitie, no doubt. But whats the point in which my Honour stands endanger'd I pray?   65

Ars. In care of that Madam, I have presum'd to offend your chast eies with my presence. Hearing it reported for truth and generally, that your Honor will take to husband a yong Gentleman of this Citie called *Tharsalio*.

Eud. I take him to husband?   70

Ars. If your Honour does, you are vtterly vndone, for hees the most incontinent, and insatiate Man of Women that euer *Venvs* blest with abilitie to please them.

Eud. Let him be the Deuill; I abhorre his thought, and could I be inform'd particularly of any of these slanderers of mine Honour, he   75 should as dearely dare it, as any thing wherein his life were endanger'd.

Ars. Madam, the report of it is so strongly confident, that I feare the strong destinie of marriage is at worke in it. But if it bee Madam: Let your Honours known vertue resist and defie it for him: for not a hundred will serue his one turne. I protest to your Honour, when   80 (*Venvs* pardon mee) I winckt at my vnmaidenly exercise, I haue knowne nine in a Night made mad with his loue.

Eud. What tell'st thou mee of his loue? I tell thee I abhorre him; and destinie must haue an other mould / for my thoughts, then Na-   [D4] ture or mine Honour, and a Witchcraft aboue both, to transforme mee   85 to another shape, as soone as to an other conceipt of him.

Ars. Then is your good Honour iust as I pray for you, and good Madam, euen for your vertues sake, and comfort of all your Dignities, and Possessions; fixe your whole Woman-hood against him. Hee will so inchant you, as neuer man did woman: Nay a Goddesse (say his   90 light huswives) is not worthie of his sweetnesse.

Eud. Goe to, be gone.

Ars. Deare Madam, your Honours most perfect admonitions haue brought mee to such a hate of these imperfections, that I could not but attend you with my dutie, and vrge his unreasonable manhood to   95 the fill.

Eud. Man-hood, quoth you?

Ars. Nay Beastly-hood, I might say, indeede Madam, but for sauing your Honour; Nine in a night said I?

Eud. Goe to, no more.   100

Ars. No more Madame? that's enough one would thinke.

Eud. Well be gone I bid thee.

80 when] When ‖

Ars. Alas Madam, your Honour is the chiefe of our Citie, and to whom shall I complaine of these inchastities, (being your Ladiships reform'd Tennant) but to you that are chastest? 105

Eud. I pray thee goe thy waies, and let me see this reformation you pretend continued.

Ars. I humbly thanke your good Honour, that was first cause of it.

Eud. Here's a complaint as strange as my Suiter.

Ars. I beseech your good Honour thinke vpon him, make him an 110
example.

Eud. Yet againe?

Ars. All my dutie to your Excellence. *Exit. Ars.*

Eud. These sorts of licentious persons, when they are / once re- [D4ᵛ]
claim'd, are most vehement against licence. But it is the course of the 115
world to dispraise faults and vse them; that so we may vse them the
safer. What might a wise Widdow resolue vpon this point now? Contentment is the end of all worldly beings: Beshrow her; would shee
had spared her newes.

[*Eudora, Sthenio, and Ianthe exit as Rebus, Hiarbas, Psorabeus enter.*]

Reb. See if shee take not a contrarie way to free her selfe of vs. 120

Hiar. You must complaine to his Altitude.

Psor. All this for triall is; you must indure
That will have wiues, nought else, with them is sure. *Exeunt.*

[II.iii]

Tharsalio, Arsace.

Thar. Hast thou beene admitted then?

Ars. Admitted? I, into her heart, Ile able it; neuer was man so
prais'd with a dispraise; nor so spoken for in being rail'd on. Ile giue
you my word; I have set her hart vpon as tickle a pin as the needle of
a Diall; that will neuer let it rest, till it be in the right position. 5

Thar. Why dost thou imagine this?

Ars. Because I saw *Cupid* shoot in my words, and open his wounds
in her lookes. Her bloud went and came of errands betwixt her face
and her heart; and these changes I can tell you are shrewd tell-tales.

Thar. Thou speak'st like a Doctrisse in thy facultie; but howsoeuer, 10
for all this foile, Ile retriue the game once againe, hee's a shallow gam-
ster that for one displeasing cast gives vp so faire a game for lost.

Ars. Well, 'twas a villanous inuention of thine, and had a swift operation, it tooke like sulphure. And yet this vertuous Countesse hath

to my eare spun out many a tedious lecture of pure sisters thred against   15
concupiscence. But euer with such an affected zeale, as my minde
gaue me, shee had a kinde of secret titillation to grace my poore house
sometimes; but that shee fear'd a spice of the Sciatica, which as you
know ever runs in the bloud. /

Thar. And as you know, sokes into the bones. But to say truth,   [E1] 20
these angrie heates that breake out at the lips of these streight lac't
Ladies, are but as symptoms of a lustfull feuer that boiles within them.
For wherefore rage wiues at their husbands so, when they flie out, for
zeale against the sinne?

Ars. No, but because they did not purge that sinne.   25

Thar. Th'art a notable Syren, and I sweare to thee, if I prosper,
not only to giue thee thy mannor-house gratis, but to marrie thee to
some one Knight or other, and burie thy trade in thy Ladiship: Goe
be gone.   *Exit. Ars.*

Enter Lycus.

Thar. What newes *Lycus*? where's the Ladie?   30

Lyc. Retir'd into her Orchard.

Thar. A pregnant badge of loue, shee's melancholy.

Lyc. 'Tis with the sight of her Spartane wooer. But howsoeuer tis
with her, you haue practis'd strangely vpon your Brother.

Thar. Why so?   35

Lyc. You had almost lifted his wit off the hinges. That sparke
ielousie falling into his drie melancholy braine, had well neare set the
whole house on fire.

Thar. No matter, let it worke; I did but pay him in's owne coine;
Sfoot hee plied me with such a volley of vnseason'd scoffs, as would   40
have made Patience it selfe turne Ruffine, attiring it selfe in wounds
and bloud: but is his humour better qualified then?

Lyc. Yes, but with a medicine ten parts more dangerous then the
sicknesse: you know how strange his dotage euer was on his wife; taking speciall glorie to have her loue and loialtie to him so renown'd   45
abrode. To whom shee oftentimes hath vow'd constancie after life, till
her owne death had brought forsooth, her widdow-troth to bed. This
he ioi'd in strangely, and was therein of infallible beliefe, till your surmise began to shake it; which hath loos'd it so, as now there's nought
can settle it, but a trial, which hee's resolu'd vpon.   50

Thar. As how man? as how? /

Lyc. Hee is resolu'd to follow your aduise, to die, and make triall of   [E1ᵛ]
her stablenesse, and you must lend your hand to it.

Thar. What to cut's throat?

---

33 howsoeuer] how-/soeuer ‖ **37** braine] *Q(c)*; braines *Q(u)* ‖ **40** vnseason'd] vn-/season'd ‖
44 you know how] *Q(c)*; how know you *Q(u)* ‖ **46** oftentimes] often-/times ‖

Lyc. To forge a rumour of his death, to vphold it by circumstance, 55
maintaine a publicke face of mourning, and all thinges appertaining.

Thar. I, but the meanes man: what time? what probabilitie?

Lyc. Nay, I thinke he has not lickt his Whelpe into full shape yet,
but you shall shortly heare ant.

Thar. And when shall this strange conception see light? 60

Lyc. Forthwith: there's nothing staies him, but some odde businesse
of import, which hee must winde vp; least perhaps his absence by occasion of his intended triall bee prolonged aboue his aimes.

Thar. Thankes for this newes i'faith. This may perhaps proue
happie to my Nephew. Truth is I loue my sister well and must ac- 65
knowledge her more then ordinarie vertues. But shee hath so possest
my brothers heart with vowes, and disauowings, seal'd with oathes of
second nuptialls; as in that confidence, hee hath inuested her in all his
state, the ancient inheritance of our Familie: and left my Nephew
and the rest to hang vpon her pure deuotion; so as he dead, and shee 70
matching (as I am resolu'd shee will) with some yong Prodigall; what
must ensue, but her post-issue beggerd, and our house alreadie sinking,
buried quick in ruin. But this triall may remoue it, and since tis come
to this; marke but the issue *Lycus,* for all these solemne vowes, if I doe
not make her proue in the handling as weake as a wafer; say I lost my 75
time in trauaile. This resolution then has set his wits in ioynt againe,
hee's quiet.

Lyc. Yes, and talkes of you againe in the fairest manner, listens
after your speede.

Thar. Nay hee's passing kinde, but I am glad of this triall for 80
all that.

Lyc. Which he thinkes to be a flight beyond your wing. /

Thar. But hee will change that thought ere long. My Bird you saw [E2]
euen now, sings me good newes, and makes hopefull signes to me.

Lyc. Somewhat can I say too, since your messengers departure, her 85
Ladiship hath beene something alter'd, more pensiue then before, and
tooke occasion to question of you, what your addictions were? of what
tast your humor was? of what cut you wore your wit? and all this in a
kind of disdainefull scorne.

Thar. Good Callenders *Lycus.* Well Ile pawne this iewell with 90
thee, my next encounter shall quite alter my brothers iudgement.
Come lets in, he shall commend it for a discreet and honourable
attempt.

          Mens iudgments sway on that side fortune leanes,
          Thy wishes shall assist me.

Lyc.   And my meanes.   *Exeunt.*

57 probabilitie?] ~. ‖ 88 wit?] ~, ‖ 95 me.] ~: ‖

[II.iv]

Argus, Clinias, Sthenio, Ianthe.

Arg. I must confesse I was ignorant, what 'twas to court a Ladie till now.

Sthe. And I pray you what is it now?

Arg. To court her I perceiue, is to woo her with letters from Court, for so this Spartane Lords Court discipline teacheth.   5

Sthe. His Lordship hath procur'd a new Pacquet from his Altitude.

Clin. If he bring no better ware then letters in's pacquet, I shall greatly doubt of his good speede.

Ian. If his Lordship did but know how gracious his Aspect is to my Ladie in this solitarie humour.   10

Clin. Well these retir'd walkes of hers are not vsuall; and bode some alteration in her thoughts. What may bee the cause *Sthenio?*

Sthe. Nay twould trouble *Argus* with his hundred eies to descrie the cause.

Ian. Venus keepe her vpright, that shee fall not from / the state of [E2ᵛ] 15 her honour; my feare is that some of these Serpentine suiters will tempt her from her constant vow of widdow-hood. If they doe, good night to our good daies.

Sthe. 'Twere a sinne to suspect her; I haue been witnesse to so many of her fearfull protestations to our late Lord against that course;   20 to her infinite oathes imprinted on his lips, and seal'd in his heart with such imprecations to her bed, if euer it should receiue a second impression; to her open and often detestations of that incestuous life (as shee term'd it) of widdowes marriages; as being but a kinde of lawfull adulterie; like vsurie, permitted by the law, not approv'd. That to wed   25 a second, was no better then to cuckold the first: That women should entertaine wedlocke as one bodie, as one life, beyond which there were no desire, no thought, no repentance from it, no restitution to it. So as if the conscience of her vowes should not restraine her, yet the worlds shame to breake such a constant resolution, should represse any   30 such motion in her.

Arg. Well, for her vowes, they are gone to heauen with her husband, they binde not vpon earth: And as for Womens resolutions, I must tell you, The Planets, and (as *Ptolomie* saies) the windes haue a great stroke in them. Trust not my learning if her late strangenesse,   35 and exorbitant solitude, be not hatching some new Monster.

Ian. Well applied *Argus*; Make you husbands Monsters?

Arg. I spoke of no husbands: but you Wenches haue the pregnant

---

II.iv] *Parrott* ‖ **7** letters] *Dodsley*; letrers ‖ **12** *Sthenio?*] ∼. ‖ **20** course;] *Q(c)*; ∼, *Q(u)* ‖ **24** marriages;] *Q(c)*; ∼, *Q(u)* ‖ **25** vsurie,] *Q(c)*; ∼∧ *Q(u)* ‖ **38** husbands:] *Q(c)*; ∼, *Q(u)* ‖

wits, to turne Monsters into husbands, as you turne husbands into
monsters. 40

Sthe. Well *Ianthe,* 'twere high time we made in, to part our Ladie
and her Spartane wooer.

Ian. We shall appeare to her like the two fortunate Stars in a tempest, to saue the shipwrack of her patience.

Sthe. I, and to him to, I beleeue; For by this time he hath spent the 45
last dramme of his newes.

Arg. That is, of his wit.

Sthe. Iust good wittals.

Ian. If not, and that my Ladie be not / too deep in her new dumps, [E3]
we shall heare from his Lordship; what such a Lord said of his wife 50
the first night hee embrac't her: To what Gentleman such a Count
was beholding for his fine children. What yong Ladie, such an old
Count should marrie; what Reuells: what presentments are towards;
and who penn'd the Pegmas; and so forth: and yet for all this, I
know her harsh Suiter hath tir'd her to the uttermost scruple of her 55
forbearance, and will doe more, vnlesse we two, like a paire of Sheres,
cut a-sunder the thred of his discourse.

Sthe. Well then, lets in; But my masters, waite you on your charge
at your perils. See that you guard her approch from any more in-
truders. 60

Ian. Excepting yong *Tharsalio.*

Sthe. True, excepting him indeede, for a guard of men is not able to
keepe him out ant please your Honour.

Arg. O Wenches, that's the propertie of true valour, to promise like
a Pigmey, and performe like a Giant. If he come, Ile bee sworne Ile 65
doe my Ladies commandement vpon him.

Ian. What? beate him out?

Sthe. If hee should, *Tharsalio* would not take it ill at his handes,
for he does but his Ladies commandement.

Enter Tharsalio.

Arg. Well, by *Hercules* he comes not here. 70

Sthe. By *Venus* but hee does: or else shee hath heard my Ladies
praiers, and sent some gracious spirit in his likenesse to fright away
that Spartane wooer, that hants her.

Thar. There stand her Sentinells.

Arg. Slight the Ghost appeares againe. 75

Thar. Saue yee my qondam fellowes in Armes; saue yee; my women.

Sthe. Your Women Sir?

Thar. 'Twill be so. What no courtesies? No preparation of grace?
Obserue me I advise you for your owne sakes.

---

49 not, and that my Ladie] *Q(c)* (La:); not, that my Ladie *Q(u)* ∥ 52 fine] *Q(c)*; fiue *Q(u)* ∥
56 forbearance] *Q(c)*; forbearances *Q(u)* ∥ 59 perils.] ∼, ∥ 64-65 like a Pigmey] *Q(c)*; like
Pigmey *Q(u)* ∥

Ian. For your owne sake, I aduise you to pack hence, lest / your [E3ᵛ] 80
impudent valour cost you dearer then you thinke.

Clin. What senselesse boldnesse is this *Tharsalio?*

Arg. Well said *Clinias,* talke to him.

Clin. I wonder that notwithstanding the shame of your last entertainment, and threatnings of worse; you would yet presume to trouble   85
this place againe.

Thar. Come, y'are a widgine; Off with your hat Sir, acknowledge:
forecast is better then labour. Are you squint ey'd? can you not see
afore you? A little foresight I can tell you might sted you much as the
Starres shine now.   90

Clin. 'Tis well sir, tis not for nothing your brother is asham'd on
you. But Sir, you must know, wee are chardg'd to barre your entrance.

Thar. But Wifler, know you, that who so shall dare to execute that
charge, Ile be his Executioner.

Arg. By *Ioue, Clinias,* me thinks, the Gentleman speakes very hon-   95
ourably.

Thar. Well I see this house needes reformation, here's a fellow
stands behind now, of a forwarder insight then yee all. What place
hast thou?

Arg. What place you please Sir.   100

Thar. Law you Sir. Here's a fellow to make a Gentleman Vsher
Sir; I discharge you of the place, and doe here inuest thee into his
roome: Make much of thy haire, thy wit will suit it rarely. And for
the full possession of thine office; Come, Vsher me to thy Ladie: and
to keep thy hand supple, take this from me.   105

Arg. No bribes Sir, ant please your Worship.

Thar. Goe to, thou dost well; but pocket it for all that; it's no impaire to thee: the greatest doo't.

Arg. Sir, tis your loue onely that I respect, but since out of your
loue you please to bestow it vpon me, it were want of Courtship in mee   110
to refuse it; Ile acquaint my Ladie with your comming.   *Exit. Arg.*

Thar. How say by this? haue not I made a fit choise, that hath so
soone attain'd the deepest mysterie of his profession: Good sooth
Wenches, a few courtsies had not / beene cast away vpon your new   [E4]
Lord.   115

Sthe. Weele beleeue that, when our Ladie has a new Sonne of your
getting.

Enter Argus, Eudora, Rebus, Hiar. Psor.

Eud. Whats the matter? whose that, you say, is come?

Arg. The bold Gentleman, ant please your Honour.

89 you?] ∼. ‖ 91 on] *Q(c)*; in *Q(u)* ‖ 102 Sir;] ∼, ‖ 103 roome:] ∼, ‖ 110 it were] It ∼ ‖

Eud. Why thou flering Asse thou.   120

Arg. Ant please your Honour.

Eud. Did not I forbid his approch by all the charge and dutie of thy seruice?

Thar. Madam, this fellow only is intelligent; for he truly vnderstood your command according to the stile of the Court of *Venus*; that is,   125
by contraries: when you forbid you bid.

Eud. By heauen Ile discharge my house of yee all.

Thar. You shall not neede Madame, for I haue alreadie casheer'd your officious Vsher here, and chos'd this for his Successor.

Eud. O incredible boldnesse!   130

Thar. Madam, I come not to command your loue with enforst letters, not to woo you with tedious stories of my Pedigree, as hee who
drawes the thred of his descent from *Ledas* Distaffe; when 'tis well
knowne his Grandshire cried Coniskins in Sparta.

Reb. Whom meane you Sir?   135

Thar. Sir, I name none, but him who first shall name himselfe.

Reb. The place Sir, I tell you still; and this Goddesses faire presence, or else my reply should take a farre other forme vpon't.

Thar. If it should Sir, I would make your Lordship an anser.

Arg. Anser's Latine for a Goose, ant please your honor.   140

Eud. Well noted Gander; and what of that?

Arg. Nothing, ant please your Honor, but that he said he / would   [E4ᵛ]
make his Lordship an answere.

Eud. Thus euery foole mocks my poore Suiter. Tell mee thou most
frontlesse of all men, did'st thou (when thou had'st meanes to note me 145
best) euer obserue so base a temper in mee, as to giue any glance at
stooping to my Vassall?

Thar. Your drudge Madam, to doe your drudgerie.

Eud. Or am I now so skant of worthie Suiters,
That may aduance mine honour; aduance my estate;   150
Strengthen my alliance (if I list to wed)
That I must stoop to make my foot my head?

Thar. No but your side, to keepe you warme a bed.
But Madame vouchsafe me your patience to that points serious answere. Though I confesse to get higher place in your graces, I could   155
wish my fortunes more honourable; my person more gratious, my
minde more adorn'd with Noble and Heroicall vertues; yet Madame
(that you thinke not your bloud disparadg'd by mixture with mine)
daine to know this: howsoever I once, only for your loue, disguis'd my
selfe in the seruice of your late Lord and mine; yet my descent is as   160

149-53 Or . . . bed.] *as prose* (that . . . strengthen . . . that) ‖ **152** head?] ∼. ‖ **157** vertues;]
Q*(c)*; ∼, Q*(u)* ‖

honourable as the proudest of your Spartane attempters; who by unknown quills or conduits under ground, drawes his Pedigree from
Lycurgus his great Toe, to the Viceroies little finger, and from thence
to his owne elbow, where it will neuer leaue itching.

Reb. Tis well Sir, presume still of the place.   165

Thar. Sfoot Madame, am I the first great personage that hath
stoopt to disguises for loue? what thinke you of our Countrie-man
Hercules; that for loue put on *Omphales* Apron, and sate spinning
amongst her Wenches, while his Mistris wore his Lyons skin and
Lamb-skin'd him, if he did not his businesse?   170

Eud. Most fitly thou resembl'st thy selfe to that violent outlaw, that
claim'd all other mens possessions as his owne by his meere valour.
For what lesse hast thou done? Come into my house, beate away these
Honourable persons?

Thar. That I will Madam. Hence ye Sparta-Veluets. /   175

Psor. Hold, shee did not meane so.   [F1]

Thar. Away I say, or leaue your liues I protest here.

Hiar. Well Sir, his Altitude shall know you.

Reb. Ile doe your errand Sir.   *Exeunt.*

Thar. Doe good Cosen Altitude; and beg the reuersion of the next   180
Ladie: for *Dido* has betrotht her loue to me. By this faire hand
Madam, a faire riddance of this Calidonian Bore.

Eud. O most prodigious audaciousnesse!

Thar. True Madam; O fie vpon am, they are intollerable. And I
can not but admire your singular vertue of patience, not common in   185
your sexe; and must therefore carrie with it some rare indowment of
other Masculine and Heroicall vertues. To heare a rude Spartane
court so ingenuous a Ladie, with dull newes from Athens, or the Vi-
cerois court; how many dogs were spoil'd at the last Bull-baiting; what
Ladies dub'd their husbands Knights, and so forth.   190

Eud. But hast thou no shame? No sense of what disdain I shew'd
thee in my last entertainment? chacing thee from my presence, and
charging thy dutie, not to attempt the like intrusion for thy life; and
dar'st thou yet approch mee in this vnmannerly manner? No question
this desperate boldnesse can not choose but goe accompanied with   195
other infinite rudenesses.

Thar. Good Madam, giue not the Child an vnfit name, terme it not
boldnes, which the Sages call true confidence, founded on the most
infallible Rocke of a womans constancie.

Eud. If shame can not restraine thee, tell mee yet if any brainlesse   200
foole would have tempted the danger attending thy approch.

---

170 businesse?] ~. ‖ **171** outlaw,] *Q(c)*; *Atlas*∧ *Q(u)* ‖ **175** ye Sparta-Veluets] *Q(c)*; yee
Sparta Veluet *Q(u)* ‖

Thar. No Madam, that proues I am no Foole: Then had I been
here a Foole, and a base low-sprited Spartan, if for a Ladies froune,
or a Lords threates, or for a Guard of Groomes, I should have shrunke
in the wetting, and suffer'd such a delicious flower to perish in the   205
stalke, or to be sauadgely pluckt by a prophane finger. No Madam:
First / let me be made a Subiect for disgrace; let your remorselesse   [F1ᵛ]
Guard seaze on my despised bodie, bind me hand and foot, and hurle
me into your Ladiships bed.

Eud. O Gods: I protest thou dost more and more make me admire   210
thee.

Thar. Madam, ignorance is the mother of admiration: know me
better, and youle admire me lesse.

Eud. What would'st thou haue mee know? what seekes thy com-
ming? why dost thou hant me thus?   215

Thar. Only Madam, that the *Ætna* of my sighes, and *Nilus* of my
teares, pour'd forth in your presence, might witnesse to your Honor
the hot and moist affection of my hart, and worke me some measure of
fauour, from your sweete tongue, or your sweeter lips, or what else
your good Ladiship shall esteeme more conducible, to your diuine   220
contentment.

Eud. Pen and Inck-horne I thanke thee. This you learn'd when
you were a Serving-man.

Thar. Madam, I am still the same creature; and I will so tie my
whole fortunes to that stile, as were it my happinesse (as I know it will   225
be) to mount into my Lords succession, yet vow I never to assume
other Title, or State, then your seruants: Not approching your boord,
but bidden: Not pressing to your bed, but your pleasure shall be first
known if you will command me any seruice.

Eud. Thy vowes are as vaine as a Ruffins othes; as common as the   230
aire; and as cheape as the dust. How many of the light huswiues, thy
Muses, hath thy loue promist this seruice besides, I pray thee?

Thar. Compare shadowes to bodies, Madam; Pictures to the life;
and such are they to you, in my valuation.

Eud. I see wordes will neuer free me of thy boldnesse, and will   235
therefore now vse blowes; and those of the mortallest enforcement.
Let it suffice Sir, that all this time, and to this place, you enioy your
safetie; keepe backe: No one foote follow mee further; for I protest to
thee, the next threshold past, lets passe a prepar'd Ambush to thy
latest / breath.   *Exit. Eud.*   [F2]

Thar. This for your Ambush! *He drawes.* Dare my loue with
death?   [*Exit.*]

242 SD *Exit.*] *Reed* ||

Clin. Slight; follow ant please your Honour.
Arg. Not I by this light.
Clin. I hope Gentle-women you will.   245
Sthe. Not we Sir, we are no parters of fraies.
Clin. Faith nor Ile be any breaker of customes.   *Exeunt.*

Finis Actus Secundi.

Actus Tertij. Scœna Prima.

Enter Lysander and Lycus booted.

Lyc. Would any heart of Adamant, for satisfaction of an vn-
grounded humour, racke a poore Ladies innocencie as you intend to
doe? It was a strange curiositie in that Emperour, that ript his
Mothers wombe to see the place he lay in.

Lys. Come do not lode me with volumes of perswasion; I am re-   5
solu'd, if shee be gold shee may abide the tast; lets away. I wonder
where this wild brother is.

Enter Cynthia, Hylus, and Ero.

Cynth. Sir —
Lys. I pray thee wife shew but thy selfe a woman;
And be silent: question no more the reason   10
Of my iourney, which our great Viceroies charge
Vrg'd in this letter doth enforce me to.
Cynth. Let me but see that letter, there is somthing
In this presaging bloud of mine, tells me
This sodaine iourney can portend no good;   15
Resolue me sweet, haue not I giuen you cause
Of discontent, by some misprision,
Or want of fit obseruance? let mee know
That I may wreake my selfe vpon my selfe. /
Lys. Come wife, our loue is now growne old and staid,   [F2ᵛ] 20
And must not wanton it in tricks of Court,
Nor enterchang'd delights of melting louers;
Hanging on sleeues, sighing, loth to depart;
These toies are past with vs; our true loues substance
Hath worne out all the shew; let it suffice,   25
I hold thee deare: and thinke some cause of weight
With no excuse to be dispenst with all,

3 doe?] ∼. ‖ **6** tast; . . . away.] ∼, . . . ∼, ‖ **8** Sir—] ∼. ‖ **9-12** I . . . to.] *as prose* (and . . . of
. . . vrg'd) ‖ **13-19** Let . . . selfe.] *Parrott; as prose* (in . . . this . . . resolue . . . of . . . or . . . that) ‖
15 good;] ∼, ‖ **18** obseruance?] ∼, ‖ **25** shew;] ∼, ‖

Compells me from thy most desir'd embraces;
I stay but for my Brother, came he not in last night?

Hyl. For certaine no sir, which gaue vs cause of wonder, what acci-   30
dent kept him abrode.

Cynth. Pray heauen it proue not some wild resolution, bred in him
by his second repulse from the Countesse.

Lys. Trust me I something feare it, this insatiate spirit of aspiring,
being so dangerous and fatall; desire mounted on the wings of it, de-   35
scends not but headlong.

Hyl. Sir, sir, heres my Vncle.

Enter Thars.

Lys. What wrapt in carelesse cloake, face hid in hat vnbanded!
these are the ditches brother, in which outraging colts plunge both
themselues and their riders.   40

Thar. Well, wee must get out as well as wee may, if not, there's the
making of a graue sau'd.

Cynth. That's desperately spoken brother, had it not been happier
the colt had beene better broken, and his rider not fallen in?

Thar. True sister, but wee must ride colts before wee can breake   45
them, you know.

Lys. This is your blind Goddesse *Confidence.*

Thar. Alas brother, our house is decaid, and my honest ambition to
restore it, I hope be pardonable. My comfort is: the Poet that pens
the storie wil write ore my head *magnis tamen excidit ausis*;   50
Which in our natiue Idiome, lets you know,
His mind was high, though Fortune was his Foe.

Lys. A good resolue brother, to out-iest disgrace: come, I had been
on my iourney but for some priuate speech with you: lets in. /

Thar. Good brother stay a little, helpe out this ragged colt out of   [F3] 55
the ditch.

[*Uncloaks and reveals a splendid suit.*]

Lys. How now.

Thar. Now I confesse my ouersight, this haue I purchas'd by my
confidence.

Lys. I like you brother, 'tis the true Garb you know,   60
What wants in reall worth supply in show.

Thar. In show? alas 'twas euen the thing it selfe,
I op't my counting house, and tooke away
These simple fragments of my treasurie,
Husband my Countesse cri'd take more, more yet,   65
Yet, I in hast, to pay in part my debt,

---

29 night?] ∼. ‖ 38 vnbanded!] *Shepherd*; vn-/banded, ‖ 44 in?] ∼. ‖ 51-52 Which . . . Foe.]
Reed; *as prose* (which) ‖ 53 come,] ∼∧ ‖ 56 SD *Uncloaks . . . suit.*] *Parrott* ‖

And proue my selfe a husband of her store,
Kist and came of; and this time tooke no more.
   Cynth. But good brother —
   Thar. Then were our honor'd spousall rites perform'd,   70
Wee made all short, and sweet, and close, and sure.
   Lys. Hee's wrap't.
   Thar. Then did my Vshers, and chiefe Seruants stoope,
Then made my women curtsies, and enuied
Their Ladies fortune: I was magnified.   75
   Lys. Let him alone, this spirit will soone vanish.
   Thar. Brother and sister as I loue you, and am true servant
To *Venus,* all the premises are serious and true,
And the conclusion is: the great Countesse is mine,
The Palace is at your seruice, to which I invite   80
You all to solemnize my honour'd nuptialls.
   Lys. Can this be credited!
   Thar. Good brother doe not you enuie my fortunate atchieuement?
   Lys. Nay I euer said, the attempt was commendable.
   Thar. Good.   85
   Lys. If the issue were successefull.
   Thar. A good state-conclusion, happie euents make good the worst
attempts. Here are your widdow-vowes sister; thus are yee all in your
pure naturalls; certaine morall disguises of coinesse, which the ignorant
cal modestie, ye bor- / row of art to couer your buske points; which a [F3ᵛ] 90
blunt and resolute encounter, taken vnder a fortunate aspect, easily
disarms you off; and then alas what are you? poore naked sinners,
God wot: weake paper walls thrust downe with a finger; this is the
way on't, boile their appetites to a full height of lust; and then take
them downe in the nicke.   95
   Cynth. Is there probabilitie in this; that a Ladie so great, so vertuous, standing on so high termes of honour, should so soone stoope?
   Thar. You would not wonder sister, if you knew the lure shee
stoop't at: greatnesse? thinke you that can curb affection? no, it
whets it more; they haue the full streame of bloud, to beare them: 100
the sweet gale of their sublim'd spirits to driue them: the calme of ease
to prepare them: the sun-shine of fortune to allure them: Greatnesse
to waft them safe through all Rocks of infamie: when youth, wit, and
person come aboord once, tell me sister, can you chuse but hoise saile,
and put forward to the maine?   105
   Lys. But let me wonder at this frailtie yet; would shee in so short
time weare out his memorie, so soone wipe from her eies, nay, from her
heart, whom I my selfe, and this whole Ile besides, still remember with

---

69 brother—] *Parrott;* ∼. ‖ **77-81** Brother . . . nuptialls.] *as prose* (to . . . and . . . the . . . you)
‖ **83** atchieuement?] ∼. ‖ **99** stoop't . . . affection?] stoo'pt . . . ∼; ‖

griefe, the impression of his losse taking worthily such roote in vs; howe
thinke you wife? 110

Cynth. I am asham'd ant, and abhorre to thinke,
So great and vow'd a patterne of our sexe,
Should take into her thoughts, nay to her bed,
(O staine to woman-hood) a second loue.

Lyc. In so short time.

Cynth. In any time.

Lys. No, wife? 115

Cynth. By *Iuno* no; sooner a lothsom Tode.

Thar. High words beleeue me, and I thinke sheele keep them; next
turne is yours Nephew; you shall now marrie my noblest Ladie-
Daughter; the first marriage in *Paphos* next my nuptialls shall be
yours; these are strange occur- / rents brother, but pretie and patheti- [F4] 120
call: if you see mee in my chaire of Honour; and my Countesse in
mine armes; you will then beleeue, I hope, I am Lord of the Palace,
then shall you trie my great Ladies entertainement; see your handes
free'd of mee, and mine taking you to aduancement.

Lys. Well, all this rids not my businesse; wife you shall bee there to 125
partake the vnexpected honour of our House. *Lycus,* and I will make
it our recreation by the way, to thinke of your Reuells and Nuptiall
sports; Brother my stay hath beene for you; Wife pray thee bee gone,
and soone prepare for the solemnitie, a Moneth returnes mee.

Cynth. Heauens guide your iourney. 130

Lys. Fare-well.

Thar. Fare-well Nephew; prosper in virilitie, but doe you heare;
keepe your hand from your voice, I haue a part for you in our Hy-
meneall shew.

Hyl. You speake too late for my voice, but Ile discharge the part. 135

Exit. Cyn. Hyl. and Ero.

Lys. Occurrents call yee them; foule shame confound them all; that
impregnable Fort of chastitie and loyaltie, that amazement of the
world, O yee Deities could nothing restraine her? I tooke her spirit to
bee too haughtie for such a depression.

Thar. But who commonly more short heeld; then they that are high 140
'ith in-step?

Lys. Mee thinkes yet shame should have controul'd so sodaine an
appetite.

Thar. Tush, shame doth extinguish lust as oile doth fire,
The bloud once het, shame doth enflame the more, 145
What they before by art dissembled most,
They act more freely; shame once found is lost;

---

115 No, wife?] *Parrott;* ∼∧ ∼. ‖ **119** *Paphos*] ∼; ‖ **131** Fare-well] Fare-will ‖ **135** SD *Hyl.*
and Ero.] *Parrott; Hyl.* ‖ **141** in-step?] ∼. ‖

And to say truth Brother; what shame is due to't? or what congruence doth it carrie? that a yong Ladie, Gallant, Vigorous, full of Spirit, and Complexion; her appetite newe whetted with Nuptiall delights; / to [F4ᵛ] 150 be confind to the speculation of a deaths head, or for the losse of a husband, the world affording flesh enough, make the noone-tide of her yeares, the sunne-set of her pleasures.

Lyc. And yet there haue been such women.

Thar. Of the first stamp perhaps, when the mettal was purer then   155
in these degenerate daies; of later yeares, much of that coine hath beene counterfait, and besides so crackt and worne with vse, that they are growne light, and indeede fit for nothing, but to be turn'd ouer in play.

Lys. Not all brother.   160

Thar. My matchlesse sister only excepted: for shee, you know is made of an other mettall, then that shee borrow'd of her mother. But doe you brother sadly intend the pursuite of this triall?

Lys. Irreuocably.

Thar. Its a high proiect: if it be once rais'd, the earth is too weake   165
to beare so waightie an accident; it cannot bee coniur'd downe againe, without an earth-quake, therefore beleeue shee will be constant.

Lys. No, I will not.

Thar. Then beleeue shee will not be constant.

Lys. Neither, I will beleeue nothing but what triall enforces; will   170
you hold your promise for the gouerning of this proiect with skill, and secrecie?

Thar. If it must needes bee so. But hearke you brother; haue you no other Capricions in your head to intrap my sister in her frailtie, but to proue the firmenesse of her widdow vowes after your suppos'd   175
death?

Lys. None in the world.

Thar. Then here's my hand, Ile be as close, as my Ladies shoe to her foote that pinches and pleases her, and will beare on with the plot, till the vessell split againe.   180

Lys. Forge any death, so you can force beliefe. Say I was poison'd, drown'd —

Thar. Hang'd.

Lys. Any thing, so you assist it with likely circumstance, / I neede   [G1]
not instruct you: that must bee your imploiment *Lycus.*   185

Lyc. Well Sir.

Thar. But brother you must set in to; to countenance truth out, a herse there must be too; Its strange to thinke how much the eie preuailes in such impressions; I haue marckt a Widdow, that iust before

---

149 carrie?] ∼, ‖ **166** accident;] ∼, ‖ **176** death?] ∼. ‖ **182** drown'd—] ∼. ‖

was seene pleasant enough, follow an emptie herse, and weepe de-   190
uoutly.

Lyc. All those thinges leaue to me.

Lys. But brother for the bestowing of this herse in the monument of
our Familie, and the marshalling of a Funerall —

Thar. Leaue that to my care, and if I doe not doe the mourner, as   195
liuely as your Heire, and weepe as lustily as your Widdow, say there's
no vertue in Onions; that being done, Ile come to visit the distrest widdow; apply old ends of comfort to her griefe, but the burden of my
song shall be to tell her wordes are but dead comforts; and therefore
counsaile her to take a liuing comfort, that might Ferrit out the thought   200
of her dead husband, and will come prepar'd with choise of suiters;
either my Spartane Lord for grace at the Viceroies Court, or some
great Lawyer that may soder vp her crackt estate, and so forth. But
what would you say brother, if you should finde her married at your
arriuall?   205

Lys. By this hand — split her Wezand!

Thar. Well, forget not your wager, a stately chariot with foure
brave Horses of the Thracian breede, with all appurtenances. Ile prepare the like for you, if you proue Victor; but well remembred, where
will you lurke the whiles?   210

Lys. Mewd vp close, some short daies iourney hence, *Lycus* shall
know the place; write still how all things passe. Brother adiew; all ioy
attend you.

Thar. Will you not stay our nuptiall now so neare?

Lys. I should be like a man that heares a tale   215
And heedes it not; one absent from himselfe.
My wife / shall attend the Countesse, and my Sonne.   [G1^v]

Thar. Whom you shal here at your returne call me
Father; adiew: *Ioue* be your speede.
My Nuptialls done, your Funeralls succeed.   *Exeunt.*

[III.ii]

Enter Argus barehead.

Arg. A Hall, a hall: who's without there?

Enter two or three with cushions.

Come on, y'are proper Groomes, are yee not? Slight I thinke y'are all
Bridegroomes, yee take your pleasures so. A companie of dormice.
Their Honours are vpon comming, and the roome not readie. Rushes
and seates instantly.   5

---

200 comfort,] ~; ‖ **205** arriuall?] ~. ‖ **206** hand— . . . Wezand!] ~∧ . . . ~. ‖ **212** place;
. . . passe.] ~, . . . ~, ‖ **214** neare?] ~. ‖ **216** himselfe.] ~, ‖ **216-17** And . . . Sonne.] *Collier;*
as prose (my) ‖ **218-19** Whom . . . speede.] *Parrott; as prose* (father) ‖ **III.ii]** *Parrott* ‖

[*Enter Tharsalio.*]

Thar. Now, alas fellow *Argus*, how thou art comberd with an office?

Arg. Perfume sirrha, the roome's dampish.

Thar. Nay you may leaue that office to the Ladies, theyle perfume it sufficiently.

Arg. Cry mercie Sir, here's a whole *Chorus* of *Syluans* at hand, 10
cornetting, and tripping ath' toe, as the ground they troad on were too hot for their feete. The deuice is rare; and there's your yong Nephew too, he hangs in the clouds Deified with *Hymens* shape.

Thar. Is he perfect in's part? has not his tongue learn'd of the *Syluans* to trip ath' Toe? 15

Arg. Sir, beleeue it, he does it pretiously for accent and action, as if hee felt the part he plaid: hee rauishes all the yong Wenches in the Palace: Pray *Venus* my yong Ladie *Laodice* haue not some little prick of *Cupid* in her, shee's so diligent at's rehearsall.

Thar. No force, so my next vowes be heard, that if *Cupid* haue 20
prickt her, *Hymen* may cure her.

Arg. You meane your Nephew Sir that presents *Hymen*.

Thar. Why so, I can speake nothing but thou art within me: fie of this wit of thine, 'twill be thy destruction. But howsoever you please to vnderstand, *Hymen* send the boy / no worse fortune: And where's [G2] 25
my Ladies honour?

Arg. At hand Sir, with your vnparagond sister, please you take your chaire of Honour Sir?

Thar. Most seruiceable *Argus*, the Gods reward thy seruice; [*Aside.*] for I will not. 30

Enter Eudora, leading Cynthia, Laodice, Sthenio, Ianthe,
Ero, with others following.

Eud. Come sister, now we must exchange that name
For stranger Titles, let's dispose our selues
To entertaine these *Syluane* Reuellers,
That come to grace our loued Nuptialls.
I feare me we must all turne Nymphs to night, 35
To side those sprightly wood-Gods in their dances;
Can you doo't nimbly sister? slight what ails you,
Are you not well?

Cynth.   Yes Madam.

Eud.   But your lookes,
Mee thinkes, are cloudie; suiting ill the Sunne-shine
Of this cleare honour to your husbands house. 40
Is there ought here that sorts not with your liking?

---

5 SD *Enter Tharsalio.*] *Parrott* ‖ 21 may] *Dodsley*; my ‖ 23 within] *Dodsley*; with in ‖ 29 thy] *Q(c)*; they *Q(u)* | SD *Aside.*] ‖ 33 Reuellers,] ~. ‖ 34 Nuptialls.] ~, ‖ 37-38 Can . . . well?] *Dodsley*; *as prose* (are) ‖ 37 ails] *Parrott*; aile ‖ 38-40 But . . . house.] *Reed*; *as prose* (mee . . . of) ‖ 39 ill] *Shepherd*; all ‖

Thar. Blame her not Mistris, if her lookes shew care.
Excuse the Merchants sadnesse that hath made
A doubtfull venture of his whole estate;
His liuelyhood, his hopes, in one poore bottome,   45
To all encounters of the Sea and stormes.
Had you a husband that you lou'd as well,
Would you not take his absent plight as ill?
Cauill at every fancie? not an obiect
That could present it selfe, but it would forge   50
Some vaine obiection, that did doubt his safetie;
True loue is euer full of iealousie.
   Eud. Iealous? of what? of euery little iourney?
Meere fancie than is wanton; and doth cast
At those sleight dangers there, too doting glances; /   55
Misgiuing mindes euer prouoke mischances: [G2ᵛ]
Shines not the Sunne in his way bright as here?
Is not the aire as good? what hazard doubt you?
   Arg. His horse may stumble if it please your Honour;
The raine may wet, the winde may blow on him;   60
Many shrewd hazards watch poore trauailers.
   Eud. True, and the shrewdest thou hast reckend vs.
Good sister, these cares fit yong married wiues.
   Cynth. Wiues should be stil yong in their husbands loues.
Time beares no Sythe should bear down them before him.   65
Our liues he may cut short, but not our loues.
   Thar. Sister be wise, and ship not in one Barke,
All your abilitie: if he miscarrie,
Your well tried wisedome should look out for new.
   Cynth. I wish them happie windes that runne that course, 70
From me tis farre; One Temple seal'd our troth
One Tomb, one houre shall end, and shroud vs both.
   Thar. Well, y'are a *Phoenix*; there, be that your cheere:
Loue, with your husband be, your wisedome here.
Hearke, our sports challenge it; Sit dearest Mistris.   75
   Eud. Take your place worthiest seruant.
   Thar. Serue me heauen,
As I my heauenly Mistris; Sit rare sister.

      Musique: Hymen descends; and sixe Syluanes enter beneath,
                  with Torches.

   Arg. A hall, a hall: let no more Citizens in there.
   Laod. O, not my Cosen see; but *Hymens* selfe.   80
   Sthe. He does become it most enflamingly.

---

69 out] *Dodsley;* ont ‖ **73** *Phoenix;* there, . . . cheere:] *Parrott;* ∼, ∼∧ . . . ∼∧ ‖ **77** heauen,]
∼. *Musique.* ‖ **78** Mistris;] ∼, │ SD *Musique: . . . Torches.*] *in roman except for Musique, Hymen,*
and Syluanes ‖ **80** not] *Not* ‖

Hym. Haile honor'd Bridegroom, and his Princely bride,
With the most fam'd for vertue, *Cynthia;*
And this yong Ladie, bright *Laodice,*
One rich hope of this noblest Familie. 85
    Sthe. Hearke how he courts: he is enamour'd too.
    Laod. O grant it *Venus,* and be ever honour'd.
    Hym. In grace and loue of you, I *Hymen* searcht
The groues and thickets that embrace this Palace
With this clear-flam'd, and good aboding Torch / 90
For summons of these fresh and flowrie *Syluans,* [G3]
To this faire presence; with their winding Haies,
Actiue and Antique dances to delight
Your frolick eies, and helpe to celebrate
These noblest nuptialls; which great Destinie, 95
Ordain'd past custome and all vulgar obiect
To be the readuancement of a house,
Noble and Princely, and restore this Palace
To that name, that six hunderd Summers since
Was in possession of this Bridegroomes Ancetors, 100
The ancient and most vertue-fam'd *Lysandri.*
Syluans! the Courtships you make to your Dryads,
Vse to this great Bride, and these other Dames,
And heighten with your sports, my nuptiall flames.
    Laod. O would himselfe descend, and me command. 105
    Sthe. Dance; and his heart catch in an others hand.

       Syluans, take out the Bride and the rest: They dance,
         after which, and all set in their places, Hymen.

Hym. Now, what my Power and my Torches influence
Hath in the blessings of your Nuptiall ioyes
(Great Bride and Bridegroome) you shall amply part
Betwixt your free loues, and forgoe it neuer. 110
    Omn. Thankes to great *Hymen,* and faire *Syluanes* euer.   *Exeunt.*

               Finis Actus Tertij.

Actus Quarti. Scœna Prima.

      Tharsalio, Lycus, with his Arme in a skarfe, a night-
              cap on's head.

Lyc. I hope Sir by this time —
Thar. Put on man, by our selues.

---

82 bride,] ∼∧ ‖ 106 SD *places,] Shepherd;* ∼. ‖ 107 my Power] *G. B. Evans;* the Power ‖ 1 time
—] ∼. ‖

Lyc. The edge of your confidence is well taken off; would you not bee content to with-draw your / wager?   [G3ᵛ]

Thar. Faith fellow *Lycus,* if my wager were weakely built, this vn-   5
expected accident might stagger it. For the truth is, this strain is extraordinarie, to follow her husbands bodie into the Tombe, and there for
his companie to burie her selfe quick: it's new and stirring, but for all
this, Ile not despaire of my wager.

Lyc. Why Sir, can you thinke such a passion dissembl'd?   10

Thar. All's one for that, what I thinke I thinke; In the meane time
forget not to write to my Brother, how the plot hath succeeded, that
the newes of his death hath taken; a funerall solemnitie perform'd, his
suppos'd Corse bestow'd in the monument of our Familie, thou and I
horrible mourners: But aboue all that his intollerable vertuous Widow,   15
for his loue; and (for her loue) *Ero* her hand-maid, are discended with
his Corse into the vault; there wipe their eies time out of minde, drinke
nothing but their own teares, and by this time are almost dead with
famine. There's a point will sting it (for you say tis true); where left
you him?   20

Lyc. At Dipolis Sir, some twentie miles hence.

Thar. He keepes close.

Lyc. I sir, by all meanes; skulks vnknowne under the name of a
strange Knight.

Thar. That may carrie him without discrying, for there's a number   25
of strange Knights abroad. You left him well?

Lyc. Well Sir, but for this iealous humour that hants him.

Thar. Well, this newes will absolutely purge that humor. Write all,
forget not to describe her passion at thy discouerie of his slaughter:
did shee performe it well for her husbands wager?   30

Lyc. Performe it, call you it? you may iest; men hunt Hares to
death for their sports, but the poore beasts die in earnest: you wager
of her passions for your pleasure, but shee takes little pleasure in those
earnest passions. I never saw such an extasie of sorrow, since I knew
the name of / sorrow. Her hands flew vp to her head like Furies, hid [G4] 35
all her beauties in her discheuel'd haire, and wept as she would turne
fountaine. I would you and her husband had beene behind the Arras
but to haue heard her. I assure you Sir, I was so transported with the
spectacle, that in despight of my discretion, I was forc't to turne
woman, and beare a part with her. Humanitie broke loose from my   40
heart, and stream'd through mine eies.

11 what] What ‖ **16** and (for] *Q(c)*; (∼ ∧∼ *Q(u)* ‖ **17** wipe] *Q(c)*; ∼: *Q(u)* ‖ **19** true);]
∼)∧ ‖ **26** well?] ∼. ‖

516

Thar. In prose, thou weptst. So have I seen many a moist Auditor doe at a play; when the storie was but a meere fiction: And didst act the Nuntius well? would I had heard it: could'st thou dresse thy lookes in a mournefull habite?   45

Lyc. Not without preparation Sir; no more then my speech, twas a plaine acting of an enterlude to me, to pronounce the part.

Thar. As how for heauens sake?

Lyc. Phœbus addrest his chariot towards the West
To change his wearied Coursers, and so forth.   50

Thar. Nay on, and thou lou'st me.

Lyc. Lysander and my selfe beguild the way
With enterchang'd discourse, but our chiefe Theame,
Was of your dearest selfe, his honour'd wife;
Your loue, your vertue, wondrous constancie.   55

Thar. Then was her Cu to whimper; on.

Lyc. When sodainly appear'd as far as sight
A troope of horse, arm'd as we might descerne,
With Iauelines, Speares, and such accoutrements.
He doubted nought (As Innocencie euer   60
Is free from doubting ill.)

Thar. There dropt a teare.

Lyc.   My minde misgaue me.
They might be mountaners. At their approch
They vs'd no other language but their weapons,
To tell vs what they were; *Lysander* drew,   65
And bore him selfe *Achilles* like in fight,
And as a Mower sweepes off t'heads of Bents,
So did *Lysanders* sword shaue off the points /
Of their assaulting lances. His horse at last,   [G4ᵛ]
Sore hurt, fell vnder him; I seeing I could   70
Not rescue, vs'd my spurres to flie away.

Thar. What from thy friend?

Lyc. I in a good quarrell, why not?

Thar. Good; I am answer'd.

Lyc. A lance pursued me, brought me back againe;   75
And with these wounds left me t'accompanie
Dying *Lysander*: Then they rifl'd us, and left us.
They gone; my breath not yet gone, gan to striue
And reuiue sense: I with my feeble ioynts

---

44 well?] ∼, ‖ **69-71** Of . . . away.] Of . . . lances. / His . . . him; / I . . . spurres / To . . . away. Q (sore . . . not) ‖ **77** and . . . us.] *on separate line* (And) ‖

Crawl'd to *Lysander,* stirr'd him, and withall 80
He gaspst; cried *Cynthia*! and breath'd no more.
   Thar. O then shee howl'd out right.
   Lyc. Passengers came and in a Chariot brought vs
Streight to a Neighbour Towne; where I forthwith
Coffind my friend in leade; and so conuaid him 85
To this sad place.
   Thar. 'Twas well; and could not show but strangely.
   Lyc. Well Sir, this tale pronounc't with terrour, suited with action,
clothed with such likely circumstance; My wounds in shew, her hus-
bands herse in sight, thinke what effect it wrought: And if you doubt, 90
let the sad consequence of her retreat to his Tombe, bee your wofull
instructer.
   Thar. For all this, Ile not despaire of my wager:
These Grieues that sound so lowd, proue alwaies light,
True sorrow euermore keepes out of sight. 95
This straine of mourning wi'th' Sepulcher, like an ouer-doing Actor,
affects grosly, and is indeede so farre forc't from the life, that it bewraies it selfe to be altogether artificiall. To set open a shop of mourning! Tis palpable. Truth, the substance, hunts not after the shadow of
popular Fame. Her officious ostentation of sorrow condemnes her sin- 100
ceritie. When did euer woman mourne so vnmeasura- / bly, but shee [H1]
did dissemble?
   Lyc. O Gods! a passion thus borne; thus apparell'd with teares,
sighes, swownings, and all the badges of true sorrow, to be dissembl'd!
by *Venus* I am sorrie I ever set foot in't. Could shee, if shee dissembl'd, 105
thus dally with hunger, be deafe to the barking of her appetite, not
hauing these foure daies relieu'd nature with one dramme of sustenance?
   Thar. For this does shee looke to bee Deified, to haue Hymnes made
of her, nay to her: The Tomb where she is to be no more reputed the 110
ancient monument of our Familie the *Lysandri*; but the new erected
Altar of *Cynthia*: To which all the Paphian widdowes shall after
their husbands Funeralls, offer their wet muckinders, for monuments
of the danger they haue past, as Sea-men doe their wet garments at
Neptunes Temple after a shipwracke. 115
   Lyc. Well, Ile apprehend you, at your pleasure: I for my part will
say; that if her faith bee as constant as her love is heartie, and vnaf-
fected, her vertues may iustly challenge a Deitie to enshrine them.

93-94 For ... light,] *Dodsley*; For ... These / Grieues ... light, ‖ **96** wi'th'] *Parrott* (*Brereton conj.*); with ‖ **107-8** sustenance?] ∼. ‖

Thar. I, there's an other point too. But one of those vertues is
enough at once. All natures are not capable of all gifts. If the braine   120
of the Wise were in the heads of the learned; then might Parish-
Clerkes be common counsaile men, and Poets Aldermens deputies.
My sister may turne *Niobe* for loue; but till *Niobe* bee turn'd to a
Marble, Ile not despaire but shee may proue a woman. Let the triall
runne on, if shee doe not out-runne it, Ile say Poets are not Prophets,   125
Prognosticators are but Mountibankes, and none tell true but wood-
mongers.   *Exit.*

    Lyc. A sweet Gentleman you are. I meruaile what man? what
woman? what name? what action doth his tongue glide ouer, but it
leaues a slime vpon't? Well, Ile presently to Dipolis, where *Lysander*   130
staies; and will not say but shee may proue fraile:
But this Ile say, if she should chance to breake,
Her teares are true, though womens truths are weake.   *Exit. /*

[IV.ii]   [H1ᵛ]

*Enter Lysander like a Souldier disguisde at all parts, a
halfe Pike, gorget, &c; he discouers the Tombe, lookes in
and wonders, &c.*

O Miracle of nature! womens glorie;
Mens shame; and enuie of the Deities!
Yet must these matchlesse creatures be suspected;
Accus'd; condemn'd! Now by th'immortall Gods,
They rather merit Altars, Sacrifice,   5
Then loue and courtship.
Yet see the Queene of these lies here interred;
Tearing her haire, and drowned in her teares.
Which *Ioue* should turne to Christall; and a Mirrour
Make of them; wherein men may see and wonder   10
At womens vertues. Shall shee famish then?
Will men (without disswasions) suffer thus
So bright an Ornament to earth, tomb'd quick,
In Earths darke bosome? Ho! who's in the Tombe there?
    Ero. Who calls? whence are you?   15
    Lys. I am a Souldier of the watch and must enter.
    Ero. Amongst the dead?

---

121 Wise] *Parrott (Deighton conj.)*; West, ‖ **130** vpon't?] ∼. ‖ **132-33** But . . . weake.] *Dodsley;*
as prose (If) ‖ IV.ii] *Parrott* ‖ SD &c;] ∼, ‖ **4** Accus'd; . . . Gods,] *Collier*; Accus'd condemn'd
/ Now . . . Gods, ‖ **13** quick,] ∼. ‖ **14** bosome?] ∼: | In . . . there?] *Collier*; In . . . Ho! / Who's
. . . there? ‖

Lys. Doe the dead speake? ope or Ile force it open.

Ero. What violence is this? what seeke you here
Where nought but death and her attendants dwell?   20

    Lys. What wretched soules are you that thus by night
Lurke here amongst the dead?

    Ero.   Good Souldier doe not stirre her,
Shee's weake, and quickly seiz'd with swowning and passions,
And with much trouble shall we both recall
Her fainting spirits.   25
Fiue daies thus hath shee wasted; and not once
Season'd her Pallate with the tast of meate;
Her powers of life are spent; and what remaines
Of her famisht spirit, serues not to breath but sigh.
Shee hath exil'd her eies from sleepe, or sight,   30
And giuen them wholly vp to ceaselesse teares
Ouer that ruthfull herse / of her deare Spouse,   [H2]
Slaine by Bandittos, Nobly borne *Lysander.*

    Lys. And hopes shee with these heauie notes and cries
To call him from the dead? In these fiue daies   35
Hath shee but made him stirre a finger or fetch
One gasp of that forsaken life shee mournes?
Come, honour'd Mistris; I admire your vertues;
But must reproue this vaine excesse of mone;
Rowse your selfe Ladie, and looke vp from death,   40
Well said, tis well; stay by my hand and rise.
This Face hath beene maintain'd with better huswiferie.

    Cynth. What are you?

    Lys.   Ladie, I am Sentinell,
Set in this hallowed place, to watch and guard
On forfait of my life, these monuments   45
From Rape, and spoile of sacrilegious handes,
And saue the bodies, that without you see
Of crucified offenders; that no friends
May beare them hence, to honour'd buriall.

    Cynth. Thou seem'st an honest Souldier; pray thee then   50
Be as thou seem'st; betake thee to thy charge
And leaue this place; adde not affliction
To the afflicted.

    Lys.   You misname the children.
For what you terme affliction now, in you
Is but selfe-humour; voluntaire Penance   55

---

20 dwell?] ∼. ‖ **21-22** What . . . dead?] *Collier; as prose* (lurke) ‖ **22-23** Good . . . *Lysander.*]
Parrott; as prose sentences in separate paragraphs: Shee's . . . Spirits / Fiue . . . sigh. / Shee . . .
Lysander. Q (and . . . her . . . season'd . . . her . . . of . . . and . . . ouer . . . slaine); *Collier*
prints Shee . . . *Lysander as verse* ‖ **33** Bandittos] *Reed;* Banditos ‖ **34-37** And . . . mournes?]
Collier; as prose (to . . . in . . . hath . . . one) ‖ **46** spoile] *Dodsley;* spoil'd ‖

Impos'd vpon your selfe: and you lament
As did the *Satyre* once, that ran affrighted
From that hornes sound that he himselfe had winded.
Which humour to abate, my counsaile tending your term'd affliction,
What I for Phisicke giue, you take for poison.   60
I tell you honour'd Mistris, these ingredients
Are wholesome, though perhaps they seeme vntoothsome.
    Ero. [*Aside.*] This Souldier sure, is some decai'd pothecarie.
    Lys. Deere Ghost be wise, and pittie your faire selfe
Thus, by your selfe vnnaturally afflicted: /   65
Chide back, heart-breaking grones, clear vp those lamps,   [H2ᵛ]
Restore them to their first creation:
Windowes for light; not sluces made for teares.
Beate not the senselesse aire with needlesse cries,
Banefull to life, and bootlesse to the dead.   70
This is the Inne, where all *Deucalions* race
Sooner or later, must take vp their lodging;
No priuiledge can free vs from this prison;
No teares, no praiers, can redeeme from hence
A captiu'd soule; Make vse of what you see: 75
Let this affrighting spectacle of death
Teach you to nourish life.
    Ero. Good [Mistris] heare him: this is a rare Souldier.
    Lys. Say that with abstinence you should vnlose
The knot of life: Suppose that in this Tombe   80
For your deare Spouse, you should entomb your selfe
A liuing Corse; Say that before your houre
Without due Summons from the Fates, you send
Your hastie soule to hell: can your deare Spouse
Take notice of your faith and constancie?   85
Shall your deare Spouse reuiue to giue you thankes?
    Cynth. Idle discourser.
    Lys.   No, your moanes are idle.
Goe to I say, be counsail'd; raise your selfe:
Enioy the fruits of life, there's viands for you,
Now, live for a better husband. No? will you none?   90
    Ero. For loue of courtesie, good Mistris, eate,
Doe not reiect so kinde and sweet an offer,
Who knowes but this may be some *Mercurie*
Disguis'de, and sent from *Iuno* to relieue vs?

---

63 SD *Aside.*] *Parrott* ‖ **78** Good Mistris heare] *Parrott* (*Gilchrist conj. in Collier*); Good heare ‖
79-86 Say … thankes?] *Reed*; *as prose* (the … for … a … without … your … take) ‖ **90**
Now … none?] *Parrott*; Now … husband. / No? … none? ‖

Did ever any lend vnwilling eares   95
To those that came with messages of life?
   Cynth. I pray thee leave thy Rhetorique.
   Ero. By my soule; to speake plaine truth, I could rather wish t'em-
ploy my teeth then my tongue, so your example would be my warrant.
   Cynth. Thou hast my warrant. /
   Lys.   Well then, eate my wench,   [H3] 100
Let obstinacie starue. Fall to.
   Ero.   Perswade
My Mistris first.
   Lys.   Slight tell me Ladie,
Are you resolu'd to die? If that be so,
Choose not (for shame) a base, and beggars death:
Die not for hunger, like a Spartane Ladie;   105
Fall valiantly vpon a sword, or drinke
A noble death, expell your griefe with poison,
There 'tis, seize it. [*offering his sword.*] Tush you dare not die.
Come, Wench, thou hast not lost a husband;
Thou shalt eate, th'art now within the place   110
Where I command.
   Ero.   I protest sir.
   Lys. Well said; eate, and protest, or Ile protest
And doe thou eate; thou eat'st against thy will,
That's it thou would'st say.
   Ero.   It is.
   Lys. And vnder such a protestation   115
Thou lost thy Maiden-head.
For your owne sake good Ladie forget this husband,
Come you are now become a happy Widdow,
A blessednesse that many would be glad of.
That and your husbands Inventorie together,   120
Will raise you vp husbands enow. What thinke you of me?
   Cynth. Trifler, pursue this wanton Theame no further;
Lest (which I would be loth) your speech prouoke
Vnciuill language from me; I must tell you,
One ioynt of him I lost, was much more worth   125
Then the rackt valew of thy entire bodie.
   Ero. O know what ioynt shee meanes.
   Lys.   Well, I haue done.
And well done frailtie; proface, how lik'st thou it?

---

101 Let . . . to.] *Collier*; Let . . . starue. / Fall to. ‖ **101-2** Perswade . . . first.] *one line* ‖ **107** A noble] *Reed*; Noble ‖ **108** SD *offering his sword.*] *Parrott*; it. ——————Tush ‖ **109** Come, Wench,] ∼∧ ∼∧ ‖ **110-11** Thou . . . command.] Thou . . . within / The . . . command. ‖ **116** lost] lost' ‖ **121** Will . . . me?] *Collier*; What . . . me? *on separate line* ‖ **128** it?] ∼. ‖

Ero. Very toothsome Ingrediens surely sir,

Want but some lycor to incorporate them. / 130

    Lys. There tis, carouse.   [H3ᵛ]

    Ero.   I humbly thanke you Sir.

    Lys. Hold pledge me now.

    Ero.   Tis the poison Sir,

That preserues life, I take it.   *bibit Ancill.*

    Lys.   Doe so, take it.

    Ero. Sighing has made me somthing short-winded.

Ile pledge y'at twice.   135

    Lys. Tis well done; doe me right.

    Ero. I pray sir, have you beene a Pothecarie?

    Lys. Marrie haue I wench; A womans Pothecarie.

    Ero. Haue you good Ingredients?

I like your Bottle well. Good Mistris tast it.   140

Trie but the operation, twill fetch vp

The roses in your cheekes againe.

Doctor *Verolles* bottles are not like it;

There's no *Guaicum* here, I can assure you.

    Lys. This will doe well anone.

    Ero.   Now fie vpon't.   145

O I haue lost my tongue in this same lymbo.

The spring an't's spoil'd me thinkes; it goes not off

With the old twange.

    Lys. Well said wench, oile it well; twill make it slide well.

    Ero. Aristotle saies sir, in his Posterionds —   150

    Lys. [*Aside.*] This wench is learned; — And what saies he?

    Ero. That when a man dies, the last thing that moues is his heart,

in a woman her tongue.

    Lys. Right; and addes further, that you women are

A kind of spinners; if their legs be pluckt off,   155

Yet still they'le wag them; so will you your tongues.

[*Aside*] With what an easie change does this same weaknesse

Of women, slip from one extreame t'another?

All these attractions take no hold of her;

No not to take refection; 'T must not be thus —   160

Well said wench; Tickle that Helicon.

But shall we quit the field with this disgrace

Giuen to our Oratorie? Both not gaine /

So much ground of her as to make her eate?   [H4]

---

147 an't's] *Parrott subs.*; ants, ‖ **150** Posterionds—] ∼. ‖ **151** SD *Aside.*] | learned; —] ∼;∧ ‖
154-56 Right; . . . tongues.] *Reed; as prose* (a . . . yet) ‖ **157** SD *Aside.*] *Parrott* ‖ **160** thus—] ∼. ‖

Ero. Faith the truth is sir; you are no fit Organe   165
For this businesse;
Tis quite out of your Element:
Let vs alone, sheele eate I haue no feare;
A womans tongue best fits a womans eare.
Ioue neuer did employ *Mercurie,*   170
But *Iris* for his Messenger to *Iuno.*
    Lys. Come, let me kisse thee wench; wilt vndertake
To make thy Mistris eate?
    Ero.   It shall goe harde Sir
But I will make her turne flesh and bloud,
And learne to liue as other mortalls doe.   175
    Lys. Well said: the morning hasts; next night expect me.
    Ero. With more prouision good Sir.
    Lys.   Very good.   *Exiturus.*
    Ero. And bring more wine.   *Shee shuts vp the Tomb.*
    Lys.   What else; shalt haue enough:
O *Cynthia,* heire of her bright puritie,
Whose name thou dost inherit; Thow disdainst   180
(Seuer'd from all concretion) to feede
Vpon the base foode of grosse Elements.
Thou all art soule; All immortalitie.
Thou fasts for *Nectar* and *Ambrosia,*
Which till thou find'st, and eat'st aboue the starres,   185
To all foode here thou bidd'st celestiall warrs.   *Exit.*

[IV.iii]

Cynthia, Ero, the Tombe opening.

    Ero. So; lets aire our dampish spirits, almost stifl'd in this grose
muddie Element.
    Cynth. How sweet a breath the calmnesse of the night inspires the
aire withall?
    Ero. Well said; Now y'are your selfe: did not I tell you how sweet   5
an operation the Souldiers bottle had? And if there be such vertue in
the bottle; what is there in the Souldier? know, and acknowledge his
worth when hee comes in any case Mistris.
    Cynth. So Maide. /
    Ero. Gods my patience? did you looke forsooth that *Iuno* should [H4ᵛ] 10
haue sent you meate from her owne Trencher, in reward of your widdowes teares? you might sit and sigh first till your heart-strings broke,
Ile able't.

IV.iii] *Parrott* ‖

524

Cynth. I feare me thy lips have gone so oft to the bottle, that thy tongue-strings are come broken home. 15

Ero. Faith the truth is, my tongue hath beene so long tied vp, that tis cover'd with rust, and I rub it against my pallat as wee doe suspected coines, to trie whether it bee currant or no. But now Mistris for an vpshot of this bottle; let's haue one carouse to the good speede of my old Master, and the good speede of my new. 20

Cynth. So Damzell.

Ero. You must pledge it, here's to it. Doe me right I pray.

Cynth. You say I must.

Ero. Must? what else?

Cynth. How excellent ill this humour suites our habite? 25

Ero. Goe to Mistris, do not thinke but you and I shall haue good sport with this iest, when we are in priuate at home. I would to *Venus* we had some honest shift or other to get off withall; for Ile no more ant; Ile not turne Salt-peeter in this vault for never a mans companie liuing; much lesse for a womans. Sure I am the wonder's ouer, and 30 'twas only for that, that I endur'd this; and so a my conscience did you. Neuer denie it.

Cynth. Nay pray thee take it to thee.

Enter Lysander.

Cynth. Hearke I heare some footing neare vs.

Ero. Gods me 'tis the Souldier Mistris, by *Venus* if you fall to your 35 late black *Santus* againe, Ile discouer you.

Lys. [*Aside.*] What's here? The maid hath certainly preuail'd with her; mee thinkes those cloudes that last night couer'd her lookes are now disperst: Ile trie this further — Saue you Lady.

Ero. Honourable Souldier? y'are welcome; please you step in sir? 40

Lys. With all my heart sweet heart; by your patience Ladie; why this beares some shape of life yet. Damzell, th'ast / performd a service [11] of high reckoning, which cannot perish vnrewarded.

Ero. Faith Sir, you are in the way to doe it once, if you haue the heart to hold on. 45

Cynth. Your bottle has poisond this wench sir.

Lys. A wholsome poison it is Ladie, if I may iudge; of which sort here is one better bottle more.

    Wine is ordaind to raise such hearts as sinke,

    Whom wofull starres distemper; let him drinke. 50

I am most glad I have beene some meane to this part of your recouerie, and will drinke to the rest of it.

Ero. Goe to Mistris, pray simper no more; pledge the man of Warre here.

---

37 SD *Aside.*] *Parrott* ‖ **39** further—] ∼. ‖ **42** performd] per formd ‖

Cynth. Come y'are too rude. 55

Ero. Good.

Lys. Good sooth Ladie y'are honour'd in her seruice; I would haue you liue, and shee would haue you liue freely; without which life is but death. To liue freely is to feast our appetites freely; without which humanes are stones; to the satisfaction whereof I drinke Ladie. 60

Cynth. Ile pledge you Sir.

Ero. Said like a Mistris; and the Mistris of your selfe; pledge him in loue too: I see hee loues you; Shee's silent, shee consents sir.

Lys. O happy starres. And now pardon Ladie; [*kisses her.*] me thinks these are all of a peece. 65

Ero. Nay if you kisse all of a peece wee shall n'ere haue done: Well twas well offer'd, and as well taken.

Cynth. If the world should see this.

Lys. The world! should one so rare as your selfe, respect the vulgar world? 70

Cynth. The praise I haue had, I would continue.

Lys. What, of the vulgar? Who hates not the vulgar, deserues not loue of the vertuous. And to affect praise of that we despise, how rediculous it is?

Ero. Comfortable doctrine, Mistris, edifie, edifie. Me thinkes euen 75
thus it was when *Dido* / and *Aeneas* met in the Caue; And hearke me [I1ᵛ]
thinks I heare some of the hunters. *She shuts the tomb.*

Finis Actus Quarti

Actus Quinti Scœna Prima:

Enter Tharsalio, Lycus.

Lyc. Tis such an obstinacie in you Sir,
As neuer was conceipted, to runne on
With an opinion against all the world,
And what your eies may witnes; to aduenture
The famishment for griefe of such a woman 5
As all mens merits met in any one,
Could not deserue.

Thar. I must confesse it *Lycus,*
Weele therefore now preuent it if we may,
And that our curious triall hath not dwelt
Too long on this vnnecessarie hant: 10
Griefe, and all want of foode, not hauing wrought
Too mortally on her diuine disposure.

---

64 SD *kisses her.*] *Parrott* ‖ 72 What,] ∼∧ ‖ 75-77 Comfortable ... hunters.] *Shepherd*; Comfortable ... edifie. / Me ... *Dido* / And ... hearke / Me ... hunters. Q (and) ‖ 11 foode,]
∼; ‖

Lyc. I feare they haue, and shee is past our cure.

Thar. I must confesse with feare and shame as much.

Lyc. And that shee will not trust in any thing   15
What you perswade her to.

Thar.   Then thou shalt hast
And call my brother from his secret shroude,
Where he appointed thee to come and tell him
How all thinges have succeeded.

Lyc.   This is well.
If (as I say) the ill be not so growne,   20
That all help is denied her. But I feare
The matchlesse Deme is famisht.   *Thar. looks into the tomb.*

Thar.   Slight, whose here?
A Souldier with my sister? wipe, wipe, see! /
Kissing by *Ioue*; shee, as I lay tis shee.   [12]

Lyc. What? is shee well Sir?

Thar.   O no, shee is famisht;   25
Shee's past our comfort, shee lies drawing on.

Lyc. The Gods forbid.

Thar.   Looke thou, shee's drawing on.
How saist thou?

Lyc.   Drawing on? Illustrious witchcrafts.

Thar. Lies shee not drawing on?

Lyc.   Shee drawes on fairely.
Your sister Sir? This shee? can this be shee?   30

Thar. She, she, she, and none but she.   *He dances and sings.*
Shee only Queene of loue, and chastitie,
O chastitie; This women be.

Lyc. Slight tis prodigious.

Thar.   Horse, horse, horse,
Foure Chariot Horses of the Thracian breede,   35
Come, bring me, brother. O the happiest euening,
That euer drew her vaile before the Sunne.
Who is't canst tell?

Lyc.   The Souldier Sir that watches
The bodies crucified in this hallow'd place.
Of which to lose one, it is death to him,   40
And yet the lustfull knave is at his Venerie,
While one might steale one.

Thar.   What a slaue was I
That held not out my mindes strength constantly,
That shee would prove thus? O incredible?
A poore eight-pennie Souldier? Shee that lately   45

23 see!] ~∧ ‖ 30 Your] *Parrott*; Our ‖ 36 me,] ~∧ ‖ 43 mindes] *Parrott*; windes ‖

Was at such height of interiection,
Stoope now to such a base coniunction?
By heauen I wonder now I see't in act,
My braine could euer dreame of such a thought.
And yet, tis true: Rare, pereles, is't not *Lycus*?   50
   Lyc. I know not what it is; Nor what to say.
   Thar. O had I held out (villaine that I was,)
My blessed confidence but one minute longer,
I should have beene eternis'd. Gods my fortune, /
What an vnspeakable sweet sight it is?   [I2ᵛ] 55
O eies Ile sacrifice to your deare sense.
And consecrate a Phane to Confidence.
   Lyc. But this you must at no hand tell your brother.
Twill make him mad: For he that was before
So scurg'd but only with bare iealousie,   60
What would he be, if he should come to know it?
   Thar. He would be lesse mad: for your only way
To cleare his iealousie, is to let him know it.
When knowledge comes suspicion vanishes.
The Sunne-beames breaking forth swallow the mists.   65
But as for you Sir Gallant; howsoeuer
Your banquet seemes sweet in your lycorous pallat,
It shall be sure to turne gall in your maw.
Thy hand a little *Lycus* here without.
   Lyc. To what?
   Thar.   No bootie serue you sir Soldado   70
But my poore sister? Come, lend me thy shoulder,
Ile climb the crosse; it will be such a cooler
To my Venerean Gentlemans hot liuer,
When he shall finde one of his crucified
Bodies stolne downe, and he to be forthwith   75
Made fast in place thereof, for the signe
Of the lost Sentinell. Come glorifie
Firme Confidence in great Inconstancie.
And this beleeue (for all prou'd knowledge sweares)
He that beleeues in errour, neuer errs.   *Exeunt.*

[V.ii]

The Tomb opens, Lysander, Cynthia, Ero.

   Lys. Tis late; I must away.
   Cynth.   Not yet sweet loue.

---

60 iealousie,] ∼. ‖ **74-76** When … signe] *Parrott*; When … bodies / Stolne … fast / In … signe ‖

Lys. Tempt not my stay, tis dangerous. The law is strict, and not to bee dispenst with. If any Sentinell be too late in's watch, or that by his neglect one of the crucified bodies should be stollen from the crosse, his life buyes it.	5

Cynth. A little stay will not endanger them.
The daies proclaimer has not yet giuen warning.
The Cock yet has not beate his third alarme. /

Lys. What? shall we euer dwell here amongst	[13]
Th'Antipodes? Shall I not enioy	10
The honour of my fortune in publique?
Sit in *Lysanders* chaire? Raigne in his wealth?

Cynth. Thou shalt, thou shalt; though my loue to thee
Hath prou'd thus sodaine and for hast lept ouer
The complement of wooing,	15
Yet only for the worlds opinion —

Lys.					Marke that againe.

Cynth. I must maintaine a forme in parting hence.

Lys. Out vpon't, Opinion the blind Goddesse of Fooles, Foe to the vertuous; and only friend to vndeseruing persons, contemne it. Thou know'st thou hast done vertuously; thou hast strangly sorrow'd for thy	20 husband, follow'd him to death; further thou could'st not; thou hast buried thy selfe quick, [*Aside.*] (O that 'twere true) — spent more teares ouer his carcase, then would serue a whole Citie of saddest widdowes in a plague time; besides sighings, and swownings, not to be credited.	25

Cynth. True; but those complements might haue their time for fashion sake.

Lys. Right, Opinion and Fashion. Sfoot what call you time? t'hast wept these foure whole daies.

Ero. Nay berladie almost fiue.	30

Lys. Looke you there; nere vpon fiue whole daies.

Cynth. Well goe and see; Returne, weele goe home.

					[*Exeunt Cynthia and Ero into the tomb.*]

Lys. Hell be thy home, Huge Monsters damne yee, and your whole creation! O yee Gods; in the height of her mourning in a Tomb, within sight of so many deaths! her husbands beleeu'd bodie in her eie.	35 He dead, a few daies before; this mirrour of Nuptiall chastitie; this Votresse of widdow-constancie: to change her faith; exchange kisses, embraces, with a stranger; and but my shame with-stood, to giue the vtmost earnest of her loue, to an eight-pennie Sentinell: in effect, to prostitute her selfe vpon her husbands Coffin! Lust, impietie, hell,	40 womanhood it selfe, adde if you can one step to this.

9-12 What? ... wealth?] *as prose* (th' ... the ... sit) ‖ 15-16 The ... opinion—] *Dodsley*; *one line* ‖ 16 opinion—] ∼. ‖ 21-22 not; ... quick,] ∼, ... ∼. ‖ 22 SD *Aside.*] *Parrott* | true) —] ∼) ∧ ‖ 32 SD *Exeunt ... tomb.*] *Parrott* ‖

Enter Captaine with two or three Souldiers.

Cap. One of the crucified bodies taken downe!

Lys. [*Aside.*] Enough.   (*slincks away.*)

Cap. And the Sentinell not to be heard off?

1. No sir. /   45

Cap. Make out; hast, search about for him; does none of you know   [13ᵛ]
him? nor his name?

2. Hee's but a stranger here of some foure daies standing; and we
neuer set eie on him, but at setting the watch.

Cap. For whom serues he? you looke well to your watch masters.   50

1. For *Seigneur Stratio,* and whence he is, tis ignorant to vs; we are
not correspondent for any, but our owne places.

Cap. Y'are eloquent. Abroad I say, let me haue him.   *Exeunt the souldiers.*
This negligence will by the Gouernour be wholly cast on me, he hereby
will suggest to the Viceroy, that the Citie guards are very carelessly   55
attended.
He loves mee not I know; because of late
I knew him but of meane condition;
But now by fortunes iniudicious hand,
Guided by bribing Courtiers, hee is rais'd   60
To this high seate of honour. Nor blushes he,
To see him selfe aduanc't ouer the heads
Of ten times higher worths; but takes it all
Forsooth, to his merits; and lookes (as all
Vpstarts doe) for most huge obseruance.   65
Well, my minde must stoope to his high place,
And learne within it selfe to seuer him
From that, and to adore Authoritie
The Goddesse, how euer borne by an vnworthie beast;
And let the Beasts dull apprehension take   70
The honour done to *Isis,* done to himselfe.
I must sit fast, and bee sure to give
No hold to these fault-hunting enemies.   *Exit.*

[V.iii]

Tomb opens, and Lysander within lies along, Cynthia and Ero.

Lys. Pray thee disturbe me not; put out the lights.

Ero. Faith Ile take a nap againe.

---

43 SD *Aside.*] *Parrott* ‖ **53** SD *Exeunt . . . souldiers.*] *Parrott subs.; Exeunt.* ‖ **55** carelessly] *Dodsley;*
caresly ‖ **57-73** He . . . enemies.] *as prose* (but . . . guided . . . to . . . to . . . of . . . forsooth
. . . vpstarts . . . and . . . from . . . the . . . and . . . the . . . no) ‖ V.iii] *Parrott as V.ii* ‖

Cynth. Thou shalt not rest before I be resolu'd
What happy winde hath driven thee back to harbour?
Was it my loue?
    Lys.   No.
    Cynth.   Yet say so (sweet)   5
That with the thought thereof I may enioy
All that I wish in earth.
    Lys.   I am sought for.
A crucified body is stolne while I
Loiter'd here; and I must die for't.
    Cynth.   Die?
All the Gods forbid; O this affright   10
Torments me ten parts more then the sad losse
Of my deare husband.
    Lys. [*Aside.*] (Damnation) — I beleeue thee. /
    Cynth. Yet heare a womans wit,   [14]
Take counsaile of Necessitie and it.   15
I haue a bodie here which once I lou'd
And honour'd aboue all; but that time's past.
    Lys. [*Aside.*] It is, reuenge it heauen.
    Cynth. That shall supply at so extrem a need
The vacant Gibbet.
    Lys.   Cancro! What? thy husbands bodie?   20
    Cynth. What hurt is't, being dead it saue the liuing?
    Lys. O heart hold in, check thy rebellious motion.
    Cynth. Vexe not thy selfe deare loue, nor vse delay.
Tempt not this danger, set thy handes to worke.
    Lys. I can not doo't; my heart will not permit   25
My handes to execute a second murther.
The truth is I am he that slew thy husband.
    Cynth. The Gods forbid.
    Lys. It was this hand that bath'd my reeking sword
In his life bloud, while he cried out for mercie,   30
But I remorselesse, panch't him, cut his throat,
He with his last breath crying, *Cynthia.*
    Cynth. O thou hast told me newes that cleaues my heart,
Would I had never seene thee, or heard sooner
This bloudie storie; yet see, note my truth;   35
Yet I must loue thee.
    Lys.   Out vpon thee Monster.
Goe, tell the Gouernour; Let me be brought

5-12 Yet . . . husband.] *as prose* (that . . . all . . . loiter'd . . . torments . . . of) ‖ 9 for't.] ∼,
‖ 13 SD *Aside.*] *Dodsley* | Damnation) —] ∼) ∧ ‖ 18 SD *Aside.*] *Parrott* ‖ 19-20 That . . . Gibbet.]
Reed; one line (the) ‖ 20 Cancro!] *Dodsley;* Cancro. ‖ 35 truth;] ∼∧ ‖ 36 thee] *Reed;* the ‖

To die for that most famous villanie;
Not for this miching base transgression
Of [truant] negligence.
    Cynth.   I can not doo't.   40
Loue must salue any murther: Ile be iudge
Of thee deare love, and these shall be thy paines
In steede of yron, to suffer these soft chaines.
    Lys. O I am infinitely oblig'd.
    Cynth. Arise I say, thou sauer of my life.   45
Doe not with vaine-affrighting conscience
Betray a life, that is not thine but mine:
Rise and preserue it.
    Lys.   Ha? thy husbands bodie?
Hang't vp you say, in steede of that that's stolne; /
Yet I his murtherer, is that your meaning?   [I4ᵛ] 50
    Cynth. It is my Loue.
    Lys.   Thy loue amazes me,
The point is yet how we shall get it thither,
Ha? Tie a halter about's necke, and dragge him to the Gallowes:
Shall I my loue?
    Cynth.   So you may doe indeede,
Or if your owne strength will not serue, wee'le aide   55
Our handes to yours, and beare him to the place.
For heauens loue come, the night goes off apace.
    Lys. [*Aside.*] All the infernall plagues dwell in thy soule —
Ile fetch a crow of yron to breake the coffin.
    Cynth. Doe loue, be speedie.
    Lys. [*Aside.*]   As I wish thy damnation.   *Shut the Tomb.*
O I could teare my selfe into Atomes; off with this Antick, the shirt
that *Hercules* wore for his wife, was not more banefull. Is't possible
there should be such a latitude in the Sphere of this sexe, to entertaine
such an extention of mischiefe, and not turne Deuill? What is a
woman? what are the worst when the best are so past naming? As   65
men like this, let them trie their wiues againe. Put women to the test;
discouer them; paint them, paint them ten parts more then they doe
themselues, rather then looke on them as they are; Their wits are but
painted that dislike their painting.
Thou foolish thirster after idle secrets,   70
And ills abrode; looke home, and store and choke thee;
There sticks an Achelous horne of ill,
Copie enough;

40 truant] *Dodsley*; tenant ‖ **53-54** Ha? . . . loue?] *Parrott; as prose* (shall) ‖ **58** SD *Aside.*] *Dodsley* ǀ
soule—] ∼; ‖ **60** SD *Aside.*] *Parrott* ‖ **64** Deuill?] ∼. ‖ **66** this,] ∼∧ ‖ **70-71** Thou . . . thee;]
Shepherd; as prose ‖ **72-73** There . . . enough;] *Parrott; as prose* (*See Textual Note*) ‖ **72** Achelous]
Dodsley subs.; Achelons ǀ ill] *Parrott* (*Deighton conj.*); all ‖ **73** enough;] ∼. ‖

As much as Alizon of streames receiues,
Or loftie Ida showes of shadie leaues.   75

Enter Tharsalio.

Who's that?

Thar. I wonder *Lycus* failes me. Nor can I heare whats become of
him. Hee would not certaine ride to Dipolis to call my brother back,
without my knowledge.

Lys. [*Aside.*] My brothers voice; what makes he here abouts so   80
vntimely? Ile slip him.   *Exiturus.*

Thar. Who goes there?

Lys. A friend.

Thar. Deare friend, lets know you. A friend least look't for but
most welcome, and with many a long looke expected here. What sir   85
vnbooted? haue you beene long arriu'd?

Lys. Not long, some two houres before night. /

Thar. Well brother, y'haue the most rare, admirable, vnmatchable   [K1]
wife, that euer suffer'd for the sinne of a husband. I cannot blame
your confidence indeede now: 'tis built on such infallible ground;   90
Lycus I thinke be gone to call you to the rescue of her life; why shee!
O incomprehensible!

Lys. I haue heard all related since my arriuall, weele meet to
morrow.

Thar. What hast brother? But was it related with what vntollerable   95
paines, I and my Mistris, her other friends, Matrones and Magistrates,
labour'd her diuersion from that course?

Lys. Yes, yes.

Thar. What streame of teares she powr'd out; what tresses of her
haire she tore! and offer'd on your suppos'd herse!   100

Lys. I have heard all.

Thar. But aboue all; how since that time, her eies neuer harbour'd
winck of slumber, these six daies; no nor tasted the least dramme of
any sustenance.

Lys. How, is that assurd?   105

Thar. Not a scruple.

Lys. Are you sure there came no Souldier to her nor brought her
victualls?

Thar. Souldier? what Souldier?

Lys. Why some Souldier of the watch, that attends the executed   110
bodies: well brother I am in hast; to morrow shall supply this nights
defect of conference; Adieu.   *Exit. Lys.*

75 Ida] *Dodsley*; Ilea ‖ 80 SD *Aside.*] *Parrott* ‖ 105 How,] ∼∧ ‖

Thar. A Souldier? of the watch? bring her victualls? Goe to brother I haue you in the winde; hee's vnharnest of all his trauailing accoutrements. I came directly from's house, no word of him there;   115 he knowes the whole relation; hee's passionate: All collections speake he was the Souldier. What should be the riddle of this? that he is stolne hether into a Souldiers disguise? he should haue staid at Dipolis to receiue news from vs. Whether he suspected our relation; or had not patience to expect it, or whether that furious, frantique capricious   120 Devill iealousie hath tost him hether on his hornes, I can not coniecture. But the case is cleare, hee's the Souldier. Sister, looke to your fame, your chastetie's vncouer'd. Are they here still? here beleeue it both most wofully weeping ouer the bottle.   *He knocks.*

Ero. Who's there?   125

Thar. Tharsalio, open.

Ero. Alas Sir, tis no boote to vexe your sister, and your selfe, she is desperate, and will not heare perswasion, she's very weak. /

Thar. [*Aside.*] Here's a true-bred chamber-maid. — Alas, I am   [K1ᵛ] sorrie for't; I haue brought her meat and Candian wine to strengthen   130 her.

Ero. O the very naming an't, will driue her into a swowne; good Sir forbeare.

Thar. Yet open sweet, that I may blesse mine eies with sight of her faire shrine; and of thy sweetest selfe (her famous Pandresse) open I   135 say. Sister? you heare me well, paint not your Tomb without; wee know too well what rotten carcases are lodg'd within; open I say.

      Ero opens, and hee sees her head layd on the coffin, &c.

Sister I haue brought you tidings to wake you out of this sleeping mummerie.

Ero. Alas shee's faint, and speech is painefull to her.   140

Thar. Well said frubber, was there no Souldier here lately?

Ero. A Souldier? when?

Thar. This night, last night, tother night; and I know not how many nights and daies.

Cynth. Whose there?   145

Ero. Your brother Mistris, that asks if there were not a souldier here.

Cynth. Here was no souldier.

Ero. Yes Mistris I thinke here was such a one though you tooke no heede of him.   150

Thar. Goe to sister; did not you ioyne kisses, embraces, and plight indeede the utmost pledge of Nuptiall love with him? Deni't, deni't;

---

125 there?] ∼. ‖ **129** SD *Aside.*] | maid. —] ∼.∧ ‖ **137** SD *Ero . . . &c.*] roman, *as part of Tharsalio's speech* ‖ **152** indeede the] *Dodsley*; indeede with him, the ‖

but first heare me a short storie. The Souldier was your disguis'd husband, dispute it not. That you see yonder, is but a shadow, an emptie
chest containing nothing but aire. Stand not to gaze at it, tis true.   155
This was a proiect of his owne contriving to put your loialtie and constant vowes to the test; y'are warned, be arm'd.   *Exit.*

    Ero. O fie a these perils.

    Cynth. O *Ero*! we are vndone.

    Ero. Nay, you'd nere be warn'd; I ever wisht you to withstand the   160
push of that Souldiers pike, and not enter him too deep into your
bosom, but to keep sacred your widowes vowes made to *Lysander*.

    Cynth. Thou did'st, thou did'st.

    Ero. Now you may see th'euent. Well our safetie lies in our speed:
heele doe vs mischiefe, if we preuent not his comming. Lets to your   165
Mothers: and there cal out your mightiest friends to guard you from
his furie. Let them begin the quarrell with him for practising this villanie on your sexe to intrappe your frailties. /

    Cynth. Nay I resolue to sit out one brunt more;   [K2]
To trie to what aime heele enforce his proiect: 170
Were he some other man, vnknowne to me,
His violence might awe me; but knowing him
As I doe, I feare him not. Do thou
But second me, thy strength and mine shall master
His best force, if he should proue outragious.   175
Despaire they say makes cowardes turne couragious.
Shut up the Tomb.   *Shut the Tomb.*

[V.iv]

Enter one of the Souldiers sent out before to seeke the
Sentinell.

    1. All paines are lost in hunting out this Souldier; his fear (adding
wings to his heeles) out-goes vs as farre as the fresh Hare the tir'd
hounds. Who goes there?

    Enter 2. Souldier another way.

    2. A friend.

    1. O, your success and mine touching this Sentinell, tells, I suppose,   5
one tale; hee's farre enough I vndertake by this time.

    2. I blame him not: the law's seuere (though iust and can not be
dispenc'd.)

    1. Why should the lawes of Paphos, with more rigour, then other

---

169-71 Nay, . . . me,] *Parrott*; *as prose* (to . . . were . . . his) ‖ **172-76** His . . . couragious.] *as*
prose (his . . . as . . . but . . . his) ‖ V.iv] *Parrott as V.iii* ‖

Citie lawes, pursue offenders? that not appeas'd with their liues forfait,   10
exact a justice of them after death? And if a Souldier in his watch forsooth lose one of the dead bodies, he must die for't: It seems the State
needed no souldiers when that was made a law.

2. So we may chide the fire for burning vs; or say the Bee's not good
because she stings; Tis not the body the law respects, but the souldiers   15
neglect; when the watch (the guard and safetie of the Citie) is left
abandon'd to all hazards. But let him goe; and tell me if your newes
sort with mine, for *Lycus*; apprehended they say, about *Lysanders*
murther.

1. Tis true; hee's at the Captaines lodge vnder guard, and tis my   20
charge in the morning to vnclose the leaden coffin, and discouer the
bodie; The Captaine will assay an old conclusion often approu'd; that
at the murtherers sight the bloud reuiues againe, and boiles a fresh;
and euery wound has a condemning voice to crie out guiltie gainst the
murtherer.   25

2. O world, if this be true; his dearest friend, his bed companion,
whom of all his friends he cull'd out for his bosome!

1. Tush man, in this topsie turuy world, friendship and bosom kindnes, are but made couers for mischief, meanes to compasse il. Near-
allied trust, is but a bridge for treson. The presumptions / crie loud [K2ᵛ] 30
against him; his answeres found disionted; crosse-legd tripping vp one
another. He names a Town whether he brought *Lysander* murther'd
by Mountainers; thats false, some of the dwellers haue been here, and
all disclaim it. Besides, the wounds he bears in show, are such as shrews
closely giue their husbands, that neuer bleede, and finde to be coun-   35
terfait.

2. O that iade falshood is neuer sound of all;
But halts of one legge still.
Truth's pace is all vpright; sound euery where,
And like a die, sets euer on a square.   40
And how is *Lycus* his bearing in this condition?

1. Faith (as the manner of such desperate offenders is till it come to
the point) carelesse, and confident, laughing at all that seeme to pittie
him. But leaue it to th'euent. Night, fellow Souldier, youle not meet
me in the morning at the Tomb, and lend me your hand to the vn-   45
rigging of *Lysanders* herse?

2. I care not if I do, to view heauens power in this unbottomd seller.
Bloud, though it sleep a time, yet neuer dies.
The Gods on murtherers fixe reuengefull eies.   *Exeunt.*

31 crosse-legd] crosse-/legd ‖ 33 Mountainers;] ∼, ‖ 37-38 O . . . still.] *Shepherd; as prose*
(but) ‖ 39 Truth's] *Parrott (Collier conj.)*; Truth ‖ 39-40 Truth's . . . square.] *Reed; as prose* ‖
44 Night,] ∼∧ ‖ 46 herse?] ∼. ‖

[V.v]

Lysander solus with a crow of yron, and a halter which he laies
downe, and puts on his disguise againe.

Come my borrow'd disguise, let me once more
Be reconcild to thee, my trustiest friend;
Thou that in truest shape hast let me see
That which my truer selfe hath hid from me,
Helpe me to take reuenge on a disguise,   5
Ten times more false and counterfait then thou.
Thou, false in show, hast been most true to me;
The seeming true hath prou'd most false in her.
Assist me to behold this act of lust,
Note what a Scene of strange impietie.   10
Her husbands murtherd corse! O more then horror!
Ile not beleeue't vntri'd; If shee but lift
A hand to act it; by the fates her braines flie out,
Since shee has madded me; let her beware my hornes,
For though by goring her, no hope be showne   15
To cure my selfe, yet Ile not bleede alone.   *He knocks.*
   Ero. Who knocks?
   Lys. The souldier; open.   *She opens and he enters.*
See sweet, here art the engines that must doo't, /
Which with much feare of my discouerie   [K3] 20
I have at last procur'd.
Shall we about this worke? I feare the morne
Will ouer-take's; my stay hath been prolong'd
With hunting obscure nookes for these emploiments,
The night prepares a way; come, art resolu'd?   25
   Cynth. I, you shall finde me constant.
   Lys. I, so I haue, most prodigiously constant,
Here's a rare halter to hugge him with.
   Ero. Better you and I ioyne our handes and beare him thether, you
take his head.   30
   Cynth. I, for that was alwaies heauier then's whole bodie besides.
   Lys. [*Aside.*] You can tell best that loded it.
   Ero. Ile be at the feet; I am able to beare against you I warrant you.
   Lys. Hast thou prepar'd weake nature to digest
A sight so much distastfull; hast ser'd thy heart   35
T'bleede not at the bloudie spectacle?

8 true] ∼; | most false in] more false then (*See Textual Note*) ‖ **10** what] with ‖ **18** SD *enters.*]
∼∧ ‖ **25** a way] *Reed*; away | resolu'd?] ∼. ‖ **32** SD *Aside.*] *Parrott* ‖ **36** T'] I ‖

Hast arm'd thy fearefull eies against th'affront
Of such a direfull obiect? Thy murther'd husband
Ghastly staring on thee; his wounds gaping
To affright thee; his bodie soild with gore? fore heaven   40
My heart shruggs at it.
    Cynth.   So does not mine,
Loue's resolute; and stands not to consult
With pettie terrour; but in full carrier
Runnes blind-fold through an Armie of misdoubts,
And interposing feares; perhaps Ile weepe   45
Or so, make a forc't face and laugh againe.
    Lys. O most valiant loue! I was thinking
With my selfe as I came; how if this brake
To light; his bodie knowne; (as many notes
Might make it) would it not fixe vpon thy fame,   50
An vnremoued Brand of shame and hate;
They that in former times ador'd thy vertue;
Would they not abhorre thy lothest memorie?
    Cynth. All this I know. But yet my loue to thee /
Swallowes all this; or whatsoeuer doubts   [K3ᵛ] 55
Can come against it.
Shame's but a feather ballanc't with thy loue.
    Lys. Neither feare nor shame? you are steele toth'proofe
[*Aside.*] (But I shall yron you) : — Come then lets to worke.
Alas poore Corps how many martyrdomes   60
Must thou endure? mangl'd by me a villaine,
And now expos'd to foule shame of the Gibbet?
Fore pietie, there is somewhat in me striues
Against the deede, my very arme relents
To strike a stroke so inhumane,   65
To wound a hallow'd herse? suppose twere mine,
Would not my Ghost start vp and flie upon thee?
    Cynth. No, Ide mall it down againe with this.

              She snatches up the crow.

Lys. How now?   *He catches at her throat.*
    Cynth. Nay, then Ile assay my strength; a Souldier and afraid of a   70
dead man? A soft-roed milk-sop? come Ile doot my selfe.
    Lys. And I looke on? giue me the yron.
    Cynth. No, Ile not lose the glorie ant. This hand, *&c.*

38-41 Of ... it.] Of ... obiect? / Thy ... thee; / His ... with / Gore? ... it *Q* (ghastly ...
to ... my) ‖ **47-53** O ... memorie?] O ... loue! / I ... this / Brake ... knowne; / (As ...
fixe / Vpon ... Brand / Of ... times / Ador'd ... abhorre / Thy ... memorie? *Q* (with
... to ... might ... an ... They ... would) ‖ **54** All ... thee] *Reed*; All ... know. / But
... thee ‖ **58-59** Neither ... worke.] *Dodsley*; Neither ... toth' / Proofe ... worke. ‖ **59** SD
Aside.] *Parrott* | you): —] ∼): ∧ ‖ **63** Fore] ∼, ‖ **71** soft-roed] *Collier*; soft-r'ode ‖ **73** This
hand, *&c.*] *See Textual Note* ‖

Lys. Pray thee sweet, let it not bee said the sauage act was thine; deliuer me the engine.   75

    Cynth. Content your selfe, tis in a fitter hand.

    Lys. Wilt thou first? are not thou the most —

    Cynth. Ill-destin'd wife of a transform'd monster;
Who to assure him selfe of what he knew,
Hath lost the shape of man.

    Lys.   Ha? crosse-capers?   80

    Cynth. Poore Souldiers case; doe not we know you Sir?
But I have giuen thee what thou cam'st to seeke.
Goe *Satyre,* runne affrighted with the noise
Of that harsh sounding horne thy selfe hast blowne,
Farewell; I leave thee there my Husbands Corps,   85
Make much of that.   *Exit. cum Er.*

    Lys.   What have I done?
O let me lie and grieue, and speake no more.

    Enter Captaine, Lycus with a guard of three or foure
                        Souldiers.

    Cap. Bring him away; you must haue patience Sir: If you can say
ought to quit you of those presumptions / that lie heauie on you, you   [K4]
shall be heard. If not, tis not your braues, nor your affecting lookes   90
can carrie it. We must acquite our duties.

    Lyc. Y'are Captaine ath' watch Sir.

    Cap. You take me right.

    Lyc. So were you best doe mee; see your presumptions bee strong;
or be assured that shall proue a deare presumption, to brand me with   95
the murther of my friend. But you haue beene suborn'd by some close
villaine to defame me.

    Cap. Twill not be so put off friend *Lycus,* I could wish your soule
as free from taint of this foule fact; as mine from any such vnworthy
practise.   100

    Lyc. Conduct mee to the Governour him selfe; to confront before
him your shallow accusations.

    Cap. First Sir, Ile beare you to *Lysanders* Tombe, to confront the
murther'd body; and see what evidence the wounds will yeeld against
you.   105

    Lyc. Y'are wise Captaine. But if the bodie should chance not to
speake; If the wounds should bee tongue-tied Captaine; where's then

---

77 most—] ∼. ‖ **86-87** What . . . more.] *Parrott; as prose* ‖ **87** SD *Enter Captaine*] *Parrott; Captaine*
‖ **91** We . . . duties.] *on separate line* ‖

your euidence Captaine? will you not be laught at for an officious
Captaine?

Cap. Y'are gallant Sir.　　　　　　　　　　　　　　　　　　110

Lyc. Your Captainship commands my seruice no further.

Cap. Well Sir, perhaps I may, if this conclusion take not; weele
trie what operation lies in torture, to pull confession from you.

Lyc. Say you so Captaine? but hearke you Captaine, Might it not
concurre with the qualitie of your office, ere this matter grow to the　　115
height of a more threatning danger; to winck a little at a by slip, or so?

Cap. How's that?

Lyc. To send a man abroad vnder guard of one of your silliest
shack-rags; that he may beate the knaue, and run's way. I meane this
on good termes Captaine; Ile be thankfull.　　　　　　　　　　120

Cap. Ile thinke ont hereafter. Meane time I haue other emploiment
for you.

Lyc. Your place is worthily replenisht Captaine. My dutie Sir;
Hearke Captaine, there's a mutinie in your Armie; Ile go raise the
Gouernour.　　　　　　　　　　　　　　　　　　*Exiturus.* /

Cap. No hast Sir; heele soone be here without your summons.　　[K4ᵛ]

　　　　Souldiers thrust vp Lysander from the Tomb.

1. Bring forth the Knight ath' Tomb; haue we met with you Sir?

Lys. Pray thee souldier vse thine office with better temper.

2. Come convay him to the Lord Gouernour.

[*Lys.*] First afore the Captaine Sir. [*Aside.*] Haue the heauens　　130
Nought else to doe, but to stand still, and turne
All their malignant aspects vpon one man?

2. Captaine here's the Sentinell wee sought for; hee's some new prest
Souldier, for none of us know him.

Cap. Where found you him?　　　　　　　　　　　　　　135

1. My truant was mich't Sir into a blind corner of the Tomb.

Cap. Well said, guard him safe, but for the Corps?

1. For the Corps Sir? bare misprision, there's no bodie, nothing. A
meere blandation; a *deceptio visus.* Vnlesse this souldier for hunger
haue eate vp *Lysanders* bodie.　　　　　　　　　　　　　140

Lyc. Why, I could haue told you this before Captaine; the body was
borne away peece-meale by deuout Ladies of *Venus* order, for the man
died one of *Venus* Martyrs. And yet I heard since 'twas seene whole
ath' other side the downes vppon a Colestafe betwixt two huntsmen,
to feede their dogges withall. Which was a miracle Captaine.　　145

Cap. Mischiefe in this act hath a deepe bottom; and requires more
time to sound it. But you Sir, it seemes, are a Souldier of the newest

---

129 Gouernour.] ~, ‖ **130-32** Haue . . . man?] Haue . . . malignant *as prose* / Aspects . . .
man? (nought . . . all) ‖ **130** *Lys.*] *Shepherd* | SD *Aside.*] *Parrott* ‖ **137** but] bur | Corps?] ~. ‖
143 Martyrs.] *Dodsley*; Martys ‖

stamp. Know you what tis to forsake your stand? There's one of the
bodies in your charge stolne away; how answere you that? See here
comes the Gouernour. 150

> *Enter a Guard bare after the Gouernour: Tharsalio, Argus,*
> *Clinias, before Eudora, Cynthia, Laodice, Sthenio,*
> *Ianthe, Ero, &c.*

Guard. Stand aside there.

Cap. [*Aside.*] Roome for a strange Gouernour. The perfect draught
of a most brainelesse, imperious vpstart. O desert! where wert thou,
when this woodden dagger was guilded over with the Title of
Gouernour? 155

Guard. Peace Masters; heare my Lord.

Thar. [*Aside.*] All wisedome be silent; Now speakes Authoritie.

Gouer. I am come in person to discharge Iustice. /

Thar. [*Aside.*] Of his office. [L1]

Gouer. The cause you shall know hereafter; and it is this. A villaine, 160
whose very sight I abhorre; where is he? Let mee see him.

Cap. Is't *Lycus* you meane my Lord?

Gouer. Goe to sirrha y'are too malipert; I have heard of your
Sentinells escape; looke too't.

Cap. My Lord, this is the Sentinell you speake of. 165

Gouer. How now Sir? what time a day ist?

Arg. I can not shew you precisely, ant please your Honour.

Gouer. What? shall we have replications? Reioinders?

Thar. [*Aside.*] Such a creature, [a] Foole is, when hee bestrides the
back of Authoritie. 170

Gouer. Sirrha, stand you forth. It is supposed thou hast committed
a most inconuenient murther upon the body of *Lysander.*

Lyc. My good Lord, I have not.

Gouer. Peace varlet; dost chop with me? I say it is imagined thou
hast murther'd *Lysander.* How it will be prou'd I know not. Thou 175
shalt therefore presently bee had to execution, as justice in such cases
requireth. Souldiers take him away: bring forth the Sentinell.

Lyc. Your Lordship will first let my defence be heard.

Gouer. Sirrha; Ile no fending nor prouing. For my part I am satisfied, it is so: thats enough for thee. I had euer a Sympathy in my 180
minde against him. Let him be had away.

Thar. [*Aside.*] A most excellent apprehension. Hee's able yee see
to iudge of a cause at first sight, and heare but two parties. Here's a
second *Solon.*

---

152 SD *Aside.*] *Collier* ‖ 157 SD *Aside.*] ‖ 159 SD *Aside.*] ‖ 169 SD *Aside.*] *Parrott* | a Foole]
Parrott (*Collier conj.*); Foole ‖ 181 Let . . . away.] *separate line* ‖ 182 SD *Aside.*] *Parrott* ‖ 183
heare but two parties] *stet* (*See Textual Note*) ‖

Eud. Heare him my Lord; presumptions oftentimes, 185
(Though likely grounded) reach not to the truth.
And truth is oft abus'd by likelyhood.
Let him be heard my Lord.

Gouer. Madam, content your selfe. I will doe iustice; I will not
heare him. Your late Lord was my Honourable Predecessour: But 190
your Ladiship must pardon me. In matters of iustice I am blinde. /

Thar. [*Aside.*] Thats true. [L1ᵛ]

Gouer. I know no persons. If a Court fauorite write to mee in a
case of iustice; I will pocket his letter, and proceede. If a Suiter in
a case of iustice thrusts a bribe into my hand, I will pocket his bribe, 195
and proceede. Therefore Madam, set your heart at rest: I am seated
in the Throne of iustice; and I will doe iustice; I will not heare him.

Eud. Not heare him my Lord?

Gouer. No my Ladie: and moreover put you in mind, in whose
presence you stand; if you Parrat to me long; goe to. 200

Thar. [*Aside.*] Nay the Vice must snap his Authoritie at all he
meetes, how shalt else be knowne what part he plaies?

Gouer. Your husband was a Noble Gentleman, but alas hee came
short, hee was no Statesman. Hee has left a foule Citie behinde him.

Thar. [*Aside.*] I, and I can tell you twill trouble his Lordship and 205
all his Honorable assistants of Scauingers to sweepe it cleane.

Gouer. It's full of vices, and great ones too.

Thar. [*Aside.*] And thou none of the meanest.

Gouer. But Ile turne all topsie turuie; and set vp a new discipline
amongst you. Ile cut of all perisht members. 210

Thar. [*Aside.*] Thats the Surgeons office.

Gouer. Cast out these rotten stinking carcases for infecting the
whole Citie.

Arg. Rotten they may be, but their wenches vse to pepper them;
and their Surgeons to perboile them; and that preserues them from 215
stinking, ant please your Honour.

Gouer. Peace Sirrha, peace; and yet tis well said too. A good pregnant fellow yfaith. But to proceede. I will spew drunkennesse out
ath' Citie.

Thar. [*Aside.*] In to th' Countrie. 220

Gouer. Shifters shall cheate and sterue; And no man shall doe good
but where there is no neede. Braggarts shall live at the head a' the
tumult that hant Tauernes. Asses shall beare good qualities, and wise
men shall vse them. I will whip lecherie out ath' Citie, there shall be

---

192 SD *Aside.*] *Parrott* ‖ **201** SD *Aside.*] *Parrott* ‖ **203** alas] Alas ‖ **205** SD *Aside.*] *Parrott* ‖ **208**
SD *Aside.*] *Parrott* ‖ **211** SD *Aside.*] *Parrott* ‖ **220** SD *Aside.*] *Parrott* ‖ **222** head a'] head; and
(*See Textual Note*) ‖

no more Cuckolds. They that heretofore were errand Cornutos, shall 225
now bee honest shop-keepers, and iustice shall take place. I will hunt
ielousie / out of my Dominion.   [L2]

   Thar. [*Aside to Lysander.*] Dee heare Brother?

   Gouer. It shall be the only note of loue to the husband, to loue the
wife: And none shall be more kindly welcome to him then he that 230
cuckolds him.

   Thar. [*Aside.*] Beleeue it a wholsome reformation.

   Gouer. Ile haue no more Beggers. Fooles shall haue wealth, and
the learned shall liue by their wits. Ile haue no more Banckrouts.
They that owe money shall pay it at their best leisure: And the rest 235
shall make a vertue of imprisonment; and their wives shall helpe to
pay their debts. Ile haue all yong widdowes spaded for marrying
againe. For the old and wither'd, they shall be confiscate to vnthriftie
Gallants, and decai'd Knights. If they bee poore they shall bee burnt
to make Sope ashes, or giuen to Surgeons Hall, to bee stampt to salue 240
for the French mesells. To conclude, I will Cart pride out ath' Towne.

   Arg. Ant please your Honour Pride ant be nere so beggarly will
looke for a Coch.

   Gouer. Well said a mine Honour. A good significant fellow yfaith:
What is he? he talkes much; does he follow your Ladiship? 245

   Arg. No ant please your Honour, I goe before her.

   Gouer. A good vndertaking presence; A well-promising forehead,
your Gentleman Vsher Madam?

   Eud. Yours if you please my Lord.

   Gouer. Borne ith' Citie? 250

   Arg. I ant please your Honour, but begot ith' Court.

   Gouer. Tressellegg'd?

   Arg. I, ant please your Honour.

   Gouer. The better, it beares a bredth; makes roome a both sides.
Might I not see his pace? 255

   Arg. Yes ant please your Honour.   *Argus stalkes.*

   Gouer. Tis well, tis very well. Giue me thy hand: Madame I will
accept this propertie at your hand, and wil weare it thred-bare for
your sake. Fall in there, sirrha. And for the matter of *Lycus* Madam,
I must tell you, you are shallow: there's a State point in't! hearke 260
you: The Viceroy has giuen him, and / wee must vphold correspon- [L2ᵛ]
dence. Hee must walke; say one man goes wrongfully out ath' world,
there are hundreds to one come wrongfully into th' world.

   Eud. Your Lordship will give me but a word in priuate.

---

228 SD *Aside to Lysander.*] *Parrott subs.* | Dee] Doe ‖ **232** SD *Aside.*] *Parrott* ‖ **256** SD *Argus stalkes.*] *Dodsley; on preceding line* ‖ **258** thred-bare] thred-/bare ‖ **260** in't] ∼? ‖

Thar. Come brother; we know you well: what meanes this habite?   265
why staid you not at Dipolis as you resolu'd, to take advertisement
from vs of your wiues bearing?

Lys. O brother, this iealous phrensie has borne mee headlong to
ruine.

Thar. Go to, be comforted; vncase your selfe; and discharge your   270
friend.

Gouer. Is that *Lysander* say you? And is all his storie true? Berladie
Madam this iealousie will cost him deare: he undertooke the person
of a Souldier; and as a Souldier must haue iustice. Madam, his Altitude in this case can not dispence. *Lycus,* this Souldier hath acquited   275
you.

Thar. And that acquitall Ile for him requite; the body lost is by this
time restor'd to his place.

Soul. It is my Lord.

Thar. These are State points, in which your Lordships time   280
Has not yet train'd your Lordship; please your Lordship
To grace a Nuptiall we have now in hand,

       Hylus and Laodice stand together.

Twixt this yong Ladie and this Gentleman.
Your Lordship there shall heare the ample storie.
And how the Asse wrapt in a Lyons skin   285
Fearefully rord; but his large eares appeard
And made him laught at, that before was feard.

Gouer. Ile goe with you. For my part, I am at a non plus.

      Eudora whispers with Cynthia.

Thar. Come brother; thanke the Countesse: she hath swet
To make your peace. Sister give me your hand.   290
      So; brother let your lips compound the strife,
      And thinke you have the only constant Wife.   *Exeunt.*

FINIS

267 from] *Parrott*; for ‖ **268** headlong] head-/long ‖ **280-82** These ... hand,] *Shepherd*; *as prose* (has ... to) ‖ **282** hand,] ∼. ‖

HISTORICAL COLLATION

[Editions collated: Dodsley (=*Do*, in *A Select Collection of Old Plays*, 1st ed., 1744, IV, pp. 231-306); Reed (=*R*, in *A Select Collection of Old Plays*, 2nd ed., 1780, VI, pp. 134-231); Collier (=*C*, in *A Select Collection of Old Plays*, 3rd ed., 1825, VI, pp. 115-202); Shepherd (=*S*, in *The Works of George Chapman: Plays*, 1875, pp. 307-40); Parrott (=*P*, in *The Plays and Poems of George Chapman: The Comedies* [1914], pp. 365-434). Only substantive and semi-substantive variants are recorded; obvious errors are not recorded. The lemmata are taken from the present text. Omission of siglum indicates agreement with lemma.]

Dedication

[Omitted *Do*, *R*]
Mitton] Milton *C*
4 Iniusti sdegnij] Injusti Sdegni *C*; Gli Ingiusti Sdegni *P*
  Amorose] Amoroso *C*, *P*
4-5 Calisthe] Calisto *P*
5 &c.] *om. C*
6 *therefore I only*] *P*; *therefore only Q*, *C*, *S*
7 *disposition. This*] *P*; *disposition, this C*, *S*; *disposition; This Q*

Actors

3 Gouernour] *R*, *C*; *The ~ P*; *Thir. Gouern. Q*, *Do*, *S*
4 Lycus] *Do*, *R*, *C*; *Lycas Q*, *S*, *P*
6 Clinias . . . Eudora.] *P*; *om. Q*, *Do*, *R*, *C*, *S*
7-9 Rebus . . . friends.] *P*; *3. Lords suiters to Eudora the widdow Countesse Q*, *Do*, *R*, *C*, *S*
15 Sthenio] *Sthenia Do*, *R*, *P* (*See Textual Note*)
15-16 Sthenio . . . Eudora.] *P*; *Sthenio. / Ianthe Gent. attending on Eudora Q*; *Sthenio / Ianthe gentlewoman attending on Eudora Do*, *R*, *C*, *S*
18-20 Laodice . . . courtesan.] *P*; *om. Q*, *Do*, *R*, *C*, *S*

I.i

SD] *A Room in the House of* Lysander. *P*
1 delights] delight'st *S*
17-18 how, are] ~∧ ~ *Do*, *R*, *C*, *S*, *P*
60 becke] back *R*
83-84 done) . . . interred,] *P*; ~, . . . ~) *Q*, *Do*, *R*, *C*; ~, . . . ~), *S*
93 amongst] among *S*
95 adhorne] adorne *Do*, *R*, *C*, *S*

98 ere] e'er *R* (*not hereafter recorded*)
101 Ruffine] ruffian *Do, R, C, S, P* (*not hereafter recorded*)
104 mine.] ∼— *Do, R, C, P*
110 Fort] sort *C*
112 should] shall *S*
113 Nature had made] nature made *R, C*

I.ii

SD] *A Room in the House of* Eudora. *P*
9 as] *om. S*
24 sai't] say it *Do, R, C*
32 SD *barehead*] bareheaded *Do, R*
   SD *Vsher Lycus*] ∼, ∼∧ *S*; ∼, ∼, *P*
54 can want] want *Do, R, C*
59 whether] whither *Do, R, C, S, P* (*not hereafter recorded*)
88 *Reb.*] *Reb. drawing P*
97 Lordship] ladyship *Do, R, C*
99 SD *to Hiar.*] *om. Q, Do, R, C, S, P*
102 Whores-sonne] whore's son *Do, R, C*; whoreson *S, P*
105 dub'd] daub'd *C conj.*
108 in's] in his *Do, R, C* (*not hereafter recorded*)
120 'thead] th'head *Do, R, C, P*; the head *S*
   Shoulders] *Do, R, C, S, P*; Soulders *Q*
143 dores] the ∼ *Do*; The ∼ *R, C*
151 *Pso.*] *P*; Lord *Do, R, C, S*; *Lurd Q*
   SD *to Rebus*] *om. Q, Do, R, C, S, P*
   poison'd] poisoned *S, P*
152 begg'd] begged *S, P*; beg't [beg it] *Brereton conj.* (*in P*)
   SD *Exeunt.*] *Exit. Q, Do, S*; *Exit* Eudora *with the others. P*

I.iii

SD] *Before the House of* Eudora. *P*
7 SD *Aside.*] *P*; *om. Q, Do, R, C, S*
23-24 (I . . . long.)] *aside* ∧∼ . . . ∼.∧ *P*; ∧∼ . . . ∼.∧ *S*
30-31 All . . . engender?] *italics Do, R, C*; *in quotes P*
55 further] farther *Do, R, C* (*not hereafter recorded*)
67 mysticall] *Q(u)*; yong *Q(c), Do, S, P*
72 lease] leaf *S*
74 that] their *Do, R*
75 not-headed] knot-headed *Do, R, C*; nott-headed *S*
77 beholding] beholden *Do, R*
92 SD *Aside.*] *P*; *om. Q, Do, R, C, S*
100 SD *Aside.*] *P*; *om. Q, Do, R, C, S*
103 it but was] *Q* (*c second state*); but it was *Do, R, C*; it was but *S*; but vpon *Q*
   (*u second state*)
125 sometimes] sometime *Do, R, C*
151 fledge] fledg'd *Do, R, C*

167 manner] manor *Do, R*
176 *Exeunt.*] *Exit with* Arsace. *P*; *Exit. Q, Do, R, C, S*

II.i

SD] *A Room in the House of* Lysander. *P*
1 our selues] by ourselves *R, C, S*
7 pray] pr'y *Do, R, C*
15 SD *Exiturus*] *Going R, C*; *om. Do*
16 tis] it is *Do, R, C*
34 h'as] he as *Do*; he has *R, C*
   giuen] giv'n *Do, R, C*
39 priuat'st] privatest *Do, R, C, S*
42 Squires] 'squires *Do, R, C*
54 a strange] strange *Do, R, C*
56 a work] ∼-∼ *S, P*
58 vertues] virtue's *Do, R, C*

II.ii

SD] *A Room in the House of* Eudora. *P*
5 Lets] *Sthe.* ∼ *Q*; *Ian.* ∼ *Do, R, C, S, P*
9 *Ian.*] *Sthe. Do, R, C, S, P*
23 SD *Laodice, Argus*] *Laodice, Reb, Hiar Psor. comming after, Argus Q, Do, R, C, S, P*
29 SD *sheestrikes.*] *she strikes him. P (after l. 26)*
36 SD *walks aside.*] *om. Q, Do, R, C, S, P*
43 importance.] ∼— *Do, R, C, P*
50 SD *Arsace . . . Eudora.*] *Arsace advances. P*; *Enter Arsace. Q, Do, R, C, S*
69 *Tharsalio.*] ∼— *Do, R, C, P*
79 vertue] virtues *S, P*
119 SD *Eudora . . . enter.*] *Exit. Q, Do, R, C, S, P*
123 SD *Exeunt.*] *Exit* Rebus *with the others. P*; *Exit. Q, Do, R, C, S*

II.iii

SD] *Before the House of* Eudora. *P*
4 tickle] ticklish *Do, R, C*
26 Th'art] Thou'rt *Do, R, C*
33 tis] it is *Do, R, C*
76 trauaile] travel *Do, R, C, P*; travail *S*
77 quiet.] ∼? *Do, R, C, P*

II.iv

23 detestations] detestation *Do, R, C*
52 beholding] beholden *Do, R, C*
87 widgine] widgeon *Do, R, C, S, P*
87-88 acknowledge: forecast] ∼∧ ∼ *Do, R, C, S*; ∼! Forecast *P*
93 Wifler] whisler *Do, R, C*; whiffler *S, P*
125 your] his *S*
129 chos'd] chose *Do, R*; choose *C*; choosed *S, P*

168 sate] sat *Do, R, C, S*
174 persons?] ∼. *Do, R, C;* ∼— *S, P*
175 Sparta-Veluets.] Sparta-velvets! *Beating them. P*
227 seruants] servant's *Do, R, C, P*
237 it] is *Do*
239 lets] let's *Do*
240 SD *Exit.] R, C, P; om. Q, Do, S*
247 Ile] will I *Do, R, C*

III.i

SD] *Before the House of* Lysander. *P*
6 tast] test *Do, R, C, S*
19 wreake] wreck *Do;* wreack *R*
22 enterchang'd] interchanged *S*
37 SD *Enter Thars.] Enter* Tharsalio *cloaked. P*
38 vnbanded!] *S, P;* ∼? *Do, R, C;* ∼, *Q*
49 be] is *Do, R, C*
55 helpe out this] help this *Do, R, C*
56 SD *Uncloaks . . . suit.] P; om. Q, Do, R, C, S*
63 counting house] compting-house *Do, R, C*
70 spousall] 'spousal *Do, R, C*
72 wrap't] rapt *Do, R, C, P;* wrapt *S*
92 off] of *Do, R, C, S, P*
104 hoise] hoist *Do, R, C*
135 SD *Hyl. and Ero.] P; Hyl. Q, Do, R, C, S*
139 depression] impression *Do, R, C*
145 het] hot *Do, R, C, S*
174 Capricions] Capricorns *Do, R*

III.ii

SD] *A Room in the House of* Eudora. *P*
SD *barehead.]* bareheaded. *Do, R, C*
5 SD *Enter Tharsalio.] P; om. Q, Do, R, C, S*
10 *Arg.* Cry] ∼. *perceiving* Tharsalio ∼ *P*
11 cornetting] curvetting *Do, R, C, S*
21 may] *Do, R, C, S, P;* my *Q*
29 SD *Aside.] om. Q, Do, R, C, S, P*
37 ails] *P;* aile *Q, Do, R, C, S*
39 suiting] unsuiting *Do, R*
  ill] *S, P;* all *Q, Do, R, C*
47 you lou'd] lov'd you *Do, R, C*
69 out] *Do, R, C, S, P;* ont *Q*
73 *Phoenix;* there, . . . cheere:] *P;* ∼; ∼, . . . ∼; *Do, R, C;* ∼, ∼, . . . ∼: *S;* ∼,
  ∼∧ . . . ∼∧ *Q*
74 Loue,] ∼∧ *Do, R, C, S, P*
77 heauen,] ∼. *Musique Q, Do, R, C, S, P*
91 flowrie] flowery *R, C, S, P*
93 Antique] antic *S, P*

106 SD *after which, and all set*] ∼ ∼, *all sit Do, R*; ∼ ∼∧ *all sit C*
  SD *places, Hymen.*] *S; places./ Hymen. Q, Do, R, C* (*Hymen as speech head, centered*); *places,* Hymen *speaks P*
107 what my Power] *G. B. Evans*; ∼ the ∼ *Q, Do, R, C, S*; ∼ e'er ∼ *P*

IV.i

SD] *A Room in the House of* Eudora. *P*
14, 17 Corse] corpse *Do, R, C*
51 lou'st] lovest *S*
60 Innocencie] innocence *Do, R*
67 t'heads] th'heads *Do, R, C, P*
96 wi 'th'] *P* (*Brereton conj.*); with *Q, Do, R, C*; within a *S*
107-8 sustenance?] *Do, R, C, S, P*; ∼. *Q*
121 Wise] *P* (*Deighton conj.*); West *Q, Do, R, C, S*; wisest *S, P conj.*
130 vpon't?] *S, P*; ∼! *Do, R, C*; ∼. *Q*

IV.ii

SD] *The Graveyard. P*
1 O Miracle] Lysander. [*speech head*] ∼ ∼ *Do, R, C*
15 *Ero.* Who] ∼. *within* ∼ *P*
19 *Ero.* What] ∼. *opening the door of the tomb* ∼ *P*
32 ruthfull] ruthless *S*
33 Bandittos] *R, C, S, P*; Banditto's *Do*; Bantditos *Q*
43 *Cynth.* What] ∼. *at the door of the tomb* ∼ *P*
46 spoile] *Do, R, C, S, P*; spoil'd *Q*
63 SD *Aside.*] *P; om. Q, Do, R, C, S*
78 Good Mistris heare] *P* (*Gilchrist conj. in C*); Good∧ heare *Q, S*; Good, hear *Do*; Good; hear *R, C*
107 A noble] *R, C, S, P*; Noble *Q, Do*
108 it. *offering his sword.* Tush] *P*; ∼. ────── ∼∧ *Q*; ∼. ────── ∼! *Do, R, C*; ∼∧ ────── ∼! *S*
127 O know] O I know *Do, R, C*
128 proface] profess *Do, R*
133 SD *bibit Ancill.*] *She drinks Do, R, C*
147 an't's] on't's *P*; ants *Q, S*; of't's *Do, R, C*
151 SD *Aside.*] *om. Q, Do, R, C, S, P*
157 SD *Aside.*] *P; om. Q, Do, R, C, S*
174 turne] turn to *S*
177 SD *Exiturus.*] *Is going. Do, R; Going C*

IV.iii

SD] *The same. P*
36 *Santus*] *Sanctus R, C, P*
37 SD *Aside.*] *P; om. Q, Do, R, C, S*
42 th'ast] thou'st *Do, R, C*
  performd] *Do, R, C*; per formd *Q*; performed *S, P*
61 Sir.] Sir. *She drinks P*

64 SD *kisses her.*] P; *om. Q, Do, R, C, S*
75 edifie, edifie.] edify. *Do*

V.i

SD] *The Graveyard. P*
12 disposure.] ∼, *P*
22 whose] who's *S, P*
30 Your] *P;* Our *Q, Do, R, C, S*
36 me] my *Brereton conj.*
43 mindes] *P;* windes *Q, Do, R, C, S*
67 lycorous] liquorish *Do, R*

V.ii

SD *opens,*] *opens, disclosing P*
14 lept] leapt *Do, R, C, S, P*
22 SD *Aside.*] *P; om. Q, Do, R, C, S*
23 carcase] carcass *Do, R*
24 plague time] ∼-∼ *P*
30 nere] near *Do, R, C, S, P*
31 Well] We'll *Do, R*
   SD *Exeunt . . . tomb.*] *P; om. Q, Do, R, C, S*
42 SD *Aside.*] *P; om. Q, Do, R, C, S*
43 off] of *Do, R, C, S, P*
47 some] *om. Do, R, C*
50 *Seigneur*] signior *Do, R, C*
52 SD *Exeunt the souldiers.*] *Exeunt Soldiers. P; Exeunt. Q, Do, R, C, S*
54 carelessly] *Do, R, C, S, P;* caresly *Q*

V.iii

7 in] on *Do, R, C*
13 SD *Aside.*] *Do, R, C, S, P; om. Q*
   I . . . thee.] *as aside P*
17 past.] ∼— *Do, R, C, P*
18 SD *Aside.*] *P; om. Q, Do, R, C, S*
20 Cancro!] *Do, R, C, P; Cancro. Q;* Canero. *S*
21 saue] saves *Do, R, C*
36 vpon thee] *R, C, P;* ∼ the *Q, Do, S*
40 truant] *Do, R, C, P;* tenant *Q, S*
43 chaines.] chains. *Embracing him. P*
55 aide] add *Do, R, C*
58 SD *Aside.*] *Do, R, C, P; om. Q, S*
60 SD *Aside.*] *P; om. Q, Do, R, C, S*
   SD *Shut*] Shuts *Do, R, C*
62 banefull. Is't] ∼ *throwing off his armour* ∼ *P*
67 paint them, paint them ten] paint them ten *S*
71 store] stare *Deighton conj. (in P)*
72 Achelous] Acheloüs' *Do, R, C, S, P;* Achelons *Q*
   ill] *P (Deighton conj.);* all *Q, Do, R, C, S*
72-73 horne of ill, / Copie] *P;* ∼ₐ ∼ all, Copie *Q;* ∼, ∼ allₐ copia *Do, R, C;*
       ∼ₐ ∼ all, copie *S*

74 Alizon] Amazon *P conj.*
75 Ida] *Do, R, C, S, P;* Ilea *Q*
80 SD *Aside.*] *P; om. Q, Do, R, C, S*
    here abouts] hereabouts *S, P;* here about *Do, R, C*
81 SD *Exiturus.*] *Is Going Do, R; Going C*
84 you. A] you. *recognizing* Lysander A *P*
91 be] is *Do, R, C*
93-94 to morrow.] to-morrow. *going P*
129 SD *Aside.*] *om. Q, Do, R, C, S, P*
130 Candian] Canadian *C*
151 indeede the] *Do, S, P;* indeed with him, the *Q, R, C*
157 a] o' *Do, R, C, P*
176 SD *Shut the Tomb.*] *She shuts the tomb. Do, R, C*

V.iv

SD] *The Graveyard P*
7-8 (though iust . . . dispenc'd)] ($\sim \sim$) . . . dispensed$_\wedge$ *C, P*
18 apprehended] is $\sim$ *Do, R, C*
30 loud] aloud *Do, R, C*
31 found] sound *Do, R, C, S*
35 finde] found *P*
37 sound] found *Do, R*
39 Truth's] *P* (*C conj.*); Truth *Q, Do, R, C, S*
41 *Lycus* his] Lycus' *C*

V.v

1 Come] *Lys.* Come *Do, R, C, P*
2 reconcild] reconciled *Do, R, C, S*
8 The] She *Brereton conj.* (*in P*)
    most false in her] more false then her *Q, Do, R, C, S;* more false than thee
    Gilchrist conj. (*in C*), *P;* more false than thou *Brereton conj.* (*in P*)
10 Note what] $\sim_\wedge$ with *Q, Do, R, C, S;* $\sim$, with *P* (*Brereton conj.*)
24 emploiments] implements *Do*
25 prepares a way] *R, C, P;* $\sim$ away *Q, S;* wears away *Do*
32 SD *Aside.*] *P; om. Q, Do, R, C, S*
36 T'] I *Q;* It *Do, R, C, S, P*
43 carrier] career *Do, R, C, S, P*
48 brake] break *Do, R, C*
53 lothest] loathed *Do, R, C*
59 SD *Aside.*] *P; om. Q, Do, R, C, S*
65 inhumane] in human *S, P*
68 SD *He . . . throat.*] *after l. 78 R, C*
70 assay] essay *Do, R, C*
71 soft-roed] *C, S, P;* soft-r'ode *Q;* soft-toed *Do, R*
73 hand, & c.] hand— *S*
86 SD *Exit. cum Er.*] *Exit with Ero. Do, R, C*
87 more.] more. *Tomb closes. P*
114 hearke you] $\sim$ ye *Do, R, C*

119 run's way] run way *R*; run away *C*

124 Hearke] Heark ye *Do, R, C*

125 SD *Exiturus.*] *Is going. Do, R*; *Going. C*

130 *Lys.* First afore] *S, P*; First afore *Q*; *1 Sol.* Afore *Do, R, C*
    SD *Aside.*] *P*; om. *Q, Do, R, C, S*

148 tis] it is *Do, R, C*

152 SD *Aside.*] *C, P*; om. *Q, Do, R, S*

157 SD *Aside.*] om. *Q, Do, R, C, S, P*

159 SD *Aside.*] om. *Q, Do, R, C, S, P*

169 SD *Aside.*] *P*; om. *Q, Do, R, C, S*
    a Foole] *P* (*C conj.*); Foole *Q, Do, R, C, S*

182 SD *Aside.*] *P*; om. *Q, Do, R, C, S*

183 but two] not ∼ *P conj.*

192 SD *Aside.*] *P*; om. *Q, Do, R, C, S*

200 Parrat] prate *Deighton conj.* (*in P*)

201 SD *Aside.*] *P*; om. *Q, Do, R, C, S*

205 SD *Aside.*] *P*; om. *Q, Do, R, C, S*

208 SD *Aside.*] *P*; om. *Q, Do, R, C, S*

211 SD *Aside.*] *P*; om. *Q, Do, R, C, S*

220 SD *Aside.*] *P*; om. *Q, Do, R, C, S*

222 head a'] ∼; and *Q, Do, R*; ∼, and *C, S, P*

225 errand] arrant *Do, R, C, S*; errant *P*

228 SD *Aside to Lysander.*] *Aside. P*; om. *Q, Do, R, C, S*
    Dee] Doe *Q*; Do you *Do, R, C*; Do ye *S, P*

232 SD *Aside.*] *P*; om. *Q, Do, R, C, S*

234 their] his *Do, R, C*

237 spaded] spayed *C conj.*

238 confiscate] confiscated *Do, R, C*

244 a] o' *Do, R, C, P*
    yfaith] 'faith *Do, R, C*; i'faith *S, P*

254 a] o' *Do, R, C, P*

256 SD *Argus stalkes.*] *Do, R, C, S, P*; *on preceding line Q*

263 th'] the *Do, R, C*

264 priuate.] ∼. *Whispers to the* Governor *P*

267 from] *P*; for *Q, Do, R, C, S*

272 Berladie] By'r lady *Do, R, C*; By'rlady *S, P*

283 Gentleman.] ∼? *Do, R, C*

288 a] an *Do, R*

PRESS-VARIANTS

[Copies collated: Bodl¹ (Bodleian Library Mal. 240.7), Bodl² (Bodleian Library Mal. 162.4), Bodl³ (Bodleian Library Douce C.245), CSmH (Huntington Library), DFo (Folger Shakespeare Library), IU (University of Illinois), MB (Boston Public Library, wants L1ᵛ, L2), MH (Harvard University), NNP (Pierpont Morgan Library), Ryl (John Rylands Library)]

Sheet C (outer forme)

Corrected: Bodl¹, Bodl², IU, MB, MH, NNP
Uncorrected: Bodl³, CSmH, DFo, Ryl

Sig. C1
    I.ii.77 Giant,] By but,
       84 Madam?] Madam,
Sig. C2ᵛ
    I.iii.11 erection] direction
         lowe] loued
      27 like] tooke
      31 engender?] engender.
      38 Well] What
Sig. C3
    I.iii.67 yong] mysticall

Sheet C (inner forme)

First State Corrected: CSmH
Uncorrected: DFo

Sig. C4
    I.iii.119 speeding place] place speeding
Second State Corrected: Bodl¹, Bodl², Bodl³, IU, MB, MH, NNP, Ryl
Sig. C3ᵛ
    I.iii.103 it but was] but vpon
Sig. C4
    I.iii.123 so] so;

Sheet D (outer forme)

Corrected: Bodl¹, Bodl², CSmH, DFo, IU, MB, MH, NNP
Uncorrected: Bodl³, Ryl

Sig. D1
    I.iii.176 seeme] few
    II.i.12 to you, and] too, and
         shal] shall
      13 firmely] firme

Sig. D2ᵛ
    II.ii.SD *Sthenio*] *Sthenia*
        9 Who?] Who
Sig. D3
    II.ii.41 *Sthenio*] *Sthenia*
        49 that,] that

Sheet E (outer forme)

Corrected: Bodl¹, Bodl², Bodl³, CSmH, MB, MH, Ryl
Uncorrected: DFo, IU, NNP

Sig. E1
    II.iii.37 braine] braines
        44 you know how] how know you
Sig. E2ᵛ
    II.iv.20 course;] course,
        24 marriages;] marriages,
        25 vsurie,] vsurie
        38 husbands:] husbands,
        49 not, and that] not, that
Sig. E3
    II.iv.52 fine] fiue
        56 forbearance] forbearances
        64-65 like a Pigmey] like Pigmey
Sig. E4ᵛ
    II.iv.157 vertues;] vertues,
        171 outlaw,] *Atlas*,
        175 ye Sparta-Veluets] yee Sparta Veluet

Sheet E (inner forme)

Corrected: Bodl¹, Bodl², Bodl³, CSmH, DFo, MB, MH, Ryl
Uncorrected: IU, NNP

Sig. E3ᵛ
    II.iv.91 on] in

Sheet G (inner forme)

Corrected: Bodl¹, Bodl², Bodl³, CSmH, IU, MB, MH, NNP, Ryl
Uncorrected: DFo

Sig. G2
    III.ii.29 thy] they
Sig. G3ᵛ
    IV.i.16 and (for] (and for
        17 wipe] wipe:

TEXTUAL NOTES

The Actors

15 *Sthenio*] Both *Sthenio* and *Sthenia* appear in Q. *Sthenia* appears in
I.ii.32 SD and in the uncorrected states of II.ii.SD and II.ii.41. *Sthenio* appears
in the list of Actors and six times in the stage directions and text, including
the corrected states of II.ii.SD and II.ii.41. That *Sthenio* is not simply an
erroneous correction imposed by the proofreader is apparent from the fact
that it appears in the uncorrected as well as the corrected state of G2
(III.ii.30 SD). Dodsley, Reed, and Parrott adopt *Sthenia,* the correct classical
spelling, but the quarto text would seem to authorize *Sthenio.*

I.iii

67 mysticall] Dodsley, Shepherd, and Parrott adopted the corrected reading
"yong." But the correction was, I think, a gratuitous alteration of the copy-
text. "Mysticall" evidently means "secretive," "hidden," or "unknown."
Cf. the phrase "Confesse thou misticall *Pandress —* " in *The Second Maiden's
Tragedy* (l. 993, Malone Society Reprints).

II.ii

5-8 *Sthe.* A . . . her.] Q has *"Sthe.* A . . . comparison. / *Sthe.* Lets . . . her."
Shepherd and Parrott change the second speech-prefix to *Ian.* and alter the
succeeding ones (see Historical Collation). This emendation is dubious. The
repeated speech-prefix, I suppose, was added by Chapman or the bookkeeper
to erase the ambiguity caused by a marginal insertion above the line in Sthenio's
speech.

23 SD *Enter . . . Eudora.*] The action of this scene indicates that the Spartan
lords enter at line 119 (as Eudora exits) since they do not speak or take part
in the preceding action. Q's stage direction *"Reb., Hiar Psor comming after"*
at line 23 merely anticipates their entrance later in the scene, a practice that
also occurs in the stage directions of *The Gentleman Usher.*

29 SD *shee strikes.*] Parrott unnecessarily advances this SD to the preceding
line. But apparently Eudora is angered more by Argus' stupidity than by
Arsace's presence.

V.iii

72-73 There . . . enough;] Although this passage, with its succeeding lines,
makes a rough kind of sense, it is, as Parrott remarks, corrupt and has probably been cut after "Copie enough."

V.v

8 false in her.] Parrott, following Gilchrist's suggestion in Collier's edition, emends the line to read "more false than thee." Although this emendation forms lines 7 and 8 into a couplet, it also makes line 8 a lame repetition of line 6, which has the more natural construction "then thou." It seems to me that lines 7 and 8 are parallel in construction, but that the compositor erroneously recalled the "more false . . . then" construction of line 6.

73 This hand, &c] Parrott believed that the "etc." "denotes that the speech was cut here, or perhaps that Chapman left it unfinished." More likely, I think, the "etc." is a kind of stage direction (cf. IV.ii.SD) indicating that here Cynthia gestures heroically with her hand.

183 heare but two parties.] The phrase is puzzling and probably corrupt. Parrott suggests the possibility of "hear not two parties"; perhaps more fitting to the context would be "hear not the parties."

222-23 the . . . tumult] The passage is corrupt and in all probability part of a line has been omitted in Q. But the emendation of "and" to "a' " makes sense. Under the proposed new discipline, braggarts will be forced to lead the tavern rabble and shout above their tumult.

The Memorable Masque

edited by G. Blakemore Evans

❖

TEXTUAL INTRODUCTION

Two editions of *The Memorable Maske,* both undated, were printed for George
Norton after 15 February 1612/13, when, as the title page notes, the *Maske*
was presented[1] by "the two Honorable Houses or Inns of Court; the Middle
Temple, and Lyncolns Inne . . . before the King at White-Hall . . . At the
Princely celebration of the most Royall Nuptialls of the Palsgraue, and his
thrice gratious Princesse Elizabeth. . . ." Together with Francis Beaumont's
masque, which was performed on 20 February, it was entered by Norton in
the *Stationers' Register* on 27 February 1612/13,[2] a date close enough to the

[1] John Chamberlain in a letter to Alice Carleton (18 February 1612/13) has left an
eyewitness account of the performance of the *Maske (The Letters of John Chamberlain,* ed. N. E. McClure [Memoirs, XII, The American Philosophical Society], I, 425):
"On Monday night was the Middle Temple and Lincolns Ynne maske presented in the
hall at court, wheras the Lords was in the bancketting roome. Yt went from the
Rolles all up Fleet-street and the Strand, and made such a gallant and glorious shew
that yt is highly commended. They had forty gentlemen of best choise out of both
houses rode before them in theyre best array, upon the Kings horses: and the twelve
maskers with theyre torch-bearers and pages rode likewise upon horses excedingly well
trapped and furnished: besides a dousen litle boyes, dresst like babones that served for
an antimaske, (and they say performed yt exceedingly well when they came to yt),
and three open chariots drawne with fowre horses a peece that caried theyre musicians,
and other personages that had parts to speake: all which together with theyre trumpetters and other attendants were so well set out, that yt is generally held for the best
shew that hath ben seen many a day. The Kinge stood in the gallerie to behold them
and made them ride about the tilt-yard, and then were receved into St. James Parke
and went all along the galleries into the hall, where themselves and their devises
(which they say were excellent) made such a glittering shew that the King and all
the companie were excedingly pleased, and specially with theyre dauncing, which was
beyond all that hath ben yet. The King made the maskers kisse his hand at parting,
and gave them many thanckes, sayeng he never saw so many proper men together, and
himself accompanied them at the banket, and tooke care yt shold be well ordered, and
speakes much of them behind their backes, and strokes the master of the rolles and
Dick Martin who were the cheife dooers and undertakers." See, also, E. K. Chambers,
The Elizabethan Stage (Oxford, 1923), III, 261-62, for other contemporary comment.
[2] See the entry quoted in W. W. Greg, *A Bibliography of the English Printed Drama
to the Restoration,* I (London, 1939), 452. The *SR* dates the entry as "27 Januarij," but
since the preceding entry is for "26 ffebruarij" it seems clear that the month is wrongly
given. Moreover, the masque was not presented at court until 15 February 1612/13.

productions of the masques to suggest a desire for haste in getting the two masques into print. The bookseller's haste is further evidenced by Chapman's complaint in the introductory material printed before the *Maske* proper:

These following should in duty haue had their proper places, after euery fitted speech of the Actors; but being preuented by the vnexpected haste of the Printer [George Eld], which he neuer let me know, and neuer sending me a proofe, till he had past those speeches; I had no reason to imagine hee could haue been so forward.

It seems highly likely, then, that the first edition (Q1) appeared in 1613, and probable that the second edition (Q2) was published later in the same year.[3]

Q1 was printed by George Eld; Q2 by "F.K." (Felix Kingston). The question of priority between what are here called Q1 and Q2 has been dealt with in detail by W. W. Greg in his *Bibliography of the English Printed Drama to the Restoration* (1939).[4] The "F.K." edition (Q2) is shown to be the later on the evidence of its collational pattern, the lack of the errata list, and the missigning of sig. D2 as B. To Greg's evidence may be added the appearance of fairly extensive stop-press corrections in Q1, all of which readings appear in their corrected states in Q2. Curiously, Greg, in his much earlier *A List of Masques* (1902), had reversed the order of editions, a decision first challenged by T. M. Parrott in his 1914 edition of the masque. At the time Parrott wrote, apparently only a single imperfect copy of Q2 was known (British Museum C.34.b.41), and, although several copies (Folger, Harvard, Huntington, Yale) have since turned up, it is considerably more scarce than Q1.

A collation of sixteen copies of Q1 shows press-variants in sheets ¶ (outer and inner formes), a (outer and inner formes), B (outer forme), D (outer forme), and E (outer forme).[5] Although several sets of running titles are employed, parts of the same set appear regularly on both outer and inner formes of the same sheet. This disposition of the running titles, together with the survival of corrected states of both inner and outer formes of sheets ¶ and a, rules out printing by the method known as simultaneous imposition. The work of at least two compositors can be distinguished sporadically throughout the volume from the evidence of spellings,[6] speech heads, and verse setting, but no very definite pattern of work stints seems to emerge.

There is no reason to doubt that at least part, and probably all, of the copy for Q1 was in Chapman's autograph. His complaint quoted above about the printer's haste shows that he was at least cognizant of the plans to print the masque, and the appearance of this passage within the descriptive introduction itself proves Chapman's immediate concern with the copy. Thus, "The Epistle Dedicatorie" (sig. ¶), the descriptive introductory materials (sigs. A-a2ᵛ), Chapman's "*To answer certaine insolent obiections made against the*

---

[3] Greg (*Bibliography*, I, 452-53) is noncommital about the date of Q2, listing it as "N.D." *STC*, however, lists Q1 as "[1613?]" and Q2 as "[1614?]."

[4] I, 452-53. Q1 is described under No. 310 (a) ; Q2 under No. 310 (b).

[5] See Press-Variants in Q1.

[6] Since, as I argue below, Q1 was set from Chapman's autograph, some of the unusual forms may represent characteristic Chapman spellings ("gould," "lardges," "boarn," etc.). If so, this fact does not seriously disturb their value in a compositor test; it merely means that one compositor followed his copy more closely than the other.

length of my speeches" (sig. a3), and, probably, "The aplicable argument of the Maske" (sig. a4) are almost certainly based directly on Chapman's own manuscript copy.

There is, perhaps, more room for question so far as the immediate copy for the masque proper is concerned. There can be no doubt that the masque itself (sigs. B-E, including part of "A hymne to Hymen") was set first and run off before the various parts of the preliminary materials (sigs. ¶, A-a) were set up in type. The "Errata" list,[7] which appears (in all but one copy) on sig. a4, and which makes corrections only in the text of the masque, is sufficient to establish this order. There is also, however, the evidence of Chapman's complaint, already quoted, that he had seen no proofs until a certain point had been reached in the printing of the masque. What that point was may be judged by the extra rubrics he then inserted, rubrics which have reference to speeches in the masque through sig. D. And since the "Errata" list contains corrections only through sig. D, corrections we may suppose insisted upon by Chapman himself, it seems likely that Chapman did see proofs of sigs. E and F, and there is no reason to question his personal intervention in the proof correction of at least sig. ¶, with its obviously authorial change in the complimentary close of "The Epistle Dedicatorie," and sig. a, with its added phrase at the conclusion of "The aplicable argument."

One puzzling aspect of Chapman's added rubrics is the appearance of similar, though, to be sure, somewhat less detailed, rubrics in the printed text of the masque. In other words, the rubrics which Chapman here included and which "should in duty haue had their proper places, after euery fitted speech of the Actors" are essentially already in place in the text of the masque as printed, including one which occurs as early as sig. B2 (ll. 15-18 in the present text). This state of affairs might be taken to imply that the manuscript copy from which the masque was set up was not Chapman's own, but an unauthorized transcript of some kind, and that Chapman in his rewriting of the rubrics is registering his annoyance. I suspect, however, that the new rubrics are simply a case of an author's second thoughts, second thoughts which he, like many a writer, had been lazy about conveying to the printer. I see, therefore, no serious reason to question autograph copy-text for the whole of Q1.

Four of the copies of Q1 here collated (British Museum[3], Huntington, Dyce[1], and University of Illinois) contain manuscript corrections. All these corrections are, I believe, in the same hand.[8] Those in the British Museum[3], the Huntington, and Dyce[1] copies are limited, with one exception,[9] to remedying the errors pointed out in the "Errata" list, but the corrections in the

---

[7] The "Errata" list is as follows:

   "*In* Capri. *first speech, for many, read maine, in c.1. for Pot, re. post, in c.3. for answer, re. austerity, for purposes, re. purses, in c.3. for seemingly, re. securely, in d. 2. for law, and vertue, re. loue and beauty, in the first stance of the second song, for this re. his. for sweet deuotions, re. fit deuotions.*" "Errata" list is omitted in Q2.

[8] It is possible, of course, that the hand is Chapman's. Unfortunately, the autograph remains we possess of Chapman's two different scripts are not very helpful in this case.

[9] The Q1 reading "seate" (The Maske [introductory description], 1.194) has been altered to "state" in British Museum[3] and Dyce[1], as well as in the Illinois copy.

Illinois copy are much more significant. Like the other three it corrects the readings singled out in the "Errata" (except for the first), but it also makes a number of other corrections, both substantive and accidental. Several of these suggested readings are, I feel, unquestionably right, and none shows what might be called mere unwarranted meddling with the text. In a case of this kind the question of authority immediately arises. Is an editor justified in disturbing his copy-text (Q1) on the strength of such anonymous manuscript corrections? Under ordinary circumstances the answer has to be that he is not, but in this particular case there is enough evidence, I believe, almost to guarantee the authority of the manuscript readings. In two substantive corrections the writer shows a knowledge of the corrected state of sigs. a2^v and D3, and in the second of these ("al nightes" for the uncorrected reading "the nightes") there is nothing immediately suspicious in the uncorrected reading and nothing to point to the correct reading. Add to this the evidence of authority suggested by the common hand found in all four copies, and the case for accepting the readings in the Illinois copy becomes a strong one. I have, therefore — though still not without occasional qualms — admitted into my text all the substantive and semi-substantive corrections, and several of the corrections of the accidentals where they clearly improve or sharpen the sense of the passage. A separate, complete list of all the manuscript corrections in the Illinois copy will be found following the listing of the press-variants in Q1.

Only two copies of Q2 have been collated. It is printed from a copy of Q1 made up of the corrected states,[10] even reproducing the obvious error in the catchword on sig. B3^v (D2^v in Q2). Textually, Q2 offers nothing significant, although it corrects a few simple errors in Q1's spelling and punctuation. Curiously, it fails to correct any of the errors listed in the Q1 "Errata" except for one ("watering post" for "watering pot").[11] That it was, nevertheless, printed from a copy of Q1 containing the "Errata" list is proved by its inclusion of the added phrase in "The aplicable argument" found only in the corrected state of sig. a4, which state also includes the "Errata." Any possibility that the text of the masque in Q2 was set up first, before the preliminary materials, from the sheets of Q1 as they were printed (a possible publisher's move to ensure a large stock on publication) is ruled out by the continuous signing of the sheets (A through G) and by the fact that the text of the masque itself begins on sig. C4. The few substantive variants which occur in Q2 suggest nothing but compositorial meddling or error. Three spellings in Q2 deserve notice: Q1's "Maske," "Antemaske," and "Stance" are regularly altered to "Masque," "Anti-masque" (once "Anti-maskes"), and "Stanze."

The following edited texts of *The Memorable Maske* have been collated and their substantive and semi-substantive variants (obvious errors aside) recorded in the Historical Collation:

(1) John Nichols, in *The Progresses of King James the First* (1828), II, 566-86. Nichols' text, typical of its time, is a weird mixture of old-spelling

---

[10] I.e., so far as we know the corrected states. No press-variants have been discovered for sheets A and C.

[11] Greg (*Bibliography*, I, 453) is mistaken, therefore, when he claims that none of the corrections in the "Errata" list are made in Q2.

and modernized forms, but Nichols made a serious attempt to edit the text and some of his readings deserve notice.

(2) Richard Herne Shepherd, in *Works of George Chapman: Plays* (1875), pp. 341-50; and "A Hymne to Hymen" in *Works of George Chapman: Poems* (1875), pp. 176-77. This is a modernized text in spelling and punctuation, but it is *not* a mere modernized reprint of the so-called Pearson (1873) old-spelling reprint, as T. M. Parrott affirms.

(3) Thomas Marc Parrott, in *The Plays and Poems of George Chapman: The Comedies* [1914], pp. 435-60. This, a modernized text in spelling and punctuation, has been for many years the standard edition. It was, unfortunately, printed from a corrected copy of Shepherd's edition, thus perpetuating a number of Shepherd's errors. Despite this lapse, Parrott examined some nine copies of Q1 and recorded a number of press-variants. With its valuable annotation, it is in many respects a remarkable edition.

(4) Phyllis B. Bartlett, in *The Poems of George Chapman* (1941), pp. 365-67 (includes "A Hymne to Hymen" only). Miss Bartlett chooses to print her text from Q2.

The present text of the *Maske* has been edited in accordance with the principles outlined in the General Introduction, but the use of italic and roman in the descriptive rubrics of the *Maske* proper has been silently regularized. The compositors of Q1 tended to alternate lines of italic and roman, or to set the first line in italic and the remainder in roman.

THE
MEMORABLE MASKE

of the two Honorable Houses or Inns of
Court; the Middle Temple, and
Lyncolns Inne.

As it was performd before the King, at
White-Hall on Shroue Munday at night;
being the 15. of February. 1613.

At the Princely celebration of the moſt Royall
Nuptialls of the Palſgraue, *and his thrice gratious*
Princeſſe Elizabeth.&c.

With a deſcription of their whole ſhow; in the manner
of their march on horſe-backe to the Court from
the Maiſter of the Rolls his houſe : with all
their right Noble conſorts, and moſt
ſhowfull attendants.

Inuented, and faſhioned, with the ground, and
ſpeciall ſtructure of the whole worke,

By our Kingdomes moſt Artfull and Ingenious
Architect INNIGOIONES.

Supplied, Aplied, Digeſted, and written,
By GEO: CHAPMAN.

AT LONDON,
Printed by *G. Eld*, for *George Norton* and are to be
ſould at his ſhoppe neere Temple-bar.

TO THE MOST NOBLE,
and constant Combiner of Honor,
and Vertue, Sir EDWARD PHILIPS,
Knight, M^r. of the Rolls.

This Noble and Magnificent performance, renewing the ancient spirit, and Honor of the Innes of Court; being especially furthered and followed by your most laborious and honored endeuors, (for his Maiesties seruice; and honour of the all-grace-deseruing Nuptialls, of the thrice gracious Princesse Elizabeth, *his Highness daughter) deserues especially to be in this sort consecrate, to your worthy memory and honor. Honor, hauing neuer her faire hand more freely and nobly giuen to Riches (being a fit particle of this Inuention) then by yours, at this Nuptiall solemnity. To which assisted, and / memorable ceremony; the ioin'd hand and industry, of the worthely honour'd Knight, Sir H. Hubberd, his Maiesties Atturny generall, deseruing, in good part, a ioint memory with yours; I haue submitted it freely to his noble acceptance. The poore paines I added to this Royall seruice, being wholly chosen, and commanded by your most constant, and free fauour; I hope will now appeare nothing neglectiue of their expected duties. Hearty wil, and care enough, I am assured was employ'd in me; and the onely ingenuous will, being first and principall step to vertue; I beseech you let it stand for the performing vertue it selfe. In which addition of your euer-honour'd fauours, you shall euer binde all my future seruice to your most wished Commandement.*

    God send you long health, and your Vertues will endue you with honor enough,

By your free merits euer vow'd honorer,
and most vnfainedly affectionate
Obseruant.
GEO. CHAPMAN.

Line numbers: 5, [¶2ᵛ] 10, 15, 20, 25

---

4 all-grace-deseruing] *Q1 (c), Q2; all-gracefull-deseruing Q1 (u)* ‖ **7** hand more] *Q2;* (?) ∼, ∼ *Q1 (the comma is very doubtful)* ‖ **12** part,] *Q1 (c), Q2;* ∼∧ *Q1 (u)* | yours;] *Q1 (c), Q2;* ∼, *Q1 (u)* ‖ **24-25** affectionate Obseruant.] *Q1 (c, 2nd state);* affectioned, *Q1 (u);* ∼, ∼. *Q1 (c, 1st state), Q2* ‖

THE MASKE OF THE

Gentlemen of the two combin'd houses,
or Inns of Court, the Middle-Temple,
and Lincolns Inne.

At the house of the most worthely honour'd preferrer and gracer of
all honorable Actions, and vertues, (sir *Edward Philips* Knight, Master
of the Rolls) al the Performers and their Assistents made their *Rendes
vous,* prepar'd to their performance, and thus set forth.

Fiftie Gentlemen, richly attirde, and as gallantly mounted, with 5
Foot-men perticularly attending, made the noble vant-guarde of these
Nuptiall forces. Next (a fit distance obseru'd betweene them) marcht
a mock- / Maske of Baboons, attir'd like fantasticall Trauailers, in [A1ᵛ]
Neapolitane sutes, and great ruffes, all horst with Asses; and dwarfe
Palfries, with yellow foot-cloathes, and casting Cockle-demois about, in 10
courtesie, by way of lardges; Torches boarn on either hand of them;
lighting their state as ridiculously, as the rest Nobly. After them were
sorted two Carrs Triumphall, adornd with great Maske heads, Festones, scroules, and antick leaues, euery part inricht with siluer and
golde. These were through-varied with different inuention, and in 15
them aduanc't, the choice Musitions of our Kingdome, six in each;
attir'd like Virginean Priests, by whom the Sun is there ador'd; and
therfore called the *Phœbades.* Their Robes were tuckt vp before;
strange Hoods of feathers, and scallops about their neckes, and on their
heads turbants, stucke with seuerall colour'd feathers, spotted with 20
wings of Flies, of extraordinary bignesse; like those of their countrie:
And about them march't two ranks of Torches. Then rode the chiefe
Maskers, in In- / dian habits, all of a resemblance: the ground cloath [A2]
of siluer, richly embroidered, with golden Sunns, and about euery
Sunne, ran a traile of gold, imitating Indian worke: their bases of the 25
same stuffe and work, but betwixt euery pane of embroidery, went
a rowe of white Estridge feathers, mingled with sprigs of golde plate;
vnder their breasts, they woare bawdricks of golde, embroidered high
with purle, and about their neckes, Ruffes of feathers, spangled with

---

18 *Phœbades*] Phœbades *Q1-2* ‖ **25** worke:] *Q2;* ∼,: *Q1* ‖

pearle and siluer. On their heads high sprig'd-feathers, compast in   30
Coronets, like the Virginian Princes they presented. Betwixt euery set
of feathers, and about their browes, in the vnder-part of their Coronets,
shin'd Sunnes of golde plate, sprinkled with pearle; from whence
sprung rayes of the like plate, that mixing with the motion of the
feathers, shew'd exceedingly delightfull, and gracious. Their legges   35
were adorn'd, with close long white silke-stockings: curiously embroidered with golde to the Midde-legge. /

And ouer these (being on horse backe) they drew greaues or bus-   [A2ᵛ]
kins embrodered with gould, and enterlac't with rewes of fethers; altogether estrangfull, and *Indian* like.   40

In their Hands (set in seueral postures as they rode) they brandisht
cane darts of the finest gould. Their vizerds of oliue collour; but pleasingly visag'd: their hayre, blacke and lardge, wauing downe to their
shoulders.

Their Horse, for rich show, equalld the Maskers them-selues; all   45
their caparisons being enchac't with sunnes of Gould and Ornamentall
Iewells. To euery one of which, was tackt a Scarffing of Siluer; that
ran sinnuousely in workes ouer the whole caparison, euen to the dasel-
ing of the admiring spectators.

Their heads, no lesse gracefully and properly deckt with the like   50
light skarffing that hung about their eares wantonly dangling.

Euery one of these horse, had two Moores, attir'd like *Indian* slaues,
that for state sided them; with swelling wreaths of gould, and watshed
on their heads, which arose in all to / the number of a hundred.   [A3]

The Torch-bearers habits were likewise of the *Indian* garb, but more   55
strauagant then those of the Maskers; all showfully garnisht with
seueral-hewd fethers. The humble variety whereof, stucke off the
more amplie, the Maskers high beauties, shining in the habits of themselues; and reflected in their kinde, a new and delightfully-varied
radiance on the beholders.   60

All these sustaind torches of *Virgine* wax, whose staues were great
canes al ouer gilded; And these (as the rest) had euery Man his
Moore, attending his horse.

The Maskers, riding single; had euery Masker, his Torch-bearer
mounted before him. The last Charriot, which was most of all adornd;   65
had his whole frame fill'd with moulded worke; mixt all with paint-
ings, and glittering scarffings of siluer; ouer which was cast a Canopie
of golde, boarne vp with antick figures, and all compos'd *a la Grotesca.*
Before this in the seate of it, as the Chario- / tere; was aduanc't a   [A3ᵛ]

---

37 Midde-legge] *Q2;* Midde- / legge *Q1* ‖ **39** altogether] Al- / together *Q1;* Altogether *Q2* ‖ **68**
Grotesca] *Nichols;* Grotesea *Q1-2* ‖

strange person, and as strangely habited, half French, halfe Swizz; his 70
name *Capriccio*; wearing on his head a paire of golden Bellowes, a
guilt spurre in one hand, and with the other mannaging the reignes
of the fowre Horses that drewe it.

On a seate of the same Chariot, a little more eleuate, sate *Eunomia,*
the Virgine Priest of the Goddesse *Honor,* together with *Phemis,* her 75
Herald: The habite of her Priest, was a Robe of white silke, gathered
about the necke; a pentacle of siluered stuffe about her shoulders,
hanging foldedly downe, both before and behind.

A vestall vaile on her head of Tiffany, strip't with siluer, hanging
with a trayne, to the earth. 80

The Herrald was attyr'd in an Antique Curace of siluer stuffe, with
labells at the wings and basses; a short gowne of gould stuffe; with
wide sleeues, cut in panes: a wreath of gould on his head, and a Rod
of gould in his hand. /

Highest of all in the most eminent seate of the Tryumphall sat, [A4] 85
side to side, the cœlestiall Goddesse, *Honour*; and the earthy Deity,
Plutus; or Riches. His attire; a short robe of gould, frindg'd; his wide
sleeues turn'd vp, and out-showd his naked armes: his Head and
Beard sprinckl'd with showrs of gould: his Buskins, clinckant, as his
other attire. The Ornaments of *Honor* were these: a rich full robe of 90
blew silke girt about her, a mantle of siluer worne ouer-thwart, ful
gathered, and descending in folds behind: a vaile of net lawne, en-
brodered with Oos and Spangl'd; her tresses in tucks, braided with
siluer: the hinder part shadowing in waues her shoulders.

These, thus perticularly, and with proprietie adorn'd, were strongly 95
attended with a full Guard of two hundred Halbardiers: two Marshals
(being choice Gentlemen, of either house) Commaunder-like attir'd,
to and fro coursing, to keepe all in their orders. /

A showe at all parts so nouell, conceitfull and glorious, as hath not [A4ᵛ]
in this land, (to the proper vse and obiect it had porpos'd) beene euer 100
before beheld. Nor did those honorable Inns of Court, at any time in
that kinde, such acceptable seruice to the sacred Maiesty of this kingdome, nor were return'd by many degrees, with so thrice gratious, and
royall entertainment and honor. But, (as aboue sayd) all these so
marching to the Court at White Hall, the King, Bride, and Bride- 105
groom, with all the Lords of the most honord priuy Councel, and our
chief Nobility, stood in the Gallery before the Tilt-yeard, to behold
their arriuall; who, for the more ful satisfaction of his Maiesties view,
made one turn about the yeard, and dismounted: being then honor-

---

79 strip't with] *Q2*; strip'twith *Q1* ‖ **83** a wreath] A ∼ *Q1-2* ‖ **90** *Honor*] Honor *Q1-2* ‖ **94** the]
The *Q1-2* ‖ **95** strongly] *Q2*; 'strongly *Q1* ‖ **105-6** Bride- / groom] Bridegroom *Q1-2* ‖

ably attended through the Gallery to a Chamber appointed, where   110
they were to make ready for their performance in the Hall, &c.

The King beeing come forth, the Maskers ascended vnseene to their
scœne. Then for the works.

First there appear'd at the lower end of the / Hall, an Artificiall   [a1]
Rock, whose top was neere as high as the hall it selfe. This Rock, was   115
in the vndermost part craggy, and full of hollow places, in whose con-
caues were contriv'd, two winding paire of staires, by whose greeces
the Persons aboue might make their descents, and all the way be
seene: all this Rocke grew by degrees vp into a gold-colour; and was
run quite through, with veines of golde: On the one side whereof,   120
eminently raised on a faire hill, was erected a siluer Temple of an
octangle figure, whose Pillars were of a compos'd order, and bore
vp an Architraue, Freese, and Cornish: Ouer which stood a continued Plinthe; whereon were aduaunc't Statues of siluer: Aboue
this, was placed a bastarde Order of Architecture, wherein were keru'd   125
Compartements: In one of which was written in great golde Capitalls,
HONORIS FANVM: Aboue all, was a *Coupolo,* or Type, which
seem'd to be scal'd with siluer Plates.

For finishing, of all, vpon a Pedistall, was fixt a round stone of
siluer, from which grew a paire of golden wings; both faign'd to   130
bee / Fortunes: the round stone (when her feet trod it) euer affirm'd   [a1ᵛ]
to be rouling, figuring her inconstancy: the golden wings, denoting
those nimble Powres, that pompously beare her about the world; on
that Temple (erected to her daughter, *Honor*; and figuring this kingdome) put off by her, and fixt, for assured signe she would neuer for-   135
sake it.

About this Temple, hung Festones wreath'd with siluer from one
Pillars head to another. Besides, the Freese was enricht with keruings,
all shewing Greatnes and Magnificence.

On the other side of the Rocke, grewe a Groue, in whose vtmost   140
part appear'd a vast, wither'd, and hollow Tree, being the bare re-
ceptacle of the Baboonerie.

These following should in duty haue had their proper places, after
euery fitted speech of the Actors; but being preuented by the vnexpected haste of the Printer, which he neuer let me know, and neuer   145
sending me a proofe, till he had past those speeches; I had no reason
to imagine hee could haue been so forward. His fault is therfore to
be supplied by the obserua- / tion, and reference of the Reader, who   [a2]
will easily perceiue, where they were to bee inserted.

130 wings;] *Q1(c), Q2;* ~, *Q1(u)* ‖ 132 rouling,] *Q2;* ~; *Q1* ‖ 133 world;] *Q1(c);* ~. *Q1(u)*;
~: *Q2* | on] On *Q1-2* ‖

After the speech of *Plutus* (who as you may see after, first entred)   150
the middle part of the Rocke began to moue, and being come some fiue
paces vp towards the King, it split in peeces with a great crack; and
out brake *Capriccio,* as before described. The peeces of the Rocke
vanisht, and he spake as in his place.

At the singing of the first Song, full, which was sung by the Virginian   155
Priests; called the *Phœbades,* to sixe Lutes (being vsed as an Orphean
vertue, for the state of the Mines opening): the vpper part of the
Rock was sodainly turn'd to a Cloude, discouering a rich and refulgent
Mine of golde; in which the twelue Maskers were triumphantly
seated: their Torch-bearers attending before them. All the lights   160
beeing so ordred, that though none were seen, yet had their lustre
such vertue, that by it, the least spangle or spark of the Maskers rich
habites, might with ease and cleerenesse be discerned as far off as the
state. /

Ouer this golden Mine, in an Euening sky, the ruddy Sunne was [a2ᵛ] 165
seen ready to set; and behind the tops of certaine white Cliffes, by
degrees descended; casting vp a banke of Cloudes; in which, a while
hee was hidden: but then gloriously shining, gaue that vsually-
obseru'd good Omen, of succeeding faire weather.

Before he was fully set, the *Phœbades* (shewing the custome of the   170
Indians to adore the Sunne setting) began their obseruance with the
Song, to whose place, wee must referre you for the manner and words;
All the time they were singing; the Torch-bearers holding vp their
Torches to the Sun; to whome the Priests themselues, and the rest,
did (as they sung) obeisance: Which was answred by other Musique   175
and voices, at the commandement of *Honor,* with al obseruances vs'd
to the King &c. As in the following places. /

To answer certaine insolent obiections made against the length of   [a3]
my speeches, and narrations; being (for the probability of all accidents,
rising from the inuention of this Maske; and their aplication, to the   180
persons, and places: for whome, and by whome it was presented) not
conuenient, but necessary; I am enforct to affirme this; That: as there
is no Poem nor Oration so generall; but hath his one perticular proposi-
tion; Nor no riuer so extrauagantly ample, but hath his neuer-so-narrow
fountaine, worthy to be namd; so all these courtly, and honoring inuen-   185
tions (hauing Poesie, and Oration in them, and a fountaine, to be
exprest, from whence their Riuers flow) should expressiuely-arise out
of the places, and persons for and by whome they are presented; with-
out which limits, they are luxurious, and vaine. But what rules soeuer

---

156 *Phœbades*] Phœbades *Q1-2* | an] *Q1(c), Q2*; in *Q1(u)* ‖ **164** state] *MS correction IU copy;*
seate *Q1-2 (See Textual Note)* ‖ **166** to set] *Q1(c), Q2*; to be set *Q1(u)* ‖ **167** descended;]
Q1(c), Q2; ~, *Q1(u)* ‖ **168-69** vsually-obseru'd] vsually- / obseru'd *Q1*; vsually obser- / ued
Q2 ‖ **170** *Phœbades*] Phœbades *Q1*; Phæbades *Q2* ‖ **174** and] aud *Q1*; & *Q2* ‖ **175** (as they
sung)] *Q2*; ∧~~~∧ *Q1* ‖ **176** obseruances] *Q2*; obseᵣuances *Q1* ‖ **187** *expressiuely-arise*]
Q1(c); ~-~; *Q1(u)*; ~∧~ *Q2* ‖ **188** for] *Q1(c), Q2*; ~; *Q1(u)* ‖ **189** vaine] *Q1(c), Q2; paine*
Q1(u) ‖

are set downe, to any Art, or Act (though, without their obseruation; 190
No Art, nor Act, is true, and worthy) yet are they nothing the more
followd; or those few that follow them credited. Euery vulgarly-
esteemd vpstart; dares breake the dreadfull dignity of antient and
autenticall Poesie: and presume Luciferously, to proclame in place
thereof, repugnant precepts of their owne spaune. Truth, and Worth, 195
haue no faces, to enamour the Lycentious, but vaine-glory, and humor.
The same body: the same beauty, a thousand men seeing: Onely the
man whose bloud is fitted, hath that which hee calls his soule, enam-
ourd. And this, out of infallible cause; for, men vnderstand not these
of Mænander ———— ———— est mor- / bus oportunitas [a3ᵛ] 200

Animæ, quod ictus, vulnus accipit graue.

But the cause of some Mens being enamourd with Truth, and of her
slight respect, in others; is the diuine Freedom; *one touching with his*
aprehensiue finger, the other, passing. The Hill of the Muses (which
all men must clime in the regular way, to Truth) is said of ould, to 205
be forcked. And the two points of it, parting at the Top; are Insania,
and, diuinus furor. Insania, *is that which euery Ranck-brainde writer;*
and iudge of Poeticall writing, is rapt withal; when hee presumes either
to write or censure the height of Poesie; and that transports him with
humor, vaine-glory and pride, most prophane and sacrilegious: when 210
diuinus furor, *makes gentle, and noble, the neuer so truly-inspired*
writer ——— ———

Emollit mores nec sinit esse feros.

And the mild beames of the most holy inflamer; easely, and sweetly
enter, with all vnderstanding sharpenesse, the soft, and sincerely hu- 215
mane; but with no Time; No Study; No meanes vnder heauen: any
arrogant, all-occupation deuourer (that will Chandler-like set vp with
all wares; selling, Poesies Nectar and Ambrosia; as wel as musterd, and
vineagar) the chast and restraind beames of humble truth will euer
enter; but onely grase, and glaunce at them: and the further fly 220
them. /

The aplicable argument of [a4]
the *Maske.*

Honor, is so much respected, and ador'd; that shee hath a Temple
erected to her, like a Goddesse; a Virgine Priest consecrated to her 225
(which is *Eunomia,* or Lawe; since none should dare accesse to Honor,
but by Vertue; of which Lawe being the rule, must needes be a chiefe)
and a Herrald (call'd *Phemis,* or Fame) to proclame her institutions,

200 oportunitas] *Q1(c), Q2; ~. Q1(u)* ‖ **202** some] *Parrott; all Q1-2* | Truth, and] *Truth. And Q1-2* ‖ **203** slight] *Q1(c), Q2; sleight Q1(u)* | Freedom] *Q1(c), Q2; freedom Q1(u)* ‖ **209** write] *Q1(c), Q2; writ Q1(u)* ‖ **211** furor,] *~; Q1-2* ‖ **219** vineagar) the] *vineagar.) The Q1-2* ‖ **224** Honor] *Honor Q1-2* ‖

and commandements. To amplefie yet more the diuine graces of
this Goddesse; *Plutus,* (or Riches) being by *Aristophanes, Lucian. &c.*   230
presented naturally blind, deformd, and dull witted; is here by his loue
of *Honor,* made see, made sightly, made ingenious, made liberall: And
all this conuerted and consecrate to the most worthy celebration of
these sacred Nuptialls; all issuing (to conclude the necessary application) from an honorable Temple. &c.   235

Non est certa fides, quam non Iniuria versat.
——— ——— Fallit portus & ipse fidem. /

THE NAMES OF THE SPEAKERS.   [B1]

Honour, a Goddesse.

Plutus, (or Riches) a God.

Eunomia, (or Law) Priest of *Honor.*

Phemis, Honors Herrald.

Capriccio, a man of wit, &c.

THE PRESENTMENT.

Plutus appear'd suruaying the worke with this speech.

PLVT.

Rockes? Nothing but Rockes in these masking deuices? Is Inuention so poore shee must needes euer dwell amongst Rocks? But it may
worthily haue chaunc'd (being so of- / ten presented) that their vaine   [B1ᵛ] 5
Custome is now become the necessarie hand of heauen, transforming
into Rocks, some stonie-hearted Ladies, courted in former masks; for
whose loues, some of their repulst seruants haue perisht: or perhaps
some of my flintie-hearted Vsurers haue beene heere metamorphosed;
betwixt whom and Ladies, there is resemblance enough: Ladies vsing   10
to take interest, besides their principall, as much as Vsurers. See, it
is so; and now is the time of restoring them to their naturall shapes:
It moues, opens, excellent! This metamorphosis I intend to ouer-
heare. /

A Rock, mooving and breaking with a cracke about   [B2] 15
Capriccio, he enters with a payre of Bellows on

---

230 *Aristophanes*] *Q1(c), Q2; Arisiophanes Q1(u)* ‖ **231** witted;] *Q1(c), Q2;* ~, *Q1(u)* ‖ **232**
Honor] Honor *Q1-2* | ingenious,] ~; *Q1-2* ‖ **234-37** *Nuptialls; . . . fidem.*] *Q1 (c, 2nd state), Q2;*
Nuptialls; . . . versat. *Q1 (c, 1st state);* Nuptialls. *Q1(u)* ‖ **234** issuing] *Q2;* issning *Q1* ‖ Riches)
a God.] *Q1(c), Q2;* Riches.) *Q1(u)* ‖ *Eunomia,*] ~∧ *Q1-2* | Law] law *Q1-2* | *Honor*] honor *Q1-2* ‖
Honors] Honors *Q1-2* ‖ **7** stonie-hearted] stonie hearted *Q1-2* ‖ **13-14** ouer-heare] ouer-heare
Q1; ouer- / heare *Q2* ‖ **16** *Capriccio*] Capriccio *Q1-2*

his head, a spur in one hand, and a peece of golde
Ore in the other, &c.

He speakes, vt sequitur.

CAPR.

How hard this world is to a man of wit? hee must eate through 20
maine Rockes for his food, or fast; a restles and tormenting stone,
his wit is to him: the very stone of *Sisyphus* in hell; nay, the Philosophers stone, makes not a man more wretched: A man must be
a second *Proteus,* and turne himselfe into all shapes (like *Vlisses*) to
winde through the straites of this pinching vale of miserie; I haue 25
turn'd my selfe into a Tailor, a Man, a Gentleman, a Nobleman, a
Worthy man; but had neuer the witte to turne my selfe into an
Alder-man. There are manie shapes to perish in, but one to liue in,
and that's an Aldermans: / Tis not for a man of wit to take any [B2ᵛ]
rich Figure vpon him: your bould, proud, ignorant, that's braue and 30
clinkant, that findes crownes put into his shooes euery morning by
the Fayries and will neuer tell; whose Wit is humor, whose Iudgement
fashion, whose Pride is emptinesse, Birth his full man; that is in all
things something, in Sum totall, nothing: He shall liue in the land
of *Spruce,* milke and hony flowing into his mouth sleeping. 35

PLVT.

This is no transformation, but an intrusion into my golden mines:
I will heare him further.

CAPR.

This breach of Rockes I haue made, in needy pursuite of the blind
Deity, Riches: who is myraculously ariued here. For (according to
our rare men of wit) heauen standing, and earth mouing, her motion 40
(being circular) hath brought one of the most re- / mote parts of the [B3]
world, to touch at this all-exceeding Iland: which a man of wit would
imagine must needs moue circularly with the rest of the world, and
so euer maintaine an equal distance. But, Poets (our chiefe men of
wit) answere that point directly; most ingeniously affirming: That 45
this Ile is (for the excellency of it) diuided from the world (*diuisus
ab orbe Britannus*) and that though the whole World besides moues;
yet this Ile stands fixt on her owne feete, and defies the Worlds muta-
bility, which this rare accident of the arriuall of Riches, in one of his
furthest-off-scituate dominions, most demonstratiuely proues. 50

PLVT.

This is a man of wit indeede, and knows of all our arriuals.

---

17 peece] *Q2;* peeee *Q1* ‖ **21** maine] *Q1 errata;* manie *Q1-2 text* ‖ **26** Nobleman] Noble- / man
Q1-2 ‖ **29** that's] *Q2;* tha's *Q1* ‖ **32-33** Iudgement fashion] *MS correction IU copy;* Iudgement is
fashion *Q1-2* (*See Textual Note*) ‖ **33** man;] *MS correction IU copy;* ∼, *Q1-2* ‖ **34** He] *Q1(c),*
Q2; hee *Q1(u)* ‖ **37** him] *Q2;* him- *Q1* ‖ **42** all-exceeding] all- / exceeding *Q1-2* ‖

CAPR.

With this dull Deity Riches, a rich Iland lying in the South-sea, called *Pæana*, of the *Pæans* (or songs) sung to the Sun, whom they / there adore (being for strength and riches, called the Nauill of that South-sea) is by earths round motion mou'd neere this Brittan Shore. In which Island (beeing yet in command of the Virginian continent) a troupe of the noblest Virginians inhabiting; attended hether the God of Riches, all triumphantly shyning in a Mine of gould. For hearing of the most royal solemnity, of these sacred Nuptialls; they crost the Ocean in their honor, and are here arriu'd. A poore snatch at some of the goulden Ore, that the feete of Riches haue turnd vp as he trod here, my poore hand hath purchast; and hope the Remainder of a greater worke, wilbe shortly extant.

[B3ᵛ]
55

60

PLVT.

You Sir, that are miching about my goulden Mines here.

CAPR.

What, can you see Sir? you haue heretofore beene presented blinde: like your Mo- / ther Fortune; and your Brother Loue.

65
[B4]

PLVT.

But now Sir, you see I see.

CAPR.

By what good meanes, I beseech you Sir.

PLVT.

That meanes, I may vouchsafe you hereafter; meane space, what are you?

70

CAPR.

I am Sir a kinde of Man; A Man of wit: with whom your worship has nothing to do I thinke.

PLVT.

No Sir, nor will haue any thing to doe with him: A Man of wit? what's that? A Begger?

CAPR.

And yet no Diuell Sir. /

75
[B4ᵛ]

PLVT.

As I am, you meane.

CAPR.

Indeede sir your Kingdome is vnder the Earth.

53 *Pæana . . . Pæans*] *Nichols*; *Pæana . . . Pæans Q1-2* | of] *Q2*; (of *Q1* ‖ **57** continent) a] ∼.) A *Q1-2* ‖ **61** Riches] *Q2* (*Riches*); riches *Q1* ‖ **69** hereafter] here- / after *Q1-2* ‖ **74** what's] whats *Q1-2* | Begger?] ∼. *Q1-2* ‖

PLVT.

That's true, for Riches is the *Atlas* that holdes it vp, it would sinke else.

CAPR.

Tis rather a wonder, it sinks not with you Sir, y'are so sinfully, and   80
damnably heauy.

PLVT.

Sinfull? and damnable? what, a Puritane? These Bellowes you
weare on your head, shew with what matter your braine is pufft vp
Sir: A Religion-forger I see you are, and presume of inspiration from
these Bellowes; with which yee study to blow vp the setled gouern-   85
ments of kingdomes. /

CAPR.   [C1]

Your worship knockes at a wrong dore Sir, I dwell farre from the
person you speak of.

PLVT.

What may you be then, beeing a man of wit? a Buffon, a Iester.
Before I would take vpon mee the title of a man of wit, and bee   90
baffl'd by euery man of wisedome for a Buffon; I would turne Banckrout, or set vp a Tobacco shop; change clokes with an Alchemist,
or serue an Vsurer; bee a watering post for euery Groome; stand the
push of euery rascall wit; enter lists of iests with trencher-fooles, and
bee foold downe by them, or (which is worse) put them downe in   95
fooling: are these the qualities a man of wit should run proud of?

CAPR.

Your worship I see has obtaind wit, with sight, which I hope yet
my poor wit wil well be able to answer; for touching my iesting, I /
haue heard of some Courtiers, that haue run themselues out of their   [C1ᵛ]
states with Iusting; and why may not I then raise my selfe in the State   100
with iesting? An honest Shoomaker, (in a liberall Kings time) was
knighted for making a cleane boote, and is it impossible, that I for
breaking a cleane Iest, should bee aduaunc't in Court, or Counsaile?
or at least, serued out for an Ambassador to a dull Climate? Iests, and
Merriments are but wild weedes in a rank soile, which being well   105
manured, yield the wholesom crop of wisdome and discretion at time
ath'yeare.

PLVT.

Nay, nay, I commend thy iudgement for cutting thy cote so iust
to the bredth of thy shoulders; he that cannot be a courser in the field,

---

82 what,] *Shepherd*; ∼∧ *Q1-2* ‖ **92** shop;] *MS correction IU copy*; ∼, *Q1-2* ‖ **93** Vsurer;] *MS correction IU copy*; ∼, *Q1-2* | post] *Q1 errata, Q2*; pot *Q1 text* ‖ **101** in] *Q2*; in in *Q1* ‖

let him learne to play the Iack-an-Apes in the Chamber, hee that   110
cannot personate the wise-man well amongst wisards, let him learne
to play the foole well amongst dizzards. /

CAPR.

[C2]

Tis passing miraculous, that your dul and blind worship should so
sodainly turne both sightfull, and witfull.

PLVT.

The Riddle of that myracle, I may chance dissolue to you in se-   115
quell; meane time, what name sustain'st thou? and what toies are
these thou bear'st so phantastically about thee?

CAPR.

These toies, Sir, are the Ensignes that discouer my name and qualitie: my name being *Capriccio,* and I weare these Bellowes on my
head, to shew I can puffe vp with glory all those that affect mee: 120
and besides, beare this spurre, to shew I can spur-gall, euen the best
that contemne me.

PLVT.

A dangerous fellowe; But what makest thou (poore man of wit) at
these pompous Nuptials? /

CAPR.

[C2ᵛ]

Sir, I come hether with a charge; To doe these Nuptialls, I hope,   125
very acceptable seruice; And my charge is; A company of accomplisht
Trauailers; that are excellent at Antemaskes; and will tender a tast of
their quallity, if your worship please.

PLVT.

Excellent well pleasd; of what vertue are they besides?

CAPR.

Passing graue Sir, yet exceeding acute: witty, yet not ridiculous   130
(neuer laugh at their owne iests) laborious, yet not base; hauing cut
out the skirts of the whole world, in amorous quest of your gould and
siluer.

PLVT.

They shal haue enough; cal them: I beseech thee call them: how
farre hence abide they? /   135

CAPR.

[C3]

Sir (being by another eminent qualitie the admired souldiers of the
world) in contempt of softnes, and delicacie, they lie on the naturally

---

118 These toies,] ∼, ∼∧ *Q1-2* ‖ **123** fellowe;] ∼, *Q1-2* ‖ **124** Nuptials?] *Q2;* ∼; *Q1* ‖ **129** besides?] *MS correction IU copy;* ∼. *Q1-2* ‖ **130-31** ridiculous (. . . iests)] *MS correction IU copy;* ridiculous; . . . iests: *Q1-2 (See Textual Note)* ‖ **131** laborious,] *Q2;* ∼∧ *Q1* | base;] *MS correction IU copy;* ∼, *Q1-2* ‖

hard boords of that naked tree; and will your worship assure them rewards fit for persons of their freight?

PLVT.

Dost thou doubt my reward beeing pleased?   140

CAPR.

I know Sir, a man may sooner win your reward, for pleasing you, then deseruing you. But you great wise persons, haue a fetch of State; to employ with countenance, and encouragement, but reward with austerity and disgrace; saue your purses, and lose your honours.

PLVT.

To assure thee of reward, I will now sa- / tisfie thee touching the   [C3ᵛ] miraculous cause, both of my sight and wit, and which consequently moues mee to humanity, and bounty; And all is, onely this; my late being in loue, with the louely Goddesse *Honor.*

CAPR.

If your Worshipp loue *Honor,* indeed Sir, you must needes be boun- tifull. But where is the rare Goddesse you speake of to be seene?   150

PLVT.

In that Rich Temple, where Fortune fixt those her goulden wings, thou seest; And that rowling stone she vs'd to tread vpon, for signe shee would neuer for-sake this Kingdome; There is ador'd, the worthy Goddesse *Honor.* The swetnesse of whose voice, when I first heard her perswasions, both to my self, and the *Virginian* Princes arriu'd here,   155 to doe honor and homage, to these heauenly Nuptialls, so most power- fully enamour'd mee, that the fire of my loue flew vp to the sight / of mine eyes: that haue lighted within mee a whole firmament of   [C4] Bounty, which may securely assure thee, thy reward is certaine: and therefore call thy accomplisht company to their Antemaske.   160

CAPR.

See Sir, the time, set for their apperance, being expir'd; they appeere to their seruice of them-selues.

Enter the Baboones, after whose dance, being
Anticke, and delightful, they returned to their
Tree, when Plutus *spake to* Capriccio.   165

PLVT.

Gramercy now *Capriccio,* take thy men of complement, and trauaile

139 freight?] *Q2;* ∼. *Q1* ‖ **144** austerity] *Q1 errata;* answer *Q1-2 text* | disgrace;] *MS correction IU copy;* ∼, *Q1-2* | purses] *Q1 errata;* purposes *Q1-2 text* ‖ **148, 149** Honor] Honor *Q1-2* ‖ **149** indeed Sir,] *MS correction IU copy;* ∼, ∼∧ *Q1-2* ‖ **154** Honor] Honor *Q1-2* ‖ **159** securely] *Q1 errata;* semingly *Q1 text;* seemingly *Q2 text* | thee] *Q2;* the *Q1* ‖ **161** the] The *Q1-2* ‖ **162** to ... them-selues.] *Q1-2 divide this line from the following SD by two parallel rules running across the width of the type-page* ‖ **163** Baboones,] ∼∧ *Q1-2* ‖ **165** Capriccio] *MS correction IU copy;* Capriccius *Q1-2* ‖

with them to other marriages. My Riches to thy Wit; they will get
some thing some-where. /

CAPR. [C4ᵛ]

What's this?

PLVT.

A straine of Wit beyond a Man of Wit. I haue imployd you, and   170
the grace of that, is reward enough; hence; packe, with your comple-
mental Fardle: The sight of an attendant for reward, is abominable
in the eyes of a turne-seru'd Politician, and I feare, will strike me
blinde againe. I can not abide these bellowes of thy head, they and
thy men of wit haue melted my Mines with them, and consum'd me;   175
yet take thy life and be gone. *Neptune* let thy predecessor, *Vlysses,*
liue after all his slaine companions, but to make him die more miser-
ably liuing; gaue him vp to ship-wracks, enchantments; men of wit
are but enchanted, there is no such thing as wit in this world. Go,
take a tree, inure thy souldiers to hardnes, tis honorable, though not   180
clinkant. /

CAPR. [D1]

Can this be possible?

PLVT.

Alas! poore man of wit, how want of reward daunts thy vertue?
But because I must send none away discontented, from these all-
pleasing Nuptials; take this wedge of golde, and wedge thy selfe into   185
the world with it, renouncing that loose wit of thine, t'will spoile
thy complexion.

CAPR.

Honor, and all *Argus* eyes, to Earths all-commaunding Riches.
Pluto *etiam cedit* Iupiter.   *Exit Capr. /*

> After this lowe Induction, by these succeeding   [D1ᵛ] 190
> degrees, the chiefe Maskers were aduanc't to their
> discouerie.

PLVT.

These humble obiects can no high eyes drawe.
Eunomia? (or the sacred power of Lawe)
Daughter of *Ioue,* and Goddesse *Honors* Priest;   195
Appeare to *Plutus,* and his loue assist.

169 What's] Whats *Q1-2* ‖ 175 me;] *MS correction IU copy;* ~, *Q1-2* ‖ 179 Go] *MS correction*
IU copy; So *Q1-2* ‖ 184-85 all-pleasing] all- / pleasing *Q1-2* ‖ 188 *Honor*] Honor *Q1-2* | all-
commaunding] all- / commaunding *Q1-2* ‖ 189 Iupiter.] *Q2;* ~∧ *Q1* ‖ 192 discouerie.] *Q2;*
~∧ *Q1* ‖ 193 drawe.] *Parrott;* ~, *Q1-2* ‖ 195 *Honors*] Honors *Q1-2* ‖

EVN.

Eunomia
in the
Temple
gates.

What would the god of Riches?

PLVT.

          Ioine with *Honor*:
In purpos'd grace of these great Nuptials;
And since to *Honor* none should dare accesse,
But helpt by vertues hand (thy selfe, chaste *Lawe*   200
Being *Vertues* Rule, and her directfull light)
Help me to th'honor of her speech and sight.

EVN.

Thy will shal straight be honour'd; all that seek
Accesse to *Honor,* by cleer virtues beame,
Her grace preuents their pains, and comes to them. /   205

      Loud Musick, and *Honor* appears, descending with   [D2]
      her Herrald *Phemis,* and *Eunomia* (her Priest) be-
      fore her. The Musique ceasing *Plutus* spake.

PLVT.

Crowne of all merit, Goddess, and my Loue;
Tis now high time, that th'end for which we come   210
Should be endeuor'd in our vtmost right,
Done to the sweetnes of this Nuptiall night.

HON.

Plutus? The Princes of the Virgine land,
Whom I made crosse the Britan Ocean
To this most famed Ile, of all the world,   215
To do due homage to the sacred Nuptials
Of *Loue,* and *Beauty,* celebrated here,
By this Howre of the holy Eeuen I know,
Are ready to performe the rites they owe
To setting *Phœbus*; which (for greater State   220
To their apparance) their first act aduances,
And with songs Vshers their succeeding dances:
Herrald! giue summons to the Virgine Knights,
No longer to delay their purpos'd Rites.

HER.

Knights of the Virgine Land, whom bewties lights   225
Would glorifie with their inflaming sights;
Keep now obscur'd no more your faire intent, /
To adde your Beames to this nights ornament,   [D2ᵛ]

197, 199 *Honor*] Honor *Q1-2* ‖ **200** *Lawe*] Law *MS correction IU copy*; Loue *Q1-2* ‖ **204, 206**
Honor] Honor *Q1-2* ‖ **217** *Loue,* and *Beauty*] loue and beauty *Q1 errata; Lawe,* and *Vertue Q1-2*
text ‖ **221** aduances,] *MS correction IU copy, Q2;* ∼. *Q1* ‖ **222** dances:] *MS correction IU copy;* ∼,
Q1-2 ‖

The golden-winged *Howre* strikes now a Plaine,
And calls out all the pompe ye entertaine; 230
The Princely Bride-groome, and the Brides bright eyes,
Sparkle with grace to your discoueries.

> At these words, the *Phœbades* (or Priests of the
> Sunne) appear'd first with sixe Lutes, and sixe
> voices, and sung to the opening of the Mine and 235
> Maskers discouery, this ful Song.

The first Song.

Ope Earth thy wombe of golde,
   Shew Heauen thy cope of starres.
All glad Aspects vnfolde, 240
   Shine out, and cleere our Cares:
      Kisse Heauen and Earth, and so combine
      In all mixt ioy our Nuptiall Twine.

> This Song ended, a Mount opened, and spred like
> a Skie, in which appear'd a Sunne setting; beneath 245
> which, sate the twelue Maskers, in a Mine of golde;
> twelue Torch-bearers holding their torches before
> them, after which *Honor, &c.*

HON.

See now the setting Sun, casts vp his bank,
And showes his bright head at his Seas repaire, 250
For signe that all daies future shall be faire. /

PLVT. [D3]

May he that rules al nightes and dayes confirme it.

HON.

Behold the Sunnes faire Preists the *Phœbades,*
Their euening seruice in an Hymne addresse
To *Phœbus* setting; which we now shall heare, 255
And see the formes of their deuotions there.

The Phœbades *sing the first Stance of the* second song, *vt sequitur.*

One alone. 1.

Descend (faire Sun) and sweetly rest,
   In Tethis *Cristal armes, thy toyle,* 260
Fall burning on her Marble brest,
   And make with Loue her billowes boyle.

---

233 *Phœbades*] Phœbades *Q1-2* ‖ 249 See] *Q2*; Se *Q1* ‖ 252 al] *Q1(c), Q2*; the *Q1(u)* ‖ 253
Phœbades] *Q2*; *Phæbades Q1* ‖ 257 The] *Q2*; Thc *Q1* | Phœbades] *Phœbades Q1-2* ‖ 258 alone.] ∼∧
Q1-2 ‖

Another alone. 2.

Blow blow, sweet windes, O blow away,
    Al vapours from the fined ayre: 265
That to his golden head no Ray,
    May languish with the least empaire.

CHO.

Dance Tethis, *and thy loues red beames,*
    Embrace with Ioy, he now discends: /
Burnes burnes with loue to drinke thy streames,   [D3ᵛ] 270
    And on him endles youth attends.

After this Stance, *Honor* &c.

HON.

This superstitious Hymne, sung to the Sunne,
Let vs encounter with fit duties done
To our cleere *Phœbus*; whose true piety,   275
Enioyes from heauen an earthly deity.

Other Musique, and voyces; and this second
Stance was sung, directing their obseruance to the
King.

One alone. 1.   280

Rise, rise O Phœbus, *euer rise,*
    Descend not to th'inconstant streame,
But grace with endles light, our skyes,
    To thee that Sun is but a beame.

Another. 2.   285
Dance Ladies in our Sunnes bright rayes,
    In which the Bride and Bridegroome shine:
Cleere sable night with your eyes dayes,
    And set firme lights on Hymens *shrine.*

CHO.

O may our Sun not set before,   290
    He sees his endles seed arise:
And deck his triple crowned shore,
    With springs of humane Deities. /

This ended the *Phœbades* sung the third Stance.   [D4]

1.

Set Set (great Sun) our rising loue   295
    Shall euer celebrate thy grace:

---

266 *his*] *Q1 errata; this Q1-2 text* ‖ **269** *Ioy,*] *MS correction IU copy;* ∼∧ *Q1-2* ‖ **271** *And*] *and Q1-2*
‖ **272** *Honor*] Honor *Q1-2* ‖ **275** *Phœbus*] Phœbus *Q1-2* ‖ **280** *alone.*] ∼∧ *Q1-2* ‖ **281** Phœbus]
Phœbus *Q1-2* ‖ **282** *Descend*] descend *Q1-2* ‖ **284** *To*] to *Q1-2* ‖ **285** *Another.*] ∼∧ *Q1-2* ‖ **287** *In*]
in *Q1-2* ‖ **289** *And*] and *Q1-2* | Hymens] *Hymens Q1-2* ‖ **291** *He*] he *Q1-2* ‖ **293** *With*] with *Q1-2*
‖ **296** *Shall*] shall *Q1-2* ‖

Whom entring the high court of Ioue,
　Each God greetes, rising from his place.

2.

When thow thy siluer bow dost bend,
　All start aside and dread thy draughtes:　　　　　　　300
How can we thee enough commend,
　Commanding all worlds with thy shafts?

CHO.

Blest was thy mother bearing thee,
　And Phœbe *that delights in darts:*
Thou artful Songes dost set; and shee　　　　　　　305
　Winds horns, loues hounds, and high pallmd harts.

After this, *Honor.*

HON.

Againe our Musique and conclude this Song,
To him, to whom all *Phœbus* beames belong:

　　The other voyces sung to other Musike the fourth　　310
　　stance.

1.

Rise stil (cleere Sun) and neuer set,
　But be to Earth her only light:
All other Kings in thy beames met,
　Are cloudes and darke effects of night. /　　　　　315

2.　　　　　　　　　　　　　　　　　[D4ᵛ]

As when the Rosie Morne doth rise,
　Like Mists, all giue thy wisedome waie:
A learned King, is, as in skies,
　To poore dimme stars, the flaming day.

CHO.

Blest was thy Mother, bearing Thee,　　　　　　　320
　Thee only Relick of her Race,
Made by thy vertues beames a Tree,
　Whose armes shall all the Earth embrace.

This done *Eunomia* spake to the Maskers set yet
aboue.　　　　　　　　　　　　　　　　　　325

EVN.

Virginian Princes, ye must now renounce
Your superstitious worship of these Sunnes,

---

298 *Each*] each *Q1-2* | *greetes,*] *MS correction IU copy*; ∼∧ *Q1-2* ‖ **300** *All*] all *Q1-2* ‖ **302** *Commanding*] commanding *Q1-2* ‖ **304** *And*] and *Q1-2* | Phœbe] *Phœbe Q1-2* ‖ **306** *Winds*] winds *Q1-2* | *harts.*] ∼∧ *Q1-2* ‖ **307** this,] *MS correction IU copy*; ∼∧ *Q1-2* | *Honor*] Honor *Q1-2* ‖ **309** *Phœbus*] Phœbus *Q1-2* ‖ **310** *fourth*] Parrott; third *Q1-2* ‖ **313** *But*] but *Q1-2* ‖ **315** *Are*] are *Q1-2* ‖ **327** these Sunnes] *stet (See Textual Note)* ‖

Subiect to cloudy darknings and descents,
And of your fit deuotions, turne the euents
To this our Britan *Phœbus,* whose bright skie   330
(Enlightned with a Christian Piety)
Is neuer subiect to black Errors night,
And hath already offer'd heauens true light,
To your darke Region; which acknowledge now;
Descend, and to him all your homage vow. /   335

[Loude Mus⟨ick.⟩] With this the Torch-bearers de-   [E1]
scended, and performed another Antemaske, dancing with Torches lighted at both ends; which done,
the Maskers descended, and fell into their dances,
two of which being past, and others with the Ladies,   340

Honor spake.

The Bride
and Bride-
groome
were fig-
ured in
Loue and
Beauty.
Twinns
of which
Hippoc-
rates
speakes.

Musique! your voyces, now tune sweet and hie,
And singe the Nuptiall *Hymn* of *Loue,* and *Beauty.*
Twinns, as of one age, so to one desire
May both their bloods giue, an vnparted fire.   345
And as those twinns that Fame giues all her prise,
Combind their lifes pow'rs in such *Sympathies;*
That one being merry; mirth the other grac't:
If one felt sorrow, th'other griefe embrac't.
If one were healthfull; Health the other pleasd: 350
If one were sicke: the other was diseasd;
And all waies ioynd in such a constant troth
That one like cause had like effect in both,

Called
Twynns
being
both of
an Age.

So may these Nuptiall Twynnes, their whole liues store,
Spend in such euen parts, neuer grieuing more,   355
Then may the more set off their ioyes diuine;
As after clouds, the Sunne, doth clerest shine. /

This sayd, this Song of *Loue,* and *Bewty* was sung;   [E1ᵛ]
single.

[1.]

Bright Panthæa *borne to* Pan,   360
Of the Noblest Race of Man,
Her white hand to Eros *giuing,*

329 fit] *Q1 errata;* sweet *Q1-2 text* ‖ **334** Region;] *Q1(c), Q2;* ~, *Q1(u)* ‖ **336** Loude Mus⟨ick.⟩]
MS addition IU copy; om. Q1-2 ‖ **340** Ladies,] ~. *Q1-2* ‖ **343** *Loue,* and *Beauty*] Loue, and Beauty
Q1-2 ‖ **345** May both] Mayboth *Q1-2* ‖ **347** pow'rs] *MS correction IU copy;* power *Q1-2* ∣ *Sym-
pathies*] *Q2;* Symphathies *Q1* ‖ **359** 1.] *om. Q1-2* ‖

With a kisse, ioin'd Heauen to Earth
And begot so faire a birth,
　　As yet neuer grac't the liuing.　　　　　　　　　　365

CHO.

A Twinne that all worlds did adorne,
For so were Loue *and* Bewty *borne.*

2.

Both so lou'd, they did contend
Which the other should transcend,
　　Doing either, grace, and kindnes;　　　　　　　370
Loue *from* Bewty *did remoue*
Lightnes, call'd her staine in loue,
　　Bewtie *took from* Loue *his blindness.* /

CHO.　　　　　　　　　　　　　　[E2]

Loue *sparks made flames in* Bewties *skie,*
And Bewtie *blew vp* Loue *as hie.*　　　　　　375

3.

Virtue then commixt her fire;
To which Bountie *did aspire,*
　　Innocence *a* Crowne *conferring;*
Mine, and Thine, were then vnusde,
All things common: Nought abusde,　　　　　380
　　Freely earth her frutage bearing.

CHO.

Nought then was car'd for, that could fade,
And thus the golden world was made.

This sung, the Maskers danc't againe with the
Ladies, after which *Honor*.　　　　　　　　　　385

HON.

Now may the blessings of the golden age,
Swimme in these Nuptials, euen to holy rage:
A Hymn to Sleep prefer, and all the ioyes
That in his Empire are of dearest choice, /
Betwixt his golden slumbers euer flow,　　　　[E2ᵛ] 390
In these; And Theirs, in Springs as endless growe.

371-72 *remoue Lightnes,*] *Nichols;* ∼, ∼∧ *Q1-2* ‖ **375** 3.] *Q2;* ∼∧ *Q1* ‖ **387** rage:] *MS correction*
IU copy; ∼, *Q1-2* ‖ **391** these; And Theirs] *Q1(c), Q2;* these, and theirs *Q1(u)* ‖ .

This sayd, the last Song was sung full.

The last Song.

Now sleepe, binde fast, the flood of Ayre,
    Strike all things dumb and deafe,   395
And, to disturbbe our Nuptiall paire,
    Let stir no Aspen leafe.
Send flocks of golden Dreames
    That all true ioyes presage,
Bring, in thy oyly streames,   400
    The milke and hony Age.
        Now close the world-round sphere of blisse,
        And fill it with a heauenly kisse.

After this *Plutus* to the Maskers.

PLVT.

Come Virgine Knights, the homage ye haue done,   405
To *Loue* and *Bewty,* and our Britan Sun,
Kinde *Honor,* will requite with holy feasts
In her faire Temple; and her loued Guests,
Giues mee the grace t'inuite; when she and I
(*Honor* and *Riches*) will eternally /   410
A league in fauour of this night combine,   [E3]
In which *Loues* second hallowed Tapers shine;
Whose Ioies, may Heauen and Earth as highly please
As those two nights that got great *Hercules.*

The speech ended; they concluded with a dance,   415
that brought them off; *Plutus,* with *Honor* and
the rest conducting them vp to the Temple of
Honor.

FINIS. /

A Hymne to Hymen for the most time-   [E4]
fitted Nuptialls of our
thrice gracious Princesse
Elizabeth. *&c.*

Singe, Singe a Rapture to all Nuptial eares,
Bright *Hymens* torches, drunke vp *Parcæs* tears:
Sweete *Hymen; Hymen,* Mightiest of Gods,

---

395 *Strike*] strike *Q1-2* ‖ 409 t'inuite;] *MS correction IU copy;* ∼, *Q1-2* ‖ 2 Bright . . . tears:] *stet (See Textual Note)* ‖

Attoning of all-taming blood the odds;
Two into One, contracting; One to Two 5
Dilating, which no other God can doe.
Mak'st sure, with change, and lett'st the married try,
Of Man and woman, the Variety.

mil.   And as a flower, halfe scorcht with daies long heate
Thirsts for refreshing, with Nights cooling sweate, 10
The wings of *Zephire,* fanning still her face,
No chere can ad to her heart-thirsty grace;
Yet weares she gainst those fires that make her fade,
Her thicke hayrs proofe, al hyd, in Midnights shade;
Her Helth, is all in dews; Hope, all in showres, 15
Whose want bewailde, she pines in all her powres:
So Loue-scorch't Virgines, nourish quenchles fires; /
The Fathers cares; the Mothers kind desires; [E4ᵛ]
Their Gould, and Garments, of the newest guise,
Can nothing comfort their scorcht Phantasies, 20
But, taken rauish't vp, in *Hymens* armes,
His Circkle holds, for all their anguish, charms:

mil. ad   Then, as a glad Graft, in the spring Sunne shines,
ndem   That all the helps, of Earth, and Heauen combines
plicat.   In Her sweet grouth: Puts in the Morning on 25
Her cherefull ayres; the Sunnes rich fires, at Noone;
At Euen the sweete deaws, and at Night with starrs,
In all their vertuous influences shares;
So, in the Bridegroomes sweet embrace; the Bride,
All varied Ioies tasts, in their naked pride: 30
To which the richest weedes: are weedes, to flowres;
Come *Hymen* then; com close these Nuptial howres
With all yeares comforts. Come; each virgin keepes
Her odorous kisses for thee; Goulden sleepes
Will, in their humors, neuer steepe an eie, 35
Till thou inuit'st them with thy Harmony.
Why staiest thou? see each Virgin doth prepare
Embraces for thee; Her white brests laies bare
To tempt thy soft hand; let's such glances flie
As make starres shoote, to imitate her eye. 40
Puts Arts attires on, that put Natures doune:
Singes, Dances, sets on euery foote a Crowne,
Sighes, in her songs, and dances; kisseth Ayre
Till Rites, and words past, thou in deedes repaire;
The whole court Io sings: Io the Ayre: 45
Io, the flouds, and fields: Io, most faire,

18 desires;] ∼. *Q1-2* ‖ **41** attires] *Q1(c), Q2;* attire *Q1(u)* ‖ **43** dances;] *Q1(c), Q2;* ∼, *Q1(u)* ‖

Most sweet, most happy *Hymen*; Come: away; /
With all thy Comforts come; old Matrons pray,   [F1]
With young Maides Languors; Birds bill, build, and breed
To teach thee thy kinde, euery flowre and weed   50
Looks vp to gratulate thy long'd for fruites;
Thrice giuen, are free, and timely-granted suites:
There is a seed by thee now to be sowne,
In whose fruit Earth, shall see her glories show'n,
At all parts perfect; and must therfore loose   55
No minutes time; from times vse all fruite flowes;

Simil.   And as the tender Hyacinth, that growes
Where *Phœbus* most his golden beames bestowes,
Is propt with care; is water'd euery howre;
The sweet windes adding their encreasing powre,   60
The scattered drops of Nights refreshing dew,
Hasting the full grace, of his glorious hew,
Which once disclosing, must be gatherd straight,
Or hew, and Odor both, will lose their height;
So, of a Virgine, high, and richly kept,   65
The grace and sweetnes full growne must be reap't,
Or, forth her spirits fly, in empty Ayre;
The sooner fading; the more sweete and faire.
Gentle, O Gentle *Hymen*, be not then
Cruell, that kindest art to Maids, and Men;   70
These two, One Twynn are; and their mutuall blisse,
Not in thy beames, but in thy Bosome is.
Nor can their hands fast, their harts ioyes make sweet;
Their harts, in brests are; and their Brests must meete.
Let, there be Peace, yet Murmur: and that noise,   75
Beget of peace, the Nuptiall battailes ioyes.
Let Peace grow cruell, and take wrake of all, /
The warrs delay brought thy full Festiuall.   [F1ᵛ]
Harke, harke, O now the sweete Twyn murmur sounds;
Hymen is come, and all his heate abounds;   80
Shut all Dores; None, but *Hymens* lights aduance.
No sound styr; let, dumb Ioy, enioy a trance.
Sing, sing a Rapture to all Nuptiall eares,
Bright *Hymens* Torches, drunke vp *Parcæs* teares.

FINIS.

70 that] That *Q1-2* | art] *Nichols*; arts *Q1-2* ‖ 84 Torches,] ∼∧ *Q1-2* ‖

HISTORICAL COLLATION OF Q2
AND EDITED TEXTS

[Editions collated: Q2 (n.d.), Yale and Huntington copies; Nichols (=*N*, in *The Progresses . . . of King James the First*, 1828, II, 566-86); Shepherd (=*S*, in *The Works of George Chapman: Plays*, 1875, pp. 341-50; *Poems and Minor Translations*, 1875, pp. 176-77); Parrott (=*P*, in *The Plays and Poems of George Chapman: The Comedies*, [1914], pp. 435-60); Bartlett (=*B*, in *Poems of George Chapman*, 1941, pp. 365-67; for "A Hymne to Hymen" only). Only substantive and semi-substantive variants are recorded; obvious errors are not recorded. Lemmata are taken from the present text. Where lemma represents the reading of Q copy-text, omission of siglum indicates agreement with lemma.]

Epistle Dedicatorie
11 Hubberd] Hobart *P*

The Maske [introductory description]
12 were] was *Q2*
14 antick] ~ [antique] *N*; antic *S, P*
23 ground cloath] ground-cloth *S, P*
30 pearle] pearles *N*
31 presented] [re]presented *N*
42 cane darts] cane-darts *Q2*
45 Horse] horses *N*
57 stucke] strucke *N*
61 of *Virgine* wax] of the Virgine-wax *N*
66 his] its *N*
68 *Grotesca*] *N, S, P*; *Grotesea Q1-2*
74 On a] On the *N*
85 Tryumphall] Triumphal car *S, P*
86 earthy] earthly *Q2*
100 porpos'd] purpos'd *Q2, N*; proposed *S, P*
111 &c.] *om. N*
128 scal'd] seal'd [ceiled] *N*
146 those] their *N*
152 vp] *om. N*
157 Mines] mine's *N*
164 state] *MS correction IU, BM³, Dyce¹ copies*; seate *Q1-2, N, S*; s[t]ate *P*
180 *rising*] arising *N*
181-82 *not conuenient*] not [only] convenient *N*

187 *expressiuely-arise*] *expressively arise Q2, N, S, P*
191 *are they*] they are *S, P*
192 *those few that*] the few who *N*
202 *some*] *P; all Q1-2, N, S*
    Truth,] *N, S, P;* ~. *Q1-2*
204 *passing. The*] ~∧ *the Q2*
206 *at the Top*] *om. N*
210 *vaine-glory*] vain glory *P*
211 *truly-inspired*] *truely inspired Q2, N, S, P*
215-16 *humane;*] humane, *S*
217 *all-occupation*] all occupation *Q2*
218 *Poesies*] ~, *Q2*
219 *vineagar) the*] *P; vineagar.) The Q1-2;* vineager. The *N;* vinegar, the *S*
    beames] beame *N*
    euer] never *N*
236 versat.] ~, *N*

The Maske

35 *Spruce*] spruce *S*
    PLVT.] *Plu. [aside] P*
50 PLVT.] *Plu. [aside] P*
53-54 they there] there they *S, P*
57 continent) a] *N, P;* continent.) A *Q1-2;* continent), a *S*
61 *Riches*] *Q2, N, S, P;* riches *Q1*
62 he] she *N*
63 PLVT.] *Plu. [advancing] P*
64 Mines] mine *N*
82 Sinfull?] ~; *Q2*
93 watering post] *Q1 errata, Q2;* watering pot *Q1 text;* watering-po[s]t *N;* watering-post *S, P*
    for] to *N*
100 states] 'states *N*
101 in] *Q2, N, S, P;* in in *Q1*
107 ath'] o'th' *N, P*
112 well] *om. S, P*
144 austerity . . . purses] *N reads* answers *for the erroneous Q1* answer *and glosses as* excuses; *he also reads* purposes (*following the erroneous Q1 reading*), *but suggests* purses *as an emendation (see footnote on p. 559).*
159 securely] *N reads* seemingly (*the erroneous Q1 reading*) *and glosses as* clearly (*see footnote on p. 559*).
165 Capriccio.] *MS correction IU copy, N;* Capriccius *Q1-2, S, P*
166 Gramercy now *Capriccio,*] ~, ~, ~, *N;* ~ ~, ~, *S;* ~, ~ ~, *P*
177-78 but to . . . liuing; gaue] but, to . . . living, gave *P*
178 ship-wracks] shipwrack *N*
188 Riches] riches *S*
193 drawe.] *P;* ~, *Q1-2, N, S*
198 these] those *P*
200 *Lawe*] Law *MS correction IU copy, P; Loue Q1-2, N, S*
201 light] right *N*

211 right] rite *S, P*
213 *Plutus?*] ~; *Q2*; ~, *N, S, P*
218 Eeuen] eve *N*
221 aduances,] *MS correction IU copy, Q2, N, P*; ~. *Q1, S*
222 dances:] *MS correction IU copy*; ~, *Q1-2, N*; ~. *S, P*
229 a Plaine] a-plaine *N*
257 *Stance*] Stanze *Q2*
265 *fined*] 'fined *N*
268-69 *beames, . . . Ioy, . . . discends:*] *MS correction IU copy*; beames . . . joy; . . .
    descends, *N, P*; beams . . . joy, . . . descends; *S*
272 Stance] Stanze *Q2*
277 this] the *N*
278 Stance] Stanze *Q2*
294 Stance] Stanze *Q2*
310 *fourth*] *P*; third *Q1-2, N, S*
311 *stance*] stanze *Q2*
327 these Sunnes] the sunne *N*
340 Ladies,] *P*; ~. *Q1-2, N, S*
347 lifes] liues *Q2*; life's *N, S, P*
352 all waies] allwaies *Q2, N*; always *S, P*
354 liues] lives' *N, S, P*
355 neuer] ne're *Q2*
371-72 *remoue Lightnes,*] *N, S, P*; ~, ~∧ *Q1-2*
387 rage:] *MS correction IU copy*; ~, *Q1-2, N, S*; ~; *P*
412 hallowed] hallow'd *S, P*
417 conducting] conducted *N*

A Hymne to Hymen

2 torches, drunke] *torche has drunke N*
7 Mak'st] Makest *S*
18 desires;] ~. *Q1-2, B*; ~, *N, S, P*
27 Euen] eve *N*
31 weedes: are weedes,] ~; ~ ~, *Q2, B*; *weedes are weedes N, S, P*
37 staiest] stay'st *S*
40 eye.] ~, *P*
41 attires . . . put] *attire . . . puts N*
43 dances;] *dancing N*
61 scattered] scatter'd *S*
70 art] *N, S, P, B*; arts *Q1-2*
74 Brests] Brest *Q2*
81 aduance.] advance, *N, P*; advance; *B*
84 Torches, drunke] ~∧ ~ *Q1-2, S, P, B*; *torche has drunke N*

PRESS-VARIANTS IN Q1

[Copies collated: BM¹ (British Museum C.34.c.56), BM² (C.12.g.6), BM³ (G. 11214), BM⁴ (Ashley 380), Bodl¹ (Bodleian Library Malone 241[2]), Bodl² (Malone 172[4]), Bodl³ (T.37 ART [5]), Camb (Cambridge University Library), CSmH (Huntington Library), Dyce¹ (Victoria and Albert 26. Box. 5.5), Dyce² (Victoria and Albert Museum), Eton (College Library), DFo (Folger Shakespeare Library), IU (University of Illinois Library, lacks sigs. E4, F1), MH (Harvard University Library), NNP (Pierpont Morgan Library).]

Sheet ¶ (outer forme)

Corrected: BM¹, BM², BM³, BM⁴, Bodl¹, Bodl², Camb, CSmH, Dyce¹,
    Dyce², Eton, DFo, IU, MH
Uncorrected: Bodl³, NNP

Sig. ¶2

    4 *all-grace-deseruing*] *all-gracefull-deseruing*

Sheet ¶ (inner forme)

First State Corrected: Bodl²
Uncorrected: BM², Camb, Eton

Sig. ¶2ᵛ

    12 *part,*] *part*
      yours;] *yours,*
    24 affectionate, Obseruant.] affectioned,
Second State Corrected: BM¹, BM³, BM⁴, Bodl¹, Bodl³, CSmH, Dyce¹, Dyce²,
    DFo, IU?, MH, NNP

Sig. ¶2ᵛ

    24 affectionate Obseruant.] affectionate, Obseruant.

Sheet a (outer forme)

Corrected: BM¹, BM³, BM⁴, Bodl¹, Bodl², Bodl³, Camb, CSmH, Dyce¹,
    Dyce², DFo, Eton, MH, NNP
Uncorrected: BM², IU

Sig. a1

    130 wings;] wings,

Sig. a2ᵛ

    166 to set] to be set
    167 descended;] descended,

Sig. a3

    187 *-arise*] *-arise;*
    188 *for*] *for;*
    189 *vaine*] *paine*

Sheet a (inner forme)

First State Corrected: BM⁴
Uncorrected: Bodl¹
Sig. a1ᵛ
    133 world;] world.
Sig. a2
    156 an] in
Sig. a3ᵛ
    200 oportunitas] oportunitas.
    203 *slight*] *sleight*
        Freedom] *freedom*
    209 *write*] *writ*
Sig. a4
    230 *Aristophanes*] *Arisiophanies*
    231 witted;] witted,
    234-36 Nuptialls; . . . versat.] Nuptialls.
    Errata *list added*] *no* Errata *list*
    Second State Corrected: BM¹, BM², BM³, Bodl², Bodl³, Camb, CSmH, Dyce¹,
        Dyce², DFo, Eton, IU, MH, NNP
Sig. a4
    236-37 versat. ——— ——— Fallit . . . fidem.] versat.
    catchword *omitted*] THE

Sheet B (outer forme)

Corrected: BM¹, BM², BM³, BM⁴, Bodl¹, Bodl², Camb, CSmH, Dyce¹,
    Dyce², DFo, Eton, IU, MH, NNP
Uncorrected: Bodl³
Sig. B1
Names of the Speakers Riches) a God.] Riches.)
Sig. B2ᵛ
    34 He] hee

Sheet D (outer forme)

Corrected: BM¹, BM², Bodl¹, Bodl³, Camb, CSmH, Dyce¹, Dyce², DFo,
    Eton, NNP
Uncorrected: BM³, BM⁴, Bodl², IU, MH
Sig. D3
    252 al] the
Sig. D4ᵛ
    334 Region;] Region,

Sheet E (outer forme)

Corrected: BM¹, BM², BM³, BM⁴, Bodl¹, Bodl², CSmH, Dyce¹, Dyce², DFo,
    Eton, IU (-E4, F1), MH, NNP
Uncorrected: Bodl³, Camb
Sig. E2ᵛ
    391 these; And Theirs] these, and theirs
Sig. E4ᵛ
    41 attires] attire
    43 dances;] dances,

MANUSCRIPT CORRECTIONS IN
UNIVERSITY OF ILLINOIS
COPY OF Q1

[The manuscript corrections of errors noted in the Q1 "Errata" list are not recorded. Lemmata are taken from Q1, not from the present text.]

The Maske [introductory description]

164 seate] state (*first* e *altered to* t; *same correction also in* BM³ *and* Dyce¹)
166 to be set (*Q1* [*u*])] to set (be *deleted*)

The Maske

32-33 Iudgement is fashion] Iudgement fashion (is *deleted*)
33 man, that] man; That
34 nothing:] nothing;
92 shop,] shop;
93 Vsurer,] Vsurer;
94 wit;] wit? (*or perhaps* wit!)
95 them,] them? (*or perhaps* them!)
96 fooling:] fooling? (*or perhaps* fooling!)
102 boote,] boote;
129 besides.] besides?
130-31 ridiculous; . . . iests:] rediculous (neuer laught at their owne iests)
131 base,] base;
139 freight.] freight, (*period appears to have been converted into a comma; what is needed is a question mark*)
144 disgrace,] disgrace;
146 wit,] wit;
149 indeed, Sir] indeed Sir,
165 *Capriccius*] *Capricci*o (o *written over* u *and* s *deleted*)
167 marriages.] marriages:
173 Politician,] Politician;
175 me,] me;
179 So] Go (*reading very blurred, but* S *has definitely been written over*)
200 *Loue*] Law
221 aduances.] aduances,
222 dances,] dances:
252 the nightes (*Q1* [*u*])] All nightes
269 *Ioy*] *Ioy,*
298 *greetes*] *greetes,*

307 this] this,
332 night,] night;
334 Region, (*Q1*[*u*])] Region;
336] *MS corrector places* Loude Mus⟨ick⟩ *in right margin opposite* Ma- / skers.
347 power] pow'rs
385 *Honor.*] *MS corrector appears to delete period, not clear, however.*
387 rage,] rage:
409 t'inuite,] t'inuite;

TEXTUAL NOTES

The Maske [introductory description]

164 state] The reading of Q1-2 ("seate") means essentially the same as "state" (i.e., a throne, chair of state, seat-royal [*NED*]), but the authority I have attached to the MS corrections in the IU copy warrants the change. Parrott made the emendation independently. It is worth noticing, perhaps, that "seate" had been used by Chapman three times earlier (ll. 69, 74, 85) to refer to positions in the several masque "chariots."

The Maske

32-33 Iudgement fashion] I have accepted the IU MS correction (the omission of "is" after "Iudgement"). It can be defended, I believe, first, as the sort of change only an author would be likely to be concerned with; and, second, on the grounds of rhetorical parallelism: "Iudgement fashion" balancing "Birth his full man," the first preceded by "whose Wit is humor," the second by "whose Pride is emptinesse."

131 (neuer . . . iests)] The pointing of the IU MS correction clarifies, which otherwise is not very clear, the relationship of this clause to "ridiculous," making it a parenthetical gloss.

327 these Sunnes] Nichols' emendation to "the sunne" makes excellent sense in itself, but the next line ("Subiect to cloudy darknings and descents") makes it, I think, unacceptable. To what "these Sunnes" refers is not very apparent, since the songs sung by the Phœbades have both been addressed to *the* sun. The only suns which appear are the "golden Sunns" and "Sunnes of golde plate" which adorned the "Indian habits" and "Coronets" of the "chiefe Maskers," the Virginean Princes (introductory description, ll. 24, 33).

A Hymne to Hymen

2 Bright . . . tears:] This line, repeated as the final line (84) of the "Hymne," is grammatically awkward, forcing the reader to take "drunke" with the force of 'have drunk' — a usage not vouched for by *NED*. Nichols' emendation, by which in both lines he reads "torche has drunke," has the merit of clarity, and Q1's "torches, drunke" would be an easy misreading from a carelessly written MS. Q1's plural "torches," however, is strongly supported by the reference to "*Hymens* lights" in line 81.